Juvenile Justice in America

Juvenile Justice in America

SEVENTH EDITION

Clemens Bartollas
- University of Northern Iowa

Stuart J. Miller
- Washington & Jefferson College

PEARSON

Boston   Columbus   Indianapolis   New York   San Francisco   Upper Saddle River
Amsterdam   Cape Town   Dubai   London   Madrid   Milan   Munich   Paris   Montréal   Toronto
Delhi   Mexico City   São Paulo   Sydney   Hong Kong   Seoul   Singapore   Taipei   Tokyo

Editorial Director: Vernon Anthony
Acquisitions Editor: Gary Bauer
Editorial Assistant: Tanika Henderson
Director of Marketing: David Gesell
Senior Marketing Manager: Mary Salzman
Senior Marketing Coordinator: Alicia Wozniak
Senior Marketing Assistant: Les Roberts
Senior Managing Editor: JoEllen Gohr
Production Project Manager: Jessica H. Sykes
Senior Operations Supervisor: Pat Tonneman
Senior Art Director: Diane Ernsberger

Text and Cover Designer: Wanda Espana at Wee Design
Cover Art: Shutterstock
Editor, Digital Projects: Nichole Caldwell
Lead Media Project Manager: Karen Bretz
Full-Service Project Management: Kelli Jauron/S4Carlisle
Publishing Services
Composition: S4Carlisle Publishing Services
Printer/Binder: Courier/Kendallville
Cover Printer: Courier/Kendallville
Text Font: ITC Century Std

Library of Congress Cataloging-in-Publication Data
Bartollas, Clemens.
  Juvenile justice in America/Clemens Bartollas, University of Northern Iowa,
Stuart J. Miller Washington & Jefferson College.—Seventh Edition.
    p. cm.
  ISBN 978-0-13-297830-9
  1. Juvenile justice, Administration of—United States. 2. Juvenile delinquency—United States.
  3. Juvenile delinquents—United States. I. Miller, Stuart J., 1938- II. Title.
  HV9104.B347 2013
  364.360973—dc23

                                                        2012051584

10 9 8 7 6 5 4 3

ISBN 10:   0-13-297830-X
ISBN 13: 978-0-13-297830-9

**To the Parents and Children
of Newtown, Connecticut.**

Your grief is felt by all.

Preface

Juvenile justice is part of a broader human rights movement that is concerned with far more than society's response to juvenile lawbreaking. Indeed, as globalization, urbanization, industrialization, and communications quickly spread across the globe, the world's attention increasingly is directed to the plight of all children, regardless of circumstances. This concern is extremely late in coming. Approximately twenty-five percent of the world's population today is age 15 or younger, and the magnitude of the problems these youths face is staggering. Poverty, racism, sexism, ethnocentrism, and religious differences all influence how children are treated. The reality is that in many societies, children are considered to be economic hindrances and expendable. Local, municipal, state, provincial, territorial, and national governments often lump together the needy, the dependent and neglected, the status offender, those who are mentally ill or violent, and the victims of abuse. These children are discriminated against, victimized, persecuted, and sometimes executed by citizens, police, and paramilitary forces. The problems youths face go to the core of cultural thinking, far beyond the needs of societies simply to fine-tune agencies and the rules already in place for the handling of youths in need.

English-speaking countries such as the United States provide many of the ideals that are behind current worldwide efforts to reform the world's approach to juvenile justice. Unfortunately, even world leaders often fall far short of their own ideals. In this regard, the United States is an excellent case study of what is and what could be in juvenile justice in the world today.

Goals and Objectives

Our primary purposes in writing this edition are as follows:

1. To give students an intimate look at the lives of juveniles, their experiences in society, and the consequences of those experiences

2. To present the structures, procedures, and philosophies of juvenile justice agencies in the United States

3. To explore and define the important components of and debates over juvenile justice in the United States

4. To examine the issues and challenges facing juvenile justice agencies today

5. To maintain a balance between theory, evidence-based findings, law, and practice in our examination of juvenile justice

6. To provide the most up-to-date materials possible and, at the same time, to make this text interesting for the student.

Although no author is totally value-free, every attempt has been made to be fair and provide a balanced presentation of the juvenile justice system. Before juvenile justice can develop more just systems and a more humane present and future for juveniles, its characteristics, procedures, policies, and problems must be carefully examined. That is the task of this text.

What's New in This Edition

- Evidence-based practices and programs are featured in every chapter.
- New chapter openers and learning objectives are provided for each chapter.
- More concepts are now presented in both narrative and graphical form.
- New Juvenile Justice Video descriptions with assignment questions related to issues discussed in the chapter have been added at the end of each chapter. The videos can be found at www.pearsonhighered.com/careers for *Juvenile Justice in America*, 7th edition.
- The history of the development of the juvenile justice system has been expanded in Chapter 1.
- Along with the completely updated statistics on the measurement of juvenile crime, Chapter 2 has an expanded section on bullies and a new section on brothels and the streets.
- Chapter 3 has been divided into two chapters. Chapter 3 now provides a broad review of the causes of juvenile crime as well as the causes of juvenile offending.
- Chapter 4 now examines gender, race/ethnicity, and class correlates of delinquency including new coverage of the causes of African American and Hispanic youthful offending.
- A final section on how police handle juveniles in the community has been added to Chapter 5.
- Chapters 5 and 6 from the 6th edition are now combined into a new Chapter 6 on the juvenile court. Chapter 6 also has a new section on crossover youth.
- Chapter 7 has been considerably updated with materials recently published on transfer from juvenile court to an adult court. New materials are also provided on the controversial issue of juveniles who are sentenced to life without parole.
- Chapter 8 has been totally updated. It includes a Technocorrections feature on the use of technology in juvenile probation and an expanded discussion on the roles of the probation officer.
- The new features of Chapter 9 include the continuum of sanctions, an examination of Project CRAFT, and discussion of youth courts, drug courts, and teen courts.
- Chapter 10 has a new Focus on Practice, *Indiana Implements a Faith- and Character Based Housing Program*, and includes updated data and discussion on juvenile institutions.
- Chapter 11 focuses on aftercare in juvenile justice and uses current research to place a major emphasis on reentry programs and has a new section on the characteristics of those receiving aftercare.
- Chapter 12 includes a new table on risk assessment instruments, in which several instruments are described. In addition, the organization of treatment is divided into insight and group therapies, and a much greater emphasis is placed on cognitive-based therapy.
- Chapter 13 has been reorganized to improve the flow of topics and make it more student friendly.
- Chapter 14 has new sections on explanations for the onset of drug use and solutions to the drug problem.
- Chapter 15 now discusses juvenile justice in Somalia and Sweden in addition to the countries covered in the 6th edition.
- Chapter 16 is essentially a new chapter. It begins with an overview of the problems in modern society that affect youths at risk, has expanded coverage of issues facing juvenile justice, and discusses the changing face of juvenile justice. Discussion of the growth of professionalism in juvenile justice and what juvenile justice will look like in the twenty-first century has also been expanded.

Organization of the Text

The seventh edition of *Juvenile Justice in America* has sixteen chapters:

- Chapter 1 presents the history of juvenile justice and several historical themes of juvenile justice, examines juvenile justice agencies and functions, and reviews the most widely held philosophies and strategies on correcting juveniles.
- Chapter 2 examines the measurement of juvenile crime, considers the dimensions of law-violating behaviors, and takes a look at the victimization of children at home and in the school.
- Chapter 3 provides a broad review of the causes of juvenile crime as they developed over the past century.
- Chapter 4 examines gender, race/ethnicity, and class correlates of delinquency. Such subjects as the causes of African American and Hispanic youthful offending are examined.
- Chapter 5 discusses the role of the police in dealing with juveniles. It covers police attitudes, the legal rights of juveniles in dealing with the police, how police process juveniles, and the role of community-oriented policing.
- Chapter 6 examines the main U.S. Supreme Court cases related to the handling of juveniles who come before the juvenile court, considers how status offenders have been handled, presents information on the judge and other key personnel in the juvenile court, and discusses the pretrial procedures of the juvenile court. This chapter also focuses on the adjudicatory hearing, disposition hearing, and judicial alternatives of the juvenile court and looks at the rights of appeal a juvenile has and the current juvenile sentencing structure. Then it provides a defense of the juvenile court and suggestions concerning what is needed for the juvenile court to achieve excellence.
- Chapter 7 extends the discussion to juveniles who are waived to adult court. The issue of transfer receives major attention, but discussions are also provided on the youthful offender system, life for a juvenile in prison, changes in the death penalty for juveniles, and current evaluation of the situation in which juveniles are sentenced to life without the possibility of parole.
- Chapter 8 considers the administration, functions, and risk control focus of probation today. The job of the probation officer is described, and the rights of probationers, the role of volunteers, and the effectiveness of probation are considered.
- Chapter 9 examines the various aspects of community-based programs, including prevention, diversion, day treatment, and residential programs.
- Chapter 10 evaluates the various aspects of institutionalization, both short term and long term, for juveniles.
- Chapter 11 delves into aftercare in juvenile justice. Using current research, it places a major emphasis on reentry programs.
- Chapter 12 considers and evaluates the various types of treatment modalities.
- Chapter 13 extends the discussion to juvenile gangs, revealing their history, the types and background of urban and emerging gangs, and the toxicity of gang involvement. The chapter concludes by considering what communities can do to prevent and control youth gangs.
- Chapter 14 examines drugs and youthful offending. The main types of drugs, the extent of drug use among juveniles, the relationship between drug use and delinquency, and an explanation of why youngsters use drugs are some of the subjects of this chapter.
- Chapter 15 discusses juvenile justice in Somalia, China, India, Brazil, Canada, England/Wales, and Sweden.
- Chapter 16 provides a review of the text, considers the major issues facing juvenile justice now, considers what juvenile justice will look like in the future, looks at the new technologies emerging in corrections and security procedures, examines how professionalism impacts juvenile justice, and discusses whether juvenile justice is a good career.

Learning Tools

This text contains a number of features that are designed to help students in the learning process.

For Students

Evidence-Based Practice Boxes. A new box in each chapter (except for Chapter 1) highlights real-life examples of evidence-based practices and programs currently in operation.

Focus Boxes. Each chapter contains one or more boxes relating to aspects of juvenile justice, such as laws, social policy, intervention programs, and insights into offenders' thoughts and motivations.

Summary. The chapter concepts are summarized and organized according to the chapter's learning objectives to help students learn the material.

Juvenile Justice Videos. Most chapters now ask students to view specific video clips related to juvenile justice at www.pearsonhighered.com. These clips take students into the world of the juvenile justice system in a way that simple text cannot achieve. Following the description of each video, several analytical review questions encourage students to engage themselves further in the subject matter.

Critical Thinking and Review Questions. These are found at the end of some boxes and at the end of each chapter.

Group Exercises. Each chapter includes exercises for small group discussions, writing exercises, and/or suggestions for class debate topics.

Student Resources Online

The Video Case Studies at the end of each chapter that highlight real-life cases of juveniles in contact with the justice system along with Links to Web Extras and Library Extras can be accessed by going to www.pearsonhighered.com/careers.

Instructor Resources

Voices in the Juvenile Justice System are referenced in the margins of the text as they relate to each topic throughout the text. Victims, delinquents, and professionals contribute thirty-five "stories"; twenty-one are from individuals who talk about their childhoods, the crimes they committed, the contacts they had with the police and juvenile justice system and a victim of sex slavery. The other statements are from those who either have worked or presently work with youthful offenders, ranging from police officers to a juvenile court judge, a chief of juvenile probation, a deputy director of a detention center, a community mental health coordinator, a forensic psychiatrist, and a practicing clinical psychologist. The founder and director of a residential facility, two staff members in residential facilities, a therapist who has worked with sex offenders, a former juvenile court prosecutor from New York City, and a Deputy Commissioner of Probation in New York City. These are identified in the margins of the text and can be accessed from www.pearsonhighered.com/careers.

eBooks

Juvenile Justice is available in two eBook formats, *CourseSmart* and Adobe Reader. *CourseSmart* is an exciting new choice for students looking to save money. As an alternative to purchasing the printed textbook, students can purchase an electronic version of the same content. With a *CourseSmart* eTextbook, students can search the text, make notes online, print out reading assignments that incorporate lecture notes, and bookmark important passages for later review. For more information, or to purchase access to the *CourseSmart* eTextbook, visit **www.coursesmart.com**.

TestBank *and* MyTest

These supplements represent a new standard in testing material. Whether you use the basic *TestBank* or generate questions electronically through *MyTest*, every question is linked to the text's learning objective, page number, and level of difficulty. This allows for quick reference in the text and is an easy way to check the difficulty level and variety of your questions. *MyTest* can be accessed at **www.PearsonMyTest.com**.

Interactive Lecture PowerPoints

This supplement will enhance lectures like never before. Award-winning presentation designers worked with our authors to develop *PowerPoints* that truly engage the student. Much like the text, the *PowerPoints* are full of instructionally sound graphics, tables, charts, and photos that do what presentation software was meant to do: support and enhance your lecture. Data and difficult concepts are presented in a truly interactive way, helping students connect the dots and stay focused on the lecture. The *Interactive Lecture PowerPoints* also include in-depth lecture notes and teaching tips so you have all your lecture material in one place.

The Pearson Criminal Justice Online Community

Available at www.mycriminaljusticecommunity.com, this site is a place for educators to connect, and to exchange ideas and advice on courses, content, interactive multimedia, and so much more.

To access these supplementary materials online, instructors need to request an instructor access code at www.pearsonhighered.com/irc. Within 48 hours after registering, you will receive a confirmation e-mail that includes an instructor access code. When you receive your code, go to the site and log on for full instructions on downloading materials you wish to use.

Acknowledgments

Many individuals have contributed to the writing of this book. We are profoundly grateful to our wives, Linda Dippold Bartollas and JoAnn Miller. Both were constant sources of support and encouragement throughout the many phases involved in the publication of this seventh edition. Linda Bartollas also conducted interviews with juvenile offenders in three states.

We are grateful to those participants of the juvenile justice system who were willing to be interviewed, who contributed materials for this edition, or who assisted us in replicating scenes from the halls of justice for photographs for this volume. Special thanks are due to Police Chief Richard Horner, Lt. Kirk Hessler, and mall security officers Rich Keys, Willard (Buzz) Holbert, and Shane Bane. Special thanks are also due to Trevor Onest and David Kraueter, former reference librarians at Washington & Jefferson College, as well as to those neighbors and students who were willing to be models for various photographs throughout this book, and Jessica Melody, and Thomas Butterfield. Kate O'Lare, James Scheengost, and Dr. Constinia Charbonnette provided photos for this edition, as did the Washington County, Pennsylvania, Juvenile Probation Department's Leader program. Special thanks are due to Lynette-Drawn-Williamson of the Allenghany County Shuman Center for obtaining its permission to use specific photos in the text.

Thanks to the following reviewers: Maldine "Beth" Bailey, University of North Florida; Scott William Bowman, Texas State University–San Marcos; Tiffany Cox, San Antonio College; Denise D. Dyer, LeMoyne College; Susan S. Hodge, University of North Carolina–Charlotte; Kareem L. Jordan, University of North Florida; Mahfuzul Khondaker, Kutztown University of Pennsylvania; and Barry S. McCrary, Western Illinois University.

At the University of Northern Iowa, we thank Wayne Fauchier for all the tasks that he and his staff performed to keep the manuscript moving without interruption. At Washington & Jefferson College, Alanna Santee, Allyson Kolljeski, Desiree Dornetta, Marissa Stephens, Alyssa Zrimchek, Stephanie Brunermer, Larissa Grudi, Lauren Horning, and James Schreengost diligently performed research and sent out permission requests throughout a number of editions to sources that in some cases are still used. Alanna Santee also typed, developed questions for the test manuals, and assisted in writing several boxes. Debbie Trent, Margie Mahramus, Barbara Rea, and Doree Baumgart provided invaluable assistance in preparation of the text, instructor's manual, "Voices," and index. Special recognition for this edition goes to Corey Young of Clemenson University for his assistance and insights on Somalia and to James Schrecengost and Lauren Horning for their research and writing about Sweden. Mr. Schrecengost, especially, was invaluable in copyediting, searching out videos, and helping organize various components and obtaining permissions for this text. Finally, we are grateful to our development editor, Elisa Rogers, and our editor, Gary Bauer.

Brief Contents

Contents

PART II   *The Causes of Delinquency*

CHAPTER 3 **Causes of Juvenile Crime** 47

CHAPTER 15 International Juvenile Justice 303

Juvenile Justice
An Overview

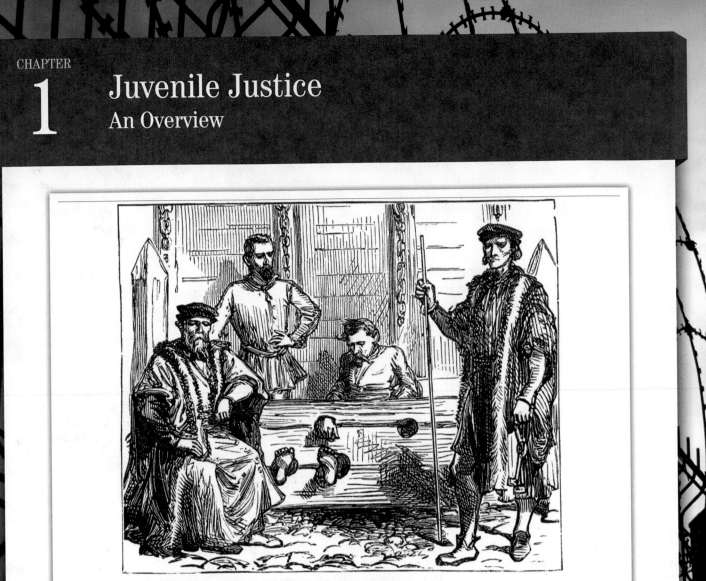

THE STOCKS (16TH CENTURY).

19th era/Alamy

Learning Objectives

1. Retrace the journey of juvenile justice in the United States.

2. Explain the concept of *parens patriae*.

3. Summarize the historical themes that guided the development of juvenile justice in the United States.

4. Present the structure and procedures of juvenile justice agencies in this nation.

5. Examine the various philosophies and strategies for correcting juveniles.

In 2010, Mark W. Lipsey and colleagues published Improving the Effectiveness of Juvenile Justice Programs[1]:

> *We now have research on best practices for juvenile justice–involved youth and the policies that support the practices. We find this reflected in the increased use of evidence-based practices and programs, in the growth of the science of risk and protective factors and criminogenetic factors and characteristics, and in the development and use of validated risk and needs assessment instruments. We have learned about the importance of advancing our work on an ecological platform, serving youth closer to home, and better connecting youth to family, school, community, and pro-social peers while utilizing a strength-based approach. The true challenge is not, therefore, a lack of knowledge of what works, but rather is in translating the robust body of knowledge into practice.[2]*

Evidence-based research provides reason to be positive about the future of juvenile justice in the United States. All of the remaining chapters of this text discuss evidence-based practices in juvenile justice. "Gold standard" programs that have recently been developed to benefit youthful lawbreakers are Blueprints for Violence Prevention developed by Dr. Delbert Elliott, the Office of Juvenile Justice and Delinquency Prevention's Model Programs guide, or the Substance Abuse and Mental Health Services Administration's National Registry of Evidence-based Programs and Practices.[3]

In the midst of these hopeful program innovations in the juvenile justice system, there remains wide criticism of juvenile justice in the United States. Some of the criticism focuses on the juvenile court, as well as on the court's rehabilitative **parens patriae** ("the state as parent") philosophy. Indeed, one characteristic of juvenile justice today is the proposal, from both liberals and conservatives, to reduce the scope of the juvenile court's responsibilities. Conservatives want to refer more law-violating youths to adult court, while many liberals recommend divesting the juvenile court of its jurisdiction over **status offenders** (juveniles who have engaged in behaviors for which adults would not be arrested). Some also believe that the adult court could do a much better job than the juvenile court with youthful offenders. Juvenile offenders, according to this position, would at least receive their constitutionally guaranteed due process rights.

Voices of Delinquency: I Am Just a Small Town Girl

The fact is that the juvenile justice system will experience major changes in the next few years. How it will change and whether the changes will be helpful to the youth of this nation are critical questions to be answered. In a number of chapters of the current volume, positive changes are recommended to improve the functioning of the juvenile justice system.

The juvenile justice system is responsible for controlling and correcting the behavior of troublesome juveniles. What makes this mission so difficult to accomplish in the twenty-first century are the complex forces that intrude on any attempt either to formulate goals or to develop effective programs. Juvenile violence remains a serious problem, although homicides committed by juveniles began to decline in the mid-1990s. Even though juvenile gangs declined in numbers and membership across the nation in the final four years of the twentieth century, these gangs continue to be a problem in many communities. Juveniles' increased use of weapons has also become a serious concern, and there are those who believe that "getting the guns out of the hands of juveniles" is the most important mandate that the juvenile justice system currently has. The use of drugs and alcohol among the juvenile population declined in the final decades of the twentieth century, but beginning in the mid-1990s and continuing to the present, there is evidence that the use of alcohol and drugs, especially marijuana and methamphetamine, is rising in the adolescent population. Furthermore, conflicting philosophies and strategies for correcting juvenile offenders have combined with the social, political, and economic problems that American society faces today—this combination presents other formidable challenges to the juvenile justice system.

Yet, let it be clear that while presenting the challenges of juvenile justice and the often disturbing results of working with youth in trouble, the authors are not promoting a "nothing works" thesis. There are stirring accounts of youths who started out in trouble and were able to turn things around. In some cases, it was a program that worked with them; in others, it was an adult who made a difference in their lives; and in still others, it was the youths themselves who made the decision to live a crime-free life. As previously noted, with the

Focus on Offenders 1–1
I Am Determined to Make Something of Myself

I returned to Cincinnati when I left TICO [Training Institution, Central Ohio, a maximum security training school of the Ohio Youth Commission] in August 1977. Since I was 18, I opted for independent status and stayed at the Fryar's Club for six months and then moved into my own apartment that I shared with a friend. I had a regular job, both while I was staying at the Fryar's Club and after I moved out. I started college at Thomas More College in Erlanger, Kentucky, in the fall of 1978, and commuted from Cincinnati.

I applied for and received a grant but finally started to run out of money. I majored in chemistry and was hoping to get a job working in a lab. I was not able to find anything local, so after a year and a half at Thomas More, I moved to New Jersey, where my mother lived with my two younger sisters. I got a job as a chemist. My mother was able to get me a job at the company she worked for. I had only intended to stay for a year and then return to school. Somehow, that never happened.

I got laid off from the one company and landed a job with another chemical company. After a little over a year and a half, I was in a motorcycle accident and was out of work for three months. When I was ready to return, they had filled my position. I decided that I would go back to school, but I would do it in New Jersey. I went to the local two-year school, which was where I met my wife. I then landed a job in chemistry with Colgate-Palmolive [which] had come recruiting on campus. [It was] located very close to Rutgers, and my intention was to work and go to school at night. School and work proved to be a bit more than I could deal with, so I stopped going to school after about a year.

I stayed at Colgate for about six years, during which time my wife and I were married in May of 1987. I left Colgate and went to work for another chemical company. After being there only a short time, I decided that I was tired of working in a lab, so I went back to school at night for a degree in Information Systems.

My wife and I bought our house in the late fall of 1990. Our daughter was born in April of 1992. I finished my B.S. [Bachelor of Science degree] in the spring of 1993. I was able to make the transition from the lab to IT [information technology] while I was at FMC. That fall I decided to go to graduate school and get an M.B.A. Our son was born in January of 1994. There was a change in management at the company I was with, so I left and joined a consulting firm doing IT consulting. I finished my graduate degree in 1996.

I was promoted and moved to a more senior-level position within the consulting firm I was working for. I had started to specialize in pharmaceutical clinical data management systems and was leading a team of six other consultants. I left that firm and joined another consulting firm that I am currently with now. I am currently consulting for a major pharmaceutical company as an IT project manager.

CRITICAL THINKING QUESTIONS:

Why do you believe that this person turned his life around? What attributes does he appear to have that many delinquents who go on to criminal careers do not have? Does the focus have any lessons for those in the juvenile justice system?

Source: Letter received from a former institutionalized delinquent. Used with permission; the writer chooses to remain anonymous.

---

current emphasis on evidence-based practices and other model programs, it is hoped that juvenile justice programs will be more effective in the future.

A heartwarming success story is found in Focus on Offenders 1–1. The youth in this case had more than his share of troubles with the law as an adolescent. He ended up being sent to one of the toughest juvenile correctional institutions in the United States. Upon his release at the age of eighteen, this youth could have continued his law-violating activities into his adult years and spent the remainder of his life in and out of prison. Instead, he was motivated to make something of himself. His goals were not always achieved in the ways he intended, but he persisted. He earned a B.S. degree and eventually was awarded an M.B.A. With his educational achievements came job success, a happy marriage, and the joys of fatherhood.

This chapter examines four topics: a historical sketch of juvenile justice, several historical themes, the organizational structure of juvenile justice agencies, and the philosophical approaches to treating youthful offenders. What these topics have in common is that they present the contexts (past and present) that have shaped juvenile justice in the United States.

What Are the Roots of Juvenile Justice?

Throughout history, there has rarely been an emphasis on the special needs of juveniles. Adults and juveniles who violated the law were typically processed in the same manner and were subject to the same types of punishments, including whippings, mutilation, banishment, torture, and death.

Early Europe

In the fifth century A.D., the age was fixed at seven for determining whether youths would be exempted from criminal responsibility under certain conditions. With the onset of puberty, at the age of twelve for girls and fourteen for boys, youths were held totally responsible for their socially unacceptable behaviors.

This understanding of children and criminal responsibility continued in medieval Europe. For example, during the entire period between 700 and 1500 A.D., children were not viewed as a distinct group with special needs and behaviors. Although little is known about the peasant families of the Middle Ages, it is clear that children were expected to assume adult roles in the family early in life and apprentice themselves in crafts or trades to wealthier families. The landowners of the country, then, assumed control over children and their welfare and, at the same time, lifted the burden of child care from their parents.

These early medieval traditions eventually influenced the shaping of juvenile justice in England. Both the Chancery court, which eventually became responsible for overseeing the general welfare of the citizenry, and the concept of *parens patriae*, which focused on the sovereign as the one who protected his or her subjects, played a prominent role in the shaping of English juvenile justice.

Because children and other incompetents were under the protective control of the sovereign, it was not difficult for English kings to justify interventions in their lives. With the passage of time, the concept of *parens patriae* was increasingly used to justify interventions in peasants' families.

The common law tradition in England eventually concurred with earlier law that children under seven should not face legal penalties. Children between seven and fourteen were deemed another matter, and their responsibility was determined by other considerations: severity of the crime, maturity, capacity to distinguish between right and wrong, and evidence of blatant malice.

A sad page in the history of English juvenile justice is that some 160 to 200 capital offenses were listed in the statutes for which children could be executed. Although many juveniles sentenced to die were later pardoned or transported to another country, some children were executed. For example, eighteen of the twenty people executed in London in 1785 were under the age of eighteen.[4] The executions of children continued, but only occasionally, into the 1800s.

▲ Beheadings and the amputations of limbs of adults and children were undertaken in public squares to act as deterrents to crime in the middle ages—and even today in some countries.

Washington & Jefferson College

The Colonies and Later

Juvenile justice in the United States began in the colonial period and continued English practices. In the colonial period, juvenile justice was shaped principally by the cultural and religious ideas of the Puritans. The family, the cornerstone of the community in colonial times, was the source and primary means of social control of children. The law was uncomplicated; the only law enforcement officials were town fathers, magistrates, sheriffs, and watchmen; and the only penal institutions were jails for prisoners awaiting trial or punishment. Juvenile lawbreakers did not face a battery of police, probation, or **aftercare officers** (the juvenile equivalent of adult parole officers), nor did they have to worry that practitioners of the juvenile justice system would try to rehabilitate or correct them. They only had to concern themselves with being sent back to their families for punishment.[5]

As children got older, however, the likelihood increased that they would be dealt with more harshly by colonial law. The state, even in those early days, clearly was committed to raising its children correctly and making them follow society's rules. If children were still recalcitrant after harsh whippings and other forms of discipline from their families, they could be returned to community officials for more punishment, such as public whippings, dunkings, or the stocks, or in more serious cases, expulsion from the community or even the use of capital punishment.[6]

The state became even more concerned about the welfare of its children in the 1800s. Increased urbanization, industrialization, and bureaucratization were changing the face of America. In the cities particularly, increasing numbers of youths were seemingly out of control. Reformers searched for ways to teach them traditional values, and the asylum and the training school were developed to help the state maintain its control.

The courts were by now heavily involved with the juvenile problem. The concept of *parens patriae* was formalized by *ex parte Crouse* in 1838 and gave the courts a legal basis for intervening in the lives of children. The Bill of Rights, the court ruled, did not apply to minors, and the state could legitimately confine minors, who, according to the ruling, did not have the right to counsel or trial by jury, and who could be confined even in the absence of criminal behavior.

By the end of the 1800s, much of the U.S. population lived in urban areas and worked in factories. Cities were large and growing, and waves of immigration were inundating the nation's shores with millions of people destined to remain poor. Conditions in the cities were shocking; there was much poverty, crime, disease, mental illness, and dilapidation. The cities' children were viewed as unfortunate victims of the urban scene.

How Did the Juvenile Court Develop?

Anthony Platt, in *The Child Savers*, adds greatly to our understanding of the origins of the first juvenile court in Chicago. The Chicago court was created, he argues, partly because the middle and upper classes wanted to control the increasing numbers of immigrants and the poor. Platt claims that the juvenile court was established in Chicago and later elsewhere because it satisfied several middle-class interest groups. He sees the juvenile court as an expression of middle-class values and of the philosophy of conservative political groups.[7]

There is a somewhat different interpretation of the development of the juvenile court. The conditions of the Cook County Jail and the Chicago House of Correction, in which children were placed with adults, were deplorable. Increased numbers of youths were being confined with hardened adult felons who corrupted and exposed them to debauchery, crime, and sin. A group of middle- and upper-class women who had achieved a certain amount of power and freedom wanted to relieve children from confinement with adults in deplorable conditions. Women such as Jane Addams, Louise Bowen, and Julia Lathrop were committed to rescuing the urban American family and its youth by restoring rural values to them. They wanted to reaffirm parental authority, restore the role of the woman in the home, ensure the proper training of youths, and, most important, save youths from the sins they were exposed to on the streets.[8] Focus on the Law 1–2 reveals the prohibited behaviors that the early juvenile courts attempted to correct in the youth brought before them.

The reformers were aided in their quest by a new emerging philosophy. In the past, the classical school of criminology had argued that laws were violated because people willfully chose to violate them. People were presumed to operate on the basis of free will, having total control over their actions; punishment was required to get them to follow the law. The emerging **positivist** school, in contrast, contended that people were pushed into crime by forces beyond their control. It argued that the causes of crime could be discovered through the use of the scientific method and that the biological, psychological, social, economic, political, and other environmental causes of crime could be discovered through rigorous and precise measurement. Once the causes of crime were discovered, this school argued, experts could then step in and cure the offender of his or her problem. Proponents of this philosophy believed that the juvenile court should use these assumptions in attacking the problems of youth.

Everything was in place. The *parens patriae* doctrine had been accepted by the courts for more than a half century. Social conditions had generated an underclass of people who appeared unable to help themselves. Conservative, humanitarian, and religious philosophies had justified the need and had provided the power necessary for change. Jails and prisons clearly were no places for children. And finally, the positivist philosophy held out the promise that if the right mechanism could be developed, wayward children could be saved.

The Cook County Juvenile Court was founded in 1899. Its premises were that the *parens patriae* doctrine permitted it to take charge of children in need, that the causes of the

Focus on the Law 1–2
Prohibited Behaviors in Early Juvenile Codes

- Violating any law or ordinance
- Being habitually truant from school
- Associating with vicious or immoral persons
- Being incorrigible
- Demonstrating behavior that is beyond parental control
- Leaving home without consent of parents
- Growing up in idleness or crime
- Participating in behavior that injures or endangers the health, morals, or safety of self or others
- Using vile, obscene, or vulgar language in public
- Entering or visiting a house of ill repute
- Patronizing a place where liquor is sold
- Patronizing a gaming place
- Wandering in the streets at night not on lawful business (curfew violations)
- Engaging in immoral conduct at school or in other public places

- Smoking cigarettes or using tobacco in any form
- Loitering
- Sleeping in alleys
- Using intoxicating liquor
- Begging
- Running away from a state or charitable institution
- Attempting to marry without consent, in violation of law
- Indulging in sexual irregularities
- Patronizing public pool rooms
- Wandering about railroad yards or tracks
- Jumping a train or entering a train without authority
- Refusing to obey a parent or guardian

CRITICAL THINKING QUESTIONS

Which of these offenses do you believe should be defined as delinquent behavior today? How many of these behaviors did you engage in when you were a teenager. How should you have been punished?

children's problems could be discovered and treated, and that the court had to develop a different set of procedures and terminology from those of the adult courts to achieve these goals.

Accordingly, the Illinois court was set up to operate on an *informal* basis. First, this meant that traditional courtrooms were not used; all that was actually required were a table and chairs where the judge, the child, and his or her parents and probation officers could sit together and discuss the case. Second, children could be brought before the court on the basis of complaints of citizens, parents, police, school officials, or others. Third, the children's hearings were not public, and their records were kept confidential because children coming before the court were not considered criminal. Fourth, proof of the child's criminality was not required for the child to be considered in need of the court's services. Fifth, the court had great discretion in determining what kinds of services the child required and had wide latitude in determining a disposition. Sixth, lawyers were not required because the hearings were not adversarial. Finally, the standards and procedures long in use in adult courts were missing in the juvenile courts; the standard of proof beyond a reasonable doubt was not required, and hearsay evidence was permitted.

The attractiveness of the juvenile court philosophy resulted in almost all states setting up juvenile courts. In fact, by 1928, only two of thirty-one states had not passed a juvenile court statute.[9] Those that did closely followed the wording and intent of the Chicago statute and its amendments. These were civil courts, usually a family court, and their purpose was rehabilitation, not punishment. The neglected, the dependent, the misbehaving youngster, the status offender, and the delinquent were all subject to the courts' dictates. But the public was assured that programs would be developed to solve the problems of wayward youth so that they would be released to the community as respectable citizens.

Juvenile courts attempted to live up to their mandate for the next sixty years. For about the first twenty years, the court was aided by religiously motivated volunteers who brought strong moral commitments to their work with juveniles. Confidence in the juvenile court began to erode in 1911 and 1912, with exposés detailing the court's deplorable conditions and practices.[10] Another negative influence on the juvenile court following World War I was the general disenchantment with the idea that society was improving.

Immediately following World War I, volunteers were replaced with paid social work professionals called "social adjusters." The social work orientation of these professionals enabled them to help redefine the juvenile court as a social agency and to lobby successfully for more paid social workers. In the 1920s, the field of social work adopted Freudian psychoanalysis, which focused on the client's emotional feelings. Thus, instead of attempting to deal with social environmental problems as the cause of delinquency, as the earlier reformers did, social workers began to focus on the inner mental workings of the child.

What Is the History of Juvenile Confinement?

At the time of the American Revolution, the penal system in the colonies was modeled after the one in England. The larger urban jails, county jails, and prisons contained men, women, and juveniles, whether they were felons or misdemeanants, insane or sane—sometimes all mixed together. Smaller rural counties, however, had less need for large jails and prisons and temporarily housed their wayward citizens in small rural jails.

In neither city nor county, however, were youths expected to get into trouble. If they did, they were subject to the same punishments as were adults. Beyond that, normal community processes were thought to be sufficient to keep them in line. Community norms were enforced through gossip, ridicule, and other informal social pressures, and little formal social control was needed. Local enforcers consisted of watchmen, magistrates, and sheriffs. All those who were caught, including youths, received fines, beatings, and floggings; were put in stocks; were driven through town in carts to be ridiculed by the citizenry; and in extreme cases were hanged, burned, mutilated, or banished from the community. After punishment, some youths were apprenticed to local craftsmen; until the mid-1800s others were sent on extended whaling voyages; and still others were placed with relatives or farm families.[11]

In the late 1700s and early 1800s, the United States was in a period of transition. The rural way of life was threatened, and the changes were having an irreversible effect on the structure of society. Concern about what to do with the growing number of juveniles who were abandoned, were runaways, or had run afoul of community norms increased and placed the young nation in a dilemma. On the one hand, thinkers reasoned that the natural depravity of humans made attempts at rehabilitation useless and that banishing the guilty was simpler than either punishment or rehabilitation. On the other hand, some hoped to find specific causes for deviancy, and the family was believed to be the primary source of the problem. Common sense and the examination of case histories indicated that older offenders usually had been problem children. The idea emerged that if institutions could be used for the poor, perhaps similar institutions could be set up for children using the well-adjusted family as the model.[12]

Regardless of the source of the problem, the situation demanded a solution. The growing number of delinquents and other children running in the streets of larger cities, the increasing population, and the changing character of U.S. society were all putting greater pressure on existing facilities. Conditions in the jails and prisons were deplorable. Youths were sentenced for fixed periods of time and were confined with the worst criminals society had to offer. Some youths died of disease, and morals were corrupted as children ten to eighteen years old were confined with adult felons.

The House of Refuge

When citizens and reformers first became concerned about these inhumane conditions, their solution was the **house of refuge**. This facility was for all children, not just delinquents. Benevolence and compassion, along with concern over the degrading conditions in the jails and prisons, motivated the reformers to establish the houses of refuge.

New York City started the first school for males in 1825, followed by Boston in 1826 and Philadelphia in 1828. Other cities, including Bangor, Richmond, Mobile, Cincinnati, and Chicago, followed suit over the years. Twenty-three houses of refuge were built in the 1830s and thirty more in the 1840s. Of these, the vast majority were for males, with an occasional institution reserved for females. Their capacity ranged from ninety at Lancaster, Massachusetts, to 1,000 at the New York House of Refuge, with a median number of 210. The promise of these institutions seemed so great that youths with every type of problem were placed in them. The New York House of Refuge accepted children adjudicated guilty of committing crimes as well as those who simply were in danger of getting into trouble. The poor, the destitute, the incorrigible, and the orphaned were all confined. Admission policies were obviously quite flexible, and little concern was shown for due process; some youths simply were kidnapped off the streets. Not until later did these institutions begin to limit their rosters to those who had committed crimes.

The children generally were confined for periods ranging from less than six weeks to about twenty-four months, although some stayed longer. In some institutions the youths were taught trades, such as manufacturing shoes, brushes, and chairs, or were readied for apprenticeships to local craftsmen. Sentences were indeterminate, and superintendents of the institutions decided whether the apprenticed youths would be released or returned to the institution.

These juvenile institutions accepted the family model wholeheartedly, for reformers desired to implant the order, discipline, and care of the family in institutional life. The institution, in effect, would become the home, peers would become the family, and staff would become the parents. Orphanages and houses of refuge substituted a rigorous system of control and discipline for the disordered life of the community.

Discipline was severe when the rules were disobeyed, but the reformers believed that once the authority of the superintendents was established, they would be looked on admiringly and as friends. Belief in these principles was so great that parents for the first time had to surrender their authority to superintendents and could not participate in the upbringing of their unruly children.

Treatment of the youths paralleled the routine nature of the facility's physical plant. When the youths entered, they were dressed in institutional clothing and given identical haircuts. Troublemakers were punished; placing offenders on a diet of bread and water or depriving them of meals altogether were milder forms of discipline, but they were coupled with solitary confinement if a severe punishment was deemed necessary. Corporal punishments, used alone or in combination with other corrections, consisted of whipping with a cat-o'-nine-tails or manacling with a ball and chain. The worst offenders were shipped off to sea.

The specific order of daily events varied from institution to institution, but all followed the same basic schedule and routine. In some, youths were counted frequently to make sure that none had escaped, and in many facilities silence was maintained at all times, even during the recreation and exercise periods. Eating at times other than regularly scheduled mealtimes was forbidden, and youths who wanted extra food had to raise their hands. In school everyone recited in unison.

Reformers were enthusiastic about the houses of refuge, but the residents apparently did not share their positive feelings. Hutchins Hapgood, sent to the New York House of Refuge in the nineteenth century, viewed this setting as a "school for crime," because "unspeakably bad habits were contracted there. The older boys wrecked the younger ones," and children who were orphans had an especially hard time. The residents, he added, were overworked while making overalls and were beaten frequently. He bluntly concluded, "I say without hesitation that lads sent to an institution like the House of Refuge, the Catholic Protectory, or the Juvenile Asylum might better be taken out and shot."[13]

The Reformatory or Training School

Reformatories, also called *training schools* or *industrial schools*, developed in the midnineteenth century. The new reformatories were essentially a continuation of the houses of refuge, although they did stress a longer period of schooling, usually half a day. Another change was that the contracting of inmates' labor became more exploitative, as manufacturers often inflicted cruelty and violence on juveniles during working hours. The cat-o'nine-tails, for example, was used on youths who slacked off on their work in the reformatory shops.

In spite of the questionable nature of these institutions, states continued to build reformatories or training schools. In 1847 Massachusetts opened the first state-operated training school, the Lyman School for Boys, and in 1856 established the State Industrial School for Girls at Lancaster. New York built an industrial school in 1849, and by 1870 Connecticut, Indiana, Maryland, Nevada, New Hampshire, New Jersey, Ohio, and Vermont had opened training schools for delinquents. By 1890 nearly every state outside of the South had established a training school.[14]

The Cottage System

Introduced in 1854, the **cottage system** spread throughout the country. Reformers had succeeded in placing the industrial schools outside cities, their rationale being that youths on farms would be reformed when exposed to the rural virtues, the simple way of life, and the bounty of Mother Nature. With the new cottage system, the process of individual reform could be furthered, as residents were housed in separate buildings, usually no more than twenty to forty per cottage. The training schools were no longer supposed to be fortresslike either in physical design or in the relationships among residents and staff. The first cottages were log cabins; later ones were made of brick or stone. This form of organization was widely accepted and is the basic design for many juvenile facilities even today.

Three major changes began to affect juvenile institutions in the closing decades of the nineteenth century: the increasing size of institutional populations, a decrease in funding from state legislatures, and the admission of more dangerous offenders. As a result, the industrial school became custodial, and superintendents had to accept custodianship as an adequate goal.[15] Yet faith in the industrial school continued into the twentieth century.

How Did Probation Develop?

John Augustus, a Boston cobbler, is considered to be the father of probation in this country. He spent considerable time in the courtroom and in 1841 accepted his first probation client, whose offense was "yielding to his appetite for strong drink."[16] Beginning with this "common drunkard," he was able to devote himself to the cause of probation as he became convinced that many lawbreakers needed only the interest and concern of another to be able to stop drinking, straighten out their lives, and become model citizens. Augustus worked with women and children as well as with male offenders; in fact, he was willing to work with all types of offenders—drunkards, petty thieves, prostitutes, and felons—as long as he met a contrite heart. Augustus instigated such services as investigation and screening, supervision of probationers, interviewing, and arranging for relief, employment, and education—all of which are still provided today.

The state of Massachusetts, very much impressed with Augustus's work, established a visiting-probation-agent system in 1869. The philosophy of this system, which was set up to assist both youths and adults, was that first offenders who showed definite promise should be released on probation. Youths would be allowed to return to their parents and to live at home as long as they obeyed the injunction "Go and sin no more."[17]

Probation was regulated by statute for the first time in 1878, when the mayor of Boston was authorized to appoint a paid probation officer to the police force, to serve under the police chief. In 1880, the authority to appoint probation officers was extended to all cities and towns in Massachusetts. By 1890, probation had become statewide, with the authority to appoint officers resting with the courts rather than with municipal authorities. Soon thereafter, Vermont, Missouri, Illinois, Minnesota, Rhode Island, and New Jersey enacted probation statutes.

Although probation was radically extended in the wake of the juvenile court movement, probation systems varied from one jurisdiction to another. Probation officers generally considered themselves servants of the juvenile court judge rather than defenders of the rights of children. Thus, they would gather relevant facts and opinions on each case to help the judge make his decision, sometimes blatantly disregarding the due process safeguards of the law. Judges, in turn, saw nothing objectionable about returning children to the care of the probation officer who had placed them at the court's mercy in the first place. Most juvenile courts relied at first on volunteer juvenile probation officers. One observer said that their work "is the chord upon which all the pearls of the Juvenile Court are strung. It is the keynote of a beautiful harmony; without it the Juvenile Court could not exist."[18] Probation volunteers, however, largely disappeared by the second decade of the twentieth century, not to return until the late 1950s.

The spread of probation was marked by the founding in 1907 of the National Association of Probation Officers (renamed the National Probation Association in 1911). Homer Folks, one of the early advocates of probation, summarized the perception of probation in the early twentieth century: "Probation provides a new kind of reformatory, without walls and without much coercion."[19] Nevertheless, the idea of coercion lurked close to the surface, and force was used without hesitation if the delinquent continued to disobey the law. "When sterner treatment was demanded," said one officer, "the friendly advisor became the official representative of the court with the demand that certain conditions be observed or that the probationer be returned to the court."[20]

After World War I, there was an ever-increasing demand for trained social workers to serve as probation officers. In addition to a greater concern for treating children's problems, twentieth-century probation theory also includes the idea of more responsibility for the delivery of services to probationers, a greater consciousness of standards, and a desire to upgrade the probation officer and restore the volunteer to probation services.

What Is the History of Aftercare?

Juvenile aftercare is as old as the juvenile institution. Superintendents of the early houses of refuge had the authority to release youths when they saw fit. Some youths were returned directly to their families; others were placed in the community as indentured servants and apprentices. After such service, they were released from their obligations and reentered the community as free citizens. For some, placement amounted to little more than slavery. They were sent to stores, factories, or farms that needed cheap labor. For others, the situation was more favorable, and some youths in trouble benefited from placement with caring and responsible families. Nevertheless, the system was not at all formalized; only in the 1840s did states begin to set up inspection procedures to keep watch on those with whom youths were placed.[21]

Parole, the period of time after institutional release when offenders are still under the control of the courts or state, continued to be used throughout the 1800s and into the 1900s. With the formation of the juvenile court, parole generally was called *aftercare*. In the early 1900s, professionally trained individuals were added to the juvenile court to deal with released juveniles. In addition, aftercare officers generally mirrored probation officers in trying to utilize current popular treatment modalities. Aftercare officers' caseloads were generally extremely high, and few resources were available to them. Even today, aftercare officers in many jurisdictions have the task of monitoring extremely large caseloads.

The development of aftercare programs was far from rapid, and the system remains underdeveloped even today. Citizens and professionals perhaps thought that institutionalization was sufficient for youth, or they might have been more concerned about adults, whom they feared and mistrusted more. Whatever the reason, not until fairly recently have innovative efforts been undertaken to improve juvenile aftercare systems. See Figure 1–1 for the historical stages in the development of juvenile justice.

FIGURE 1–1
Historical Stages in the Development of Juvenile Justice

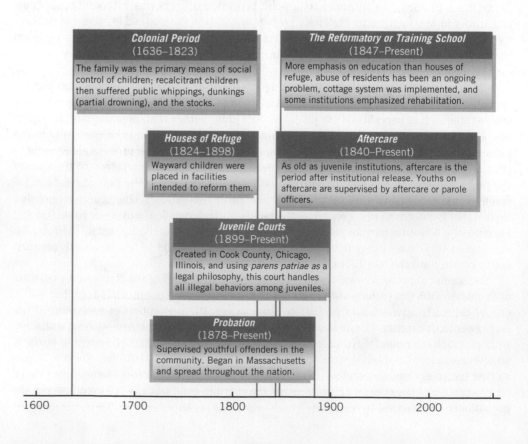

Colonial Period (1636–1823)
The family was the primary means of social control of children; recalcitrant children then suffered public whippings, dunkings (partial drowning), and the stocks.

The Reformatory or Training School (1847–Present)
More emphasis on education than houses of refuge, abuse of residents has been an ongoing problem, cottage system was implemented, and some institutions emphasized rehabilitation.

Houses of Refuge (1824–1898)
Wayward children were placed in facilities intended to reform them.

Aftercare (1840–Present)
As old as juvenile institutions, aftercare is the period after institutional release. Youths on aftercare are supervised by aftercare or parole officers.

Juvenile Courts (1899–Present)
Created in Cook County, Chicago, Illinois, and using *parens patriae* as a legal philosophy, this court handles all illegal behaviors among juveniles.

Probation (1878–Present)
Supervised youthful offenders in the community. Began in Massachusetts and spread throughout the nation.

1600   1700   1800   1900   2000

What Are the Historical Themes of Juvenile Justice?

The roots of today's juvenile justice extend back through the European experience and the norms and values of agricultural societies. As societies change socially, technologically, and economically, from nomadic communities to agricultural societies, from villages to cities, from feudal systems to industrialized societies and into the "postindustrial" world, their structures change as do their citizens' assumptions and perceptions about youths, their roles, and motivations. Of concern in all societies is what causes misbehavior on the part of youths and what should be done to solve the problem. Some of the major themes that run through this history include discovering the child, the rising power of the state, reform and retrenchment, the get-tough and go-slow approaches, the threat of the dangerous poor, and the unsolvable nature of youth crime.

Discovering the Child

The background of juvenile justice illustrates well the difficulties societies faced in defining children and their place in society. For most of history, the special needs of juveniles were never considered, with the possible exception of children ages two and under in the earliest eras and under the age of seven later in history. Subsistence living in the earliest societies required children to take on whatever productive roles necessary to help their families and themselves survive. In some societies, children were looked upon as adults in miniature and were subject to the same punishments as were adults. Eventually, children were classified by whether they were under the age of seven, between seven and fourteen years of age, or fourteen and older. Members of society began to debate children's "age of responsibility" in considering the seriousness and extent of their undesirable behavior.

Increased Authority of the State

Ever since the colonial period, society has gradually *taken authority away from the family* and given it to the state for correcting the behavior of children. There is little reason to believe that the three-hundred-year-old legacy of taking authority away from the family is likely to change in the near future. Even if the state were receptive to relinquishing some of its power (all indicators point to the fact that the state wants to increase rather than decrease its power over citizens), the American family is under greater pressure now than ever before. Its mounting problems include high rates of divorce and single-parent families, alarming rates of abuse and neglect of children, problems with drug and alcohol abuse among both parents and children, and large numbers of adolescent and out-of-wedlock births.

Reform and Retrenchment

It is sometimes claimed that the history of juvenile justice has been a steady march toward more humane and enlightened conceptions of childhood and democracy, but a more reliable reading of history shows that a period of reform has inevitably led to a period of retrenchment.[22] To express this another way, the history of juvenile justice appears to go through cycles of reform and retrenchment. Thomas J. Bernard's *The Cycle of Juvenile Justice* is a perceptive analysis of what drives these cycles of reform and retrenchment. According to Bernard, a cycle begins when both juvenile officials and the general public believe that youth crime is at an exceptionally high level and that many harsh punishments are used but few lenient treatments exist for youthful offenders. In this context, many minor offenders avoid punishment because justice officials believe that harsh punishment will make them worse. A period of reform arrives when the solution is seen as introducing lenient treatments for youthful offenders.[23]

The period from the 1960s to the mid-1970s was characterized by a liberal agenda. This reform agenda emphasized the reduced use of training schools, the diversion of status offenders and minor offenders from the juvenile justice system, and the reform of the juvenile justice system.

The liberal agenda ended in the 1990s and was followed by a get-tough approach. One of the contributing causes of this shift from reform to repression was the failure of the reform agenda of the 1970s to address violent youth crime and repeat offenders. Thus, the inability of the reformers to provide meaningful programs and policies aimed at persistent and serious youth crime proved to be the Achilles heel of the reform process.[24] The get-tough approach continued into the 1980s. The main thrusts of the Reagan administration's crime control policy for juveniles were preventive detention, transfer of violent and repeat juvenile offenders to the adult court, mandatory and determinate sentences for serious and repeat juvenile offenders, increased long-term confinement for juveniles, and enforcement of the death penalty for juveniles who commit "brutal and senseless" murders.

The get-tough attitude toward youth crime led to a number of federal juvenile justice initiatives in the 1990s that went beyond those implemented in the 1980s. These initiatives consisted of (1) establishing curfews, (2) passing parental responsibility laws, (3) increasing efforts to combat street gangs, (4) moving toward graduated sanctions, (5) creating juvenile boot camps, (6) maintaining and strengthening current laws restricting juveniles' use of guns, (7) opening juvenile proceedings and records, (8) transferring juveniles to criminal or adult courts, and (9) expanding sentencing authority over juveniles. The popularity of the get-tough approach was reflected in the fact that in the 1990s nearly every state enacted legislation incorporating these federal initiatives into the social policy for handling juveniles.[25]

In sum, the cyclical relationship between reform and retrenchment in juvenile justice seems to hinge upon society's dissatisfaction with the ill-fated promises of reform, followed, a generation or two later, by rejection of retrenchment's lack of benevolence. Perhaps the key to this shift is that society and its policy makers want social order, but, at the same time, they want special treatment for children.

Get-Tough and Go-Soft Approaches

Although reform and retrenchment alternate as official policies for juvenile justice in this nation, the get-tough approach for serious juvenile offenders and the go-soft strategy for minor offenders and status offenders have characterized the sentencing practices of juvenile courts in recent decades. The **least-restrictive** (or go-soft) **approach** first became popular in the 1960s. When professionals and students became aware of the extent of youth crime, the negative impact of delinquency labels, and the criminogenic and violent nature of juvenile institutions, many of them began to reappraise what should be done with juvenile lawbreakers. Studies on hidden delinquency and middle-class lawbreaking also taught a valuable lesson—nearly all juveniles break the law, but only a few are caught.[26]

For these reasons, supporters of this approach urge a least-restrictive philosophy—do not do any more than necessary with youthful offenders. If possible, leave them alone.[27] If their offense is too serious to permit this course of action, use every available resource before placing them in detention or in institutions. Keeping status offenders (juveniles who run away, violate a curfew, are ungovernable at home, or are truant from school) out of the juvenile justice system is one of the predominant concerns of proponents of this philosophy. Providing juveniles with all the procedural safeguards given to adults is also a vital concern. Adherents, of course, urge the use of community resources in working with juvenile offenders, an approach believed by many to be the best for juvenile justice.

On the other end of the spectrum, however, juveniles who commit serious crimes or continue to break the law are presumed to deserve punishment rather than treatment because they possess free will and know what they are doing. Their delinquencies are viewed as purposeful activity resulting from rational decisions in which the pros and cons are weighed and the acts that promise the greatest potential gains are performed. See Figure 1–2 for three approaches to delinquency control.

Threat of the Dangerous Poor

Early in the history of this nation, crime was blamed on the poor, especially on those who were newcomers to America. The fact that these individuals came from different cultural, ethnic, and religious backgrounds also made them appear dangerous. It was reasoned that institutions were needed to protect society against the behavior of these so-called **dangerous poor**.

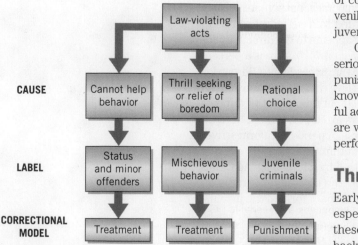

FIGURE 1–2
Three Approaches to Delinquency Control

Significantly, until the late nineteenth century, each succeeding wave of immigration that brought impoverished newcomers was perceived as threatening a new crime wave. Anthony Platt's classic work, *The Child Savers*, makes the point that the behaviors the child savers selected to be penalized—sexual license, roaming the streets, drinking, begging, fighting, frequenting dance halls and movies, and staying out late at night—were found primarily among lower-class children. From the very beginning, according to this interpretation, juvenile justice engaged in class favoritism that resulted in poor children being processed through the system while middle-class children were more likely to be excused.[28] The association of poverty with dangerousness has continued to the present day. It is expressed, especially, with the fear of violence and gang behaviors from African American and Hispanic underclass children.

The Unsolvable Nature of Youth Crime

The get-tough and go-soft policies illustrate that the United States has a history of seeking cure-alls to solve the crime problem. Unfortunately, no simple solution to this age-old problem exists. The search for a panacea began in the early nineteenth century—the Jacksonian period—when the young American nation was thought to have an unlimited capacity to solve its social problems.[29] The institutions that emerged to create better environments for deviants represented an attempt to promote the stability of society at a time when traditional ideas and practices seemed to be outmoded, constricted, and ineffective.

Legislators, philanthropists, and local officials were all convinced that the nation faced both unprecedented dangers and unprecedented opportunities. It was hoped that the penitentiary for adults and the house of refuge for juveniles, as well as the almshouse for the poor, the orphan asylum, and the insane asylum, would restore a necessary balance to the new republic and, at the same time, eliminate long-standing problems. The fact that these institutions eventually came to be viewed as failures did not prevent another generation of reformers from seeking new ways to cure the crime problem.[30] Table 1–1 summarizes the historical themes of juvenile justice.

TABLE 1–1
Historical Themes of Juvenile Justice

Theme	What Has Taken Place in Society	Effects on Juvenile Justice
Discovering the Child	Society began the process of defining children and their place in society	Enabled the development of the juvenile system, where juveniles would be treated differently than adults
Increased Authority of the state	Society took authority away from the family and gave it to the state	With the development of the juvenile court and its *parens patriae* philosophy, the state assumed authority over juveniles
Reform and Retrenchment	Society changed its mind about the juvenile justice system depending upon which cycle of reform and retrenchment currently seemed effective	Juvenile justice appears to go through cycles of reform and retrenchment
Get-Tough and Go-Soft Approaches	Society is apt to excuse the behavior of minor forms of delinquency and to desire punishment for serious forms	The juvenile justice system likewise excuses or punishes depending on the seriousness of delinquent acts
Threat of the Dangerous Poor	Beginning with immigration, certain groups are perceived as the dangerous class	African Americans and Hispanic children are more likely to be given this label
Unsolvable Nature of Youth Crime	Society has long pursued solutions to both juvenile and adult crime	No panacea has been found

What Are the Juvenile Justice Agencies and Functions?

The Constitution of the United States gives both the federal government and the states the authority to draw up laws and the mechanisms for enforcing those laws. The primary laws with which this book is concerned are laws governing delinquent and criminal behaviors and the three subsystems—the police, the courts, and correction departments—that carry out the mandates of the laws.

These three subsystems have between ten thousand and twenty thousand public and private agencies, with annual budgets totaling hundreds of millions of dollars. Many of the forty thousand police departments have juvenile divisions, and more than three thousand juvenile courts and about one thousand juvenile correctional facilities exist across the nation. More than thirty thousand of the fifty thousand employees in the juvenile justice system are employed in juvenile correctional facilities; sixty-five hundred are juvenile probation officers, and the remainder are aftercare officers and residential staff in community-based programs. Several thousand more employees work in diversion programs and privately administered juvenile justice programs.[31]

The Police

The functions of the three subsystems are somewhat different. The basic responsibilities of the police consist of enforcing the law and maintaining order. The law enforcement function requires that the police deter crime, make arrests, obtain confessions, collect evidence for strong cases that can result in convictions, and increase crime clearance rates. The maintenance of order function involves such tasks as settling family disputes, directing traffic, furnishing information to citizens, providing emergency ambulance service, preventing suicides, giving shelter to homeless persons and alcoholics, and checking the homes of families on vacation. Police–juvenile relations require the police to deal with juvenile lawbreaking and to provide services needed by juveniles.

The Juvenile Courts

The juvenile courts must dispose of cases referred to them by intake divisions of probation departments, make detention decisions, deal with child neglect and dependency cases, and monitor the performance of juveniles who have been adjudicated delinquent or status offenders. The *parens patriae* philosophy, which has undergirded the juvenile court since its founding at the end of the nineteenth century, charges that juvenile judges treat rather than punish juveniles appearing before them. This treatment arm of the juvenile court generally does not extend to those committing serious crimes or persisting in juvenile offenses, however; such hard-core juveniles may be sent to training schools or transferred to the adult court.

Correction Departments

The agency responsible for the care of juvenile offenders sentenced by the courts is called a variety of names—one of the more popular ones is the Department of Youth Services. Juvenile probation departments supervise offenders released to probation by the courts, ensuring that they comply with the courts' imposed conditions of probation and refrain from unlawful behavior in the community. Day treatment and residential programs have the responsibility of preparing juveniles for their return to the community.

Training schools have similar responsibilities, but the administrators of these programs are generally also charged with deciding when each juvenile is ready for institutional release and with ensuring that residents receive their constitutionally guaranteed due process rights. Aftercare officers are delegated the responsibility of supervising juveniles who have been released from training schools to ensure that they comply with the terms of their

FIGURE 1–3
Basic Subsystem of the Juvenile Justice System

Subsystem	Function
Police	Maintaining order and enforcing the law
Juvenile Court	Disposing of cases referred to them by intake divisions of probation departments, supervising juvenile probationers, making detention decisions, dealing with cases of child neglect and dependency, monitoring the performance of youths who have been adjudicated delinquent or status offenders
Corrections	Caring for youthful offenders sentenced by the courts, supervising offenders released to probation by the courts, and using day-treatment and residential programs, as well as short- and long-term juvenile facilities, to prepare youths for release to the community

aftercare agreements and avoid unlawful behavior. See Figure 1–3 for the basic subsystem of the juvenile justice system.

Juvenile justice agencies, because they have been developed by more than fifty state and federal government legislative bodies, do differ rather significantly across the nation. The structure of the juvenile court, as well as its administrative responsibilities, varies widely from one state to the next. Most juvenile probation departments emphasize restitution and community service programs as conditions of probation, but some provide intensive supervision programs and may even have house arrest and electronic monitoring programs. Some states hire private agencies to implement community-based programs, and most states are increasingly using private institutional placements for status offenders. Finally, a number of organizational structures are in use to administer juvenile correctional institutions and aftercare services.

Much similarity exists between the juvenile and adult justice systems. Both consist of three basic subsystems and interrelated agencies. The flow of justice in both is supposed to be from law violation to police apprehension, judicial process, judicial disposition, and rehabilitation in correctional agencies. The basic vocabulary is the same in the juvenile and adult systems, and even when the vocabulary differs, the intent remains the same.

The following terms refer to both the juvenile and adult systems:

An **adjudicatory hearing** is a trial that can result in a conviction.

Aftercare is parole.

A **commitment** is a sentence to confinement.

Detention is holding in jail.

A **dispositional hearing** is a sentencing hearing.

Juvenile court officer is a probation officer.

A **minor** is a defendant.

A **petition** is an indictment.

A **petitioner** is a prosecutor.

A **respondent** is a defense attorney.

Taking into custody is the act of **arresting** a suspect.

Both the juvenile and adult systems are under fire to get tough on crime, especially on offenders who commit violent crimes. Both must deal with excessive caseloads and institutional overcrowding, must operate on fiscal shoestrings, and face the ongoing problems of staff recruitment, training, and burnout. Focus on Practice 1–3 further describes the common ground and differences between the juvenile and adult justice systems.

Focus on Practice 1–3
Similarities and Differences Between the Juvenile and Adult Justice Systems

SIMILARITIES

- Police officers use discretion with both juvenile and adult offenders.
- Juvenile and adult offenders receive *Miranda* and other constitutional rights at time of arrest.
- Juveniles and adults can be placed in pretrial facilities.
- The juvenile court and the adult court use proof beyond a reasonable doubt as the standard for evidence, except when a juvenile court hears matters such as status offenses, beyond a reasonable doubt is not required.
- Plea bargaining may be used with both juvenile and adult offenders.
- Convicted juvenile and adult offenders may be sentenced to probation services, residential programs, or institutional facilities.
- Boot camps are used with juvenile and adult offenders.
- Released institutional juvenile and adult offenders may be assigned to supervision in the community.

DIFFERENCES

- Juveniles can be arrested for acts that would not be criminal if they were adults (status offenders).

- Age determines the jurisdiction of the juvenile court; age does not affect the jurisdiction of the adult court.
- Parents are deeply involved in the juvenile process but not in the adult process.
- Juvenile court proceedings are more informal, whereas adult court proceedings are formal and open to the public.
- Juvenile court proceedings, unlike adult proceedings, are not considered criminal; juvenile records are generally sealed when the age of majority is reached. Adult records are permanent.
- Juvenile courts cannot sentence juveniles to jail or prison; only adult courts may issue such sentences.

CRITICAL THINKING QUESTIONS

How much harm would it do to juveniles if juvenile proceedings were abolished and juveniles were handled in adult court? What would the advantages be to juvenile offenders if they were handled with adult proceedings and procedures?

How Are Juvenile Offenders Processed?

The means by which juvenile offenders are processed by juvenile justice agencies are examined throughout this text. The variations in the juvenile justice systems across the nation make describing this process difficult. The process begins when the youth is referred to the juvenile court; some jurisdictions permit a variety of agents to refer the juvenile, whereas others charge the police with this responsibility. The more common procedure is that the youth whose alleged offense has already been investigated is taken into custody by the police officer who has made the decision to refer the juvenile to the juvenile court. After adjudication, a youth is placed in juvenile detention or moved out of detention and into probation, residential placement, or the adult system, and then released (see Figure 1–4).

The intake officer, usually a probation officer, must decide whether the juvenile should remain in the community or be placed in a shelter or detention facility. A variety of options exist for determining what to do with the youth, but in more serious cases, the juvenile generally receives a petition to appear before the juvenile court.

The juvenile court judge, or the referee in many jurisdictions, hears the cases of those juveniles referred to the court. The transfer of a juvenile to the adult court must be done before any juvenile proceedings take place. Otherwise, an adjudicatory hearing, the primary purpose of which is to determine whether the juvenile is guilty of the delinquent acts alleged in the petition, takes place. The court hears evidence on these allegations. The *In re Gault* case (see Chapter 6) usually guarantees to juveniles the right to representation by counsel, freedom from self incrimination, the right to confront witnesses, and the right to cross-examine witnesses. Some states also give juveniles the right to a jury trial.

A disposition hearing takes place when a juvenile has been found delinquent in the adjudicatory stage. Most juvenile court codes now require that the adjudicatory and disposition hearings be held at different times. The number of dispositions juvenile judges have available to them varies from one jurisdiction to the next. In addition to the standard dispositions of warning and release, placement on juvenile probation, or adjudication to the department of youth services or corrections, some judges can place juveniles in a publicly or privately

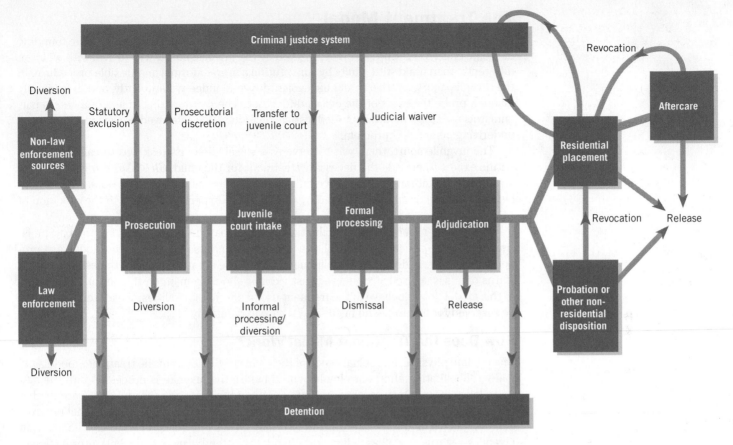

FIGURE 1–4

The Stages of Delinquency Case Processing in the Juvenile Justice System

Note: This chart gives a simplified view of case flow through the juvenile justice system. Procedures vary among jurisdictions.

Source: Howard N. Snyder and Melissa Sickmund, *Juvenile Offenders and Victims: 2006 National Report* (Washington, DC: Office of Juvenile Justice and Delinquency Prevention, 2006), p. 105.

administered day treatment or residential program. Some jurisdictions even grant juvenile judges the authority to send a juvenile to a particular correctional facility.

A juvenile adjudicated to a training school is generally treated somewhat differently in small and large states. In small states with one training school for males and usually one for females, a youth adjudicated to a training school is usually sent directly to the appropriate school. But large states that have several facilities for males and perhaps more than one for females may send the youth to a classification, or diagnostic, center to determine the proper institutional placement. Training school residents currently are not confined for as long a period as they were in the past and are often released within a year. Institutional release takes place in a variety of ways, but a juvenile released from a training school is generally placed on aftercare status. To be released from this supervision, the juvenile must obey the rules of aftercare and must avoid unlawful behavior.

What Are the Most Widely Held Philosophies and Strategies on Correcting Juveniles?

Four basic correctional models exist in juvenile justice: the treatment model, the justice model, the crime control model, and the balanced and restorative justice model. These conflicting strategies handicap juvenile justice and are a major reason why no single policy or set of policies presently guides the handling of offenders. Indeed, nearly everyone has an opinion on what can be done to correct the behavior of law-violating youths; pet theories and folk remedies abound throughout society.

Voices of Delinquency: A Person of Great Promise

The Treatment Model

Parens patriae, the philosophical basis of the **treatment model**, emerged with the founding of the juvenile court. The state, represented by the juvenile court, was to deal with children differently than it did with adults by substituting a more informal and flexible procedure. In the juvenile court, a fatherly and benevolent juvenile judge would gently, and in a friendly manner, probe the roots of the child's difficulties. The court, acting in lieu of a child's parents, was to engage in individualized justice; delinquency was viewed as a symptom of some underlying personality problem.

The juvenile court, then, was to serve as a social clinic. Its task was to call up the scientific expert to provide the necessary treatment for the child. *Child-saving reformers*, a term used by Anthony Platt, were confident that the combination of *parens patriae* philosophy and the treatment provided by the scientific expert would lead to the salvation of wayward children.[32]

The treatment model, or rehabilitation model, is based on the belief that the basic mission of juvenile justice is to rehabilitate youthful offenders. The treatment model also proposes that the legal definition of delinquency should be broad and that victimless crimes and status offenses, as well as crimes against victims, should remain on the books. Proponents of this model do not believe in the frequent use of detention facilities; these facilities should be reserved for children who need special care and custody.

How Does the Treatment Model Work?

The mental, physical, and social needs of the child are the focus of the treatment model, and many rehabilitation efforts are implemented before the juvenile is processed into the system. Police officers may recommend community programs to youths and their parents that help youths in need with their specific problems. Intake officers, probation officers, prosecutors, judges, and aftercare officers also may either informally or formally request that juveniles—status as well as delinquent offenders—attend drug and alcohol, tutoring, anger management, and other after-school programs; youths who are institutionalized also often receive drug and alcohol, sexual offending, and other treatment modalities. The treatment model encountered considerable criticism in the late twentieth century, but it is experiencing a resurgence of research and interest in the early twenty-first century.

The Justice Model

The *parens patriae* philosophy has been challenged by due process philosophy since the very founding of the juvenile court. Those promoting the due process approach wanted to give juveniles better protection through due process provisions and procedural safeguards. In the 1970s, proponents of due process were troubled by the contradictions of juvenile justice philosophy and by the inequities and inadequacies of juvenile justice law, policy, and practice.[33] These reformers turned to David Fogel's **justice model** and its concept of **just deserts**. Fogel believes that both juvenile and adult offenders are volitional and responsible human beings and, consequently, deserve to be punished if they violate the law. The punishment they receive, however, must be proportionate to the seriousness of the offense. Fogel also proposed the end of the indeterminate sentence and parole, the initiation of uniform sentencing, and the establishment of correctional programming based solely on the compliance of inmates.[34] Fogel reasons, "If we cannot coercively treat with reliability, we can at least be fair, reasonable, humane, and constitutional in practice."[35]

How Does the Justice Model Work?

Proponents of the justice model are now advocating a number of changes to bring more fairness to juvenile justice:

- Limit the enormous discretion granted to juvenile justice practitioners.
- Divert increasing numbers of youthful offenders from the justice system to voluntary services.
- Remedy common deficiencies in due process to ensure greater fairness in the transactions among the justice system, the family, and the juvenile offender.

- Curb indeterminate sentencing practices of juvenile courts and give juveniles a fixed sentence by the court at the time of disposition.
- Decriminalize status offenses.
- Change the governing principle of sentencing to one of *proportionality*, which means that there must be a relationship between the seriousness of the offense committed and the severity of the sanction imposed.
- Make training schools safer and more humane.
- Allow programs offered in training schools to be voluntary in nature and to have nothing to do with the release of a youth.
- Require restitution and community service sanctions of more juvenile lawbreakers; these sanctions have the potential for fairness because they give youthful offenders opportunities to atone or make amends for the damage or harm they have inflicted on others.[36]

The mandatory sentencing law for violent juvenile offenders in the state of New York, the determinate sentencing law for juveniles in the state of Washington, and the institutional release policy adopted in the state of Minnesota are other indicators of the national acceptance of the justice model.

The Crime Control Model

The **crime control model** emphasizes punishment as the remedy for juvenile misbehavior. Punishment philosophy actually originated well before the eighteenth century, but it gained popularity in the 1970s because of the assumed rise of youth crime. Although this approach has had different connotations at various times, supporters today maintain that punishment is beneficial because it is educative and moral. Offenders are taught not to commit further crimes, whereas noncriminal citizenry receive a demonstration of what happens to a person who breaks the law; punishment, proponents believe, deters crime.

The supporters of punishment philosophy claim that the juvenile court has abandoned punishment in favor of individual rehabilitation. They argue for severity and certainty of punishment and advocate a greater use of incarceration. Other fundamental assumptions of punishment philosophy propose that those who become involved in unlawful behavior are abnormal and few in number; that this unlawful behavior reflects a character defect that punishment can correct; that punishment can be helpful in teaching a youth to be responsible, diligent, and honest; and that the deterrence of youth crime depends on the juvenile justice system apprehending and punishing youthful offenders with greater speed, efficiency, and certainty.

How Does the Crime Control Model Work?

The crime control model holds that the first priority of justice should be to protect the life and property of the innocent. Accordingly, proponents of this model support the police and are quick to isolate juvenile offenders, especially those who have committed serious crimes, in detention homes, jails, and training schools. The increased use of transfers to adult court and the adoption of mandatory sentencing laws specifying extended confinements for serious crimes are recent crime control policies. Many states are now using a combination of the crime control and justice models to deal with violent and hard-core juvenile offenders.

The Balanced and Restorative Justice Model

A traditional New Zealand approach to juvenile offending, the **balanced and restorative justice model**, is rapidly expanding throughout the United States and, indeed, throughout the world. "Balanced" refers to system-level decision making by administrators to "ensure that resources are allocated equally among efforts to ensure accountability to crime victims, to increase competency in offenders, and to enhance community safety." These three goals are summarized in the terms *accountability*, *competency*, and *community protection*.[37]

Accountability refers to a sanctioning process in which offenders must accept responsibility for their offenses and the harm caused to victims, and make restitution to the

Focus on Practice 1–4
Balanced and Restorative Justice Model

Restorative Justice intervention includes a wide array of programs and practices that may be applied at virtually any point in the juvenile justice process, or in the community.

Objective/Focus	Practice	Location
Conflict resolution; prevention; peacemaking	Community mediation; alternative dispute resolution, school and neighborhood conferencing; victim awareness education; youth development	Schools; neighborhoods; churches; civic groups
Provide decision-making alternatives to formal court or other adversarial process for determining obligations for repairing harm	Victim offender dialog; family group conferencing circles; reparation boards: other restorative conferencing	Police and community diversion; court diversion; dispositional/sentencing alternatives; post-dispositional planning; residential alternative discipline; conflict resolution; post-residential reentry
Victim and community input to court or formal decision making	Written or oral impact statement to court or other entity	Court; probation; residential
Provide reparative sanctions or obligation in response to crime or harmful behavior	Restitution, community service to victims, and payment to victims service funds.	Diversion; court sanction; probation condition; residential program; post-incarceration
Offender treatment; rehabilitation; education	Victim impact panels; victim awareness education; Mothers Against Drunk Driving panels; community service learning project designed to build offender competency and strengthen relationships with law-abiding citizens	Probation; residential facilities; diversion program; jails
Victim services and support groups	Counseling; volunteer support groups; faith community groups	Multiple settings
Community building	Family support and discussion groups	Neighborhood and community

Source: Gordon Bazemore, Jay S. Zaslaw, and Danielle Riester, "Behind the Walls and Beyond: Restorative Justice, Instrumental Communities, and Effective Residential Treatment," *Juvenile and Family Court* (Winter 2005), p. 58.

victims, assuming that community members are satisfied with the outcome. *Competency* refers to the rehabilitation of offenders, that is, when offenders improve their educational, vocational, emotional, social, and other capabilities and can perform as responsible adults in the community. *Community protection* refers to the ability of citizens to prevent crime, resolve conflict, and feel safe because offenders have matured into responsible citizens. Subsequently, the overall mission of the balanced and restorative justice model is to develop a community-oriented approach to the control of offenders rather than rely solely either on punishment by confinement or on individual rehabilitation through counseling. The juvenile justice system, in implementing this model, meets the needs of the community, the victim, and the offender in the most cost-effective manner possible. See Focus on Practice 1–4 for the objective, practice, and location of the balanced and restorative justice model.

How Does the Balanced and Restorative Justice Model Work?

This approach is an alternative to processing youths through the juvenile justice systems of their communities. Once a juvenile is identified as being a perpetrator of a delinquent act, a police officer, probation officer, community volunteer, or other designated person initiates the restorative process. The victim, the offender, the offender's family, a law enforcement representative, or a volunteer brings all the parties together to begin discussing the problem at hand.

This model, in other words, calls for a new framework of community organization and a restructuring of practitioner roles throughout the juvenile justice system. It calls for a new set of values that emphasize a commitment to all—the offender, the victim, and the community. Importantly, offenders are viewed as clients whose crime is a symptom of family breakdown, community disorganization, and community conflict, and these problems must be addressed if juvenile crime is to be reduced.

Comparison of the Four Models

The treatment model, or rehabilitation model, is most concerned that juvenile offenders receive therapy rather than institutionalization. The crime control model emphasizes punishment because it argues that juveniles must pay for their crimes. Proponents of this model support long-term, rather than short-term, confinements for juvenile offenders. The justice model strongly supports the granting of procedural safeguards and fairness to juveniles who have broken the law. Yet proponents of this model also believe that the punishment of juveniles should be proportionate to the gravity of their crimes. The balanced and restorative justice model also contends that juveniles have free will and know what they are doing and, therefore, should receive punishment for their antisocial behavior. The advantages of this model, according to its proponents, are that it includes the punishment approach of the crime control and justice models, supports the due process emphasis of the justice model, and places consequences on behavior to encourage juveniles to become more receptive to treatment.

Each of the models has supporters. The crime control model, or the hard line, is used with violent and repetitive juvenile offenders. The treatment model, or the soft line, is primarily used with status offenders and minor offenders. Some jurisdictions show support for the justice model in juvenile justice, but the balanced and restorative justice model is making the most extensive advances. Nevertheless, on a day-to-day basis, juvenile justice practitioners continue to pick and choose from each of the four models in designing how they work with juvenile offenders. These conflicting approaches, as well as the intolerance of those who follow a different course of action, create inefficiency and confusion in juvenile justice. Table 1–2 compares the key elements of the rehabilitation, justice, balanced and restorative, and crime control models.

TABLE 1–2
Comparison of Key Elements of the Rehabilitation, Justice, Balanced and Restorative, and Crime Control Models

	Models			
Elements	**Rehabilitation**	**Justice**	**Crime Control**	**Balanced and Restorative**
Theory of why delinquents offend	Behavior is caused or determined; based on positivism	Free will; based on the classical school	Free will; based on the classical school	Free will; based on the classical school
Purpose of sentencing	Change in behavior or attitude	Justice	Restoration of law and order	Community protection
Type of sentencing advocated	Indeterminate	Determinate	Determinate	Determinate
View of treatment	Goal of correctional process	Voluntary but necessary in a humane system	Ineffective and actually coddles offenders	Voluntary but necessary in a humane system
Crime control strategy	Use therapeutic intervention to eliminate factors causing crime	Provide fairness for victims, for offenders, and for practitioners in the system	Declare war on youth crime by instituting "get-tough" policies	Make juvenile offenders accountable for their behavior

Juvenile Justice Videos

KIDS TODAY

Kids Today focuses on the goals of the juvenile court and the ideology of working in the best interests of juvenile delinquents as well as juvenile victims. Based on the video and the readings from this chapter, discuss how the early juvenile justice system differs from the evolved juvenile justice system of today. How are the two systems similar? How does focusing on the best interest of the child impact the juvenile justice system? What are the pros and cons of this approach?

AT A GLANCE: THE JUVENILE JUSTICE PROCESS

At a Glance depicts a youth offender starting through the juvenile justice system beginning with the intake process. Based on the readings in this chapter, discuss which steps of the justice system are present in the video. How are these processes designed to protect the rights of the child while also reaching the goals of the court? Are these processes established by *parens patriae*? Why or why not?

SUMMARY

LEARNING OBJECTIVE 1 Retrace the journey of juvenile justice in the United States.

- The influences affecting the juvenile justice system can be traced back to the Middle Ages.

- The common law tradition in England eventually concluded that children under age seven should not face legal penalties.

- However, the responsibility of children between ages seven and fourteen was determined by such considerations as the severity of the crime, maturity, capacity to distinguish between right and wrong, and evidence of blatant malice.

- The family was the source and primary means of social control of children in the colonial period.

- The concept of *parens patriae* gave the courts a legal basis for intervening in the lives of children.

- The premises of the *parens patriae* doctrine permitted the juvenile court to take charge of children in need so that the causes of their problems could be discovered and treated.

- The juvenile courts had to develop different procedures and terminology from those of the adult courts to achieve their goals.

- The attractiveness of the juvenile court philosophy resulted in almost all states setting up juvenile courts.

- Juvenile confinement goes back to the nineteenth century, when houses of refuge were established to separate juveniles from adult offenders in jails and prisons.

- The cottage system, in which residents were housed in separate buildings, usually included no more than twenty to forty juveniles per cottage.

- Later nineteenth-century juvenile institutions were called *reformatories* or *industrial schools.*

- Probation and aftercare were also early developments of juvenile justice; their focus was on treating youthful offenders in the community.

LEARNING OBJECTIVE 2 Explain the concept of *parens patriae*.

The Cook County Juvenile Court was founded in 1899. Its premises were that the *parens patriae* doctrine permitted it to take charge of children in need, that the causes of the children's problems could be discovered and treated, and that the court had to develop a different set of procedures and terminology from those of the adult courts to achieve these goals.

LEARNING OBJECTIVE 3 Summarize the historical themes that guided the development of juvenile justice in the United States.

The historical themes of juvenile justice include discovering the child, increased authority of the state, reform and retrenchment, get-tough and go-soft approaches, threat of the dangerous poor, and the unsolvable nature of youth crime.

LEARNING OBJECTIVE 4 Present the structure and procedures of juvenile justice agencies in this nation.

- The juvenile justice system has been given the mandate to correct and control youthful offenders. The U.S. Constitution gives both the federal government and the states the authority to make laws and the mechanisms for enforcing the law. The primary laws with which this book is concerned are laws governing delinquent and criminal behaviors in the three subsystems—the police, the courts, and correction departments—that carry out the mandates of the laws.

- The juvenile is typically referred to the juvenile court, which first decides whether to leave the juvenile in the system or not. The juvenile court decides in what is called an adjudicatory hearing whether the juvenile is guilty of the delinquent acts alleged in the petition. A disposition hearing takes place when a juvenile has been found delinquent in the adjudicatory stage. A delinquent youth might be referred to probation or one of the residential programs in the community or might be referred to a training school.

LEARNING OBJECTIVE 5 Examine the various philosophies and strategies for correcting juvenile offenders.

- The treatment model is most concerned that juvenile offenders receive therapy rather than institutionalization.

- The justice model supports the granting of procedural safeguards and fairness to juveniles who have broken the law.

- The crime control model emphasizes punishment because it argues that juveniles must pay for their crimes. The crime control policies of the past twenty years have proposed a get-tough strategy, especially with violent juveniles.

- The balanced and restorative justice model called for a new framework of community organization and a new set of values that emphasizes a commitment to all—the offender, the victim, and the community.

- The conflicting philosophies and methods of correcting juvenile offenders make it difficult to succeed in correcting juveniles in trouble.

KEY TERMS

adjudicatory hearing, p. 15	dangerous poor, p. 12	*parens patriae*, p. 2
aftercare, p. 15	detention, p. 15	parole, p. 10
aftercare officers, p. 4	dispositional hearing, p. 15	petition, p. 15
approach, p. 12	house of refuge, p. 7	petitioner, p. 15
arrest, p. 15	just deserts, p. 18	positivist, p. 5
balanced and restorative justice model, p. 19	justice model, p. 18	respondent, p. 15
commitment, p. 15	juvenile court officer, p. 15	status offenders, p. 2
cottage system, p. 8	least-restrictive approach, p. 12	taking into custody, p. 15
crime control model, p. 19	minor, p. 15	treatment model p. 18

GROUP EXERCISES

1. Write a single paragraph describing each of the following: the history of the juvenile court, probation, juvenile confinement, and aftercare. Critique and revise.
2. *Group Work:* Describe each of the juvenile justice agencies and their functions.
3. *Class Debate:* Divide the class into four groups. Each group will be assigned one of the four models found in juvenile justice today. Each group should learn its essentials and argue for its model as being the best model for the United States today. Groups may not compromise in the defense of their models.

REVIEW QUESTIONS

1. The juvenile justice system has devised four ways to deal with youth crime: the treatment model, the justice model, the crime control model, and the balanced and restorative justice model. Which do you think works the best? Why?
2. Why is justice so important to the juvenile justice system? How can the juvenile justice system become more just, fair, and effective?
3. What do you believe can be done about reconciling the different approaches to juvenile justice?
4. What do you think would be the result of abolishing the juvenile justice system and having the adult courts deal with all youthful offenders?

NOTES

1. Mark W. Lipsey, James C. Howell, Marion R. Kelly, Gabrielle Chapman, and Darin Carver, *Improving the Effectiveness of Juvenile Justice Programs: A New Perspective on Evidence-Based Practice* (Washington, DC: Georgetown University, Center for Juvenile Justice Reform, 2010).
2. Ibid., 1.
3. S. Mihalic, K. Irwin, D. Elliott, A. Fagan, and D. Hansen, *Blueprints for Violence Prevention* (Washington, DC: U.S. Department of Justice, Office of Justice Programs, Office of Juvenile Justice and Delinquency Prevention, 2001); Office of Juvenile Justice and Delinquency Prevention, *Model Programs Guide (MPG)*, http://www.ojjdp.gov/mgg; and

Substance Abuse and Mental Health Services Administration, *SAMHSA Bulletin: National Registry of Evidence-Based Programs and Practices* (Washington, DC: SAMHSA, 2009).

4. Leon Radzinowicz, *A History of English Criminal Law and Its Administration from 1750–1833* (London: Stevens and Sons, 1948), 14.

5. David Rothman, *The Discovery of the Asylum* (Boston: Little, Brown, 1971), 46–53.

6. Ibid.

7. Anthony M. Platt, *The Child Savers* (Chicago: University of Chicago Press, 1969), 121–36.

8. Ibid.

9. Ibid., 98.

10. Sanford J. Fox, "Juvenile Justice Reform: An Historical Perspective," *Stanford Law Review* 22, no. 6 (June 1970), 1187–239.

11. Rothman, *The Discovery of the Asylum.* See also Barbara M. Brenzel, *Daughters of the State* (Cambridge, MA: MIT Press, 1983) and Alexander W. Pisciotta, "Treatment on Trial: The Rhetoric and Reality of the New York House of Refuge, 1857–1935," *American Journal of Legal History* 29 (1985), 151–81.

12. Rothman, *The Discovery of the Asylum*, 53–54. For the origins of juvenile justice in California, see Daniel Macallair, "The San Francisco Industrial School and the Origins of Juvenile Justice in California: A Glance at the Great Reformation," *UC Davis Journal of Juvenile Law & Policy* 7 (Winter 2003), 1–60.

13. Hutchins Hapgood, *Autobiography of a Thief* (New York: Fox, Duffield, 1903), 71–72.

14. National Conference of Superintendents of Training Schools and Reformatories, *Institutional Rehabilitation of Delinquent Youth: Manual for Training School Personnel* (Albany, NY: Delmar, 1962).

15. For this same tendency in the State Industrial School for Girls in Lancaster, Massachusetts, see Brenzel, *Daughters of the State.*

16. John Augustus, *John Augustus: First Probation Officer* (Montclair, NJ: Patterson-Smith Company, 1972), 4–5.

17. Board of State Charities of Massachusetts, *Sixth Annual Report, 1869,* 269.

18. Robert M. Mennel, *Thorns and Thistles* (Hanover: University of New Hampshire Press, 1973), 140.

19. Homer Folks, "Juvenile Probation," *NCCD Proceedings, 1906,* 117–22.

20. Mennel, *Thorns and Thistles,* 142.

21. Frederick Howard Wines, *Punishment and Reformation: Rise of the Penitentiary System* (Boston: Thomas Y. Crowell, 1985), 222.

22. Barry Krisberg and James Austin, *The Children of Ishmael: Critical Perspectives on Juvenile Justice* (Palo Alto, CA: Mayfield, 1978), 569.

23. Thomas J. Bernard, *The Cycle of Juvenile Justice* (New York: Oxford University Press, 1992), 3.

24. Barry Krisberg et al., "The Watershed of Juvenile Justice Reform," *Crime and Delinquency* 32 (January 1986), 40.

25. National Crime Justice Association, *Juvenile Justice Reform Initiatives in the States, 1994–1996* (Washington, DC: Office of Juvenile Justice and Delinquency Prevention, 1997), 9.

26. See David Matza, *Delinquency and Drift* (New York: Wiley, 1964); Edwin M. Schur, *Radical Non-Intervention: Rethinking the Delinquency Problem* (Upper Saddle River, NJ: Prentice Hall, 1973).

27. Schur, *Radical Non-Intervention.*

28. Platt, *The Child Savers.*

29. Rothman, *The Discovery of the Asylum*, 78.

30. Ibid.

31. *Sourcebook of Criminal Justice Statistics—2009* (Washington, DC: Bureau of Justice Statistics, 2010).

32. Anthony M. Platt, *The Child Savers*, 2d ed. (Chicago: University of Chicago Press, 1977).

33. Charles Shireman, "The Juvenile Justice System: Structure, Problems and Prospects," in *Justice as Fairness,* edited by David Fogel and Joe Hudson (Cincinnati: W. H. Anderson, 1981), 136–41.

34. David Fogel, *"… We Are the Living Proof …": The Justice Model for Corrections* (Cincinnati: W. H. Anderson, 1975).

35. Fogel, "Preface," in *Justice as Fairness,* viii.

36. Adapted from Shireman, "The Juvenile Justice System."

37. Adapted from D. Maloney, D. Romig, and T. Armstrong, "Juvenile Probation: The Balanced Approach," *Juvenile and Family Court Journal* 39 (1988), 5; G. Bazemore, "On Mission Statements and Reform in Juvenile Justice: The Case for the Balanced Approach," *Federal Probation* 56 (1992), 64–70. G. Bazemore, "What's 'New' about the Balanced Approach?" *Juvenile and Family Court Journal* 48 (1997), 2, 3.

The National Assessment of Delinquency and Victimization

Karramba Production/Shutterstock

Learning Objectives

1. Identify the different methods juvenile crime data is categorized, measured, and reported.
2. Summarize juvenile crime rates and trends.
3. Summarize juvenile victimization, including school violence.
4. Describe the limitations and problems of measuring juvenile crime.
5. Describe the factors that lead to career escalation and/or a transition to adult crime.

The data collected by police departments, victimization surveys, self-report studies, and by governmental agencies such as the National Center for Juvenile Justice, National Center for Educational Statistics and university and private foundations have some good strengths and provide us with some very good knowledge, particularly at the national level.

But one of the problems with a number of those sources is where the data comes from. Some comes from surveys and some from the police. That is ok, but much of it is at the national level, which is helpful, and they do give us sort of overall depictions of a phenomenon over time. That, I think, is really important and I think will continue to be important.

There are, however, other weaknesses in that type of data. For example, the Uniform Crime Reports don't allow us to look very closely at individual characteristics of cities— and much crime is local. As a result, you don't get enough in-depth information to really understand what's going on at the local level. Similarly, survey data can tell us how many people do such-and-such but the data aren't nuanced enough to understand things at the individual level. In other words, would this individual be so inclined to do this as opposed to another individual? Why would girls do this as opposed to boys? We need to understand local contexts and individual performers. In neighborhoods, for example, we need to know not just how many people live there, but the type of movement in and out of the neighborhood.

You don't know how many properties are abandoned and how that occurred; you don't know how many people know each other on those blocks or how many people are moving in and out. How many people know each other and as a result have some sort of control over their neighborhood? How many people really do care about their neighborhoods?

You don't find that kind of information in any of the national databases. Survey data might indicate that a sexually assaulted victim is a 15-year-old girl from a single-parent household. But we also don't know what the resilient factors are in this individual girl that protect her from becoming delinquent, even though those are high predictors of delinquency. We also don't know whether she's got a close friend outside the family who's a good mentor or a good influence who might be an extraordinary support person.

The family could be single parent and a great parent at that. The sexual assault may have been once out on the street, and has no relationship to what the family was. The family may be a very resilient family for this girl. You can't really understand the individual very well by just looking at survey data and we've relied a lot on survey data.

—Margaret A. Zahn[1]

The chapter-opening quote from Margaret A. Zahn, one of the most highly respected researchers in juvenile justice, is a reminder that all statistical measurements of crime have strengths and weaknesses. After pointing out the weaknesses of each type of measurement, she draws the conclusion that one of the serious problems is the difficulty of obtaining accurate information about the people involved in crime. A simple enumeration of the data is interesting and sometimes illuminating, but it is often notable for the information *not* conveyed.

A responsible researcher must make use of many different sources of data to understand fully the crime problem. Nowhere is this more true than with respect to juvenile crime. Debates persist over what juvenile crime is and should be, where the causes of crime originate, and what special issues, such as gangs, drugs, guns, and schools, concern juveniles. The result is that many different sources of information are available today to provide us with insights into juvenile misbehaviors. All sources must be studied, their strengths and weaknesses analyzed, and their contributions to understanding stated clearly.

Our understanding starts with distinguishing between juveniles who are **status offenders** and juveniles who are **delinquent offenders**. Early juvenile courts did not make this distinction, as all youths coming before them were considered in need of care. Today, however, abused and neglected youths, and those who are incorrigible, run away, talk back to their parents, smoke cigarettes, and engage in other behaviors for which adults would not be arrested are called *status offenders*; society is not quite certain what to do with these youths, but more and more frequently, they are kept out of the juvenile justice system. On the other hand, youths who commit crimes such as murder, robbery, burglary, auto theft, and other serious crimes for which they can be arrested the same way as adults can are considered *delinquents*. This chapter and book focus primarily on delinquents, but we also consider the plight of status offenders, for many still end up behind bars with delinquents and, sometimes, with adult felons.

The purpose of this chapter is to unmask the amount, the nature, and the extent of juvenile lawbreaking in the United States. Official juvenile lawbreaking is youthful misbehavior violating the legal norms of society that comes to the attention of justice authorities and is recorded. Unofficial juvenile lawbreaking is youthful misbehavior that does not result in youths' names or behaviors being recorded in official records; these youths are handled informally by those in the justice system.

The various studies on officially undetected delinquency find that adolescents should not be divided into offenders and nonoffenders, because the majority of youths occasionally commit minor offenses.[2] The evidence, in fact, suggests that the youth who never violates the law is a rarity. Some are minor offenders, some break the law regularly, a few commit violent or predatory crimes, and a few support themselves through crime and are committed to crime as a way of life.[3] Studies also demonstrate that the victims of crime frequently are juveniles. Whether minority or white, male or female, infant or adolescent, the very young often carry their histories with them throughout life, often in the form of permanent brain damage, brain function disruption, or brain rewiring.

In this chapter, we identify the main tools used to measure juvenile crime, and we discuss the problems with these statistical approaches. Finally, we examine juvenile victims and address the dimensions of law-violating behavior.

The Measurement of Juvenile Crime

Juveniles are studied by a wide variety of agencies. Traditionally, the **Uniform Crime Reports**, collated by the Federal Bureau of Investigation (FBI), were known as **official statistics** and were the primary source of our knowledge. Today, these data are referred to as the CIUS or *Crime in the United States*. During the past seventy-five years, however, many more data collection sources have been developed that contribute to our knowledge of juveniles and their problems. **Juvenile Court Statistics** were developed to show what happens to juveniles who come to the attention of authorities. Victimization surveys focus on "hidden" or non-reported crime. Other governmental agencies such as the National Center for Education Statistics, the National Clearinghouse on Child Abuse and Neglect, and the Office of Juvenile Justice and Delinquency Prevention also do research on juveniles. In addition, research funded by federal and state governments and private foundations takes place in private research institutes and in universities and hospitals across the nation. This chapter looks at these research efforts and their findings on children in trouble. Table 2–1 lists major sources of data about juvenile delinquency.

Uniform Crime Reports

The *Uniform Crime Reports*, the statistics of which now are called the CIUS, have been our major source of information since 1930 on the amount of crime in the United States. In an effort to better understand the nature and extent of crime, the International Association of Chiefs of Police recommended that national crime statistics be collected and reported. The FBI was chosen as the clearinghouse for these data, and police departments across the United States were requested to report all arrests to the FBI. This information is currently published by the FBI on both a quarterly and a yearly basis and is probably the most popular of all the crime statistics. Reports of offenses, however, are not always sent from the local police directly to the FBI. Some states have state reporting agencies; the local police report to the state agency, which, in turn, reports to the FBI.

The UCRs classify crimes into Part I and Part II offenses. This classification is used to differentiate very serious from less serious crimes for the purpose of national statistics.

TABLE 2–1
Major Sources of Data About Delinquency

Data Source	Sponsoring Agency	Type of Information	General Findings
Uniform Crime Reports program *National Crime Victimization Study*	Federal Bureau of Investigation Statistics	Arrest Statistics Interview data	Youth crime is widespread in U.S. society. The number of victimization discovered is much higher than the number of offenses reported to the police.
Juvenile Court Statistics	Office of Juvenile Justice and Delinquency Prevention	Delinquency cases processed in juvenile courts	Most youths come into juvenile court as a result of the filing of a petition or complaint.
Self-report surveys	Universities/ academic researchers and crime	Individual self-report involvement in delinquency	A large amount of hidden delinquency occurs and is not reported to the police.

Part I offenses include murder, rape, aggravated assault, robbery, burglary, larceny, auto theft, and arson. Part II offenses include all crimes not listed as Part I, such as simple assaults; buying, receiving, and possessing stolen property; carrying and possessing weapons; fraud; forgery; and counterfeiting. All states classify these behaviors as crimes and call for their prosecution.

In addition to reporting arrest data, the UCRs provide data on the age, sex, and race of offenders, as well as on the amount of crime they commit. Information is available on whether the total amount of crime is increasing or decreasing, as well as on the amount of crime by size of city and by the gender and race of the offenders. In addition to the FBI, the Office of Juvenile Justice and Delinquency Prevention and the Bureau of Justice Statistics use these data in their analysis of juvenile crime.

The CIUS program examines the extent of juvenile crime; compares youth crime to adult crime; considers gender and rural variations in youth crime; and presents urban, suburban, and ruled differences in youth crime. Following are the chief findings of the CIUS 2010 data reporting on juveniles[4]:

1. Youth crime is widespread in U.S. society. For example, the CIUS 2010 data reveal that 1,288,615 juveniles under age eighteen were arrested that year. Youths between the ages of ten and seventeen constituted about 24 percent of the total population of the United States.[5] Of those arrested, 13.7 percent were arrested for violent crimes and 22.5 percent for property crimes.[6]

2. The percentages of total arrests involving juveniles are highest for curfew breaking, loitering, disorderly conduct, liquor law violations, drug abuse violations, vandalism, and larceny-theft.[7]

3. Juveniles are arrested for serious offenses as well. Juveniles were arrested for 22.7 percent of all burglaries, 24.1 percent of robberies, 19.8 percent of weapons offenses, 9.0 percent of murders, and 11.0 percent of aggravated assaults in 2010.[8]

4. Juvenile murder rates increased substantially between 1987 and 1993. In the peak year of 1993, approximately 3,800 juveniles were arrested for murder; between 1993 and 2003, however, juvenile arrests for murder declined, with the number of arrests in 2010 (627) representing a drop of 11.7 percent from 2001.[9]

5. Juvenile female arrests in 2010 represented 14.5 percent of all female arrests that year.[10]

▲ White Supremacists are potentially the most dangerous "home grown" terrorists in the United States. Many want to overthrow the U.S. Government.
Jerry Cavanaugh

6. Drug arrests increased by 3.7 percent from 2001 to 2010.[11] During these years, arrests for male drug offenses dropped 14.1 percent, while that for females increased 14.7 percent.[12]

7. According to these official statistics, between 2001 and 2010, for all offenses involving juveniles under the age of eighteen, youth crime trends declined 23.5. During these same years, the percentage of violent arrests declined 9.6 percent, but the percentage of property crimes increased 3.3 percent. Interestingly, motor vehicle thefts declined 48.3 percent between 2001 and 2010.[13]

Juvenile Court Statistics

Most information about the number of children appearing before the juvenile court each year comes from the *Juvenile Court Statistics* publication, released annually by the Office of Juvenile Justice and Delinquency Prevention, an arm of the U.S. Department of Justice. The number of children appearing before the juvenile court significantly increased from 1960 until the early 1980s, when it began to level off. It then started to rise again and continued to rise until the late 1980s, when it began to level off again. In 2009, juvenile courts in the United States handled an estimated 1,504,100 delinquency cases; 39 percent of these were property cases, 24 percent were person offenses, 27 percent were public order offenses, and 11 percent were drug offenses. The largest percentage of person offenses consisted of simple assaults, followed by aggravated assaults, and then robberies. Larceny-theft made up the largest number of property offenses, followed by burglary and vandalism; and obstruction of justice and disorderly conduct comprised the largest percentage of public order offenses.[14]

Juvenile Court Statistics 2009 describes what happens to the cases brought into the system. For example, 55 percent of the delinquency cases were petitioned. That is, these youths came into the juvenile court system as a result of someone filing a petition or issuing a complaint requesting the court to declare the youths delinquent or dependent or to transfer the youths to an adult court. In terms of nonpetitioned cases, 45 percent were informally handled cases in which authorized personnel for the court screened the cases prior to the filing of a formal petition and decided not to prosecute the offenders.[15] Figure 2–1 shows the case processing of delinquency cases in juvenile courts nationwide in 2009, and Figure 2–2 shows the general downward trend of offenses, especially property offenses from 1985 through 2009.[16]

A summary of the findings of the juvenile court statistics is as follows:

1. Older delinquents are referred to the court more often than are younger delinquents.

2. The number of cases appearing before the juvenile court increased until the mid-1970s, leveled off until the late 1980s, rose dramatically from the late 1980s to the mid-1990s, and then declined 11 percent to the 2008 level (see Figure 2–3).

3. Of status offenses, truancy and ungovernability rates peak at age sixteen, while liquor law violations increase continuously with age.

4. Males are more frequently referred to the juvenile court than are females.

5. Females are referred to juvenile court for truancy and ungovernability at about the same rate as males; across the board, female rates are increasing relative to male rates.

6. White males are referred to the juvenile court roughly in proportion to their numbers in the population; black males are referred to the juvenile court at rates highly disproportionate to their numbers in the population.

The findings of juvenile court statistics parallel those of the UCRs. The advantage of the court statistics, however, is that they reveal not only who the offenders are but also what types of dispositions are handed down. The juvenile court statistics are also able to track the number of offenders coming to the courts over specific periods of time and to follow trends in the changing characteristics of offenders and the dispositions handed down. The

FIGURE 2–1
Juvenile Arrests

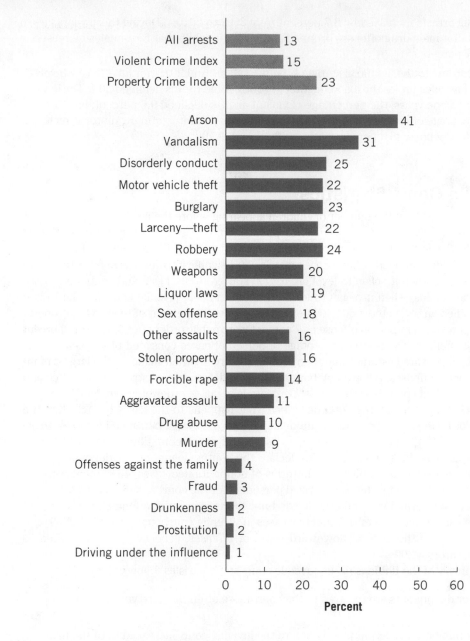

Voices of Delinquency: "I Never Got
Caught"

latter data are helpful in determining the success of suggested and mandated social policy changes that determine who should come to court and what should happen to them.

Juvenile court statistics do have serious limitations. The usual time lag in the publication of the statistics lessens their usefulness. In addition, these cases make up only a small percentage of the total number of juvenile offenses. Moreover, the data collected by the Office of Juvenile Justice and Delinquency Prevention represent only an estimate of the total number of juvenile crimes that come to the attention of juvenile courts. Finally, juvenile court statistics provide limited information about juvenile court transactions and the characteristics of referred juveniles. Yet these statistics still provide a useful means by which researchers can examine youths and what happens to them relative to juvenile court.

Victimization Surveys

In 1972, the U.S. Bureau of the Census began victimization studies to determine as accurately as possible the extent of crime in the United States. This type of data was needed because the UCRs measured police activity, that is, the number of arrests that police made, not the actual amount of crime committed. The volume of "hidden crime" has long been

Juvenile court processing for a typical 1,000 delinquency cases, 2009

Total delinquency [Opens a new window]
1,504,100 Estimated Cases

| Intake decision | Intake disposition | Judicial decision | Judicial disposition |
[Opens a new window]

			Waived	5
				Placed	89
				Probation	194
Petitioned	547		Adjudicate	325	Other sanction	42

1,000 Cases

		Nonadjudicated	217
			Probation	50
			Other sanction	30
Nonpetitioned	453		Dismissed	137

Probation	116
Other sanction	151
Dismissed	186

Detail may not add to total because of rounding.

- Cases referred to juvenile court are first screened by an intake department (either within or outside the court). The intake department may decide to dismiss the case for lack of legal sufficiency or to resolve the matter formally (**petitioned**) or informally (**nonpetitioned**).

  - In 2009, 55% (547 of 1,000) of all delinquency cases disposed by juvenile courts were handled formally while 45% (453 of 1,000) were handled informally.

  - Among nonpetitioned cases, 41% (186 of 453) were dismissed at intake, often for lack of legal sufficiency. In the remaining cases (59%, or 266 of 453), youth voluntarily agreed to informal sanctions, including referral to a social service agency, informal probation, or the payment of fines or some form of voluntary restitution.

- If the intake department decides that a case should be handled formally within the juvenile court, a petition is filed and the case is placed on the court calendar (or docket) for an adjudicatory hearing. On the other hand, the intake department may decide that a case should be removed from juvenile court and handled instead in criminal (adult) court. In these cases, a petition is usually filed in juvenile court requesting a waiver/transfer hearing, during which the juvenile court judge is asked to waive jurisdiction over the case.

  - In 2009, 59% (325 of 547 cases) of all formally processed delinquency cases resulted in the youth being adjudicated delinquent. In 40% (217 of 547) of these cases, the youth was not adjudicated and 1% (5 of 547) were judicially waived to criminal court.

- At the disposition hearing, the juvenile court judge determines the most appropriate sanction, generally after reviewing a predisposition report prepared by the probation department. The range of options available to a court typically includes commitment to an institution; placement in a group or foster home or other residential facility; probation (either regular or intensive supervision); referral to an outside agency, day treatment, or mental health program; or imposition of a fine, community service, or restitution.

  - Youth in 27% (89 of 325) of adjudicated delinquency cases were placed in a residential facility. In another 60% (194 of 325) of these adjudicated cases, youth were placed on formal probation.

FIGURE 2–2
Case Flow by Detailed Offense

Source: OJJDP Statistical Briefing Book, released May 1, 2012 Accessed at http://www.ojjdp.gov/ojstatbb/court/JCSCF_Display.asp?ID=qa06601&year=2009&group=1&estimate=1. Data Source: National Juvenile Court Data Archive, National Center for Juvenile Justice, Pittsburgh, PA.

FIGURE 2–3
Breakdown of Juvenile Placements

*Source: OJJDP Statistical Briefing
Book*, released May 1, 2012. Accessed at http://www.ojjdp
.gov/ojstatbb/court/qa06205
.asp?qaDate=2009. Adapted from
Juvenile Court Statistics 2009
(Pittsburgh, PA: National Center
for Juvenile Justice, 2012).

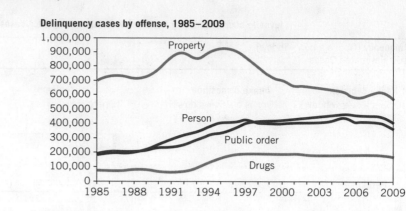

Delinquency cases by offense, 1985–2009

- Between 1985 and 2009, the total number of delinquency cases handled by juvenile courts increased 30%.

- During this period, the number of drug offense cases increased 117%, public order offense cases increased 108%, and person offense cases increased 99%. In comparison, the number of property offense cases declined 19%.

- Compared with 1985, the 2009 delinquency caseload contained greater proportions of person (24% versus 16%), drugs (11% versus 7%), and public order (27% versus 17%) offense cases and a smaller proportion of property (38% versus 61%) offense cases.

known to be great, because many crimes go unreported to the police. The *National Crime Victimization Survey* was set up to overcome this problem and it gives policy makers a better idea of just how much crime is actually committed.

The *National Crime Victimization Survey* is conducted annually by the Bureau of Justice Statistics and administered by the U.S. Census Bureau. The 2010 survey shows that persons twelve years or older suffered more than 18.7 million crime victimizations, of which 14.8 million were property crimes, 3.8 million were violent crimes, and 138,000 were crimes of theft.[17] Overall, the number of victimizations discovered was much higher than the number of offenses reported to the police. Figure 2–4 shows changes in reported property and violent crime victimization rates between 1999 and 2010. Data from these individuals reported by the NCR were used to measure all crimes—whether or not reported to the police—in the previous six-month period. To collect the data, representatives of the Bureau of the Census interviewed all household residents twelve years of age or older in the selected sample.

The *National Crime Victimization Survey* reported that in 2010 juveniles were highly overrepresented in comparison to other age groups in the population of those victimized. Juveniles between the ages of twelve and fourteen experienced the highest rape victimization rate of any age group for all violent crimes, and youths between the ages of fifteen and seventeen have the next highest rate, with rates dropping as the victims' age increased. Data also showed that adolescents are more likely than adults to commit violent crimes

FIGURE 2–4
Juvenile Victimization in Recent Years

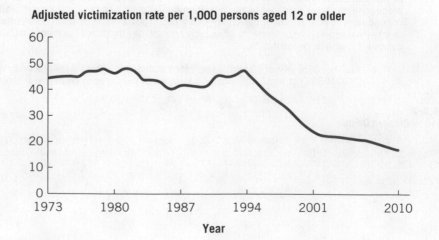

Adjusted victimization rate per 1,000 persons aged 12 or older

Year

against peers and to report knowing their assailants. Crimes against adolescents are also less likely to be reported to the police than are crimes against adults.[18]

Within the adolescent population, males are more likely than females to become victims of violent crime, but females are much more likely to be victims of sexual assault (see Figure 2–5). The survey also revealed that African Americans are several times more likely than Caucasians to be victims of violence overall, including rape, sexual assault, aggravated assault, and robbery.[19]

Victimization surveys are not as widely used in analyzing youth crime as are the other means of measuring youth crime, but they do add to what is known about delinquency in the United States. Some of the principal findings of victimization surveys are as follows:

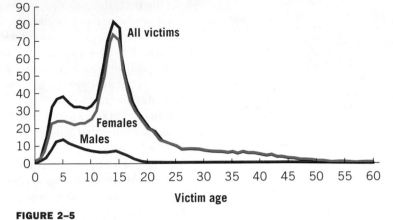

Victims (per 1,000 total sexual assault victims)

FIGURE 2–5
Victimization and Assaults

1. Much more crime is committed than is recorded.

2. The discrepancy between the number of people who say they have been victimized and the number of crimes known to the police varies with the type of offense.

3. The probability of being victimized varies with the type of crime and one's place of residence. The centers of U.S. cities are the more probable sites of violent crimes.

4. Juveniles are more likely to be victimized than any other age group.

Victimization studies do have limitations: information on status offenses is not included, victims may forget the victimization they experienced, or victims may state that a specific crime took place within the research year when it took place before or after that period.

Contexts of Juvenile Victimization

Victimization surveys indicate that children too frequently are the targets of crime. In many countries throughout the world, attention to the plight of children is increasing the focus on the victimization of youths in dysfunctional families, in schools, in neighborhoods, in brothels and on the streets, by terrorist groups looking for child soldiers, and by authorities. Emotionally damaged as a result of neglect and abuse, these children are often unable to relate to adults and peers, to perform in school, and to make realistic plans for the future. Many of these juveniles are imprisoned as adults.

The Family and the Victimization of Children

As an indication of the extent of maltreatment of children, an estimated 3.3 million referrals involving the maltreatment of approximately 6 million children were made to child protective services during the 2009 fiscal year, and of that number, one-quarter were found to be victims.[20]

The demographics of child maltreatment show that younger children make up the largest percentage of victims. Just over 33 percent of all victims of maltreatment were younger than three years of age, an additional 23.3 percent were ages four to seven, and 18.8 percent were ages eight to eleven. Victimization was split almost evenly between the sexes: 51.1 percent of the victims were girls and 48.2 percent were males. Less than one-half of all victims were white (44 percent), one-fifth (22.3 percent) were African Americans, and one-fifth (20.7 percent) were Hispanic.[21]

The problem of parental maltreatment of children is divided into several different categories. The Children's Bureau reports that in 2009, 78.3 percent of reported maltreatment stemmed from neglect, 17.8 percent from physical abuse, 9.5 percent from sexual abuse, and less than 7.6 percent from emotional maltreatment.[22] Homicide is the most serious form of victimization of children. An estimated 1,770 children died in 2009 due to child abuse or neglect.[23]

Voices of Delinquency: The Coal Miner's Daughter

The School and Victimization

In the past, the major problems faced by teachers and administrators in the nation's school systems were those of juveniles running the halls, leaving class without permission, writing graffiti on the walls, and occasionally fighting. Today's students, however, are likely to experience the same problems in the schools as they do on the streets. Drugs, alcohol, suicide, rape, robbery, assault, arson, and bomb threats have combined with knives and guns to change the atmosphere of schools and to generate fear on the part of parents, who worry about their children's safety. A 2011 report on school crime and **school safety** by the Bureau of Justice Statistics and the National Center for Education Statistics titled *Indicators of School Crime and Safety: 2011* report found the following[24]:

- Between July 1, 2009, and June 30, 2010, seventeen homicides and one suicide of school-age youth (ages five to eighteen) occurred at schools. The total number of school-associated violent deaths of nonstudents was thirty-three.
- In 2010, among students ages twelve to eighteen, there were about 828,000 nonfatal victimizations including 470,000 victims of theft and 359,000 victims of simple assaults and serious violence.
- About 74 percent of public schools reported one or more violent incidents of crime.
- Higher percentages of black students and Hispanic students (11 percent each) reported being the targets of hate-related words at school than white students (7 percent) in 2009.
- In 2009, about 28 percent of twelve- to eighteen-year-old students reported having been bullied at school during the school year and 6 percent reported having been cyberbullied.
- Eleven percent of students in 2009 said they had been in a fight on school property during the previous twelve months.
- In 2009, a higher percentage of students ages twelve to eighteen reported that they were afraid of attack or harm at school (4 percent) than away from school (3 percent) during the school year.

This report helps put the amount of crime in schools into perspective. Males are more likely to be victims of theft than are females, but males and females are the victims of violence about equally. Students in the higher grades are more likely to be victims of violence than are younger youths, and Hispanic students are less likely than whites to be victims of theft. Somewhat predictably, students from urban schools are exposed to greater amounts of victimization than those in rural schools; suburban schools have the highest number of victimizations.[25]

Death in the Schools

Death in the schools is a rarity. For example, from July 1, 2009, through June 30, 2010, seventeen homicides and one suicide occurred of school-age youth (ages five through eighteen) at school. During the 2008–2009 school year, as previously suggested, 1,579 homicides occurred among school-age youth ages five to eighteen, while during the 2008 calendar year, 1,344 suicides of youth ages five to eighteen took place. Combining these figures translates into about one homicide or suicide of school-age youth at school per 2.7 million students enrolled during the 2009–2010 school year.[26] The small number of child deaths that takes place in the schools as opposed to those occurring in the community is considerable.[27] Unfortunately, the few acts of murder that do happen dramatically color our perception of the safety of schools.

▲ Younger and weaker children are sometimes taken advantage of by older and stronger children.
Keith Publicover/Shutterstock

Critical Thinking Question: Look through the data, think through your own experiences in schools in your home community, and draw some conclusions about how safe the schools you went to were.

Bullying

Bullying by individuals and groups as a major problem burst onto the scene in the 1990s because of its apparent connection with school shootings by bullying victims. Traditional **bullying** is direct, face-to-face, and physical in nature and occurs when a stronger, more aggressive child hits, pushes, slaps, or beats other children with the intent to produce bodily injury and pain. A second bullying technique is verbal and consists of youths teasing, calling their targets names, and making fun of their victims' families, clothes, faces, and friends, usually with untrue statements, in order to affect the victims' thinking, feeling, and acting. Closely related to verbal abuse is the third technique of emotional or psychological abuse, which generates fear, distress, or anxiety in a weaker child.[28] Although much bullying consists of all three types of victimization, the consequences of bullying may have different effects on different types of children. A common theme running through bullying is the desire to exercise power and to feel superior over victims (see Exhibit 2–1).[29]

The vast majority of adults is uninvolved and uninformed about the online social networks used by children and thus have no real ability to understand or intervene when children are bullied. Children, as might be expected, are more likely to tell their friends than their parents when contacted by a bully and may feel victimized on many separate occasions when other youths place unwanted messages, photos, or videos online again and again. The result is a perceived lack of balance of power on the part of the victim and some youths. Although research is as yet inconclusive on the roles that gender and age play in the bully/victim interactions, some observers suggest that bullied females are likely to become emotionally upset, whereas males tend to deny bullying's effects on them. These observations, however, need much more research because they may simply reflect gender stereotyping.

Studies show that students are able to discount cyberbullying more than traditional bullying. Nonetheless, severe and prolonged bullying does result in embarrassment, stress, depression, and loneliness; if youths are unable to resolve these issues, the pressures on them build, eventually resulting in low self-worth, low confidence in their social competence, and an increase in self-blame for their victimization.[30] The results are a "loss of face, reputation damage, public humiliation, damage to self-esteem, impact on schoolwork and rejection."[31] An inability to retaliate keeps the victim feeling helpless, and the result for some victims

---

Exhibit 2–1
Nine Adolescents Charged After Suicide of Classmate

In 2010, a prosecutor brought charges against nine juveniles at South Hadley High School in western Massachusetts who subjected a classmate to relentless taunting and physical threats. This bullying, according to the prosecutor, led the freshman, Phoebe Prince, to hang herself from a stairwell at her home following school. In this case, two boys and four girls, ages sixteen to eighteen, face a variety of felony charges including statutory rape, violation of civil rights with bodily injury, harassment, stalking, and disturbing a school assembly. Prince's family had recently moved to the United States from Ireland. Investigators found that the abuse took place in the school library, the lunchroom, and the hallways. Phoebe went to school officials, but she told a friend that no action was taken. This pattern of abuse included text messages, Facebook postings, threats, and efforts to corner Phoebe, whose actions were described as fearful, distraught, and panicked. She endured three months of it and then hanged herself.

CRITICAL THINKING QUESTIONS

Why do you think that school administrators did nothing about this ongoing abuse? Do you think that this lack of response is a typical response of school administrators? How frequently do you believe that students' lives are made miserable by bullies at school? What punishment do you believe that bullies in this case should receive?

Source: Carlin DeGuerin Miller, "Phoebe Prince's Final Days: Bullied Girl Suffered 'Intolerable' Abuse Before Suicide, Say Court Documents," accessed at http://www.cbsnews.com/8301-504083_162-20002132-504083 .html, February 13, 2012; Helen Kennedy, "Phoebe Prince, South Hadley High School 'New Girl,' Driven to Suicide by Teenage Cyber Bullies," *Daily News,* March 29, 2010; and Erik Eckholm and Katie Zezima, "9 Teenagers Are Charged After Suicide of Classmate," *The New York Times,* March 30, 2010, A14.

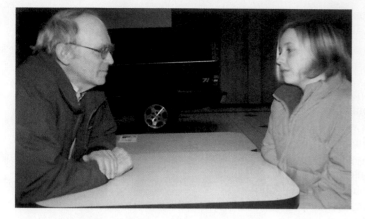

▲ Lured to the mall after several
months of contact on the Internet, this
young girl could be in extreme danger.
Kathryn O'Lare

**Voices of Delinquency: A Voice
for the Enslaved**

**Voices of Delinquency: A Researcher
Speaks Out**

is an increase in thinking about suicide and suicide attempts.[32] Others move from their homes, neighborhoods, towns, and schools to escape their victimization.

Brothels and the Streets

A hidden side of U.S. culture is child prostitution. The sexual and physical abuse of children outside of their homes is no less devastating than that by parents and relatives. Children coming home from school are picked up on the streets, kidnapped from their driveways and front yards, lured out of malls, and enticed by pimps who prowl bus stations and train terminals. Yet others are recruited from the Internet, by cell phone, by youths who know of vulnerable "candidates," and on Facebook and MySpace. Some children are smuggled into the United States from other countries for purposes of prostitution and almost all girls are kept captive by illegal drugs that make them into addicts. Ninety percent of the children brought into the United States for prostitution are female and 10 percent are male.[33]

Although estimates vary, in 2010 the United States was estimated by some to have three hundred thousand child prostitutes, although the United Nations estimates that the United States has six hundred thousand.[34] These numbers are qualified by the fact that no central clearinghouses for the statistics on child prostitutes exist, by the fact that the numbers likely include youths who have been hidden away by pimps and enslaved for several years, and by statements that the United States has one hundred thousand children who are "at risk" for being turned into sex slaves. Regardless of the actual numbers, the trauma experienced by these juveniles is real and severe; some children are forced to service hundreds of clients a year.

On occasion, some children ages two and three are used as prostitutes and in the pornography industry, and some who are even younger are occasionally discovered. As children's ages increase, researchers find that the numbers of children exploited also increase, with the ages of six and seven appearing all too frequently. The average age for a girl to become involved in prostitution is around thirteen or fourteen. Unfortunately, that age is slowly lowering because males who use prostitutes, generally males ranging in age from their twenties through their sixties, are tending to prefer younger and younger girls because of the possibility of contracting HIV/AIDS.[35]

What Are Self-Report Measures of Juvenile Crime?

Self-report and cohort studies are other main sources of information on delinquent behavior. Self-report studies ask juveniles to tell about offenses they committed in a previous period of time. Cohort studies utilize raw police files along with a variety of other data.

Self-Report Studies

Self-report studies have been used since the 1940s to measure hidden youth crime. The reason for their use is to obtain a fuller and more accurate picture of the amount of crime than can be obtained through the UCRs. The UCRs, for example, generally show that lower-class youths commit more crime than do middle- or upper-class youths. Researchers can test this finding by going to different classes of youths and asking them about the number and type of offenses they have committed. Researchers also can obtain considerable information on offender characteristics such as age, gender, and race, as well as on the amount of gang delinquency and the extent of drug and alcohol abuse. In this section, we look at self-reporting and offenders' demographic characteristics.

One of the most significant findings of all of the self-report studies is that the amount of youth crime is much greater than that indicated by the UCRs. Indeed, practically every youth commits some type of crime. Very few, however, ever come to the attention of the authorities. This means that little reason exists for dividing youths into offenders and nonoffenders, as many students of the juvenile justice system are prone to do. The self-report studies contradict or expand on the UCRs in other ways as well.

Self-Report Studies and Race

Official statistics tend to show that the differences between African Americans and whites are greater than self-report studies indicate. In looking at race, for example, David Huizinga and Delbert S. Elliott's examination of the National Youth Survey concluded that "there are few if any substantial and consistent differences between the delinquency involvement of different racial groups."[36] Two other national studies reported involvement in seventeen delinquent behaviors with similar frequencies, but further analysis of the data revealed that the seriousness of self-reported delinquency was slightly greater for African American males than for white males.[37] Elliott and Suzanne Ageton's study revealed that the offense rate was greater for African Americans because they were more likely to be involved in serious property crime and because they were more likely to be chronic or repeat offenders.[38]

Self-Report Studies and Gender

Similar discrepancies appear between official data and self-report studies when examining the gender of youthful offenders. Self-report studies show that female delinquency is higher than reported in official data.[39] Between 1989 and 1993, the relative growth in juvenile arrests for females was more than double the growth for males (23% vs. 11%). Self-report studies do show that females are less likely to be involved in serious crime.

Social Class and Delinquency

The finding that unlawful behavior is unrelated or only slightly related to a juvenile's social class is one of the most significant findings of self-report studies.[40] Travis Hirschi's survey of four thousand junior and senior high school students in Richmond, California, found little association between self-reported delinquencies and income, education, and occupation.[41] Richard E. Johnson, in redefining social class as underclass and earning class, added: "The data provide no firm evidence that social class, no matter how it is measured, is a salient factor in generating delinquent involvement."[42]

Elliott and Ageton's national study, however, found a different pattern when youths were asked how many times they had violated the law during the previous year. The average number of delinquent acts reported by lower-class juveniles, according to these researchers, exceeded that reported by working- or middle-class youths. Indeed, the average number of crimes against persons reported by lower-class youths was one and one-half times greater than that reported by working- or middle-class youths.[43]

Evaluation of Self-Report Studies

The realization that official statistics on juvenile delinquency have serious limitations led to a growing reliance on the use of self-report studies. These studies have revealed the following conclusions:

1. A significant amount of undetected delinquency exists in the United States, and police apprehension is low—probably less than 10 percent.

2. Juveniles in both the middle and lower classes are involved in considerable illegal behavior.

3. Not all hidden delinquency involves minor offenses; a significant number of serious crimes are committed each year by juveniles who elude apprehension by the police.

4. The differences between the offenses of African Americans and those of whites are less visible in self-reports than in official statistics.

5. Girls commit more delinquent acts than official statistics indicate, but boys commit more delinquent acts and commit more serious youth crimes than girls do.

Cohort Studies

Cohort studies are another valuable tool for researchers. These studies do not start by counting offenses or by asking who has been victimized. Rather, they identify every juvenile born in a certain time frame in a particular city and then follow those juveniles for many years. Depending on the goals of the study, police files, school records, and/or socioeconomic data are collected and then scrutinized for all the juveniles. These data and any evidence that the youths have gotten into trouble are collected by the researchers for their study. The result is a wealth of information not attainable through the use of official statistics.[44] Four of the most important older cohort studies involve data collected on cohorts of youths in Philadelphia; London, England; Racine, Wisconsin; and Columbus, Ohio.[45] Table 2–2 compares the findings of these four cohort studies.

In the 1990s, a number of studies were done documenting the lives of adolescents over the life course. See Focus on Research 2–1 for highlights from three of the more highly cited recent cohort studies, the Denver, Pittsburgh, and Rochester Youth Surveys.

TABLE 2–2
Comparison of Four Cohort Studies

	Philadelphia Cohorts	London Cohort	Racine Cohorts	Columbus Cohort
Sample	Males born in 1945 and males and females born in 1958	Males born between 1951 and 1954	Males and females born in 1942, 1949, and 1955	Males and females born between 1956 and 1960
Delinquent population	32.6 percent in first cohort and 34.9 percent in second cohort	About one-third of the cohort	90 percent of males and 65 to 70 percent of females in each cohort	1,138 youths born during these years committed a violent offense
Gender	Females not as delinquent	N.A.	White females had least involvement with the police	Males outnumbered females by almost 6 to 1
Race	Nonwhites committed more serious crimes and were more likely to be recidivists	N.A.	Afro-American males had more police contacts and committed more serious crimes	Afro-Americans were more likely to commit violent offenses than were whites
Chronic offenders	6.3 percent of first cohort and 7.5 percent of males in second cohort	6 percent; 23 boys of the 396 had 6 or more convictions	N.A.	Nearly one-third of the violent offenders were arrested 5 or more times
Patterns of delinquent behavior	Reasonably constant	Chronics exhibited high and stable recidivism rates through sixth involvement of 72 percent	Declining seriousness and discontinuation after teenage period	Did not progress from less to more serious crimes
Impact of intervention by justice system	Profitable if early in a delinquent career	Early discrimination and treatment of persisters can help prevent adult criminality	Increase in seriousness and involvement following sanctions	Length of time outside an institution between arrests reduced after each commitment

Focus on Research 2–1
Highlights from the Denver, Pittsburgh, and Rochester Youth Surveys

DENVER

The Denver study follows 1,527 boys and girls from high-risk neighborhoods in Denver who were seven, nine, eleven, thirteen, and fifteen years old in 1987. In exploring the changes in the nature of delinquency and drug use from the 1970s to the 1990s, the Denver study's findings are as follows:

- Overall, there was little change in the prevalence rates of delinquency, including serious delinquency and serious violence. However, the prevalence rate of gang fights among males doubled (from 8 to 16 percent).
- The level of injury from violent offenses increased substantially.
- The prevalence of drug use decreased substantially: alcohol, from 80 percent to 50 percent; marijuana, from 41 percent to 18 percent; and other drug use, from 19 percent to 4 percent.
- The relationships between drug use and delinquency have changed in that a smaller percentage (from 48 percent to 17 percent) of serious delinquents are using hard drugs other than marijuana, and a greater percentage (from 27 percent to 48 percent) of hard drug users are serious offenders.
- More than half (53 percent) of the youth in the study ages eleven through fifteen in 1987 were arrested over the next five years.

PITTSBURGH

The Pittsburgh study, a longitudinal study of 1,517 inner-city boys, followed three samples of boys for more than a decade to advance knowledge about how and why boys become involved in delinquency and other problem behaviors. Its chief findings are as follows:

- There were no differences between African American and white boys at age six, but differences gradually developed, the prevalence of serious delinquency at age sixteen reaching 27 percent for African American boys versus 19 percent for white boys.
- As prevalence increased, so did the average frequency of serious offending, which rose more rapidly for African American boys than for white boys.
- The onset of offending among the boys involved in serious delinquency occurred by age fifteen, when 51 percent of African American boys and 28 percent of white boys committed serious delinquent acts.
- The boys generally developed disruptive and delinquent behavior in an orderly, progressive fashion, with less serious problem behaviors preceding more serious problem behaviors.

- Three groups of developmental pathways were identified that displayed progressively more serious problem behaviors:

  Authority Conflict: Youths on this pathway exhibit stubbornness prior to age twelve, then move on to defiance and avoidance of authority.

  Covert: This pathway includes minor acts, such as lying, followed by property damage and moderately serious delinquency.

  Overt: This pathway includes minor aggression followed by fighting and violence.

ROCHESTER

The Rochester study, a longitudinal study of one thousand urban adolescents, investigates the causes and consequences of adolescent delinquency and drug use by following a sample of high-risk urban adolescents from their early teenage years through their early adult years. Its chief findings are as follows:

- Attachment and involvement were both significantly related to delinquency. Children who were more attached to and involved with their parents were less involved in delinquency.
- The relationship between family process factors and delinquency was bidirectional—poor parenting increased the probability of delinquent behavior, and delinquent behavior further weakened the relationship between parent and child.
- The impact of family variables appeared to fade as adolescents became older and more independent of their parents. Weak school commitment and poor school performance were associated with increased involvement in delinquency and drug use.
- Associating with delinquent peers was strongly and consistently related to delinquency, in part because peers provide positive reinforcements for delinquency. There is a strong relationship between gang membership and delinquent behavior, particularly serious and violent delinquency.

CRITICAL THINKING QUESTIONS

What do the findings of these three studies have in common? How do they differ? What would you say are the most important finding overall?

Sources: Katharine Browning, Terence P. Thornberry, and Pamela K. Porter, "Highlights of Findings from the Rochester Youth Development Study," *OJJDP Fact Sheet* (Washington, DC: Office of Juvenile Justice and Delinquency Prevention, 1999); Katharine Browning and Rolf Loeber, "Highlights from the Pittsburgh Youth Study," *OJJDP Fact Sheet* (Washington, DC: Office of Juvenile Justice and Delinquency Prevention, 1999); and Katharine Browning and David Huizinga, "Highlights from the Denver Youth Study," *OJJDP Fact Sheet* (Washington, DC: Office of Juvenile Justice and Delinquency Prevention, 1999).

Evaluation of Cohort Studies

The cohort studies conducted in Columbus, Ohio, and Racine, Wisconsin, as well as the newer ones, generally agree with the following:

1. A few youths commit at least half of all juvenile offenses and an even higher percentage of the violent juvenile offenses.

2. African American urban youths as a group commit more frequent and more serious delinquent offenses than do whites.

3. Females typically have fewer contacts and less serious involvement with the police than do males.

4. The more frequent and more serious the police contacts that a juvenile has, the more likely that youth is to continue on to commit adult crime.

5. Interventions by the justice system appear to raise the likelihood of the frequency and seriousness of unlawful behavior in the future.

Cohort studies, like other forms of crime statistics, have two major problems. First, their findings cannot be generalized confidently beyond the persons in the cohort. Second, cohort studies are extremely expensive and time consuming. Indeed, keeping track of a sample of individuals even up to age thirty-five is almost impossible because names and addresses change, some people die, and others simply drop out of sight. Still, even with these drawbacks, cohort studies remain a useful addition to other official and unofficial measurements of crime.

What Are the Dimensions of Law-Violating Behaviors?

A century of study has enabled researchers to identify variables and patterns that are important to the understanding of juvenile crime. The age of onset, escalation of offenses, specialization of offenses, desistance from crime, and transition to adult crime all help focus attention on some key patterns in juvenile crime and provide some guidelines for understanding the causes of crime and the recidivism of offenders.

Age of Onset

Several studies have found that the earlier the juveniles began law-violating behaviors (the **age of onset**) the more likely they were to continue such behaviors. Marvin E. Wolfgang, Terence P. Thornberry, and Robert M. Figlio followed a 10 percent sample of Cohort I (of the Philadelphia cohort study) to the age of thirty and found that the average number of offenses tended to decline almost uniformly as the age of onset increased.[46] Alfred Blumstein, David P. Farrington, and Soumyo Moitra also showed that one of the factors predicting who became chronic offenders was offending at an early age.[47] Farrington further found that those who were first convicted at the earliest age (ten to twelve years) consistently offended at a higher rate and for a longer time period than did those who were first convicted at later ages.[48]

Escalation of Offenses

The findings on **escalation of offenses** (an increase in the number of crimes committed by an individual) are less consistent than those on age of onset. Official studies have typically found that the incidence of arrest accelerates at age thirteen and peaks at about age seventeen, but this pattern is less evident in self-report studies. For example, Ageton and Elliott found that the incidence of some offenses, such as assault and robbery, increased with age, whereas that of others peaked between ages thirteen and fifteen.[49]

Specialization of Offenses

The findings on **specialization of offenses** (the tendency to repeat one type of crime) are more consistent than those on escalation. The cohort studies, especially, revealed little or no specialization of offenses among delinquents.[50] Some evidence exists, however, that specialization is much more typical of status offenders. Susan K. Datesman and Michael Aickin's examination of a sample of status offenders found that the majority, regardless of gender and race, were referred to court within the same offense category 50 to 70 percent of the time. Females, especially white females, were referred to court for the same offenses, a sizable proportion of them for running away.[51]

Desistance from Crime

Desistance from crime, or the age of termination of delinquency, has become a recent concern of researchers. A major problem in establishing desistance is the difficulty of distinguishing between a gap in a delinquent career and true termination. Crime-free intervals are bound to be present in the course of delinquent careers. Two of the most popular theories of desistance are (1) the maturation and aging out of deviance, which suggests that individuals pursue a conventional lifestyle when they deal with the undesirability of continuing with unlawful activities; and (2) the decision to give up or continue with crime is based on a person's conscious reappraisal of the costs and benefits of criminal activity. See Table 2–3 for the dimensions of delinquent behavior.

Transition to Adult Crime

Studies have identified three groups of criminal offenders. One group offends only during their juvenile years; a second group offends only during adult years; and a third group persistently offends during both periods.[52] Some scholars argue that juvenile offenders' **transition to adult crime** is due to their prior participation in unlawful activities. This prior participation, according to this position, reduces inhibitions against engaging in future unlawful behavior. Other scholars contend that some individuals have a higher propensity to delinquency than do others and that this higher propensity persists over time. This higher propensity is related to such factors as poor parental supervision, paretal rejection, parental criminality, delinquent siblings, and low IQ.[53] For an examination of chronic offenders, the group of youthful offenders who violate the law more frequently and seriously and are more likely to go on to adult crime, see Focus on Offenders 2–2.

Evidence-based practices in juvenile justice are featured throughout this text. Evidence-based practice (EBP) forms an important part of the knowledge of what we know and do not know about the efficacy of juvenile justice programs. The EBP feature for this chapter, however, alerts the reader to the limits of these best practice research programs.

Voices of Delinquency: I Could Be in Deep Trouble Now

TABLE 2–3
Dimensions of Delinquent Behavior

Dimensions of Behavior	Finding	Consensus
Age of onset	It is the best predictor of length of continuity of delinquent behavior	Mixed
Escalation of Offenses	Offense studies have generally found that the instance of arrest accelerates at age 13 and peaks about age 17	Mixed
Specialization	The majority of studies have found little or no specialization	Fairly strong
Chronic offender	A small group of offenders commits the most serious offenses	Strong
Youth crimes and adult criminality	Some childhood factors have been identified as contributing to the continuity of criminality	Very mixed
Lengths of criminal careers	Careers tend to be longer for violent offenses, for those with early convictions, and for minority offenders	More studies are needed to determine outcomes

Focus on Offenders 2–2
Chronic Offenders: Notes on Their Backgrounds

The **chronic offender** is known by many labels: *serious delinquent, repeat offender, violent offender, dangerous offender, hard-core delinquent*, and *career delinquent.* Whatever the label, the predominant characteristics of these youths are their commitment to crime and their involvement in one crime after another, often very serious crimes against persons and property. Their initial participation in crime constitutes the budding of a lifestyle centered on violence and "making it big" in the criminal world. Chronic offenders expect to engage in criminal careers for at least several years, if not for the rest of their lives.

Chronic offenders become committed to criminal careers through one of two routes. In the first, noncriminal and situational offenders move from casual involvement with other offenders on the streets, to being processed with them through the system, to perceiving crime as a way of life, and finally to being willing to stand up for this involvement. Usually these youths have been picked up by the police many times, have been in courts and detention halls several times, and have had one or more institutional stays. The decisions they make at each stage move them closer to a delinquent career.

The second route is quite different. Some youths become absorbed in crime before they have contact with the justice system. These offenders often grow up in a ghetto area and, surrounded by vice and crime, become involved, along with peers, in unlawful acts at an early age. Frequently, they come from impoverished families. They tend to feel that life is a struggle and that only the strong survive; therefore, they are always on guard against being hurt or exploited by others, and they develop a hostile and suspicious view of the world around them. They seem to accept a commitment to crime without any apparent episodes of decision making.

Chronic offenders typically come from lower-class backgrounds and in many cases have grown up in urban pockets of poverty. They most often are minority males who have lived on the streets with insufficient parental support and with a history of failure in social institutions. An inability to function in school either in acceptable academic performance or in satisfactory relationships with teachers and peers characterizes their school experiences. A history of school dropout is followed by a pattern of unemployment. Part of this inability to find jobs is the lack of marketable skills. These juveniles contribute to the disturbingly high rates of unemployment among urban African Americans.

The attitudes of chronic offenders, of course, do vary. Some are more bitter or angry than others, and this variation seems to be affected greatly by the amount of love and acceptance they received at home and the injustices they experienced. In addition, some chronic offenders have more hope than others. Youths with histories of drug addiction generally do not demonstrate the positive attitudes of those without such histories. Chronic offenders who are closest to institutional release, not surprisingly, are more hopeful than those who face long periods of confinement. Chronic offenders who have developed positive goals for the future are also more hopeful than those who lack such goals. Finally, the more the chronic offenders see life as a "give me" experience, the less they seem able to develop positive relationships with others or to pursue noncrime options.

CRITICAL THINKING QUESTIONS

Why is the chronic offender so difficult to treat in the juvenile justice system? Why does this category of offenders so frequently go on to commit adult crime? Is long-term incarceration the only possible means to deter their criminal behaviors as juveniles and adults?

Source: One of the authors of this textbook has formed these impressions of chronic offenders, based on his work with them in both institutional and community-based contexts over the past forty years.

Evidence-Based Practice
Evidence, Emotions, and Criminal Justice: The Limits to Evidence-Based Policy

In 2008, Australian Prime Minister Kevin Rudd, in addressing the heads of agencies and members of the senior executive of the Commonwealth Public Service, set out as one of his goals a "robust, evidence-based policy making process" that would lead to government by reason rather than ideology, "by facts rather than fads."

In making this commitment, the prime minister was joining a long line of politicians and other policy makers who had shared similar ideas before him. In one way or the other, evidence-based policy is as old as the state itself. For example, Davies, Nutley, and Smith have charted its history from Bacon's seventeenth-century vision of the New Atlantis where "policy is formed by knowledge, truth, reason and facts." Evidence-based policy can be described as an approach that "helps people make well-informed decisions about policies, programs and projects by putting the best available evidence from research at the heart of policy development and implementation."

There is no question that the phenomenon of evidence-based policy has truly arrived. Evidence-based policy and practice have spawned dozens of specialist journals, and evidence-based institutes, generally attached to universities, have also flourished in recent times. The more self-conscious approaches to evidence-based policy in criminology can probably be traced to the development of an evaluation literature, especially the meta-analysis evaluation studies of correctional effectiveness. The theory of evidence-based policy, however, has been most fully developed in the field of crime prevention where the cycle of experimentation/evaluation/improvement has been most widely used and resourced.

Reasons exist to explain why the rational model in itself is inadequate to describe the policy process:

- *Economic and financial factors:* In view of the limits on resources, the decision for policy makers is not just "What works," but "How much does it cost and can we afford it?"
- *Time and tactical versus strategic factors:* Decision makers often operate in conditions of uncertainty and must make their decisions within strict time constraints that may be related to budget cycles, electoral cycles, or institutional requirements.
- *Lack of a research-oriented culture:* There may not be a culture in the organization that understands the nature of research and its role in policy development.

- *Habit, tradition, and bureaucratic logic:* It is more comfortable to hold to the old rather than venture out into the new.
- *Politics:* Decision makers have the right to reject or ignore evidence if there are other more pressing or politically convincing reasons to act in a particular way.

In the field of policy studies, the role of emotion in the shaping of governmental decisions must be taken into account. The point is made that criminal justice policies are more likely to be adopted if they recognize the importance of the roles of emotions, symbols, faith, belief, and religion in the criminal justice system.

CRITICAL THINKING QUESTION

What insights does this paper leave to the person committed to using evidence-based practices in juvenile justice?

Source: Arie Freiberg and W. W. (Kit) Carson, "Evidence, Emotion and Criminal Justice: The Limits to Evidence-Based Policy," paper presented before the New South Wales Bureau of Crime Statistics and Research, 40th Anniversary Symposium, February 18–19, 2009.

Juvenile Justice Videos

STATUS OFFENDER

Status Offender looks at the intake process and the initial detention hearing for a seventeen-year-old female status offender. The juvenile was brought into the intake facility for running away. At both stages of the justice system, the court attempts to make decisions that would be in the best interest of the child. In the video two recommendations are made concerning whether or not the youth is mature enough to understand what is in her own best interests; the first was given at the youth's initial detention hearing, the other was given at the second hearing. Discuss both recommendations and the changes displayed by the youth between the two hearings. Based on the readings and the videos, explain and discuss status offenses. What makes a behavior a status offense? How does the juvenile justice system handle status offenses? What treatment model best handles status offenses? Explain.

DELINQUENT OFFENDER

Delinquent Offender displays a juvenile detention hearing. The judge discusses the proceedings with the delinquent juvenile, including his rights, the methods for determining probable cause for trying the offenses brought before the court, and the petition for the youth's delinquency. Throughout the case professionals within the juvenile court and juvenile care agencies recommend different proposals for dealing with the youth, all of which are intended to be in the best interest of the child. Based on the charges filed against the juvenile in the video, what options does the court have in treating the youth? What kinds of recommendations are made to the judge for dealing with the youth? How do these recommendations treat the juvenile's risk factors and delinquency? Based on your readings discuss other methods not mentioned in the video that could be used to treat a juvenile with a similar record.

SUMMARY

LEARNING OBJECTIVE 1 Identify the different methods used to categorize, measure, and report juvenile crime data.

The *Uniform Crime Reports, Juvenile Court Statistics, National Crime Victimization Data,* and self-report surveys are the major sources of data on juvenile crime.

LEARNING OBJECTIVE 2: Summarize juvenile crime rates and trends.

Official statistics have contributed important findings about youth crime in American society:

- Juveniles commit a disproportionate number of property and violent offenses.

- Lower-class youths are involved in slightly more frequent and more serious offenses than are middle-class youths.
- African American youths commit more frequent and more serious offenses than do white youths.
- Urban youths commit more frequent and more serious offenses than do suburban or rural youths.
- A small group of youthful offenders, primarily lower-class minority youths, commit at least half of the serious offenses in urban areas.
- The interventions by the juvenile justice system frequently make youths worse rather than better.

The findings of unofficial studies of juvenile lawbreaking include the following:

- Self-report studies have revealed that most youths are involved in delinquent behavior and that almost 90 percent of delinquent acts are undetected or ignored.

- Self-report studies also indicate that girls commit more delinquent acts than are recorded in official accounts of delinquency, but boys still appear to commit more serious crimes than girls do.

- Victimization surveys reveal nearly four times as many victims each year as the UCR statistics show.

- Surveys also reveal that juveniles are more likely than adults to become victims.

- Together, these unofficial measurements of delinquency add to what is known officially about juvenile crime in the United States. As we continue to seek out the parameters of youth crime, important data are being developed in the area of drug use, and comprehensive data are beginning to emerge on school violence and bullying.

LEARNING OBJECTIVE 3 Summarize juvenile victimization, including school violence.

- Much more crime is committed than is recorded.

- The discrepancy between the number of people who say they have been victimized and the number of crimes known to the police varies with the type of offense.

- The probability of being victimized varies with the type of crime and one's place of residence. The centers of U.S. cities are the more probable sites of violent crimes.

- Juveniles are more likely to be victimized than any other age group.

- Males are more likely to be victims of violence in school than are females, but males and females are the victims of theft about equally.

- Students in the higher grades are less likely to be the victims of violence than are younger youths.

- Bullying in schools has created a climate of fear and discomfort.

LEARNING OBJECTIVE 4 Describe the limitations and problems of measuring juvenile crime.

Official statistics, such as the *Uniform Crime Reports*, depend on the accurate reporting of official agencies. Statistics from the *Juvenile Court Statistics* have the limitation of the time lag until publication, which lessens their usefulness, and the data collected by the Office of Juvenile Justice and Delinquency Prevention represent only an estimate of the total number of juvenile crimes that come to the attention of juvenile courts. Both victimization and self-report surveys depend on the reliability of what juveniles remember and report.

LEARNING OBJECTIVE 5 Describe the factors that lead to career escalation and/or a transition to adult crime.

Research has revealed that the most important factors that lead to career escalation and/or a transition to adult crime are the age of onset, escalation of offenses, specialization of offenses, chronic offending, and length of criminal careers.

KEY TERMS

age of onset, p. 40
bullying, p. 35
chronic offenders, p. 42
cohort studies, p. 37
delinquent offenders, p. 26
desistance from crime, p. 41

escalation of offenses, p. 40
Juvenile Court Statistics, p. 27
National Crime Victimization Survey, p. 32
official statistics, p. 27
school safety, p. 34

self-report studies, p. 36
specialization of offenses, p. 40
status offenders, p. 26
transition to adult crime, p. 41
Uniform Crime Reports, p. 27

REVIEW QUESTIONS

1. What do the UCRs generally show about youth crime in the United States?
2. What do juvenile court statistics show about youth crime in the United States?

3. What can self-report studies tell us that official accounts of youth crime cannot?
4. What do you believe the connection is between the maltreatment of children in their homes and on the streets and their involvement in crime and delinquency?

GROUP EXERCISES

1. *Group Work:* First identify and describe the different types of research methodologies used to collect data on crime and offenders. After discussions die down, you may open your books and spell out in considerably more detail the different types of research methodologies used to collect data.
2. *Group Work:* First, all groups are, without looking at the data in the text, to discuss with each other the findings of the different research methods. After initial discussions,

open the text and describe the findings of the different research methodologies.
3. *Writing to Learn:* Write on one or more of the following topics: the UCRs, victimization surveys, self-report studies, or cohort studies. Critique and revise.
4. *Class Debate:* Divide the class into two parts. Assign one group to argue the benefits and advantages of the UCRs, victimization studies, and *Juvenile Court Statistics* in

understanding crime. Assist the other group to argue, supported by the chapter's introductory comments by Dr. Zahn and her excerpt in *Voices of Delinquency: A Researcher Speaks Out*, that the data on school and family victimization are the most worthwhile data for use in juvenile justice.

5. ***Writing to Learn:*** Write on the nature of juvenile victimization in the school and in the family (about 10 minutes for a paragraph on each). Critique and revise.

NOTES

1. Interview with Margaret A. Zahn, April 2009.
2. LaMar T. Empey, *Studies in Delinquency: Alternatives to Incarceration* (Washington, DC: U.S. Department of Health, Education and Welfare, Office of Juvenile Delinquency and Youth Development, 1967), 27–32; Maynard L. Erickson and LaMar T. Empey, "Court Records, Undetected Delinquency and Decision-Making," *Journal of Criminal Law, Criminology and Police Science* 54 (December 1963), 456–69.
3. William T. Pink and Mervin F. White, "Delinquency Prevention: The State of the Art," in *The Juvenile Justice System,* edited by Malcolm W. Klein (Beverly Hills, CA: Sage Publications, 1976), 9.
4. Federal Bureau of Investigation, *Crime in the United States, 2010,* accessed at http://www.fbi.gov/about-us/cjis/ucr/crime-in-the-u.s/2010/crime-in-the-u.s.-2010/persons-arrested.
5. Ibid., Table 41.
6. Ibid., Table 41.
7. Ibid., Table 38.
8. Ibid., Table 41.
9. Ibid., Table 32.
10. Ibid., Table 40.
11. Ibid., Table 32.
12. Ibid., Table 33.
13. Ibid., Table 32.
14. Adapted from *Juvenile Court Statistics 2009* (Pittsburgh, PA: National Center for Juvenile Justice, 2012). Accessed at http://www.ojjdp.gov/ojstatbb/court/qa06201.asp?qaDate=2009. Released on May 1, 2012. Special thanks goes to Benjamin Adams for his assistance in directing the authors to these data sets.
15. Adapted from *Juvenile Court Statistics 2009* (Pittsburgh, PA: National Center for Juvenile Justice, 2012). Accessed at http://www.ojjdp.gov/ojstatbb/court/qa06205.asp?qaDate=2009. Released on May 1, 2012.Special thanks goes to Benjamin Adams for his assistance in directing the authors to these data.
16. Ibid.
17. Jennifer Truman, *Criminal Victimization, 2010* (Washington, DC: Bureau of Justice Statistics, 2011).
18. Ibid.
19. Ibid.
20. Children's Bureau, *Child Maltreatment 2009* (Washington, DC: U.S. Department of Health and Human Services, 2010), viii.
21. Ibid., 22.
22. Ibid., 23.
23. Ibid., 54.
24. All of the data above are excerpted or quoted from Simone Robers, Jijun Zhang, Jennifer Truman, and Thomas D. Snyder, *Indicators of School Crime and Safety, 2011* (NCES 2012-002/NCJ 236021) (Washington, DC: Bureau of Justice Statistics, National Center for Education Statistics, 2012), iii–vii. Accessed at http://nces.ed.gov/pubs2012/2012002.pdf.
25. Ibid., 97.
26. Ibid., 6.
27. Ibid.
28. D. P. Farrington, "Understanding and Preventing Bullying," in *Crime and Justice: A Review of Research*, Vol. 17, edited by M. Tonray (Chicago: University of Chicago Press, 1993), 381–458, cited in U.S. Department of Education, National Center for Education Statistics, *Are America's Schools Safe? Students Speak Out: 1999 School Crime Supplement* (NCES 2002–331), by Lynn A. Addington et al., *Project Officer: Kathryn A. Chandler* (Washington, DC: U.S. Department of Education, 2002), 55.
29. Some observers do not distinguish between verbal and emotional abuse.
30. David Perry, Ernest Hodges, and Susan Egan, "Determinants of Chronic Victimization by Peers: A Review and a New Model of Family Influence," in *Peer Harassment in School: The Plight of the Vulnerable and Victimized* (New York: Guilford, 2001), 73–104. Thanks to Alexis Geeza of Washington and Jefferson College for pulling together much of the research in this section on bullying.
31. Barbara Speers, Phillip Slee, Larry Owens, and Bruce Johnson, "Behind the Scenes and Screens: Insights into the Human Dimension of Covert and Cyberbullying," *Zeitschrift fur Psychologie/Journal of Psychology* 217, no. 4 (2012), 189–96.
32. Anat Brunstein Klomek, Andre Sourander, and Madelyn Gould, "The Association of Suicide and Bullying in Childhood to Young Adulthood: A Review of Cross-Sectional and Longitudinal Research Findings," *Canadian Journal Of Psychiatry* 55, no. 5 (2010), 282–88; Perry et al., "Determinants of Chronic Victimization."
33. Polaris Project, accessed at http://www.polarisproject.org/human-trafficking/overview accessed 05/06/2012; BellaOnline: The Voice of Women, "Human Trafficking in America," accessed May 5, 2012, at http://www.bellaonline.com/articles/art175483.asp. A number of children, usually smuggled in from Mexico, are used as laborers and janitors in homes, stores, agricultural enterprises, and businesses in need of cheap labor; these are often brutal experiences. A rather large number of children smuggled into the United States are brought in by well-off parents who are too impatient to wait for legal adoptions to take place. Many children smuggled out of a country end up in international sex pedophile organizations.
34. Change Starts with One, Child Prostitution: A Global Epidemic" accessed May 6, 2012, at http://changestartswithone

.wordpress.com/02/07/2012/child-prostitution-a-global-epidemic; U.S. Department of Justice OJP Bureau of Justice Statistics, "The Human Trafficking Project: USDOJ Releases Trafficking Victim Statistics for the U.S.," accessed May 6, 2012, at http://www.traffickingproject.org01/2009/usdoj-releases-trafficking-victim.html.

35. BellaOnline, "Human Trafficking," 1. For a good overview of the problem, see International Crisis Aid, "Sex Trafficking in the United States," accessed August 22, 2012, at http://www.crisisaid.org/ICAPDF/Trafficking/traffickstats.pdf

36. David Huizinga and Delbert S. Elliott, "Juvenile Offenders: Prevalence, Offender Incidence, and Arrest Rates by Race," *Crime and Delinquency* 33 (April 1987), 208, 210; Franklin W. Dunford and Delbert S. Elliott, "Identifying Career Offenders Using Self-Report Data," *Journal of Research in Crime and Delinquency* 21 (February 1984), 57–82, 215.

37. J. R. Williams and Martin Gold, "From Delinquent Behavior to Official Delinquency," *Social Problems* 20 (1972), 202–29; Martin Gold and David J. Reimer, *Changing Patterns of Delinquent Behavior Among Americans 13 to 16 Years Old* (Ann Arbor: Institute for Social Research, University of Michigan, 1974).

38. Delbert S. Elliott and Suzanne S. Ageton, "Reconciling Race and Class Differences in Self-Reported and Official Estimates of Delinquency," *American Sociological Review* 45 (February 1980), 103.

39. Gary Jensen and Raymond Eve, "Sex Differences in Delinquency: An Examination of Popular Sociological Explanations," *Criminology* 13 (1976), 427–88; Michael Hindelang, "Age, Sex, and the Versatility of Delinquent Involvements," *Social Problems* 18 (1979), 522–35; Short and Nye, "Reported Behavior as a Criterion of Deviant Behavior."

40. James F. Short, Jr. and F. Ivan Nye, "Reported Behavior as a Criterion of Deviant Behavior"; *Social Problems* 5 (Winter 1957–58), p. 211; F. Ivan Nye, James Short, Jr., and Virgil Olsen, "Socio-Economic Status and Delinquent Behavior," *American Journal of Sociology* 63 (1958), 381–89; Robert Dentler and Lawrence Monroe, "Social Correlates of Early Adolescent Theft," *American Sociological Review* 26 (1961), 733–43.

41. Travis Hirschi, *Causes of Delinquency* (Berkeley: University of California Press, 1969).

42. Richard E. Johnson, "Social Class and Delinquent Behavior: A New Test," *Criminology* 18 (May 1980), 91.

43. Elliott and Ageton, "Reconciling Race and Class Differences."

44. For a more complete examination of cohort studies, see Clemens Bartollas, *Juvenile Delinquency*, 7th ed. (Boston: Allyn & Bacon, 2006), 41–42.

45. Marvin E. Wolfgang, Robert M. Figlio, and Thorsten Sellin, *Delinquency in a Birth Cohort* (Chicago: University of Chicago Press, 1972); Donna Martin Hamparian et al., *The Violent Few: A Study of Dangerous Juvenile Offenders* (Lexington, MA: Lexington Books, 1980); Lyle W. Shannon, *Assessing the Relationships of Adult Criminal Careers to Juvenile Careers: A Summary* (Washington, DC: U.S. Government Printing Office, 1982).

46. Marvin E. Wolfgang, Terence P. Thornberry, and Robert M. Figlio, eds., *From Boy to Man, from Delinquency to Crime* (Chicago: University of Chicago Press, 1987), 37, 39.

47. Alfred Blumstein, David P. Farrington, and Soumyo Moitra, "Delinquency Careers: Innocents, Amateurs, and Persisters," in *Crime and Justice: An Annual Review*, 6th ed., edited by Michael Tonry and Norval Morris (Chicago: University of Chicago Press, 1985), 187–220.

48. D. P. Farrington, "Offending from 10 to 25 Years of Age," in *Prospective Studies of Crime and Delinquency*, edited by K. T. Van Dusen and S. A. Mednick (Boston: Kluwer-Nijhoff, 1983).

49. Suzanne S. Ageton and Delbert S. Elliott, *The Incidence of Delinquent Behavior in a National Probability Sample of Adolescents* (Boulder, CO: Behavioral Research Institute, 1978).

50. See Wolfgang et al., *Delinquency in a Birth Cohort* and Hamparian et al., *The Violent Few*.

51. Susan K. Datesman and Michael Aickin, "Offense Specialization and Escalation Among Status Offenders," *Journal of Criminal Law and Criminology* 75 (1984), 1260–73.

52. See Wolfgang et al., *From Boy to Man*, 21.

53. Daniel S. Nagin and Raymond Paternoster, "On the Relationship of Past to Future Participation in Delinquency," *Criminology* 29 (May 1991), 163, 165.

3 Causes of Juvenile Crime

David Grossman/Alamy

Learning Objectives

1. Explain the role of theory and research pertaining to causes of juvenile crime.
2. Summarize the principles and influences of the classical school of criminology.
3. Describe biological theories of juvenile crime and delinquency.
4. Describe psychological theories of juvenile crime and delinquency.
5. Describe sociological theories of juvenile crime and delinquency.
6. Summarize integrated theories of juvenile crime and delinquency.

If you or I committed a crime we would be irrational, because we stand a great deal to lose and relatively little to gain. But most of the people who commit crime have very little to lose and a lot to gain. They know that the chances of being punished are very small, so crime for them is perfectly rational.

Let me conclude by saying that currently crime pays. Crime pays for adults. It pays even more for juveniles. Juveniles will take things seriously only when crime stops paying. Hard-core offenders know the chances of being punished are very small, so crime for them is perfectly rational. We must make crime irrational, it is not the criminal who is irrational; it is society.

—Ernest Van den Haag[1]

The late Ernest Van den Haag made this statement to one of the authors in 1984. His contention was that we need to get tough on juvenile crime, and in the past three decades we have done that. We have increased the penalties for lawbreaking among juveniles, especially for those who commit serious offenses. This is documented throughout this text.

Still, considerable questions remain about whether getting tough, or making it costly to commit crime, is working. As a result, this text suggests other means of working with juveniles who have the promise of more effective outcomes. A future chapter examines positive youth development (PYD), one of these approaches. Other chapters look at other approaches.

But first, let's consider this question: Why do juveniles violate the law? As we will see, experts offer at least four basic explanations. First, some hold that juveniles commit crimes because youths have free will and rationally choose to do so. Second, biological and psychological causes have long offered support for those seeking other explanations for youth crime. This position supports the view that juvenile offenders either are biologically different from other youths or have experienced emotional damage in their early years. Third, social structural explanations argue that these youths are out of step with the norms of society because some are inadequately socialized, are negatively influenced by antisocial peers, or are poor and have no possibilities for good jobs later in life. Finally, some experts argue that multidimensional explanations are needed to understand why juveniles violate the law. Integrated explanations of delinquent behavior argue for the combination of two or more existing theories on the basis of their perceived commonalities.

However, whether talking about youth crime arising from free will, biological or psychological inferiority, social causes, or integrated explanations (two or more existing theories), it is clear that any particular theory only accounts for some of the reasons for juvenile offenses. Some explanations are more powerful than others in explaining youth crime, but even the most powerful amounts to only a small piece in the larger puzzle of juvenile offending.

Do juveniles understand why they are violating the law? The majority of those with whom the authors have worked during the past forty years did not know why they got into trouble. Occasionally, some did have insight into their behavior. For example, in Focus on Offenders 3–1, one youth first suggested that he committed an armed robbery because his mother became sick and, as the oldest sibling, he felt responsible for putting food on the table. The second offender was aware that she committed crimes to support her drug habit. With the assistance of another youth, the third offender committed an armed robbery because it made sense to rob a store of which the owner had poor sight and was old. More typically, however, juvenile offenders do not know why they break the law.

Even adult offenders are frequently unable to explain why they broke the law. Richard Speck, the murderer of seven student nurses in Chicago during the mid-1960s, reported to one of the authors: "I don't remember the crime. I don't remember killing those girls. I was stoned and drunk at the time. People think I'm some kind of monster. I don't know why I did it."[3]

This chapter examines the traditional theoretical approaches to the explanation of youth crime; the next chapter will examine explanations based on gender, race/ethnicity, and class.

Focus on Offenders 3–1
Staying Out of Trouble

I made up my mind the last time I was released from Fairfield that I was going to stay out of trouble. I went home and told my friends that I was going to stay clean. Then, my mother got sick, needed an operation, and couldn't work. I am older than my brothers and sisters and someone had to put food on the table. Instead of telling my friends to stay out of my face, I agreed to pull an armed robbery with them. We got caught and here I am.

—Nineteen-year-old institutionalized male

I got to the point that I was drug dependent. I went from pot to pills. Crystal (meth) is what really hooked me. To get money for drugs, I sold drugs, robbed houses, and did everything but sell my body. When you are drug dependent, you are willing to do anything to get your drugs. Even when I was arrested and sat in jail at 18 for a drug bust, I didn't know if I could walk away from drugs. But I knew if I didn't, the next step was the penitentiary.

—Twenty-two-year-old female college senior

We robbed the liquor store because we knew we wouldn't get caught. The owner of this store was half blind and old. He didn't move too good. He had a gun, but we knew there was no way he could hit us. If he went for his gun, we would have blown him away. Man, robbing that place was like taking candy from a baby.

—Seventeen-year-old male on aftercare[2]

CRITICAL THINKING QUESTION

To these three adolescents, crime was rational activity. How many adolescents do you believe are guided by rationality in what they do? Are there degrees of rationality?

What Is the Relationship Between Theory and Research?

Throughout history, civilizations have developed many techniques for seeking truth. Magic and superstition; the divine right of kings; the guidance of prophets, priests, and philosophers; intuition; and common sense have all been called on to provide the answers to the great questions. The failure of these methods to provide reliable and valid knowledge has led thinkers to search for other, better sources of truth. The contemporary solution is called *science*, the proponents of which contend that it provides more accurate answers than any other method yet discovered.

The two basic tools of science are theory and research, which are inextricably bound. Each helps to guide and direct the other. Research uses methods to collect data, helps to identify variables to be studied, tests variables for their worth, analyzes related variables, and suggests new directions for theory. Theory points the way to new research, helps derive new variables, builds interconnections among variables, interprets new and old ideas, builds systems of thought, and leads the way to new social and theoretical conclusions. Research collects and theory analyzes; research discovers and theory explains; research disproves and theory reorders. The process is never-ending. Without it, we would be likely to wallow in ignorance, personal prejudice, and inaccurate information. We would also be doomed to repeat harmful and even dangerous practices.

Thus, the main task of a theory is to explain the events in the world. A theory attempts to explain the cause of past events and predict when, where, and how future events will occur.[4] A theory is a basic building block indispensable for the advancement of human knowledge, but because social science theories can rarely be proven or rejected with the same finality as can theories in the natural sciences, several theories compete with each other.

One of the most critical debates in the study of crime is that of determinism versus free will. The basic issue is whether humans freely choose or whether other factors determine their choices. The concept of **free will** is based on the notion that we choose how to act. Crime or delinquency is viewed as purposeful activity resulting from rational decisions in which the pros and cons are weighed and the acts that promise the greatest potential gains are performed. Because juveniles and adults possess free will, make choices, and know what they are doing, those who commit crime are presumed to deserve punishment rather than treatment.

Focus on Theory and Research 3–2
What Is Empirically Based Juvenile Justice?

Historically, people have responded to troublesome youths by drawing on tradition, the dictates of priests and sovereigns, and what their "gut" told them—usually that the youths should be punished. This still happens, but the continued development of science is allowing researchers and those in the justice system to develop scales and other assessment instruments that measure more precisely the characteristics and needs of juveniles. From an historical perspective, this science is still new, but progress is being made.

A brief journey into the nature of science illustrates some of the issues facing it. Qualitative research, which is often based on clinical verbal descriptions of youths and their problems and characteristics, is still useful. Quantitative methods are what we call objective research, and involve asking questions and collecting data that can have numbers assigned to them and then be analyzed statistically. Generally, many scientists like the quantitative approach much more than the qualitative approach because of the opportunity to do statistical analysis on the data.

The ideal with both types of data collection is to achieve validity and reliability. Validity is when the researchers truly are studying what the researchers believe they are studying, and it is very difficult to achieve. Reliability is gained when different researchers using the same instruments come up with the same results. Scientists are making strides in achieving both valid and reliable data and this progress is very important, because economics dictates that money only be spent on therapies and programs that restore youths to health, reduce recidivism, integrate youths into their families and communities, and protect society. This book illustrates some of the research and assessment that is occurring today.

CRITICAL THINKING QUESTION

Why is it important for juvenile justice to be based on a sound empirical basis?

In contrast, the **deterministic view** holds that individuals cannot help committing criminal or delinquent acts because they are controlled either by internal factors (biological or psychological imbalances) or by external factors (poverty, learning crime from others, strain, or societal labeling). To put it another way, offenders are objects that react like billiard balls in response to different forces.[5] The youths are presumed to need treatment rather than punishment when internal and/or external factors force them into crime. Our interpretation of this free-will debate determines how we explain why individuals commit crime and what can be done about crime. See Figure 3–1 and Focus on Research 3–2.

Is Juvenile Crime Rational Behavior?

The association between criminal behavior and the rationality of crime has its roots in the eighteenth-century classical school of criminology. More recently, a number of approaches to the rationality of crime, especially the rational choice theory, have emerged.

Classical School of Criminology

Cesare Beccaria and Jeremy Bentham were the founders of the classical school of criminology. These scholars viewed humans as rational creatures who are willing to surrender enough liberty to the state so that society can establish rules and sanctions for the preservation of the social order.

In 1763, Cesare Bonesana Beccaria, Marquis of Beccaria, then only twenty-six and just out of law school, published *On Crimes and Punishment*. This essay was read avidly and

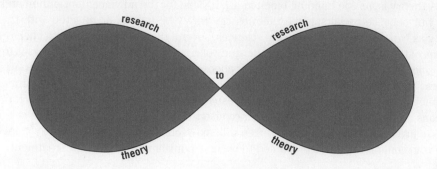

FIGURE 3–1
The Relationship Between Theory and Research

translated into the languages of Europe.[6] Beccaria based the legitimacy of criminal sanctions on the social contract. The authority of making laws rested with the legislator, who should have only one view in sight: "the greatest happiness of the greatest number." Beccaria also saw punishment as a necessary evil and suggested that "it should be public, immediate, and necessary: the least possible in the case given; proportioned to the crime; and determined by the laws."[7] He then defined the purpose and consequences of punishment as being "to deter persons from the commission of crime and not to provide social revenge. Not severity, but certainty and swiftness in punishment best secure this result."[8]

In 1780, the Englishman Jeremy Bentham published *An Introduction to the Principles of Morals and Legislation*, which further developed the philosophy of the classical school. Believing that a rational person would do what was necessary to achieve the maximum pleasure and the minimum pain, Bentham contended that punishment would deter criminal behavior, provided it was made appropriate to the crime. He stated that punishment has four objectives: (1) to prevent all offenses if possible, (2) to persuade a person who has decided to commit an offense to commit a less rather than a more serious one, (3) "to dispose [a person who has resolved upon a particular offense] to do no more mischief than is necessary to his purpose," and (4) to prevent the crime at as small a cost to society as possible.[9] See Figure 3–2.

The basic theoretical constructs of the classical school of criminology were developed from the writings of Beccaria and Bentham:

- Human beings were all looked on as rational creatures who, being free to choose their actions, could be held responsible for their behavior. This doctrine of **free will** was substituted for the widely accepted concept of theological determinism, which saw humans as predestined to do certain actions.

- Punishment was justified because of its practical usefulness, or utilitarianism. No longer was punishment acceptable on the grounds of vengeful retaliation or as expiation on the basis of superstitious theories of guilt and repayment. The aim of punishment was the protection of society, and its dominant theme was deterrence.

- The human being was presumed to be a creature governed by a **felicific calculus** oriented toward obtaining a favorable balance of pleasure and pain.

- A rational scale of punishment was proposed that should be painful enough to deter the criminal from further offenses and to prevent others from following his or her example of crime.

- Sanctions should be proclaimed in advance of their use; these sanctions should be proportionate to the offense and should outweigh the rewards of crime.

- Equal justice should be offered to everyone.

- Proponents of the classical school urged that individuals should be judged by the law solely for their acts, not for their beliefs.

According to the principles of the classical school then, juveniles who commit serious crimes or continue to break the law are presumed to deserve punishment rather than treatment, because they possess free will and know what they are doing. Their delinquencies are viewed as purposeful activity resulting from rational decisions in which the pros and cons are weighed and the acts that promise the greatest potential gains are performed.[10]

1747	1764	1780
Charles de Secondat, Baron De Montesquieu argued against severe punishments for crime in the book, *On the Spirit of the Laws*.	**Cesare Bonesana, Marquit of Beccaria** developed the notion of the social contract, and suggested that the purpose of punishment should be "to deter persons from the commission of crime and not to provide social revenge."	**Jeremy Bentham** contended that punishment would deter criminal behavior, provided it was made appropriate to the crime.

FIGURE 3–2
Founders of the Classical School

▲ The purchasing of drugs between two adolescents. Is this rational behavior?

Marie-Reine MATTERA/Glow Images

Rational Choice Theory

Rational choice theory, largely borrowed primarily from the utility model in economics, is one of the hottest present-day topics in criminology. This approach makes the assumption that the delinquent chooses to violate the law and has free will. In its pure form, rational choice theory is reviewed, at least in part, as an extension of the deterrence doctrine found in the classical school to include incentives as well as deterrence and to focus on the rational calculation of payoffs and costs before delinquent and criminal acts are committed.[11]

Lawrence E. Cohen and Marcus Felson are guided by ecological concepts and the presumed rationality of offenders in developing a **routine activity approach** for analyzing crime rate trends and cycles. This approach links the dramatic increase in crime rates since 1960 to changes in the routine activity structure of U.S. society and to a corresponding increase in target suitability and a decrease in the presence of "guardians," such as neighbors, friends, and family. The decline of the daytime presence of adult caretakers in homes and neighborhoods is partly the result of a trend toward increased female participation in the labor force.[12]

Steven F. Messner and Kenneth Tardiff used the routine activities approach to help interpret patterns of homicides in Manhattan (New York City) and found that the routine activities approach does indeed provide a useful framework for interpreting the social ecology involved in urban homicides. They found that people's lifestyles affected their chances of being victimized. People who tended to go out frequently were more often victimized by strangers, whereas those who preferred to stay at home were more likely to be killed by someone they knew.[13]

In sum, rational choice theory in criminology has recently moved away from the strictly rational, reasoning model of behavior to a more limited and constrained role for rational thought. Rational choice theory does not even assume that all or even most delinquent or criminal acts result from clear, planned, well-informed, and calculated choices.[14] It can still be argued, of course, that the rational choice model places more emphasis on rationality and free will than do other theories of delinquent behavior and that this degree of rationality is not present in most juvenile crimes.[15]

Beginning with a brief introduction to the theoretical constructs of the positivist school, we examine the biological, psychological, and sociological explanations of delinquency and crime in this section.

Development of Positivism

According to **positivism**, human behavior is but one more facet of a universe that is part of a natural order, but human beings can study behavior and discover how natural laws operate. Two positions diverge at this point of natural law. One view states that, because a natural order with its own laws exists, to change human behavior is impossible. The other view is that, just as laws operate in the medical, biological, and physical sciences, laws govern human behavior, and these laws can be understood and used. The causes of human behavior, once discovered, can be modified to eliminate or ameliorate many of society's problems. This second position is the one most scientists accept. The concept, as it applies to juvenile justice, is called positivism.

Positivism became the dominant philosophical perspective of juvenile justice at the time the juvenile court was established at the beginning of the twentieth century. During the Progressive Era (the period from about 1890 to 1920), the wave of optimism that swept through

TABLE 3–1
Three Assumptions of the Positivist Approach

- First, the character and personal backgrounds of individuals explain delinquent behavior. Positivism, relegating the law and its administration to a secondary role, looks for the cause of deviancy in the actor.

- Second, the existence of scientific determinism is a critical assumption of positivism. Delinquency, like any other phenomenon, is seen as determined by prior causes; it does not just happen. Because of this deterministic position, positivism rejects the view that the individual exercises freedom, possesses reason, and is capable of making choices.

- Third, the delinquent is seen as fundamentally different from the nondelinquent. The task then is to identify the factors that have made the delinquent a different kind of person. In attempting to explain this difference, positivism has concluded that wayward youths are driven into crime by something in their physical makeup, by aberrant psychological impulses, or by the meanness and harshness of their social environment.

Source: Donald C. Gibbons, "Differential Treatment of Delinquents and Interpersonal Maturity Level: A Critique," *Social Services Review* 44 (1970), 68.

U.S. society led to the acceptance of positivism. The doctrines of the emerging social sciences assured reformers that through positivism their problems could be solved. The initial step was to gather all the facts of the case. Reformers were then expected to analyze the important questions in a scientific fashion and discover the right solution using objective data.[16]

Armed with these principles, reformers set out to deal with the problem of delinquency, feeling confident that they knew how to find its cause. Progressives looked first to environmental factors, pinpointing poverty as the major cause of delinquency. Some progressives were attracted also to the doctrine of eugenics and believed that the biological limitations of youthful offenders drove them to delinquency. But eventually the psychological origins of delinquency came to be more widely accepted than either the environmental or the biological origins.[17] Table 3–1 lists three assumptions of positivism.

Biological Positivism

The belief that there is a biological explanation for criminality has a long history. For example, the study of physiognomy, which attempts to discern inner qualities through outward appearance, was developed by the ancient Greeks. The attention given to **biological positivism** in the United States can be divided into two periods.

Early Forms of Biological Positivism

The first period was characterized by the nature–nurture debate during the latter part of the nineteenth century and the early twentieth century. Cesare Lombroso's theory of physical abnormalities, genealogical studies, and theories of human somatotypes represent early approaches relating crime and delinquency to biological factors to the study of crime.

- *Lombroso and biological positivism.* Lombroso, a nineteenth-century Italian forensic psychiatrist, is frequently regarded as the father of criminology and the founder of biological positivism. In the process of examining prisoners before and after their deaths, he became convinced that there was a "criminal man" distinct from other human beings. According to Lombroso, the **born criminal** was atavistic, someone who reverts to an earlier evolutionary form or level; in other words, the characteristics of primitive men periodically reappeared in certain individuals.[18]

- *Genealogical studies and delinquency.* Henry Goddard's finding that at least half of all juvenile delinquents had mental deficits sparked intense debate for more than a decade.[19] But the findings of Edwin Sutherland discouraged future investigations of the correlation between intelligence and delinquency. Sutherland, evaluating IQ studies of delinquents and criminals, concluded that the lower IQs of offenders were related more to testing methods and scoring than the offenders' actual mental abilities.[20]

- *Body type theory.* Ernst Kretschmer, a German, first developed the theory that people have one of two body types: the schizothyme or the cyclothyme. Schizothymes are strong and muscular, and according to Kretschmer, they are more likely to be delinquent than are cyclothymes, who are soft skinned and lack muscle.[21] William Sheldon,[22] Sheldon Glueck and Eleanor Glueck,[23] and Juan B. Cortes and Florence M. Gatti also supported body type theory. Cortes and Gatti even drew on body type theory to develop a biopsychosocial theory of delinquency.[24]

Biological Positivism Today: Sociobiology

In the second half of the twentieth century, **sociobiologists** began to link genetic and environmental factors; they claimed that criminal behavior, like other behaviors, has both biological and social aspects. These sociobiologists have investigated the relationship between antisocial behavior and biological factors and the environment through studies of twins and adoption, chromosomal abnormalities, electrodermal activity, chemical imbalances, and psychopathy. The focus of these studies were on minimal functioning, intelligence, and physique.

In the twenty-first century, the two areas of sociobiology that are receiving the most attention are neuropsychological factors and delinquency and the relationship between temperament and negative behavior. Activity and emotionality are two behaviors that identify a child's temperament. *Activity* refers to motor movements, such as the movement of arms and legs, crawling or walking. Children who exhibit an inordinate amount of movement as compared with peers are often labeled *hyperactive* or as having an attention deficit disorder (generally referred to as *attention deficit hyperactivity disorder* or ADHD). *Emotionality* ranges from very little reaction to intense emotional reactions that are out of control.

The hyperactive child remains a temperamental mystery. Three common behaviors in such children are impulsivity (shifts quickly from one activity to another), inattention (is easily distracted and does not want to listen), and excessive motor activity (cannot sit still, runs about, is talkative and noisy). Educators note that ADHD children have difficulty staying on task, sustaining academic achievement in school, maintaining control over their behavior, and remaining cognitively organized.[25]

In sum, early biological positivism was replaced by sociobiology, which has more support in the criminological community. However, criminologists generally are reluctant to place much credence in biological explanations of delinquent behaviors because social factors are often needed to trigger and/or interact with the physiological characteristics of the brain and nervous system.

Psychological Positivism

Psychological factors have always been more popular in the United States in explaining juvenile offending than were biological or sociobiological factors. An early psychological explanation of juvenile offending was the psychoanalytic explanation. More recently, sensation seeking, reinforcement theory and psychopathic indicators are receiving considerable attention.

Psychoanalytic Explanations

Sigmund Freud's psychoanalytic theory, although not positivistic because of the inability to measure his concepts, was based on a biological determinist view of human behavior. In developing **psychoanalytic theory**, he contributed three insights that have shaped the handling of juvenile delinquents: (1) Children who have not yet learned to control primitive drives are pushed by the raw instincts and primitive drives of the id and cannot distinguish socially acceptable behavior from socially unacceptable behavior.[26] (2) Children must learn to control their sexual and aggressive drives, which create inner tensions that children must learn to resolve in socially acceptable ways.[27] (3) What a child has experienced emotionally by the age of five affects that child for the rest of his or her life. Emotional traumas experienced in childhood are especially likely to cause lifelong psychological problems.[28]

Voices of Delinquency: It Was the Rush

Voices of Delinquency: Understanding Red Flags in the Development of Delinquency: A Counselor's Perspective

Other psychologists have taken the insights of psychoanalysis and applied them to the situations of delinquents:

- William Healy focused on mental conflicts that originate in unsatisfactory family relationships.[29]
- August Aichhorn thought that delinquents had considerable hatred toward their parents because of the conflicted nature of family relationships and that children transfer this hatred to other authority figures.[30]
- Kate Friedlander focused on the development of antisocial characteristics in the personality, such as selfishness, impulsiveness, and irresponsibility, which she defined as the results of disturbed ego development in early childhood.[31]

Sensation Seeking and Delinquency

Sensation seeking is defined "as an individual's need for varied, novel, and complex sensations and experiences and the willingness to take physical and social risks for the sake of such experience."[32] Derived from optimal arousal theory, this construct assumes that organisms are driven or motivated to obtain an optimal level of arousal.[33]

Jack Katz's controversial book, *Seductions of Crime*, conjectures that individuals who commit crime are involved in "an emotional process—seductions and compulsions that have special dynamics." It is this "magical" and "transformative" experience that makes crime "sensible," even sensually "compelling." For example, he states that for many adolescents, shoplifting and vandalism offer an exciting experience, not because of the act, but because if adults see the youths do something wrong and the kids still can get away with it, the youths will feel they have proved their competence in society.[34]

Katz is arguing that instead of approaching criminal or delinquent behavior from the traditional focus on background factors, what needs more consideration are the foreground or situational factors that directly precipitate antisocial acts and reflect crimes' sensuality. According to Katz, offenders' immediate social environment and experiences encourage them to conceive of crimes as sensually compelling.[35]

The Psychopath

The psychopath (also known as the **sociopath**, *person with a conduct disorder*, and a host of other names) is acknowledged as the personality of the hard-core juvenile offender. According to the DSM-IV, these individuals are usually diagnosed with a conduct disorder. The claim is made that these are chiefly the unwanted, rejected children, who grow up but remain undomesticated "children" and never develop trust in or loyalty to other adults.[36] Hervey Cleckley gave a very complete clinical description of this type of personality.[37] More recently, Robert D. Hare developed a new checklist for the antisocial personality; some of the most significant items on the list are the following:

- Cunning and manipulativeness
- Giving false impressions to others
- Lack of remorse or guilt
- Callousness and lack of empathy
- Lack of realistic long-term goals
- Impulsivity
- Failure to accept responsibility for their actions.[38]

The continuity between childhood symptoms of emotional problems and adult psychopathic behavior emerged in Lee N. Robins' thirty-year follow-up of 526 white children who were patients in a St. Louis, Missouri, guidance clinic in the 1920s. Robins was looking for clues to the adult "antisocial personality," or "sociopathy."[39] Excluding cases involving organic brain damage, schizophrenia, mental retardation, or symptoms that appeared only after heavy drug or alcohol use, she found that the adult sociopath is almost invariably an antisocial child who has grown up. Indeed, she found no case of adult sociopathy without antisocial behavior before the age of eighteen. Over 50 percent of sociopathic males showed an onset of symptoms before the age of eight.[40]

What percentage of the juvenile offender population can be classified as psychopathic? It depends on what population of delinquents is being considered. The percentage is very low with status offenders and youthful offenders with minor violations and it increases as hard-core youthful offenders sentenced to long-term training schools come under examination. One study of adult prison inmates found that only 15 to 25 percent met the criteria for psychopathy.[41] Based on the experience of working with inmates for several years in a maximum-security juvenile institution, one of the authors would agree that those numbers seem reasonable for delinquents who commit serious personal and property offenses.

Reinforcement Theory

James Q. Wilson and Richard Herrnstein's *Crime and Human Nature* combines biosocial factors and psychological research with rational choice theory to redevelop reinforcement theory.[42] Wilson and Herrnstein consider potential causes of crime and of noncrime within the context of **reinforcement theory**, that is, the theory that behavior is governed by its consequent rewards and punishments, as reflected in the history of the individual.

The rewards of crime, according to Wilson and Herrnstein, are found in the form of material gain, revenge against an enemy, peer approval, and sexual gratification. The consequences of crime include pangs of conscience, disapproval of peers, revenge of the victim, and, most important, the possibility of punishment. The rewards of crime tend to be more immediate, whereas the rewards of noncrime generally are realized in the future. The authors are quick to dismiss evidence that is inconsistent with their theoretical framework but, as few have done in the field of criminology, they are able to show how gender, age, intelligence, families, schools, communities, labor markets, mass media, and drugs, as well as variations across time, culture, and race, influence the propensity to commit crimes, especially violent offenses.[43]

Wilson and Herrnstein's theory does have serious flaws. Most important, it consistently shows a disdain for the social context in which crime occurs. What Wilson and Herrnstein do, in effect, is to factor society out of their considerations of crime. Instead of examining criminal behavior as part of complex social mechanisms and attempting to understand the connection, they typically conclude that no conclusion is possible from the available data, and therefore no programs for reducing criminality among groups perceived as major sources of crime are worth their costs.[44]

Sociological Positivism

Social structure, social process, and conflict theories are the three main divisions of the sociological explanations of crime and delinquency. The basic flaw of explanations based on the individual, according to these sociological theories, is that such interpretations fail to come to grips with the underlying social and cultural conditions giving rise to youthful offending. These sociological theories add that the overall crime picture reflects conditions requiring collective social solutions; therefore, social reform, rather than individual counseling, must be given the highest priority in efforts to reduce crime problems.

Social Structural Theories

Using official statistics as their guide, social structure theorists claim that such forces as social disorganization, cultural deviance, and status frustration are so powerful that they induce lower-class individuals to become involved in criminal and delinquent behaviors. Social structural theories include the following:

1. *Social disorganization theory.* Clifford R. Shaw and Henry D. McKay's **social disorganization theory** views crime as resulting from the breakdown of social control by the traditional primary groups, such as the family and the neighborhood, because of the social disorganization of the community. Shaw and McKay's studies revealed that high-delinquency areas are found in disorganized communities characterized by physically deteriorated and condemned buildings, economic dependence, population

mobility, heterogeneous populations, high rates of school truancy, infant mortality, and tuberculosis.[45]

2. *Cultural deviance theory.* Walter B. Miller contends that the lower class has its own cultural history and that the motivation to become involved in criminal activities is intrinsic in lower-class culture. Miller's **cultural deviance theory** argues that the lower-class culture is characterized by a set of focal concerns, or values, that command widespread attention and a high degree of emotional involvement. The focal concerns consist of trouble, toughness, smartness, excitement, fate, and autonomy.[46]

▲ Disorganized, dilapidated and unkempt areas of cities both produce and attract delinquency and violent behaviors.
Kathryn O'Lare

Trouble: Getting into and out of trouble represents a major preoccupation of the lower class, and fighting, drinking, and sexual adventures are basic causes of trouble for this class.

Toughness: The "tough guy" who is hard, fearless, undemonstrative, and a good fighter is the ideal personality in the eyes of lower-class males.

Smartness: This value among the lower class involves the desire to outsmart, outfox, con, and dupe others.

Excitement: The quest for excitement leads to the widespread use of alcohol and drugs by both genders and to extensive gambling.

Fate: Lower-class individuals feel that their lives are subject to a set of forces over which they have little control.

Autonomy: Desire for personal independence is an important concern for lower-class persons because they feel controlled so much of the time.[47]

3. *Status frustration theory.* In an early version of **strain theory**, Robert K. Merton theorized that cultural goals and the means to achieve these goals must be reasonably well integrated if a culture is to be stable and smooth running. If individuals feel that a particular goal is important, they should have legitimate means of attaining it. The cultural goal of American society, according to Merton, is success, but the inequality of life in this nation produces structural pressures toward deviation to criminal behavior. In Table 3–2, types of individual adaptation are listed: a plus (+) signifies acceptance, a minus (−) signifies rejection, and a plus-and-minus (±) signifies a rejection of the prevailing values and a substitution of new ones.

Two of the most important delinquency theories are those by Cloward and Ohlin and by Cohen. Richard A. Cloward and Lloyd E. Ohlin's insight is that lower-class cultures are asked to orient their behavior toward the prospect of accumulating wealth while being denied the means of doing so legitimately. Thus, delinquent subcultures develop as collective social adjustments to the strains of blocked opportunity.[48] See Figure 3–3. Albert K. Cohen's status

TABLE 3–2
Merton's Theory of Anomie

	Means	Ends
1. Conformity	+	+
2. Innovation	−	+
3. Ritualism	+	−
4. Retreatism	−	−
5. Rebellion	±	±

Source: This material appears in Robert K. Merton, "Social Structure and Anomie," *American Sociological Review* 3 (1938), 676.

FIGURE 3–3
Cloward and Ohlin's Opportunity Theory

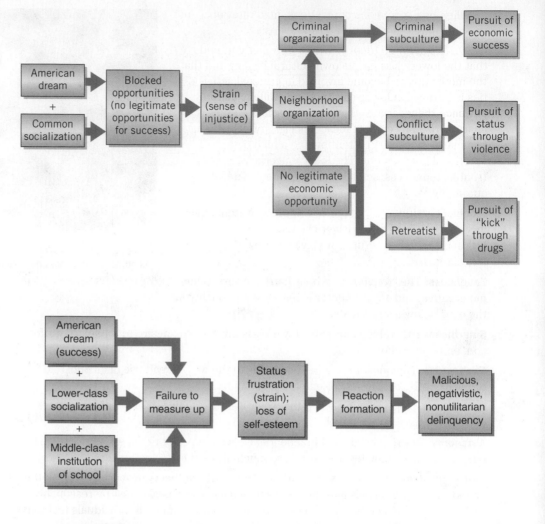

FIGURE 3–4
Cohen's Theory of Delinquent Subcultures

frustration (or strain) theory suggests that the destructive and malicious behavior of lower-class delinquent subcultures is a reaction to their failure to achieve middle-class norms and values.[49] See Figure 3–4.

▲ Lil' MoJo. Children growing up in a culture of gangs are quickly socialized into gang life. This young boy knew how to "blood up" at the young age of ten.
Constinia Charbonnette

Social Process Theories

Social process theories examine the interactions between people and their environment that influence individuals to become involved in criminal or delinquent behaviors. These sociopsychological theories became popular in the 1960s because they provided a mechanism for understanding how environmental factors influence individual decision making. Differential association, containment, social control, and labeling theories are the social process theories that have been the most widely received.

1. *Differential association theory.* According to Edwin H. Sutherland's **differential association theory**, criminals and youthful offenders learn crime from others. Thus, crime, like any other form of behavior, is a product of social interaction. Sutherland began with the notion that criminal behavior is to be expected of those individuals who have internalized a preponderance of definitions favorable to law violations. That is, individuals are taught their

basic values, norms, skills, and perceptions of self from others; therefore, it makes sense that they also learn crime from "significant others."[50]

2. *Containment theory.* Walter C. Reckless developed **containment theory** in order to explain why individuals do not commit crime and delinquent acts. He argued that individuals are affected by a variety of forces, some driving them toward—and others restraining them from—crime. As a control theory, which can explain both conforming behavior and deviance, containment theory has two elements: an internal control system and an external control system. Internal containment is made up of self-control, a positive self-concept, ego strength, a well-developed superego, high frustration tolerance, and a high sense of responsibility. External containment represents the buffers in the person's immediate environment that are able to hold him or her within socially acceptable bounds. The assumption is that strong internal containment and reinforcement of external containment provide insulation against delinquent or criminal behavior.[51]

3. *Social control theory.* Travis Hirschi developed another version of control theory that examines the individual's ties to conventional society. In *Causes of Delinquency*, Hirschi outlined **social control theory**, in which he linked delinquent behavior to the bond an individual has with conventional social groups, such as the family and the school. The social bond, according to Hirschi, is made up of four main elements: attachment, commitment, involvement, and belief.[52] See Figure 3–5.

An individual's attachment to conventional others is the first element of the social bond. Sensitivity toward others, argues Hirschi, relates to the ability to internalize norms and to develop a conscience.[53] Attachment to others also includes the ties of affect and respect children have to parents, teachers, and friends. The stronger the attachment to others, the more likely an individual is to take this into consideration when and if he or she is tempted to commit a delinquent act.[54]

Commitment to conventional activities and values is the second element of the bond. An individual is committed to the degree that he or she is willing to invest time, energy, and the self in conventional activities, such as educational goals, property ownership, or reputation building. When a committed individual considers the cost of delinquent behavior, he or she uses common sense and thinks of the risk of losing the investment already made in conventional behavior.[55]

Involvement also protects an individual from delinquent behavior. Because time and energy are limited, involvement in conventional activities leaves no time for delinquent behavior. "The person involved in conventional activities is tied to appointments, deadlines, working hours, plans, and the like," reasoned Hirschi, "so the opportunity to commit deviant acts rarely arises. To the extent that he is engrossed in conventional activities, he cannot even think about deviant acts, let alone act out his inclinations."[56]

The fourth element is belief. Delinquency arises from the absence of effective beliefs that forbid socially unacceptable behavior. Respect for the law and for the social norms of society is an important component of belief. This respect for the values of the law and legal system is derived from intimate relations with other people, especially parents.[57]

4. *Labeling perspective.* Labeling theory contends that society creates deviants by labeling those who are apprehended as "different" from others, when in reality the youths are different only because authorities "tagged" them with a criminal label. Edwin Lemert and Howard Becker are the chief proponents of the view that formal and informal societal reactions to criminal behavior can influence the subsequent attitudes and behaviors of criminals and delinquents.[58]

Lemert focused attention on the interaction between social control agents and rule violators and

Voices of Delinquency: Peers Created Some Grief for Me

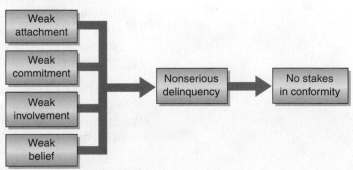

ELEMENTS OF THE BOND

FIGURE 3–5
Elements of Travis Hirschi's Social Bond

the way certain behavior came to be labeled "criminal" or "deviant." His concept of primary and secondary deviation is regarded as one of the most important insights of this **labeling perspective**. According to Lemert, *primary deviation* refers to the behavior of the individual, and *secondary deviation* is behavior resulting from society's response to that behavior. Lemert contended that society's reaction—use of the "deviant" label—forces a change in the status or role of the individual and, in effect, pressures the person to pursue deviant or criminal behavior.[59] Thus, the social reaction to the criminal is crucial in understanding the progressive commitment of a person to a criminal way of life.

Becker adds that once a person is caught and labeled, that person becomes an outsider and gains a new social status, with consequences for both one's self-image and one's public identity. The person is regarded as a different kind of person, and he or she finds it difficult to regain social acceptance. Hence, society's labeling ultimately forces a juvenile or an adult into a deviant career.[60]

Conflict Theory

A great deal of variation exists among conflict theories. Some theories emphasize the importance of socioeconomic class; other theories emphasize power and authority, and others, group and cultural conflict.

1. *Socioeconomic class and Marxist criminology.* Karl Marx, who wrote very little on the subject of crime as the term is defined today, inspired a new school of criminology that is variously defined as "Marxist," "radical," "critical," "left-wing," "socialist," or "new." The **Marxist perspective** views the state and the law itself as ultimate tools of the economic interests of the ownership class. It is capitalism, rather than human nature, that produces egocentric, greedy, and predatory human beings. The ownership class is guilty of the crime of the brutal exploitation of the working class. Conventional crime, according to this perspective, is caused by extreme poverty and economic alienation, products of the dehumanizing and demoralizing capitalist system.

2. *Power and authority relationships.* Ralf Dahrendorf and Austin T. Turk have emphasized the relationships between authorities and their subjects. They contend that power is the critical variable explaining crime. These authors argue that although Marx built his theory on only one form of power (property ownership), a more useful perspective could be constructed by incorporating broader concepts of power.[61]

3. *Group and cultural conflict.* Another dimension of the conflict perspective focuses on group and cultural conflict. Thorsten Sellin and George Vold advocated this approach to the study of crime, the causes of crime, necessary to understand the concept of *conduct norms*. This concept refers to the rules of a group concerning how its members should act under particular conditions. The violation of these rules guiding behavior arouses a group reaction.[62]

   Vold views society "as a congeries [an aggregation] of groups held together in a shifting, but dynamic equilibrium of opposing group interests and efforts."[63] He formulated a theory of group conflict that contends that "the whole political process of law making, law breaking, and law enforcement directly reflects deep-seated and fundamental conflicts between interest groups and the more general struggles for the control of the police power of the state."[64]

See Table 3–3 for a comparison of the biological, psychological, and sociological theories.

In sum, when social structural, social process, and social conflict theories are considered separately, a piece of the puzzle of how the environment influences a youth to become involved in crime is missing. Together, they provide a more satisfactory explanation than does each separately for why juveniles become involved in delinquency. This realization led to the development of integrated theory.

TABLE 3–3
Comparison of Biological, Psychological, and Sociological Theories

Theory	Proponents	Causes of Crime Identified
Atavistic, or born criminal	Lombroso	The atavistic criminal is a reversion to an earlier evolutionary form.
Developmental	Moffitt	Delinquent behavior proceeds along two developmental paths: On one path, early-age delinquents develop a lifelong pattern of delinquency; on the other, the adolescent develops a limited path and desists from delinquency around eighteen years of age.
Psychoanalytic	Freud	Unconscious motivations result from early childhood experiences.
Emotional process and situational factors	Katz	Delinquency becomes an emotional process that is seductive and sensually compelling.
Psychopathic personality	Hare	Lack of affect, impulsiveness, and aggression.
Reinforcement	Wilson and Herrnstein	Several key constitutional and psychological factors.
Social disorganization	Shaw and McKay	Delinquent behavior becomes an alternative mode of socialization through which youths who are part of disorganized communities are attracted to delinquent values and traditions.
Cultural deviance	Miller	The lower class has a distinctive culture of its own, and its local concerns, or values, make lower-class boys more likely to become involved in delinquent behavior.
Strain	Merton	Social structure exerts pressure on those individuals who cannot attain the cultural goal of success to engage in nonconforming behavior.
Delinquency opportunity	Cloward and Ohlin	Lower-class boys seek out illegitimate means to attain middle-class success goals if they are unable to attain them through legitimate means.
Status frustration	Cohen	Lower-class boys are unable to attain the goals of middle-class culture, and therefore they become involved in nonutilitarian, malicious, and negative behavior.
Differential association	Sutherland	Criminal behavior is learned by individuals through interaction with others who hold attitudes and definitions favorable to the violation of the law.
Containment	Reckless	Strong inner and reinforced external containment provide insulation against delinquent behavior.
Social control	Hirschi	Delinquent acts result when an individual's bond to society is weak or broken.
Labeling	Lemert and Becker	Society creates deviants by labeling those who are apprehended as different from other juveniles, when in reality, the youths are "different" only because they have been given the label "deviant."
Marxist perspective	Marx	Conventional delinquency and crime are caused by extreme poverty and economic alienation.
General theory of crime	Gottfredson and Hirschi	Lack of self-control is the common factor underlying problem behaviors.
Integrated social process theory	Elliott and colleagues	Integrates the strongest elements of strain, social control, and social learning perspectives into a single paradigm that accounts for delinquent behavior and drug use.
Interactional theory	Thornberry	Associations with delinquent peers and delinquent values make up social delinquency; especially prolonged serious delinquency is learned and reinforced.

How Does Integrated Theory Explain Juvenile Crime?

Several integrated theories for delinquent behavior have been developed. Three of the most important are Michael Gottfredson and Travis Hirschi's general theory of crime, Delbert Elliott's integrated social process theory, and Terence P. Thornberry's interactional theory[65]:

1. *Gottfredson and Hirschi's general theory of crime.* In their 1990 publication, *A General Theory of Crime*, Gottfredson and Hirschi define lack of self-control as the common factor underlying problem behaviors.[66] Self-control is the degree to which an individual is "vulnerable to the temptations of the moment."[67] The other pivotal construct in this theory of crime is crime opportunity, which is a function of the structural or situational circumstances encountered by the individual. In combination, these two constructs are intended to capture the simultaneous influence of external and internal restraints on behavior.[68] More than two dozen studies have been conducted on general theory, and the vast majority are largely favorable.[69]

2. *Elliott and colleagues' integrated social process theory.* Delbert Elliott and colleagues offer "an explanatory model that expands and synthesizes traditional strain, social control, and social learning perspectives into a single paradigm that accounts for delinquent behavior and drug use."[70] Integrating the strongest features of these theories into a single theoretical model, Elliott and colleagues contend that the experience of living in socially disorganized areas leads youths to develop weak bonds with conventional groups, activities, and norms. High levels of strain, as well as weak bonds with conventional groups, lead some youth to seek out delinquent peer groups. These antisocial peer groups provide both positive reinforcement for delinquent behavior and role models for this behavior. Consequently, Elliott and

---

Evidence-Based Practice
Targeting the Programs That Show Particular Promise

Lipsey, et.al. summarize some of the research recognized for about a decade that shows that some popular programs simply do not work. Public and professional favorites such as "Scared Straight," and DARE cost millions of hours in time wasted and dollars lost, even though the programs have a "feel good" aura and a mantel of plausibility about them.

A metanalysis by Lipsey and his colleagues is allowing professionals and practitioners to sharpen their focus on just what works best and plan accordingly. Their findings focus on the risk level of juveniles, therapeutic versus control treatment philosophies, generic programs types and embedded model programs, and amount and quality of service.

Target High Risk Cases. Their findings make it clear that high risk rather than low risk juveniles should be the focus of attention. Studies indicate that juveniles unlikely to get into trouble anyway will absorb time and funds without significant payback. High risk juveniles, on the other hand, are well worth the time and cost and many studies report the important recidivism reductions.

Use Programs That Calli on Constructive Personal Development. Analyses of therapeutic programs as opposed to control programs also show considerable differences. Youths who are the subjects of discipline instilling programs, those who are expected to be deterred from crime and those kept under close surveillance to keep them from bad behavior—or under control types of programs—recidivate more than those who are on treatment programs. For example, youths who undergo skills development,

relationship building, insight, counseling and case management improve significantly more than those under the control programs.

Favor Those Program Types that Have Shown the Largest Effects in Research Studies. Generic types of programs, such as different types of counseling, all show positive gains by juveniles. Group programs, mentoring, mixed methods, family and family crisis programs are are successful and do include such "brand name" techniques as Functional Family Therapy and Multisystemic Therapy. Cognitive-behavioral therapy, behavioral techniques, and social skills training rate well in the analyses. As might be expected, variations across therapies are found, but the overall impact of the programs is positive.

Implement the Selected Programs Well. The quality and amount of service provided is important. Neither too little nor too much "medicine" must be dispensed for youths to receive maximum benefit without undue costs and, the quality of the programs, although not well reported, can be measured by factors such as dropout rates, staff turnover and poorly trained staff. These latter factors must be singled out for further attention.

Source: Adapted and quoted from Mark W. Lipsey, James C. Howell, Marion R. Kelly, Gabielle Chapman, and Darin Carver, "Improving the Effectiveness of Juvenile Justice Programs: A New Perspective on Evidence-Based Practice," *Center for Juvenile Justice Reform: Working across Systems of Care,* (Washington, D.C.: Georgetown University, December 2010), pp. 22–28.

colleagues theorize, there is a high probability of involvement in delinquent behavior when bonding to delinquent groups is combined with weak bonding to conventional groups.[71] Tests of these proportions are generally supportive of the theory.[72]

3. *Thornberry's interactional theory.* In Thornberry's interactional theory of delinquency, the initial impetus toward delinquency comes from a weakening of the person's bond to conventional society, represented by attachment to parents, commitment to school, and belief in conventional values. Associations with delinquent peers and delinquent values make up the social setting in which delinquency, especially prolonged serious delinquency, is learned and reinforced. These two variables, along with the delinquent behavior itself, form a mutually reinforcing causal loop that leads toward increasing delinquency involvement over time.[73] Moreover, this interactive process develops over the person's life cycle. Thornberry's theory essentially views delinquency as the result of events occurring in a developmental fashion. Delinquency is not viewed as the end product; instead, it leads to the formation of delinquent values, which then contribute to disconnections in social bonds, more attachments to antisocial peers, and further involvement in delinquent behavior. As found in other developmental theories, some variables affect unlawful behavior at certain ages and other factors at other ages.[74]

Best practice programs and their application to juvenile justice have considerable promise in promoting a more effective juvenile justice system. In this chapter, in the Evidence-Based Practice feature, we examine the more promising interventions for reducing aggression and violence.

Why Has Delinquency Across the Life Course Become so Important in Studying the Theories of Juvenile Crime?

Delinquency across the life course (DLC), or life-course criminology, is particularly concerned with documenting and explaining within-individual changes in offending throughout life. Robert J. Sampson and John H. Laub's analysis of the Gluecks' classic longitudinal study of one thousand men has been a major impetus to the life-course perspective.[75] Using life history data drawn from the Gluecks' longitudinal study, Laub and Sampson found that although adult crime is connected to childhood behavior, both incremental and abrupt changes still take place through changes in adult social bonds. The emergence of strong social bonds to work and family among adults deflects early behavior trajectories. Laub and Sampson also argue that the events that trigger the formation of strong adult bonds to work and family commonly occur by chance or luck.[76]

The concept of a **turning point** in the life course is one of the fascinating contributions of Laub and Sampson's research. A turning point involves a gradual or dramatic change and may lead to "a modification, reshaping, or transition from one state, condition, or phase to another."[77] In seeking to unravel the mechanisms that operate at key turning points to shift a risk trajectory to a more adaptive path, Laub and Sampson found that stable employment and a good marriage, or changing roles and environment, can lead to investment of social capital or relations among persons.[78]

Longitudinal studies usually reveal that delinquent careers differ by gender. Male careers usually begin earlier and extend longer into the adult years. Studies of youth gangs reveal that female members are more likely than male members to leave the gang if they have a child. Also, conventional life patterns—particularly marriage, parenting, and work—draw both males and females away from gangs and offending behaviors, but do so more completely and quickly for females.[79]

Rebecca S. Katz, using waves 1 and 7 of the National Longitudinal Survey of Youth, found that, similar to other studies, childhood victimization, sexual discrimination, adult racial discrimination, and the experience of domestic violence largely explained women's involvement in crime and deviance.[80] John Hagan and Holly Foster, based on their analysis of data from the first two waves of the National Longitudinal Study of Adolescent Health, found that the life-course consequences of experiences with violence, especially violence in intimate adolescent relationships, result in special difficulties for female juveniles, including depression and teenage pregnancy.[81]

Alex R. Piquero, Robert Brame, and Terrie E. Moffitt, using data from the Cambridge Study of males and from the Dunedin, New Zealand, birth cohort found that the vast majority of both males and females never experience a conviction, and for those who do, the number of convictions is quite small. They also found that boys, more than girls, tend to become involved in crime when measured by conviction experience, and once involved, boys exhibit more variations in conviction activity than do girls. The data further revealed that boys can be separated into low-, medium-, and high-frequency offender groups, whereas girls can be separated into low- and medium-frequency groups. Finally, their analysis found "that the process of continuity in criminal activity is formed by the end of adolescence similarly for both males and females" and that "there appear to be more similarities than differences across gender in how adolescent and adult patterns of offending are linked."[82]

At least three studies have examined the desistance process among women. Ira Sommers, Deborah R. Baskin, and Jeffrey Fagan found that quality marriages led women to desist from crime, with some variation depending on the class and race of the women being studied.[83] A later study by Sommers and Baskin revealed that the desistance process was quite different for inner-city women of color. These women were more likely to desist as the result of receiving alcohol and drug treatment or because they grew tired or fearful of repeated imprisonments.[84] Finally, as will be discussed in Chapter 4, Peggy C. Giordano and colleagues followed up on a sample of serious adolescent female delinquents and found neither marital attachment nor job stability to be strongly related to female desistance. Instead, desisters underwent a cognitive shift, or transformation, in which they experienced successful "hooks for change." These hooks "facilitated the development of an alternative view of self that was seen as fundamentally incompatible with criminal behavior."[85]

Conclusions

The authors draw three conclusions regarding the prospects of being able to reduce established patterns of aggressive and personal violence.

First, large amounts of evidence show that it is possible to reduce the rate of occurrence of violent patterns among individuals identified with these violent characteristics. Beyond the methodological weaknesses, encouraging trends are still present. Emotional self-management, social problem solving, and interpersonal skills show mainly positive effects with a reasonably high degree of reliability.

Second, with regard to almost all issues, a need is present for more and better quality research if reducing violence and aggression is not to remain an underdeveloped area of correctional rehabilitation.

Third, in relation to practice, increasing the duration and intensity of treatment above presently inadequate levels is necessary if intended effects are to be achieved.

CRITICAL THINKING QUESTION

To what extent do you believe this review of existing research provides hope for working with offenders who have histories of violent behaviors or tendencies?

What Is the Application of Theory to Practice?

One advantage of the *Voices in the Juvenile Justice System*, a supplement to this text, is that some of the stories record the accounts of individuals across their life course. A few stories describe how individuals made decisions that resulted in their being arrested, adjudicated delinquent, sent to jail or detention, and placed in residential programs. A couple of stories include accounts of how decision making resulted in a prison sentence.

With nearly every story, ask yourself the following questions: How did this person's family background influence the course of his or her behaviors? How did success or failure in school influence subsequent behaviors? How was he or she affected by the environment? Why did he or she become involved in a youth gang? Why did this person become a drug user? What influenced this person to stop taking drugs or becoming involved in other illegal behaviors?

Also, ask yourself which theory or theories found in this chapter seem to apply closely to the choices that this person made? If more than one theory is required to explain behavior, what theories would you use? If none of the theories found in this chapter seem to apply to a particular story, what theoretical constructs are needed to understand this behavior?

Juvenile Justice Videos

MENTAL ILLNESS

Mental Illness focuses on the complicated issues the juvenile court system handles when dealing with juveniles who have mental illnesses. In the video a situation arises where an institutionalized offender engages in the abnormal behavior of self-mutilation and extreme anger. The individual injures himself repeatedly and has a long history of violent outbursts, often victimizing himself as well as others. How does the facility handle the situation? The individual has difficulty following orders; what does the institution do to assist the youth? Based on the readings, how do the juvenile court systems assess and handle youths who suffer from mental illnesses? Discuss what treatments juvenile institutions may use to deal with these children.

SUMMARY

LEARNING OBJECTIVE 1 Explain the roles of theory and research as they pertain to causes of juvenile crime.

Theory and research are the two basic tools of science, and they are inextricably bound. Each helps to guide and direct the other.

LEARNING OBJECTIVE 2 Summarize the principles and influences of the classical school of criminology.

The classical school believed that individuals needed to have free will to possess the rationality that is necessary to choose whether to commit criminal behavior or not. The classical school in recent decades has influenced both juvenile and adult justice in perceiving that offenders, especially hard-core ones, have rationality when they commit crime and deserve to be punished for their behaviors.

LEARNING OBJECTIVE 3 Describe biological theories of juvenile crime and delinquency.

A number of early theories relate crime and delinquency to biological factors. More recently, sociobiologists have linked genetic and environmental factors claiming that delinquent behavior, like other behaviors, has both biological and social aspects.

LEARNING OBJECTIVE 4 Describe psychological theories of juvenile crime and delinquency.

Early on, psychoanalytic explanations received great attention, but more recently, a number of psychological factors, including psychopathic factors, sensation seeking, and delinquency and reinforcement theory, have been examined for their contributions in understanding delinquent behavior.

LEARNING OBJECTIVE 5 Describe sociological theories of juvenile crime and delinquency.

The sociological theories of juvenile crime and delinquency can be divided into structural and social process theories. The most important social structural theories are social disorganization theory, cultural deviance theory, and status frustration theory. Differential association, containment, social control, and labeling theories are the social process theories that have been the most widely received.

LEARNING OBJECTIVE 6 Summarize integrated theories of juvenile crime and delinquency.

The most widely hailed integrated theories are Gottfredson and Hirschi's general theory of crime, Elliott's integrated social process theory, and Thornberry's interactional theory. Each of these theories draws from various theories, typically strain, to generate an integrated theory that captures a larger number of delinquent behaviors.

KEY TERMS

autonomy, p. 57

biological positivism, p. 53

born criminal, p. 53

containment theory, p. 58

cultural deviance theory, p. 57

delinquency across the life course (DLC), p. 63

deterministic view, p. 50

differential association theory, p. 58

excitement, p. 57

fate, p. 57

felicific calculus, p. 51

free will, p. 49

labeling perspective, p. 60

Marxist perspective, p. 60

positivism, p. 52

psychoanalytic theory, p. 54

REVIEW QUESTIONS

1. What is the labeling perspective's definition of why adolescents become delinquent? Do you agree with this interpretation?
2. Which of the three integrated theories makes the most sense to you? What are the advantages of integrated theory? What are its disadvantages?
3. Should poverty exclude an adolescent from responsibility for delinquent behavior? Why or why not?
4. Why have the juvenile courts been so quick to apply the concept of free will and rationality to violent juvenile criminals?
5. To what extent do you believe juveniles are rational in their behavior? What are the implications of your answer for the justice system?

GROUP EXERCISES

1. **Writing to Learn:** Write an essay in class that explains the nature and types of biological positivism. Critique and revise.
2. **Writing to Learn:** Write an essay in class that explains the nature and types of psychological positivism. (Skip the psychoanalytic approach for this particular exercise unless requested by the instructor.) Critique and revise.
3. **Writing to Learn:** Write an essay that explains the nature and types of sociological positivism. Critique and revise.
4. **Class Presentations:** Divide the class into three groups. Ask each group to report on one of the major ideas of structural functionalism, social process, and conflict theories. Let each group defend its ideas against the other approaches as to why their ideas are the strongest.
5. **Group Work:** Divide the class into three groups. Each group should develop one of the three following approaches: the major and minor ideas of Gottfredson and Hirschi's general theory of crime, Elliott's integrated social process theory, and Thornberry's interactional theory. After identifying the components of each theory, have each group pull together all of the ideas of each theory into a schema of the whole theory and present the ideas to the class.

NOTES

1. Interview by one of the authors with Ernest Van den Haag in 1984.
2. Interview by one of the authors in the 1970s.
3. Interview by one of the authors with Richard Speck in 1977.
4. Jonathan H. Turner, *The Structure of Sociological Theory* (Homewood, IL: Dorsey, 1974), 2.
5. Michael Phillipson, *Understanding Crime and Delinquency* (Chicago: Aldine, 1974), 18.
6. Cesare Bonesana Beccaria, *On Crimes and Punishment*, translated by H. Paolucci (1764), reprinted ed. (Indianapolis, IN: Bobbs-Merrill, 1963).
7. Ysabel Rennie, *The Search for Criminal Man: A Conceptual History of the Dangerous Offender* (Lexington, MA: Lexington Books, 1978), 15.
8. Beccaria, *On Crimes and Punishment*, 179.
9. Rennie, *The Search for Criminal Man*, 22.
10. Edward Cimler and Lee Roy Bearch, "Factors Involved in Juvenile Decisions About Crime," *Criminal Justice and Behavior* 8 (September 1981), 275–86.
11. Ronald L. Akers, "Deterrence, Rational Choice, and Social Learning Theory: The Path Not Taken," paper presented at the annual meeting of the American Society of Criminology, Reno, NV, November 1989, 2–3.
12. Lawrence E. Cohen and Marcus Felson, "Social Change and Crime Rate Trends: A Routine Activity Approach," *American Sociological Review* 44 (August 1979), 588–609.
13. Steven F. Messner and Kenneth Tardiff, "The Social Ecology of Urban Homicides: An Application of the 'Routine Activities' Approach," *Criminology* 23 (1985), 241–67.
14. Akers, "Deterrence, Rational Choice, and Social Learning Theory," 12.
15. Akers, however, questions this in his paper, "Deterrence, Rational Choice, and Social Learning Theory," 11.
16. See David J. Rothman, *Conscience and Convenience: The Asylum and Its Alternatives in Progressive America* (Boston: Little, Brown, 1980), 32.
17. Ibid., 43–60.
18. Cesare Lombroso, Introduction to C. Lombroso-Ferrero, *Criminal Man According to the Classification of Cesare Lombroso* (New York: Putnam, 1911), xiv.
19. Henry Goddard, *Efficiency and Levels of Intelligence* (Princeton, NJ: Princeton University Press, 1920).
20. Edwin Sutherland, "Mental Deficiency and Crime," in *Social Attitudes*, edited by Kimball Young (New York: Henry Holt, 1926).

21. William Sheldon, *Varieties of Delinquent Youth* (New York: Harper & Row, 1949).

22. Ibid.

23. S. Glueck and E. Glueck, *Physique and Delinquency* (New York: Harper & Row, 1956), p. 9.

24. Juan B. Cortes and Florence M. Gatti, *Delinquency and Crime: A Biopsychosocial Approach: Empirical, Theoretical, and Practical Aspects of Criminal Behavior* (New York: Seminar Press, 1972), 18–19.

25. Curt R. Bartol and Anne M. Bartol, *Delinquency and Justice: A Psychosocial Approach,* 2d ed. (Upper Saddle River, NJ: Prentice Hall, 1998), 89.

26. Sigmund Freud, *An Outline of Psychoanalysis*, translated by James Strachey (1940 reprint, New York: W. W. Norton, 1963).

27. Ibid.

28. Ibid.

29. William Healy, *Twenty-Five Years of Child Guidance Studies from the Institute of Juvenile Research,* Series C, no. 256 (Chicago, IL: Department of Public Welfare, 1914).

30. August Aichhorn, *Wayward Youth* (New York: Viking Press, 1963).

31. Kate Friedlander, *The Psychoanalytic Approach to Juvenile Delinquency* (London: Routledge and Kegan Paul, 1947).

32. Marvin Zuckerman, *Sensation Seeking Beyond the Optimal Level of Arousal* (Hillsdale, NJ: Lawrence Erlbaum, 1979), 10.

33. Ibid.

34. Jack Katz, *Seductions of Crime: Moral and Sensual Attractions in Doing Evil* (New York: Basic Books, 1988).

35. Ibid.

36. Richard L. Jenkins, "Delinquency and a Treatment Philosophy," in *Crime, Law and Corrections*, edited by Ralph Slovenko (Springfield, IL: Charles C Thomas, 1966), 135–36.

37. Hervey M. Cleckley, *The Mask of Sanity* 3rd ed (St. Louis, MO: Mosley Company, 1955), 132–37.

38. Robert Hare, " Psychopathy: A Clinical Construct Whose Time Has Come," *Criminal Justice and Behavior* 23 (1996), 25–54.

39. Lee N. Robins, *Deviant Children Grown Up: A Sociological and Psychiatric Study of Sociopathic Personality* (Baltimore, MD: Williams & Wilkins, 1966), 256.

40. Lee N. Robins et al., "The Adult Psychiatric Status of Black Schoolboys," *Archives of General Psychiatry* 24 (1971), 338–45.

41. Rolf Holmqvist, "Psychopathy and Affect Consciousness in Young Criminal Offenders," *Journal of Interpersonal Violence* 23 (February 2008), 209–24.

42. James Q. Wilson and Richard J. Herrnstein, *Crime and Human Nature* (New York: Simon & Schuster, 1985).

43. Ibid.

44. Edgar Z. Friedenberg, "Solving Crime," *Readings: A Journal of Reviews* (March 1986), 21.

45. Clifford R. Shaw and Henry D. McKay, *Juvenile Delinquency and Urban Areas* (Chicago: University of Chicago Press, 1942).

46. Walter B. Miller, "Lower-Class Culture as a Generating Milieu of Gang Delinquency," *Journal of Social Issues* 14 (1958), 9–10.

47. Ibid.

48. Richard A. Cloward and Lloyd E. Ohlin, *Delinquency and Opportunity: A Theory of Delinquency* (New York: Free Press, 1960).

49. Albert K. Cohen, *Delinquent Boys: The Culture of the Gang* (New York: Free Press, 1955).

50. Edwin H. Sutherland, *Principles of Criminology* (Philadelphia: J. B. Lippincott Company, 1947).

51. The principles of containment theory are described in Walter C. Reckless, "A New Theory of Delinquency and Crime," *Federal Probation* 24 (December 1952), 133–38.

52. Travis Hirschi, *Causes of Delinquency* (Berkeley: University of California Press, 1969).

53. Ibid., 18.

54. Ibid., 83.

55. Ibid., 20.

56. Ibid., 22.

57. Ibid., 198.

58. Edwin L. Lemert, *Social Pathology* (New York: McGraw-Hill, 1951); and Howard S. Becker, *Outsiders* (New York: Free Press, 1958).

59. Lemert, *Social Pathology.*

60. Becker, *Outsiders.*

61. Ralf Dahrendorf and Austin T. Turk, *Class and Class Conflict in Industrial Society* (Palo Alto, CA: Stanford University Press, 1959).

62. Thorsten Sellin, *Culture, Conflict, and Crime* (New York: Social Science Research Council, 1938), 28.

63. George B. Vold, *Theoretical Criminology*, 2d ed., prepared by Thomas J. Bernard (New York: Oxford University Press, 1979), 283.

64. Ibid., 288.

65. Michael G. Gottfredson and Travis Hirschi, *A General Theory of Crime* (Stanford, CA: Stanford University Press, 1990); Delbert S. Elliott, David Huizinga, and Suzanne S. Ageton, *Explaining Delinquency and Drug Use* (Beverley Hills, CA: Sage, 1985); Delbert S. Elliott, Suzanne S. Ageton, and Rachelle J. Canter, "An Integrated Theoretical Perspective on Delinquent Behavior," *Journal of Research in Crime and Delinquency* 16 (1979), 3–27; Terence P. Thornberry, "Toward an Interactional Theory of Delinquency," *Criminology* 25 (1987), 862–91; Terence P. Thornberry et al., "Testing Interactional Theory: An Examination of Reciprocal Causal Relationships among Family, School and Delinquency," *Journal of Criminal Law and Criminology* 82 (1991), 3–35.

66. Gottfredson and Hirschi, *A General Theory of Crime.*

67. Ibid., 87.

68. Ibid., 87.

69. For a review of these studies, see T. David Evans et al., "The Social Consequences of Self-Control: Testing the General Theory of Crime," *Criminology* 35 (1997), 476–77.

70. Delbert S. Elliott, Suzanne S. Ageton, and Rachelle J. Canter, "An Integrated Theoretical Perspective on Delinquent

Behavior," *Journal of Research in Crime & Delinquency* 16 (1979), 862–91.

71. Ibid.

72. Cynthia Chien, "Testing the Effect of the Key Theoretical Variable of Theories of Strain, Social Control and Social Learning on Types of Delinquency," paper presented at the annual meeting of the American Society of Criminology, Baltimore, November 1990.

73. Terence P. Thornberry, "Toward an Interactional Theory of Delinquency," *Criminology* 25 (1987): 886.

74. Donald J. Shoemaker, *Theories of Delinquency: An Examination of Explanations of Delinquent Behavior* (New York: Oxford University Press, 2005), 161–63.

75. Robert J. Sampson and John H. Laub, *Crime in the Making: Pathways and Turning Points Through Life* (Cambridge, Mass.: Harvard Press, 1993) ; and John H. Laub and Robert J. Sampson, *Shared Beginnings, Divergent Lives, Delinquent Boys to Age 70*. (Cambridge, mass.: Harvard Press, 2003).

76. John H. Laub and Robert J. Sampson, "Turning Points in the Life Course: Why Change Matters to the Study of Crime," *Criminology* 31 (August 1993), 309.

77. Ibid., 309.

78. Ibid., 310.

79. J. Bottcher, "Social Practices of Gender: How Gender Relates to Delinquency in the Everyday Lives of High-Risk Youths," *Criminology* 39 (2001), 893–932, 899.

80. Rebecca S. Katz, "Explaining Girls' and Women's Crime and Desistance in the Context of Their Victimization Experiences," *Violence Against Women* 6 (2000), 633–60.

81. John Hagan and Holly Foster, "Youth Violence and the End of Adolescence," *American Sociological Review* 66 (2001), 874–900.

82. Alex R. Piquero, Robert Brame, and Terrie E. Moffitt, "Extending the Study of Continuity and Change: Gender Differences in the Linkage Between Adolescent and Adult Offending," *Journal of Quantitative Criminology* 21 (June 2005), 219–43.

83. Ira Sommers, Deborah R. Baskin, and Jeffrey Fagan, "Getting Out of the Life: Crime Desistance by Female Street Offenders," *Deviant Behavior* 15 (1994), 125–49.

84. Ira Sommers and Deborah R. Baskin, "Situational or Generalized Violence in Drug Dealing Networks," *Journal of Drug Issues* 27 (1997), 833–49.

85. Peggy C. Giordano, Stephen A. Cernkovich, and Jennifer L. Rudolph, "Gender, Crime, and Desistance: Toward a Theory of Cognitive Transformation," *American Journal of Sociology* 107 (January 2002), 990–1064, 1038.

Gender, Race/Ethnicity, and Class Correlates of Delinquency

LUIS ROMERO/AP Images

Learning Objectives

1. Outline the various explanations for why adolescent females become involved in offending
2. Describe a feminist theory of delinquency
3. Identify the relationship between adolescent male and female offending
4. Describe how gender affects the processing of adolescent females in the juvenile justice system
5. Identify the relationship between class and delinquency
6. Identify how race/ethnicity affects the handling of juveniles in the juvenile justice system

Society struggles with ways to distribute resources and opportunities among its members. Some societies are more equitable in their distribution than others. In the United States, we focus on gender, race and class in order to value an individual and afford or deny them resources and opportunities. For example, from birth, when a child is assigned to a category of either male or female, the rules and values associated with that gender are applied. Difference, based in Biology, in and of itself is not necessarily a bad thing. However, as a society, we place differential values on physical & emotional traits, based on sex. As a society, we value masculine traits such as independence and strength more than stereotypically feminine traits like nurturance and compassion. As a result of this polarization of two genders and resulting inequalities, women generally fare poorly in the workplace and economy, relative to men. The undervaluing of traditionally labeled, "women's work," a lack of work opportunities for mothers (who still carry the burden of the majority of childcare), and discrimination by employers, all contribute to the wage gap in this country.

Race is another categorization that we use to label individuals at birth. It is also another way in which difference equals inequality. Based on the considerable variation among societal categories of race, one could argue that race is socially constructed. Race as a construction has real consequences in the workplace, housing market, department store, virtually every aspect of daily life. Race, like gender, indicates difference in status in a very obvious and immutable manner.

As a society, we also classify people based on shared economic conditions or social class. Class status, although possibly less visually salient, is used to rank individuals in terms of power, prestige, and financial status. Social class stereotypes plague our society and have far reaching ramifications in life chances. For example, the stereotype of lower class people as lazy, irresponsible, and morally reprehensible may squelch support for policies aimed to help the impoverished to improve their situation.[1]

The theories reviewed in Chapter 3 largely reflect social thought from the late 1800s, up through the 1900s, and into the 2000s. Throughout much of that time period, males were considered the primary culprits in committing crime and delinquency. Critics of these early opinions, however, had their doubts because they recognized that different explanations could be applied to why females, delinquents in the lower classes, and members of various racial and ethnic groups got involved in juvenile delinquency. Indeed, as the collection of data and consideration of the social circumstances of different groups involved with delinquency increased, attention shifted. Social observers began calling attention to extreme social circumstances, such as poverty or violent neighborhoods, as possible contributors to delinquency. Other observers noted the possible effects of social values and norms that led to discrimination against females, African Americans, Hispanics, and lower-class youths. Research began in an effort to sort out the basis for the differences among these groups and began to become more nuanced in its observations and thinking. This chapter on causation begins to sort through those issues.

The chapter initially compares the explanations of why males and females become involved in antisocial behaviors and presents a feminist theory of delinquency. The next section considers the various types of female delinquent offending following an examination of how gender affects the processing of the female delinquent. The final two sections investigate the influence of class and race/ethnicity on the handling of male and female youthful offenders and explore how the categories of gender, class, and race are interlocked and influence both delinquent behavior and how this behavior is handled by the juvenile justice system.

The Female Delinquent

Female delinquency, like all other social behaviors, takes place in a world where gender still shapes the lives of adolescents in powerful ways. Feminist theory starts with the assumption that juvenile females are positioned in society in ways that produce vulnerability to victimization by males, including abuse and the negative effects of poverty.[2] In addition, the variable of class cannot be ignored in understanding the behavior of juveniles. In all dimensions of their lives, class is important in determining how juveniles perceive themselves, are responded to by others, and are treated by the juvenile justice system. The middle-class male youthful offender typically is treated very differently by the police and court officials than is his lower-class counterpart. Finally, one of the most serious indictments of the juvenile justice system is the mounting evidence of its unfair treatment of African American, Native American, and Hispanic adolescent males and females.

A growing body of research is devoted to the study of the characteristics of delinquent girls.[3] Researchers have identified basic demographic and offense patterns as well as background characteristics such as family dysfunction, trauma, physical abuse, mental health issues, substance abuse, risky sexual behavior, academic problems, and delinquent peers as common features among girls in custody.[4]

Until recently, the study of female delinquency has been largely the study of male delinquency.[5] Things changed, however, in 2003 when the Office of Juvenile Justice and Delinquency Prevention awarded a grant to the North Carolina Research Triangle Institute (RTI) to study female delinquency and its consequences. RTI formed the Girls Study Group with the goal of developing a research foundation that will enable communities to make sound decisions about how best to prevent and reduce delinquency and violence by girls. The work of the Girls Study Group is guided by the following research questions:

- Who is the delinquent girl?
- What are the risks and protective factors associated with girls' delinquency?
- What are the pathways to girls' delinquency?
- What programs can prevent girls from becoming delinquent?
- What are the system responses to girls' delinquency?
- What are the life consequences of girls' delinquency?

The Girls Study Group is currently involved in giving presentations and authoring papers about the issue of female delinquency and promises to be helpful in better understanding the female delinquent in the future.[6]

The profile of at-risk adolescent females that emerges from this and other studies identifies common characteristics, including stories of victimization, unstable family life, school failure, repeated status offenses, and mental health and substance abuse problems.[7] These risk factors are similar to those for boys but different in terms of intensity for girls, except for school failure. Further female gender risk factors singled out by the National Juvenile Justice Networking Forum, a project of the Girl's Study Group, are early puberty and physical development, sexual assault, depression and anxiety, mother–daughter conflict, and cross-gender peer influence. For example, girls may be more influenced by romantic partners and boys, especially in the commission of minor delinquent acts.[8] B. Bloom and S. Covington offer a profile of female juvenile offenders in Figure 4–1.

One of the most significant and potentially useful criminological research findings in recent years is the recognition of girls' and women's pathways into delinquency.[9] Researchers generally believe that the first step along females' pathway into the juvenile justice system is victimization. Parents, siblings, or relatives may have sexually abused them at home, and the girls run away.

The second step along females' pathway into the juvenile justice system involves substance abuse. Substance abuse is highly correlated with early childhood sexual victimization, especially among white females. The literature also consistently reports a strong link between childhood abuse and the later development of alcoholism and other drug problems.[10] Significantly, at about the same age as the victimization occurred (usually when the girls were between thirteen and fourteen years old), the girls started using addictive substances.

- She is 13 to 18 years old.
- She has experienced academic failure, truancy, and dropping out.
- She has a history of repeated victimization, especially physical, sexual, and emotional abuse.
- She is from an unstable family background that includes involvement in the criminal justice system, lack of connectedness, and social isolation.
- She has a history of unhealthy dependent relationships, especially with older males.
- She has mental health issues, including a history of substance abuse.
- She is apt to be a member of a community of color.

FIGURE 4–1
The Typical Female Juvenile Offender

FIGURE 4–2
Pathways to Delinquency

A third step along females' pathway into the juvenile justice system involves girls acting out at home, in school, in sexual activity, in law-violating acts, and in gang involvement. Emotional problems and drugs tend to influence their negative behavior and, as a result, girls do poorly in school, are sometimes suspended or expelled, or drop out and often run away from home. Once caught, the girls come before the juvenile court, or they are referred to the court for their involvement in gangs or delinquent behaviors. Figure 4–2 illustrates the pathways to delinquency.

Why Do Adolescent Females Become Involved in Offending?

One of the research questions frequently raised is whether female delinquency has different explanations than does male delinquency. Little disagreement exists on whether adolescent females experience life differently than adolescent males. Researchers commonly agree that females are more controlled than males, enjoy more social support, are less disposed to crime, and have fewer opportunities to commit certain types of crimes.[11]

Three different opinions document the approaches to male–female delinquency. One approach focuses on the question of generalizability. Those who support this **gender-neutral** position usually examine social learning, delinquent peer relationships, social bonding, the family, and deterrence and strain.[12] The researchers claim to see no reason to develop theories to account for female and male delinquency and criminality because female delinquents and offenders are pressured into delinquency in the same way as are male delinquents and criminals.[13]

In contrast, the second approach argues that new theories are needed to account for female delinquency and criminality. Eileen Leonard, for example, questions whether common explanations such as differential association, anomie, labeling, subcultural, and Marxist theories can be used to explain the crime patterns of adolescent females and adult women.[14] Meda Chesney-Lind also suggests that existing theories of delinquency are inadequate for explaining female delinquency. Instead, she proposes a **feminist theory of delinquency**, which examines adolescent females' sexual and physical victimization at home and the relationship between these experiences and their crimes.[15] This position argues that the structural categories of gender, class, and race are more helpful than individual or sociopsychological explanations in understanding women's involvement in crime.

In the face of these divergent positions—one seeking to explain away gender gaps and to be gender-neutral and the other focusing on the importance of gender in understanding delinquency and crime—Darrell Steffensmeier and Emilie Allen attempted to put the two approaches together. They contend that there "is no need for gender-specific theories," although they acknowledge that "qualitative studies reveal major general differences in the context and nature of offending."[16] These researchers are developing a third, or "middle-of-the-road," position.

Biological and Constitutional Explanations

More recently, the focus has been on biopsychological vulnerability factors that are related to girls' delinquency. Five general categories are considered: (1) stress and anxiety, (2) attention deficit/hyperactivity disorder and conduct disorder, (3) intellectual deficits, (4) early pubertal maturation, and (5) mental health issues.[17] For example, recently discovered gender-related biological process differences may account for gender differences in stress reactivity, which, in turn, contribute to a heightened vulnerability to behavioral problems with traumatized females.[18]

Psychological Explanations

Psychological explanations of female delinquency also vary between the early and the more recent studies. The early studies addressed the "innate" female nature and its relationship to deviant behavior, but more recent studies focus on psychiatric disorders and female delinquency:

- Gisela Konopka's 1966 study of delinquent females linked a poor home life with a deep sense of loneliness and low self-esteem. Her conception of delinquency relied heavily on the notion of individual pathology, as she concluded that only a female who is "sick" can become delinquent.[19] Konopka identified four key factors contributing to female delinquency: (1) a uniquely dramatic biological onset of puberty, (2) a complex identification process because of a girl's competitiveness with her mother, (3) the changing cultural position of females and the resultant uncertainty and loneliness, and (4) the hostile picture that the world presents to some young females.[20]

- A more recent study, consistent with the other studies, found that along with their physical and sexual abuse, female delinquents tend to exhibit psychopathology, including post-traumatic stress disorder, suicidal behavior, dissociative disorder, and borderline disorder.[21]

In sum, psychological studies of female delinquency shifted in the 1950s from the psychoanalytical to the familial-social and today to the neuropsychological. As Chapter 3 noted, advances in both the neurological sciences and developmental psychology reflect a much greater understanding of why both male and female delinquents become involved in crime.

Sociological Explanations

Since the late 1970s, numerous studies proceeded from the assumption that sociological processes traditionally related to males could also affect the delinquent involvement of females. General agreement exists among feminists and nonfeminists that literature approaching female delinquency from a sociological perspective offers more promise than literature about biological or psychological causes. Sociological factors focus on blocked opportunity, the women's liberation movement, social bonding, masculinity, power control, and peer group influence to explain much of the gender gap in delinquency.[22]

- *General strain theory (GST).* Males may be more likely to become involved in delinquency than females because males tend to experience strains such as high aspirations but poor schools and a lack of opportunity. They cope with these strains through delinquency. Females, in turn, may experience other strains that may induce other-directed delinquency. For example, GST explains female delinquency by contending that many females experience harsh discipline, parental rejection, peer abuse, negative secondary school experience, homelessness, and a strong need for money.[23]

- *Blocked opportunity theory.* The role of blocked or limited opportunity has received considerable attention in the sociological analysis of male delinquency. The usefulness of such variables in studying female delinquency is largely neglected. This is because males are viewed as being concerned with achieving short- and long-term status and economic success, whereas juvenile females are seen as possessing no such aspirations; females are believed to be satisfied to occupy a role that is dependent on males.[24] Several studies have found that such perception of limited opportunity was more strongly related to female delinquency than it was to male delinquency. Both African American and white female delinquents regarded their opportunities less positively than did the male delinquents in studies' samples.[25]

- *Social learning theory.* This theory contends that males have higher rates of delinquency than that of females primarily because males tend to be associated with delinquent peers and belong to gangs more often than do females. Some researchers argue that female peer groups are less conducive to delinquency than are mixed-gender or all-male peer groups. However, according to social learning theory, some females tend to associate with others who provide exposure to delinquent models, reinforce delinquent behaviors, and teach identities that are favorable to delinquency. In addition, research studies add that females are inclined to engage in delinquency if they associate with older males or are part of mixed-sex or all-male peer groups.[26]

- *Social control theory.* Proponents of social control theory contend that females are less involved in delinquency than are males because **gender-role socialization** results in more social bonds for females than for males.[27] In addition, adolescent females may have less opportunity to engage in delinquent behavior because, in general, young girls are more closely supervised by parents. Adolescent females are also more dependent on others, whereas adolescent males are encouraged to be more independent and achievement oriented.[28] Those females who are delinquent, according to social control theory, have less parental supervision, are less tied to their homes and families, are weakly bonded to parents and teachers, perform poorly in school, spend less time on homework, are involved in delinquent peer groups, and have less self-control.[29]

- *Masculinity hypothesis.* Several studies of female delinquents have proposed a **masculinity hypothesis**. Freda Adler contended that if females become more malelike in their roles and acquire more "masculine" traits, in the process, they become more delinquent.[30] Francis Cullen and coworkers found that the more male and female adolescents possessed "male" personality traits, the more likely the girls were to become involved in delinquency, but that the relationship between masculinity and delinquency was stronger for males than for females.[31] William E. Thornton and Jennifer James found a moderate degree of association between masculine self-expectations and delinquency but concluded that males were still more likely to be delinquent than were females, regardless of their degree of masculinity.[32]

- *Power-control theory.* John Hagan and colleagues proposed a power-control theory to explain female delinquency.[33] Using a class-based framework and data collected in Toronto, Ontario, the research team contended that as mothers gain power relative to their husbands, usually by employment outside the home, daughters and sons alike are encouraged to be more open to risk taking. Parents in egalitarian families, then, redistribute their control efforts so that daughters are subjected to controls more like those imposed on sons. In contrast, daughters in patriarchal families are taught by their parents to avoid risks.[34] Hagan and colleagues concluded that "patriarchal families will be characterized by large gender differences in common delinquent behavior while egalitarian families will be characterized by smaller gender differences in delinquency."[35] Power-control theory thus concludes that daughters who are freed from patriarchal family relations more frequently become delinquent.[36]

- *Labeling theory.* Labeling theory focuses on the reaction to delinquency, both the formal reaction by the justice system and the informal reaction by parents, teachers, community residents, and friends. Labeling theorists claim that males are more likely to be labeled as delinquents than are females because of the cultural stereotype that views males as troublemakers and the fact that males engage in more delinquency. Labeling theory does argue that some females are more delinquent than others because they have been informally labeled as delinquents by parents, teachers, and others and formally labeled by the juvenile justice system.[37]

- *Interactionist theory of delinquency.* Karen Heimer reported that delinquency for both females and males occurred through a process of role taking in which youths considered the perspectives of significant others; and among both boys and girls, attitudes favoring deviance encouraged delinquency. She also found that "girls' misbehavior can be controlled by inculcating values and attitudes, whereas more direct controls may be necessary to control boy's deviance."[38]

- *Deterrence, rational choice, and routine activities theories.* Females have a higher level of supervision, more self-control, less time spent in unstructured and unsupervised activities, and less prior delinquency, and this makes them less vulnerable to delinquency than males. In contrast, females that spend more unstructured and unsupervised time with peers have higher rates of delinquency. This is particularly true of those females who run away from home and spend a lot of time on the streets.[39]

Evaluating Explanations of Female Delinquency

The discussion of female delinquency readily leads to the conclusion that biological explanations are the less predictive factors. Personal maladjustment hypotheses may have some predictive ability in determining the frequency of delinquency in girls, but sociological theories appear to be able to explain female delinquency far more adequately. Some feminists are satisfied with the conclusions of sociological studies that males and females are differentially exposed to or affected by the same criminogenic associations.[40] Strain theory, general theory, social learning theory, social control theory, differential association theory, power-control theory, and labeling theory all have received some support.[41] Other feminists, as the next two sections will show, contend that the unique experiences of females require gender-specific theories. Table 4–1 summarizes the explanations for female delinquency.

What Is a Feminist Theory of Delinquency?

The feminist theory of delinquency mentioned earlier argues that girls' victimization and the relationship between that experience and girls' crime are largely ignored. Meda Chesney-Lind, one of the main proponents of this position, states that it has long been understood

TABLE 4–1
Summary of Types of Explanations for Female Delinquency

Types	Explanation
Biological and constitutional explanations	Biopsychological vulnerability factors related to girls' delinquency
Psychological explanations	Focus on psychiatric disorders
Sociological explanations	Focus on social structure and relationships among groups
General strain theory	Females can experience strain, especially in the family and school, conducive to female delinquency.
Blocked opportunity theory	Some evidence has been found that the perception of limited opportunity is more strongly related to female delinquency than it is to male delinquency.
Social learning theory	Some females are more likely than others to become involved in delinquent behavior because of their exposure to delinquent models.
Social control theory	Females who are delinquent have less parental supervision and bonding to the school.
Differential association	Emotional bonds to families are negatively related to the learning of violent definitions for girls but not for boys.
Masculinity hypothesis	Some studies have found that as females become more male like and acquire more masculine traits, they become more delinquent.
Power-control theory	When daughters are freed from patriarchal family relations, this theory concludes that they become more delinquent.
Labeling theory	Males are more likely to be labeled as delinquent than females, but some females—especially the more delinquent girls—can be informally labeled by parents, the school, and the justice system.
Interactionist theory of delinquency	For both males and females, delinquency occurs through a process of role taking.
Deterrence, rational choice, and routine activities theories	Some females see the costs of crime as low and the rewards as high. They usually spend more unstructured and unsupervised activities with peers.

| Girls are frequently the victims of sexual abuse. | → | Victimizers (often fathers) may utilize official agencies (like the police and the juvenile court) to keep victims at home and vulnerable. | → | As girls run away from home, they are forced to survive on the streets and become involved in various forms of crime. | → | On the streets, they become involved in various forms of criminal activity that exploits their sexuality. |

FIGURE 4–3
Chesney-Lind's Four Propositions on the Feminist Theory of Delinquency

that a major reason for girls' presence in juvenile court is their parents' insistence on their arrest. Those who study female offending, as well as those who work with female offenders, have discovered that a substantial number are victims of both physical and sexual abuse.[42]

Chesney-Lind developed a number of propositions on the causes of female delinquency. First, girls are often the victims of violence and sexual abuse (estimates are that up to three-quarters of sexual abuse victims are girls); but, unlike those of boys, girls' victimization and their responses to that victimization are shaped by their status as young women. Second, their victimizers (generally male caretakers) have the ability to invoke official agencies of social control to keep daughters or stepdaughters at home and vulnerable. Third, as girls run away from abusive homes characterized by sexual abuse and parental neglect, they are forced into the life of an escaped prisoner. Unable to enroll in school or take a job to support themselves because of fear of detection, female runaways are forced to engage in panhandling, petty theft, and, often, prostitution to survive. Finally, it is no accident that girls on the run from abusive homes or on the streets because of impoverished homes become involved in criminal activities that exploit their sexuality. Apart from their sexuality, these females have little value to trade and feel compelled to utilize their one resource.[43] Figure 4–3 shows Chesney-Lind's four propositions on the feminist theory of delinquency.

What Are the Most Important Dimensions of Female Delinquent Behavior?

The studies of female delinquents have examined several dimensions of delinquent behavior: females' involvement in offenses; their use of drugs and alcohol; their participation in illegal behaviors, including prostitution and violence; their experiences across the life course; and their desistance and persistence as offenders. Gang behavior among female delinquents is addressed in Chapter 13. A feminist theory of delinquency addresses childhood victimization and the ways in which discrimination and oppression, based on a juvenile's race or gender, can shape experiences, options, and identity.

Relationship Between Male and Female Patterns of Adolescent Offending

Early cohort studies provide some evidence of the relationship between male and female patterns of delinquency. Delinquency cohort studies generally include all people born in a particular year in a city or county and follow this group, or cohort, through part or all of their lives. The second Philadelphia cohort study examined all males and females born in 1958 in that city. It found that males were two and a half times more likely than females to become involved in delinquent acts. Law-violating females were much more likely to be one-time offenders and less likely to become chronic offenders.[44] The Columbus cohort study found that males outnumbered females by almost six to one in the delinquent population. The violent cohort consisted of 84.6 percent boys and 15.7 percent girls.[45]

Moffitt, Lynam, and Silva's examination of the neuropsychological status of several hundred New Zealand males between the ages of thirteen and eighteen revealed that poor neuropsychological scores "were associated with early onset of delinquency" but were "unrelated to delinquency that began in adolescence."[46] Moffitt's developmental theory views delinquency as proceeding along two developmental paths. On one path, the **early-onset, persistent offenders (life-course persistent [LCP])** develop a lifelong course of delinquency and crime at an early age. On the other path, that of **adolescence-limited (AL) delinquents**, the majority of male delinquents begin offending during the adolescent years and desist from delinquent behaviors around their eighteenth birthday. The early and persistent problems found in members of the LCP group are not found in the AL delinquents.[47]

Female Use of Drugs and Alcohol

Comparative studies reveal a marked decrease in the use of drugs as well as a decrease in gender differences among adolescent drug users during the past decade and a half. An exception to this general trend is that the use of marijuana and ecstasy increased from 2009 to 2011 among both males and females.[48] Data indicate that female high school seniors are slightly more likely than male high school students to smoke cigarettes, although males may be switching to smokeless tobacco, hookah pipes, and snuff instead of cigarettes; on the positive side, cigarette and tobacco use are at their lowest levels for all youths since 1975.[49] Females use alcohol and marijuana at about the same rates as male high school seniors. Male adolescents, conversely, are more likely than female adolescents to be involved in heavy, or binge, drinking.

The primary difference between males and females, according to Patrick Zickler, is that males have greater access to drugs than females but, once given access to drugs, both males and females are equally likely to try the drugs. Presented with the opportunity to use, males tended to use at relatively higher rates than females.[50] The significance of these findings for females is that delinquency may lead to pregnancy, drug-induced dependency of fetuses in the womb, having to raise children without the presence of the father, fetal alcohol syndrome, malnourished and damaged fetuses, the death of fetuses, and having to drop out of school. Some girls become involved with gangs, theft, and prostitution; experience early deaths from overdoses; and contract hepatitis and HIV/AIDS as a result of their problems. Knowing the paths young women take to drugs may assist in developing prevention strategies. For example, the latest publication of the *Monitoring the Future* study indicates that the nation has experienced a "generation history gap" in people's understanding of the harmful effects of drugs. Society must develop a comprehensive plan to make students aware of the risks of using drugs to reduce the demand side of addiction.[51]

Adolescent Females and Prostitution

Silbert and Pines's study found that a high percentage of street prostitutes had been abused sexually as juveniles.[52] Chesney-Lind and Rodriguez's investigation of the backgrounds of adult women in prison underscored the links between victimization as children and later careers as prostitutes.[53] Furthermore, R. J. Phelps and colleagues' survey of 192 female youths in the Wisconsin juvenile justice system revealed that 79 percent of them had been subjected to physical abuse that resulted in some form of injury.[54]

Adolescent Females and Violent Behavior

Since the late 1960s, the media have been quick to identify the violent female criminal, a type not previously supported by research on females and crime.[55] In the late 1980s, the media focused on the rise of violence among juvenile girls when reporting increased arrest trends. Between 1992 and 2003, juvenile females' arrests increased by 6.4 percent, while arrests of adolescent boys decreased by 16.4 percent. While decreases were present across many crimes of violence for both juvenile males and females, the period saw a 7 percent increase in girls' arrests for aggravated assault and a 29.1 percent decrease in boys' arrests for this offense. Similarly, arrests of juvenile girls for simple assaults climbed 40.9 percent, while arrests of juvenile males rose only 4.3 percent.[56]

Brown, Chesney-Lind, and Stein's article, "Patriarchy Matters: Toward a Gendered Theory of Teen Violence and Victimization," challenges this notion of a rise of violence among juvenile females. They claim that self-report data sources reveal that juvenile girls' and boys' violence *decreased* dramatically in the late 1990s. They also cite the findings of the Youth Risk Behavior Survey, the biennial survey of the Centers for Disease Control and Prevention. In this survey, 34.4 percent of girls surveyed in 1991 said that they had been in a physical fight the previous year; by 2001 this figure had dropped to 23.9 percent, a 10.5 percent decrease in girls' fighting. Furthermore, these researchers are skeptical of arrest data reporting rises in violence among young women, because studies of other systems that monitor injury and mortality do not show dramatic increases in violent victimization. Finally, in considering other forms of violence, such as robbery and murder, no data show that girls are becoming more violent. Instead, arrests of juvenile girls for other crimes of violence, including the most lethal, have shown decreases rather than increases.[57]

Brown, Chesney-Lind, and Stein conclude that "someone's behavior has been changing, but it is likely not the behavior of girls, but rather that of police and those who monitor youthful behavior, including the behavior of girls."[58] They believe that three factors are at work in this social construction of crime data on juvenile females' increased rates of violence. The first is *relabeling,* often called *bootstrapping,* of female girls' status offense behavior from noncriminal charges like incorrigibility to assaultive charges. The second factor involves a rediscovery of girls' violence, especially in the arrests of both girls and women for domestic violence. These researchers have found that a closer reading of the available studies reveals that most of these juvenile female assaults are "the result of nonserious, mutual combat situations with parents."[59] The third factor is the *upcriming* of minor forms of youth violence (including juvenile females' physical aggression). Upcriming refers to policies, such as "zero tolerance policies," which have the effect of increasing the severity of criminal penalties associated with particular offenses, such as minor forms of fighting and school bullying.[60]

Gender Across the Life Course

Longitudinal studies usually reveal that delinquent careers differ by gender. Male careers usually begin earlier and extend longer into the adult years. Studies of youth gangs reveal that female members are more likely than male members to leave the gang if they have a child. Also, conventional life patterns—particularly marriage, parenting, and work—draw both males and females away from gangs and offending behaviors, but do so more completely and quickly for females.[61]

Amy V. D'Unger and colleagues' follow-up of the second Philadelphia cohort study found the presence of both LCP and AL delinquents (see Moffitt's classification scheme earlier in the chapter) among the males. There was a higher and lower category for each group. Among the females were comparable AL groups as with the boys, though with lower overall offending levels. The high-rate AL female offenders did share marked similarities with low-rate chronic male offenders. Yet the chronic or persistent category of offenders was less prominent among the females.[62]

Desistance from Crime

In their follow-up of a sample of serious adolescent female delinquents, Peggy C. Giordano and her colleagues developed a theory of cognitive transformation to explain desistance, or the dropping out of committing crime. They found that neither marital attachment nor job stability was strongly related to female desistance. Instead, desisters underwent a **cognitive transformation**. These researchers found that four types of cognitive transformation take place as an integral part of the desistance process: (1) a shift takes place in the actor's openness to change; (2) the individual is exposed to a hook or set of hooks for change; (3) the individual begins to envision and fashion an appealing and conventional "replacement self"; and (4) a transformation takes

▲ A juvenile suspect is arrested by a police officer. His arrest may be dismissed or he could end up in juvenile court and even sent to an institution. A few arrested juveniles are transferred to an adult court.

Radius Images/Alamy

place in the way the actor views the former deviant lifestyle. These cognitive transformations or shifts not only influence receptivity to one or more hooks of change but also inspire and direct behavior. These hooks "facilitated the development of an alternative view of self that was seen as fundamentally incompatible with criminal behavior[63]

Gender Inequality and Processing of the Female Delinquent

Several reasons exist as to why the juvenile justice system treats female adolescent offenders unfairly, especially those who end up in juvenile institutions:

- Adolescent females receive discriminatory treatment because of society's disapproval of sexual activity.[64]

- Rosemary C. Sarri concludes that juvenile law has long penalized females. She claimed that although the law may not be discriminatory on its face, the attitudes and ideologies of juvenile justice practitioners administering it may result in violations of the equal protection clause of the Fourteenth Amendment, by leading them to commit females to longer sentences than males are committed to, under the guise of "protecting" the female juveniles.[65] She added that "females have a greater probability of being detained and held for longer periods than males, even though the overwhelming majority of females are charged with status offenses.[66]

- According to another perspective, the oppressive treatment of adolescent females is hidden in the juvenile justice system. Many girls appear in court for criminal-type offenses that had previously been classified as status offenses. This suggests that juvenile justice officials may have redefined these girls to be eligible for the kinds of protectionist sanctions that have been traditionally applied.[67] This permits juvenile judges to use their contempt power to confine repeat status offenders. If a runaway girl, for example, was ordered by the court to remain at home, and she chose to run away again, she might be found in contempt of court—a criminal-type offense.

- Finally, the early studies in particular found that police officers, intake personnel, and judges supported a sexual double standard. Female status offenders, as previously indicated, were more likely than their male counterparts to be petitioned to formal court proceedings, to be placed in preadjudicatory detention confinements, and to be confined in juvenile institutions.

See Focus on Practice 4–1.

On balance, some evidence does exist that the discriminatory treatment of female status offenders may be declining since the passage of the Juvenile Justice and Delinquency Prevention Act.[68] No longer do many states send status offenders to training schools with delinquents. But the long tradition of sexism in juvenile justice will be difficult to change. Due process safeguards for female delinquents, as well as for female status offenders, must be established to ensure them greater social justice in the juvenile justice system. The intrusion of extralegal factors into the decision-making process in the juvenile court has led to discrimination against the adolescent female, which must become a relic of the past.

What Is the Influence of Class on the Handling of Juvenile Offenders?

Decades of debate still have not produced consensus on the true relationship between social class and youthful offending behavior. The early studies of the 1950s and 1960s found that middle- and upper-class juveniles were as delinquent as their lower-class peers. Then, Richard Johnson in 1980, in redefining social class as "underclass" and "earning class," concluded: "The data provides no firm evidence that social class, no matter how it is measured,

Focus on Practice 4–1
Gender-Specific Services in the Juvenile Justice System: A Critical Examination

Sara Goodkind refers to the 1992 Juvenile Justice and Delinquency Prevention Act's appropriations authorization, which states that "the term 'gender-specific services' means services designed to address needs unique to the gender of the individual to whom such services are provided." She adds that "the term *gender specific* has been interpreted to mean 'for girls' and that gender-specific programming refers to a comprehensive approach to female delinquency rooted in the experience of girls."

Goodkind found four fundamental critiques of the literature of gender-specific programming for female delinquency:

1. The need for gender-specific services is demonstrated and justified by frequent citations of increased rates of arrest and confinements for girls. However, Goodkind concludes that self-report and other sources have indicated that girls' delinquent behavior may not be on the rise.
2. An essentialized notion of gender is used that serves to reify socially constructed categories and ignore intersections of gender with race, ethnicity, class, sexuality, and other axes of difference.
3. The focus on the individual is too great. Efforts should instead be geared toward institutional or structural change.
4. Her final critique is that girls' delinquency is frequently tied to their victimization, especially physical and sexual abuse.

This approach ignores girls' agency and neglects the fact that girls continue to be punished for behavior that is considered to be acceptable among boys.

Goodkind's concern is to shift the way treatment agents, such as social workers, think about and engage gender. She is proposing an understanding of gender that is part of a framework for designing services for boys and girls that address their differential social locations without reifying socially constructed gender differences. This framework is based on the following seven principles, which she developed through her critical review:

1. Deconstruct and move beyond false dichotomies.
2. Adopt an interpretivist or constructionist epistemology that recognizes categories as socially constructed and presents a vision for social change.
3. Uncover assumptions and identify interests and goals.
4. Attend to the importance of context.
5. Balance structure and agency and think in terms of interdependence.
6. Focus on progress.
7. Rethink difference.

Source: Sara Goodkind, "Gender-Specific Services in the Juvenile Justice System: A Critical Examination," *Affifia* 20 (Spring 2005), 52–70.

---

is a salient factor in generating delinquent involvement."[69] Charles Tittle and colleagues' 1978 review of thirty-five studies examining the relationship between class and crime concluded that little support existed for the contention that delinquency is basically a lower-class phenomenon.[70]

Critics charged that self-report studies tended to overload their questionnaires with trivial offenses. Thus, when middle- and upper-class youths recorded their participation in such offenses as swearing or curfew violations, they were found to be as delinquent as lower-class youths. However, Ageton and Elliott's 1978 national study found that a different pattern emerged when juveniles were asked how many times they had violated the law during the previous year. They found that the average number of delinquent acts reported by lower-class youths exceeded the average number reported by working-class youths. The average number of crimes against person reported by lower-class juveniles was one and one-half times greater than that reported by the working-class group and nearly four times greater than that reported by the middle-class group. The average number of reported crimes against property was also slightly higher for lower-class than for working-class or middle-class youth.[71]

Margaret Farnworth and colleagues' examination of the first four waves of data from the Rochester Youth Development Study found that the "strongest and most consistent class–crime associations are found between measures of continuing underclass status and sustained involvement in street crimes."[72] Their 1994 article further explored the possibility that "inadequate measurement may explain past findings indicating no relationship between class and delinquency."[73]

Class Oppression

As part of the female delinquent's "multiple marginality," **class oppression** is another form of exploitation experienced by an adolescent female.[74] In a number of ways, serious problems of childhood and adolescence related to poverty set the stage for the young person's entry into homelessness, unemployment, drug use, survival sex and prostitution, and, ultimately, even more serious delinquent and criminal acts. Even adolescents from middle-class homes may be thrust into dire situations for economic survival if they choose to run away from abusive environments.

Traditional theories fail to address the life situations of girls on the economic and political margins, because researchers fail to examine the situations or talk with these girls. For example, nearly all urban females identified by police as gang members have been drawn from low-income groups.[75] Lee Bowker and Malcolm Klein's examination of girls in gangs in Los Angeles revealed the importance of class as well as racism:

▲ The party has been broken up and several juveniles are arrested. There was alcohol and drugs present, but the parents were out of town.
Thomas Allison/Associated Press

> We conclude that the overwhelming impact of racism, sexism, poverty and limited opportunity structure is likely to be so important in determining the gang membership and juvenile delinquency of women and girls in urban ghettos that personality variables, relations with parents and problems associated with heterosexual behavior play a relatively minor role in determining gang membership and juvenile delinquency.[76]

Class becomes important in shaping the lives of adolescent females in a number of ways. Lower-class adolescent females tend to confront higher risks than middle- and upper-class adolescent females. They tend to have more unsatisfactory experiences at school, to lack educational goals beyond high school, to experience higher rates of physical and sexual abuse, to deal with pregnancy and motherhood more frequently, to be involved in higher rates of drug and alcohol dependency, and to lack supportive networks at home.[77] Not all adolescent females at risk end up in the juvenile justice system, but the likelihood of such a placement is greater for lower-class girls.

What Is the Influence of Race on Juvenile Justice?

Race has been examined in terms of discrimination, gender, and its effect on the processing of minorities in the juvenile justice system. The disproportionate confinement of minorities has become one of the most serious indictments of juvenile justice policy and has led to the enforcement of federal law to attain more fair treatment of minorities by the justice system. But first let us turn to a preliminary examination of causation and African American and Hispanic youths.

How Can African American Delinquency be Explained?

Criminologists frequently have reduced the race–crime debate to simplistic arguments about culture versus social structure. On one side of the debate, structuralists argue that African American crime can be understood through "relative deprivation," even though the social and class evidence is weak. On the other side, cultural theorists tend to focus on the indigenous culture of violence in black ghettoes; and here the evidence is weak as well.[78]

Robert J. Sampson and William J. Wilson, two of the most respected authorities on race and crime, argue that the above stalemate can be broken by a theoretical strategy that incorporates both structural and cultural arguments regarding crime, race, and social inequality. They argue "that macro-social patterns of residential inequality give rise to the social isolation and ecological concentration of the truly disadvantaged, which in turn leads to structural barriers and cultural adaptations that undermine social organization and hence the control of crime."[79]

These researchers support their thesis with a macrosocial, or community level, explanation. This explanation questions what it is about community structures and cultures that produces differential rates of crime.[80] Sampson and Wilson raise two questions that still appear to be relevant today:

1. To what extent do African American rates of crime vary by types of ecological area?
2. Is it possible to reproduce in white communities the structural circumstances in which many African Americans live?

Sampson and Wilson proceed to argue that African Americans are no more of a homogeneous group than are whites. As Sampson and Wilson point out, the heterogeneity among African Americans in crime corresponds to community context. They argue that the sources of violent crime seem to be remarkably invariant across race and are rooted in the structural differences among communities, cities, and states in terms of economic and family organization.[81]

To the second question, Sampson and Wilson challenge whether African Americans and whites share a similar environment, particularly with regard to concentrated urban poverty. They add that while the majority of poor African Americans live in communities characterized by high rates of family disruption, poor whites—even those from broken homes—live in areas of relative family stability.[82] Or, to express this in another way, the racial differences in poverty and family disruption are so strong that the "worst" urban contexts in which whites live are considerably better than the average context of African American communities.[83]

Wilson has labeled the effects of living in a neighborhood that is overwhelmingly impoverished as "concentration effects." In recent decades, the social transformation of the inner city has resulted in an increased concentration of the most disadvantaged segments of the urban African American population—particularly poor, female-headed families with children.[84] These macrostructural factors—which include, but are not limited to, racial segregation, structural economic transformation, joblessness among African American males, housing discrimination, and class-linked outmigration from the inner city—have combined to concentrate urban black poverty and family disruption.[85] Thus, Sampson and Wilson's explanation of African American crime rejects both the "individualist" and "materialist" fallacies and instead develops a theoretical strategy that incorporates both cultural and structural arguments regarding race, crime, and urban inequality in U.S. cities.[86]

Sampson and Wilson's theoretical findings have received support in the literature. Charis E. Kubrin and Ronald Weitzer found that what they refer to as "cultural retaliatory homicide" is more common in some neighborhoods than in others because of the combined effects of economic disadvantage, neighborhood cultural responses to disadvantage, and questionable policing.[87]

Stacy De Coster, Karen Heimer, and Stacy M. Wittrock's analysis of data from the National Longitudinal Study of Adolescent Health revealed that status characteristics, such as race, poverty, and female households, restrict the residential choices of families. Residence in these extremely disadvantaged communities, in turn, increases the likelihood of violent behavior by youths by influencing the development and maintenance of community and family social capital and by influencing the chances that children are exposed to a criminogenic street context.[88] Finally, Sampson and Wilson found that black family disruption has a stronger effect on juvenile violence than on adult violence, which supports the idea that the effects of family structure are related to macrolevel patterns of guardianship and social control, particularly for juveniles and their peers.[89]

How Can Hispanic Delinquency Be Explained?

Although many Hispanics are born in the United States, the vast majority still come from a relatively recent immigrant background. By official U.S. Census count, 50.5 million Hispanic-origin persons, which is equivalent to 16 percent of the total population, resided in the United States in 2010. Thirty-one percent of Hispanics in 2000 were foreign-born, 28 percent were native-born of foreign or mixed percentage, and the remainder 33 percent were born in the United States.[90] Widespread beliefs that Hispanics have high or perhaps very high crime rates seem to exist. As Latino gangs have gained notoriety in the United States, especially MS-13, a perception that has taken place in the minds of the American public and many elected officials is that the greatest threat posed by mass immigration is crime.[91]

One of the arguments about immigration is that allowing more low-skilled workers, particularly Spanish-speaking ones, into the United States or legalizing their presence here will swell the ranks of the underclass, with people who have low earnings, a minimal education, and who in the worst cases exhibit such dysfunctional behavior as drug addiction and higher illegitimacy rates. Thus, our immigration regime is said to "import poverty," bringing in its wake rising rates of crime and social chaos.[92] However, this can be balanced by the fact that immigrants are less prone to commit crimes and land behind bars than their native-born counterparts. One striking fact about low-skilled immigrants in America today, whether legal or illegal, is their propensity to work. In 2008, the rate of labor-force participation of foreign-born Hispanics was 71 percent, while that of native-born Americans was 66 percent. Immigrant dropouts—who were 25 years or older without a high-school diploma—were far more likely than native-born dropouts to be participating in the labor force—61 percent versus 28 percent. In fact, according to the Pew Hispanic Center, male illegal immigrants, who are ages 18 to 64, had a labor-force participation rate in 2004 of a remarkable 92 percent. So the fact may be that illegal immigrants are typically poor, but they are almost all working poor.[93] Once they are able to help their families back home, the vast majority return home themselves.

Crime rates are even lower than average among the poorly educated and Hispanic immigrants. Rubēn Rumbaut analyzed census data from the year 2000 and found that incarceration rates among illegal and legal immigrants from El Salvador, Mexico, and Guatemala were less than half the rate of U.S.-born whites. Without a high school diploma immigrants had an incarceration rate that was only one-seventh that of native-born high school dropouts.[94]

It is true that Hispanic/Latino youths involved in gangs have high crime rates and spend extensive periods in institutionalization, both juveniles and adults. These gangs can be divided into Mexican American, Cuban, Puerto Rican, Dominican, Jamaican, and Central American members. Yet, no evidence exists that, other than perhaps MS-13, the gangs are any more prone to crime or violence than other youth and adult gangs.

Michael F. de Vries, a former Hispanic gang member who spent a number of years in prison, proposed that researchers need an integrated approach to understand why juveniles become involved with gangs, stating that for African American youths, strain theory is "the heart of why African-Americans find gang associations worthwhile." Gangs offer deprived African-American youths some opportunities to obtain status and financial gain that are denied to them in the larger culture. Asian immigrants are more "likely to engage in licit drug distribution to counteract their inherited inferior position in society. Asian immigrants are also more apt to engage in home invasions, theft, and intimidation as their way of coping with a similar strain."[96] According to de Vries, subculture theory appears to be helpful in explaining Hispanic gangs, which are largely separated from Anglo-American culture by their own traditions; he stated that "this subcultural group places a high degree of value on an individual's prowess (machismo), territorial identity, pride, and loyalty to their own group identity."[97]

Gender and Racial Discrimination

Young women of color, as well as other minority girls, frequently grow up in contexts very different from those of their white counterparts. Signithia Fordham's "Those Loud Black Girls" showed that young African American women resisted the norms of femininity of white culture as they became loud or asserted themselves vocally. Yet, this behavior led to negative school experiences, and it did not take long for these juvenile females to discover that the quiet ones were those who did well in school. Some of these young women decided to "pass for white" or to adopt more acceptable norms of femininity in order to succeed in school. Others refused to adopt this survival strategy, and their tool for liberation contributed to their lack of school success.[95]

The fact that racism and poverty often go hand in hand means that girls are forced by their minority status and poverty to deal early and on a regular basis with problems of abuse, drugs, and violence.[96] Minority girls' strategies for coping with these problems, as well as their gang membership, increases the likelihood that they will come to the attention of the juvenile justice system.[97]

Finally, there is the belief that girls of color enjoy the benefits of chivalry much less than white girls do. Middle- and upper-class white girls, especially those who have committed minor offenses, not sexual ones, may be given greater latitude by the police and by court intake and juvenile court workers than their minority counterparts. Like male minority offenders, female minority offenders are likely to be viewed as more dangerous to society and more likely to require long-term confinement.

Racial Differences in Juvenile Justice Processing

When racial/class gender disparities do occur, they take place at any stage of processing within the conviction and incarceration rates with respect to their population base. A serious issue, of course, is whether this disproportionate representation in the juvenile justice system is due to a pattern of racist decision making.

Janet L. Lauritsen, in examining what is known about racial and ethnic differences in juvenile offending, offers the following conclusions, which have wide support in the literature:

- Rates of juvenile homicide are higher for minorities than for white youthful offenders. Variations do exist in rates of lethal violence among minority groups.

- Official data suggest disproportionate involvement in nonlethal violence on the part of African American youth. When arrest data are restricted to specific forms of nonlethal violence, African American youth appear to be disproportionately involved in robbery, aggravated assault, and rape.

- Juvenile property crime data show that African American youths are slightly more involved than white youths, although the level of disproportionate involvement varies by type of property crime.

- Arrest data show that white youths are disproportionately involved in alcohol offenses, and that American Indian youths are slightly more likely than African American or Asian youths to be arrested for these crimes.

- African American youths are disproportionately arrested for drug abuse violations and drug use, but data from juveniles on their own drug use and selling do not confirm the differences between African American and white youths suggested by the arrest data. Indeed, white youths are somewhat more likely to report using marijuana (ever and in the past thirty days), selling any drugs, and selling marijuana.

- The arrest data for weapons violations indicate that African American youths are disproportionately likely to be arrested for weapon violations.[98]

Lauritsen contends that the empirical evidence suggests that the relationship between race and ethnicity and juvenile involvement in delinquency is complex and contingent on the type of offense. Although the most commonly occurring crimes exhibited few group differences, the less frequent and serious crimes of violence showed generally higher levels of African American and Latino youth involvements.[99]

Donna Bishop, in what will likely become a definitive article on race and ethnicity in juvenile justice, concludes that minority overrepresentation is attributable to inequities in the juvenile justice process rather than the incidence, seriousness, and persistence of their offending. Minorities are overrepresented among youths held in secure detention, petitioned to juvenile court, and adjudicated delinquent. Among those who are adjudicated delinquent, minorities are more often committed to the "deep end" of the justice system. When confined, they are more likely to be housed in large public institutions rather than privately run, specialized treatment facilities or group homes. Furthermore, at "the end of the line," prosecutors and judges are quicker to relinquish jurisdiction over minorities, transferring them to criminal court for prosecution and punishment as adults.[100]

Carl E. Pope and William H. Feyerherm's highly regarded assessment of the issue of discrimination against minorities reveals that two-thirds of the studies they reviewed found "both direct and indirect race effects or a mixed pattern [being present at some stages and not at others]."[101] They add that selection bias can take place at any stage and that small racial differences may accumulate and become more pronounced as minority youth are processed into the juvenile justice system.[102]

The Coalition for Juvenile Justice (the former National Coalition of State Juvenile Justice Advisory Groups) brought national attention to this problem of **disproportionate minority confinement** in their 1988 annual report to Congress. In that same year, Congress responded to this evidence of disproportionate confinement of minority juveniles in secure facilities by amending the Juvenile Justice and Delinquency Prevention Act (JJDPA) of 1974 by mandating that states participating in the Formula Grants Program must address efforts to reduce the proportion of the youth detained or confined in secure detention facilities, secure correctional facilities, jails, and lockups who are members of minority groups if such proportion exceeds the proportion such groups represent in the general population.[103]

During the 1992 reauthorization of the JJDPA, Congress substantially strengthened the effort to address disproportionate confinement of minority youth in secure facilities. Disproportionate minority confinement was elevated to the status of a "core requirement" alongside deinstitutionalization of status offenders, removal of juveniles from adult jails and lockups, and separation of youthful offenders from adults in secure institutions.[104]

The JJDPA was reauthorized in late 2002 and took effect in October 2003. The first three mandates, for the most part, stayed the same. The fourth mandate was changed from disproportionate minority confinement to **disproportionate minority contact**. The focus is currently on efforts to reduce minority contact with the system. Programs geared to delinquency prevention, as well as a multipronged approach to DMC, are encouraged.[105]

Prior to 2002, the JJDPA required states to assess their level of disproportionate minority confinement (DMC) by using a statistic dividing the proportion of a given minority group of youths who were detained or confined in a state's secure detention facilities, secure correctional facilities, jails, and lockups by the proportion that group represented in the general population. If this DMC Index was significantly greater than 1.0, the state was required to develop and implement a plan to reduce the disproportionality.[106]

However, it was soon evident that problems existed in interpreting the DMC Index. First, comparing one jurisdiction's index to another was difficult. The value of the DMC Index was related in part to the proportion of minority youths in the general population. Those communities with low minority proportions could have very high DMC Indexes, in contrast with communities with high proportions. Another problem, even more critical, was that the index provided limited guidance on where to look for the source(s) of disparity. Was disparity introduced at all stages of the system? Or did it accumulate from beginning to end? Or was it introduced only at the earliest stage and then remained through the end stages?[107]

Measuring the disparity at each decision point gives a better understanding of where disparity is introduced and/or magnified in the handling of cases by the juvenile justice system. To address problems with the DMC Index, the Office of Juvenile Justice and Delinquency Prevention developed a tool, called the **DMC Relative Rate Index**, to measure the level of disparity at each decision point.[108]

In sum, the disproportionate numbers of minority youths confined in long-term training facilities, as well as the disproportionate numbers of these youths processed through the juvenile justice system, is a serious issue. Hopefully, the recent federal intervention will, in the long run, result in the reduction of minority representation in long-term institutional care.

Although the DMC initiative was begun with great promise, the following Evidence-Based Practice feature shows that achieving racial justice can often be a difficult path.

Evidence-Based Practice
Disproportionate Minority Confinement/Contact

The disproportionate minority confinement/contact (DMC) directive was designed to ensure that youthful offenders, regardless of their race or position in the social structure, receive equitable treatment within the juvenile justice system. Recently Michael Leiber and his associates examined the impact of the DMC on the processing of juvenile offenders within a state juvenile justice system. They chose Iowa for their study because it is one of the states that was selected to serve as a model for the implementation of strategies to reduce DMC. Their research focused on the extent that race influences decision makers and whether the implementation of the DMC effort would result in the reduction or elimination of a race effect on decision-making outcomes. After controlling for a wide array of variables, they found that African Americans were more likely than whites to be referred at intake for further proceedings both before and after the implementation of the DMC initiative. The relative influence of race on intake decision making did not change following the implementation of the DMC initiative.

In some instances the researchers found that the DMC created an effect in opposition to what was intended. During the decade prior to the implementation of the DMC mandate, white adolescents who committed property offenses were less likely than African Americans to be referred to juvenile court for further proceedings. However, during the decade after the implementation of the DMC mandate, whites who committed property offenses were more likely than African Americans to be referred to juvenile court for further proceedings. While this change can be viewed as a movement toward equality, it was actually an overcorrection. Rather than helping African American youths it penalized white offenders.

Decision making was influenced by gender and family household structure. African American males were more likely than their white males to receive a court referral, and this racial disadvantage remained in the post-DMC period. After DMC was in place, African Americans who came from single-parent households were more likely to be referred to juvenile court than those who resided in two-parent households, although this was not the case for whites. Stated differently, after the DMC mandate, the effects of race became more covert and indirect, operating through family structure. One might conclude that this result reflects decision makers' reliance on stereotypes involving assessments of the African American single-parent family as dysfunctional and less able than either the white single-parent household or the African American two-parent household to supervise and socialize children effectively. In sum, there was little to no evidence that the DMC legislation impacted decision makers to rely less on race and more on legal and extralegal considerations at intake. The DMC initiative, to some extent, may have reduced the influence of being African American on the judicial decision-making process, but not quite in the manner anticipated.

Source: Michael Leiber, Donna Bishop, Mitchell Chamlin, "Juvenile Justice Decision-Making Before and After the Implementation of the Disproportionate Minority Contact (DMC) Mandate," *Justice Quarterly* 28, no. 3 (2011), 460–92.

Juvenile Justice Videos

DISPROPORTIONATE MINORITY CONFINEMENT AND CONTACT (DMC)

Disproportionate Minority Confinement and Contact (DMC) discusses the overrepresentation of nonwhite juveniles within the justice system. DMC calls for proper precautions to be taken to keep these juveniles out of the system to provide them the opportunity for a better future. How can DMC be detrimental to the goals of the justice system? Based on the readings in this chapter as well as this video, what steps can be taken to decrease the proportion of nonwhite juveniles within institutions? What theories of crime might explain the disproportionate number of minorities within the justice system? Discuss.

DIFFERENTIAL ASSOCIATION

Differential Association discusses the criminological theory of differential association for the causation of crime. The video explains that Edwin Sutherland's work of differential association argues that crime is a learned behavior from peers. An individual becomes delinquent through an excess of exposure to behavior that violates the law. Explain the theory of differential association. How would differential association explain the criminal behavior of a juvenile? From the readings in this chapter and this video, do you believe that differential association can be used in all situations to explain the causation of crime? Why or why not?

INTRODUCTION TO SOCIAL CONTROL THEORY

Introduction to Social Control Theory describes the philosophy behind social control theory, which explains trends of criminal behavior. Social control theory states that individuals are restrained by social norms and values that prevent the naturally occurring deviant behavior that exists out of human self-interest. How would social control theory explain crime trends? Why would females be less involved in crime than males? From the readings in this chapter as well as this video, do you believe that social control theory can be used in all situations to explain criminal behavior? Why or why not?

SUMMARY

LEARNING OBJECTIVE 1: Outline the Various Explanations for Why Adolescent Females Become Involved in Offending.

The focus has been on biopsychological vulnerability factors related to girls' delinquency. In terms of psychological explanations, the early studies addressed the "innate" female nature and its relationship to deviant behavior, but more recently the focus has been on psychiatric disorders and female delinquency. Researchers have also focused on sociological factors such as blocked opportunity, social bonding, masculinity, power control, and peer group influence. Research has discovered that the causal factors identified by these theories can explain much of the gender gap in delinquency.

LEARNING OBJECTIVE 2: Describe a Feminist Theory of Delinquency.

The feminist theory of delinquency argues that girls' victimization, especially physical and sexual abuse, and the relationship between that experience and girls' crime have been continually ignored. In addition, their victimizers have the ability to invoke official agencies of social control to keep girls home and vulnerable. Further, girls on the run from abusive homes become involved in criminal activities that exploit their sexuality and, as a result, bring them to the attention of the juvenile and adult justice systems.

LEARNING OBJECTIVE 3: Identify the Relationship Between Adolescent Male and Female Offending.

Gender still shapes the lives of adolescents in powerful ways. Males are more likely to become involved in delinquent behavior, but female adolescents are also involved in the use of alcohol and drugs, especially alcohol and marijuana, at about the same rates as male high school seniors. Females who become prostitutes are likely to be victimized at home, and the data do not show that girls are becoming more violent.

LEARNING OBJECTIVE 4: Describe How Gender Affects the Processing of Adolescent Females in the Juvenile Justice System.

Female offending, like all other social behavior, takes place in a world where gender still shapes the lives of adolescents in powerful ways. Female adolescent offenders have been treated unfairly, particularly those who end up in juvenile institutions. This is so because of society's disapproval of sexual activity; because of the tendency to give females longer sentences than males, under the guise of "protecting" the female juveniles; because of keeping girls longer in detention and juvenile institutions, as compared to males detained for similar offenses; and because the juvenile justice officials sometimes redefine girls to make them eligible for the kinds of protectionist sanctions that have been traditionally applied.

LEARNING OBJECTIVE 5: Identify the Relationship Between Class and Delinquency.

The influence of class cannot be ignored in the handling of youthful offenders by police officers and officials of the juvenile justice system. An examination of how the categories of gender, class, and race are interlocked and influence delinquency across the life course will lead to needed insights into the problems female delinquents face in the United States.

LEARNING OBJECTIVE 6: Identify How Race/Ethnicity Affects the Handling of Juveniles in the Juvenile Justice System.

Race can affect African American and Hispanic/Latino youths in terms of why they become delinquent. Evidence supports the thinking that minority overrepresentation is attributable to inequities in the juvenile justice process rather than the incidence, seriousness, and persistence of their offending.

KEY TERMS

adolescence-limited (AL) delinquents, p. 77
class oppression, p. 81
cognitive transformation, p. 78
disproportionate minority confinement, p. 85

disproportionate minority contact, p. 85
DMC Relative Rate Index, p. 85
early-onset, persistent offenders
  (life-course persistent [LCP]), p. 77

feminist theory of delinquency, p. 72
gender-neutral, p. 72
masculinity hypothesis, p. 74
gender-role socialization, p. 74

REVIEW QUESTIONS

1. How has the social context affected the legal context in terms of female delinquency?
2. Why is the interlocking nature of gender, class, and race so important in understanding female delinquency?

3. Has your experience led to the conclusion that social class matters in the way individuals are perceived and handled in this society?
4. Why is racial disparity such a serious issue for the juvenile justice system?

GROUP EXERCISES

1. *Group Work:* All members of the class should look up what is meant by the social definition of reality. Then, probably the next day, form small groups or whatever works best to discuss whether the differences among males, females, blacks, ethnic groups, or social classes are real or are the result of a social definition of reality based on social values.

2. *Writing to Learn:* Write three fairly long paragraphs of about half a page each that describe the biological, psychological, and sociological causes of the behavior of delinquent girls.

3. *Class Presentations:* Break the class up into groups for presentations on gender, social class, and race/ethnicity. Have each group summarize what the book—and outside sources if time permits—states about each. What are the unique problems faced by each social construction?

4. *Group Work:* Have students discuss what the social definition of reality was like in their family, neighborhoods, schools, and communities concerning the behavior of girls, blacks, whites, and social classes. In other words, what were the social realities that everyone grew up with? How about at their current college or university?

5. *Writing to Learn:* Have each member of the class write a paragraph on the area of causation on which they are the weakest and then, in small groups or before the class as a whole, read their answers and revise them on the basis of suggestions made by other students.

NOTES

1. Danielle Ficco, Department of Sociology and Gender and Women's studies, Washington and Jefferson College, contributed this statement for this book in September 2012.

2. Donald J. Shoemaker, *Theories of Delinquency: An Examination of Delinquent Behavior,* 5th ed. (New York: Oxford University Press, 2005), 266.

3. C. S. W. Lederman, G. A. Dakof, M. A. Larreal, and L. Hua, "Characteristics of Adolescent Females in Juvenile Detention," *International Journal of Law and Psychiatry* 27 (2004), 321–27; and M. Zahn, "The Causes of Girls' Delinquency and Their Program Implications," *Family Court Review* 45 (2007), 456–65.

4. Lederman et al., "Characteristics of Adolescent Females."

5. Meda Chesney-Lind has articulated this point in her publications through the years.

6. See http://girlsstudygroup.rti.org.

7. B. Bloom and S. Covington, "Effective Gender Responsive Interpretations in Juvenile Justice: Addressing the Lives of Delinquent Girls," paper presented at the Annual Meeting of the American Society of Criminology, Atlanta, Georgia, 2001. See also B. Bloom. "Gender Responsive Treatment Services in Correctional Settings," in *Inside and Out: Women, Prison, and Therapy*, edited by E. Leeder (London: Haworth Press, 2006). Also published as *Women and Therapy*, Vol. 29, nos. 3/4. With B. Bloom, "Creating Gender-Responsive Services in Correctional Settings: Context and Considerations," paper presented at the American Society of Criminology Annual Meeting, Nashville, TN, November 2004.

8. National Juvenile Justice Networking Forum, *Girls Study Group* (Washington, DC: Research Triangle Institute, 2007), accessed at http://girlsstudygroup.rtl.lorg/docs/GSG_NJJNC_June_2007.pdf.

9. Meda Chesney-Lind's feminist theory of delinquency identified these pathways.

10. W. R. Downs, T. Capshew, and B. Rindels, "Relationships Between Adult Men's Alcohol Problems and Their Childhood Experiences of Parental Violence and Psychological Aggression," *Journal of Studies on Alcohol 65* (2004), 336–45.

11. *Juvenile Female Offenders: A Status of the States Report* (Washington, DC: Office of Juvenile Justice and Delinquency Prevention, 1998).

12. Jody Miller, *One of The Guys: Girls, Gangs, and Gender* (New York: Oxford University Press, 2001), 3–4.

13. Kathleen Daly, "Looking Back, Looking Forward: The Promise of Feminist Transformation," in *The Criminal Justice System and Women: Offenders, Victims, and Workers,* edited by B. R. Price and N. J. Sokoloff (New York: McGraw-Hill, 1995), 447–48.

14. Eileen Leonard, "Theoretical Criminology and Gender," in *The Criminal Justice System and Women ,* 54–70.

15. Meda Chesney-Lind, *The Female Offender*: *Girls, Women, and Crime* (Thousand Oaks, CA: Sage Publications, 1997).

16. D. Steffensmeier and E. Allen, "Gender and Crime: Toward a Gendered Theory of Female Offending," *Annual Review of Sociology* 22 (1996), 459–87.

17. Diana Fishbein et al., "Biopsychological Factors, Gender, and Delinquency," in *The Delinquent Girl,* edited by Margaret A. Zahn (Philadelphia: Temple University Press, 2008), 84.

18. Diana Fishbein, Shari Miller, Donna Marie Winn, and Gayle Dakof, "Biopsychological Factors, Gender, and Delinquency," in *The Delinquent Girl*, edited by Margaret A. Zahn (Philadelphia: Temple University Press, 2008), 84–106.

19. Gisela Konopka, *The Adolescent Girl in Conflict* (Englewood Cliffs, NJ: Prentice-Hall, 1966).

20. These key factors from Gisela Konopka's *The Adolescent Girl in Conflict* are listed in Peter C. Kratcoski and John E. Kratcoski, "Changing Patterns in the Delinquent Activities of Boys and Girls: A Self-Reported Delinquency Analysis," *Adolescence* 18 (Spring 1975), 83–91.

21. Ossai Miazad, *High Rights*, Brief 10, Washington College of Law, accessed April 17, 2012, at http://www.wel.american.edu//hrbrief/10gender.cfm.

22. Robert Agnew, "The Contribution of 'Mainstream' Theories to the Explanation of Female Delinquency," in *The Delinquent Girl,* 7.

23. Ibid., 9–11.

24. Talcott Parsons, "Age and Sex in the Social Structure of the United States," *American Sociological Review* 7 (October 1942), 604–16; James S. Coleman, *The Adolescent Society* (New York: Free Press, 1961); Ruth Rittenhouse, "A Theory and Comparison of Male and Female Delinquency" (Ph.D. dissertation, University of Michigan, Ann Arbor, 1963).

25. Susan K. Datesman, Frank R. Scarpitti, and Richard M. Stephenson, "Female Delinquency: An Application of Self and Opportunity Theories," *Journal of Research in Crime and Delinquency* 12 (1975), 120; Jeffery O. Segrave and Douglas N. Hastad, "Evaluating Three Models of Delinquency Causation for Males and Females: Strain Theory, Subculture Theory, and Control Theory," *Sociological Focus* 18 (January 1985), 13; Stephen A. Cernkovich and Peggy C. Giordano, "Delinquency, Opportunity, and Gender," *Journal of Criminal Law and Criminology* 70 (1979), 150.

26. Agnew, "The Contribution of 'Mainstream' Theories," 11–14.

27. Ibid.

28. William E. Thornton Jr., Jennifer James, and William G. Doerner, *Delinquency and Justice* (Glenview, IL: Scott Foresman, 1982), 268.

29. Agnew, "The Contribution of 'Mainstream' Theories," 11–14.

30. Freda Adler, *Sisters in Crime* (New York: McGraw-Hill, 1975).

31. F. T. Cullen, K. M. Golden, and J. B. Cullen, "Sex and Delinquency: A Partial Test of the Masculinity Hypothesis," *Criminology* 15 (1977), 87–104.

32. William E. Thornton and Jennifer James, "Masculinity and Delinquency Revisited," *British Journal of Criminology* 19 (July 1979), 225–41.

33. John Hagan, John Simpson, and A. R. Gillis, "Class in the Household: A Power-Control Theory of Gender and Delinquency," *American Journal of Sociology* 92 (January 1987), 788–816; John Hagan, A. R. Gillis, and John Simpson, "The Class Structure of Gender and Delinquency: Toward a Power-Control Theory of Common Delinquent Behavior," *American Journal of Sociology* 90 (1985) 1151–78.

34. Hagan et al., "Class in the Household," 791–92.

35. Ibid., 793.

36. Ibid., 813–14.

37. Agnew, "The Contribution of 'Mainstream' Theories," 17–18.

38. Karen Heimer, "Gender, Interaction, and Delinquency: Testing a Theory of Differential Social Control," *Social Psychology Quarterly* 59 (1996), 57.

39. Agnew, "The Contribution of 'Mainstream' Theories."

40. Ibid.

41. Peggy C. Giordano and Stephen A. Cernkovich, "Changing Patterns of Female Delinquency," research proposal submitted to the National Institute of Mental Health, February 28, 1979, 24–28.

42. Chesney-Lind, *The Female Offender.*

43. See Clemens Bartollas, *Juvenile Delinquency,* 7th ed. (Boston: Allyn & Bacon, 2006), 211–12.

44. M. Wolfgang, R. M. Figlio, and T. Sellin, *Delinquency in a Birth Cohort* (Chicago: University of Chicago Press, 1972).

45. D. Hamparian, R. Schuster, S. Dinitz, and J. P. Conrad, *The Violent Few: A Study of Dangerous Juveniles* (Lexington, MA: D. C. Heath, 1980).

46. T. E. Moffitt, M. Lynam, and P. A. Silva, *Sex Differences in Antisocial Behavior: Conduct Disorder, Delinquency, and Violence in the Dunedin Longitudinal Study* (Cambridge: Cambridge University Press, 2001).

47. T. E. Moffitt, "Adolescent-Limited and Life-Course Persistent Antisocial Behavior: A Developmental Taxonomy," *Psychological Review* 100 (1993), 674–701.

48. See http://archives.drugabuse.gov/NIDA_notes/nnv5n4/prevalence.html, accessed May 20, 2012. Please note that the data are not entirely consistent. Recent upturns in the use of certain drugs may be significant or simply a "blip" in the sociocultural patterns of behavior. See L. D. Johnston, P. M. O'Malley, J. G. Bachman, and J. E. Schulenberg, Between *Monitoring the Future National Results on Adolescent Drug Use: Overview of Key Findings, 2010* (Ann Arbor, MI: Institute on Drug Abuse of the National Institutes of Health, 2011)

49. Johnson, et al., 2011.

50. See http://archives.drugabuse.gov/NIDA_notes/nnv5n4/prevalence.html, accessed May 20, 2012.

51. Monitoring the Future. 2010.

52. Mini Silbert and Ayala Pines, "Entrance into Prostitution." *Youth and Society* 13 (1982), p. 476.

53. Cited in Meda Chesney-Lind, "Girls, Crime, and Women's Place: Toward a Feminist Model of Female Delinquency" Paper presented at the Annual Meeting of the American Society of Criminology, Montreal, Canada (November 1987), p. 16.

54. Ibid.

55. Federal Bureau of Investigation, *Uniform Crime Reports* (Washington, DC: U.S. Government Printing Office, 2003).

56. L. Brown, M. Chesney-Lind, and N. Stein, *Patriarchy Matters: Toward a Gendered Theory of Teen Violence and Victimization,* Working Paper No. 417 (Wellesley, MA: Center for Research on Women, Wellesley College, 2004), 5.

57. Ibid., 6.

58. Ibid.

59. Ibid., 8.

60. Ibid.

61. J. Bottcher, "Social Practices of Gender: How Gender Relates to Delinquency in the Everyday Lives of High-Risk Youths," *Criminology* 39 (2001), 899.

62. A. V. D'Unger, K. C. Land, and P. L. McCall, "Sex Differences in Age Patterns of Delinquent Criminal Careers: Results from Poisson Latent Class Analysis of the Philadelphia Cohort Study," *Journal of Quantitative Criminology* 18 (2002), 371–73.

64. Etta A. Anderson, "The 'Chivalrous' Treatment of the Female Offender in the Arms of the Criminal Justice System: A Review of the Literature," *Social Problems* 23 (1976), 350–57. See also Chesney-Lind, "Judicial Enforcement of the Female Sex Role: The Family Court and Female Delinquency," *Issues in Criminology* 8 (1973), 57–59; Kristine

Olson Rogers, "For Her Own Protection, . . . Conditions of Incarceration for Female Juvenile Offenders in the State of Connecticut" *Law and Society Review* 7 (1973), 223–46; and John M. MacDonald and Meda Chesney-Lynd, "Gender Bias and the Juvenile Justice Revisited: A Multiyear Analysis," *Crime and Delinquency* 47 (2001), 173–95.

65. Rosemary C. Sarri, "Juvenile Law: How It Penalizes Females," in Crites, ed., *The Female Offender*, 68–69.

66. Ibid., 76.

67. Ibid.

68. Ibid.

69. Richard E. Johnson, "Social Class and Delinquent Behavior: A New Test," *Criminology* 18 (1980), 91.

70. Charles Tittle, Wayne Villemez, and Douglas Smith, "The Myth of Social Class and Criminality: An Empirical Assessment of the Empirical Evidence," *American Sociological Review* 43 (1978), 643–56.

71. Suzanne S. Ageton and Delbert S. Elliott, *The Incidence of Delinquent Behavior in a National Probability Sample of Adolescents* (Boulder, CO: Behavioral Research Institute, 1978).

72. Margaret Farnworth, Terence P. Thornberry, Marvin D. Krohn, and Alan J. Lizotte, "Measurement in the Study of Class and Delinquency: Integrating Theory and Research," *Journal of Research in Crime and Delinquency* 31 (1994), 32.

73. Ibid.

74. Chesney-Lind, *The Female Offender*.

75. Lee H. Bowker and Malcolm M. Klein, "Female Participation in Delinquent Gang Activities," *Adolescence 15:* 509–519.

76. Ibid.

77. J. G. Dryfoos, *Adolescents at Risk: Prevalence and Prevention* (New York: Oxford University Press, 1990).

78. Robert J. Sampson and William Julius Wilson, "Toward a Theory of Race, Crime, and Urban Inequality," in *Crime and Inequality,* edited by John Hagen and Ruth D. Peterson (Stanford, CA: Stanford University Press, 1995), 38.

79. Ibid., 38.

80. Ibid.; Robert J. Bursik, Jr., "Social Organization and Theories of Crime and Delinquency: Problems and Prospects," *Criminology* 26 (November 1988), 522.

81. Sampson and Wilson, "Toward a Theory of Race, Crime, and Urban Inequality," 41.

82. Ibid., 54. See also Robert J. Sampson, "Urban Black Violence: The Effect of Male Joblessness and Family Disruption," *American Journal of Sociology* 93 (1987), 348–82.

83. Sampson, "Urban Black Violence."

84. Sampson and Wilson, "Toward a Theory of Race, Crime, and Urban Inequality," 52.

85. Ibid., 54.

86. Ibid., 53.

87. Charis E. Kubrin and Ronald Weitzer, "Retaliatory Homicide: Concentrated Disadvantage and Neighborhood Culture," *Social Problems* 50 (2003), 157–80.

88. Stacy De Coster, Karen Heimer, and Stacy M. Wittrock, *Sociological Quarterly* 47 (2006), 723–53.

89. Sampson and Wilson, "Toward a Theory of Race, Crime, and Urban Inequality," 40.

90. Published by U.S. Census, 2012, Orlando Rodriguez, *The Criminal Justice System as an Assimilation Milieu for the Hispanic Immigrant*, accessed April 22, 2012, at http:P//cnz.org/content/m33211/latest, p. 2.

91. Ron Uznz, "Hispanic Crime: A Postscript," *The American Conservative (*September 4, 2012).

92. Daniel Griswold, "Higher Immigration, Lower Crime," *Commentary* (December 2009), 1. Accessed April 22, 2012, at http://www.commentarymagainze.com/article/higher-immigration-lower-crime.

93. Ibid., 5.

94. Ibid., 6.

95. Signithia Fordham, "'Those Loud Black Girls': (Black) Women, Silence and Gender 'Passing' in the Academy," in *Beyond Black and White: New Faces and Voices in U.S. Schools,* edited by Maxine Seller and Lois Weis (Albany: State University of New York Press, 1997), 81–111.

96. Chesney-Lind, *The Female Offender,* 23.

97. Ibid.

98. Janet L. Lauritsen, "Racial and Ethnic Differences in Judicial Offending," in *Our Children, Their Children: Confronting Racial and Ethnic Differences in American Juvenile Justice,* edited by Darrell F. Hawkins and Kimberly Kempf-Leonard (Chicago: University of Chicago Press, 2005), 91–95.

99. Ibid., 99.

100. Donna M. Bishop, "The Role of Race and Ethnicity in Juvenile Justice Processing," in *Our Children,* 23. See also *Federal Advisory Committee on Juvenile Justice: Annual Report 2010* (Washington, DC: U.S. Government Printing Office, 2010)

101. Carl E. Pope and William H. Feyerherm, "Minority Status and Juvenile Justice Processing: An Assessment of the Research Literature," *Criminal Justice Abstract* (June 1990), 333–34. See also Donna Bishop and Charles E. Frazier, "The Influence of Race in Juvenile Justice Processing," *Journal of Research in Crime and Delinquency* 25 (August 1988), 242.

102. Pope and Feyerherm, "Minority Status and Juvenile Justice Processing."

103. Donna Hamparian and Michael J. Leiber, *Disproportionate Confinement of Minority Juveniles in Secure Facilities: 1996 National Report* (Champaign, IL: Community Research Associates, 1997), 1.

104. Ibid.

105. Howard N. Snyder and Melissa Sickmun, *Juvenile Offenders and Victims: 2006 National Report*, (Washington, D.C. National Center for Juvenile Justice and Office of Juvenile Justice and Delinquency Prevention, 2006), 189.

106. Ibid.

107. Ibid, 190.

108. Ibid.

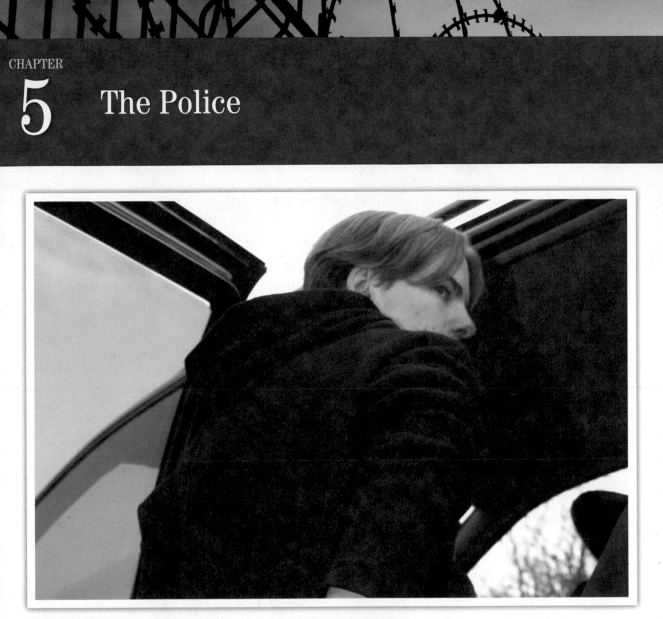

ACE STOCK LIMITED/Alamy

Learning Objectives

1. Summarize the history of police–juvenile relationships.
2. Summarize juveniles' attitudes toward the police.
3. Describe police discretion and the factors that influence discretion.
4. Summarize how police process juveniles.
5. Describe the legal rights of arrested juveniles.
6. Describe how police agencies are structured to deal with juvenile crime.
7. Summarize developing trends in how police deal with juveniles.

How does one explain the raw excitement of being a cop? This is an excitement so powerful that it consumes and changes the officer's personality. For the officer all five senses are involved, especially in dangerous situations. They are stirred in a soup of emotions and adrenaline and provide an adrenaline rush that surpasses anything felt before. You are stronger and more agile; your mind functions on a higher level of quickness and alertness. Afterwards, the grass seems greener; the air fresher; food tastes better; and the spouse and children are even more precious. It is an addictive feeling that makes the runner's high in comparison feel like a hangover. Police work gets into the blood and possesses the spirit. You become the job and the job becomes you, until the day you die.[1]

—Veteran police officer

In the chapter-opening quote, the veteran police officer makes a passionate statement about the joys of becoming a police officer. He clearly sees policing more as a calling than as a job or a set of bureaucratically defined duties. He believes that policing demands the very best that a person has to offer. Once it gets into your blood, he warns, it will change your identity and self-image and will stay with you for the rest of your life.

This officer, despite his positive attitude about a police career, has little interest in working with juveniles. With him, as well as with many officers, many problems exist in policing juveniles. Juvenile crimes are viewed as minor, and the arrest of a juvenile is not considered a real arrest. The due process rights accorded juveniles in recent decades also make the police feel that their crime-fighting hands are tied. Furthermore, police officers are distrusted by many juveniles, some of whom view the police as the enemy. The police, then, must deal with juveniles' hostile attitudes, which can become explosive and violent at a moment's notice. Finally, the nature of juvenile crime is changing; the spread of malls, the explosion of drug use, and the proliferation of gangs have complicated the lives of police officers across the country.

Police officers are faced with juveniles whose misbehaviors range from drinking in parks to murder. At one end of the spectrum are status offenders who have conflicts with their parents, schools, and community but who are not true criminals in either behavior or intent. At the other end are the violent, repetitive offenders. These youths commit murder, aggravated assault, rape, and grand theft; some are in organized crime, and some deal in drugs. Between these extremes are varieties of runaways and mentally ill, dependent, neglected, abused, victimized, and delinquent youths.

The history of police–juvenile relationships in the United States is reviewed in this chapter, followed by juveniles' attitudes toward the police, the cycle of alienation, factors that influence police discretion, the informal and formal dispositions of juvenile offenders, and the changing legal rights of juveniles. The final sections of this chapter consider police organizations and functions as they relate to juveniles, as well as the special challenges that juveniles' drug use, gang involvement, and gun possession bring to community-based policing.

What Is the History of Police–Juvenile Relations?

The earliest Puritan communities in the United States used informal methods of controlling juveniles. Probably the most effective of these informal methods was *socialization*, by which youths were taught the rules of society from the time they were born until the rules became internalized. If a youth violated a law, the family, church, and community stepped in to bring the youth back into line. The family was expected to punish the youth, and if the family failed, church and community elders assumed the task of punishment.

The industrialization and urbanization that began in the late 1700s reduced the effectiveness of informal social controls. As the population increased and cities grew, the traditional tight-knit family and community structures became disorganized and street crime increased. Religious, ethnic, and political violence also increased, leading the society to look for other methods of social control.[2] Police forces were created to help solve the problem.

In the 1830s and 1840s, full-time police forces were established in larger cities, such as Boston, New York, and Philadelphia; by the 1870s, all the major cities had full-time forces, and many of the smaller cities had part-time forces. Social control had moved from the family to police officers walking the beat. The police emerged as a coercive force employed to keep youthful criminals, gangs, ethnic minorities, and immigrants in line.

Police officers had the power to arrest juveniles, but they still used many informal techniques of social control. Some officers undoubtedly were effective in striking up friendships with juveniles and convincing them to mend their ways. In other cases, police reprimanded juveniles verbally or turned them over to their parents or parish priests. Unfortunately, the power of police officers at this time was virtually unlimited; some officers talked abusively to children, roughed them up, or beat them in alleys. The result was that, added to the corruption found in many police departments, considerable tension existed between police officers and the communities they patrolled. Few, if any, efforts to remedy this problem occurred before the 1900s.

In the first three decades of the twentieth century, the Portland, Oregon; New York City; and Washington, D.C., police departments started to address the problem of juvenile crime. Police chiefs began to think in terms of prevention instead of mere control. Policewomen were hired to deal with delinquents and runaway and truant children by patrolling amusement parks, dance halls, and other places where juveniles might be corrupted. The job of these officers was to dissuade the youths from engaging in a life of crime.[3]

The idea of prevention was so popular that 90 percent of the nation's largest cities had instituted some type of juvenile program by 1924.[4] The Police Athletic League was launched in the 1920s to provide children with safe playgrounds, and by the 1930s, most large police departments had either assigned welfare officers to difficult districts, initiated employment bureaus for youthful males, assigned officers to juvenile courts, or set up special squads to deal with juvenile crime.[5] Other innovative actions included instituting relief programs, giving poor children gifts at Christmas, and developing programs whereby police spoke to various groups of youths, such as the Boy Scouts and Campfire Girls.[6]

A major development occurred in the mid-1920s. Until this time, departments had not effectively organized their juvenile crime prevention efforts. Chief August Vollmer of the Berkeley, California, Police Department is credited with being the first chief to bring together the various segments of a police force to form a youth bureau.[7] The concept spread to other urban areas, and soon youth bureaus, often called *youth aid bureaus, juvenile bureaus, juvenile control bureaus, juvenile divisions,* or *crime prevention bureaus,* were founded throughout major cities in the United States. The police in these bureaus were the forerunners of the modern juvenile officers.

Two developments formalized the increasingly important role of juvenile officers in the United States. In 1955, the Central States Juvenile Officers Association was formed, followed soon after by the International Juvenile Officers Association in 1957. Meetings were held by these and similar groups at regional, national, and international levels. For the first time, the responsibilities, standards, and procedures necessary in juvenile work began to be developed. In addition, the increase in social science research on youths highlighted the necessity of training juvenile officers better, because these officers were expected to help, rather than punish, youthful offenders.

Preventive police work with juveniles continued through the 1960s. Programs were developed to reduce delinquency and to improve the way youths viewed the police. Police officers volunteered to speak to elementary, junior high, and high school students, and some departments developed special programs for these purposes. The Police Athletic League expanded its athletic programs and set up courses in leadership and moral training for youths. Furthermore, some police agencies helped youths find jobs and worked with schools to reduce truancy. Programs to fight drugs and alcohol and to show the consequences of drinking and driving were also developed.

In the 1970s, 1980s, and 1990s, severe budgetary restrictions forced many police departments to reduce their emphasis on juvenile programs. Some dropped their juvenile divisions altogether, whereas others limited their programs to dependent, neglected, and abused children; these programs had commenced in response to the increasingly recognized problems of domestic violence. By the late 1990s and the first decade of the twenty-first century,

FIGURE 5–1
Timeline of Police–Juvenile Relations

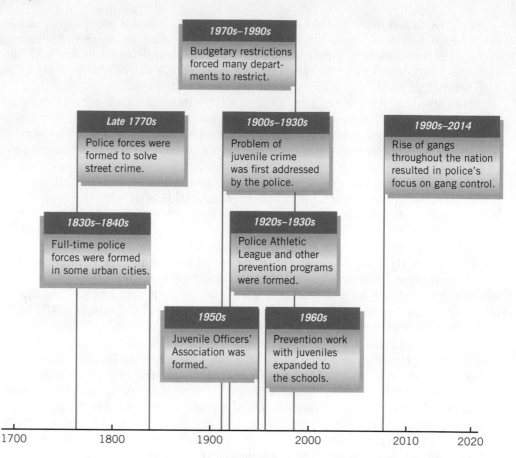

some police departments were experimenting with community-based or **problem-oriented policing** as well as restorative justice practices.

Beginning in the late 1980s and continuing to the present, youth gangs have developed in nearly every urban and suburban area of the nation, as well as in some rural areas. The problems created by these gangs have resulted in the police being given the responsibilities of identifying and controlling these gangs. Gang divisions were developed in many departments, and other law enforcement emphases were designed to control gangs. Figure 5–1 illustrates the timeline of police–juvenile relations.

What Are Juveniles' Attitudes Toward the Police?

Researchers began studying the public's attitudes toward the police more than forty years ago and came to these conclusions about juveniles:

- Several studies have reported that juveniles who have had contact with the police have more negative attitudes toward them than those who have not had contact.[8] This seems to be especially true of African American youth whose cultural accepted view of police is independent of their arrest experience.[9]

- Scott H. Decker's 1981 review of literature on attitudes toward the police concluded that youths had more negative attitudes toward the police than did older citizens and that race, the quality of police services, and previous experiences with the police also affected citizens' attitudes.[10]

- Komanduri S. Murty, Julian B. Roebuck, and Joann D. Smith found in a 1990 Atlanta study that "older, married, white-collar, highly educated, and employed respondents reported a more positive image of the police than did their counterparts—younger, single, blue-collar, poorly educated, unemployed/underemployed respondents."[11]

- Michael J. Leiber, Mahesh K. Nalla, and Margaret Farnworth challenged the traditional argument that juveniles' interactions with the police are the primary determinant of

TABLE 5–1
Attitudes Toward the Police

Favorable Attitudes Toward Police	Less Favorable Attitudes Toward Police
younger children	older children
Caucasians	African Americans
girls	boys
middle- and upper-class youngsters	lower-class youngsters

their attitudes toward law enforcement officers. Instead, they saw juveniles' attitudes toward authority and social control developing in a larger sociocultural context, and global attitudes toward police affecting youths' assessment of specific police contacts.[12]

- Data from the *Monitoring the Future* survey of high school seniors from the late 1980s through the mid-1990s indicated that high school seniors' attitudes toward the police became more negative during that period across all subsets of the sample. However, the *Monitoring the Future* data for 2007 revealed that when high school seniors were asked their opinions of the police and other law enforcement agencies, 35.8 percent (up from 26.6 percent in 1996) responded either "good" or "very good." If the 30.2 percent of "fair" responses were added to the "good" and "very good" categories, roughly 61 percent of high school seniors could be considered to have a positive attitude toward law enforcement.[13]

- Susan Guarino-Ghezzi and Bryan Carr contend, based on the basis of a study conducted in Boston, that the way police interact with juveniles alienates youths who are already alienated from the wider society, and that the results are incorporated into the youths' subculture. This sets the stage for what Guarino-Ghezzi and Carr call a **cycle of alienation**.[14]

- Research continues today into subcultural theory and the relations of juveniles with the police. Terry Nihar and colleagues predictably find that juveniles' attitudes toward the police are positively correlated with the youths' attitudes toward parents and teachers.[15] In a different type of study, Yoland G. Hurst found that rural youths exhibit a more positive attitude toward the police than do urban youths and that whites did not have a significantly more positive view than did African Americans.[16]

To sum up: As Leiber and colleagues point out, juveniles' attitudes toward the police are formed in a larger sociocultural context. Guarino-Ghezzi and Carr's study finds that police interactions with youths alienated from the wider society often results in a cycle of alienation resulting in their greater alienation from society. Generally, most youths appear to have positive attitudes toward the police. Younger juveniles are more positive than older ones, white juveniles are more positive than African Americans, and female juveniles are more positive than males. A positive attitude also seems to be influenced by social class, because middle-class youths tend to be more positive than lower-class youths. Generally, juveniles who have not had contact with the police are more positive than those who have had police contact. The most hostile attitudes are typically those of youths with extensive histories of law-violating activities, those who have had contact with the police, or those involved in youth gangs. See Table 5–1.

How Does Police Discretion Affect the Police Response to Juveniles?

Police **discretion** can be defined as the choice between two or more possible means of handling a situation confronting the police officer. By exercising discretion, the police officer can use various methods to keep juveniles out of the juvenile justice system or to involve them in it. Although it is sometimes argued that the police abuse their broad powers of discretion with juveniles, studies generally estimate that only 10 to 20 percent of police–juvenile encounters become official contacts.[17] Two major aspects of policing are the factors that influence police discretion, discussed in this section, and the ways in which police process juveniles who come to their attention, discussed in the next section.

The police officer's disposition of the juvenile is largely determined by nine factors: the nature of the offense; citizen complaints; the juvenile's sex, race, socioeconomic status, and other individual characteristics; the nature of the interaction between the police officer and the juvenile; departmental policy; and external pressures in the community.

The Nature of the Offense

The most important factor that influences the disposition of the youthful offender is the seriousness of the offense. Research has consistently documented that the probability of arrest increases with the legal severity of the alleged offense.[18]

Citizen Complaints

Another important factor influencing the disposition of the youth is a citizen's presence or filing of a complaint against a youth.[19] If a citizen initiates a complaint, remains present, and wishes the arrest of a juvenile, the likelihood increases that the juvenile will be arrested and processed.[20]

Sex

Police officers generally are less likely to arrest a young female than a young male if she has committed an offense, but they are more likely to arrest a female if she violates traditional role expectations for females, such as failing to obey parents, being sexually promiscuous, or running away from home.[21]

Race

Studies differ in their findings on the importance of race in determining juvenile dispositions.[22] One of the problems in appraising the importance of race is that African Americans and members of other minority groups appear to be involved in more serious crimes more often than whites are. Nevertheless, it does seem that racial bias makes minority juveniles the special targets of the police.[23]

Socioeconomic Status

What makes it difficult to establish the effect of class on the disposition of cases involving juveniles is that most studies examine race and socioeconomic status together. Nevertheless, some evidence supports the long-standing conclusion that lower-class juveniles receive different justice than do middle- or upper-class juveniles. Lower-class youths are dragged into the net of the system for the same offenses for which middle- and upper-class juveniles are often sent home.

Individual Characteristics

A prior arrest record, previous offenses, prior police contacts, age, peer relationships, family situation, and the conduct of parents also may influence how the police officer handles a juvenile offender.[24] The juvenile most likely to be arrested is older, has a serious record, and fits the image of a delinquent and dangerous person.[25]

Nature of Police–Juvenile Interaction

Juveniles who defer to a police officer reduce the likelihood of a formal disposition.[26] Juveniles who are hostile increase the likelihood that they will be referred to the juvenile court.[27] One study found that in encounters in which no evidence linked a juvenile to an offense, the demeanor of the juvenile was the most important determinant of whether formal action was taken.[28]

Departmental Policy

Departmental policy also may influence police handling of juveniles.[29] Some evidence suggests that the more professional departments had higher numbers of juveniles referred to the juvenile court because they used discretion less often than did the departments that were not as professional.[30]

Focus on Practice 5–1
Age and Race Differences in Police Searches of Younger and Older Male Drivers

In recent years, researchers have found considerable empirical support that African American and Hispanic motorists stopped by the police are more likely than white motorists to be subjected to a search. Most would agree that little dispute exists regarding the fact of race and ethnic disparities in police searches. Disagreement, however, arises about whether these disparities constitute impermissible discrimination.

According to Richard Rosenfeld, Jeff Rojeck, and Scott Decker, who studied traffic searches in St. Louis, the driver's age has contrasting effects on race differences during traffic searches. They found that African American drivers over the age of 30 are no more likely than whites to be subjected to discretionary searches by the police; some evidence even exists that African American males age 30 and over are significantly less

likely than whites of the same age to be searched. However, the opposite result holds for younger African American male drivers, who are more likely than younger whites to be searched when stopped by the police, regardless of the discretionary quality of the search. As the authors note, this study is consistent with studies of young African American males' negative experience with and attitudes toward the police.

CRITICAL THINKING QUESTION:

Are you surprised by this research finding of the importance of age?

Source: Richard Rosenfeld, Jeff Rojeck, and Scott Decker, "Age Matters: Race Differences in Police Searches of Young and Older Male Drivers," *Journal of Research in Crime and Delinquency* 25 (2011), 1–25.

External Pressures in the Community

The status of the complainant or victim, the attitudes of the press and the public, and the philosophy and available resources of referral agencies also may influence the disposition of the law-violating youth. See Focus on Practice 5–1.

In sum, this portrait of police–juvenile contacts reveals that the seriousness of the offense and complaints by citizens appear to be the most important factors influencing police action toward juveniles. Other, less influential factors are the individual characteristics of the juvenile, departmental policy, and external pressures in the community. The sex, race, and socioeconomic status of the offender do not appear to be as influential today as they were in the past (see Table 5–2).

How Do Police Process Juveniles?

The studies on police discretion reveal many inconsistencies, some legitimate and some not. For example, few would argue that true justice should not take into consideration factors such as the friendliness of juveniles or their race, sex, social class, or community reputations; nevertheless, these biases do creep into police work and are under much

TABLE 5–2
Factors That Influence the Disposition of Juvenile Offenders

Individual Factors
Personality characteristics of the juvenile
Personality characteristics of the police officer
Interaction between the police officer and the juvenile

Sociocultural Factors
Citizens' complaints
Gender of the juvenile
Race/ethnicity of the juvenile
Socioeconomic status of the juvenile
The influence of cultural norms in the community and values of the wider society on both
    juveniles and police officers

Organizational Factors
Nature of the offense
Departmental policy

Police officers are required to "know their beats," which includes knowing the people and what is "normal" for their neighborhoods. List some options you might have as a police officer in meeting these youths on your beat.

Constinia Charbonnette

criticism today. On the other side of the coin is the complexity of police work. Police working their beat come into daily contact with many different types of juveniles in various situations. Some youths obviously have a mental illness; some come from families torn apart by alcohol, drugs, and other addictive disorders; some youths are neglected; and some are abused physically, emotionally, or sexually. Some youths have no family members to turn to in times of need, and some find school a frightening, frustrating, and valueless experience; conversely, many find gang experiences rewarding, emotionally satisfying, and a way to gain the respect of peers. Police officers must deal effectively with all of these youths.

Informal Options: On the Streets

Police view youths in the context of their community. This means that officers see how youths interact in their neighborhoods with friends and family and witness the many different ways the youths get along with others. The good beat officer knows who belongs to various peer groups and gangs, who is stable and who is unstable, who is belligerent and who is not; these officers also often know the circumstances of youths' lives. These factors affect how the **police process** a particular event or incident. For example, some of the following police actions are informal responses to youthful misbehavior and no permanent record of the incident will be kept, nor will juveniles be held for further actions by the juvenile court:

- Kids clowning around on the sidewalk are simply ignored by a passing officer.
- Police officers suggest that youths take their sidewalk soccer game into a nearby playground or vacant lot if they are bothering people, if someone could get hurt, or if a citizen has complained.
- An officer might talk to a youth bullying others and suggest that the bully change his or her ways.
- Some officers strike up friendships with local youths, sit and talk with them, and sometimes go to their school or sporting events.
- Officers who see youths fighting or stealing something might talk to them about the harm they are causing and how they might get into trouble as a result.
- An officer might write down the juvenile's name and address in a notepad for future reference.

Informal Options: At the Station (Station House Adjustment)

- Youths are taken to the police station, where their situation is discussed with them and their parents; the youths are then sent home with their parents.
- In larger departments, youths are sent to a police youth bureau that consists of specially trained officers or other personnel who counsel the youths and their parents but who permit the youths to remain in the community.
- Police officers or youth bureau personnel unofficially refer or direct youths and/or their parents or guardians to anger management classes, vocational training programs, shelters, or counseling programs for alcohol, drug, mental illness, or other problems.
- Police or youth service personnel contact and work with school personnel in getting truant youths back in schools or into special programs. (School personnel may initiate these contacts, and special programs may be set up in cooperation with police departments.)
- Police contact the probation department informally to access probation department programs for a youth in question. (The probation department also handles many cases informally.)
- Police unofficially contact children and youth services to get proper care for dependent and neglected or other children in need of supervision.

Combined Informal and Formal Processing

- A youth is taken into custody or arrested; he or she is then booked, talked to, and released without further action.

- A youth is taken into custody or arrested and booked and then released with the firm warning that any further problems will be dealt with by arrest and prosecution.

- Once a youth is in custody, officers officially notify community agencies such as children and youth services that a youth needs their services and either send the youth to the agency or have the agency pick up the youth.

Formal Processing: At the Station

- The parents of arrested youths are called to the police station and, after booking, have their child released to their care and supervision. The case may end at that point or may be referred to juvenile court for further consideration.

- The youth is taken into custody, booked, fingerprinted, and then referred to juvenile intake, which has both informal and formal options. After evaluation by either the police or the court intake personnel, youths may be placed in secure detention awaiting their preliminary hearing and trial. This secure detention may, in some cities, be in the local jail or a youth detention center.

- Police in states with legislative waiver will, after arresting and booking a youth, automatically waive the youth directly to adult court, which further evaluates the youth.

The further youths are processed into the system, the less discretionary authority the police have. On the street, the amount of discretion a police officer has is considerable; in states with legislative waiver, police discretion is limited, especially as it pertains to violent crimes. In addition, police discretion is governed to a considerable extent by departmental policy.

What Legal Rights Do Juveniles Have with the Police?

Juveniles were at the mercy of the police for much of the twentieth century. Few or no laws protected juveniles in trouble because of the rehabilitative ideal in juvenile justice. Police officers, whose primary mission was to maintain law and order, used whatever tactics seemed appropriate to restore the peace. Friendliness, persuasion, threats, coercion, and force were all used to gain the compliance of juveniles. If these tactics failed, juveniles were taken into juvenile court or, depending on the laws of the state and the seriousness of the crimes, to adult court for prosecution. Few protections were granted to juveniles in the areas of search and seizure, interrogation, fingerprinting, lineups, or other procedures.

In the 1960s, the U.S. Supreme Court's decisions began to change this relationship between the police and juveniles. Although not all police departments have endorsed or adhered to the guidelines laid down by the courts, most departments have made a conscientious effort to abide by the standards of justice and fairness implied by these decisions.[31]

Search and Seizure

The Fourth Amendment to the Constitution of the United States protects citizens from unauthorized **search and seizure**. This amendment states:

> The right of the people to be secure in their persons, houses, papers, and effects, against unreasonable searches and seizures, shall not be violated, and no Warrants shall issue, but upon probable cause, supported by Oath or affirmation, and particularly describing the place to be searched, and the persons or things to be seized.

▲ Private security police face multiple problems with juveniles in the malls including drugs, theft, fights, and behaving in ways that make senior citizens feel uncomfortable. Here a security officer escorts a female shoplifter to the security office where her parents will be called.
Kathryn O'Lare

The issue here is the right to privacy. All citizens are guaranteed the right by the Constitution to feel secure in their person and home. Law enforcement officers may not abridge that right without following very strict due process guidelines. In 1961, the Supreme Court decision in *Mapp v. Ohio* affirmed Fourth Amendment rights for adults. This decision stated that evidence gathered in an unreasonable search and seizure—that is, evidence seized without probable cause and without a proper search warrant—was inadmissible in court.[32] This inadmissibility of illegally obtained evidence is referred to as the *exclusionary rule.* In the 1967 *State v. Lowery* case, the Supreme Court applied the Fourth Amendment ban against unreasonable searches and seizures to juveniles:

Is it not more outrageous for the police to treat children more harshly than adult offenders, especially when such is violative of due process and fair treatment? Can a court countenance a system, where, as here, an adult may suppress evidence with the usual effect of having the charges dropped for lack of proof, and, on the other hand, a juvenile can be institutionalized—lose the most sacred possession a human being has, his freedom—for "rehabilitative" purposes because the Fourth Amendment right is unavailable to him?[33]

Juveniles, therefore, are protected from unreasonable searches and seizures. Juveniles must be presented with a valid search warrant unless they have either waived that right, have consented to having their person or property searched, or have been caught in the act. If these conditions have not been met, courts have overturned rulings against the juveniles. For example, evidence was dismissed in one case when police entered a juvenile's apartment at 5:00 A.M. without a warrant to arrest him.[34] In another case, Houston police discovered marijuana on a youth five hours after he had been stopped for driving a car without lights and a driver's license. Confined to a Texas training school for this drug offense, the youth was ordered released by an appellate court because the search took place too late to be related to the arrest.[35] The least right to privacy is on the street, followed generally by the automobile and school; the greatest right to privacy is in the home.[36]

On the Streets

Voices of Delinquency: Police Interrogation and Victimization

When a crime is committed in the community, the job of the police officer is to solve the crime and make an arrest. The officer must, however, follow legal rules that guarantee that the alleged offender is treated fairly. How do police proceed?

Consider a police stop as an example: the police officer has the right to stop a youth on the streets and ask questions. Juveniles, however, do not have to stop or answer any questions if they do not want to answer. The officer cannot pat them down, and they may leave if they desire.

A second example is that of the police approaching a youth with a specific and articulable suspicion that the juvenile is armed and possibly dangerous. The law enforcement experience of the police officer, a high-drug-dealing area of town, an obvious bulge in clothing, or the presence of another officer who may have arrested the youth previously and found a weapon on the youth may all lead to reasonable suspicion justifying a pat down. In this case, the officer may do a *Terry* search; that is, pat down the youth's outer clothing in a search for weapons only.[37] Police may not do pat downs as part of their routine stops or in order to find contraband. The pat down is for weapons only. However, in doing the pat down, if the police find an illegal weapon, they may take the weapon and arrest the youth for possessing it; then, they legally may search the youth for other contraband.[38]

A third scenario illustrates another type of concern. A police officer temporarily detains a youth on the street or takes the youth to the station. When is the juvenile actually under arrest? Some jurisdictions consider an arrest as occurring whenever the person stopped does not feel free to leave the presence of the police officer. Indeed, youths in any of the above examples could be taken or asked to come to the police station, be interviewed, and then be allowed to leave; this would be perfectly legal and within the juveniles' rights in some states and jurisdictions. The clearest indicator, of course, is when an offender officially is charged with a crime and given notice to appear at further hearings. A juvenile may, in fact, ask the officer if it is permissible to leave. The options for the police officer here are to release the juvenile immediately, detain the juvenile longer and let him or her go after further questioning and satisfying their concerns, or arrest the youth.

In the Vehicle

Officers cannot pull over youths driving a vehicle and search the vehicle without a reason. The reason can be something simple, like a broken taillight or muffler, but an officer must have an articulable reason to stop the car. The juveniles being nervous or making nervous movements when stopped is not usually sufficient reason to search the car.[39]

Once the car is pulled over, officers may look into it from the outside for anything that is illegal and "in plain view," particularly weapons.[40] If nothing is visible, the officers may not search the car. A 2009 Supreme Court decision, *Arizona v. Gant*, held that police may search the passenger compartment of an arrested offender's vehicle only if the police reasonably believe that the arrestee might grab something in the passenger compartment at the time of the search or that the vehicle contains evidence relevant to the arrest. But if the officers have information from reliable sources that the youths have contraband, they can search for the contraband. Also, if alcohol or marijuana can be smelled, the officers have a reasonable or articulable suspicion that a crime is occurring and can push their search to the next level, because they now have a reasonable suspicion or probable cause for doing so.

If a weapon or other contraband is visible from outside the car and is within the reach of the juvenile, the officers will ask the youth to get out of the car, and search the areas of the car in view, including the glove compartment, for other weapons and contraband. The police officers can search all areas in the interior of the car that the juvenile could reach into and possibly grab a weapon or attempt to dispose of contraband. Police may not, however, search the trunk of the car without a warrant because the trunk is out of reach of the juvenile.[41] If contraband is found, the police officers can then take the juvenile into custody or make an arrest and take the juvenile to the station; there the youth will be processed either formally or informally.

At Home

Police officers may come into a home without a warrant for a number of reasons. First, they may enter a home if a person authorized to let them in gives them permission or invites them in. They may even search a youth's room if they ask permission of the youth's parents, but many police officers still take the precaution of getting a warrant before going to the house. Police may also enter a home without a warrant if they have a reasonable or articulable reason or probable cause to suspect that a crime is being or will be committed. For example, if police are in "hot pursuit," believe that someone will be hurt or killed, or believe that contraband will be disposed of before they can get a warrant, then they may enter a home without a warrant.[42]

Officers may also go into a home if they are standing in the doorway and see illegal substances "in plain view." Now they may enter the house (or dorm room) and conduct a search relevant to only the contraband, as well as to the possibility that weapons may be within reach of the offenders. Any further searches are contingent on getting a warrant.

In the School

Juveniles' use of weapons and drugs is changing the nature of police–student relations in schools. The police are being called on in increasing numbers of communities to enforce drug-free school zone laws. Drug-free zones generally are defined as the school property and the area within a one-thousand-foot radius of the property's boundaries. The police are also called on to enforce the 1990 federal Gun-Free School Zones Act.

The use of dogs to sniff for drugs; the administration of a Breathalyzer test; the installation of hidden video cameras; and the routine searches of students' purses, pockets, school lockers, desks, and vehicles on school grounds are increasing as school officials struggle to control crime in schools. In some cases, school officials conduct their own searches; in other cases, the police are brought in to conduct the searches.[43]

In *New Jersey v. T. L. O.* (1985), the U.S. Supreme Court examined whether the Fourth Amendment right against unreasonable searches and seizures applies to the school setting.[44] The facts of this case are the following: A teacher at Piscataway High School in Middlesex County, New Jersey, discovered on March 7, 1980, that two girls were smoking in a bathroom. He reported this violation of school rules to the principal's office, and the two students were summoned to meet with the assistant vice principal. T. L. O., one of the two, claimed that she had done no wrong, and the assistant principal demanded to see her purse. His examination discovered a pack of cigarettes and cigarette rolling papers, some marijuana, a pipe, a considerable amount of money, a list of students who owed T. L. O. money, and letters implicating her in marijuana dealing. T. L. O. confessed later at the police station to selling drugs on school grounds.[45]

The juvenile court found T. L. O. delinquent and sentenced her to probation for one year. She then appealed her case to the New Jersey Supreme Court on the grounds that the search of her purse was not justified in the circumstances of the case. When the court upheld her appeal, the state appealed to the U.S. Supreme Court, which ruled that school personnel have the right to search lockers, desks, and students as long as they believe that the law or the school rules have been violated. The importance of this case is that the Court defined that the legality of **school searches** need not be based on obtaining a warrant or on having probable cause that a crime has taken place. Instead, the legality of the search depends on its reasonableness, considering the scope of the search, the student's gender and age, and the student's behavior at the time.[46] See Focus on Law 5–2.

School officials' searches of students suspected of violating school rules, especially regarding drugs and guns, have continued to be upheld by the courts since the *T. L. O.* decision. Indeed, of the eighteen cases decided since 1985, state appellate decisions applied the *T. L. O.* decision in fifteen.[47]

School officials, however, do not have unlimited search and seizure rights. The June 2009 Supreme Court decision in *Safford Unified School District v. Redding* placed limitations on strip searches of students. School officials in Safford, Arizona, strip searched a thirteen-year-old girl, forcing her to expose her breasts and pelvic area in a search for two Advils. The court ruled that the search was unreasonable because school officials had not demonstrated that either the power of the drugs and/or their quantity was sufficiently dangerous such as to warrant a search that was intrusive, humiliating, frightening, and embarrassing.[48]

Interrogation and Confession

The Fifth and Fourteenth Amendments to the Constitution address standards of fairness and due process in obtaining confessions. The significant statement in the Fifth Amendment relevant to juvenile interrogations is that no person

> shall be compelled in any criminal case to be a witness against himself, nor be deprived of life, liberty, or property, without due process of law. . . .

Two concerns arise here. First, no one can be "compelled" to testify or incriminate himself or herself. Second, all persons must be afforded due process of law if they might lose their freedom. For the courts, the key issue is whether juveniles are in custody at the time they make any statements to the police.[49] If we look at some of the previous examples of police stops on the streets or brief detainments in the police station, the issue is whether the juvenile feels free to leave. Juveniles who are not in custody, that is, who feel free to leave, can and will have anything incriminating they say held against them; that is, they can and will be arrested and charged and their comments held against them in court.

If juveniles are in custody or arrested, their strongest option is not to say anything or answer any questions until their parents or a lawyer is present. At this point, the now familiar *Miranda* warnings are relevant. A typical *Miranda* warning is:

> You have the right to remain silent. If you give up that right, anything you say can and
> will be used against you in a court of law. You have the right to an attorney and to have

Focus on Law 5–2
Search and Seizure in the Wisconsin Schools

The Wisconsin Department of Justice has summarized Fourth Amendment requirements for search and seizure rules as applicable to Wisconsin schools.* These rules are as follows:

SCHOOL OFFICIALS

- The Fourth Amendment restricts public school officials, but to a lesser degree than the police. The Fourth Amendment does not apply to private or parochial school officials.
- School officials may search students and their belongings if they have reasonable suspicion.
- The police may also search with reasonable suspicion (as opposed to their usual probable cause standard) if they are working at the request of, and in conjunction with, school officials.

CONSENT SEARCHES

- In order for consent to be valid, it must be voluntary and the person giving consent must have the authority to do so.
- Consent does not have to be in writing, but this form is preferable.
- A refusal to consent does not give a school official reasonable suspicion to believe that the student is hiding something.
- It is recommended that the student be advised what a school official is searching for prior to asking for consent to search.
- Consent to search a generalized area is consent to search any items found in that area.

NONCONSENSUAL SEARCHES OF THE STUDENT'S PERSON AND PERSONAL BELONGINGS

- A school official may search a student or his or her belongings if the official has a reasonable suspicion that the area being searched contains contraband or evidence of a violation.
- School officials should balance the intrusion of the search with the severity of the violation involved.
- A school official of the same gender as the student should do any physical search of a student.
- School officials may not strip search students.

LOCKER SEARCHES

- School officials may make random searches of lockers if the school has a written policy on this practice and the policy is widely disseminated to the student body.
- The Wisconsin legislature recently passed Wisconsin Statutes Section 118.325, which codifies the school's right to conduct random searches of lockers.

VEHICLE SEARCHES

- School officials may search a vehicle parked on school premises if they have a reasonable suspicion that the vehicle contains contraband or evidence of a violation.
- School officials may also search a vehicle with the consent of the student.

DRUG-DETECTION CANINES

- Random canine searches on school property are permissible, as they do not constitute a search within the meaning of the Fourth Amendment.
- If a properly trained canine alerts officials to the presence of drugs in an area, this constitutes probable cause to justify a search of the area.

POINT OF ENTRY/EXIT INSPECTIONS

- Random inspection of student items at specific locations is permitted if the school has a clear policy on this practice, clearly marks the area involved, and performs these inspections in a fair and even-handed way.

METAL DETECTORS

- Metal detectors are considered minor intrusions; thus, their use can be justified without reasonable suspicion or consent.
- The wand metal detector is more intrusive than a stationary unit, and its use should be limited to those occasions when the school official has an articulable suspicion.

SURVEILLANCE TECHNOLOGY AND SEARCH ISSUES

- School officials may use visual surveillance in any area where a student does not have a reasonable expectation of privacy.
- School officials should refrain from visual surveillance in areas where it is likely that students could be observed in a partially nude state.
- Audio surveillance is a Fourth Amendment intrusion, and schools should not monitor telephone conversations without the consent of one of the participants in the conversation.

CRITICAL THINKING QUESTION:

What is your evaluation of these search and seizure requirements?

*Some of these requirements will vary by state.

Source: For the complete Search and Seizure statement by the Department of Justice for the state of Wisconsin, see http://www.doj.state.wi.us.

---

an attorney present during questioning. If you cannot afford an attorney, one will be provided to you at no cost. During any questioning, you may decide at any time to exercise these rights, not answer any questions, or make any statements.[50]

At this stage of processing, the police have probable cause that the youth is a suspect and has information important to the case. Youths inadvertently can say something that ties them to a crime and results in their prosecution. For this reason, police are required to warn the juvenile against self-incrimination and, if the juvenile requests, make certain that a lawyer is present to discuss with the youth the answers to any questions the police might ask.

For the police to use a confession by a youth in court it must be obtained legally; that is, the youth must have been informed of his or her *Miranda* rights before giving the confession. Otherwise, the confession may not be used as evidence, because the youth's statements are inadmissible under the exclusionary rule.

At what age does a juvenile become capable of intellectually understanding the importance of the *Miranda* rights? Are juveniles under the influence of drugs or alcohol capable of legally waiving their rights? Should youths with mental illness be able to waive their rights? What about youths who do not understand English well?

These issues have been coming before various state courts for a number of years. In one case, the state of California upheld the confessions of two Spanish-speaking youths, one of whom had a mental age of slightly over ten years.[51] A North Carolina court upheld the confession of a twelve-year-old.[52] In another case, a Maryland appeals court upheld the confession of a sixteen-year-old high school dropout with an eighth-grade education.[53]

The questions raised by these court decisions require careful consideration. A study by T. Grisso found that almost all the juveniles questioned by St. Louis police in 1981 had waived their *Miranda* rights. Yet Grisso questioned whether these juveniles were able to understand the significance of the *Miranda* warnings. Grisso also concluded, after conducting a survey of juveniles, that almost all fourteen-year-olds and one-half of fifteen- and sixteen-year-olds were too young to understand the importance of their *Miranda* rights.[54] In addition, the police must stay within certain standards of fairness in their questioning.

The Supreme Court ruled in *Brown v. Mississippi* (1936) that force may not be used to obtain confessions.[55] In the *Brown* case, police used physical force in extracting an admission of guilt from a suspect. Other confessions have been ruled invalid because the accused was too tired; was questioned too long; or was not permitted to talk to his wife, friends, or lawyer either while being interrogated or until he confessed.[56]

The *Haley v. Ohio* case (1948) is another early example of police **interrogation** excesses.[57] Haley, a fifteen-year-old juvenile, was arrested five days after a robbery and shooting of a store owner. The youth confessed after five hours of interrogation (i.e., formal questioning) by five or six police officers with neither parents nor a lawyer present. During the questioning, the officers showed him alleged confessions of two other youths. The Supreme Court responded by stating:

> The age of the petitioner, the hours when he was grilled, the duration of his quizzing, the fact that he had no friend or counsel to advise him, the callous attitude of the police toward his rights combine to convince us that this was a confession wrung from a child by means which the law should not sanction. Neither man nor child can be allowed to stand condemned by methods which flout constitutional requirements of due process of law.[58]

The *Fare v. Michael C.* decision (1979) applies the "totality of the circumstances" approach to juveniles' interrogations. In this case, sixteen-year-old Michael C. was implicated in a murder that took place during a robbery. The police arrested the youth and brought him to the station. After he was advised of his *Miranda* rights, he asked to see his probation officer. When this request was denied, he proceeded to talk with the police officer, implicating himself in the murder. The Supreme Court ruled that Michael seemed to understand his rights, and even when his request to talk with his probation officer was denied, he still was willing to waive his rights and continue the interrogation.[59]

The states have passed statutes to force the police and the courts to comply with the standards of a constitutional interrogation of juveniles. Among these requirements are that parents or attorneys must be notified and present during questioning and that questioning should take place in an area other than the police station. In *Commonwealth v. Guyton* (1989), a Massachusetts motion appeals judge held that no other minor, not even a relative, can act as an interested adult.[60] Some states require that questioning occur at a juvenile detention facility, at the juvenile court, or at some other neutral place where the juvenile will not be intimidated by the surroundings. Figure 5–2 summarizes important police court cases about interrogation of juveniles, and the Evidence-Based Practice feature highlights a study about interrogation policies and practices.

TIMELINE

1936	1948	1966	1967	1979	1989
Brown v. Mississippi: Confessions cannot be extracted by police violence.	**Haley v. Ohio:** Methods used in obtaining juvenile's confession violated the Due Process Clause of the Fourteenth Amendment.	**Miranda v. Arizona:** This prohibits the use of a confession in court unless the individual was advised of his or her rights before interrogation.	**In re Gault:** This made the right against self-incrimination and the right to counsel applicable to juveniles.	**Fare v. Michael C.:** This applied the "totality of the circumstances" approach to the interrogation of juveniles.	**Commonwealth v. Guyton:** No other minor, not even a relative, can act as an interested adult (acting *in loco parentis*).

FIGURE 5–2
Timeline of Important Police Court Cases on the Police Interrogation of Juveniles

Evidence-Based Practice
Police Interrogation of Juveniles: An Empirical Study of Policy and Practice

The Supreme Court does not require any special procedural safeguards when police interrogate juveniles and use the adult standard—"knowing, intelligent, and voluntary under the totality of the circumstances"—to gauge the validity of juveniles' waivers of *Miranda* rights. Developmental psychologists, as Chapter 7 will discuss, have questioned whether juveniles possess the cognitive ability and competence necessary to exercise legal rights and have argued that immaturity and vulnerability make juveniles uniquely susceptible to police interrogation tactics. In the more than five decades since the Court decided *Miranda*, there has been almost no empirical research about what actually occurs when police interview criminal suspects and no research about how police routinely interrogate delinquents.

Since 1994, the Minnesota Supreme Court has required the police to record all interrogations of criminal suspects, including juveniles. Barry C. Feld's analysis of these data has begun to fill the empirical void about adolescents' competence in the interrogation room. He analyzed quantitative and qualitative data—interrogation tapes and transcripts, juvenile court filings, police reports, and probation and sentencing reports—of routine police interrogations of fifty-three juveniles, sixteen years of age and older, who had been charged with felony-level offenses and had waived their *Miranda* rights. This study provided the first empirical analyses of the tactics and techniques police use to interrogate juveniles and how youths respond to them.

Males comprised 86 percent of the questioned youth. About two-thirds (65 percent) were sixteen years of age at the time of their questioning. Over half of the youths were charged with crimes against the person—murder, armed robbery, aggravated assault, and criminal sexual conduct. Furthermore, these offenders were criminally experienced: almost half (42 percent) had one or more felony arrests prior to their current felony referrals; nearly two-thirds (62 percent) had prior juvenile court referrals. The majority of juveniles whom police questioned (68 percent) were members of ethnic and racial minority groups.

In the vast majority of cases (89 percent), a single officer conducted the interrogation. Police used the *Miranda* warning process subtly in order to predispose juveniles to waive their rights and talk with the police. Police interrogators used a two-pronged strategy to overcome suspects' resistance and to enable them to admit responsibility. Maximization techniques intimidate suspects and impress on them the futility of denial; in addition, they also provide moral justifications or face-saving alternatives that enable them to confess.

Police may overstate the seriousness of the crime or make exaggerated or false claims about the evidence. Police confront suspects with statements of witnesses or co-defendants, physical evidence, and fingerprints. They most typically (70 percent) refer to witnesses who identified the juvenile. In more than half of the cases (55 percent) in which police confronted suspects with evidence, they referred to statements purposely made by other participants or co-defendants implicating these suspects. Officers sometimes suggest that an admission might garner leniency, while a refusal to confess could result in more punishment.

One possibility of reducing interrogation wrongdoing by the police with juveniles is mandatory recording of all interrogations. Despite the value of taping interrogations, the question still remains: Who will review the tape? Despite the burdens and the time involved in going through the tapes, recording is absolutely essential to increase the visibility and reliability of police interrogations.

Another possibility is that the courts should also consider limiting the length of time that police may interrogate suspects, especially juveniles. The fact is that the longer the interview process is, the more likely that a false confession will be made. Most of the interviews in this study were of short duration, less than one or two hours, but lengthy interrogation questioning can pose problems of juveniles falsely implicating themselves.

A third possibility of reducing interrogation surrounding police interrogations of juveniles is concerned with the willingness of police to deceive suspects. There is no way to know, according to Feld, the prevalence of false evidence tactics or false confessions, and there is also no way to know how false evidence affects the ratios of true confessions by guilty people versus false confessions by innocent ones. The unique vulnerability of youth seems to make this practice particularly undesirable.

Source: Barry C. Feld, "Police Interrogation of Juveniles: An Empirical Study of Policy and Practice," *Journal of Criminal Law and Criminology* 97 (Fall 2006), 219–316.

Fingerprinting

The **fingerprinting** of juveniles is a controversial practice. The basic concern of critics is that the juveniles' records will not be destroyed when youths no longer fall under juvenile court jurisdiction. If they are labeled as criminals early in life, social analysts fear, the juveniles will not be able to escape such a label as they mature.

Some states have passed statutes that prohibit the fingerprinting of juveniles without a judge's permission. Many of these states also require that judges control who has access to the fingerprints and further require that the fingerprints be destroyed after the juvenile becomes an adult.[61] In other states, the police control fingerprinting policy. Some police departments follow the courts' suggested guidelines, whereas others routinely fingerprint every juvenile taken into custody.

The most important fingerprinting case to reach the courts to date is *Davis v. Mississippi* (1969).[62] In that case, the U.S. Supreme Court ruled, among other things, that fingerprints taken by the police could not be used as evidence. The youth in question was detained by the police without authorization by a judicial officer, was interrogated at the time he was first fingerprinted, and was fingerprinted again at a later date. The Court ruled that the police should not have detained the youth without authorization by a judicial officer, that the youth was unnecessarily fingerprinted a second time, and that the youth should not have been interrogated at the first detention when he was fingerprinted.[63]

Lineups and Photographs

A **lineup** consists of the police placing a number of suspects in front of witnesses or victims, who then try to identify the person who committed the crime against them. If no one can be identified, the suspects are released to the community. If one of the persons is identified as the perpetrator, the police then proceed with his or her prosecution. The courts have been careful to set standards for the police to follow, because innocent youths could end up labeled as delinquents and confined in an institution.

One important standard is that the offender must have an attorney at the initial identification lineup. This is to ensure that the identification of the offender is not tainted. For example, if a single suspect is shown to a victim with the suggestion by the police that they think "they got the offender," the victim might be pressured to identify the person even though the victim had never seen the accused before. Another concern is the possibility that simply showing a single suspect is "unnecessarily suggestive" and might bias the victim or witness.[64]

In *United States v. Wade* (1967), the Supreme Court ruled that the accused has the right to have counsel present at postindictment lineup procedures.[65] In *Kirby v. Illinois* (1972), the Court went on to say that the defendant's right to counsel at postindictment lineup procedures goes into effect as soon as the complaint or the indictment is issued.[66] In *In re Holley* (1970), a youth who was accused of rape had his conviction reversed by the appellate court because of the lack of counsel during the lineup identification procedure.[67]

Photographs also can play an important part in the identification of offenders. For example, in one case, a rape victim was shown a photograph of one suspect only. She could not identify the offender from the photograph, but then later identified her attacker in a probation office. A California appellate court noted that permitting the identification of offenders on the basis of only one photograph was inappropriate because it could prejudice the victim.[68]

Another problem with photographs is their permanency and potential stigmatizing effect on youths in the community. A youth taken in for questioning who has his or her photograph taken is easily identified. Because photographs are filed and frequently reviewed by police officers, the police examine these photographs whenever something happens in the community. Innocent youths may never be able to escape the stigma of such labeling. For these reasons, some states require that judges give the police written consent to take photographs, that the photographs not be published in the media, and that the photographs be destroyed when the youths become adults. Table 5–3 summarizes our discussion of the legal rights of juveniles.

TABLE 5–3
Legal Rights of Juveniles

Category	Brief Description of Juvenile Rights with Each Category
Search and Seizure	Juveniles, like adults, are protected from unauthorized search and seizure.
Interrogation Practices	Police must adhere to standards of fairness and due process in obtaining confessions.
Fingerprinting	Police handle the fingerprinting of juveniles in a wide variety of ways; however, there is more consistency in how they destroy the records after their purpose has been served.
Pretrial Identification Practices	The photographing and placing of juveniles in lineups are controversial but are more frequently taking place today than in the past.

Social Context of Juvenile Crime: The Police and the Prevention of Juvenile Offenses

Three ways in which police departments are attempting to implement policing in the prevention and deterrence of youth crime are community-based, school-based, and gang-based interventions (see Figure 5–3).

Community-Based Interventions

Community relations are a major focus of police officers who work with juveniles. They must cultivate good relations with school administers and teachers, with the staff of community agencies, with the staff of local youth organizations and youth shelters, with the juvenile court, and with merchants and employees at popular juvenile hangouts. Of course, juvenile police officers also must develop good relations with the parents of youthful offenders as well as with the offenders themselves. The officer who has earned the respect of youth of the community will be aware of what is happening in the community and will be more likely called on for assistance by youths in trouble.

One of the important challenges police face today is finding missing children. The AMBER Alert system began in 1996 when Dallas–Fort Worth broadcasters teamed with local police departments to develop an early warning system to assist in finding abducted children, which they called the Dallas AMBER plan. AMBER, which stands for America's Missing: Broadcast Emergency Response, was named in memory of nine-year-old Amber Hagerman, who was kidnapped and brutally murdered while riding her bicycle in Arlington, Texas, in 1996. Other states and communities soon set up their own alert plans and the AMBER network was adopted nationwide.[69]

The police are called on to intercede in a variety of juvenile problems. These include enforcing the curfew ordinances that more and more communities across the nation are passing,[70] enforcing drug laws,[71] preventing hate crimes committed by teenagers against minority groups (Jews, other ethnic groups, and homosexuals),[72] focusing attention on the serious habitual offender, enhancing the quality and relevance of information

Community-Based
Community relations are a major focus of police officers who work with juveniles.

School-Based
Developing effective delinquency prevention programs in schools is one of the most important challenges facing the police today.

Gang-Based
The number of street gangs rose dramatically across the nation beginning in the late 1980s.

FIGURE 5–3
Three Types of Police Interventions

TABLE 5–4
Special Units Targeting Juvenile Concerns

	Type of Agency	
Type of Special Unit	**Local Police**	**State**
Drug education in schools	70%	30%
Juvenile crime	62	10
Gangs	45	18
Child abuse	46	8
Domestic violence	45	10
Missing children	48	31
Youth outreach	33	6

Source: Office of Juvenile Justice and Delinquency Prevention, *Juvenile Offenders and Victims: 2006 National Report* (Washington, DC: US. Government Printing

that is exchanged through active interagency collaboration, and controlling gun-related violence in the youth population.

In many larger cities, police departments formed special juvenile units to address youth crime. A 2000 survey of law enforcement agencies (those with 100 or more sworn officers) reported that a large proportion of these agencies had special units targeting juvenile justice concerns[73] (see Table 5–4).

School-Based Interventions

Developing effective delinquency prevention programs for the schools is one of the most important challenges facing the police today. Community Predelinquent Programs have included courses in high school, junior high school, and elementary school settings that address school safety, community relations, drug and alcohol abuse, city government, court proceedings, bicycle safety, and juvenile delinquency. The Officer Friendly and McGruff "Take a Bite out of Crime" programs were established throughout the nation to develop better relations with younger children.

More recently, popular prevention programs have included Gang Resistance Education and Training (G.R.E.A.T.) and Law Enforcement Education (LRE). Since the G.R.E.A.T. program began in 1991, more than twelve thousand law enforcement officers have been certified as G.R.E.A.T. instructors and close to 6 million students have graduated from the G.R.E.A.T. program.[74] This program is found in all fifty states and in the District of Columbia and is in used in over five hundred communities across the United States. During 1999–2000, the program underwent an extensive program and curriculum review. The original program was expanded to thirteen lessons, placed more emphasis on active learning, and increased teacher involvement. The G.R.E.A.T. program currently consists of a thirteen-week middle school curriculum, an elementary curriculum, a summer program, and family training.

Evaluations were conducted in 1999, 2001, 2004, and another one—of the new curriculum—was scheduled to conclude in 2012. From all of the surveys conducted, the consistent finding was that the G.R.E.A.T. program did not reduce youths' involvement in gangs and delinquent behavior, but it did help them develop positive attitudes and relationships with law enforcement.[75]

LRE is designed to teach students the fundamental principles and skills needed to become responsible citizens in a constitutional democracy. One of the few studies evaluating the LRE program found that these programs, when properly conducted, can reduce tendencies toward delinquent behavior and improve the range of attitudes relating to responsible citizenship, and have found that successful students were also less likely to associate with delinquent peers and to use violence as a means of resolving conflict.[76]

Today, the need for substance abuse prevention programs demands creativity and involvement on the part of the police. The Drug Abuse Resistance Education (D.A.R.E.) program is a widely replicated effort by the police to prevent substance abuse (see Focus on Practice 5–3).

Focus On Practice 5–3
Project D.A.R.E.

The most popular school-based drug education program in the nation is Drug Abuse Resistance Education (D.A.R.E.), a program that receives over $200 million annually in public funding despite strong evidence of its ineffectiveness.

This program is designed to equip elementary school children with skills for resisting peer pressure to experiment with tobacco, drugs, and alcohol. Using a core curriculum consisting of seventeen hour-long weekly lessons, D.A.R.E. pays special attention to fifth and sixth graders to prepare them for entry into junior high and high school, where they are most likely to encounter pressure to use drugs. Since its foundation, D.A.R.E. has expanded to encompass programs for middle and high school students, gang prevention, conflict resolution, parent education, and after-school recreation and learning. As the most popular school-based drug education program in the United States, it is administered in about 75 percent of this nation's school districts, reaching 26 million, and has been adopted in more than fifty countries.

Widely evaluated, the disappointing findings can be summarized in the following way:

- The D.A.R.E. program has some immediate beneficial effects on student knowledge of drugs, social skills, attitudes about drug use, and attitudes toward the police.
- These effects dissipate quickly and are typically gone within one to two years.
- Most importantly, the effects of D.A.R.E. on drug use behavior (measured in numerous ways) are extremely rare and when identified tend to be small in size and dissipate quickly.

Rosenbaum summarized this collective evidence:

In sum, the results were very disappointing despite high expectations for the program. Across more than 30 studies, the collective evidence from evaluations with reasonably good scientific validity suggests that the core D.A.R.E. program does not prevent drug use in the short term, nor does it prevent drug use when students are ready to enter high school or college. Students who receive D.A.R.E. are indistinguishable from students who do not participate in the program.

Rosenbaum raises a question that has been widely raised elsewhere: "How can we reconcile this state of knowledge with the reality of worldwide support for D.A.R.E.?" He goes on to say: "The irony for the drug prevention field (and other fields as well) is that a program known to be ineffective receives millions of dollars in support, whereas programs known to be effective or promising are sidelined and remain unfunded."

In the 1990s and early 2000s dozens of communities dropped the D.A.R.E. program, but the debate whether to continue funding has been waged both nationally and internationally. Proponents of the D.A.R.E. program constitute a strong interest group, and presently are able to maintain federal funding for this delinquent prevention program.

CRITICAL THINKING QUESTION:

What explains the popularity of D.A.R.E. when evaluations of this program have been far less than positive?

Source: National Institute of Justice, *The D.A.R.E. Program: A Review of Prevalence, User Satisfaction, and Effectiveness* (Washington, DC: U.S. Department of Justice, 1994); Dennis P. Rosenbaum, "Just Say No to D.A.R.E.," *Criminology & Public Policy* 6 (November 2007), 815–24.

New York City's School Program to Educate and Control Drug Abuse, Project SPECDA, a collaborative effort of the city police department and the board of education, is another highly praised drug prevention program. In this project a sixteen-session curriculum, with the units split evenly between fifth and sixth grade, imparts basic information about the risk and effects of drug abuse, makes students aware of the social pressures that lead to drug abuse, and teaches acceptable methods for resisting peer pressure to experiment with drugs.[77]

In addition to drug prevention programs, the police respond to incidents ranging from student fights and assaults to drug and weapon possession. Officers also drive by schools during night and weekend patrols to prevent vandalism and burglary to school property, and the police are responsible for providing security and safety to the schools. In some schools, this requires conducting searches of students as they come into the school, monitoring the halls, doing conflict mediation when necessary, and protecting students as they come to and go home from school. The police are frequently called on to assist the school in searching for weapons and drugs on school property and are charged to enforce drug-free school zone laws and the federal Gun-Free School Zones Act. The police are also expected to enforce school attendance programs in a few school districts across the nation.

The federal Office of Community-Oriented Policing Services (COPS) has awarded almost $715 million to more than 2,900 law enforcement agencies to fund more than 6,300 school resource officers (SROs) through the COPS in School (CIS) program. In addition, COPS has appropriated nearly $21 million to train COPS-funded SROs and school administrators in partnering school or school districts to work more collaboratively through the CIS program. SROs in schools can serve in a variety of ways: they may function not only as law enforcement officers but as problem solvers, LRE educators, and community liaisons; they may teach classes about crime prevention, substance abuse awareness, and gang resistance; they may monitor and assist troubled students through mentoring programs; and they may promote social and personal responsibility by encouraging student participation in community service activities. Moreover these officers help students develop policies to address delinquent activity and school safety.

Gang-Based Interventions

The number of street gangs rose dramatically across the nation beginning in the late 1980s. The characteristics of these gangs vary widely from one city to another. Some of these gangs are simply groups of adolescents who hang around together and who seldom get into any serious trouble; other gangs engage in extensive drug activity, and some have become involved in violent drive-by shootings in which innocent children that have been killed.

Drugs and violence have made gangs a problem for the police. For example, police officers caught a group of Los Angeles Crips conducting a drug sales seminar in St. Louis, Missouri.[78] Once a community becomes aware of the seriousness of its drug problem—usually after a violent gang incident has taken place—pressure is typically put on the police to solve the problem. Police departments have frequently responded to this pressure by setting up one of three types of intervention units to work with gangs.

A **Youth Service Program**, which is one such unit, is formed to deal with a specific gang problem and is not a permanent unit within the department; officers continue to perform their regular duties and are not exclusively concerned with gang problems. The **gang detail** is a second type of unit in which the officers are generally pulled from detective units or juvenile units. The gang detail differs from the Youth Service Program in that its officers are assigned solely to gang problems and do not routinely work on other assignments. The **gang unit** is a third type of unit that is permanent. The members of these permanent units see themselves as specialists who work on gang problems; specialists; for example, many gang units will develop extensive intelligent networks with gang members in the community.

Formalizing Police Referral Programs

The police are the first line of contact with law-violating juveniles. They frequently have the discretion to divert a youth or refer him or her to the attention of the juvenile justice system, especially when the juvenile is involved in a minor offense. As repeatedly stated in this text, there is no question that the juvenile who has an early onset of crime behavior and comes to the attention of the justice system is more likely to be involved with the justice system longer and go on to the adult system than the youth who is diverted from the system or begins his or her onset of crime at a later date in adolescence. The police, who must try everything possible to avoid contributing to the ongoing delinquency and later criminality of individuals, can undertake activities such as those shown in Figure 5–4.

Common sense drove police officers and police chiefs to support prevention and referrals to community agencies since the early 1900s, but the programs were locally administered and sporadically implemented. Some larger cities hired youth officers and juvenile specialists, put police officers in schools as truancy officers, and set up counseling services and performed referral functions.

Develop relationships with juveniles so that they can become connected with police officers and feel that they are being treated fairly.

Develop and evaluate prevention programs, especially for predelinquent youths.

Avoid any form of abusive treatment of juveniles.

Expand the ways in which police work with the community to deal with problem juveniles.

Do not target certain juveniles to avoid making them "heroes" to their peers.

FIGURE 5–4
Police Activities to Combat Delinquency

Today, federal, state, and local police departments are beginning to address childhood development and delinquency.

Tom Sanchez, captain of the Hollywood, Florida, Police Department, identifies what police departments must do to effectively set up police referral programs. Department administrators must determine how many at-risk youths require referral; how many services for youths are in existence; which programs meet the police department's standards for inclusion; determine the means and frequency of evaluating the programs; and make certain that the intervention process starts early.[79]

Project SHIELD was founded in 1996 by the Bureau of Justice Assistance and implemented in the Westminster City Police Department in Orange County, California. Two primary goals of this program included, first, to build on the long-standing recognition that police officers do much more than simply control crime through arresting and processing offenders. Officers are often the initial responders to crisis situations involving at-risk youths. The police are the first to recognize community, individual, peer group, school, and family risk factors at homes, on the streets, and in schools. Second, knowing these risk factors enables police to then utilize multidisciplinary teams consisting of community and school representatives to refer youths to the appropriate agencies. Thus, whether youths witness violence or experience neglect, emotional, or sexual abuse; drunken, mentally ill, or addicted parents; or disturbing events on the streets, police can utilize approved and formalized procedures called for by SHIELD to get the youths to appropriate agencies.

The candidates for the program are evaluated by the SHIELD resource officer (SRO) to determine a youth's appropriateness for intervention. Assessment techniques are used to place youths in low-, medium-, or high-risk categories for both delinquency and gang involvement. Different risk assessment tools are used for youths ages 6 to 11 and those 12 to 14 to analyze how youths at different developmental levels are affected by different risk factors. The youths are also analyzed to determine how many protective factors surround them in order to gain as comprehensive a view of the youth's life as possible. All the information gathered by the SROs is then sent to a multidisciplinary Youth and Family Resource Team that meets weekly to determine the appropriate agency referrals. The assignment to a specific program may or may not require parental consent, a potential problem for some youths because abusive parents often strongly oppose the participation of their son or daughter in a program. The Youth and Family Resource Team receives regular reports from the referral agencies on each youth's progress, which allows the team to track and reassess the youths when necessary.[80]

Juvenile Justice Videos

CALLING THE POLICE

In *Calling the Police*, the formal and informal interactions between juveniles and law enforcement are discussed. How can these interactions have an impact on the at-risk juvenile? Discuss the living situations that the law enforcement officers emphasize is a common factor in many of these children's lives. How does the home life of a child have an impact on his or her involvement with criminal behavior? What would cause a parent to call the police about a child? What are the aims of the police in dealing with at-risk and delinquent children?

POLICE PERSPECTIVE

Police Perspective shows police officers discussing the differences between handling children and adults. How does law enforcement deal with juveniles? Based on the video and the readings from this chapter, how does police discretion factor into juvenile interactions with law enforcement? The officers mention the different backgrounds that juveniles can come from; how does the background of a child affect an officer's decision when interacting with the juvenile? Discuss.

SUMMARY

LEARNING OBJECTIVE 1: Summarize the history of police–juvenile relationships.

In the early 1900s, police became concerned about the problem of juvenile crime. In the 1920s and 1930s, the Police Athletic League and other prevention programs were formed. In the 1950s and 1960s, juvenile police officers associations were formed and became active. In the final decades of the twentieth century, budgetary restrictions forced many departments to restrict juvenile programs, and in the past decade or so the police have focused on gang control.

LEARNING OBJECTIVE 2: Summarize juveniles' attitudes toward the police.

Younger children, whites, girls, and middle- and upper-class youngsters have more favorable attitudes toward the police, while older children, African Americans, boys, and lower-class youngsters have less favorable attitudes toward the police.

LEARNING OBJECTIVE 3: Describe police discretion and the factors that influence discretion.

Police discretion can be defined as the choice between two or more possible means of handling a situation confronting the police officers. The police officer's disposition of the juvenile is largely determined by nine factors: the nature of the offense, citizen complainants, the juvenile's sex, race, socioeconomic status, and other individual characteristics; the nature of the interaction between the police officer and the juvenile; departmental policy; and external pressures in the community.

LEARNING OBJECTIVE 4: Summarize how police process juveniles.

Police view youth in the context of their community. Informal options are available where the youth is taken to the police station and then sent home with the parents. Formal processing is also available where the youth may be referred to juvenile court for further consideration.

LEARNING OBJECTIVE 5: Describe the legal rights of arrested juveniles.

Juveniles have legal rights in terms of search and seizure, interrogation practices, fingerprinting, and pretrial identification practices. With the first two, juveniles have the constitutional rights of adults, but with the latter two, juveniles receive some protection.

LEARNING OBJECTIVE 6: Describe how police agencies are structured to deal with juvenile crime.

Police are attempting to implement juvenile policing in community-based, school-based, and gang-based interventions.

LEARNING OBJECTIVE 7: Summarize developing trends in how police deal with juveniles.

The police continue to support prevention and referrals to community agencies; today, federal, state, and local police departments are getting more organized to address childhood development and delinquency.

KEY TERMS

cycle of alienation, p. 95
discretion, p. 95
fingerprinting, p. 106
gang detail, p. 110
gang unit, p. 110

interrogation, p. 104
lineup, p. 106
photographs, p. 106
police process, p. 98
problem-oriented policing, p. 94

school searches, p. 102
search and seizure, p. 99
Youth Service Program, p. 110

REVIEW QUESTIONS

1. What could be done to improve police acceptance in the lowest income communities?
2. Should the police be more responsible for intervening in the lives of infants and children?
3. What are the most important legal rights of juveniles?
4. How would you evaluate the police's attempts to prevent and deter delinquency?

GROUP EXERCISES

1. **Group Work:** Many members of the class have experienced contact with police officers (traffic tickets, alcohol or drug queries, or other "events") or know close friends who have. Discuss the nature of those contacts, the attitudes and behaviors of the police, and whether you (usually the women in class) "got off" because you cried. What were the attitudes and feelings after that contact and how do you evaluate those experiences? After small group discussions, "report out" to the class to determine what patterns existed in the observations.

2. **Group Work:** Discuss each of the factors that influence police discretion. Which of those factors are legitimate factors that police should take into consideration and which are not? Should any special circumstances be taken into consideration when examining these factors? All groups should report out to the class as a whole for further discussion.

3. **Writing to Learn Exercise:** Everyone should write for about twenty minutes on the following topics: The nature of police–juvenile relations in the community; the different ways police can formally or informally process youths upon contact.

4. ***Writing to Learn Exercise:*** All class members are to write two to three paragraphs on the search and seizure requirements of the police. Critique and revise.
5. ***Class Debate:*** Split the class into two groups. Charge one group to develop the topic "Resolved: the police function with juveniles should be limited to order, societal protection, and control of juveniles through legal processing." Charge

the other group with the topic "Resolved: the police should focus on prevention and the referral of juveniles to appropriate community agencies." Give each group sufficient time to develop its arguments and have the groups debate the two topics in class. After one debate, have the groups switch arguments.

NOTES

1. Interview contained in Clemens Bartollas and Larry D. Hahn, *Policing in America* (Boston: Allyn & Bacon, 1999), 53.
2. David R. Johnson, *Policing the Urban Underworld: The Impact of Crime on the Development of the American Police, 1800–1887* (Philadelphia: Temple University Press, 1979), 78–89.
3. Robert M. Fogelson, *Big-City Police* (Cambridge, MA: Harvard University Press, 1977), 86–87.
4. Ibid.
5. Ibid.
6. Ibid.
7. Ibid.
8. L. Thomas Winfree, Jr., and Curt T. Griffiths, "Adolescents' Attitudes Toward the Police: A Survey of High School Students," in *Juvenile Delinquency: Little Brother Grows Up,* edited by Theodore N. Ferdinand (Beverly Hills, CA: Sage Publications, 1977), 79–99.
9. William T. Rusinko, W. Johnson Knowlton, and Carlton A. Hornung, "The Importance of Police Contact in the Formulation of Youths' Attitudes Toward Police," *Journal of Criminal Justice* 6 (Spring 1978), 65.
10. Scott H. Decker, "Citizen Attitudes Toward the Police: A Review of Past Findings and Suggestions for Future Policy," *Journal of Police Science and Administration* 9 (1981), 80–87.
11. Komanduri S. Murty, Julian B. Roebuck, and Joann D. Smith, "The Image of Police in Black Atlanta Communities," *Journal of Police Science and Administration* 17 (1990), 250–57.
12. Michael J. Leiber, Mahesh K. Nalla, and Margaret Farnworth, "Explaining Juveniles' Attitudes Toward the Police," *Justice Quarterly* 15 (March 1998), 151–71.
13. J. G. Bachman, L. D. Johnston, and P. M. O'Malley, *Monitoring the Future: Questionnaire Responses from the Nation's High School Seniors,* 2007 (Ann Arbor, MI: Institute for Social Research). Roughly 13 percent of the youths had no opinion on the question. .
14. Susan Guarino-Ghezzi and Bryan Carr, "Juvenile Offenders v. the Police: A Community Dilemma," *Caribbean Journal of Criminology and Social Psychology* 1 (July 1996), 24–43.
15. Terry Nihart et al., "Kids, Cops, Parents and Teachers: Exploring Juvenile Attitudes Toward Authority Figures," *Western Criminology Review* 6 (2005), 79–88.
16. Yolander G. Hurst, "Juvenile Attitudes Toward the Police," *Criminal Justice Review* 32 (2007), 121–41.
17. Stephanie M. Myers, *Police Encounters with Juvenile Suspects: Explaining the Use of Authority and Provision of Support* (Washington, DC: National Institute of Justice, 2004).
18. See Donald J. Black and Albert J. Reiss, Jr., "Police Control of Juveniles," *American Sociological Review* 35 (February 1979), 63–77.
19. Robert M. Terry, "Discrimination in the Handling of Juvenile Offenders by Social Control Agencies," *Journal of Research in Crime and Delinquency* 4 (July 1967), 218–30; Nathan Goldman, *The Differential Selection of Juvenile Offenders for Court Appearances* (New York: National Council on Crime and Delinquency, 1963), 35–47; Black and Reiss, "Police Control of Juveniles"; Irving Piliavin and Scott Briar, "Police Encounters with Juveniles," *American Journal of Sociology* 70 (September 1964), 206–14.
20. Terry, "Discrimination in the Handling of Juvenile Offenders"; Black and Reiss, "Police Control of Juveniles."
21. Gail Armstrong, "Females Under the Law—Protected But Unequal," *Crime and Delinquency* 23 (April 1977), 109–20; Meda Chesney-Lind, "Girls and Status Offenses: Is Juvenile Justice Still Sexist?" *Criminal Justice Abstracts* 20 (March 1988), 144–65; Meda Chesney-Lind and Randall G. Shelden, *Girls: Delinquency and Juvenile Justice* (Pacific Grove, CA: Brooks/Cole, 1992).
22. Studies that have found a racial bias in arresting juveniles include Theodore N. Ferdinand and Elmer C. Luchtenhand, "Inner-City Youths, the Police, the Juvenile Court and Justice," *Social Problems* 17 (Spring 1970), 510–27; Goldman, *The Differential Selection of Juvenile Offenders for Court Appearances;* Piliavin and Briar, "Police Encounters with Juveniles"; and Marvin E. Wolfgang, Robert M. Figlio, and Thorsten Sellin, *Delinquency in a Birth Cohort* (Chicago: University of Chicago Press, 1972), 252.
23. Philip W. Harris, "Race and Juvenile Justice: Examining the Impact of Structural and Policy Changes on Racial Disproportionality," paper presented at the annual meeting of the American Society of Criminology, Montreal, November 13, 1987.
24. James T. Carey et al., *The Handling of Juveniles from Offense to Disposition* (Washington, DC: Government Printing Office, 1976); A. W. McEachern and Riva Bauzer, "Factors Related to Disposition in Juvenile–Police Contacts," in *Juvenile Gangs in Context,* edited by Malcolm W. Klein (Upper Saddle River, NJ: Prentice Hall, 1967); Ferdinand and Luchterhand, "Inner-City Youths, the Police, the Juvenile Court and Justice," 510–17; Miriam D. Sealock and Sally S. Simpson, "Unraveling Bias in Arrest Decisions: The Role of

Juvenile Offender Type-Scripts," *Justice Quarterly* 15 (September 1998), 427–57.

25. Merry Morash, "Establishment of Juvenile Police Record," *Criminology* 22 (February 1984), 97–111.

26. Piliavin and Briar, "Police Encounters with Juveniles," 206–14.

27. Carl Werthman and Irving Piliavin, "Gang Members and the Police," in *The Police,* edited by David J. Bordua (New York: Wiley, 1967), 56–98.

28. Richard J. Lundman, Richard E. Sykes, and John P. Clark, "Police Control of Juveniles: A Replication," in *Police Behavior: A Sociological Perspective,* edited by Richard J. Lundman (New York: Oxford University Press, 1980), 147–48.

29. Malcolm W. Klein, "Police Processing of Juvenile Offenders: Toward the Development of Juvenile System Rates" (Los Angeles County Sub-Regional Board, California Council on Juvenile Justice, Part III, 1970).

30. James Q. Wilson, "Dilemmas of Police Administration," *Public Administration Review* 28 (September–October 1968), 19.

31. For a discussion of the Constitution and Supreme Court decisions relevant to the schools, see Reed B. Day, *Legal Issues Surrounding Safe Schools* (Topeka, KS: National Organization on Legal Problems of Education, 1994).

32. *Mapp v. Ohio,* 367 U.S. 643 (1961); Day, *Legal Issues Surrounding Safe Schools,* 25–38.

33. *State v. Lowery,* 230 A. 2d 907 (1967).

34. *In re Two Brothers and a Case of Liquor,* Juvenile Court of the District of Columbia, 1966, reported in *Washington Law Reporter* 95 (1967), 113.

35. *Ciulla v. State,* 434 S.W. 2d 948 (Tex. Civ. App. 1968).

36. For a good general discussion of search and seizure law, see http://law.enotes.com/everyday-law-encyclopedia/search-and-seizure. Among the Supreme Court cases relevant to privacy are *Katz v. U.S.*, 389 U.S. 347, 88 S. Ct. 507. 19 L. Ed. 2d 576 (1967) and *Hester v. U.S.*, 265 I.S. 57, 44 S. Ct. 445, 68 L. Ed. 898 (1924). See also Judge David Demers, "Search and Seizure Outline" (2002), accessed at http://www.judges.com/Demers/page153-179.htm.

37. *Terry v. Ohio,* 392 U.S. 1, 20 L 2d 889, 911 (1968), accessed at http://urban75.org/legal/rights.html.

38. Ibid.

39. For some examples of the use of reasonable suspicion in different types of cases, see Demers, "Search and Seizure Outline."

40. See, for example the plain view doctrine and search and seizure at http://dictionary.law.com/default2.asp?selected=1538 and http://dictionary.law.com/default2.asp?selected=1894.

41. Demers, "Search and Seizure Outline."

42. "Your Rights on Arrest: Legal Advice and Useful Information," accessed at http://www.urban75.org/legal/rights.html.

43. For an extensive discussion of the relevant issues and court decisions related to police in the schools, see Samuel M. Davis, *Rights of Juveniles,* 2d ed. (New York: Clark Boardman Company, 1986), Secs. 3–19 to 3–34.3.

44. *New Jersey v. T. L. O.,* 469 U.S. 325 (1985).

45. Ibid.

46. Ibid.

47. J. M. Sanchez, "Expelling the Fourth Amendment from American Schools: Students' Rights Six Years After T. L. O.," *Education Journal* 21 (1992), 381–413; Day, *Legal Issues Surrounding Safe Schools,* 9–24.

48. *Safford Unified School District v. Redding* (no. 08-479) 557 U.S. — (2009), accessed at http://www.supremecourtus.gov/gp/08-00479gp.pdf.

49. "*Miranda* Warning," accessed at http://en.wikipedia.org/wiki/Miranda_Warning.

50. Ibid. Also, see Findlaw Lawyer Directory at http://criminal.findlaw.com/articles/1387.html for a brief but good discussion of "Police Questioning Prior to Arrest."

51. *People v. Lara,* 62 Cal. Rptr. 586 (1967), cert. denied 392 U.S. 945 (1968).

52. *In re Mellot,* 217 S. E. 2d 745 (C.A.N. Calif., 1975).

53. *In re Dennis P. Fletcher,* 248 A. 2d 364 (Md., 1968), cert. denied 396 U.S. 852 (1969).

54. T. Grisso, *Juveniles' Waiver of Rights: Legal and Psychological Competence* (New York: Plenum Press, 1981).

55. *Brown v. Mississippi,* 297 U.S. 278 (1936).

56. Davis, *Rights of Juveniles,* Sec. 3–45.

57. *Haley v. Ohio,* 332 U.S. 596 (1948).

58. Ibid.

59. *Fare v. Michael C.,* 442 U.S. 23, 99 S. Ct. 2560 (1979).

60. *Commonwealth v. Guyton,* 405 Mass. 497 (1989).

61. Elyce Z. Ferster and Thomas F. Courtless, "The Beginning of Juvenile Justice, Police Practices, and the Juvenile Offender," *Vanderbilt Law Review* 22 (April 1969), 598–601.

62. *Davis v. Mississippi,* 394 U.S. 721 (1969).

63. Ibid.

64. See Davis, *Rights of Juveniles,* Sec. 3–67.

65. *United States v. Wade,* 338 U.S. 218, 87 S. Ct. 1926 (1967).

66. *Kirby v. Illinois,* 406 U.S. 682, 92 S. Ct. 1877 (1972).

67. *In re Holley,* 107 R. I. 615, 268 A. 2d 723 (1970).

68. *In re Carl T.,* 81 Cal. Rptr. 655 (2d C.A., 1969).

69. Office of Justice Programs, *America's Missing Broadcast Emergency Response, Frequency Added Question on AMBER Alert,* accessed at http://www.amberalert-gov/faqa,htm

70. Howard N. Snyder and Melissa Sickmund, *Juvenile Offenders and Victims: 2006 National Report* (Washington, DC: U.S. Department of Justice, Office of Justice Programs, Office of Juvenile Justice and Delinquency Prevention, 2006).

71. Ibid.

72. Mark S. Hamm, *American Skinheads: The Criminology and Control of Hate Crime* (Westport, CT: Praeger, 1993).

73. Snyder and Sickmund, *Juvenile Offenders and Victims,* 2006 National Report.

74. *History of the G.R.E.A.T. Program, 2012,* accessed June 12, 2012, at http://www.great.ca-org/Organizatioln/Histlory.Aspx.

75. F. A. Esbensen and D. W. Osgood, "Gang Resistance Education and Training (G.R.E.A.T.): Results from the National Evaluation," *Journal of Research in Crime and Delinquency* 36 (1999), 194–225; F. A. Esbensen, D. W. T. J. Taylor, D. Peterson, and A. Frenger, "How Great Is G.R.E.A.T. : Results from a Longitudinal Quasi-Experimental

Design," *Criminology and Public Policy* 1 (2001), 87–118; J. Ashcroft, D. J. Daniels, and S. V. Hart, *Evaluating G.R.E.A.T.: A School-Based Gang Prevention Program* (Washington, DC: U.S. Department of Justice, 2004).

76. Judith Warrant Little and Frances Haley, *Implementing Effective LRE Programs* (Boulder, CO: Social Science Education Consortium, 1982).

77. William DeJong, *Arresting the Demand for Drugs: Police and School Partnership to Prevent Drug Abuse* (Washington, DC: National Institute of Justice, 1987).

78. Ronald D. Stephens, "School Based Interventions: Safety and Security," in *The Gang Intervention Handbook,* edited by Ron Huff (Beverly Hills, CA: Sage, 1993).

79. Tom Sanchez, "Youth Referral System," *The Police Chief* 71 (September 2004), accessed at http://policechiefmagazine .org/magazine/index.cfm?fuseaction=print_display&article_ id=…np.

80. Phelan A. Wyrick, "Law Enforcement Referral of At-Risk Youth: The SHIELD Program," *Juvenile Justice Bulletin* (Washington, DC: U.S. Department of Justice, November 2000).

6 The Juvenile Court

ZUMA Wire Service/Alamy

Learning Objectives

1. Summarize the development and legal norms of the juvenile court.
2. Describe the social control of the status offender.
3. Explain the structure and key players of the juvenile court.
4. Describe pretrial procedures and decisions of the intake officer.
5. Explain plea bargaining.
6. Summarize the adjudicatory process.
7. Describe the disposition hearing.
8. Describe disposition alternatives.
9. Describe the various sentencing alternatives for juveniles

To save a child from becoming a criminal, or from continuing in a career of crime, to end in maturer years in public punishment and disgrace, the legislature surely may provide for the salvation of such a child, if its parents or guardian be unable or unwilling to do so, by bringing it into one of the courts of the state without any process at all, for the purpose of subjecting it to the state's guardianship and protection.

The action is not for the trial of a child charged with a crime, but is mercifully to save it from such an ordeal, with the prison or penitentiary in its wake, if the child's own good and the best interests of the state justify such salvation. Whether the child deserves to be saved by the state is no more a question for a jury than whether the father, if able to save it, ought to save it. The act is but an exercise by the state of its supreme power over the welfare of its children, a power over which it can take a child from its father, and let it go where it will, without committing it to any guardianship or any institution, if the welfare of the child, taking its age into consideration, can be thus best promoted.

The design is not punishment, nor the restraint imprisonment, any more than is the wholesome restraint a parent exercises over his child. The severity in either case must necessarily be tempered to meet the necessities of the particular situation. There is no probability, in the proper administration of the law, of the child's liberty being unduly involved. Every statute which is designed to give protection, care, and training to children, as a needed substitute for parental authority, and performance of parental duty, is but a recognition of the duty of the state, as the legitimate guardian and protector of children where other guardianship fails. No constitutional right is violated.

—Julian W. Mack[1]

The purpose of the court, as expressed in the chapter-opening quote from the *Commonwealth v. Fisher* decision in 1905, "is not for the punishment of offenders but for the salvation of children . . . whose salvation may become the duty of the state."[2] It is this type of statement that resulted in the juvenile court receiving fanatical support from its followers. Ever since the turn of the twentieth century, supporters have argued that the informal setting of the juvenile court, coupled with the fatherly demeanor of the juvenile judge, enables children to be treated, rather than punished, for their problems.[3] The state, the argument goes, rescues these youths from a life of trouble on the streets, rehabilitates them, protects them from placement with adult criminals in correctional facilities, and saves them from a life of crime. According to Judge Leonard P. Edwards, what is implicit in this position is that "children are different from adults, that they have developmental needs which they cannot satisfy without assistance and that care and supervision are critical to their upbringing." He then argues that "if children were no different from adults, the juvenile court would be unnecessary."[4]

Critics of the juvenile court sharply challenge these idealistic claims. They argue that the juvenile court has not succeeded in rehabilitating juvenile offenders, in reducing or even stemming the rise of youth crime, or in bringing justice and compassion to youthful offenders.[5] The juvenile court, they argue, acts in an arbitrary and whimsical fashion. It selects whom it "saves" on the basis of their sex and race, not on the basis of justice. The court harms children by processing them through its system, offering them inadequate programs, and labeling them as they return to the community.[6] Thomas F. Geraghty and Steven A. Drizin, in the introduction to a symposium on the future of the juvenile court, suggest that the future of the juvenile court "is less secure than at any point in its history." They state that part of the problem relates to the perceived seriousness of juvenile crime, and part of the problem is found in a "get-tough" attitude that is affecting the handling of juvenile as well as adult crime.[7]

This chapter describes the changing legal norms of the juvenile court, the social control of status offenders, those who are involved in the processes of the juvenile court, the pretrial procedures of its proceedings, plea bargaining, trial and disposition stages, and the changing sentencing structures of the juvenile court.

How Have Legal Norms Changed?

In the past, **constitutionalists** have argued that the juvenile court was unconstitutional because under its auspices the principles of a fair trial and individual rights were denied. This group primarily was concerned that children appearing before the juvenile court were denied their procedural rights as well as the rights to shelter, protection, and guardianship. The constitutionalists proposed that the procedures of the juvenile court be modified in three ways: (1) by the adoption of separate procedures for dealing with dependent and neglected children and those who are accused of criminal behavior; (2) by the use of informal adjustments to avoid official court actions as frequently as possible; and (3) by the provision of rigorous procedural safeguards and rights for children appearing before the court at the adjudicatory stage.[8]

A series of decisions by the U.S. Supreme Court in the 1960s and early 1970s rapidly accelerated the influence of the constitutionalists on the juvenile court. The five most important cases were *Kent v. United States* (1966), *In re Gault* (1967), *In re Winship* (1970), *McKeiver v. Pennsylvania* (1971), and *Breed v. Jones* (1975). See Figure 6–1 for a timeline of the most important Court decisions concerning juveniles.

Kent v. United States

The first major case was **Kent v. United States**.[9] In this 1966 case, the juvenile court had disregarded all of Kent's due process rights in transferring the case to the adult court. The judge of the juvenile court did not rule on Kent's lawyer's motions. The judge also did not discuss the case with either Kent or Kent's parents, did not present any findings, did not offer any reason for waiving Kent to the adult court, and, in fact, made no reference to the motions filed by Kent's attorney. The judge also apparently ignored reports from juvenile court staff and the Juvenile Probation Section that indicated that Kent's mental condition was deteriorating. Rather, the judge entered an order waiving Kent to the adult court for trial. There, Kent was indicted by a grand jury on eight counts of housebreaking, robbery,

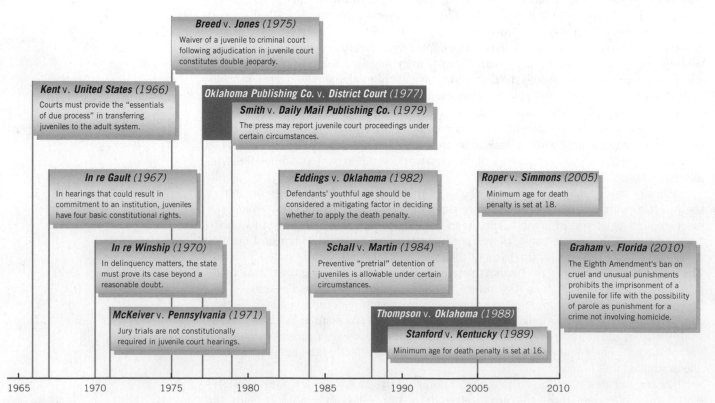

FIGURE 6–1
Timeline of Important Supreme Court Decisions Concerning Juveniles

Source: A series of U.S. Supreme Court decisions made juvenile courts more like criminal courts, but maintained some important differences.

Focus on Law 6–1
Kent v. United States

Morris A. Kent, Jr., a sixteen-year-old living in Washington, D.C., was on juvenile probation when he broke into a house and raped and robbed a woman on September 2, 1961. His fingerprints were found in the woman's apartment, and he was taken into custody by the police on September 5, 1961. He was charged with three counts each of housebreaking and robbery and two counts of rape. Kent apparently admitted not only the offense for which he was taken into custody, but other housebreaking, robbery, and rape offenses as well. He was interrogated by the police into the evening, was taken to the Receiving Home for Juveniles late that evening, and was returned to the police the next day for more questioning. No record exists as to when Kent's mother found out about his detention, but she retained counsel on the second day of Kent's detainment.

The social service director of the juvenile court discussed with Kent's counsel the possibility that Kent's case might be waived to adult court; Kent's counsel opposed the waiver and also arranged for Kent to undergo psychiatric evaluation. Kent's lawyer then filed a motion for a waiver hearing on the juvenile court's jurisdiction and provided a psychiatrist's affidavit certifying that Kent was "a victim of severe psychopathology" and recommending that he be hospitalized for psychiatric observation. The affidavit concluded that Kent could be rehabilitated if provided adequate treatment. Kent's counsel also requested a copy of Kent's social service file for use in his defense.

CRITICAL THINKING QUESTION:
What did Supreme Court Justice Fortas mean when he said "that there may be grounds for concern that the child receives the worst of both worlds?" Do you agree with his criticism of the juvenile court?

Source: Kent v. United States, 383 U.S. 541, 86 S. Ct. 1045, 16 L. Ed. 2d 84 (1966).

---

and rape, and was sentenced to a total of thirty to ninety years in prison. Focus on Law 6–1 describes the facts of this case.

Kent's counsel initiated a series of appeals that led to review of the case by the U.S. Supreme Court. The counsel argued throughout these appeals that Kent's parents had not been notified in time, that Kent's interrogation and detention were illegal because neither his parents nor his counsel was present, that probable cause for Kent's detention had not been established, that he had not been told of his right to remain silent or of his right to counsel, and that he was fingerprinted illegally.

The Supreme Court agreed that the procedures followed by the juvenile court were inadequate. In addition, the Court ruled that Kent had the right to a transfer hearing in which evidence was presented, that Kent had the right to be present at a waiver hearing, that Kent's attorney had the right to see the social service reports, and that the judge had to state the reasons for the transfer.[10] In this decision, Judge Abe Fortas stated:

There is evidence, in fact, that there may be grounds for concern that the child receives the worst of both worlds; that he gets neither the protection accorded to adults nor the solicitous care and regenerative treatment postulated for children.[11]

In re Gault

In May 1967, the U.S. Supreme Court reversed the conviction of a minor in the case of **In re Gault**.[12] This has been one of the most influential and far-reaching decisions to affect the juvenile court. In this case, the Court overruled the Arizona Supreme Court for its dismissal of a writ of habeas corpus. This writ had sought the release of Gerald Gault, who had been adjudicated to the state industrial school by the Juvenile Court of Gila County, Arizona. Focus on Law 6–2 presents the facts of this case.

In reviewing the decision of the Arizona Supreme Court, which upheld the confinement of Gault, the U.S. Supreme Court considered which of the following rights should apply to juveniles:

1. Right to receive notice of the charges
2. Right to be represented by counsel
3. Right to confront and cross-examine witnesses
4. Right to avoid self-incrimination
5. Right to receive a transcript of the proceedings
6. Right to request appellate review[13]

Focus on Law 6–2
In re Gault

Gerald Gault, a fifteen-year-old Arizona boy, and a friend, Ronald Lewis, were taken into custody on June 8, 1964, on a verbal complaint made by a neighbor. The neighbor had accused the boys of making lewd and indecent remarks to her over the phone. Gault's parents were not notified that he was taken into custody; he was not advised of his right to counsel; he was not advised that he could remain silent; and no notice of charges was made to either Gerald or his parents. In addition, the complainant was not present at either of the hearings. In spite of considerable confusion about whether or not Gerald had made the alleged phone call, what he had said over the phone, and what he had said to the judge during the course of the two hearings, Judge McGhee committed him to the State Industrial School until he reached the age of twenty-one or until he was discharged by the law.

CRITICAL THINKING QUESTION:

What due process rights did this case grant juveniles? What due process rights did juveniles still lack after the decision?

Source: *In re Gault,* 387 U.S. 1, 18 L. Ed. 2d 527, 87 S. Ct. 1428 (1967).

Justice Fortas, in delivering the Court's opinion, recalled other cases that had provided juveniles with due process of law. In both *Haley v. Ohio* (1948) and *Gallegos v. Colorado* (1962), the U.S. Supreme Court had prohibited the use of confessions coerced from juveniles; in *Kent v. United States,* the Court had given the juvenile the right to be represented by counsel.[14] Justice Fortas concluded this review of legal precedent with the sweeping statement that juveniles have those fundamental rights incorporated in the due process clause of the Fourteenth Amendment of the Constitution.

The *In re Gault* decision answered in the affirmative the question of whether a juvenile has the right to due process safeguards during confinement. But the Supreme Court did not rule that juveniles have the right to a transcript of the proceedings or the right to appellate review.

In rejecting the latter two rights, the Court clearly did not want to transform the informal juvenile hearing into an adversarial trial. The cautiousness of this decision was expressed in a footnote that indicated that the decision did not apply to preadjudication or postadjudication treatment of juveniles. Several other important issues were also left unanswered, such as the following:

1. May a judge consider hearsay in juvenile court?
2. Does the exclusionary evidence principle derived from the Fourth Amendment apply?
3. What is the constitutionally required burden of proof necessary to support a finding of delinquency?
4. Is a jury trial required?
5. Does the requirement of a "speedy and public trial" apply in juvenile court?[15]

In re Winship

The Supreme Court ruled in the **In re Winship** case (1970) that juveniles are entitled to proof "beyond a reasonable doubt."[16] The *Winship* case involved a New York boy who was sent to a state training school at the age of twelve for taking $112 from a woman's purse. The commitment was based on a New York statute that permitted juvenile court decisions on the basis of a "preponderance of evidence." The Court reasoned that "preponderance of evidence," a standard much less strict than "beyond a reasonable doubt," is not a sufficient basis for a decision when youths are charged with acts that would be criminal if committed by adults.

The findings in the *Winship* case not only expanded the implications of *In re Gault,* but also reflected other concerns of the U.S. Supreme Court. The Court desired both to protect juveniles at adjudicatory hearings and to maintain the confidentiality, informality, flexibility, and speed of the juvenile process in the prejudicial and postadjudicative states. The Court obviously did not want to bring too much rigidity and impersonality to the juvenile hearing.

Focus on Law 6–3
Right of a Jury Trial for Juveniles

MCKEIVER V. PENNSYLVANIA

Joseph McKeiver, who was sixteen years of age, was charged with robbery, larceny, and receiving stolen goods, all of which were felonies under Pennsylvania law. Found delinquent at an adjudication hearing, the youth was placed on probation after his request for a jury trial was denied.

IN RE TERRY

Edward Terry, who was fifteen years of age, was charged with assault and battery on a police officer, which were misdemeanors under Pennsylvania law. His counsel requested a jury trial, which was denied, and he was adjudicated a delinquent on the charges.

IN RE BARBARA BURRUS

Barbara Burrus and approximately forty-five other youths, ranging in age from eleven to fifteen years, received juvenile court summonses in Hyde County, North Carolina. The charges arose out of a series of demonstrations in the county in late 1968 by African American adults and children, who were protesting school assignments and a school construction plan. The youths were charged with willfully impeding traffic. The several cases were consolidated into groups for hearing before the district judge, sitting as a juvenile court. A request for a jury trial in each case was denied. Each youth was found delinquent and placed on probation.

CRITICAL THINKING QUESTION:

What is the actual difference between "preponderance of the evidence" and "proof beyond a reasonable doubt"? What was the importance of this difference in this case?

Source: McKeiver v. Pennsylvania, 403 U.S. 528 (1971); *In re Terry,* 438 Pa. 339, 265 A. 2d 350 (1970); and *In re Barbara Burrus,* 275 N.C. 517, 169 S.E. 2d 879 (1969).

McKeiver v. Pennsylvania, In re Terry, and *In re Barbara Burrus*

The Supreme Court heard three cases together (**McKeiver v. Pennsylvania**, **In re Terry**, and **In re Barbara Burrus**) to determine whether the due process clause of the Fourteenth Amendment (guaranteeing the right to a jury trial) applied to juveniles.[17] The decision, which was issued in *McKeiver v. Pennsylvania* (1971), denied the juveniles the right to have jury trials. Focus on Law 6–3 reveals the facts of these three cases.

The Supreme Court explained its ruling that juveniles do not have the right to a jury trial as follows:

1. Not all rights that are constitutionally assured for adults are to be given to juveniles.
2. If a jury trial is required for juveniles, the juvenile proceedings may become a fully adversarial process, putting an end to what has been the idealistic prospect of an intimate, informal, protective proceeding.
3. A jury trial is not necessarily a part of every criminal process that is fair and equitable.
4. If the jury trial is injected into the juvenile court system, it could bring with it the traditional delays, the formality, and the clamor of the adversarial system.
5. There is nothing to prevent an individual juvenile judge from using an advisory jury when he or she feels the need. For that matter, there is nothing to prevent individual states from adopting jury trials.[18]

Although a number of states do permit jury trials for juveniles, most states adhere to this constitutional standard set by the Supreme Court. What is significant about this decision is that the Court indicated an unwillingness to apply further procedural safeguards to juvenile proceedings. This especially appears to be true concerning the preadjudicatory and postadjudicatory treatment of juveniles.

Breed v. Jones

The **Breed v. Jones** (1975) case was slightly different from the *Kent* case. Jones was taken into custody for committing a robbery and was detained for a hearing in juvenile court. At the juvenile court hearing, the allegations against Jones were found to be true. At the disposition hearing, the court determined that Jones could not be helped by the services of the juvenile court; Jones was waived to adult court, where he was found guilty of robbery.

Jones's lawyer appealed the case, arguing that Jones had been subjected to double jeopardy; that is, this decision had violated the standard used in adult courts that prevents adults from being tried twice for the same crime. The Supreme Court concurred, stating that Jones's hearing in the juvenile court involved evidence being presented at an adjudication hearing and that his trial in adult court constituted double jeopardy.[19] For waiver to adult court to occur legally, according to the Supreme Court, juvenile courts must transfer youths to the adult court jurisdiction before any adjudicatory hearings are held on their cases.

In sum, the *In re Gault* and *In re Winship* decisions have unquestionably effected profound changes in the legal status of the juvenile justice system. The *McKeiver v. Pennsylvania* decision and the more conservative stance of the Supreme Court since 1971, however, have raised some question about whether or not this ultimate appellate court will be willing to change legal norms much more. These court decisions have, of course, received varying endorsements from juvenile courts across the United States. Some juvenile courts gave procedural rights to juveniles even before the Supreme Court decisions, but others have lagged far behind in implementing these decisions.

How Is the Status Offender Controlled?

Youths can be charged with at least three different categories of offenses:

- Offenders can be charged with a felony or misdemeanor under federal, state, and local statutes.
- Youths are subject to relatively specific statutes applying exclusively to juvenile behavior: truancy, consumption of alcoholic beverages, and running away from home are examples.
- Juveniles can be prosecuted under general omnibus statutes that include such offenses as acting beyond the control of parents, engaging in immoral conduct, and being ungovernable and incorrigible.

Offenses under both the second and third categories are status offenses. The status offense statutes pertaining to behavior for which an adult could not be prosecuted have drawn increasing attention in recent years. Status offenders can be processed through the juvenile justice system along with youths who have committed criminal offenses, or they can be handled separately from felons and misdemeanants. States that pursue the latter course usually refer to status offenders as MINS (minors in need of supervision), CINS (children in need of supervision), PINS (persons in need of supervision), FINS (families in need of supervision), or JINS (juveniles in need of supervision). Some jurisdictions handle these youths in a different court; others will not place them in detention with delinquents or send them to a juvenile correctional institution.

The handling of status offenders has focused on two questions: should status offenders be placed with delinquents in correctional settings, and should the juvenile court retain jurisdiction over status offenders?

Deinstitutionalization of Status Offenders

The **deinstitutionalization of status offenders** (to no longer confine status offenders in secure detention facilities or secure correctional facilities with delinquents) has received increased acceptance in the past couple of decades. What served as the real impetus for a nationwide deinstitutionalization of status offenders was the passage of the 1974 **Juvenile Justice and Delinquency Prevention (JJDP) Act** and its various modifications.[20] As a condition for states to continue receiving federal funding for juvenile justice programs, the JJDP Act required that status offenders be kept separate from delinquents in secure detention and institutionalization. The act also limited the placement of juveniles in adult jail facilities.[21]

The **deinstitutionalization of status offenders (DSO)** provision of the Juvenile Justice and Delinquency Prevention Act has been successful in encouraging states to amend laws, policies, and practices that led to secure confinement of juveniles who committed no criminal act. This act gave the juvenile justice system the impetus to no longer confine status offenders in secure detention facilities or secure correctional facilities with delinquents. The DSO core protection of the JJDP Act is premised on the belief that juveniles who exhibit problematic behavior but have not violated the laws are more properly served by social service, mental health, and community agencies and may actually be damaged by placement in secure detention or correctional institutions.[22] Following the adoption of the JJDP Act and its DSO requirement, the Office of Juvenile Justice and Delinquency Prevention (OJJDP) recorded approximately 171,581 violations of the DSO requirement. According to OJJDP's 2006 compliance monitoring reports, the number of DSO violations had dropped to 6,324.[23]

Jurisdiction over Status Offenders

The juvenile court's long-standing jurisdiction over status offenders is an even more volatile issue. Critics present at least four distinct arguments for the removal of status offenders from the jurisdiction of the juvenile court:

- The legal argument states that the lack of clarity of the status offender statutes makes them unconstitutionally vague in their construction; that they often are blatantly discriminatory, especially in regard to gender; and that government bodies have no legitimate interest in many of these proscribed behaviors.

- Although status offenders have not committed a criminal act, they frequently are confined with chronic or hard-core offenders.

- In keeping with the *parens patriae* philosophy of the juvenile court, the procedure of processing and confining the status offender is not in his or her best interests. Some theorists argue that the formal intervention of the juvenile court promotes rather than inhibits unlawful behavior.

- Many charge that status offenders are a special class of youth who must be treated differently from delinquents.[24]

Juvenile court judges, not surprisingly, challenge the movement to strip the court of jurisdiction over status offenders. They charge that status offenders will have no one to provide for them or to protect them if they are removed from the court's jurisdiction. The essence of this position is that other agencies will have to take over if the court relinquishes jurisdiction over these offenders and that few options are presently available for providing status offenders a nurturing environment in lieu of the home.

The states of Maine, New York, and Washington have **decriminalized status offenses**, thus removing from the juvenile court's jurisdiction youthful behavior that would not be a chargeable offense if committed by an adult.[25] However, the status offense legislation in Maine and Washington was partly repealed to give the juvenile courts a degree of jurisdiction, especially over abandoned, runaway, or seriously endangered children.[26] The most broad-based movement to strip the juvenile court of jurisdiction over status offenders took place in New York State, heralded by the passage of the 1985 PINS Adjustment Services Act. Under a new law that became effective November 1, 2001, the New York State Legislature passed a bill that raised the PINS eligibility age to eighteen. The intent of this bill was to assist and support families seeking help with troubled older children.[27]

It is unlikely that many more states will remove status offenders from the juvenile court's jurisdiction in the near future. The widespread resistance comes mainly from those who feel that status offenders need the control of the juvenile court over their lives or they will become involved in increasingly destructive behaviors. The fact is that juvenile court personnel do have jurisdiction over the status offender because they have the option of labeling youngsters downward as dependent or neglected youths, upward as delinquent youths, or laterally into private mental health facilities.[28] Thus, even in states that strongly support deinstitutionalization, the juvenile court still can institutionalize status offenders by redefining them as delinquents or as requiring mental health services. A truant may be charged with a minor delinquent offense and be institutionalized in a private facility, or a court may require school attendance as a condition of probation and then define further truancy as a delinquent offense.[29] Abuse, neglect, and delinquency cases must also be dealt with by the juvenile court and then there are those social welfare cases that cross to the juvenile justice system.

Crossover Youth

Voices of Delinquency: Scott Berry, Intersections: Cross-Over Youths and the Helping Profession

Juveniles in the child welfare system often cross into the juvenile justice system. Because these youth are known to both the child welfare system and the juvenile justice system, they are frequently referred to as "crossover youth." Other terms used to describe these youth are "dual-jurisdiction cases," "dual jurisdiction," "dually adjudicated youth," and "cross-system cases."

Crossover youth often move back and forth between a child welfare system in which they are looked on as victims, and a juvenile justice system that sees them as offenders. Yet, little integration and coordination take place between the two systems. In fact, in many jurisdictions, a common practice is for child welfare agencies to abruptly close the cases of children who become involved in the juvenile justice system.[30]

Many crossover youth experience co-occurring mental health and drug and alcohol abuse problems, which are often left unscreened and untreated in both systems. These youth frequently do poorly in school and end up being suspended or dropping out. Once in the juvenile justice system, they often continue to penetrate deeper into the system. Youth in the child welfare system who are placed in out-of-home settings are at greater risk of crossing over into the juvenile justice jurisdiction. Child welfare placements in group home settings, especially, have been found to be predictive of future involvement with the juvenile justice system.[31]

Another matter of grave concern to juvenile justice is that the disproportionate number of crossover minority youth is directly related to the disproportionate involvement of minority youth in the welfare system. Research sponsored by the Annie E. Casey Foundation

Evidence-Based Practice
Best Programs in Juvenile Court

In 1997, the federal Adoption and Safe Families Act (ASFA) established the goals of permanence, well-being, and safety for children in foster care with an emphasis on achieving "permanence" for children. In 1999, the Carolina General Assembly incorporated the ASFA standards into Chapter 7B of the North Carolina General Statutes. Child welfare agencies, as well as the courts in North Carolina, use these laws to improve how the state child welfare system responds to allegations and findings of child abuse, neglect, or dependency.

In 1996 and 2001, juvenile court improvement funds were used to conduct studies to identify methods of improving juvenile abuse, neglect, and dependency (A/N/D) proceedings in North Carolina. The 1996 study, conducted by the Research Triangle Institute, identified a number of barriers to achieving timely permanency for children and their families served by North Carolina juvenile courts. They identified the following barriers to achieving permanency:

- A shortage of adoptive homes for children with special needs
- A shortage of child welfare workers to work with parents and children in care
- Parental noncompliance with case plans
- Frequent court continuances
- Lack of supportive services for parents
- High emphasis on reuniting families that should not be reunited
- Too many court hearings for each case
- Poor court orders

A 2001 evaluation of the juvenile Court Improvement Program (CIP), conducted by the Jordan Institute for Families at the University of North Carolina–Chapel Hill, measured the effectiveness and implementation of new local court rules to juvenile CIP districts. The local rules were intended to improve the manner in which the courts process juvenile A/N/D cases. Results of the evaluation reflected that the new rules affected both positive and compelling changes in the way juvenile cases were handled. The study identified:

- Reductions in the number of cases heard by multiple judges
- Reductions in the number of continuances granted
- Reductions in time to achieve critical junctures in juvenile cases (e.g., findings, adjudications, dispositions)
- Reductions in the overall duration of cases
- Reductions in the number of out-of-home placements of children
- Accelerated time to permanency.

In 2007, the North Carolina Administrative Office of the Courts selected six judicial districts to implement juvenile case management activities, specialized training, and best practices in juvenile court. Lessons learned from these districts have been used to inform this best practices guide.

What has taken place in North Carolina with cases related to abuse, neglect, and dependency offers the promise of being extended to delinquency cases throughout the nation.

Source: North Carolina Administrative Office of the Courts, *Best Practices for North Carolina's Juvenile Abuse, Neglect, and Dependency Court Improvement Programs* (Raleigh, NC: Court Programs and Management Services Division, 2010), 3–4.

reports that although minority children are not abused more often than other children, they are put into foster care faster, receive fewer services, stay there longer, and are reunited with their families less often than white children.[32]

A question raised continually in this text is: What can be done? Researchers have identified four promising court-related practices in which family and juvenile court programs can work together to address at least some of the difficulties posed by crossover cases:

- *Routine screening and assessment.* Routine screening of youth on intake by both dependency and juvenile courts would assist in identifying the strengths and needs of these youth.

- *Case assignment.* Effective case management should include joint prehearing conferences by all parties involved and combined dependency and delinquency hearings, which will help ensure that different agencies coordinate their efforts.

- *Case planning and supervision.* Case managers should work with multidisciplinary teams of professionals with training in dual-jurisdiction matters who have the expertise and tools to develop action plans that meet the specific needs of and build on the individual strengths of crossover youth.

- *Interagency collaboration.* Judges should take the lead in making certain that the child welfare and juvenile justice systems collaborate by contributing financially in providing needed treatment and services.[33]

See the Evidence-Based Practice feature for a discussion of the safety of children in foster care.

▲ Juveniles may be brought to juvenile court by their parents, police officers, school counselors, or community helping agencies concerned over the welfare of children.
AL SCHELL/Associated Press

What Does the Juvenile Court Look Like Today?

The structure of the juvenile court varies from jurisdiction to jurisdiction. Special and separate juvenile courts in certain urban areas devote their total effort to the legal problems of children. Juveniles in smaller cities and rural areas are often tried by judges of the adult courts. A separate statewide court exists in several states, and only juvenile judges sit on cases in the various districts of those states. In other parts of the country, juvenile offenders are handled exclusively by family court judges who hear both juvenile and domestic relations cases.

More typically, juvenile courts are part of a circuit, district, county, superior, common pleas, probate, or municipal court. This broad-based trial court may be either the highest court of general trial jurisdiction or the lower trial court in which lesser criminal and limited-claim civil matters are heard.

Nationally, juvenile courts today are affected by a movement toward a single trial court, inclusive of all courts in which initial trials take place. For example, in a massive court reorganization in Cook County, Illinois, 208 courts became the circuit court for Cook County. The juvenile court of the District of Columbia was absorbed into the new single-trial court for the District.

A variety of personnel serve the juvenile court (see Table 6–1). These include the judge, who heads up the court; referees, who are assistants to the judge; the defense attorney and the prosecutor, who, respectively, defends the client and tries the case; probation officers, who investigate and supervise cases; and the nonjudicial support personnel, who do everything from providing client services to keeping the court running smoothly. The numbers and qualifications of these persons vary widely from court to court.[34]

The Judge

Juvenile court judges have an enormously important and difficult job. The most traditional role of the juvenile court judge is to decide the legal issues that appear before the court. The judge must determine, according to Leonard P. Edwards, "whether certain facts are true, whether a child should be removed from a parent, what types of services should be offered to the family and whether the child should be returned to the family and the community or placed permanently in another setting."[35]

Voices of Delinquency: Honorable Kim Berkeley Clark, A Judge Reflects from the Bench

> ### TABLE 6–1
> #### Personnel in Juvenile Court
>
> **Personnel Role**
>
> **Juvenile judge:** Most important role is to decide the legal issues that appear before the court.
>
> **Referee:** Some states use these individuals as primary hearing officers, while disposition, if necessary, is left to the judge.
>
> **Defense attorney:** Can be an adversarial advocate for the child, a surrogate guardian or parent to child, and an assistant to the court with responsibilities to the children.
>
> **Prosecutor:** Is expected to protect society, but, at the same time, to ensure that children appearing before the court receive their constitutional rights.
>
> **Probation officer:** Acts as an intake officer, assesses the needs of children, writes reports, and supervises youth.
>
> **Nonjudicial support personnel:** These include volunteers, staff from agencies providing services to the court, and paid workers who perform routine administrative functions.

The juvenile court judge also has the following responsibilities:

1. To set juvenile justice standards within the community and within the criminal and juvenile justice systems.

2. To make certain that juveniles appearing before the court receive the legal and constitutional rights to which they are entitled.

3. To ensure that the systems that detect, investigate, resolve, and bring cases to court are working fairly and efficiently.

4. To make certain that there are an adequate number of attorneys of satisfactory quality to represent juveniles in court.

5. To know how cases that do not reach the juvenile court are being resolved.

6. To monitor the progress of the child, the family, and the supervisory agency to make certain that each complies with the terms of the court's orders.

7. To be an advocate within the community on behalf of children and their families.

8. In some communities, to oversee the juvenile probation department and court staff.[36]

Juvenile judges are chosen by a variety of methods. In some states, the governor appoints candidates chosen by a screening board. In other states, judges are chosen through partisan elections, and in still other states, judges run for office without party affiliation. The legislature appoints judges in a few states. A dozen states have adopted the **Missouri Plan**, which involves (1) a commission being appointed to nominate candidates for judge vacancies; (2) an elected official, generally the governor, making judicial appointments from the list submitted by the commission; and (3) nonpartisan and uncontested elections being held (usually every three years) to give incumbent judges an opportunity to run on their records.[37]

Juvenile judges wield considerable power and, not surprisingly, a few do abuse their power as they become despots or dictators in "their courts," and some, as recently happened in Pennsylvania, engage in extreme corruption.[38] But many juvenile judges rise to the challenge and do a remarkable job. They scrupulously observe procedural safeguards and due process rights for juveniles. They are always seeking better means of detention and reserve the use of training schools as a last resort. They are extremely committed to the work of the juvenile court and sometimes even pass up promotions to more highly paid judgeships with greater prestige. The end result is that these judges change the quality of juvenile justice in their jurisdictions.

The **National Council of Juvenile and Family Court Judges**, located in Reno, Nevada, has done much to upgrade the juvenile court judiciary. This organization has sponsored research and continuing legal education efforts. It also maintains a research facility, the National Center for Juvenile Justice, in Pittsburgh, Pennsylvania. The council publishes quarterly the *Juvenile and Family Journal*; monthly, the *Juvenile and Family Law Digest*; and eight times per year, the *Juvenile and Family Court Newsletter*.

The Referee

Juvenile courts frequently employ the services of a referee, who may or may not be a member of the bar. In the state of Washington, a referee is called a *commissioner*; in Maryland, a *master*. California uses both referees and commissioners. Although a number of states use only judges in the juvenile court, other states use referees, masters, and commissioners as the primary hearing officers. All perform similar functions for the courts.

Referees generally have a fundamental grasp of juvenile law, some basic understanding of psychology and sociology, and even some experience or training in social work. In some courts, referees hear cases at the fact-finding and detention hearings and may even adjudicate cases at the discretion of the judge. If a judicial disposition is necessary, it usually is left to the juvenile judge. The use of referees appears to be on the increase in some urban areas where the caseload pressures are great.

The Defense Attorney

Defense attorneys, or *respondents*, have been part of the juvenile court structure ever since the *Gault* decision stated that juveniles have the right to be represented by an attorney. Whether they are public defenders, court-appointed attorneys, or privately retained attorneys, defense attorneys presently play an increasingly important role in juvenile trials.[39] Yet, Barry C. Feld found that nearly half of the juveniles who appeared before the juvenile courts for delinquency and status offense referrals in Minnesota, Nebraska, and North Dakota were not represented by counsel. Equally serious, Feld found that many of the juveniles who were placed out of their homes in these states also did not have counsel.[40]

Defense attorneys typically have at least three roles from which to choose: (1) an adversarial advocate for the child, (2) a surrogate guardian or parent to the child, or (3) an assistant to the court with responsibilities to the children.[41] Defense attorneys from public defenders' offices tend to do a better job of representing the rights of youth than do private and court-appointed counsel, primarily because public defenders appear in juvenile court day after day, thereby gaining valuable experience, whereas private attorneys appear only occasionally.

Some evidence suggests that juveniles who had counsel received more severe dispositions than those who did not have counsel.[42] For example, juveniles with counsel seem more likely to receive an institutional disposition than do those without counsel.[43] Such a pattern could result if juvenile judges punished youths who chose to be represented by counsel. Other studies have not found juveniles to be penalized or to fare worse in juvenile courts because they were represented by counsel.[44]

A **guardian *ad litem*** is usually a lawyer who is appointed by the court to take care of youths who need help, especially in neglect, dependency, and abuse cases, but also occasionally in delinquency cases. In delinquency cases, a guardian *ad litem* may be appointed if there is a question of a need for a particular treatment intervention, such as placement in a mental health center, and the offender and her or his attorney are resisting placement.[45]

The Prosecutor

The prosecutor, or *petitioner*, is expected to protect society and, at the same time, to ensure that children appearing before the court are provided with their basic constitutional rights. In urban courts, prosecutors typically are involved in every stage of the proceedings, from intake and detention through disposition. Prosecutors are particularly involved before the adjudication stage because witnesses must be interviewed, police investigations must be checked out, and court rules and case decisions must be researched. Prosecutors also play a role in detention decisions and represent the local or state government in all pretrial motions, probable-cause hearings, and consent decrees.

Voices of Delinquency: Peter Reinharz, Former Chief of the NYC Law Department for the Family Court Division

▲ Once juveniles are taken to court by the police, numerous and different types of hearings are used to determine what to do with them next.
Washington & Jefferson College

Voices of Delinquency: Ruth Frush, Chief Probation Officer

Prosecutors are especially involved in deciding whether juveniles should be waived to the adult court or kept in the juvenile court. In states in which certain offenses are excluded from juvenile court jurisdiction, prosecutors may send juveniles who commit those offenses to the adult court. Prosecutors further represent the county or state at the adjudication hearing and at the disposition of the case. In some urban courts, prosecutors may be involved in plea bargaining with the defense counsel. Prosecutors in some states are permitted to initiate appeals for the limited purpose of clarifying a given law or procedure. Moreover, prosecutors represent the state or county on appeals and in habeas corpus proceedings. Some critics contend that the prosecutor in some juvenile courts has come to dominate juvenile court proceedings.[46]

The Probation Officers

Probation officers have some of the most demanding jobs of any court personnel. Their functions involve developing interfaces between the probation department and community agencies that service children, and managing cases from intake through aftercare. Probation officers act as intake officers, assess the needs of youths, write reports such as predisposition reports, and supervise youths in both probation and aftercare in some jurisdictions. The officer may be given an intensive probation caseload, may be responsible for youths who are on house arrest and are monitored with electronic equipment, or may be charged with intake or secure-detention responsibilities. In addition, the probation officer is expected to be a treatment agent as well as an agent of social control.[47]

Probation officers appear to have four different orientations to their clients. First, probation officers oriented to the enforcer role perceive themselves as enforcement officers who are charged with regulating juvenile behavior. Second, probation officers oriented to the detector role attempt to identify problematic juveniles in advance on the basis of previous rule infractions. Third, probation officers oriented to the broker role refer juveniles to appropriate community services and programs—a common practice today. Finally, probation officers oriented to the educator, mediator, and enabler role are more likely to instruct and assist youthful offenders in dealing with the problems that impede their successful adjustment to the community.[48] Many of these probation officers have undergraduate backgrounds in sociology, psychology, and social work. Numerous other probation officers with these backgrounds go on to get master's degrees in social work or criminal justice to further their careers in the criminal justice system.

The Nonjudicial Support Personnel

Nonjudicial support personnel include volunteers, staff from agencies providing services to the court, and paid workers who perform routine administrative functions. Personnel from social service agencies also frequent the court as they make contact with youths and their families, but they have the job of writing reports to the courts summarizing the characteristics of youths as well as the progress youths are making. Finally, the court employs secretaries, clerks, bailiffs, legal researchers, and court administrators to perform the routine but necessary tasks of processing youths through the system.

What Are the Pretrial Procedures of the Juvenile Court?

The jurisdiction of the juvenile court, despite variations among and even within states, generally includes delinquency, neglect, and dependency cases. Children's courts may also deal with cases concerning adoption, termination of parental rights, appointment of guardians for minors, custody, contributing to delinquency or neglect, and nonsupport. The proceedings of the juvenile court can be divided into pretrial procedures and adjudicatory and dispositional hearings.

The pretrial procedures consist of the detention hearing, the intake process, and the transfer procedure. In 2005, 81 percent of delinquency cases were brought before the courts by law enforcement authorities, but there were variations across offense categories. Ninety-one percent of drug law violation cases, 91 percent of property cases, 87 percent of person offense cases, and 61 percent of public order offenses were referred by law enforcement agencies. The remaining cases resulted from complaints by parents, citizens, probation officers, victims, school officials, and others.[49]

The reasons for referring youths to the courts vary. Of the delinquency offenses, police officers brought youths to the juvenile court for property and drug offenses more than for any other category. Of the status offenses, liquor law and curfew violations headed the list for law enforcement officers. Conversely, sources other than law enforcement officers were most likely to refer youths for public order offenses and for status offenses, such as truancy, curfew violations, and ungovernability; the referral of runaways was about equally divided between law enforcement and other sources.

Detention Hearing

The use of detention has been a problem ever since the founding of the juvenile court. The original purpose of detention was to hold children securely until intake personnel reviewed the case and made a decision. The **detention hearing**, at which the decision to detain is made, must be held within a short period of time after arrest, generally forty-eight to seventy-two hours, excluding weekends and holidays. Those urban courts having intake units on duty twenty-four hours a day for detention hearings frequently act within a few hours.[50]

Detention hearings may occur at three points: (1) when the youth is taken in by the police, (2) during and after the time intake personnel review the case to decide whether to refer the case to juvenile court, and (3) after the adjudicatory hearing.

Police, as noted previously, make the first detention decision. Frequently, they must place the youth in a police lockup or local jail while they notify parents and decide what to do with the youth. The police usually exercise the option of simply releasing the youth to his or her parents. If police believe conditions warrant, as they often do with serious offenders and sometimes do with status offenders, they may hold these youths for the youths' protection or for the protection of society. In other words, the police base their decision partly on how they classify the youth.[51]

The second point at which detention may occur is after the police take the youth to the intake personnel of the juvenile court. Intake personnel then review the case to determine whether the youth should be referred to the juvenile court. They, too, often make the decision to release the youth to his or her parents, but the intake personnel may decide that the youth needs to be detained either for his or her own protection or for the protection of society (**preventive detention**), or while awaiting the adjudicatory hearing.

The third point at which a detention hearing may be held is after the adjudicatory hearing. If the youth is adjudicated delinquent, the court may in some circumstances sentence the youth to a detention center, shelter care, or in-home detention for a period of time as punishment. Detention is then used as a *sanction*, in which juveniles serve their "sentence" in detention and are released afterwards. More commonly, the court sentences the youth to a private or public residential facility.

Youths who are held in detention are assigned to one of four types of placement. The detention home is the most physically restrictive. Shelter care is physically nonrestrictive and is available for those who lack home placements or who require juvenile court intervention. The jail or police lockup is juveniles' most undesirable detention placement and is not recommended for any juvenile. The final option available in many jurisdictions is in-home detention, which restricts a juvenile to his or her home, usually under the supervision of a paraprofessional staff member.

Five states have legislated a hearing on probable cause for detained youths, and appellate courts in other states have moved in the direction of mandating a probable-cause hearing to justify further detention. Georgia and Alaska courts have ruled that a juvenile is entitled to counsel at a detention hearing and to free counsel if indigent. The supreme courts in California and Alaska, as well as a Pennsylvania appellate court, have overturned cases in which no reason or an inadequate reason was stated for continuing detention. Furthermore, courts in the District of Columbia, Maryland, and Nevada have ruled that a youth in detention is entitled to humane care.

Bail for Children

Bail is *not* a form of punishment. Rather, its purpose is to ensure that the defendant will show up at his or her adjudicatory hearing. The court usually determines the amount of bail required at an early intake hearing, which reviews such factors as the youth's behavior, past history, and relationship with parents and school authorities. Once bail is set, the defendants and their families then have to come up with a percentage (usually 10 percent) of the required amount.

The controversies over bail are similar in adult and juvenile justice. The Eighth Amendment to the U.S. Constitution states that bail shall not be excessive, but determining what is excessive is difficult. In addition, the U.S. Supreme Court in **ex parte Crouse** stated that the Bill of Rights did not apply to children. This ruling therefore implied that the states and their courts may do as they please in setting bail. The result is that few can agree whether juveniles may be released on bail, and states and courts vary widely in their practices.

For example, some states prohibit bail altogether; Hawaii, Kentucky, Oregon, and Utah fall into this category. Other states allow bail, but not for juveniles. This practice is based on the assumption that normal juvenile court procedures and due process guarantees are sufficient to protect juveniles and allow their early release. In some of these states, it should be noted, judges occasionally require a juvenile to post a bond. For the most part, however, requirements that juveniles are to be released to their parents as soon as possible are believed to be sufficient protection for juveniles.

Bail for juveniles is permitted in nine states: Arkansas, Colorado, Connecticut, Georgia, Massachusetts, Nebraska, Oklahoma, South Dakota, and West Virginia. Even though few juveniles are released on bail, most juvenile court statutes do limit the time that accused juveniles may be held in custody before their hearings.[52]

The possibility of judges setting excessive bail has led some states to require higher courts to review the bail set by lower courts. In addition, some experts suggest releasing more youths on their own recognizance or under the supervision of third parties. Some recommend that states utilize citation programs; that is, police officers simply issue youths a "ticket," or summons, that requires the youth to appear in court on a certain date. Others suggest that police should require youths to report to the station house for a consultation with officers or members of the police youth bureau. Figure 6–2 outlines the pretrial processes in a juvenile court.

Procedure / Description

Detention Hearing
The criteria for detention are based on the need to protect the youth and to ensure public safety. This decision is usually made within 48 to 72 hours.

Intake Process
This is a preliminary screening process to determine whether a court hearing should take place (and, if so, what action), or whether the matter should be referred elsewhere.

Transfer Procedure
All state legislatures have passed laws permitting juveniles to be transferred to adult court. Judicial waiver and legislative waiver are the two basic mechanisms for transferring youthful offenders to the adult court.

FIGURE 6–2
Pretrial Processes in the Juvenile Court

Preventive Detention

The 1984 *Schall v. Martin* decision of the U.S. Supreme Court represents a fundamental change that appears to be taking place in detention practices.[53] The plaintiffs originally filed a lawsuit in federal district court claiming that the New York Family Court Act was unconstitutional because it allowed for the preventive detention of juveniles:

> The District Court struck down the statute as permitting detention without due process and ordered the release of all class members. The Court of Appeals affirmed, holding . . . the statute is administered not for preventive purposes, but to impose punishment for unadjudicated criminal acts, and that therefore the statute is unconstitutional.[54]

In reversing the decision of the appeals court, Justice William Rehnquist declared that the "preventive detention under the statute serves the legitimate state objective held in common with every state, of protecting both the juvenile and the society from the hazards of pretrial crime."[55] Although the ultimate impact of this decision remains to be felt, there is reason to believe that the Court's ruling may encourage a significant expansion of preventive or secure detention for juveniles.

Preventive detention raises several controversial questions. First, laws are not supposed to be enforced against people unless some sort of overt act has occurred that violates the juvenile or criminal code. To put a youth in preventive detention under the assumption that he or she might commit an offense runs counter to the intent and, supposedly, the practice of the law. Second, preventive detention is experienced by the detainee as *punitive* confinement, regardless of the stated purpose of the practice. Finally, the propriety of incarceration before the determination of guilt and the procedural safeguards that must accompany such a practice are major issues to be considered. Indeed, evaluations of the detention process indicate that the majority of juveniles who are preventively detained are not charged with serious offenses.[56]

Intake Process

The **intake process** has several purposes: First, it screens cases to determine whether children need the help of the juvenile court. Second, it controls the use of detention, which is discussed later. Third, it reduces the courts' overwhelming caseloads. Fourth, it keeps inappropriate cases (e.g., minor cases) out of the juvenile court. Finally, it directs children to appropriate community agencies.[57]

Some probation departments have intake units, but in many departments, especially smaller ones, juvenile probation officers make intake decisions as part of their duties. When there are intake units, despite the similarity of their functions, they do not operate the same way. Juvenile court organization and available resources vary widely among the states. In addition, few states have attempted to spell out the criteria intake personnel should use to make their decisions. The result is that intake personnel exercise a great deal of discretion in deciding what to do with youths.

The first decision intake personnel must make is whether the case comes under their jurisdiction; for example, staff must determine whether the child or the child's offense falls under the appropriate age or offense category. If not, then the second decision of the staff will be either to dismiss the case or to refer it to an appropriate social agency or the adult court. Third, staff must decide whether the youth before them requires secure detention. Other options are to divert the case to a nonjudicial agency through an informal adjustment, put the youth on informal probation, issue a consent decree, or file a petition.

Case Dismissal

An intake officer reviews the cases of all youths brought to the court's attention. Often this review takes place with the police officer, the youths' parents, and perhaps the prosecutor and the youths' lawyers present. If the particular behavior in question is not an offense under the state's code, the charge will be dismissed. The case also will likely be dismissed if the case is too weak to bring before the court, if it is the youth's first offense, if the youth appears genuinely contrite, and if the parents appear concerned about the youth's behavior and promise to get the youth help. Youths whose cases are dismissed are sent home with their parents.

Informal Adjustment

This alternative, sometimes called *nonjudicial adjustment*, often is used for status and other minor offenders. One option of the intake official is simply to warn the child and release him or her to parents. A more stringent option is to require the youth to pay restitution to the victim. A third option is to refer the youth to local diversion programs, which include youth service bureaus or other social agencies that are qualified to work with the problems of youth. The agencies to which the youth is referred are then responsible for supervising the youth and reporting back to the court.

Informal Probation

Informal probation means that the youth is released back to the community but must accept certain conditions that are spelled out by the court. The youth is usually supervised for a specified period of time by either a volunteer or a probation officer. If the youth is able to stay out of trouble in the community, a report is then sent back to the court, and the case is discontinued at that time. If the youth has difficulty, a petition may be filed with the court, and the youth may be held for further adjudication.

Consent Decree

Consent decrees are intermediate steps between informal handling and probation, and the decrees are used to place the child under the jurisdiction of the court without a finding that the child is delinquent. Generally, a consent decree requires the child to agree to fulfill certain conditions in spite of the fact that he or she has not been found guilty. For informal sanctions, see Focus on Law 6-4.

Petition

The intake officer can choose to file a petition if none of the preceding options is satisfactory. There is some evidence that the broad discretionary power given to intake workers is sometimes abused. For example, Duran Bell, Jr., and Kevin Lang's study of intake in Los Angeles found that some extralegal factors, especially cooperative behavior, are important in reducing the length of detention.[58]

The Transfer Procedure

Some critics contend that the juvenile court should only work with youths who fall into the dependent/neglected and victimized/abused categories, not with those who violate the criminal code. These latter offenders, some critics believe, should be dealt with by adult courts.[59] They argue that the juvenile court not only has failed in its rehabilitative mission, but is relatively powerless to effect change in more seasoned and hard-core youthful offenders. Thus, the critics insist that offenders who commit felonies should be subject to the same punishments to which adults are subject. The popularity of this position led to an increase in the number of youths transferred to adult court in the past decade (see Chapter 7 for an expanded discussion and evaluation of transfer to adult court).

Focus on Law 6–4
Informal Sanctions

Informal processing usually is considered when the decision makers (such as the police, intake workers, probation officers, prosecutors, or other screening officers) believe that accountability and rehabilitation can be achieved without intervention from formal courts.

Informal sanctions are voluntary and, therefore, a juvenile cannot be forced to comply with an informal disposition. If a court decides to handle a matter informally (in lieu of formal prosecution), a youthful offender at that time has to agree to comply with one or more sanctions. These sanctions could include voluntary probation supervision, community service, and victim restitution. In some jurisdictions, the youth not only has to agree to sanctions but also has to agree that he or she committed the alleged act.

A case that is informally handled is usually held open pending the successful completion of the informal disposition. After the agreement on sanctions and the completion of this disposition, the charges against the offender are dismissed. But if the offender does not fulfill the court's conditions for informal handling, the case is likely to be reopened and formally prosecuted.

Informal handling has become less common but still occurs in a large number of cases. About half of the delinquency cases are handled informally. Informal handling is more likely to take place in smaller jurisdictions than in larger ones.

CRITICAL THINKING QUESTION:

What is your evaluation of informal sanctions? What do you see as their strengths and weaknesses?

Source: Howard N. Snyder and Melissa Sickmund, *Juvenile Offenders and Victims: A National Report* (Washington, DC: Office of Juvenile Justice and Delinquency Prevention, 2006), 159.

Plea Bargaining

Plea bargaining is increasingly emerging as an important issue in juvenile justice. One juvenile probation officer noted, "When I was a juvenile probation officer in a mid-sized urban county in Pennsylvania, many, if not most, of the cases were plea bargained."[60] Although little is known about how often or when it occurs, the increased trends toward "criminalization" of the juvenile court, on the one hand, and the expansion of community-based corrections, on the other, make it likely that plea bargaining will come under increased attention.[61]

A **plea bargain** is a deal made between the prosecutor and the defense attorney. The defense attorney, after consultation with his or her client, agrees that the client will admit to committing a lesser offense if the prosecutor will drop the more serious charges. The client receives a lighter sentence, and the necessity of having an adjudicatory hearing is avoided. The caseload of the court is thereby reduced.[62]

Critics of plea bargaining are concerned with its fairness. Their fear is that juveniles who are innocent of any wrongdoing may plead guilty to a lesser offense for fear that they will receive a harsh sentence if tried and found guilty of the more serious offense. This obviously is unfair to the innocent; even guilty youths may be subjected to inappropriate community referrals or placements if care is not taken to place them wisely. In addition, truly violent and dangerous youths may be able to negotiate a release back into the community when they should in all probability be placed in secure institutions. The problem at this time is that few guidelines exist to help direct prosecutors and defense attorneys in plea bargaining.

What Are Other Stages of Juvenile Court Proceedings?

After the pretrial procedures (discussed earlier in this chapter), the adjudicatory hearing, or the fact-finding stage, and the disposition hearing are the two remaining stages of the juvenile proceedings.

Adjudicatory Hearing

The **adjudicatory hearing** for juveniles is equivalent to the trial in adult court. It is the point at which the judge reviews the charges as described in the petition, hears testimony from the parties involved, and decides whether the youth committed the offense.

Adjudicatory hearings today are a blend of the old and the new. First, the hearings are still somewhat less formal than the adult trial. Second, the hearings have been traditionally closed in order to protect the juvenile's name and reputation in the community but that has been changing in many jurisdictions in terms of keeping the proceedings closed and of releasing juveniles' names to the public. Figure 6–3 indicates which states have juvenile adjudicatory hearings that are open to the public and which have confidential hearings. Third, a few juvenile courts, because they disagree strongly with the recent Supreme Court decisions, tend to ignore the new standards and operate much as in the past. Little change has occurred in these courts.

On the other side of the ledger, most states now spell out their procedural requirements very carefully. For example, all juveniles now have the right to a hearing, which is likely to be much more formal than in the past. Written petitions are required, and these may be amended if necessary. Hearsay is prohibited, and the case must be proved beyond a reasonable doubt. Youths have the right to protect themselves against self-incrimination, and they may cross-examine witnesses and victims. Attorneys and prosecutors are likely to be present. Finally, some state codes call for a separation of the adjudication and disposition hearings.

If an attorney has not been appointed or retained by the juvenile by this point in time, one will be appointed by the court and, hopefully, the date of the hearing reset to allow the attorney time to talk with the youth, review the case, and prepare the defense. Some courts may assign a public defender to the youth, allow the defender a couple of minutes to read the documents and talk with the youth, and go immediately into the adjudication hearing.

The National Council of Juvenile and Family Court Judges recommends that a script similar to that in Focus on Law 6-5 be used by the judge to ensure that the due process rights of the

FIGURE 6–3
Confidentiality of Juvenile Proceedings

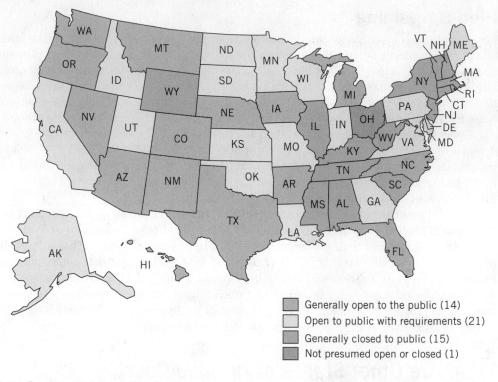

Generally open to the public (14)
Open to public with requirements (21)
Generally closed to public (15)
Not presumed open or closed (1)

juvenile are maintained. These due process rights are given to the juvenile as a result of the *Kent, Gault, Winship, Breed v. Jones*, and *McKeiver* cases discussed earlier in the chapter.

If the youth's attorney and the prosecutor have agreed on a plea bargain, the agreement is presented to the judge at this time. If the judge accepts the plea bargain, the judge will issue a predisposition at this time, a process called a *sequential hearing*, and immediately assign a disposition in the case that will likely parallel those the juvenile may already have experienced earlier in his or her career. If the judge rejects the plea bargain, the adjudicatory hearing continues.

The length of the hearings varies throughout the country from a "five-minute children's hour" to a full hour or more, possibly with continuances, if more evidence such as forensic data or social service agency data is needed. During the hearing, the prosecutor will present the facts of the case, the defense will present the youth's side of the story, and the parents will be asked for their input, as will be the probation officer and the victim. In some jurisdictions today, the judge will render a verdict immediately after the conclusion of the trial. More and more jurisdictions, however, are setting a date for a disposition hearing, often within ten days to two weeks after the adjudicatory hearing. The reason for this time frame is to keep all hearings as close to the time the offense was committed as possible in order to have the maximum impact on the juvenile.

In some jurisdictions, it is possible for juveniles to receive a jury trial. Twelve states presently mandate a jury trial for juveniles who request one during their adjudicatory hearings and who face the possibility of institutional confinement. But twenty-three states deny juveniles the right to a jury trial. South Dakota is the only state of the remaining ones that specifies whether juveniles are entitled to jury trial. In that state, a juvenile court order is required for a jury trial to be conducted in juvenile court.[63]

Disposition Hearing

Disposition hearings, which are equivalent to sentencing hearings in adult courts, are of two basic types. The first type, which is used less and less frequently in the United States, occurs at the same time as the adjudicatory hearing. The judge, after hearing the case and discussing it with the youth, the youth's parents, the prosecutor, and the defense attorney, reviews the social service report submitted by a probation officer and decides what disposition would be most effective for the youth.

The second type of disposition hearing occurs following the adjudicatory hearing. This *bifurcated system*, as it is sometimes called, has different evidentiary rules than are used

Focus on Law 6–5
Legal Rights of the Juvenile

Juvenile Delinquency Court Judge: "I am now going to advise you of your legal rights:"

1. A petition has been filed against you, and it says that you (explain the offense).
2. Do you understand what you are charged with?
3. You have the right against self-incrimination. This means that you do not have to say anything about your part in the charges or even whether you were anywhere near where the charges happened if you do not want to. If you do choose to talk about it, what you say can be used against you. Do you have any question about what this means?
4. You have the opportunity to either admit to the charges if they are true or to deny the charges if they are not true. If you deny the charges, there will be a trial to determine whether or not the charges are true. At the trial, you have the right to:
   • Confront witnesses [who] testify against you, which means your attorney gets to ask them questions to try and show that the charges are not true. Do you have any questions about what this means?
   • Compel witnesses, which means the court can require a person who your attorney thinks can help you show [that] the charges are not true to come to court and tell what they know. However, you are not required to bring any witnesses. Do you have any questions about what this means?
   • You can choose to testify or not to testify at the trial. You can remain silent and not say anything if you want. If you decide not to testify, your choice will not be held against you. Do you have any questions about what this means?
   • If you admit the charges, or if I find you are guilty at the trial, by law I can (explain what dispositions can be imposed). Do you have any questions about what this means?
5. Do you admit or deny the charges? Are the charges true or not true? If the youth denies the charge, proceed to set the trial date and deal with all pretrial issues.

If the youth admits the charges:
   • Do you understand that in saying the charges are true, you are giving up your right to a trial, which means you are also giving up your right to confront witness[es], make witness[es] testify for you, and to remain silent about the charges?
   • Has anyone made any threats or promises to you to get you to do this?
   • Have you taken any drugs, medicine, or alcohol within the last twenty-four hours? (If the youth answers yes, the judge must explore further to determine if the drug currently impairs the youth, which would mean [that] the plea should not be accepted.)
   • Are you admitting these charges to benefit yourself and nobody else?
   • At the time you did this, did you know those things were wrong? (If the youth's answers support a plea of admit, the judge should ask the parent, custodian, or [person acting] *in loco parentis* whether they know of any reason that the judge should not accept the plea.)

If the judge accepts the plea, the judge should call on the youth to explain what happened in detail. If the youth's explanation indicates that he or she is not really admitting to the offense, the judge should consider withdrawing the acceptance of the plea and setting the case for trial.

CRITICAL THINKING QUESTION:

How are the juvenile's due process rights protected by such a script? Do you believe that most youthful offenders appearing before the court in an adjudicatory hearing have any understanding of what the script means?

Source: National Council of Juvenile and Family Court Judges, *Juvenile Delinquency Guidelines* (Reno, NV: Author, 2005), Appendix.

---

in the single adjudicatory hearing. In the adjudicatory hearing, for example, the standard of "proof beyond a reasonable doubt" requires stringent rules and a limiting of the kinds of information that may be introduced. The dispositional hearing, however, calls for the judge to have as wide a range of information as possible concerning the youth; this often involves information that would be inadmissible or inappropriate in the adjudicatory hearing.[64]

The reason for separating the two hearings is to prevent judges from learning information that is prejudicial to the defendant. In a combined hearing, the judge may discover information that is not relevant to the case but nevertheless biases his or her finding of guilt or innocence. If the judge does not receive this extraneous information until after the finding of guilt, the defendant is protected from being found guilty on the basis of information unrelated to the specific allegation.

Predisposition Report

Another advantage of the bifurcated system is that it gives the probation department time to make a more comprehensive study of the youth's needs and background than is possible when presentencing reports are given at the time of the adjudicatory hearing. This, too, increases the amount of information available to the judge in making a disposition decision.

Predisposition reports are essential to defendants, defense attorneys, prosecutors, probation departments, and judges. California and Maryland Supreme Courts in fact have overturned lower-court decisions because judges have not held dispositional hearings to consider relevant sentencing information.[65] This information is crucial because the reports contain background information on defendants that helps judges make individualized decisions.

The social work perspective has helped shape the way caseworkers and probation officers develop the predisposition reports. Since the 1920s, for example, the court has used psychiatric and psychological information obtained from existing school, social agency, and medical records. If such information is not available but is believed necessary, probation officers may refer juveniles for appropriate medical, psychological, or psychiatric evaluations to determine whether they are mentally ill or restricted. Other information is collected from law enforcement agencies, social service agencies that have dealt with the juvenile previously, the juvenile, and the juvenile's family, friends, and neighbors. The object is to collect any and all information that might be relevant to the case.[66]

The written report, then, contains a description of the referral incident as well as the youth's past conduct, prior contacts with the police and courts, and family environment and relationships. Information on the youth's employment history, school records, interests, and activities is also collected. If police officers have information on special problems of the youth or if special needs of the youth are discovered, these, too, are included in the report.

Once the fact finding has been completed, probation officers recommend a course of action to the court. The predisposition report draws up a plan for what the youth needs and how he or she can be helped best. The report is submitted to the judge, who reviews the report for the dispositional hearing and usually follows the advice given in the report. The juvenile has the right to be present at this hearing.

Both formal and informal factors influence decision making at the dispositional stage. The most important formal factors are the recommendation of the probation officer and the information contained in the social study investigation, or predisposition report; the seriousness of the delinquent offense; the juvenile's previous contact with the court; and the available options. Although the recommendation of the probation officer is usually followed by the juvenile judge, the seriousness of the delinquent behavior and the previous contacts with the court probably have the greatest impact on judicial decision making at this stage.[67] M. A. Bortner found from his examination of disposition decision making in a large Midwestern county that age, prior referrals, and the detention decision were the most important influences.[68]

The informal factors that sometimes influence judicial decision making include the values and philosophy of the judge, the social and racial background of the youth, the youth's demeanor, the presence or absence of defense counsel, and political repercussions of the alleged delinquent acts. The most disturbing of these informal factors relates to the social and racial background of the youth. Ruth D. Peterson found that racial, ethnic, gender, and age disparities affected the disposition of older adolescents in New York State courts. Although race and ethnicity did not significantly influence disposition decisions in New York City, minority juveniles tended to be stereotyped and to receive harsh treatment outside the city.[69] Figure 6–4 outlines the trial proceedings in a juvenile court.

Judicial Alternatives

The alternatives that are available to different juvenile courts vary significantly. Large urban courts have all or most of the following eleven alternatives at their disposal, but rural courts may have only a few:

1. *Dismissal.* Dismissal is one of the possible dispositions for juveniles. The fact-finding stage may have shown that a juvenile is guilty, but the judge can decide, for a variety of reasons, to dismiss the case.

2. *Restitution.* One very desirable option is restitution, where youths may be required to work off their debt with a few hours each week, but their lives are not seriously interrupted.

ADJUDICATORY HEARING
This is the fact-finding stage of the court's proceedings and usually includes the youth's pleas, the presentation of evidence by the prosecution and defense, the cross-examination of witnesses, and the judge's finding.

DISPOSITION HEARING
The traditional purpose is to administer individualized justice and to set in motion the rehabilitation of the delinquent. Accordingly, the judge is not limited by constitutional safeguards as much as he or she was at the adjudication hearing.

JUDICIAL ALTERNATIVES
These alternatives available to juvenile courts vary significantly from one court to another, but most courts have a variety of choices.

RIGHT TO APPEAL
Juveniles do not have a constitutional right to make an appeal of their cases to a higher judiciary, but nearly all states permit the right to appeal by statute.

FIGURE 6–4
Trial Proceedings in the Juvenile Court

3. *Outpatient psychiatric therapy.* Whether in the court clinic, in the community mental health clinic, or with private therapists, outpatient therapy as a treatment-oriented decision and is often reserved for middle-class youths to keep them from being sent to "unfitting" placements.

4. *Probation.* As the most widely used disposition, probation seems to be a popular decision with delinquents and a good treatment alternative for the court. Probation is sometimes set for a specific length of time, usually a maximum of two years. The judge can direct the probation officer to involve the youth in special programs, such as alternative schools, speech therapy, or learning disability programs.

5. *Foster home placements.* Foster home placements are more restrictive, inasmuch as youths are removed from their natural homes. These placements are used most frequently for status offenders and dependent and eclectic youths.

6. *Day treatment programs.* Day treatment programs are a popular alternative with juveniles because youths who are assigned to these programs return home in the evening, but these programs are few in number and are available in only a few states.

7. *Community-based residential programs.* There are different types of community-based residential programs, such as group homes and halfway houses, that are available to many judges. These residential facilities may be located in the youth's community or in a nearby community, but they are not as desirable as community-based treatment programs because youths are taken from their homes to live in these facilities.

8. *Institutionalization in a mental hospital.* Institutionalization may be seen as appropriate for a youth's needs. A psychiatric evaluation is required when this alternative is chosen. After the evaluation, the doctor may recommend that the court initiate proceedings for commitment to a mental hospital.

9. *County or city institution.* Some county or city institutions are available to a few judges across the nation. Placement in these facilities may be deemed appropriate for youth who need more security than can be offered by probation offers but who do not require long-term placement in a state training school.

10. *State or private training school.* The state or private training schools usually are reserved for youths who have committed serious offenses or for whom everything else has failed. In some states, state training schools include minimum-security (forestry camps, farms, and ranches), medium-security, and maximum-security institutions.

11. *Adult facility or youthful offender facility.* In a few states, if a youth has committed serious offenses and is seen as too hard-core for a juvenile correctional institution, he or she is placed in an adult facility or youthful offender facility.

What Right Does the Juvenile Have to Appeal?

Voices of Delinquency: I Have Been Around, You Know

Juveniles do not yet have a constitutional right to appeal. Nevertheless, practically all states, following the lead of the U.S. Supreme Court, grant juveniles the right to appeal by statute for some of the following reasons. The Court pointed out in *In re Gault* that juveniles should have the same absolute right as adults have to appeal under the equal protection clause of the Constitution. Since that ruling, most state legislatures have passed laws granting juveniles the right to appeal. In addition, state courts have ruled that statutes granting the right to appeal for juveniles must be applied uniformly to all juveniles; this decision effectively undermines the tradition in some courts of giving judges the discretion to determine which juvenile cases could be appealed. The common practice today is to give juveniles the same rights to appeal as adults are given.[70]

The right to appeal is for the most part limited to juveniles and their parents. States may appeal in some circumstances, but this right is seldom exercised and few such cases have come before the courts. Some variation exists in the types of orders that may be appealed. States generally permit the appeal of "final" orders, although what is final varies from state to state. For example, some states authorize juvenile courts to order juveniles to be confined in secure facilities for a period of time. That is a final order. Nevertheless, certain states permit the youth or his or her parents to appeal that final order. States also vary in how they handle appeals. Most state statutes call for the case to be appealed to an appellate court, but a few states call for a completely new trial. Other common statutory rights of juveniles at appeal are the right to a transcript of the case and the right to counsel.[71]

Voices of Delinquency: A Longing for Street Superiority

What Is the Juvenile Sentencing Structure?

Determinate sentencing is a new form of sentencing in juvenile justice and in some jurisdictions is replacing the traditional form of indeterminate sentencing. In addition, increasing numbers of juvenile courts are using a "blended" form of sentencing.

Criticism of the decision making of the juvenile court has increased in the past thirty years. Early on, the criticism focused on the arbitrary nature of the decision making that violated the due process rights of juveniles; more recently, this criticism has been based on the belief that the juvenile court is too "soft" on crime. This latter criticism, especially, has led to a number of procedures that change sentencing and other juvenile procedures.

One of the first efforts at reform was the Juvenile Justice Standards Project, jointly sponsored by the Institute of Judicial Administration and the American Bar Association. Officially launched in 1971 by a national planning committee under the chairmanship of Judge Irving R. Kaufman, comprehensive guidelines for juvenile offenders were designed that would base sentences on the seriousness of the crime rather than on the needs of the youth. The proposed guidelines represented radical philosophical changes and still are used by proponents to attempt to standardize the handling of juvenile lawbreakers.

The belief that disparity in juvenile sentencing must end was one of the fundamental thrusts of the recommended standards. To accomplish this goal, the commission attempted to limit the discretion of juvenile judges and to make them accountable for their decisions, which would then be subject to judicial review. Also important in the standards was the provision that certain court procedures would be open to the public, although the names of juveniles still would remain confidential.

At the beginning of the twenty-first century, juvenile court judges remain quite concerned about these proposed standards. Their basic concern is that these standards attack the underlying philosophy and structure of the juvenile court. Judges also are concerned about how these standards would limit their authority. They see the influence of the hardliners behind this movement toward standardization and feel that the needs of children will be neglected in the long run. They also challenge the idea that it is possible, much less feasible, to treat all children alike.

Nevertheless, the standards are being adopted across the nation. New York State was the first to act on them through the Juvenile Justice Reform Act of 1976, which went into effect on February 1, 1977. The act orders a determinate sentence of five years for Class A felonies, which include murder, first-degree kidnapping, and first-degree arson. The initial term can be extended by at least one year. The juvenile, according to the act, should be placed in a residential facility after the first year. Then, if approved by the director of the division, the confined youth can be placed in a nonresidential program for the remainder of the five-year term. But the youth must remain under intensive supervision for the entire five-year term.

In 1977, the state of Washington also created a determinate sentencing system for juveniles in line with the recommendations of the Juvenile Justice Standards Project. Moreover, in the 1980s, a number of states stiffened juvenile court penalties for serious juvenile offenders, either by mandating minimum terms of incarceration (Colorado, Kentucky, and Idaho) or by enacting a comprehensive system of sentencing guidelines (Arizona, Georgia, and Minnesota).[72]

In 1995, the Texas legislature introduced such get-tough changes in the juvenile justice system as lowering the age at which waiver could occur to fourteen for capital, first-degree, and aggravated controlled-substance felony offenses and greatly expanding the determinate sentence statute that was first enacted in 1987. Under determinate sentences, any juvenile, regardless of age, can be sentenced for up to forty years in the Texas Youth Commission, with possible transfer to the Texas Department of Corrections. Finally, prosecutors can choose to pursue determinate sentence proceedings rather than delinquency proceedings, but they first must obtain grand jury approval.[73]

Daniel P. Mears and Samuel H. Field's examination of the determinate sentencing statute for Texas found that increased proceduralization and criminalization of juvenile courts did not eliminate consideration of age, gender, or race/ethnicity in sentencing decisions.[74]

In the 1990s, nearly every state enacted mandatory sentences for violent and repetitive juvenile offenders. The development of graduated, or accountability-based, sanctions was another means in the 1990s that states used to ensure that juveniles who are adjudicated delinquent received an appropriate disposition by the juvenile court. Several states have created a blended sentencing structure for cases involving repeat and serious juvenile offenders. Blended sentences are a mechanism for holding those juveniles accountable for their offenses. This expanded sentencing authority allows criminal and juvenile courts to impose either juvenile or adult sentences, or at times both, in cases involving juveniles.[75]

Toward Excellence in the Juvenile Delinquency Court

The National Council of Juvenile and Family Court Judges has identified the functions of the court and its judges. The council believes that the juvenile court should have exclusive jurisdiction in all matters affecting juveniles and families in delinquency cases, should have the same status as general trial courts, and should have the power and authority to "order, enforce, and review delivery of court ordered services and treatment for children and families."[76]

To overcome the many different forms and practices it has developed over the last one hundred years, the National Council on Juvenile and Family Court Judges made recommendations in 2005 to promote the best practices of the juvenile court and its personnel across the country[77] (see Figure 6–5).

Excellence in Juvenile Courts

Applies to the entire system

- Juvenile justice systems must have adequate staff, facilities, and program resources.

Applies specifically to judges

- Judges should engage in judicial leadership and encourage system collaboration. Status should be the same as other judges and judge should have multiple-year or permanent assignment.
- Judges should make certain that cases are diverted to alternative systems whenever possible and appropriate.
- Judges should make certain that victims have access to services they need.
- Judges should make certain that court dispositions are individualized and that they include graduated sanctions and incentives.
- Judges should ensure that effective post-dispositions are provided to each youth.
- Judges should ensure accountability among courtroom participants.
- Judges should ensure that an adequate information system is available to evaluate performance.
- Judges are responsible to see that all court staff are adequately trained.

Apply to other staff members

- All members of the court team should treat youths, families, crime victims, witnesses, and others with respect, dignity, courtesy, and cultural understanding.
- Youths charged in the delinquency court should have qualified and adequately compensated legal representation.
- Staff should encourage family members to participate in the development and implementation of the youth's intervention plan.

Apply to the court

- Delinquency courts and juvenile abuse courts should have integrated one-family–one-judge case assignments.
- Courts should render timely and just decisions, and trials should conclude without continuances.[78]

FIGURE 6–5
Principles of Excellence

Juvenile Justice Videos

INTAKE PROCESS 1

The first part of the *Intake Process* video showed an interaction between a juvenile offender and an intake officer. The juvenile has a history of delinquent behavior, but the intake officer focuses discussion on the personal successes and potential positive future for the youth. What motives might the intake officer have for leading the discussion in this manner? Based on what is displayed in the video and described in the readings, discuss the steps of the juvenile intake process. What are the goals of the intake process?

INTAKE PROCESS 2

In the second part of the *Intake Process* video, the intake of two juvenile brothers is shown. Describe the differences between the two brothers in regards to prior records, behaviors, and specific individual needs. Both brothers were detained prior to their hearings. Do their individual histories and personal needs validate this decision by the court? Does the decision by the court act in the children's best interest? Why or why not?

THE HEARING PROCESS

The Hearing Process video is about two brothers, both with prior records, within the beginning steps of the juvenile justice system.

What are the boys being charged with by the court? Both boys display different needs; how do the recommendations of the attorney and the judge reflect these differences? The judge discusses her faith in the juvenile justice system. Do the sentences given by the judge accommodate the needs of each youth? Why or why not?

CHILD ABUSE

Child Abuse shows a family's interaction with the juvenile justice system dealing with child abuse. The father explains his side of the story; how does the social worker deal with the possibility of child abuse? Why does the social worker take custody of the other two children? When brought before the court, what programs must the parents attend in order to keep custody of the children? Based on the video and the readings, what types of treatment and programs are used to handle this type of delicate family situation? Discuss.

CRITICAL THINKING QUESTION:

Which sentencing standards could best be required for all states?

SUMMARY

LEARNING OBJECTIVE 1: Summarize the development and legal norms of the juvenile court.

A number of cases resulted in the development of the juvenile court, ensuring that juveniles would have more constitutional rights accorded them at the time of judicial proceedings:

- *In re Gault*— This is a U.S. Supreme Court case that brought the process and constitutional procedures into juvenile courts. *In re Kent*—At the time of transfer, juveniles are accorded an evidential hearing.

- *In re Winship*—Supreme Court ruled that juveniles are entitled to proof beyond a reasonable doubt during the adjudication proceedings.

- *McKeiver v. Pennsylvania*—Juveniles are not guaranteed the right to a jury trial.

- *Breed v. Jones*—A juvenile court cannot adjudicate a case and then transfer the case over to the criminal court for adult processing on the same offense.

LEARNING OBJECTIVE 2: Describe the social control of the status offender.

There are two major decisions in terms of status offenders: (1) whether to deinstitutionalize them from delinquency youth—the majority of states have complied with the federal mandate to do this; and (2) whether the juvenile court should retain jurisdiction of status offenders—nearly all states have agreed that they should.

LEARNING OBJECTIVE 3: Explain the structure and key players of the juvenile court.

The key players of the juvenile court are the judge, the referee, the defense attorney, the prosecutor, the probation officer, and nonjudicial support personnel.

LEARNING OBJECTIVE 4: Describe pretrial procedures and decisions of the intake officer.

An intake officer reviews all cases brought before the juvenile court. At this point, the charges may be dismissed or the decision made to put a juvenile in detention or send him or her home. The decision may also be to refer the juvenile to the juvenile court. The juvenile judge may decide to grant the youth an informal adjustment, informal probation, or consent decree or he or she may be required to appear in court for an adjudicatory hearing.

LEARNING OBJECTIVE 5: Explain plea bargaining.

A plea bargain is a deal made between the prosecutor and the defense attorney. The defense attorney, after consultation with his or her client, agrees that the client will admit to committing a lesser offense if the prosecutor will drop the more serious charge.

LEARNING OBJECTIVE 6: Summarize the adjudicatory process.

The adjudicatory hearing for juveniles is equivalent to the trial in adult court. It is the point at which the judge reviews the charges as described in the petition, hears testimony from the parties involved, and decides whether the youth committed the offense.

LEARNING OBJECTIVE 7: Describe the disposition hearing.

Disposition hearings, which are equivalent to sentencing hearings in adult courts, are of two basic types. The first type occurs at the same time as the adjudicatory hearing. The judge decides what disposition would be most effective for the youth. The second type of disposition hearing occurs following the adjudicatory hearing. This *bifurcated system,* as it is sometimes called, has different evidentiary rules than are used in the single adjudicatory hearing.

LEARNING OBJECTIVE 8: Describe the disposition alternatives.

The various alternatives are dismissal, restitution, outpatient psychiatric therapy, probation, foster home placements, day treatment programs, community-based residential programs, institutionalization in a mental hospital, county or city institution, state or private training school, and adult facility or youthful offender facility.

LEARNING OBJECTIVE 9: Describe the various sentencing alternatives for juveniles.

Determinate sentencing is a new form of sentencing in juvenile justice and in some jurisdictions is replacing the traditional form of indeterminate sentencing. In addition, increasing numbers of juvenile courts are using a "blended" form of sentencing.

KEY TERMS

adjudicatory hearing, p. 133

bail, p. 130

Breed v. Jones, p. 121

constitutionalists, p. 118

decriminalized status offenses, p. 123

deinstitutionalization of status offenders, p. 122

deinstitutionalization of status offenders (DSO), p. 122

detention hearing, p. 129

disposition hearing, p. 134

ex parte Crouse, p. 130

guardian *ad litem,* p. 127

In re Barbara Burrus, p. 121

In re Gault, p. 119

In re Terry, p. 121

In re Winship, p. 120

intake process, p. 131

Juvenile Justice and Delinquency Prevention (JJDP) Act, p. 122

Kent v. United States, p. 118

McKeiver v. Pennsylvania, p. 121

Missouri Plan, p. 126

National Council of Juvenile and Family Court Judges, p. 126

plea bargain, p. 133

preventive detention, p. 129

probation officers, p. 128

REVIEW QUESTIONS

1. What is an adjudicatory hearing and what procedures does it follow?
2. What is a disposition hearing and the role of the disposition report in that hearing?
3. What range of dispositions is available to judges in the disposition hearings?
4. What are the basic arguments in favor of and in opposition to the retention of the juvenile court?
5. How did the juvenile court get to where it is today?

6. What is preventive detention? What is your evaluation of this movement in juvenile justice?
7. What role does plea bargaining play in juvenile court proceedings? What is your evaluation of plea bargaining?
8. Do you think the juvenile court should be changed? Why? How?
9. Which of the methods for appointing judges is the best? Why?

GROUP EXERCISES

1. *Writing to Learn Exercise:* Write two or three paragraphs on the nature of adjudicatory hearings today, including the reasons for the way hearings are set up and the nature of predisposition reports. Critique and revise.
2. *Group Work:* Drawing on your personal experience as a youth, "think through" the characteristics of different types of juveniles who might come into the juvenile court. Then, discuss the judicial alternatives group members would recommend to judges for the juveniles who have engaged in different types of misbehavior.
3. *Writing to Learn Exercise:* Write two paragraphs, one on "Geraghty believes that adult courts are not appropriate places to try juveniles" and another on "how Geraghty believes the juvenile court could guarantee justice for juveniles." Critique and revise.
4. *Group Work:* Spell out in detail the assumptions and procedures of the original juvenile court. Then, each group must go

through the cases highlighted in the chapter to develop the due process requirements asked for in the various court decisions.
5. *Writing to Learn Exercise:* Either after completing Exercise 4 or in place of it, have each student identify the court cases most relevant to the juvenile court and write up the due process requirements for juveniles involved in each type of circumstance.
6. *Writing to Learn Exercise:* Write one or two paragraphs identifying and describing the roles of different juvenile court personnel. Critique and revise.
7. *Group Work:* Discuss the pretrial procedures of the juvenile court, including the general process, detention hearings, bail for juveniles, and preventive detention, and the different legal issues found in each.
8. *Group Work:* Discuss the intake process and the different outcomes possible for juveniles processed through the intake process.

NOTES

1. Quoted in Julian W. Mack, "The Juvenile Court," in *Readings in Juvenile Justice Administration,* edited by Barry C. Feld (New York: Oxford University Press, 1999), 15–16.
2. G. Larry Mays, "Transferring Juveniles to Adult Courts: Legal Guidelines and Constraints," paper presented at the annual meeting of the American Society of Criminology, Reno, NV, November 1989, 1.
3. *Commonwealth v. Fisher,* 213 P. 48, 62 A, 198 (1905).
4. Leonard P. Edwards, "The Juvenile Court and the Role of the Juvenile Court Judge," *National Council of Juvenile and Family Court Judges* 43 (1992), 4.
5. Barry Krisberg, *The Juvenile Court: Reclaiming the Vision* (San Francisco: National Council on Crime and Delinquency, 1988); Arnold Binder, "The Juvenile Court: The U.S. Constitution, and When the Twain Shall Meet," *Journal of Criminal Justice* 12 (1982), 355–66; Charles E. Springer, *Justice for Children* (Washington, DC: U.S. Department of Justice, 1986).
6. Barry C. Feld, "The Transformation of the Juvenile Court," *Minnesota Law Review* 75 (February 1991), 711; Barry C. Feld, "The Juvenile Court Meets the Principle of the Offense: Legislative Changes in Juvenile Waiver Statutes," *Journal*

of Criminal Law and Criminology 78 (1987), 571–73; Barry C. Feld, "*In re Gault* Revisited: The Right to Counsel in the Juvenile Court," paper presented at the annual meeting of the American Society of Criminology, Montreal, November 1988.
7. Thomas F. Geraghty and Steven A. Drizin, "The Debate over the Future of Juvenile Courts: Can We Reach Consensus," *Journal of Criminal Law and Criminology* 88 (1998), 2–3.
8. Ellen Ryerson, *The Best Laid Plans: America's Juvenile Court Experiment* (New York: Hill and Wang, 1978), 574–75.
9. *Kent v. United States,* 383 U.S. 541, 86 S. Ct. 1045, 16 L. Ed. 2d 84 (1966).
10. Ibid.
11. Ibid.
12. *In re Gault,* 387 U.S. 1, 18 L. Ed. 527, 87 S. Ct. 1428 (1967).
13. Ibid.
14. *Haley v. Ohio,* 332 U.S. 596 (1948); *Gallegos v. Colorado,* 370 U.S. 49, 82 S. Ct. 1209 (1962); *Kent v. United States.*
15. Noah Weinstein, *Supreme Court Decisions and Juvenile Justice* (Reno, NV: National Council of Juvenile Court Judges, 1973).

16. *In re Winship,* 397 U.S. 358, 90 S. Ct. 1968, 25 L. Ed. 2d 368 (1970).

17. *McKeiver v. Pennsylvania,* 403 U.S. 528, 535 (1971). *In re Barbara Burrus,* 275 N.C. 517, 169 S.E. 2d 879 (1969).

18. Ibid.

19. *Breed v. Jones,* 421 U.S. 519, 95 S. Ct. 1779 (1975).

20. U.S. Congress, Senate Committee on the Judiciary, Subcommittee to Investigate Juvenile Delinquency, 1973, *The Juvenile Justice and Delinquency Prevention Act,* S.3148 and S.821. 92d Cong. 2d sess.; 93d Cong. 1st sess.

21. National Council on Juvenile Justice, *National Juvenile Court Case Records 1975–1992* (Pittsburgh, PA.: National Center for Juvenile Justice, 1994).

22. Federal Advisory Committee on Juvenile Justice, *Annual Report 2008* (Washington, DC: Office of Juvenile Justice and Delinquency Prevention, 2008), 1.

23. Ibid., 2.

24. Thomas, "Are Status Offenders Really So Different?" 440–42.

25. Martin Rouse, "The Diversion of Status Offenders, Criminalization, and the New York Family Court," paper presented at the annual meeting of the American Society of Criminology, Reno, NV, November 1989, 1, 2, 10–11.

26. Thomas, "Are Status Offenders Really So Different?" 179.

27. New York State Office of Children and Family Services, *PINS Reform Legislation,* accessed May 3, 2012, at http://www.olcfs.state.ny.us/main/legal/legislation/pins.

28. Bary Feld, *Bad Kids: Race and the Transformation of the Juvenile Court* (New York: Oxford University Press, 1999), 178.

29. Ibid.

30. Federal Advisory Committee on Juvenile Justice, *Federal Advisory Committee on Juvenile Justice: Annual Report 2010* (Washington, DC: U.S. Department of Justice, 2010), 3.

31. T. P. Thornberry, "Co-Occurrence of Problem Behavior Among Adolescents," paper presented at Multi-System Approaches in Child Welfare and Juvenile Justice Wingspread Conference, Milwaukee, WI, May 7–9, 2008.

32. National Resource Center for Family Centered Practice, *Minority Youth and Families Initiative (MYFI)* (Baltimore, MD: Annie E. Casey Foundation, 2005).

33. Federal Advisory Committee on Juvenile Justice, *Federal Advisory Committee on Juvenile Justice,* 5.

34. For a more expansive examination of juvenile court personnel, especially the juvenile court judge, see Ted. H. Rubin, *Behind the Black Robes: Juvenile Court Judges and the Court* (Beverly Hills, CA: Sage Publications, 1985); Ted H. Rubin, "The Juvenile Court Landscape," in *Juvenile Justice: Policies, Programs, and Services,* edited by Albert R. Roberts (Chicago: Dorsey Press, 1989); and Edwards, "The Juvenile Court and the Role of the Juvenile Court Judge."

35. Edwards, "The Juvenile Court and the Role of the Juvenile Court Judge," 25.

36. Ibid., 25–28.

37. Larry J. Siegel and Joseph J. Senna, *Juvenile Delinquency: Theory, Practice, and Law,* 7th ed. (Belmont, CA: Wadsworth, 2000), 559.

38. See Stephanie Chen, "Pennsylvania Rocked by 'Jailing Kids for Cash' Scandal," accessed at http://eee.cnn.com/2009/CRIME/02/23/PennsylvaniaCorruptJudges.

39. See Floyd Feeney, "Defense Counsel for Delinquents: Does Quality Matter?" paper presented at the annual meeting of the American Society of Criminology, Montreal, November 1987.

40. Barry C. Feld, "Criminalizing Juvenile Justice: Rules of Procedure for Juvenile Court," *Minnesota Law Review* 69 (1984), 191, 199.

41. Ted H. Rubin, *Juvenile Justice: Policy, Practice, and the Law* (Santa Monica, CA: Goodyear, 1979), 194.

42. See Charles Thomas and Ineke Marshall, "The Effect of Legal Representation on Juvenile Court Disposition," paper presented at the annual meeting of the Southern Sociological Society, Louisville, KY, 1981; and S. H. Clarke and G. G. Koch, "Juvenile Court: Therapy or Crime Control and Do Lawyers Make a Difference?" *Law and Society Review* 14 (1980), 263–308.

43. Ibid.

44. Joseph B. Sanborn, Jr., "Remnants of *Parens Patriae* in the Adjudication Hearing—Is a Fair Trial Possible in Juvenile Court?" *Crime and Delinquency* 40, no. 4 (1994), 599–615.

45. Siegel and Senna, *Juvenile Delinquency,* 561.

46. For other examinations of the prosecutor's role in the juvenile court, see John H. Laub and Bruce K. MacMurray, "Increasing the Prosecutor's Role in Juvenile Court: Expectation and Realities," *Justice System Journal* 12 (1987), 196–209; and Charles W. Thomas and Shay Bilchik, "Prosecuting Juveniles in Criminal Courts: Legal and Empirical Analysis," *Journal of Criminal Law and Criminology* 76 (1985), 438–79.

47. Lori L. Colley, Robert C. Culbertson, and Edward J. Latessa, "Juvenile Probation Officers: A Job Analysis," *Juvenile and Family Court Journal* 38 (1987), 1–12.

48. Ann Strong, *Case Classification Manual, Module One: Technical Aspects of Interviewing* (Austin: Texas Adult Probation Commission, 1981).

49. Charles Puzzanchera and Melissa Sickmund, *Juvenile Court Statistics 2005* (Pittsburgh, PA: National Center for Juvenile Justice, 2008), 31.

50. Brenda R. McCarthy, "An Analysis of Detention," *Juvenile and Family Court Journal* 36 (1985), 49–50. For other discussions of detention, see Lydia Rosner, "Juvenile Secure Detention," *Journal of Offender Counseling, Services, and Rehabilitation* 12 (1988), 77–93; and Charles E. Frazier and Donna M. Bishop, "The Pretrial Detention of Juveniles and Its Impact on Case Dispositions," *Journal of Criminal Law and Criminology* 76 (1985), 1132–52.

51. Charles P. Smith, T. Edwin Black, and Fred R. Campbell, *A National Assessment of Case Disposition and Classification in the Juvenile Justice System: Inconsistent Labeling,* Vol. III, Reports of the National Juvenile Justice Assessment Centers (Washington, DC: U.S. Government Printing Office, April 1980), 97.

52. For a discussion of the use of bail for juveniles in Massachusetts, see Alida V. Merlo and William D. Bennett, "Criteria for

Juvenile Detention: Who Gets Detained?" paper presented at the annual meeting of the American Society of Criminology, Reno, NV, November 1989.

53. *Schall v. Martin* (1984), *United States Law Review* 52 (47), 4681–96.

54. Ibid., 4681.

55. Ibid.

56. Feld, "Criminalizing Juvenile Justice," 191, 199. See also Deborah A. Lee, "The Constitutionality of Juvenile Preventive Detention: *Schall v. Martin:* Who Is Preventive Detention Protecting?" *New England Law Review* 38 (1987), 13–19.

57. See the section on intake in Patrick Griffin and Patricia Torget, *Desktop Guide to Good Juvenile Probation Practice* (Washington, DC: National Center for Juvenile Justice, 2002), 41–48.

58. Duran Bell, Jr., and Kevin Lang, "The Intake Dispositions of Juvenile Offenders," *Journal of Research of Crime and Delinquency* 2, no. 4 (1985), 309–28. See also Randall G. Sheldon and John A. Horvath, "Intake Processing in a Juvenile Court: A Comparison of Legal and Nonlegal Variables," *Juvenile and Family Court Journal* 38 (1987), 13–19.

59. Samuel M. Davis, *Rights of Juveniles: The Juvenile Justice System* (New York: Clark Boardman, 1984). Reprinted with Permission of West, a Thompson Business (St. Paul, MN: Updated March 2003), 4–26, 4–27. See also Barry C. Feld, "The Transformation of the Juvenile Court"; and Feld, "The Juvenile Court Meets the Principle of the Offense."

60. Conversation with this officer in 1990.

61. For an excellent discussion of the "criminalization" of the juvenile court, see Feld, "Criminalizing Juvenile Justice," 141–276.

62. Joyce Dougherty, "Negotiating Justice in the Juvenile Justice System: A Comparison of Adult Plea Bargaining and Juvenile Intake," *Federal Probation* 52 (1988), 72–80.

63. Kathleen Maguire and Ann L. Pastore, *Bureau of Justice Statistics: Sourcebook of Criminal Justice Statistics—1994* (Washington, DC: U.S. Government Printing Office, 1995).

64. Patrick Griffin and Patricia Torbet, eds., *Desktop to Good Juvenile Probation Practice: Mission-Driven, Performance-Based, and Outcome-Focused* (Pittsburgh, PA: National Center for Juvenile Justice, 2002), 64.

65. Ibid.

66. Ibid., 63–71.

67. Terence P. Thornberry, "Sentencing Disparities in the Juvenile Justice System," *Journal of Criminal Law and Criminology* 70 (Summer 1979), 164–71; M. A. Bortner, *Inside a Juvenile Court: The Tarnished Idea of Individualized Justice* (New York: New York University Press, 1982); Lawrence Cohen, "Delinquency Dispositions: An Empirical Analysis of Processing Decisions in Three Juvenile Courts," *Analytic Report* 9 (Washington, DC: U.S. Government Printing Office, 1975), 51.

68. Bortner, *Inside a Juvenile Court.*

69. Ruth D. Peterson, "Youthful Offender Designations and Sentencing in the New York Criminal Courts," *Social Problems* 35 (April 1988), 125–26.

70. Ibid.

71. Ibid., See *Morrissey v. Brewer,* 408 U.S. 471 (1972) and *Gagnon v. Scarpelli,* 411 U.S. 778 (1973).

72. Martin L. Forst, Bruce A. Fisher, and Robert B. Coates, "Indeterminate and Determinate Sentencing of Juvenile Delinquents: A National Survey of Approaches to Commitment and Release Decision-Making," *Juvenile and Family Court Journal* 36 (Summer 1985), 1.

73. Daniel P. Mears and Samuel H. Field, "Theorizing Sanctioning in a Criminalized Juvenile Court," *Criminology* 38 (November 2000), 985–86.

74. Ibid., 983.

75. Barry C. Feld, "Violent Youth and Public Policy: Minnesota Juvenile Justice Task Force and 1994 Legislative Reform," paper presented at the annual meeting of the American Society of Criminology, Miami, FL, 1994, 4. See also Feld, "Violent Youth and Public Policy: A Case Study of Juvenile Justice Law Reform," *Minnesota Law Review* 79 (May 1995), 965–1128. Blended sentences are discussed in greater detail in the next chapter.

76. National Council of Juvenile and Family Court Judges, *Juvenile Delinquency Guidelines: Improving Court Practice in Juvenile Delinquency Cases* (Reno, NV: Summer 1995), 37.

77. Ibid., 16.

78. Ibid.

7   Juveniles in Adult Court

Zbigniew Bzdak/MCT/Newscom

Learning Objectives

1. Explain the differences in maturity between juveniles and adults.
2. Explain how transfers to adult court take place as well as the different types of waivers.
3. Summarize blended sentencing and the different blended sentencing models.
4. Describe what an intermediate correctional system for juveniles would be like.
5. Discuss the death penalty for juveniles.
6. Summarize the debate about juveniles receiving a sentence of life without parole.

The body of Shirley Crook was found bound with electric cable and leather straps in the Meramec River in St. Louis County, Missouri, in 1993. Her head was wrapped in duct tape, her ribs were cracked and she had bruises on her body. The offender had thrown her, still alive, off a bridge and she drowned.

Christopher Simmons, aged seventeen, was arrested the next day at school and charged with the crime. He was interrogated for three hours without a parent or lawyer present and eventually confessed to the murder. Prior to the crime, Simmons had no previous criminal record.

On June 16, 1994, Christopher Simmons was convicted and sentenced to be executed for the crime.

Mr. Simmons is the product of a dysfunctional family with intergenerational psychiatric disorders and is himself predisposed to mental illness. As a child, he was the victim of severe physical and psychological abuse by his alcoholic stepfather. For example, his stepfather took him to a bar at the age of four and got him drunk to entertain the bar's patrons; his stepfather beat him severely. Mr. Simmons continued to use drugs such as LSD, marijuana, and alcohol as an adolescent and was encouraged to commit crimes by a neighbor. He viewed himself as a helpless victim unable to change. Mr. Simmons exhibited low self-esteem, impulsivity, loneliness, hopelessness, and depression.

On August 26, 2003, the Missouri Supreme Court held that to execute Simmons would violate the Eighth Amendment to the Constitution of the United States and vacated the execution of Mr. Simmons. That decision was appealed to the U.S. Supreme Court and was heard on October 13, 2004.

On March 1, 2005, the U.S. Supreme Court Ruled That the Execution of Juveniles Under the Age of Eighteen was Unconstitutional.[1]

The mission of the juvenile court, as previously discussed, is debated hotly today. Proponents contend that its original mission was to deal with all juvenile crime, from minor misbehaviors to assault, robbery, and murder. The rise in violent youth crime during the past decades, however, has increased the public's fear of juvenile crime. In addition, the emergence of a "hard line" since the late 1970s has increased the willingness of others to question the juvenile court's original mission. The result of this get-tough policy is that numerous proposals are being made that increase the chances that juvenile lawbreakers, even very young ones, will be punished with the same severity as are their adult counterparts.

This chapter examines some of the issues involved in ensuring justice for both juveniles and society. Beginning with the issue of immaturity and responsibility, this chapter considers the transfer to adult court, the 2005 *Roper v. Simmons* case that led to the abolishment of the juvenile death penalty, the sentence of a juvenile to a youthful offender system or to an adult prison, and a proposed adult court for juveniles.

Children or Adults?

As noted in Chapter 1, in terms of wrongdoing, the elusive concept of responsibility has its roots in the notions that individuals know right from wrong, have developed a social conscience, feel guilty or remorseful over their actions, are mentally sharp enough to know the rules, do not have any disease that reduces their ability to get along in society, fully understand that their actions are harming others, and are emotionally mature.

None of these criteria is measurable; but, for over a century, the assumption of the juvenile court has been that juveniles are deficient in one or more of them. Proponents of the juvenile court also assume that the court should have jurisdiction over the youths until their deficiencies are corrected and until they have developed the mental and emotional maturity of adults. What fuels the controversy over waiver to adult court is the disagreement over when youths reach this stage.

"Maturity" is a psychological term that is used to indicate when a person responds to the circumstances and environment in an appropriate manner. The fact is that this response is typically learned rather than instinctive and is determined by one's age. Maturity is involved with being aware of the correct time and place to behave and with knowing when to act appropriately, according to the situation and the culture in which a person lives.

In examining the extent to which young people should be held responsible for their criminal activity, Steven J. Morse contends that a "robust" theory of responsibility would result in most youths (in middle to late adolescence) being held responsible for their actions. He claims that there is empirical research to substantiate the position that it is often difficult to distinguish between the moral responsibility of children and young adults. Thus, he reasons, the responsibility of a juvenile should be no less than that of a similarly situated young adult. He does not believe that juveniles' susceptibility to peer pressure justifies differential allocation of responsibility.[2]

Elizabeth Scott and Thomas Grisso, in evaluating the differences between adults and youths, conclude that substantial differences exist between very young juveniles and adults in "moral, cognitive, and social development."[3] Scott and Grisso's developmental evidence does "support the argument of the post-Gault reformers of the 1970s and 1980s that a presumptive diminished responsibility standard be applied to juveniles."[4] They believe that this presumptive diminished responsibility is best applied in juvenile court systems, and they question whether the criminal justice system is able to respond to this developmental reality: "The ability or inclination of the criminal justice system to tailor its response to juvenile crime so as to utilize the lessons of developmental psychology is questionable. The evidence suggests that political pressure functions as a one-way ratchet, in the direction of ever stiffer penalties."[5]

They further question the assumption, proposed by Morse and others, that most juvenile offenders, even those in mid-adolescence, are as cognitively competent as adults are in decision-making capacity. They claim that the cognitive decision-making abilities of adolescents and adults are similar only when nondelinquent juveniles from middle-class backgrounds of above-average intelligence are compared with adults. But when children involved in the justice system, many of whom have emotional problems and learning disabilities that hinder their capacity for understanding, are compared with adults, there is real reason to question the cognitive competence of these youths.[6]

Thomas Grisso and colleagues reported that the abilities associated with competence were assessed among 927 adolescents in juvenile detention facilities and community settings. Adolescents' abilities were compared to those of 466 young adults who were in jails and in the community. Participants compared two standardized measures of abilities relevant for competence to stand trial. They found that youths ages 15 and younger performed more poorly than did young adults, with a greater proportion manifesting a level of impairment consistent with those found incompetent to stand trial. In addition, juveniles tended more often than adults to make choices in terms of plea bargaining that reflected compliance with authority and also psychological immaturity. See Table 7–1.

The fact of the matter is that some youths do commit brutal crimes, and the viciousness of their acts causes one to question the justice of their remaining in the juvenile system. Indeed, the media testify nearly daily to violent youth crime as they describe senseless killings and rapes committed by juveniles. Violent youth crime has contributed to the perception that something is seriously wrong with our society. Those who have been victims of youthful thugs feel especially vulnerable and call for stronger measures to deal with youthful predators.

Examples of savage attacks include the following: On September 24, 2009, four members of a teen gang brutally murdered Derrion Albert, an honor roll student and a bystander to gang violence in Chicago. Videotapes of the beating of Albert with two-by-fours were shown across the nation and shocked the conscience of the city of Chicago.[7] In 2011, two young men, one a seventeen-year-old, assaulted a homeless man and videos of the attacks were posted on *YouTube*. The victim is seen on tape being tackled, punched, pushed, kicked, kneed, and mocked by his assailants.[8]

▲ The formal setting of the adult court differs dramatically from the informal setting of the juvenile court and may be intimidating and scary to juveniles.

David R. Frazier Photolibrary, Inc./Alamy

TABLE 7–1
Arguments for and Against Juveniles' Diminished Responsibility

Juveniles are responsible, especially those in mid-adolescence, because
They know right from wrong.

They have developed a social conscience.

They feel guilt or remorse over their actions.

They are mentally sharp enough to know the rules.

They do not have any disease reducing their ability to get along in society.

They fully understand their actions when they harm others.

They are emotionally mature.

Juveniles lack adult maturation because
They are substantially different from adults in moral, cognitive, and social development.

They are particularly different in cognitive decision making from adults when they have low average intelligence.

They are different from adults when they have learning disabilities.

They also may not understand the language of a *Miranda* warning well enough to make a valid waiver.

They often make choices in terms of plea bargaining that reflect compliance with authority as well as psychological immaturity.

How Does Transfer to Adult Court Take Place?

Because of concern over violent juvenile offenders and the threat they pose to the community, state legislatures have passed laws permitting juveniles to be transferred or waived to adult court, where they can be tried and punished as adults. Waiver is a very serious issue because it means that a minor child can be sent to an adult prison institution where they will interact with and be influenced by experienced criminals. See Focus on Offenders 7–1 for the relationship between juvenile behavior and a life of crime.

Today, all state legislatures have passed laws permitting juveniles to be transferred to adult court. More than two hundred thousand youths are prosecuted in the adult criminal justice system each year and ten thousand children are held in adult jails and prisons.[9] Juveniles transferred to adult court are the least known group of juvenile offenders, but beginning in 2010, the Bureau of Justice Statistics funded Westat Inc. to conduct a survey of juveniles charged in adult criminal court. It is anticipated that this survey will reveal a valid estimate of how many juveniles are moved into adult courts in the United States, the demographics of these youths, the charges for which they are arraigned, and perhaps what happens after the decision is made to move a juvenile into an adult system. The results were scheduled to be published in late 2012.[10]

What is currently known is that transfer is believed to be taking place less frequently than in the early to mid-1990s. For example, in 2002, courts had fewer judicial waivers of juveniles to adult court than in 1985, and 2001 had the fewest judicial waivers of juveniles to adult court of any year since 1985.[11] In 2007, juvenile courts are estimated to have waived jurisdiction in about 8,500 cases.[12] States vary widely in the criteria they use in making the waiver decision. For example, some states focus on the age of the offender, and others consider both age and offense. For example, some states such as Kansas, Vermont (age ten), Georgia, Illinois, and Mississippi[13] (age thirteen) and others transfer children at very young ages. More states transfer juveniles at fourteen than at any other age; seven states transfer juveniles at either fifteen or sixteen years of age.

The offenses juveniles commit are also important in the waiver decision. Some states permit waiver for any criminal offense, whereas others waive only those offenses specifically mentioned in the state's statutes. Many states permit waiver to the adult court if the juvenile

---

Focus on Offenders 7–1
The Youthful Offender and a Future Life of Crime

One of the areas that has received vast examination is the relationship between juvenile behavior and adult crime. The following findings receive support:

- Adolescent gang involvement contributes to a likelihood of involvement in street crime and arrests in adulthood.
- Some evidence exists that delinquents who become adult offenders are somewhat more likely than other delinquents to have had more seriously offensive delinquent careers.
- The cumulative disadvantages of some delinquents (individual and parental deficits) make gang use, drug involvement, and gang involvement more attractive, leading to dropping out of school and unemployment into their adults years. In turn, these antisocial behaviors continue from childhood delinquency into adult crime.
- Childhood victimization with females, especially sexual victimization, can contribute to adult involvement with drugs and prostitution.

- Being institutionalized as a juvenile seriously compromises adult adjustment, especially for juveniles.
- Some studies have found a relationship among such factors as poor parental supervision, parental rejection, parental criminality, and delinquent siblings and late adult criminality.

CRITICAL THINKING QUESTION:

How will these findings impact the field of juvenile justice?

Source: Marvin D. Krohn, Jeffrey T. Ward, Terence P. Thornberry, Alan J. Lizotte, and Rebekah Chu, "The Cascading Effects of Adolescent Gang Involvement Across the Life Course," *Criminology* 49 (November 2011), 991–1025; Nadine Lanctot, Stephen A. Cernkovich, and Peggy C. Giordano, "Delinquent Behavior, Official Delinquency, and Gender: Consequences for Adult Functioning and Well-Being," *Criminology* 45 (2007), 191–222; and Brian Francis, Keith Soohill, and Alex R. Piquerro, "Estimation Issues and Generational Changes in Modeling Criminal Career Length, *Crime and Delinquency* 53 (January 2007), 3–37.

---

previously has been adjudicated delinquent or has a prior criminal conviction. Depending on the state, three major mechanisms are used to waive juveniles: judicial waiver, prosecutorial discretion, and statutorial exclusion. Table 7–2 reveals that most states have access to multiple ways of imposing adult sanctions on offenders of juvenile age.

Judicial Waiver

Except where state laws mandate that a youth be tried in adult court, someone has to make the decision to waive a youth. **Judicial waiver**, the most widely used transfer mechanism, involves the actual decision-making process that begins when the juvenile is brought to intake. Predictably, the mechanisms used vary by state. For every one thousand petitioned delinquency cases, about nine are judicially waived to criminal court.[14] In some states, intake personnel, juvenile prosecutors, or judges make the decision based, in part, on the age or offense criteria. In other states, a court other than the juvenile court makes the decision. For example, the prosecutor or judge in the adult court may decide where a juvenile is to be tried.[15] The decision is determined by the requirements of the state and the way the intake officer, prosecutor, or judge interprets the youth's background. Typically, the criteria used include the age and maturity of the child; the child's relationship with parents, school, and community; whether the child is considered dangerous; and whether court officials believe that the child may be helped by juvenile court services. Table 7–3 lists states that exclude certain serious offenses from juvenile court.

Prosecutorial Discretion

Prosecutorial discretion occurs in states with **concurrent jurisdiction** statutes. These laws give prosecutors the authority to decide whether to try juveniles in either juvenile or adult court.

Statutorial Exclusion

Some states have a **statutorial exclusion** of certain offenses from juvenile court, thereby automatically transferring perpetrators of those offenses to adult court.

Other variations on waiver also exist, some very subtle. One such variation is a state legislature lowering the age over which the juvenile court has jurisdiction. For example, if a state's

TABLE 7–2
Most States Have Multiple Ways to Impose Adult Sanctions on Juveniles

State	Judicial waiver Discretionary	Judicial waiver Presumptive	Judicial waiver Mandatory	Prosecutorial discretion	Statutory exclusion	Reverse waiver	Once an adult always an adult	Blended sentencing Juvenile	Blended sentencing Criminal
Number of states	45	15	15	15	29	24	34	14	18
Alabama	■				■		■		
Alaska	■	■			■			■	
Arizona	■			■	■	■	■		
Arkansas	■			■	■	■		■	■
California	■	■		■	■	■	■	■	■
Colorado	■	■		■	■	■	■	■	■
Connecticut			■			■		■	
Delaware	■		■		■	■	■		
Dist. of Columbia	■	■		■			■		
Florida	■			■	■		■		■
Georgia	■		■	■	■	■	■		
Hawaii	■						■		
Idaho	■				■		■		■
Illinois	■	■	■		■		■	■	■
Indiana	■		■		■		■		
Iowa	■				■	■	■		
Kansas	■	■					■	■	
Kentucky	■		■		■	■			■
Louisiana	■		■	■	■		■		
Maine	■	■					■		
Maryland	■					■	■		
Massachusetts								■	■
Michigan	■			■			■	■	■
Minnesota	■	■			■		■	■	
Mississippi	■				■	■	■		
Missouri	■						■		
Montana				■	■	■		■	
Nebraska				■		■			■
Nevada	■	■			■	■	■		
New Hampshire	■	■					■		
New Jersey	■	■	■						
New Mexico					■			■	■
New York					■	■			
North Carolina	■		■				■		
North Dakota	■	■	■		■		■		
Ohio	■		■				■	■	
Oklahoma	■			■	■	■	■		■
Oregon	■				■	■	■		
Pennsylvania	■	■			■	■	■		
Rhode Island	■	■	■				■	■	
South Carolina	■		■		■		■		
South Dakota	■				■	■	■		
Tennessee	■				■	■	■		
Texas	■						■	■	
Utah	■	■			■		■		
Vermont	■			■	■	■			■
Virginia	■		■	■		■	■		■
Washington	■				■		■		■
West Virginia	■		■						■
Wisconsin	■				■	■	■		■
Wyoming	■			■		■			

Note: Table information is as of the end of the 2009 legislative session.

Source: Patrick Griffin, Sean Addie, Benjamin Adams, and Kathy Finestine, *Trying Juveniles as Adults: An Analysis of State Transfer Laws and Reporting* (Washington, DC: Juvenile Offenders and Victims, National Report Series Bulletin, September 2011), 3.

TABLE 7–3
Many States Exclude Certain Serious Offenses from Juvenile Court Jurisdiction

State	Any criminal offense	Certain felonies	Capital crimes	Murder	Certain person offenses	Certain property offenses	Certain drug offenses	Certain weapon offenses
Alabama		16	16				16	
Alaska					16	16		
Arizona		15		15	15			
California				14	14			
Delaware		15						
Florida				16	NS	16	16	
Georgia				13	13			
Idaho				14	14	14	14	
Illinois		15		13	15			15
Indiana		16					16	16
Iowa		16					16	16
Louisiana				15	15			
Maryland			14	16	16			16
Massachusetts				14				
Minnesota				16				
Mississippi		13	13					
Montana				17	17	17	17	17
Nevada	16*	NS		NS	16			
New Mexico				15				
New York				13	13	14		14
Oklahoma				13				
Oregon				15	15			
Pennsylvania				NS	15			
South Carolina		16						
South Dakota		16						
Utah		16		16				
Vermont				14	14	14		
Washington				16	16	16		
Wisconsin				10	10			

*In Nevada, the exclusion applies to any juvenile with a previous felony adjudication, regardless of the current offense charged, if the current offense involves the use or threatened use of a firearm.

Note: An entry in the column below an offense category means that there is at least one offense in that category that is excluded from juvenile court jurisdiction. The number indicates the youngest possible age at which a juvenile accused of an offense in that category is subject to exclusion. "NS" means no age restriction is specified for an offense in that category. Table information is as of the end of the 2009 legislative session.

Source: Patrick Griffin, Sean Addie, Benjamin Adams, and Kathy Finestine, *Trying Juveniles as Adults: An Analysis of State Transfer Laws and Reporting* (Washington, DC: Juvenile Offenders and Victims, National Report Series Bulletin, September 2011), 6.

age of juvenile court jurisdiction is eighteen, the legislature may lower the age to sixteen. This approach focuses entirely on the age of the juvenile and ignores the offenses committed.

Yet other state legislatures have specified that juveniles of specific ages who commit specific crimes are to be tried in adult court. For example, until recently, Indiana statutes stated that any child age ten or older who committed murder would be tried as an adult. This method of legislative waiver focuses as much on the offense as it does on the age of the offender.

Another method of waiver is one in which the statutes simply state that anyone who commits a specific crime may be tried in adult court. No reference is made to the age of the offender. This approach is attractive to those who believe that any youth who violates the law should receive an appropriate punishment.

Reverse Waiver and Blended Sentencing

In *reverse waiver*, some state laws permit youths who are over the maximum age of jurisdiction to be sent back to the juvenile court if the adult court believes the case is more appropriate for juvenile court jurisdiction. For a reverse waiver, defense counsel and prosecutors attempt to make their case for their desired action. Some evidence and testimony are allowed, and arguments are presented. When each side has had a chance to present its case and to rebut the opponents' arguments, the judge makes the decision.[16]

A *blended sentence* is a sentence imposed by a juvenile court that blends a juvenile disposition and an adult sentence for certain serious youthful offenders. Some states permit juvenile court judges at the disposition hearing in the delinquency court to impose both an adult and a juvenile sentence concurrently. This option may be given to juveniles who have received a direct file, mandatory or a prosecutorial waiver, to the adult court. In these cases, the juvenile is given both sentences but is first given the juvenile disposition. If the juvenile fulfills the requirements of this disposition satisfactorily, the adult disposition is suspended. If the juvenile does not fulfill the conditions of the juvenile disposition, the juvenile is then required to fulfill the conditions of the adult disposition. Connecticut, Kentucky, and Minnesota are among the states adopting this sentencing authority.

In some states, the juvenile may be required to fulfill the juvenile disposition until he or she reaches the age of majority; at this point, the juvenile must begin to fulfill the adult sentence minus the time already spent fulfilling the juvenile disposition. In Texas, the juvenile court may impose a juvenile sanction that extends beyond the extended age of juvenile court jurisdiction, at which time the transfer of the youthful offender to an adult correctional facility is required. Under this form of expanded sentencing authority, the juvenile court judge or jury can impose a sentence of up to 30 years, depending on the seriousness of the offense. Legislation in 1995 added several offenses for which a juvenile may receive a determinate, fixed term of 40 years.[17] See Figure 7–1 for the types of blended sentencing:

Another common way for the adult criminal court to levy juvenile sanctions is through the creation of youthful offender programs. Otherwise known as "intermediate" or "third systems," these systems provide a mechanism that allows states to impose strict, adult sanctions on juveniles or young adults convicted of violent offenses, while maintaining a rehabilitation focus.

Since Colorado enacted the first program of this type, at least eleven other states have followed suit. These youthful offender–type programs are viewed in these states as giving juveniles one last chance before being they are sent to an adult facility.[18] See the discussion later in this chapter on these youthful offender camps.

Changing Criteria for Waiver

In the past, youths were waived to adult court without hearings, without sufficient fact finding on the part of the court, without reasons being given for the waiver, and without the youth having the benefit of an attorney. Critics fought these procedures. Their essential argument was that the decision to waive juveniles to adult court was a serious matter and that youths should be entitled to due process rights. On reviewing two cases in particular, *Kent v. United States* and *Breed v. Jones* (see Chapter 6), the U.S. Supreme Court ruled that traditional juvenile court procedures for waiver were inadequate and that juveniles were guaranteed many of the same due process rights as were adults. Since *Kent* and *Jones*, most states now require that waiver hearings be held before transferring juveniles to adult court. Yet these hearings are not required in all states; some states permit prosecutors to

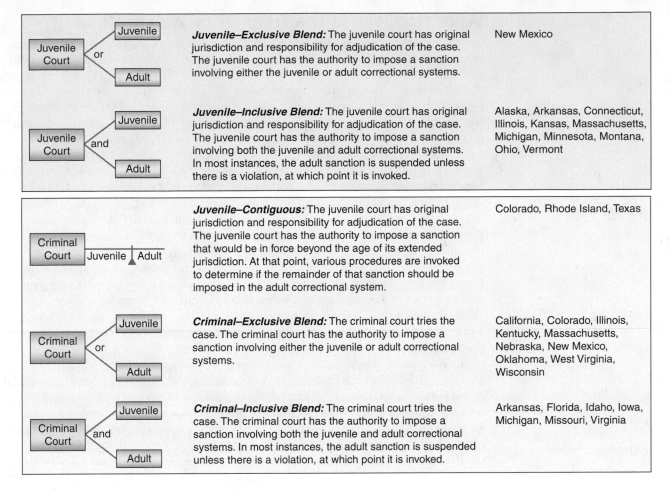

FIGURE 7–1
Types of Blended Sentencing

make the waiver decision. In addition, states that provide for mandatory legislative waiver do not have to hold such hearings.

Where juvenile courts are responsible for making the waiver decision, the Supreme Court stated in *Kent* that they must use the following criteria:

1. The seriousness of the alleged offense to the community and whether the protection of the community requires waiver

2. Whether the alleged offense was committed in an aggressive, violent, premeditated, or willful manner

3. Whether the alleged offense was against persons or against property, greater weight being given to offenses against persons, especially if personal injury resulted

4. The prosecutorial merit of the complaint, that is, whether there is evidence on which a grand jury may be expected to return an indictment

5. The desirability of trial and disposition of the entire offense in one court when the juvenile's associates in the alleged offense are adults who will be charged with a crime in the [criminal court]

6. The sophistication and maturity of the juvenile as determined by consideration of his home, environment, emotional attitude, and pattern of living

7. The record and previous history of the juvenile

8. The prospects for adequate protection of the public and the likelihood of reasonable rehabilitation of the juvenile (if he [or she] is found to have committed the alleged offense) by the use of procedures, services, and facilities currently available to the juvenile court.[19]

What Happens in the Transfer or Waiver Hearing?

Once a prosecutor has decided that a juvenile is beyond the help of the juvenile court and has reviewed the legal sufficiency of the case, the prosecutor files a motion to send the youth to adult court; this motion requires a probable-cause hearing by a juvenile judge. These hearings are required for both a mandatory judicial waiver and a discretionary judicial waiver. The judge begins either hearing by explaining the nature of the hearing and making certain that the youth and his or her parents understand the youth's rights and the consequences of the outcome. All interested parties should be present at this hearing.[20]

In a probable-cause hearing, everything said should be under oath. The prosecutor presents the state's case against the juvenile, affirming the identity of the juvenile and of witnesses and reviewing the affidavit, petition, and jurisdiction requirements—both of the age of the offender and of the geographical region from which the offender comes. The defense attorney then challenges the evidence of the prosecutor and may present witnesses; both the prosecutor and the defense attorney cross-examine the witnesses on the legal facts of the case. Both attorneys then summarize their cases at the conclusion of testimony.[21]

If the judge believes that probable cause has been established, he or she then determines whether the case satisfies the state's legally sufficient requirements for mandatory judicial waiver. If it does, the youth is transferred to criminal court. If probable cause is not established and the prosecutor's motion is denied, the National Council of Juvenile and Family Court Judges recommends the dismissal of the case. Some courts, in practice, refer the youth back to the probation department.[22]

In the judge's review of the case, the youth's dangerousness to self and others, the youth's sophistication and maturity in understanding the nature and consequences of his or her behavior, and the youth's amenability to further treatment are all evaluated. Whether to waive or retain also is based on whether the youth had a history of violent crimes, was a gang member, tested antisocial, had co-offenders, engaged in premeditated offenses, and had experienced trauma in childhood and adolescence. Very important is the availability of alternative treatments, including out-of-state placements. The youth's attorney plays a critical role in helping to evaluate the youth and in presenting alternatives that can benefit the youth. The judge must decide, if the youth is in detention, whether to continue detention or release the youth. The decision the judge finally makes should be based on clear and convincing evidence.[23]

Waiver to Criminal Court

Once the waiver decision is made, the juvenile's case is transferred to the adult court prosecutor. Prosecutors in some states may decide to send the case back to the juvenile court because the case may not meet the standards of legal sufficiency, such as probable cause. The prosecutor may confer with a judge about any legal questions the prosecutor believes the judge might have about the case before making a decision. In some states, the prosecutor takes the case to a grand jury; in other states, the prosecutor sets a date for an arraignment. There, the legal process starts all over again with the same people present, with the result that some juveniles are put on informal or formal probation and others are tried in adult court. The case now usually is tried in front of a jury, and the youth has the potential of receiving the same sentence as an adult.[24]

Evaluation of Waiver

Although waivers are still relatively infrequent and have recently increased slightly in number, they are an important issue in juvenile justice. Significantly, juveniles waived to adult court are not always the most serious and violent offenders. Examinations of waiver have found that little consensus exists today on which criteria should be used in making the waiver decision. Furthermore, although remanded youth are receiving severe penalties, waiver generally does not result in more severe penalties than juvenile offenders would have received in juvenile court. Several states have attempted to develop a process that would identify those juveniles unfit for retention in juvenile court. For example, using such criteria as age, offense, and prior record, Minnesota has codified the transfer procedures to be followed by judges and prosecutors. Given the adult courts' massive caseload and their limited judicial experience with sentencing youths, little evidence exists that adult judges know what to do with juveniles appearing before them. Finally, even when waiver does occur, some evidence exists that waiver may have the effect not of deterring crime by juveniles, but of increasing it.[25] Richard E. Redding summarized the recent Juvenile Justice and Delinquency Prevention Act–funded research on juvenile transfer by saying that transferred juveniles are more likely to offend, that they have a greater likelihood of rearrest, and that the process of transfer is found to increase recidivism.[26]

How Does a Youthful Offender System Work

Juveniles sentenced in adult courts are subject to the same range of dispositions as are adults. Cases may be dismissed or offenders may be found guilty. If found guilty, youths may be released to the care of their parents, placed on probation, fined, ordered to pay restitution, or referred to a social agency qualified to deal with their problem. But a very controversial disposition is the placement of youths in adult correctional facilities.

The crowding, violence, and exploitative relationships found in adult prisons make this disposition extremely questionable. Furthermore, although some states have attempted to develop special institutions for juveniles, even these appear to have the same characteristics as adult prisons. Youths who are placed in them can no better protect themselves than they can in adult facilities. Given the young age of even the most violent of these offenders, society has the task of deciding whether any type of adult institutional placement is appropriate for these youths.

By the year 2000, five states and the District of Columbia held no juveniles in adult prisons under the age of seventeen or younger.[27] Some variations on the practice of confining a juvenile in an adult institution do exist among the states. In some jurisdictions, states have no alternative but to place juveniles in adult institutions if the courts require incarceration. Some states can, under special circumstances, place youths in either juvenile or adult institutions; yet other states can refer juveniles back to juvenile court for their disposition. In some instances, very young juveniles are sent to juvenile facilities but then are transferred to adult institutions when they become of age. Recognizing the dangers and inadequacies of placing juveniles with adults, some jurisdictions have developed special institutions for these younger adult offenders, who are usually sixteen to nineteen years of age.

In a **youthful offender system**, as it has been proposed, programs in these institutions would emphasize work readiness, job training, and work experience. They would also attempt to establish close ties to the community to which the youth would return; employ flexible staff who would act as positive role models; enforce the rules strictly; provide opportunities for decision making, with consequences clearly and fully related to the choices made; provide opportunities to enhance self-esteem; create a continuity of care between the program or treatment sequence and integration into the community to which the youth is returning; and offer supportive services in the community after completion of the program or treatment sequence as long as the youth needs them.[28]

The California Youth Authority has long extended its jurisdiction over youthful offenders to those up to twenty-three years of age. North Carolina was one of the first states to develop youthful offender camps for sixteen- to eighteen-year-old males. In the 1990s, Colorado, New Mexico, and Minnesota also developed transitional, or intermediate, systems between the juvenile and adult systems. The Minnesota Juvenile Justice Task Force recommended the following:

> a more graduated juvenile justice system that establishes a new *transitional component between the juvenile and adult systems*. . . . [T]his new [Serious Youthful Offender] category will create viable new dispositional options for juvenile court judges facing juveniles who have committed serious or repeat offenses. It will give the juvenile *one last chance* at success in the juvenile system, with the threat of adult sanctions as an incentive not to re-offend.[29]

In 1994, the Minnesota legislature adopted the task force's recommendation but relabeled the category "extended jurisdiction juvenile" (EJJ) to make the label less attractive to delinquent "wannabes." For juveniles who are designated as EJJs, final legislation extended the juvenile court's jurisdiction until age twenty-one. The Department of Corrections was also required to license and regulate regional secure treatment facilities for EJJs.[30]

Intermediate sentencing for youthful offenders that bridges the juvenile and adult systems certainly appears to be a positive means for keeping some juveniles out of adult correctional facilities. It is hoped that the 1994 legislation in Minnesota, as well as the youthful offender systems in Colorado and New Mexico, will encourage the development of such legislation in more states.

The current get-tough mood of society does not seem to be one in which the development of youthful offender systems will be viewed as an attractive option to policy makers in many states. Yet, if the juvenile population explosion occurs in the next two decades, as predicted by some experts, and if increasing numbers of juveniles are referred to the adult systems, perhaps there will be greater receptivity toward an intermediate correctional system for youthful offenders.

What Is Life Like for a Juvenile Sent to Prison?

Adult prisons are a world apart from most training schools. Prisons are much larger, sometimes containing several thousand inmates and covering many acres of ground. Life on the inside is generally austere, crowded, and dangerous, and institutionalized juveniles are particularly subject to sexual victimization and sexual assault. Richard E. Redding concluded from his review of the programming that juveniles receive in adult correctional facilities: "Once incarcerated in adult facilities, juveniles typically receive fewer age-appropriate rehabilitative, medical, mental health and educational services, and are at greater risk of physical and sexual abuse and suicide."[31]

In 2009, state prisons held more than 2,700 juveniles. About 46 percent of these inmates were held in prisons in southern states.[32] Table 7–4 reveals that more than half of

TABLE 7–4
State Prisons and Age of Responsibility

State	Inmates*	State	Inmates*	State	Inmates*
U.S. total	2,778	Upper age 17	1,368	Montana	1
		Alabama	118	Nebraska	21
Upper age 15	737	Alaska	7	Nevada	118
Connecticut	332	Arizona	157	New Jersey	21
New York	190	Arkansas	17	New Mexico	3
North Carolina	215	California	0	North Dakota	0
		Colorado	79	Ohio	86
Upper age 16	673	Delaware	28	Oklahoma	19
Georgia	99	Florida	393	Oregon	13
Illinois	106	Hawaii	2	Pennsylvania	61
Louisiana	15	Idaho	0	Rhode Island	1
Massachusetts	8	Indiana	54	South Dakota	1
Michigan	132	Iowa	13	Tennessee	22
Missouri	31	Kansas	5	Utah	6
New Hampshire	0	Kentucky	0	Vermont	4
South Carolina	89	Maine	0	Virginia	16
Texas	156	Maryland	58	Washington	2
Wisconsin	37	Minnesota	13	West Virginia	0
		Mississippi	28	Wyoming	1

*Reported number of inmates younger than age 18 held in custody in state prisons, 2009.

Source: Authors' adaptation of West's Prison Inmates at Midyear 2009—Statistical Tables, *Prison and Jail Inmates at Midyear.*

Source: Patrick Griffin, Sean Addie, Benjamin Adams, and Kathy Finestine, *Trying Juveniles as Adults: An Analysis of State Transfer Laws and Reporting* (Washington, DC: Juvenile Offenders and Victims, National Report Series Bulletin, September 2011).

Focus on Law 7–2
You Will Spend the Remainder of Your Natural Life in Prison

In 1994, four Midwestern teenagers decided to take a Ford Bronco belonging to one of their parents and run away to Canada. The Bronco broke down in a neighboring state, and they realized that they would need to steal another car. They stopped a woman, who thought that the Bronco with lights on top was a police vehicle. One of the teenagers approached the woman and pretended to be a police officer. She demanded to see identification. He returned to the Bronco and instructed one of his companions to take the .22 rifle they had brought along and shoot her. The fifteen-year-old youth, who had committed no more serious acts than vandalism, complied. He shot her once, broke the window of her vehicle on the driver's side when she locked the door, and stabbed her thirty-one times.

The four youths called their parents after they left the crime scene. Later that night, one of their parents arrived and took them home. Within a couple of days, all four were arrested and charged with this crime. Tried in the jurisdiction where the crime was committed, the four juveniles were quickly transferred to the adult court.

During the trial of the youth who had committed the stabbing, his defense attorney attempted to explain the youth's ruthless behavior: The jury was informed that he came from a totally inadequate family background. He had been sexually abused by his natural father at the age of two and had been physically assaulted by an adopted father at the age of fifteen. His mother had been married eight times, and she failed to supply his emotional needs in a number of ways. He also did poorly in school and had failed twice. He had been charged with using marijuana on a couple of occasions but had not been involved in any serious personal or property offenses. He was particularly fearful of the youth who had instructed him to shoot the woman. In summary, the defense attorney claimed that what had taken place that night emerged from the totality of the youth's experiences, frustrations, inadequacies, and unmet needs. The child deserved punishment, the attorney admitted, but not to the extent of spending the rest of his life in prison.

Upon being sentenced to prison for life without parole, the youth admitted that he was fearful of being sexually assaulted. As a small white youth, his fears were not unreasonable. He said that he had made up his mind to be placed in the prison population (with other inmates). He did not want to be locked up twenty-four hours a day for the rest of his life. Whatever it took, he vowed, he would keep the other inmates off him. He was briefly placed in a diagnostic facility. Later, when he was transferred to an adult reformatory, it did not take him long to attack a pressuring inmate with a shank. He was charged with attempted murder and placed in administrative segregation.

CRITICAL THINKING QUESTIONS:

How much time do you believe this offender should spend in prison for a crime he committed when he was fifteen? If you were this inmate, would you want to be locked up in protective custody or try to make it in the prison population? If you chose the prison population, what would you be willing to do to protect yourself?

Source: One of the authors was involved with this defense as an expert witness.

---

inmates younger than age eighteen held in state prisons come from states with a younger age of criminal responsibility. Between 1997 and 2004, the number of inmates under age eighteen fell significantly. However, this decline of the youth proportion of prison populations was primarily the result of the large increase in the total prison population during this period.

From 1994 to 2001, almost 3,000 juveniles were committed to the custody of the federal Bureau of Prisons (BOP) for offenses committed when they were under eighteen years of age. Of these, 1,639 were committed to the BOP as delinquents and 1,346 as adults. The vast majority of these juveniles committed as delinquents (about 70 percent) were American Indians.[33] Federal prisons did not report holding any juveniles at mid-year 2007.[34]

In some states, judges opt for the **life without parole sentence** to incarcerate juveniles for the rest of their natural lives. See Focus on Law 7–2 for an Iowa case in which a fifteen-year-old received a life without parole sentence.

Providing for the care and special needs of juvenile offenders in adult facilities is proving to be a real problem. The youthful offender may be as young as thirteen and feel overwhelmed by older and more aggressive offenders. Indeed, most juvenile offenders placed in adult prisons are not violent offenders. A gang culture may be present in the prison, in which gang members pressure youthful offenders to become part of their gang, usually to exploit them. Furthermore, with their need to be part of something, youthful offenders tend to be highly impressionable and easily used or manipulated.[35]

The state of Washington has attempted to manage imprisoned youthful offenders more effectively. In 1997, the state enacted Senate Bill 3900 defining the jurisdiction, custody, and management requirements for juvenile offenders. This legislation requires juvenile offenders to be placed in adult prisons for serious offenses such as aggravated murder. In addition, it dictates the housing and educational requirements for youthful offenders within the Department of Corrections (DOC) as follows:

- An offender under the age of eighteen who is convicted in adult criminal court and sentenced to the DOC must be placed in a housing unit, or a portion of a housing unit, separated from adult inmates;

- The offender may be housed in an intensive management unit or administrative segregation unit, if necessary, for the safety or security of the offender or the staff; and

- The DOC must provide an educational program to an offender under the age of eighteen who is incarcerated at a DOC facility. The program must enable the offender to obtain a high school diploma or general equivalency diploma (GED).[36]

Female youthful offenders are placed at the Washington Corrections Center for Women (WCCW), and males are confined at the Clallam Bay Corrections Center. A multidisciplinary team was formed in September 1997 in order to meet the challenge of accommodating juveniles in adult prisons. This team has been concerned with providing a safe and secure environment, an environment distant from adult offenders' contact and influences; programs and services similar to those available to the general population; and an educational program offering credit for a high school diploma or GED.[37]

The Juvenile Death Penalty: Three Decades of Change

The most severe sentence in the adult courts is, of course, the death penalty. Much debate has centered on this issue, and in June 1989, the U.S. Supreme Court ruled that sixteen- and seventeen-year-old juveniles could be executed for their crimes.[38]

This decision generated an outburst of debate. It was applauded by conservatives, who contended that society needs the death penalty for its retributive and deterrent effects on violent crime. Conservatives also believe that juveniles are mollycoddled by the juvenile court and that juveniles who break the law deserve the same punishments as do adults. Liberals, however, decried the decision.[39] Their objections reflect, in part, the disdain that many have for the death penalty in a "civilized" society. These modern progressives also believe that youthful offenders should be rehabilitated because they are young and still in the formative years of their lives.

Victor L. Strieb traces the development of the current debate.[39] The constitutionality of the death penalty was decided in *Gregg v. Georgia* in 1976.[40] In that decision, the U.S. Supreme Court ruled that the death penalty did not violate the Eighth Amendment's prohibition against cruel and unusual punishment. The Court did stipulate that before lower courts handed down the death penalty, the special characteristics of the offender, such as his or her age, as well as the circumstances of the crime, had to be considered.[41] In later decisions, considering statutes in Ohio and other states, the Court ruled that mitigating circumstances had to be considered in any death penalty case. Accordingly, states that have handed down the death penalty without considering mitigating circumstances have had their cases overturned.[42] States that permit the death penalty today, in other words, must statutorily require that mitigating circumstances be considered.

In some ways, the debate over the death penalty for juveniles is a curious one. Strieb points out that historically, few juveniles were ever executed for their crimes. Indeed, even when juveniles were sentenced to death, few, if any, executions were carried out.[43] In the United States, for example, youths under the age of eighteen were executed at the rate of twenty to twenty-seven per decade, or about 1.6 to 2.3 percent of all executions from the 1880s to the 1920s.[44] The peak in the United States occurred in the 1940s, when fifty-three, or 4.1 percent of all those executed, were juveniles.[45]

Of the thirty-eight states that permitted capital punishment, twenty-four allowed it for individuals who were under the age of eighteen when they committed the crime. Fourteen states have never executed juveniles, but Georgia leads all states with forty-one juvenile executions, followed by North Carolina and Ohio, with nineteen each.

In 1982, in the case of *Eddings v. Oklahoma*, the Supreme Court was able to avoid directly addressing the constitutionality of the juvenile death penalty by ruling that "the chronological age of a minor is itself a relevant mitigating factor of great weight."[46] Monty Lee Eddings was sixteen when he shot and killed an Oklahoma State Highway Patrol officer, but his execution sentence was reversed in 1982 because of his age.[47]

In *Wilkins v. Missouri*, sixteen-year-old Heath A. Wilkins of Missouri stabbed Nancy Allen Moore to death on July 27, 1985, as she worked behind the counter of a convenience store. The jury found him guilty of first-degree murder, armed criminal action, and carrying a concealed weapon. During the sentencing hearing, both the prosecution and Wilkins himself urged the court to apply the death penalty. The aggravating circumstances of the case led the court to decide that the death penalty was appropriate and sentenced Wilkins to die. The Missouri Supreme Court later upheld this decision.[48] Wilkins had not been executed by the time the *Roper v. Simmons* decision was made to eliminate the juvenile death penalty.

In 1988, the U.S. Supreme Court heard the case of *Thompson v. Oklahoma.*[49] Wayne Thompson was fifteen when he was arrested, along with his twenty-seven-year-old half-brother and two other older men, for the shooting and stabbing death of Charles Keene, Thompson's former brother-in-law. The Court ruled by a five-to-three vote that "the Eighth and Fourteenth Amendment[s] prohibit the execution of a person who was under sixteen years of age at the time of his or her offense."[50]

The Supreme Court upheld the constitutionality of the death penalty for juveniles in two 1989 cases. In the case of *Stanford v. Kentucky*, Kevin Stanford, a seventeen-year-old African American youth, repeatedly raped and sodomized his victim during a robbery.[51] He then drove her to a secluded area, where he shot her point blank in the face and in the back of the head. A jury convicted Stanford of first-degree murder, first-degree sodomy, first-degree robbery, and receiving stolen property. Stanford was sentenced to death on September 28, 1989, and was transferred to death row.[52] He was not executed.

The important *Atkins v. Virginia* decision, rendered on June 20, 2002, emphasized very clearly the importance of mental retardation as a mitigating factor to be considered in sentencing juveniles. Atkins was convicted of abduction and armed robbery with a semiautomatic handgun. After the robbery, he drove the victim to a remote location and murdered him. Atkins was convicted of capital murder and sentenced to death. However, he was mentally deficient, and the Supreme Court ruled that mentally retarded juveniles could not be executed for their offenses.[53]

Individuals who were given capital sentences for crimes committed while they were juveniles continued to be executed until 2005. For example, on April 3, 2003, Scott Allen Hain was executed in Oklahoma for a murder he committed at age seventeen. Nevertheless, the juvenile death penalty had many vocal opponents. The human rights organization Amnesty International, the United Nations General Assembly, and other influential organizations continued to opt for the elimination of the juvenile death penalty in the United States. On March 1, 2005, in the case of *Roper v. Simmons* the Supreme Court ruled, in a five-to-four decision, that no juveniles who committed their crimes under the age of eighteen could be executed.[54]

The fact is that the death penalty for juveniles who commit crimes when under age eighteen has been outlawed, but, as Focus on Policy 7–3 points out, juveniles can still die in prison for crimes they have committed.

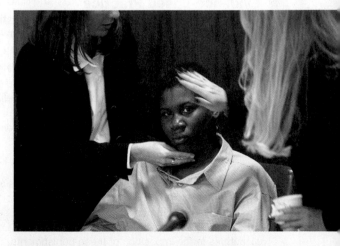

▲ The stress of being a victim or witness testifying in court is often overwhelming. Some require the assitance of their lawyers and court personnel to make it through their testimony.
LOU TOMAN/KRT/Newscom

Focus on Policy 7–3
Should Juveniles Be Allowed to Die in Prison?

Locking up a juvenile for the rest of his or her life for a crime committed while a juvenile may be cruel punishment, but it is not unusual. There are currently 2,390 people in this nation who are serving life sentences (LWOP) for crimes they committed before they turned eighteen. There are seventy-three juveniles who have committed crimes when they were thirteen or fourteen and were given this sentence. Nationally, 59 percent of the juveniles serving life without parole sentences had no prior criminal convictions before being placed in prison for life.

Forty-two states currently allow life without parole for minors. California has 225 inmates serving life sentences there for crimes committed as minors. Pennsylvania is estimated to have 360 to 443 inmates serving life without parole for crimes committed as juveniles.

In the wake of the *Roper* decision forbidding the death penalty for juvenile offenders, the next notable Eighth Amendment battleground could be LWOP sentences for juveniles. Proponents of LWOP sound much like those who favored the death penalty for juveniles in the past, and those who would abolish LWOP uses many of the same arguments that opponents of the death penalty for juvenile formerly used.

On May 18, 2010, the U.S. Supreme Court ruled, by a 5-to-4 vote, that juveniles may not be sentenced to life in prison without parole for any crime short of homicide. The majority of the Court in this ruling made clear that youthful offenders must be treated differently from adults even for heinous crimes.

Anthony M. Kennedy, writing for the majority, said states must provide juveniles who receive lengthy sentences a "meaningful" chance at some point to show that they should be released.

The case involved Terrance Jamar Graham, who was convicted of robbery in Jacksonville, Florida, when he was sixteen. He received a short jail term and probation but was arrested again at seventeen for taking part in a home invasion. The judge in the case gave him the sentence of life without the possibility of parole.

Judge Kennedy said there were 129 juveniles in eleven states, including Virginia, who had not committed homicide but were serving sentences of life without parole. The majority of them—77—were in Florida.

In the summer of 2012, the U.S. Supreme Court was scheduled to rule on *Jackson v. Hobbs* and *Miller v. Alabama*, two cases that were argued back to back. In both cases, fourteen-year-old juveniles were sentenced to life without parole. Jackson was with a couple of colleagues who were robing a video store when one of them killed the clerk. Miller, in contrast, committed a homicide, beating a man with a bat and setting fire to his trailer. In this case, one outcome could be that the Supreme Court could strike down all mandatory sentences of life without parole to juveniles, and another possibility could be that the justices will strike down life without parole for children, ages fourteen and younger, given in part their rarity (only 79 such prisoners exist). See the Evidence-Based Practice feature.

Evidence-Based Practice
The Lives of Juvenile Lifers: Findings from a National Survey

Life in prison without the possibility of parole gives no chance for fulfillment outside prison walls, no chance for reconciliation with society, no hope. Maturity can lead to that considered reflection which is the foundation for remorse, renewal, and rehabilitation. A young person who knows that he or she has no chance of leaving prison before life's ends has little incentive to become a responsible individual.

Graham v. Florida, *2010*

The United States stands alone worldwide in imposing a life without parole sentence on juveniles. Survey findings from 1,579 individuals around the country who are serving these sentences for crimes committed while juveniles demonstrate extreme racial disparities in the imposition of these punishments, high rates of social economic disadvantage, sentences often imposed without judicial discretion, and counterproductive corrections policies that make efforts at rehabilitation difficult. Highlights of this report include the following:

* Juvenile lifers experienced a high level of exposure to violence in their homes and communities. For example, 79 percent of these individuals reported witnessing violence in their homes and more than half (54.1 percent) witnessed weekly violence in their neighborhoods.

* Juvenile lifers, particularly girls, suffered high rates of abuse. Nearly half (46.9 percent) experienced physical abuse, including 79.5 percent of girls, and 77.3 percent of girls reported a history of sexual abuse. Overall, 20.5 percent of juvenile lifers reported having been victims of sexual abuse.

* Juvenile lifers generally experience significant social and economic disadvantage in their homes and communities. About a third of juvenile lifers (31.5 percent) were raised in public poverty. Juvenile lifers faced significant educational challenges. Fewer than half of these individuals had been attending school at the time of their offense, and the vast majority of juvenile lifers had been suspended or expelled from school at some point in their academic career.

* The racial dynamics of victims and offenders may play a key role in determining which offenders are sentenced to juvenile life without parole. The proportion of African Americans serving these sentences for the killing of a white person (43.4 percent) is nearly twice the rate at which white juveniles are arrested for taking a white person's life (23.2 percent).

* The majority of these sentences are imposed in states in which judges are obligated to sentence individuals without

consideration of any factors relating to a juvenile's age or his or her life circumstances. States such as Pennsylvania, which holds the nation's largest population of juvenile lifers, require that youth of any age charged with homicide be tried in adult court and, upon conviction, sentenced to life without the possibility of parole.

- Most (61.9 percent) juvenile lifers are not engaged in programming in prison, but this is generally not due to lack of interest, but because of state or prison policies.
- Many juvenile lifers are engaged in constructive change during their incarceration when they are permitted the opportunity to do so.

CRITICAL THINKING QUESTION:

Do actual differences exist between a capital sentence and a sentence of a life without parole? Discuss.

Source: Robert Barnes, "Supreme Court Restricts Life Without Parole for Juveniles," *Washington Post,* May 2010, accessed May 1, 2012, at http://www .washingtolnpost.com/wp-dyn-content-article-2010/05/17/AR2010051701355 .htm;; Lilianna Segura, "Will the Supreme Court Toss Life Without Parole for Juveniles?, *The Nation,* March 2012, accessed May 1, 2012, at http://www .thenation.com/blog/166925/2will-supreme-court-toss-life-without-parole- juveniles.; and Ashley Nellis, *The Lives of Juvenile Lifers: Findings from a National Survey* (Washington, DC: The Sentencing Project, March 2012), 2–4.

Juvenile Justice Videos

IN JUVENILE COURT AT EIGHTEEN!

In Juvenile Court at Eighteen! depicts an individual arrested for a bench warrant for failure to appear. The eighteen-year-old has a history of delinquent behavior. The video documents the intake process and the detention hearing for the case. At the detention hearing the offender's past history with criminal behavior is discussed as well as family relationships and interactions with lesser sanctions such as counseling. What was the makeup of this individual's past record? How did the home life situation affect his involvement with criminal behavior? Did being a legal adult have an impact on the judge's decision at the detention hearing? Why or why not?

SUMMARY

LEARNING OBJECTIVE 1: Explain the differences in maturity between juveniles and adults.

Defining when childhood ends and adulthood begins is a worrisome problem; unfortunately, no objective tests are available to help society draw the line. The result is much confusion from state to state over the ways in which youths and adults are defined. The basic issue is one of deciding the elusive concept of responsibility and of defining the relationship between age and mental and emotional maturity.

LEARNING OBJECTIVE 2: Explain how transfer to adult court takes place as well as the different types of waivers.

Juveniles appearing before the juvenile court can be transferred or certified to the adult court. The different types of waivers are judicial waiver, prosecutorial discretion, statutorial exclusion, reverse waiver, and blended sentencing. Proponents of the practice of transfer believe that if juveniles are processed by adult courts, punishment is ensured and society will become safer as a result.

LEARNING OBJECTIVE 3: Summarize blended sentencing and the different blended sentencing models.

A blended sentence is a sentence imposed by a juvenile court that blends a juvenile disposition and an adult sentence for certain serious youthful offenders. Some states permit juvenile court judges at the disposition hearing in the delinquency court to impose both an adult and a juvenile sentence concurrently.

LEARNING OBJECTIVE 4: Describe what an intermediate correctional system for juveniles would be like.

A youthful offender system has been developed in a number of states for young adults, ages sixteen to nineteen. These are transitional, or intermediate, systems between the juvenile and adult systems.

LEARNING OBJECTIVE 5: Discuss the death penalty for juveniles.

Up to the *Roper v. Simmons* decision, which outlawed the death penalty for juveniles for crimes committed under the age of eighteen, the most serious consequence for juveniles was the possibility of being sentenced to the death penalty.

LEARNING OBJECTIVE 6: Summarize the debate about juveniles receiving a sentence to life without parole.

Forty-two states presently allow life without parole for minors. About 2,500 people in this nation are currently serving life without parole sentences for crimes they committed before they turned eighteen. On May 18, 2010, the U.S. Supreme Court ruled, by a 5-to-4 vote, that juveniles may not be sentenced to a life in prison without parole for any crime short of homicide. In cases to be decided in the summer of 2012, *Jackson v. Hobbes* and *Miller v. Alabama,* the Supreme Court ruled on the constitutionality of life without parole for juveniles.

KEY TERMS

concurrent jurisdiction, p. 149
judicial waiver, p. 149

life without parole sentence, p. 157
prosecutorial discretion, p. 149

statutorial exclusion, p. 149
youthful offender system, p. 155

REVIEW QUESTIONS

1. At what point are children considered adults by society to-day? When do different state and local organizations in the United States consider you an adult?
2. What are the main types of waiver to the adult court?
3. Why is waiver such a controversial matter in juvenile justice?

4. What is your stand on the death penalty for juveniles? Do you support it or oppose it? Why?
5. When is treatment in the juvenile system no longer desirable for a juvenile?
6. Should any juvenile be confined for life? If so, who and why?

GROUP EXERCISES

1. *Group Work:* Discuss the different types of waivers found throughout the states and how those waivers work.
2. *Writing to Learn Exercise:* As an alternative to Exercise 1 have all students identify and describe each of the different types of waivers and then critique each others' answers for style and substance.
3. *Group Work:* Discuss the stages, issues, and court decisions involved in the evolution of the juvenile death penalty.

4. *Class Debate:* Divide the class into two groups, one of which is to argue "Resolved: juveniles receive sufficient due process and more juveniles should be sent to community-based corrections for rehabilitation and treatment." The other is to argue "Resolved: juveniles should be treated as adults, sanctions against them strengthened, and more youths should be sent to the adult court for prosecution and punishment."

NOTES

1. Compiled from the International Justice Project, "Juveniles: Christopher Simmons," accessed at http://www.internationaljusticeproject.org/juvCSimmons.cfm; Death Penalty Information Center, "U.S. Supreme Court: *Roper v. Simmons*," accessed May 5, 2006, at http://www.deathpenaltyinfo.org; American Bar Association, "Christopher Simmons," accessed May 5, 2006, at http://www.abanet.org/crimjust/juvjus/simmons.html.
2. Stephen J. Morse, "Immaturity and Responsibility," *Journal of Criminal Law and Criminology* 88 (1998), 19–20. See also Thomas F. Geraghty and Steven A. Drizin, "Foreword—The Debate Over the Future of Juvenile Courts: Can We Reach Consensus?" *Journal of Criminal Law and Criminology* 88 (1998), 6.
3. Elizabeth S. Scott and Thomas Grisso, "The Evolution of Adolescence: A Developmental Perspective on Juvenile Justice Reform," *Journal of Criminology and Criminal Justice* 88 (1998), 137, 174.
4. Ibid., 174–75.
5. Ibid., 189.
6. Ibid., 174–75.
7. "Beating Death of Derrion Albert, 16, Caught on Video," *Huffington Post,* accessed at http://huffingtonpost.com/2009/09/27/beating-death-of-derrion_n_30/319.htm. See also "Four Teens Charged in Fatal Beating of Chicago Student," *USA Today,* September 29, 2009, accessed at http://www.usatoday.com/news/nation/2009-09-28-chicago-beating_N.htm.

8. "Police: Suspects Did This for Nothing More Than Their Own Savage Amusement" (December 20, 2011), accessed at http://newyork.cbslocal.com/2011/12/202-charged-in-attack-of-nj-homeless-man-after-video-posted-on-youtube.
9. Todd D. Minton, *Jail Inmates at Midyear 2009* (Washington, DC: U.S. Department of Justice, Office of Juvenile Justice and Delinquency Prevention, June 2010).
10. John Kelly, "Justice Initiates New Study of Juveniles Transferred to Adult Court," *Youth Today* (November 2, 2010), accessed April 26, 2012, at http://www.youthtoday.org/view_article.cfm?article_id=4420.
11. Howard N. Snyder and Melissa Sickmund, *Juvenile Offenders and Victims: 2006 National Report* (Washington, DC: U.S. Department of Justice, Office of Justice Programs, Office of Juvenile Justice and Delinquency Prevention, 2006), 186.
12. Patrick Griffin, Sean Addie, Benjamin Adams, and Kathy Finestine, *Trying Juveniles as Adults: An Analysis of State Transfer Laws and Reporting* (Washington, DC: Juvenile Offenders and Victims, National Report Series, September 2011), 10.
13. For the state of Mississippi, see *OJJDP, Statistical Briefing Book,* accessed at http://ojjdp.ncjrs.org/ojstatbb/structure_process/qa04110.asp?qaDate=2004.
14. Griffin et al., *Trying Juveniles as Adults.*
15. Samuel M. Davis, *Rights of Juveniles: The Juvenile Justice System,* 2d ed. (New York: Clark Boardman, 1986), Section 4-2; see also Melissa Sickmund, *How Juveniles Get to Juvenile Court* (Washington, DC: Juvenile Justice Bulletin, 1994).

16. Davis, *Rights of Juveniles*, 24–26.

17. *Juvenile Justice Reform Initiatives in the States, 1994–1996,* accessed April 30, 2012, at http://wwwl.ojjdp .gov/pubs/reform/ch2_k.hml.

18. Ibid.

19. See the National Council of Juvenile and Family Court Judges, *Juvenile Delinquency Guidelines: Improving Court Practice in Juvenile Delinquency Cases* (Reno, NV: Summer 2005), 51.

20. Ibid, 106.

21. Ibid.

22. Ibid., 107.

23. Ibid., 108.

24. Ibid., 110.

25. Griffin et al., *Trying Juveniles as Adults.*

26. Richard E. Redding, "Juvenile Transfer Laws: An Effective Deterrent to Delinquency?" *OJJDP Juvenile Justice Bulletin* (August 2008), 5–6.

27. James Austin, Kelly Dedel Johnson, and Maria Gregoriou, *Juveniles in Adult Prisons and Jails: A National Assessment,* accessed at http://www.ncjrs/gov/pdffiles1/ bja/183503pdf.p.x.

28. Donna Martin Hamparian et al., *The Violent Few: A Study of Dangerous Juvenile Offenders* (Lexington, MA: Lexington Books, 1980), 33–34.

29. Quoted in Barry C. Feld, "Violent Youth and Public Policy: Minnesota Juvenile Justice Task Force and 1994 Legislative Reform," paper presented at the annual meeting of the American Society of Criminology, Miami, FL, 1994, 9.

30. Ibid. See also Barry C. Feld, "Violent Youth and Public Policy: A Case Study of Juvenile Justice Law Reform," *Minnesota Law Review* 79 (May 1995), 965–1128.

31. Richard E. Redding, "Juvenile Offenders in Criminal Court and Adult Prison: Legal, Psychological, and Behavioral Outcomes," *Juvenile and Family Court Journal* 50 (1999), 1–20.

32. Griffin et al., *Trying Juveniles as Adults,* 25.

33. Ibid., 117.

34. William Sabol and Heather Couture, *Prison Inmates at Midyear 2007* (Washington, DC: U.S. Department of Justice, Bureau of Justice Statistics, June 2008), 9.

35. Salvador A. Godinez, "Managing Juveniles in Adult Facilities," *Corrections Today* 61 (April 1999), 86–87.

36. Gary Fleming and Gerald Winkler, "Sending Them to Prison: Washington State Learns to Accommodate Female Youthful Offenders in Prison," *Corrections Today* 61 (April 1999), 132–33.

37. Ibid., 133.

38. The decision was rendered in two cases. One was *Stanford v. Kentucky,* No. 87–5765. See Linda Greenhouse, "Death Sentences Against Retarded and Young Upheld," *New York Times,* June 27, 1989, A1, A18.

39. Much of the current section on the development of the death penalty comes from Victor L. Strieb, *Death Penalty for Juveniles* (Bloomington: Indiana University Press, 1987), 21–40.

40. *Gregg v. Georgia,* 48 U.S. 153 (1976).

41. Ibid., 197.

42. Strieb, *Death Penalty for Juveniles,* 22.

43. Ibid., 24–25.

44. Ibid.

45. Ibid.

46. *Eddings v. Oklahoma,* 102 S. Ct. 869 (1982).

47. Ibid.

48. *Stanford v. Kentucky,* 492 U.S. 361 (1989); *Wilkins v. Missouri,* 109 S. Ct. 2969 (1989).

49. *Thompson v. Oklahoma,* 487 U.S. 815 (1988).

50. Ibid.

51. *Stanford v. Kentucky.*

52. Ibid.

53. *Atkins v. Virginia,* 536 U.S. 304 (2002).

54. *Roper v. Simmons* (03-633), 112 SW 3d 397 (2003).

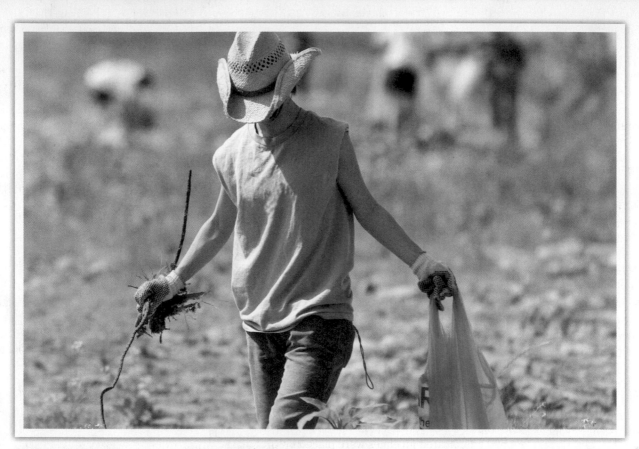

Greatbass.com/Fotolia

Learning Objectives

1. Explain how probation is administered.
2. Explain the functions of probation services.
3. Describe how classifications and risk/needs assessments are used in juvenile probation.
4. Describe the use of restitution programs.
5. Explain the use of intermediate punishments, including intensive supervision programs.
6. Describe the use of house arrest and electronic monitoring.
7. Summarize the roles and responsibilities of probation officers.
8. Explain how probation can be revoked and the rights of probationers.
9. Summarize juvenile probation's effectiveness.

At the final hearing of Attorney General Eric Holder's National Task Force on Children Exposed to Violence in Detroit, officials from the Justice Department and the city of Detroit underscored efforts to keep youth safe and prevent youth violence. At the hearing, Acting Associate General Tony West announced the release of a new Justice Department research bulletin showing that 46 percent of victimized children were known to police, school, and medical authorities.

"While more children are reporting violence to authorities, many continue to endure the pain of victimization in silence," said Acting Associate General West, "Through the work of the Attorney General's task force, we hope to find more ways to identity those children in need and make sure they have access to effective prevention and treatment options."

Composed of twelve leading experts, the task force includes practitioners, child and family advocates, academic experts, and licensed clinicians. Their findings were scheduled to be published in late 2012 as a final report to the attorney general. The report presents policy recommendations and serves as a blueprint for preventing and reducing the negative effects of such violence across the nation.[1]

Youth violence is a serious national concern, and probation officers, who can be called the "workhorses" of the juvenile justice system, have an important role in monitoring and controlling youth misbehavior, including violence. Juvenile probation officers have contact with juveniles from the time they come into the system until they are either released from the jurisdiction of the system or are sent to an institution.

Probation is a judicial disposition under which youthful offenders are subject to certain conditions imposed by the juvenile court and are permitted to remain in the community under the supervision of a probation officer. Juvenile probation has always referred to non-punitive legal disposition for delinquent youths, and has emphasized treatment without incarceration. The probation officer assists offenders in their efforts to meet the conditions of the court. As expressed vividly by the quote in Focus on Offenders 8–1, the basic goal of probation—over and above giving troublesome youths a second chance—is to provide services that will help offenders stay out of trouble with the law. Probation is the most widely used judicial disposition of the juvenile court.

About 300,000 youths are placed on formal probation each year, which amounts to more than 60 percent of all juvenile dispositions. The use of probation has increased significantly since 1993 when around 224,500 adjudicated juveniles were placed on probation.[2]

The word *probation* is used in at least four ways in the juvenile justice system. It can refer to (1) a disposition of the juvenile court in lieu of institutionalization, (2) the status of an adjudicated offender, (3) a subsystem of the juvenile justice system (the term's most common use), and (4) the activities, functions, and services that characterize this subsystem's transactions with the juvenile court, the youthful offender, and the community. The probation process includes the intake phase of the juvenile court's proceedings, preparation of the social investigation for the disposition stage, supervision of probationers, and obtaining or providing services for youths on probation.

Probation is considered a desirable alternative to institutionalization for several reasons: First, it allows offenders to retain their liberty but provides society with some protection against continued disregard for the law. Second, it promotes the rehabilitation of offenders because they can maintain normal community contacts by living at home, attending school, and participating in community activities. Third, it avoids the negative impact of institutional confinement, and furthermore, it costs less than incarceration.

How Is Probation Administered?

Two questions about the organization of the probation services have been debated for some time: Should probation administration be controlled by the judicial or the executive branch of government? Should this control be centralized in a state or in a local administration?

Focus on Offenders 8–1
One Success Story

When asked to recall a success story, a juvenile probation officer told the following:

> One success story I remember is that of a seventeen-year-old black girl who had been arrested on first-degree robbery and prostitution. She had never been referred before. What it came down to was there were two juvenile girls with two adult males who were their boyfriends, and they were in a bar trying to shake down this white guy. The girls got him up to their apartment, and they were going to get it on with him. Then their boyfriends came up and were real mad because he was with their women. The white guy said, "Take anything," and they took some money he had in his car. The robbery charge was dropped, but there was a finding of fact on the prostitution charge. She was placed on supervision until her eighteenth birthday. When I got her, the first thing we did was go out to the hospital's family practice center to have her checked and placed on birth control. But she was already pregnant. The majority of time we spent together was concentrated on job, education, getting ready for the baby, and independent living skills. It wasn't a traditional probation case. We spent a lot of time together, getting ready for her future. Her mother was dead and her father was in the Mental Health Institute. Several older sisters were already on ADC [Aid to Dependent Children], weren't married, and were not models by any means. So I felt like I'm the one she counted on. I took her to the hospital when she had her baby and was with her during delivery. It was a neat experience. She asked me to be the godmother for her baby. She's now very motivated to make something out of herself. She is now nineteen, has her own car, and keeps an apartment fairly well. She has either gone to school or worked since before she had the baby. With what she has had to work with, it's amazing she is doing so well.

Source: Interviewed by one of the authors. The interviewee is a probation officer in Waterloo, Iowa.

Locally Administered Probation Department

In those states in which probation is a local responsibility, the state is accountable only for providing financial support, setting standards, and arranging training courses. This locally based approach is used in one-third of the juvenile probation departments in the United States.

One of the most persuasive arguments for local administration of probation is that citizens and agencies in the community more readily support programs that are open to their participation and are responsive to local needs and problems. Another supporting argument is that small operations are more flexible, adjust more quickly to change, and are less encumbered by bureaucratic rigidity. Yet three arguments against local administration have won the support of many policy makers: (1) A state administrative probation system can set standards of service, thereby ensuring uniformity of procedures, policies, and services. (2) A large agency can make more effective use of funds and personnel. (3) Greater efficiency in the disposition of resources is possible when all probation officers are state employees.

State or Executive Administered Probation Departments

Assignment of probation to the executive branch on a statewide basis allows for standard policy making, recruitment, training, and personnel management. Coordination with the state department of corrections is also facilitated. The most significant disadvantage is the development of a large probation bureaucracy with echelons of decision makers shuffling memorandums from out-basket to in-basket and having little contact with the real world of the streets. Firm leadership with a grasp of sound management procedures can prevent this dismal prospect.

Combination Approach

Each of these approaches has some support because the administration of juvenile probation varies both among and within states. Juvenile probation is under the control of the juvenile court and is funded by city or county government in fifteen states and the District of Columbia. The other thirty-five states organize administered juvenile probation in a variety

TABLE 8–1
Summary of the Organization and Administration of Juvenile Probation

Type	Advantages
Local programs prefer locally administered programs	Citizens and agencies of the community respond to local
State or executive administered recruitment, training, and personnel	Allows for uniform standards of policy making, management
Combination approach	Juvenile probation is under juvenile court control but some local programs are state funded.

of ways; fourteen use a combination of approaches. The best strategy for administration of juvenile probation appears to be placing it under the control of the juvenile court and funding it through local governmental agencies while, at the same time, providing revenue support or staff from the state to those local agencies that meet state standards. Table 8–1 summarizes the various approaches to juvenile probation.

Private contractors have been used in juvenile probation, especially for providing intensive probation and aftercare services. For example, in January 2011, the Nebraska Department of Health and Human Services transferred case management functions in the eastern and southeastern service areas of the state to private contractors (who are known as family permanency specialists) in the juvenile services system as part of Nebraska's "Families Matter" reform. The goal of this reform is to improve the outcomes of child and community safety and also the permanency and well-being of children, youth, and families.[3]

To bring about greater uniformity in administration of local probation, several states offer rewards of either revenue support or manpower to local systems if they comply with state standards. Michigan, for example, assigns state-paid probation officers to work with local probation officers. Usually, though, states make direct payments to local governments to defray part of the costs of probation services. In New York State, for example, a local community that is willing to meet state staffing patterns is reimbursed up to 50 percent of its operating costs for probation services.

Other states, such as California, Nevada, Oregon, and Washington, have developed **probation subsidy programs** that encourage a decreased rate of commitment of offenders by counties to state institutions. The money saved by the state is returned to the counties. California initiated this program after a study indicated that many offenders committed to state correctional institutions could safely remain in the community under good probation supervision. With the closing of the training schools in California in 2010, county probation will assume the type of supervisory responsibility it did with the passing of the original probation subsidy programs.

What Are the Functions of Probation Services?

The four basic functions of juvenile probation are intake, management of caseloads, supervision and investigation, and reports to the court. At the intake stage of the court proceedings, the probation officer decides whether or not to file a petition on a child referred to the court. Supervision, initiated when the judge places a youth on probation, focuses primarily on risk control and crime reduction. The management of a caseload is an important responsibility of a probation officer. Investigation involves compiling a social history or study of a child judged delinquent to assist the judge in choosing the wisest disposition.

Voices of Delinquency: Patricia Brennan, Former Acting Director of Probation, NYC

Intake

During the intake stage of the court proceedings (which was discussed in Chapter 6), the probation officer carefully screens the referrals to the court. Both the statutes of the state and *interview the family for further needed in P.O.* [handwritten margin note]

the office of the state's prosecutor are helpful in determining whether or not any case referred to the court actually falls under its jurisdiction. At **intake**, the probation officer also conducts a preliminary investigation, which includes an interview during which the youth is advised of his or her legal rights. If parents or guardians have not already been contacted, the probation department gets in touch with them to discuss the status of the child and to advise them of their right to have an attorney. The intake probation officer may need to interview the family, witnesses, victims, arresting officers, peers, or neighbors to obtain sufficient information with which to make a sound determination on the necessity of filing a court petition for detention of the child. The probation officer also may need to contact the school and other agencies that have worked with the child. If the youth has been in court before or is already on probation, the intake officer must also familiarize himself or herself with the previous reports.

Casework Management

The probation officer maintains a file on each probationer for whom he or she is responsible. Within this file are the court documents that spell out the requirements of probation, chronological entries of contacts between the officer and the probationer and others whose relationship with the probationer might be sufficient, items of correspondence, and periodic reports made to the courts or to officials of the agency.

Commonly, probation officers divide probationers into several categories, based on their needs or on the risk they pose to the community. Some offenders are placed on minimum supervision status and are required only to mail in a report once a month or even less frequently. Offenders on medium supervision status must visit their probation officers at least once a month. Offenders on maximum or intensive supervision status must see their officers several times a month.

Probation officers' caseloads are so large that maintaining contact with probationers is difficult. Studies in adult probation seeking to link combined size and recidivism in probation go back forty years. Since the late 1970s, five major studies sought to identify the impact of caseloads on recidivism, and three of the five studies found evidence supporting the contention that smaller caseloads were related to lower recidivism rates. More recently, John L. Worrall and colleagues' macro-level analysis of the relationship between probation caseloads and property crime rates in California counties found over a nine-year period that as probation loads increased, so did property crime.[4] It stands to reason that this would also be true in juvenile probation.

Supervision, Investigation, and Surveillance

The length of time a juvenile must spend on probation varies among states. The maximum length in some states is until the juvenile reaches the age of majority, which is usually age sixteen or seventeen. Other states limit juvenile probation to a specific duration. In Illinois, it is limited to five years; in New York, two years; in Washington, D.C., one year; and in California, six months.

Once a youth has been placed on probation, the probation officer is required to provide the best possible **supervision**, which includes surveillance, casework services, and counseling or guidance. Surveillance involves careful monitoring of the minor's adjustment to the community. To accomplish this, the officer must establish personal contact with the minor and must learn whether the youth is attending school or is working each day, whether adequate guidance is being received from parents, and whether the child is obeying the terms of probation. At the same time, the probation officer must determine if the youth is continuing to break the law.

A popular means of probation for some departments has been team probation. Officers are divided into teams, and each team takes responsibility for a caseload and makes decisions on what community resources are needed by clients. New probationers are interviewed by a member of the team, and their needs are plotted on a needs-assessment scale. The members of the teams are usually specialists in "needs subsystems," dealing with such problems as drug abuse, alcoholism, mental illness, or runaway behavior, and the specialist links the probationer with whatever services in the community are necessary.

Concerns for public safety in the 1980s persuaded many probation departments to develop classification systems or to use the Wisconsin system or community assessment centers to place probationers under intensive, medium, or minimum supervision. Under the **Wisconsin system**, a risk/needs assessment is conducted for each probationer at regular intervals. The risk scale was derived from empirical studies that showed certain factors to be good predictors of recidivism—prior arrest record, age at first conviction, the nature of the offense for which the probationer was convicted, school or employment patterns, and so forth. The needs assessment focuses on such indicators as emotional stability, financial management, family relationships, and health. The scores derived from the risk/needs assessment are used to classify probationers by required level of supervision—intensive, medium, or minimum. Reassessment of cases takes place at regular intervals, and the level of supervision may be increased or reduced.[5]

The most widely used risk/needs assessment of human behavior is the Problem Severity Index, a screening tool that gives intake officers and others clues about the types of problems the offenders might have. Once a problem area(s) is identified, the juvenile is assessed using diagnostic tools in an attempt to identify the problem more specifically. Clinicians then can combine various diagnostic measures to develop protocols for treatment. Risk assessment today is used to classify offenders, to predict future behavior for reducing recidivism, and to plan interventions.[6] An examination of risk assessments distinguishes between risk assessments that are developed to *predict* behavior and those developed to enable probation officers to *manage* behavior.[7]

The use of risk/needs assessments in juvenile probation raises the issue of how effective they are in predicting juveniles' behaviors. The fact is that it is very difficult to predict behavior, especially for juveniles. Thus, whatever predictive techniques or classification systems are used in juvenile justice, the results are far less than desirable in forecasting juvenile behavior.[8]

There is also the issue of whether a gendered assessment instrument is needed. One study did a meta-analysis of risk assessment predictive validity with male and female offenders. Considering 20 samples, findings indicate that predictive validity is equivalent for male and female offenders. The findings also reveal that when gender differences are observed in individual studies, they provide evidence for gender biases in juvenile justice decision making and case processing rather than the ineffectiveness of risk assessment instruments with female offenders.[9]

Accountability models for supervising juvenile probationers began to be formulated in the 1980s. For example, Dennis Maloney, Dennis Romig, and Troy Armstrong developed what they called the **balanced approach to juvenile probation**. Its purpose is "to protect the community from delinquency, to impose accountability for offenses committed, and to equip juvenile offenders with the required competencies to live productively and responsibly in the community."[10] One of the popular features of this balanced approach is the equal attention it gives to the community, the victim, and the juvenile offender (see Figure 8–1). Juvenile probation departments in Oregon, Texas, and Wisconsin have implemented this accountability model in supervising juvenile probationers.[11]

The formulation of the balanced approach to juvenile probation has led to the development of the **restorative justice model**. This model, as suggested in Chapter 1, gained impetus in the 1970s and 1980s from the victim's movement, from youthful offenders' experiences with reparative sanctions, and from the rise of informal neighborhood programs and dispute resolution programs in the community.[12] The purpose of this integrated, balanced, and restorative justice model is to reconcile "the interests of victims, offenders, and the community through common programs and supervision practices that meet mutual needs."[13]

The Washington State Legislature has been funding evidence-based programs in the Washington State juvenile courts since 1999. The state-funded evidence-based programs are:

- Aggression Replacement Training (ART)
- Coordination of Services (COS)
- Functional Family Therapy (FFT)
- Family Integrated Transitions (FIT)
- Multisystemic Therapy (MST).

See the Evidence-Based Practice feature for an evaluation of the Multisystemic Therapy program.

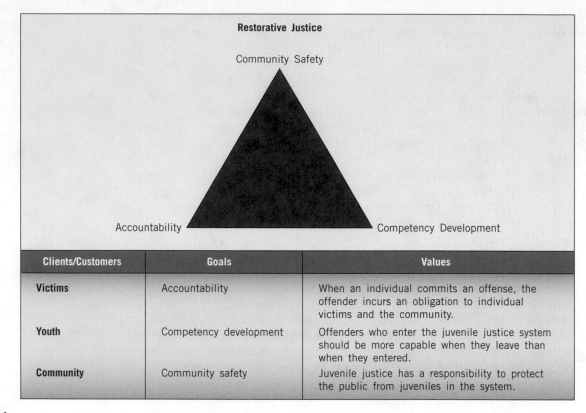

FIGURE 8–1
Graphic Representation of the Balanced Approach Mission

Source: Adapted from D. Maloney, D. Romig, and T. Armstrong, *Juvenile Probation: The Balanced Approach* (Reno, NV: National Council of Juvenile and Family Court Judges, 1998).

Evidence-Based Practice
Multisystemic Therapy for Juvenile Sexual Offenders: One-Year Results from a Randomized Effectiveness Trial

Rigorous tests of promising interventions for juvenile sexual offenders have rarely been conducted, in spite of the problems these offenders present to the community. The seriousness of this behavior has resulted in policy makers and some treatment professionals arguing for lifelong placement on sexual offender registries and extended residential treatment. Yet virtually all stakeholders agree that the scope of sexual offending by juveniles is substantial and warrants the development of effective interventions.

The primary aim of this study was to conduct a rigorous community-based effectiveness trial in which MST adapted for juvenile sexual offenders was compared with the type of group-based services that are typically provided to such offenders. The sexual offender treatment groups were led by seven specially trained probation officers, of whom three held bachelor's degrees and four held master's degrees. Three MA level treatment probation officers also held clinical licenses, and all treatment probation officers had completed a certification course for treating juvenile sexual offenders.

Participants were 127 youths referred by the county state's attorney. Inclusion criteria were (1) judicial order for outpatient sexual offender treatment either as part of postadjudication probation or preadjudication diversion; (2) presence of a local caregiver with whom the juvenile resided; (3) age of juvenile between 11 and 17 years; (4) fluency in either Spanish or English; and

(5) absence of psychotic disorders or serious mental retardation. The mean age of youth at pretreatment was 14.6 years; only three participants were female. Most youth were African American (54 percent) or white (44 percent), and 31 percent of youth had Hispanic ethnicity.

Youth were randomized to MST ($n = 67$) or treatment as usual for juvenile sexual offenders. Outcomes through twelve months postrecruitment were assessed for problem sexual behavior, substance use, delinquency, mental health functioning, and out-of-home placements. Relative to youths who received traditional treatment, those assigned to MST groups evidenced significant reductions in sexual behavior problems, substance abuse, delinquency, externalizing symptoms, and out-of-home placements. These findings suggest that family- and community-based interventions, particularly those with an established evidence base in treating adolescent antisocial behavior, hold considerable promise in meeting the clinical needs of juvenile sexual offenders.

Source: Elizabeth J. Letourneau, Scott W. Henggelder, Charles M. Borduin, Paul A. Schewe, Michael R. McCart, Jason E. Chapman, and Lisa Saldana, "Multisystemic Therapy for Juvenile Sexual Offenders: 1-Year Results from a Randomized Effectiveness Trial," *Journal of Family Psychology* 23 (February 2009), 89–102.

Reports to the Courts

If a juvenile court uses the bifurcated hearing (separation of adjudicatory and disposition stages), a **social study report** is ordered by the judge when a youth is found delinquent at the fact-finding stage of the court proceedings. Probation officers usually are given up to sixty days to make their **investigation**, but if the court combines the adjudicatory and disposition stages, the social study must be completed before a youth appears in front of the judge. The judge is not supposed to read this social study *until* the child is found to be delinquent.

The social study report details the minor's personal background, family, educational progress, present offense, previous violations of law, and employment. Also included are a description of the offender's neighborhood; the family's ability to pay court and institutionalization costs; the minor's physical and mental health; the attitude of the family, the police, neighbors, and the community toward the minor; and the attitude of the minor toward the offense in question and toward himself or herself. The social study concludes with the probation officer's diagnoses and treatment plan for the youth. An important part of this treatment plan is the probation officer's recommended course of action. In this report the officer determines whether the juvenile should remain in the community; if so, the conditions of probation are stated.

How Do Probation Officers Do Their Jobs?

The probation officer does not have an easy job. He or she is sometimes asked to supervise youths on aftercare as well as those on probation. The officer may be given a large caseload; may be responsible for youths who are on house arrest and are monitored with electronic equipment; or may be charged with intake or secure detention responsibilities. In addition, the probation officer is expected to be a treatment agent as well as an agent of social control.[14]

The juvenile probation officer plays an important role in the justice process, beginning with intake and continuing throughout the period in which a juvenile is under court supervision. Probation officers are involved at four stages of the court process. At *intake*, they screen complaints by deciding to adjust the matter, refer the juvenile to an agency for service, or refer the case to the court for judicial action. During the *predisposition* stage, they participate in release or detention decisions. At the *postadjudication* stage, they assist the court in reaching its dispositional decision. During *postdisposition*, they supervise juveniles placed on probation.

Their general duties are as follows (also see Figure 8–2):

- Provide direct counseling and casework services.
- Interview and collect social service data.
- Make diagnostic recommendations.
- Maintain working relationships with law enforcement agencies.
- Use community resources and services.
- Direct volunteer case aides.
- Write predisposition or social investigation reports.
- Work with families of children under supervision.
- Provide specialized services, such as group therapy.
- Supervise specialized caseloads involving children with special problems.
- Make decisions about the revocation of probation and its termination.

Probation
Permits juvenile offenders to remain in the community under the supervision of a probation officer, subject to certain conditions imposed by the court

Supervision
Responsible for behavior of youth violating probation

Intake
What to do with the offender

Caseload Management
Keeping a file of those on his or her caseload

Report Writing
Providing the social study report to the court

FIGURE 8–2
Duties of the Juvenile Probation Officer

Role Conflict

The nearly opposite roles of law enforcement and treatment create problems for the probation officer. The police and citizens of the community are constantly challenging the treatment role of probation officers, berating them for leaving dangerous and hard-core youths in the community. At the same time, probation officers encounter hostility from probationers because of their law enforcement role. The wide use of urinalysis testing for alcohol and drug use is evidence of this law enforcement role. Probation officers must convince the juvenile judge that they are properly filling both roles and are doling out proper portions of treatment and control.

The roles of probation officers today also are more complex than at any time in the past. The increased knowledge developed in fields that study human behavior demands that probation officers continually upgrade their knowledge and skills about child and adolescent development. In addition, schools and other community agencies that share clients with probation departments are being inundated with the same new knowledge. As these professionals become aware of cutting-edge research about potential causes of problems and their solutions, they too, are scrambling to incorporate the findings into their programs and to seek out those in their communities who can assist them. Probation officers, particularly those in the larger urban departments, often find themselves as the brokers between these organizations and the juvenile court.

Conflicting Pressures

Probation officers not only encounter role dilemmas, they must also must satisfy three needs: the juvenile justice system's needs, their own ego needs, and the human needs of the client. That the system comes first is a reality that probation officers face early in their careers. If the juvenile judge wants a youth's social study completed by next Tuesday, it must be done, regardless of the needs and problems of other probationers during that week. Similarly, probation officers know that the system will not tolerate too much adverse publicity; consequently, it is wise for them to be conservative in terms of taking chances on troublesome youths.

Probation officers, too, are human. They have ego needs and want to feel important. They want approval and acceptance from the juvenile judge; from the director of probation or court services; from other probation officers; and from clients. Even though interest in others brought many of them to their jobs, few probation officers can function effectively or happily if their own needs are not met. If an adolescent female fails to respect her probation officer, she is not likely to receive much tolerance from that officer. If an adolescent male is constantly arguing with or harassing his officer, he can expect the full weight of justice if he violates his probation terms.

The client, all too often, is considered long after the needs of the system and the officer have been satisfied. If the officer's initial job enthusiasm and involvement have waned and he or she regards the job only as one that demands much, pays little, and offers little opportunity for advancement, his or her clients may indeed be shortchanged. The endless paperwork, the hours spent on the road trying to locate clients, the broken appointments, the intractable and undependable probationers, and the hostility directed toward the probation officer also make it difficult for the officer to maintain close involvement with clients. See Focus on Practice 8–2 for characteristics of those who communicate well with clients, as well as those who do not.

A basic problem for the conscientious probation officer is disciplining the violator without alienating him or her. For example, one probation officer, in describing the problems he had working with a boy, lamented the fact that just as he began to get close to him, he would be forced to discipline him: "I can't let him go too far or you'll have to snap him back. And this destroys any kind of relationship. . . . He just clams up. . . . Underneath it all, I think he's an angry boy."[15]

But regardless of how effective and committed the probation officer may be, a number of troublesome youths will flagrantly violate their probation terms and will have to be returned to the juvenile court, which may lead to probation revocation. Before punishing a youngster who has violated the terms of his or her probation, the probation officer should make every

Focus on Practice 8–2
Communication with Clients

Probation officers who relate well and do an effective job with clients tend to have certain characteristics in common:

1. They are genuine in their relationships with probationers and do not hide behind a professional role; that is, they attempt to avoid barriers that would isolate them from their clients. Furthermore, they try to be honest with their clients and expect the juveniles to be honest in return.
2. They respond to others with respect, kindness, and compassion. Because they are caring people, they are able to listen and reach out to others.
3. They are not gullible or easily hoodwinked by probationers, because they know what life on the streets is like.
4. They are able to encourage others to pursue positive experiences; they also have an uncanny knack of knowing what to say and do when others fail.
5. They have a good understanding of themselves and have a reasonable idea of their own problems, shortcomings, and needs. They know, in addition, their biases, prejudices, and pet peeves.
6. They are very committed to their jobs, for the job to them is much more than a paycheck. Moreover, their enthusiasm does not wane following the first few weeks or months as probation officers.

Probation officers who continually have problems with clients also have certain characteristics in common:

1. They do not keep their word. Either they promise more than they are capable of delivering or they simply fail to follow through on what they have said they would do.
2. They become bored with their jobs, chiefly because they see little meaning in working with youths whom they regard as losers who will always be marginal citizens.
3. They either have unreal expectations for probationers or are inflexible in interpreting the terms of probation.
4. They permit their personality problems to affect their performance on the job, which often results in a lack of warmth, a preoccupation with self, or a sharp, biting response to others. Not surprisingly, these personality traits alienate them from both probationers and other probation staff.
5. They seem to be unable to respond to lower-class youths who do not share their own middle-class values, so they become judgmental and moralistic in dealing with clients.
6. They are unwilling to pay the price of changing their own lives in order to influence or alter the lives of juvenile offenders.

effort to gain the compliance of the youth. An understanding of the negative impact of institutionalization should compel the probation officer to return a youth to the court only as an extreme last resort.

How About Risk Control and Crime Reduction?

In the 1990s, as juvenile probation continued to face the criticism that it allowed probationers to escape punishment, reduced risk and increased surveillance models received major emphasis. Restitution and intensive supervision were the most widely used of these short-term behavior control models, but house arrest, and electronic monitoring also gained some attention.

Restitution

Restitution, a disposition that requires offenders to repay their victims or the community for their crime, began to be used widely in probation during the 1970s and 1980s. Indeed, by 1985, formal programs were known to exist in more than four hundred jurisdictions; more than thirty-five states now have statutory authority to order monetary or community service restitution.[16] Part of the reason for the skyrocketing growth of restitution programs is that the Office of Juvenile Justice and Delinquency Prevention (OJJDP) has spent some $30 million promoting the use of restitution in eighty-five juvenile courts across the nation.[17] OJJDP followed this initiative with the National Restitution Training Program in 1983 and the Restitution Education, Specialized Training, and Technical Assistance (RESTTA) Project in 1985. These initiatives are directly responsible for most of the growth of restitution programs.[18]

Three broad types of restitution obligation can be ordered by the juvenile court: straight financial restitution, community service, and direct service to victims. Community service is the most common type, probably because it is the easiest to administer. Direct service is the most rare, largely because of victims' reluctance to have contact with offenders. However, the three program types frequently blend together. For example, a local jurisdiction may organize work crews and even enter into recycling, janitorial, and other service contacts with public or private agencies in order to provide youthful offenders with jobs so that they can pay restitution. The most common goals of restitution programs are holding juveniles accountable, providing reparation to victims, treating and rehabilitating juveniles, and punishing juveniles.[19]

When it comes to making restitution and community service work, probation officers are key players, and in many jurisdictions it is up to a juvenile probation officer to handle some or all of a number of responsibilities:

- Determining eligibility for participation
- Calculating appropriate amounts
- Assessing the offender's ability to pay
- Developing a payment/work schedule
- Monitoring performance
- Closing the case.[20]

Juvenile courts have instituted job skills preparation classes to help juveniles with ordered restitution to find and hold jobs. The private and public sectors sometimes provide jobs in which youths required to make restitution can earn money and compensate victims. Juveniles failing to complete their restitution payments may have their probation term extended.

With community work restitution, probationers generally are required to work for a certain number of hours at a private nonprofit or government agency. Sites where the work may be performed include public libraries, parks, nursing homes, animal shelters, community centers, day care centers, youth agencies, YMCAs and YWCAs, and local streets. In large departments, restitution programs provide supervised work crews in which juveniles go to a site and work under the supervision of an adult. For community service in Hennepin County, Minnesota (Minneapolis), see Focus on Practice 8–3.

Intensive Supervision

In the early 1980s, **intensive supervision programs (ISPs)** began to be used in adult probation as a response to the emerging issues of prison crowding, cost escalation, and society's hard-line response to crime. It was called *intensive probation supervision* because it was operated or administered by probation offices, because it involved increased contacts, and because it generally emphasized external controls and surveillance.[21]

Juvenile justice soon followed adult justice, as so frequently happens, in implementing ISPs in juvenile probation. Georgia, New Jersey, Oregon, and Pennsylvania have experimented with or have instituted statewide ISPs for juveniles.[22] Indeed, by the end of the

---

Focus on Practice 8–3
Performing Community Service

In Hennepin County, Minnesota (Minneapolis), youthful offenders quickly discover themselves placed by the juvenile judge on a Saturday work squad for a specified amount of community service. First-time offenders usually find that they are sentenced to forty hours. Every Saturday, these youths are required to be at the downtown meeting place at 8:00 A.M. From there, five trucks are sent out with ten youths and two staff members in each truck. The coordinator of the program, who is on the staff of the probation department, then assigns each youth to a specific work detail. These details include:

- Recycling bottles and cans
- Visiting patients at a nursing home
- Doing janitorial work
- Cleaning bus stops
- Planting trees or removing barbed wire fences at a city park
- Working at a park reserve.

Source: Information gained during an onsite visit and updated in a phone call to a staff member.

1980s, juvenile judges across the nation were commonly placing high-risk offenders on small caseloads and assigning them frequent contact with a probation officer.

For example, the Juvenile Court Judges' Commission in the Commonwealth of Pennsylvania developed such a project in the 1980s because of its concern with increased commitments to training schools.[23] The standard adopted for this project included a caseload size of no more than fifteen, a minimum of three contacts per week with the youth, a minimum of one contact per week with the family or guardian, and a minimum of six months and a maximum of twelve months of intensive services.[24] Thirty-two counties in Pennsylvania had established ISPs with these standards by the end of 1989.[25]

An integrated Social Control model of intensive supervision recently has been developed to address the major causal factors identified in delinquency theory and research. This proposed model integrates the central components of strain, control, and social learning theories (see Figure 8–3). It contends that the combined forces of inadequate socialization, strains between educational and occupational aspirations and expectations, and social disorganization in the neighborhood lead to weak bonding to conventional values and to activities in the family, school, and community. Weak bonding, in turn, can lead juveniles to delinquent behavior through negative peer influence.[26]

The evaluation of adult ISPs in adult probation has received encouraging results in prevention of recidivism.[27] Two national evaluations of these programs in juvenile probation, however, have discovered that "neither the possible effectiveness nor the possible ineffectiveness of these programs had been carefully examined. As a result, their status in this regard, including their impact on recidivism, was essentially unknown."[28]

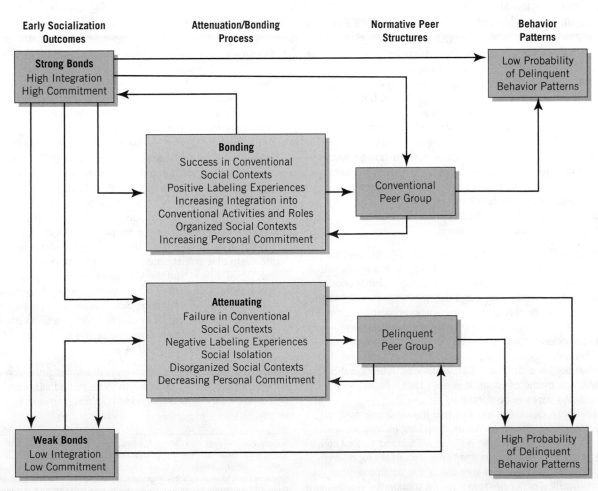

FIGURE 8–3
Integrated Strain–Control Paradigm

Source: Barry Krisberg et al., *Juvenile Intensive Supervision: Planning Guide* (Washington, DC: Office of Juvenile Justice and Delinquency Prevention, 1994), 7.

House Arrest and Electronic Monitoring

House arrest, or home confinement, is a program of intermediate punishment whereby youths are ordered to remain confined in their own residences during evening hours after curfew and on weekends.[29] Those receiving house arrest may be allowed to leave during the day for doctors' appointments, school, employment, or approved religious services. Electronic monitoring equipment may be used to verify probationers' presence in the residence in which they are required to remain.

Electronic monitoring (EM) was developed when a New Mexico district court judge read a comic strip in which the character Spider-Man was tracked by a transmitter affixed to his wrist. At the judge's request, an engineer designed an electronic bracelet to emit a signal picked up by a receiver placed in a home telephone. The design of the bracelet was such that if an offender moved more than 150 feet from his or her home telephone, the transmission signal would be broken. Authorities then would know that the offender had left his or her residence.[30] See Focus on Technology 8–4 for a discussion of the various types of electronic monitoring equipment.

More than 150,000 offenders, or approximately 20 percent of those subject to community-based supervision in the United States, are monitored at home.[31] Electronic monitoring equipment is being provided by some twenty private companies. Internationally, about 20 percent of 50,000 offenders in England and Wales who are under pre- or postrelease supervision receive electronic monitoring. In Sweden, about 25 percent of all inmates are placed on electronic

---

Focus on Technology 8–4
Technocorrections: Electronic Monitoring and GPS Systems in the Community

People generally think of electronic systems as a technological method to keep tabs on offenders in the community. However, use of the technology is expanding into a variety of applications. For example, at Bryan Adams High School in East Dallas, Texas, students who have been chronically truant are now being monitored with a global positioning system (GPS), which tracks their whereabouts 24/7 in an attempt to keep truants in school. In Midland, Texas, county officials have started using electronic ankle monitors to track the most chronically truant students.

The use of electronic monitoring to track criminal offenders who are granted community release should also expand as systems become more sophisticated. Some of the services provided by EM systems including the following:

- *Identity verification devices* can recognize different parts of the body to ensure that the reporting person is the offender.
- *Programmed contact devices* call the juvenile probationer at scheduled or random times and use various technologies to determine the identity of the person who answers, such as voice verification or a device worn by the probationer to insert in a verifier box attached to the phone, or a camera for visual verification).
- Another device is the *Tattle Tail*, which can detect alcohol or drug use by the offender. It senses these substances through the pores in perspiration.
- *Ignition interlock devices* are linked to the electronic systems of automobiles. The driver expels deep lung air into the device, and the vehicle will not start if the driver's blood alcohol content is registered above the level deemed unsafe for driving.
- *Victim notification systems* alert the victim when the offender is approaching his or her residence. A transmitter is worn by both the offender and the victim, and the receiver is placed in both residences.

- *Field-monitored devices,* or drive-by units, are used by probation or parole officers or other authorities. They are portable devices that can be handheld or used on a vehicle with a roof-mounted antenna. When within 200 to 800 feet of an offender's ankle or wrist transmitter, the portable device can detect the transmitter's radio signals.
- *Group monitoring units* permit supervisors to monitor several offenders in the same location, in order to verify attendance of multiple offenders in a day reporting program or to monitor offenders confined in a residential setting.
- *Global positioning systems* require the juvenile probationer to wear a transmitter that sends signals to a satellite and back to a computer monitor, pinpointing the offender's whereabouts at all times. *GPS location tracking systems* have receivers that detect satellite signals relating the exact time the signal is sent and the identity of the satellite sending the system. This expensive technology, which is generally used for high-risk offenders, can determine when an offender leaves an area where he or she is supposed to be (inclusion zone) or enters an area where he or she is not allowed to be (exclusion zone) as ordered by a judge.

These and other EM systems should revolutionize community supervision, allowing more people to be placed in probation and intermediate sanctions programs without compromising community safety.

Source: Sam Merton, "For Whom the Bell Tolls," *Dallas Observer,* June 16, 2008, www.dalas.observer.com/2008-06-26/news/for-whom; Secure Trac Systems, Omaha, Nebraska, www./securetrac.com/Services.aspx?-p-EMManagement; and Massachusetts Probation Service, "The Electronic Monitoring Program Fact Sheet," www.mass.gov/courts/probation/elmofactsheet.pdf (all cites accessed May 8, 2012).

monitoring.[32] The use of electronic monitoring in juvenile justice has gradually gained acceptance. For example, according to a November 1988 survey, only eleven juvenile programs used electronic monitoring.[33] Today, electronic monitoring programs are used in juvenile justice programs throughout the United States. These programs have the following goals:

- To increase the number of juveniles safely released into existing home confinement programs.
- To reduce the number of juveniles returned to juvenile detention for violating home confinement restrictions.
- To reduce the number of field contacts required of home confinement officers.
- To provide a reasonably safe alternative for lower-risk offenders.
- To provide for early reunification with the juvenile's family.
- To allow the juvenile to return to school.[34]

▲ Many probation programs involve youths in community projects to teach them marketable skills and teamwork. These youths are in a program in which they are helping to repaint a classroom of their school.
Washington County Juvenile Probation Services

What Is the Role of Volunteers in Probation?

As mentioned earlier, throughout the second half of the nineteenth century, volunteers were used widely to provide probation services, but they largely disappeared at the beginning of the twentieth century and did not reappear until the late 1950s. Indeed, only four courts were using volunteers in 1961; but today more than two thousand court-sponsored volunteer programs are in operation in this country. The use of volunteers has become one of the most valuable ways to help offenders adjust to community life.

The National Information Center on Volunteers in Court has identified several areas in which volunteers can work effectively with juvenile offenders. A volunteer can provide a one-to-one support relationship for the youth with a trustworthy adult; can function as a child advocate with teachers, employers, and the police; can be a good role model; can set limits and teach prosocial values; can teach skills or academic subjects; and can help the youth to develop a realistic response to the environment.

In addition to these areas of direct contact, volunteers can assist in administrative work. They can help recruit, train, and supervise other volunteers; can serve as consultants to the regular staff; can become advisers to the court, especially in the policy-making area; can develop good public relations with the community; and can contribute money, materials, or facilities.

Volunteers can improve the morale of the regular probation staff, because they are usually positive and enthusiastic about the services they provide. Because many volunteers are professionals (physicians, psychiatrists, psychologists, and dentists), they can provide services that the probation department may not have the financial resources to obtain. Finally, their contributions can reduce the caseload of the regular staff.

Several criticisms have been leveled at volunteer programs: The programs tend to attract a high ratio of middle-class persons, and they often create more work than they return in service. Volunteers cannot handle serious problems and sometimes in fact can harm their clients. Parents may resist the volunteer as an untrained worker. Although inappropriate volunteers clearly can do a great deal of damage, proper screening, training, and supervision can do much to ensure high-quality probation services from volunteers. See Focus on Practice 8–5 for a list of guidelines for working with juveniles.

What Programs Are Found in Juvenile Probation?

Juvenile probation usually has a number of programs available for probationers. Table 8–2 lists the types of programs to which probation officers can refer youths at the intake stage or later in the juvenile court process. Some jurisdictions, of course, have more of these programs than do others.

Focus on Practice 8–5
Considerations When Working with Juveniles

1. Keep continual contact with the child. We recommend one visit a week as a minimum.
2. Be patient. Don't expect overnight success. When things have been going wrong for years, they don't get corrected in a few weeks, or months, or even years.
3. Be ready for setbacks. Although we all like to achieve success with a child, remember [that] he or she does not owe it to us; the youth owes it only to himself or herself.
4. Give attention and affection. The child you are working with may never have known really sustained attention and affection and (at least at first) may not know how to handle it in a normal way.
5. Be prepared to listen and to understand what your child says. Too much talking on your part is more likely to break communication than enhance it.
6. Be a discerning listener; listening does not mean you have to believe everything you hear.
7. Don't prejudge. Avoid forming fixed and premature opinions until you have gathered all the background information you can.
8. Know your youngster. Get all the information you can on him or her.
9. Respect confidentiality, utterly and completely. Whatever you know about a youngster is under no circumstances to be divulged to or discussed with anyone but a person fully authorized by the court to receive this information.
10. Report violations. Confidentiality does not include keeping known violations a secret from the probation officer in charge of the youngster.
11. Be supportive, encouraging, friendly, but also firm. Although you have to report infractions, you can still be supportive, encouraging, and friendly, to the limit possible.
12. Present your ideas clearly, firmly, and simply. Always mean what you say, be consistent, and keep your promises.
13. Be a good role model. Before accepting court volunteer work, you must decide to live up to this special condition.
14. Avoid being caught in the middle. Be careful not to get caught between the child and his or her parents, the child and his or her teachers, or the child and the court.
15. Be yourself and care sincerely about the child. The more you are yourself, the easier it will be to communicate with the child.

CRITICAL THINKING QUESTIONS:

Is this a good list of considerations for working with juveniles? Would you like to be a volunteer probation officer? Which of these considerations would be most difficult for you to follow?

Source: Handout given to volunteer probation officer aides by the Black Hawk County Juvenile Court Services (Waterloo, Iowa).

Of the programs listed in Table 8–2, the most widely found would be restitution programs, in which youths are assigned to a work crew to fulfill their community service sanctions; volunteer programs in which volunteers are trained to work with probationers; mentoring programs in which youths individually or in a group are assigned mentors, especially, to work with them on their school assignments; youth courts or teen courts, in which juveniles themselves are given a voice on what happens to their peers; after-school study programs for youths doing below-average school work; drug or alcohol counseling, conducted

TABLE 8–2
Some Programs Utilized by Local Probation Departments

4-H programs	Self-improvement classes	Day schools
Social skills development	Youth courts	Evening care
School-based probation	Teen courts	Community service
Truancy programs	Drug courts	Volunteer work
After-school study programs	Positive peer groups	Big Brothers/Big Sisters
Sports programs	Reintegration programs	Volunteers in probation
After-school counseling	Faith-based initiatives	Drug counseling
Writing a paper	Treatment courts	Sex offender programs
Curfew requirements	Job training	Aggression replacement training
Restorative programs	Alcohol counseling	Runaway programs
Restitution programs	Mentoring programs	

individually or in groups; and sex offenders programs for youthful sex offenders. Some programs are established and then disappear when their funding runs out.

The Safe Houses in Minneapolis and St. Paul, Minnesota, which provide a haven for female prostitutes, constitute one such important probation program. Safe Houses' staff are particularly eager to involve adolescent females who have run away from home and ended up as prostitutes. When adolescent residents of the Safe Houses who were on probation for having committed prostitution were interviewed, they revealed that these facilities and their staff represent a hope for them to escape from street life and the inevitable drug use that accompanies street life.[35] With the downturn of the economy in the early twenty-first century in the United States, these types of programs have become more essential for dealing with increasing numbers of teenage runaways, homeless juveniles, juveniles with mental health issues, and juveniles "strung out" on drugs.

▲ Getting youths outside and engaging in constructive supervised activities is important to probation departments across the country. These are only some of the many ways youths can engage in community restitution. *Washington County Juvenile Probation Services*

What Are the Rights of Probationers?

The U.S. Supreme Court has ruled on two cases concerning probation revocation: *Mempa v. Rhay*[36] and *Gagnon v. Scarpelli*.[37] The Court held in the *Mempa* case that the Sixth Amendment's right to counsel applies to the sentencing hearing because it is an important step in criminal prosecution. The Court then extended this right to deferred sentencing and probation revocation hearings, and it reversed the decision of the lower courts because Mempa did not have counsel at his revocation hearing.

Gagnon v. Scarpelli involved an offender whose probation was revoked in Wisconsin without a hearing. Scarpelli, who had been sentenced to fifteen years of imprisonment for armed robbery, had his sentence suspended and was placed on probation for seven years. He was given permission to reside in Illinois, where he was subsequently arrested for burglary. His probation at that point was revoked without a hearing. Scarpelli appealed this revocation, claiming that his failure to receive a hearing and to have counsel violated his due process rights. Although the Supreme Court held that the right to counsel should be decided on a case-by-case basis, the Court did indicate that counsel should be provided on request when the probationer denies that he or she committed the violation or when the reasons for the violation are complex.[38]

These two adult cases have influenced what takes place during probation revocation in juvenile court, because in many jurisdictions the juvenile probationer has the same basic rights as an adult. The juvenile has the right to a hearing, the right to five-day notification of the probation revocation hearing, the right to be represented by an attorney, the right to confrontation, and the right to see the reports citing his or her violations.

"Reasonable efforts" is the standard that most juvenile judges adhere to at the probation revocation hearing. According to this standard, the probation officer must show that reasonable efforts have been made to provide different services and programs to the probationer. The standard requires that clear and convincing evidence be presented that the youth's refusal or inability to profit from these services and programs show that he or she cannot be kept in the community.[39]

Is Probation Effective?

Studies evaluating the probation efforts of the 1960s and 1970s indicated that probation was more effective than any other method for rehabilitating youthful offenders. For example, Douglas Lipton and colleagues' work reviewed the studies of adult and juvenile probation and arrived at the following conclusions: (1) evidence exists that a large proportion of offenders now incarcerated could be placed on probation without any change in the recidivism rates; (2) probationers have a significantly lower violation rate than do parolees; and

Focus on Practice 8–6
Successful Probation Practices in Adult Probation

- *The use of risk and needs assessments.* Corrections research supports the use of risk and needs assessments when offenders are first placed on probation and periodically thereafter. These assessments provide probation departments with resources to be able to prioritize intensive rehabilitation services.
- *Referral to community-based programs to reduce recidivism.* Offenders are more likely to be successful while on probation when effective treatments and assistance programs are provided. This includes drug treatment and mental health counseling, employment assistance, and anger management. In the current period of fiscal austerity being experienced in the United States, with its high rates of unemployment, jobs are particularly needed.
- *Manageable supervision caseloads.* No national standard is available for how many probationers should be on a probation officer's caseload. Supervision generally is only effective at reducing recidivism when coupled with treatment-oriented programs.

- *A system of graduated sanctions.* One of the key strategies for effectively intervening and interrupting the cycle of reoffending is to establish a system of graduated sanctions.
- *Program reviews and evaluations.* Certain programs and practices have been found to result in better outcomes and reduce recidivism. Several states, such as Oregon, utilize assessment tools to assess a program's fidelity, a measurement of how well the program or practice is implemented. In addition to measuring programs' fidelity, it is important to collect data on probationer outcomes that can indicate which programs are most effective in rehabilitating offenders.

Source: Mac Taylor, *Achieving Better Outcomes for Adult Probation: Executive Summary* (Sacramento, CA: California Legislative Analyst's Office, May 29, 2009), accessed May 20, 2012, at www.lao.ca.gov/2009/crim/probation/probation_052909.pdf.

(3) intensive probation supervision (a fifteen-ward caseload) is associated with lower recidivism rates for youths under age eighteen.[40]

But a major problem in evaluating the effectiveness of probation today is that probation has changed so much since these early evaluation studies. The risk reduction programs, such as restitution, intensive supervision, and house arrest, are still in the early stages of evaluation. Evidence suggests that restitution and intensive supervision studies are returning some positive results, but it is much too early to draw any conclusions about the present effectiveness of juvenile probation from these studies.

Two positive possibilities can be used to improve the effectiveness of juvenile probation: (1) to implement as much as possible the successful probation practices in adult probation (see Focus on Practice 8–6) and (2) to examine the juvenile probation practices that are found across the nation and to utilize those that might be helpful to your jurisdiction. For example, in the Department of Juvenile Justice in Florida, juvenile probation officers play a major role throughout the juvenile justice process because they work with youth from the time they are arrested to the time they transition back into the community. The strength of this approach to juvenile probation is that it provides a continuum of contact and services, so that juvenile probation officers continue their supervision of those with whom they have worked in the past, as they are processed through the juvenile justice system.[41]

Juvenile Justice Videos

JUVENILE PROBATION AND PAROLE 1

In the first *Juvenile Probation and Parole* video, a juvenile comes before an administrative review committee to discuss the possibility of being granted parole. The youth must "convince" the committee that his time in the facility has changed his behavior for the better and that as such he deserves a chance to be released back into the real world. Listen to the questions the committee is asking the youth in regards to his past criminal history, time in the facility, and future plans. What importance do these questions have in determining the status of the juvenile? Does the youth's gang involvement have an impact in the decision of the committee? What is the decision of the committee? What programs are suggested for the youth to engage in? Why?

SUMMARY

LEARNING OBJECTIVE 1: Explain how probation is administered.

Probation can be administered locally, state or executive administered, or a combination of both. One popular way is to place juvenile probation under the control of the juvenile court and to fund it through local government agencies.

LEARNING OBJECTIVE 2: Explain the functions of probation services.

Probation is a judicial disposition under which youthful offenders are subject to certain conditions imposed by the juvenile court and are permitted to remain in the community under the supervision of a probation officer.

LEARNING OBJECTIVE 3: Describe how classifications and risk/needs assessments are used in juvenile probation.

Concerns for public safety in the 1980s persuaded many probation departments to develop classification systems or to place probationers under intensive, medium, or minimum supervision. The most widely used risk/needs assessment of human behavior is the Problem Severity Index, a screening tool that gives intake officers and others clues about the types of problems the offenders might have.

LEARNING OBJECTIVE 4: Describe the use of restitution programs.

Restitution is a disposition of the courts that requires offenders to repay their victims or the community for their crimes. It can be either financial restitution or community service restitution.

LEARNING OBJECTIVE 5: Explain the use of intermediate punishment, including intensive supervision programs.

One of the graduated sanctions, or intermediate punishment, programs used in juvenile justice is intensive supervision programs. Probationers who are placed on intensive probation are required to have increased contacts with their probation officers, and other forms of external controls and surveillance might also be required.

LEARNING OBJECTIVE 6: Describe the use of house arrest and electronic monitoring.

House arrest is a program of intermediate sanctions whereby youths are ordered to remain confined in their own residences during evening hours after curfew and on weekends. Electronic monitoring equipment may be used to verify probationers' presence in the residence in which they are required to remain.

LEARNING OBJECTIVE 7: Summarize the roles and responsibilities of probation officers.

Probation officers' many responsibilities include intake, caseload management, supervision and investigation, and report writing.

LEARNING OBJECTIVE 8: Explain how probation can be revoked and the rights of probationers.

The juvenile has the right to a hearing, the right to five-day notification of the probation revocation hearing, the right to be represented by an attorney, the right to confrontation, and the right to see the reports citing his or her violations.

LEARNING OBJECTIVE 9: Summarize juvenile probation officers' effectiveness.

Early evaluations indicated the effectiveness of juvenile probation, but recent evaluation data are lacking. There is reason to believe that restitution and intensive supervision, as well as risk reduction programs, will reflect their effectiveness. The new methods of crime control are currently being evaluated.

KEY TERMS

balanced approach to juvenile probation, p. 169
electronic monitoring (EM), p. 176
house arrest, p. 176
intake, p. 168

intensive supervision programs (ISPs), p. 174
investigation, p. 171
probation, p. 165
probation subsidy programs, p. 167

restitution, p. 173
restorative justice model, p. 169
social study report, p. 171
supervision, p. 168
Wisconsin system, p. 169

REVIEW QUESTIONS

1. What do you feel is the most effective way to administer probation?
2. Do you believe that probation and parole should be administered together?
3. How can probation officers establish better relations with probationers?

4. Would you like to be a probation officer? Why or why not? What major problems would you face? How would you attempt to solve them?

GROUP EXERCISES

1. *Group Work:* Discuss what probation is, how it operates, and how it is organized across the nation.
2. *Writing to Learn Exercise:* Write a paragraph identifying and describing the functions of probation. Critique and revise.
3. *Group Work:* Discuss what to do with a youthful offender who commits a violent crime. If he or she sent to an adult prison, how can this offender be protected? What services does this offender need?

4. *Writing to Learn Exercise:* Write a paragraph on how the courts approach the issues of risk control and crime reduction. Critique and revise.
5. *Writing to Learn Exercise:* Write a paragraph or two on the characteristics of the best behaviors of probation officers. Critique and revise.

NOTES

1. U.S. Department of Justice, Office of Public Affairs, *Attorney General Eric Holder's Task Force on Children Exposed to Violence Holds Final Public Hearing in Detroit, Tuesday, April 24, 2012.*

2. Howard N. Snyder and Melissa Sickmund, *Juvenile Offenders and Victims: 2006 National Report* (Pittsburgh, PA: National Center for Juvenile Justice, 2006), 174–75.

3. See http://www.partnering4students.org/part-three/tool-d1.html (accessed May 19, 2012).

4. John L. Worrall, Pamela Schram, Eric Hays, and Matthew Newman, "An Analysis of the Relationships Between Probation Caseloads and Property Crime Rates in California Counties," *Journal of Criminal Justice* 32 (2004), 231–41.

5. Joan Petersilia, *The Influence of Criminal Justice Research* (Santa Monica, CA: Rand, 1987), 72.

6. K. Heilbrun, C. Cottle, and R. Lee, "Risk Assessment for Adolescents," *Juvenile Justice Fact Sheet* (Charlottesville: Institute of Law, Psychiatry, and Public Policy, University of Virginia, 2000).

7. Ibid.

8. C. Cottle, R. Lee, and K. Heilbrun, "The Prediction of Criminal Recidivism in Juveniles: A Meta-Analysis," *Criminal Justice and Behavior* 28, no. 3 (June 2001), 367–94.

9. Craig S. Schwalbe, "A Meta Analysis of Juvenile Justice Risk Assessment Instruments: Predictive Validity by Gender," *Criminal Justice and Behavior* 35 (November 2008), 1367–81.

10. See Dennis Maloney, Dennis Romig, and Troy Armstrong, "The Balanced Approach to Juvenile Probation," *Juvenile and Family Court Journal* 39 (1989), 1–49.

11. Ibid., 10. See also Gordon Bazemore and Mark S. Umbreit, *Balanced and Restorative Justice: Program Summary* (Washington, DC: Office of Juvenile Justice and Delinquency Prevention, 1994).

12. Bazemore and Umbreit, *Balanced and Restorative Justice,* 5.

13. Ibid., 7.

14. See Lori L. Colley, Robert C. Culbertson, and Edward J. Latessa, "Juvenile Probation Officers: A Job Analysis," *Juvenile and Family Court Journal* 38 (1987), 1–12.

15. Robert Emerson, *Judging Delinquents: Context and Process in the Juvenile Court* (Chicago: Aldine, 1969), 253.

16. Anne L. Schneider, "Restitution and Recidivism Rates of Juvenile Offenders: Results from Four Experimental Studies," *Criminology* 24 (1986), 533.

17. William G. Staples, "Restitution as a Sanction in Juvenile Court," *Crime and Delinquency* 32 (April 1986), 177.

18. OJJDP Model Program Guide, *Restitution/Community Service,* accessed at http://www.dsgonline.com/mpg_non_flash/restitution?community?service.htm.

19. Patrick Griffin and Patricia Torbet, eds., *Desktop Guide to Good Juvenile Probation Practice: Mission-Driven, Performance-Based, and Outcome-Focused* (Pittsburgh, PA: National Center for Juvenile Justice, 2002), 85.

20. Ibid., 85–86.

21. Ted Palmer, *The Re-Emergence of Correctional Intervention* (Newbury Park, CA: Sage Publications, 1992), 80.

22. Emily Walker, "The Community Intensive Treatment for Youth Program: A Specialized Community-Based Program for High-Risk Youth in Alabama," *Law and Psychiatry Review* 13 (1989), 175–99.

23. Cecil Marshall and Keith Snyder, "Intensive and Aftercare Probation Services in Pennsylvania," paper presented at the annual meeting of the American Society of Criminology, Baltimore, MD, November 7, 1990, 3.

24. Bernadette Jones, "Intensive Probation, Philadelphia County, November 1986–February 1989," paper presented at the annual meeting of the American Society of Criminology, Baltimore, MD, November 1990, Appendix, p. 1.

25. Marshall and Snyder, "Intensive and Aftercare Probation Services in Pennsylvania."

26. Barry Krisberg et al., *Juvenile Intensive Supervision: Planning Guide* (Washington, DC: Office of Juvenile Justice and Delinquency Prevention, 1994), 7.

27. For a review of these studies in intensive supervision programs for adults, see Clemens Bartollas and John P. Conrad, *Introduction to Corrections,* 2d ed. (New York: HarperCollins, 1992).

28. Palmer, *The Re-Emergence of Correctional Intervention,* 82.

29. J. Robert Lilly and Richard A. Ball, "A Brief History of House Arrest and Electronic Monitoring," *Northern Kentucky Law Review* 13 (1987), 343–74.

30. Richard A. Ball, Ronald Huff, and Robert Lilly, *House Arrest and Correctional Policy: Doing Time at Home* (Newbury Park, CA: Sage Publications, 1988), 35–36.

31. Jennifer Lee, "Some States Track Parolees by Satellite," *New York Times,* January 31, 2002, A3.

32. Ralph Gable and Robert Gable, "Electronic Monitoring: Positive Intervention Strategies," *Federal Probation* 69 (2005), 21–25.

33. Joseph B. Vaughn, "A Survey of Juvenile Electronic Monitoring and Home Confinement Programs," *Juvenile and Family Court Journal* 40 (1989), 4, 22. For a description of another program, see Michael T. Charles, "The Development of a Juvenile Electronic Monitoring Program," *Federal Probation* 53 (1989), 3–12.

34. Vaughn, "A Survey of Juvenile Electronic Monitoring and Home Confinement Programs."

35. One of the authors and his wife interviewed willing residents of these Safe Houses.

36. *Mempa v. Rhay,* 339 U.S. 128, 2d Cir. 3023 (1968).

37. *Gagnon v. Scarpelli,* 411 U.S. 778 (1973).

38. Ibid.

39. Information gained from an interview with a juvenile probation officer in Iowa.

40. Douglas Lipton et al., *The Effectiveness of Correctional Treatment: A Survey of Evaluation Studies* (New York: Praeger, 1975), 59–61.

41. Florida Department of Juvenile Justice, *Florida Juvenile Justice Probation and Community Intervention,* accessed May 21, 2012, a http://www.djj.state.fl.us/services/probation.

Community-Based Programs

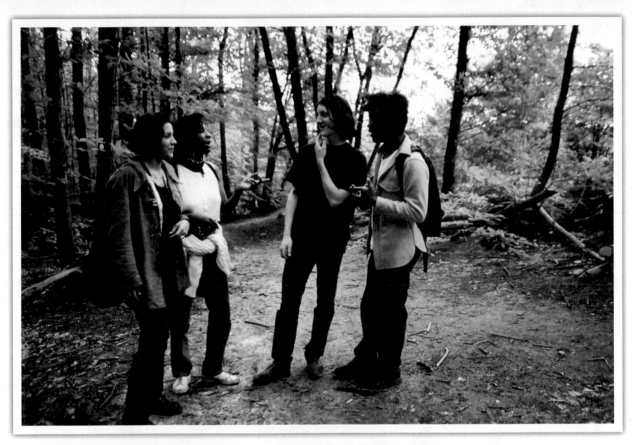

Directphoto.org/Alamy

Learning Objectives

1. Summarize the philosophy and objectives of community-based corrections.
2. Explain how community-based programs are administered.
3. Explain the importance of delinquency prevention.
4. Describe diversion and various diversion programs.
5. Describe residential programs in the community.
6. Evaluate the effectiveness of community-based programs.

From 1969 to 1973, Dr. Jerome Miller was head of the Massachusetts Department of Youth Services, during which time Miller closed the reform schools in Massachusetts and replaced them with a few small, secure units and a diverse array of community-based services.

Miller creatively and courageously acted to change Massachusetts from large state schools to one of community-based programs. He described and implemented several principles:

1. *Reform the "deep end" first. Eliminate large rural institutions and replace them with small urban-based alternatives for the "worst kids." If the least deserving youth are treated with fairness and decency, the rest of the system will follow.*

2. *Ensure that the funds follow the youth to the community; otherwise the alternatives to institutions will become supplements, increasing costs and capacity and unnecessarily isolating more youth.*

3. *Stay partially connected to the youth. Seek to understand and respect the uniqueness of each person and his or her life story.*

4. *Develop a diversity of alternative responses to youths' behavior, in a meaning-ful and dynamic process for matching youth and programs.*

5. *Seize the moment. True reform is much more a matter of messy increments through risk-taking, creative fund management, and manipulation of personnel rules and staff appointments than master planning and smooth administration.*

6. *Build broad coalitions. Seek support not only from the usual child advocacy and juvenile reform groups, but also rely heavily on groups such as the League of Women Voters.[1]*

This chapter-opening quote describes Miller's accomplishments in converting Massachusetts' juvenile justice system from one of state-dominated institutions to community-based programs and services. His principles continue to inspire those who are leading the way toward focusing on corrections and are a reminder that community-based programs offer a more effective approach to youth in trouble than long-term institutional care. Today, an impressive array of programs for juvenile offenders exists in communities across the nation. These programs include delinquency prevention, runaway facilities, foster care facilities, diversion, day treatment programs, group homes, and wilderness learning experiences. The ongoing search for solutions to the problem of juvenile crime, the popularity of deinstitutionalization in juvenile justice, and the emphasis in the past 20 years on short-term behavioral control probably best explains why there are so many programs for juvenile offenders. Community-based programs range from those focusing on delinquency prevention and diversion from the juvenile justice system to those designed for short-term residential care; the trend toward evidence-based programming continues to influence these efforts.

What Is the Philosophy Underlying Community-Based Corrections?

Three somewhat diverse philosophies guide community-based programming: (1) reintegration, (2) a continuum of sanctions, and (3) restorative justice and peacemaking.

Reintegration

Community-based programs have rested on a **reintegration philosophy** that assumes that both the offender and the receiving community must be changed. The community is as important as the client and plays a vital role in facilitating the reabsorption of offenders into its life. The task of corrections, according to this philosophy, involves the reconstruction, or construction, of ties between offenders and the community through maintenance of family bonds, employment and education, and placement in the mainstream of social life. Youths should be directed to community resources, and the community should be acquainted with the skills and needs of youthful lawbreakers.

Continuum of Sanctions

Advocates for more effective juvenile justice are increasingly calling for a range of punishment options, providing graduated levels of supervision in the community. Judges are able to exercise discretion by selecting, from a range of sentencing options, the punishment that best fits the circumstances of the offense and the youth. Intermediate sanctions are said to allow juvenile judges to match the severity of punishment with the severity of the crime. Juvenile institutions, then, are treated as backstops, rather than backbones, of the corrections systems.[2]

Providing justice through a **continuum of sanctions**, ranging from diversion programs to being placed in community correctional facilities, is one of the exciting innovations in juvenile corrections today. The intermediate sanctions can be grouped from those less intrusive to offenders to those that are most intrusive. The basic aim behind intermediate sanctions, or alternative sanctions, is to escalate punishments to fit the offense. These sanctions typically are administered by probation departments and include intensive probation (which was examined in Chapter 8), community service, house arrest, and electronic monitoring. But they also involve sentences that are administered independently of probation, such as day treatment programs, drug courts, and residential care. See Figure 9–1.

| **Less Intrusive to Offenders** |
| Prevention programs |
| Diversion programs |
| Probation |
| Day treatment programs |
| Community restitution |
| Drug courts |
| **More Intrusive to Offenders** |
| Intensive probation |
| House arrest |
| Electronic monitoring |
| Residential facilities |

FIGURE 9–1
Continuum of Sanctions

Restorative Justice

Restorative justice recently has been coupled with intermediate sanctions. Humanistic in its treatment of offenders, restorative justice has as its focus the welfare of victims in the aftermath of crime. In bringing criminal and victim together to heal the wounds of violation, the campaign for restorative justice advocates alternative methods to incarceration, such as intensive community supervision. The most popular of the restorative strategies are victim–offender conferencing and community restitution. In many states, representatives of the victims' rights movement have been instrumental in setting up programs in which victims/survivors confront their violators.[3]

Other elements are involved in most restorative justice approaches. Restorative justice processes pay attention not only to the harm inflicted on the direct victims of a crime, but also to the ways in which the crime has harmed the offender and the community. The focus, thus, is on victim healing, offender reintegration, and community restoration. This emphasis on victim healing has persuaded some to consider restorative justice to be a victim-centered approach. Yet the emphasis on providing offenders an opportunity to make amends and to increase their awareness of the consequences of their actions has persuaded others to regard restorative justice as offender focused. It is the third emphasis, community restoration, that puts victim healing and offender reparation into perspective.

How Are Community-Based Programs Administered?

Comprehensive state-sponsored, locally sponsored, and privately administered programs are the three basic types of organizational structures in community-based programs.

In California, Indiana, Kansas, Michigan, Minnesota, and Oregon, the state sponsors residential and day treatment programs under **community corrections acts**. The Minnesota Community Corrections Act, which has become a model for other community corrections acts, provides for a state subsidy to any county or group of counties that chooses to develop its own community corrections system. The costs for juvenile offenders who are adjudicated to a training school are charged back to the county, and these costs are subtracted from the county's subsidy. Counties in Minnesota have been understandably reluctant to commit youths to training schools because of the prohibitive costs and therefore have established and encouraged a wide variety of residential and day treatment programs.

Voices of Delinquency: Dr. Robert Clark: On the Firing Line

▲ Some community-based corrections have as a goal the teaching of skills to youths who may have none. Here a supervisor is working with young men teaching them the basics of cooking.

Washington County Juvenile Leader program

The deinstitutionalization movements in Maryland, Massachusetts, North Dakota, South Dakota, Utah, and a number of other states also has led to the development of a wide network of residential and day treatment programs for youths. In Massachusetts, the Department of Youth Services administers some of these programs, but more often the juvenile court sponsors these programs, or state or local agencies contract for services for those youths from private vendors in the community. Regardless of who administers these community programs, the most innovative and effective ones attempt to provide a continuum of care for youthful offenders.

Private delivery of correctional services to youthful offenders originated in the early days of juvenile justice in this nation. Most of these programs were religious or business backed, but died in the early to mid-1900s. In 1972, the private sector reentered the field of juvenile corrections in an unprecedented manner. Privatization, or placing control of facilities in the hands of the private sector, has expanded significantly in the past few decades. Privately run programs are emerging as a result of budget problems that prevent local or state agencies from supplying the services in an efficient manner. Privatization has become big business and has sparked the interests of investors from all walks of life. Those operating in the private sector receive payment for their programs through federal, state, or local funding, from insurance plans, or from the juvenile's parents.

Federal grants are the basis of the funding of many community programs. SafeFutures is a program funded by the Office of Juvenile Justice and Delinquency Prevention (OJJDP) that appears to be a model worth replicating in communities across the nation. The Safe-Futures urban sites are located in Boston, Massachusetts; Contra Costa County, California; Seattle, Washington; and St. Louis, Missouri. The other two sites are Imperial County, California (rural), and Fort Belknap Indian Community, Harlem, Montana (tribal government). SafeFutures seeks to improve the service delivery system by creating a continuum of care that is responsive to the needs of youths and their families at all points along the path toward juvenile reintegration. This coordinated approach of prevention, intervention, and treatment is designed both to serve the juveniles of a community and to encompass the human service and the juvenile justice systems. A national evaluation is being conducted to determine the success of the continuum of services in all six sites.

Project CRAFT (community restitution and apprenticeship-focused training program), a vocational training program for high-risk youths, is sponsored by the Home Builders Institute (HBI), the educational arm of the National Association of Home Builders (NAHB). Project CRAFT offers pre-apprenticeship training and job training for adjudicated juveniles referred to the program. It was started in 1994 by HBI in Bismarck, North Dakota; Nashville, Tennessee; and Sabillasville, Maryland. It has been replicated in five sites in Florida (Avon Park, Daytona Beach, Fort Lauderdale, Lantana, and Orlando), in Texas, and in Connecticut.[4] This program works in partnership with private facilities, juvenile judges, juvenile justice

Focus on Treatment 9–1
Project CRAFT

Project CRAFT has been teaching court-involved youth ages fifteen to nineteen marketable construction trade skills that help them find jobs, instill a sense of confidence and excitement about the future, and provide them with a viable career option. Once graduates earn their industry-recognized pre-apprenticeship certification, Project CRAFT staff helps them find jobs, continue their education, or join the military.

Journey-level trades instructors teach the HBI's Pre-Apprenticeship Certificate Training (PACT) curriculum in electric wiring, carpentry, landscaping, facilities maintenance, plumbing, and painting, depending on the program. Some of their accomplishments include the following:

- HBI Project CRAFT Avon Park Youth Academy students have installed solar panels on academy buildings to reduce its carbon footprint.

- Students at HBI Project CRAFT Baltimore have renovated Family League of Baltimore City office space into a state-of-the-art conference room and built a bench for a presiding Baltimore City juvenile judge.
- HBI Project CRAFT Okeechobee Girls Academy is the only juvenile justice residential program in Florida that provides career and technical education to young women.

Source: Home Builders Institute, "Project CRAFT," n.d., accessed May 12, 2012, at http://www.hbi.org/Programs/PreApprenticeship/ProjectCRAFT.aspx.

system personnel, educational agencies, and other human service agencies.[5] Although the initial sample size was small, an early study indicates that most youths, 15 percent, recidivate during their first year after release, 10 percent recidivate their second year, and 1 percent recidivate their third year after release; these data compare favorably with an untreated sample with a 50 percent recidivism rate over three years.[6] See Focus on Treatment 9–1.

What Is the Role of Delinquency Prevention?

Delinquency prevention is defined as any attempt to thwart youths' illegal behavior before it occurs. The Juvenile Justice and Delinquency Prevention Act of 1974 and the Juvenile Justice Amendments of 1977, 1980, and 1984 established the prevention of delinquency as a national priority.[7] Anne Newton has identified three levels of delinquency prevention:

- *Primary prevention* is directed at modifying conditions in the physical and social environment at large.

- *Secondary prevention* is directed at early identification and intervention in the lives of individuals or groups in criminogenic circumstances.

- *Tertiary prevention* is directed at the prevention of recidivism (after delinquent acts have been committed and detected).[8]

An example of primary prevention is the 1960s Mobilization for Youth program, which took place in a sixty-seven-block area of Manhattan's Lower East Side in New York City. This project was designed to improve educational and work opportunities for area youth, to make a variety of services available to individuals and families, and to provide assistance in community organization.[9]

A number of primary and secondary prevention programs have been conducted since the beginning of the twentieth century, using neighborhood groups, the family and school environment, youth gangs, and social and mental health agencies as points of intervention.[10] Unfortunately, the results of most of these programs have been disappointing.[11] The Chicago Area Projects, however, is one program that achieved some success in the fifty years or so that it was conducted (see Focus on Policy 9–2). More recently, a number of programs have been developed that promise to be more effective in preventing juvenile crime, including juvenile violence and drug abuse.

Focus on Policy 9–2
The Chicago Area Projects

Clifford Shaw and Henry McKay, the founders of the Chicago Area Projects (CAP) in 1934, were committed to creating community consciousness directed at solving social problems on the local level. The first projects were initiated in three areas: South Chicago, the Near West Side, and the Near North Side. Today, each project area has a committee that operates as an independent unit under the guidance of a board of directors chosen by the local community residents. Twenty such projects have functioned in Chicago, and others have formed throughout the state. In addition, other groups in Illinois have taken the projects as the model for their own delinquency control programs.

The projects have three basic goals: First, they provide a forum for local residents to become acquainted with new scientific perspectives on child rearing, child welfare, and juvenile delinquency. Second, they initiate new channels of communication between local residents and the institutional representatives of the larger community, those influencing the life chances of local youth. Third, they bring adults into contact with local youths, especially those having difficulties with the law.

The philosophy of CAP is based on the belief that instead of quickly turning over youth to the justice system, the community should deal with its own problems and intervene on behalf of its youth. Citizens of the community show up in juvenile court to speak on behalf of the youths; they organize social and recreational programs so that youths can participate in constructive activities. The leaders of the local groups, often individuals who were once in CAP programs, know how to relate to and deal with youths who are having problems at school or with the law.

More than fifty years ago, Saul Alinsky stated, "It's impossible to overemphasize the enormous importance of people doing things for themselves." What is ultimately significant about CAP is that this philosophy was its basic approach to delinquency prevention. CAP advocated grassroots leadership, neighborhood revitalization, the community's role in policing itself, and the importance of community dispute resolution. These same emphases were incorporated into most community crime prevention strategies in the late 1990s.

Source: The description of CAP is largely derived from Harold Finestone, *Victims of Change: Juvenile Delinquents in American Society* (Westport, CT: Greenwood Press, 1976), 125–30.

Promising Prevention Programs

The Blueprint for Violence Prevention, which was developed by the Center for the Study and Prevention of Violence at the University of Colorado–Boulder and supported by the OJJDP, identified eleven model programs as well as twenty-one promising violence prevention and drug-abuse programs that had been demonstrated—through rigorous empirical evaluation—to work.[12] Table 9–1 presents the complete list of models and promising programs the researchers identified; the following discussion briefly describes the eleven model programs:

- *Big Brothers Big Sisters of America (BBBSA)* With a network of more than five hundred local agencies throughout the United States that maintains more than 145,000 one-to-one relationships between youth and volunteer adults, BBBSA is the best known and largest mentoring program in the nation. The program serves youths ages six to eighteen, a significant number of whom are from disadvantaged and single-parent households.[13] An eighteen-month evaluation found that compared with a control group waiting for a match, youths in this mentoring program were 46 percent less likely to start using drugs, 27 percent less likely to start drinking, and 32 percent less likely to hit or assault someone. They also were less likely to skip school and more likely to have improved family relationships.[14]

- *Bully Prevention Program* The primary purpose of the Bully Prevention Program is to restructure the social environment and secondary schools in order to provide fewer opportunities for bullying and to reduce the peer approval and support that reward bullying behavior.[15] In a large sample evaluated in Norway and South Carolina, the Bully Prevention Program has proved effective. For example, children in thirty-nine schools in South Carolina in grades four through six reported that they experienced a 25 percent decrease in bullying by other children.[16]

- *Functional Family Therapy (FFT)* A short-term family-based prevention and intervention program, FFT has been successfully applied in a variety of contexts to treat high-risk youths and their families. Specifically designed to help underserved and at-risk youth ages eleven to eighteen, this multisystemic clinical program provides twelve one-hour family therapy sessions spread over three months. More difficult cases receive

TABLE 9–1
Model and Promising Programs and Age Groups of Juveniles Targeted

Blueprints Program	Age Group				
	Pregnancy/ Infancy	Early Childhood	Elementary School	Junior High School	High School
Model Programs					
Big Brothers Big Sisters of America (BBBSA)			X	X	X
Bullying Prevention Program			X	X	
Functional Family Therapy (FFT)				X	X
Incredible Years		X	X		
Life Skills Training (LST)				X	
Midwestern Prevention Project (MPP)				X	
Multidimensional Treatment Foster Care (MTFC)				X	X
Multisystemic Therapy (MST)				X	X
Nurse–Family Partnership	X				
Project Toward No Drug Abuse (Project TND)					X
Promoting Alternative Thinking Strategies (PATHS)			X		
Promising Programs					
Athletes Training and Learning to Avoid Steroids					X
Brief Strategic Family Therapy			X	X	X
CASASTART			X	X	
Fast Track			X		
Good Behavior Game			X		
Guiding Good Choices			X	X	
High/Scope Perry Preschool		X			
Houston Child Development Center	X	X			
I Can Problem Solve		X	X		
Intensive Protective Supervision				X	X
Linking the Interests of Families and Teachers			X		
Preventive Intervention				X	
Preventive Treatment Program			X		
Project Northland				X	
School Transitional Environmental Program				X	X
Seattle Social Development Project			X	X	
Strengthening Families Program: Parents and Children 10–14			X	X	
Student Training through Urban Strategies				X	X
Syracuse Family Development Program	X	X			
Yale Child Welfare Project	X	X			

Source: Sharon Mihalic, Abigail Fagan, Katherine Irwin, Diane Ballard, and Delbert Elliott, *Blueprints for Violence Prevention* (Washington, DC: Office of Juvenile Justice and Delinquency Prevention, 2004), table 1-1.

up to twenty-six to thirty hours of therapy.[17] The success of this program has been demonstrated and replicated for more than twenty-five years. Using controlled follow-up periods of one, three, and five years, evaluations have demonstrated significant and long-term reductions in the reoffending of youth, ranging from 25 to 60 percent.[18]

- *Incredible Years: Parent, Teacher, and Child Training Series* The Incredible Years model program has a comprehensive set of curricula designed to promote social competence and to prevent, reduce, and treat conduct problems in children ages two to eight who exhibit or are at risk for conduct problems. In the parent, teacher, and child training programs, trained facilitators use videotaped scenes to encourage problem solving and sharing of ideas.[19] The three series of this program have received positive evaluations as meeting their original goals.[20]

- *Life Skills Training (LST)* LST is a three-year intervention curriculum designed to prevent or reduce the use of "gateway" drugs, such as tobacco, alcohol, and marijuana. The lessons emphasize social resistance skills training to help students identify pressures to use drugs.[21] Using outcomes from more than a dozen studies, evaluators have found LST to reduce tobacco, alcohol, and marijuana use by 50 to 75 percent in intervention students compared to control students.[22]

- *Midwestern Prevention Project (MPP)* MPP includes school normative environment change as one of the components of a comprehensive three- to five-year community-based prevention program that targets gateway use of alcohol, tobacco, and marijuana. The school-based intervention is the central component of the program. The program begins in either sixth or seventh grade and includes ten to thirteen classroom sessions taught by teachers trained in the curriculum.[23] Researchers followed students from eight schools who were randomly assigned to treatment or control groups for three years and found that the program brought net reductions of up to 40 percent in adolescent smoking and marijuana use, with results maintained through high school graduation.[24]

- *Multidimensional Treatment Foster Care (MTFC)* MTFC has been found to be a cost-effective alternative to group or residential treatment, confinement, or hospitalization. This program provides short-term (usually about seven months), highly structured therapeutic care in foster families. Its goal is to decrease negative behaviors, including delinquency, and to increase youths' participation in appropriate prosocial activities, including school, hobbies, and sports.[25] Evaluations of MTFC demonstrated that youths who participated in the program had significantly fewer arrests (an average of 2.6 versus 5.4 offenses) and spent fewer days in lockup than youths placed in other community-based programs.[26]

- *Multisystemic Therapy (MST)* MST provides cost-effective community-based clinical treatment of chronic and violent juvenile offenders who are at high risk of out-of-home placement. The overarching goal of the intervention is to help parents understand and help their children overcome the multiple problems contributing to antisocial behavior. Treatment generally lasts for about four months, which includes about sixty hours of therapist–family contact.[27] Program evaluations have revealed 25 to 70 percent reductions in long-term rates of rearrest and 47 to 64 percent reductions in out-of-home placements. These and other positive results were maintained for nearly four years after treatment ended.[28]

- *Project Toward No Drug Abuse (Project TND)* This project targets high school youth ages fourteen to nineteen who are at risk for drug abuse. Over a four- or five-week period, twelve classroom-based lessons offer students cognitive motivation enhancement activities, information about the social and health consequences of drug use, correction of cognitive misperceptions, help with stress management, training in self-control, and instruction in active listening.[29] At a one-year follow-up, participants in forty-two schools revealed reduced use of cigarettes, alcohol, marijuana, and hard drugs.[30]

- *Promoting Alternative Thinking Strategies (PATHS)* A comprehensive program for promoting social and emotional competencies, PATHS focuses on the understanding, expression, and regulation of emotions. The yearlong curriculum is designed to be used by teachers and counselors within classrooms of children in kindergarten through fifth grade. The basic outcome goals are to provide youths with tools to achieve academically as well as to enhance the classroom atmosphere and the learning process. Evaluations have found positive behavioral changes related to hyperactivity, peer aggression, and conduct problems.[31]

Violent Juvenile and Delinquency Prevention Programs

Spearheaded by the OJJDP, the belief emerged in the 1990s that the most effective strategy for juvenile corrections is to place the thrust of the prevention and diversion emphases on high-risk juveniles who commit violent acts. These are the juveniles who commit the more serious and most frequent delinquent acts and are the youths whom officials are quick to place into the adult system. At the same time that the seriousness of their behaviors has effected changes in juvenile codes across the country, research is beginning to find that these high-risk youths can be impacted by well-equipped and well-implemented prevention and treatment programs.[32]

These programs are based on the assumption that the juvenile justice system does not see most serious offenders until it is too late to effectively intervene.[33] Advocates also presume that in order to reduce the overall level of violence in American society successful intervention in the lives of high-risk youth offenders, who commit about 75 percent of all violent juvenile offenses, is necessary.[34]

The general characteristics of these programs is that they (1) address key areas of risk in youths' lives, (2) seek to strengthen the personal and institutional factors that contribute to the development of a healthy adolescent, (3) provide adequate supervision and support, and (4) offer youths a long-term stay in the community.[35] Importantly, these prevention programs must be integrated with local police, child welfare, social services, school, and family preservation programs. Comprehensive approaches to delinquency prevention and intervention require a strong collaborative effort between the juvenile justice system and other service provision systems, such as health, mental health, child welfare, and education. An important component of a community's comprehensive plan is to develop mechanisms that effectively link these service providers at the program level.[36]

The comprehensive, or multisystemic, aspects of these programs are designed to deal simultaneously with many aspects of youths' lives. The intent is that they are intensive, often involving multiple contacts weekly, or possibly daily, with at-risk youth. They build on the strength of these youths, rather than dwell on their deficiencies. These programs operate mostly, although not exclusively, outside of the formal justice system under a variety of public, nonprofit, or university auspices. Finally, they combine accountability and sanctions with increasingly intensive treatment and rehabilitation services that are achieved through a system of graduated sanctions, in which an integrated approach is employed to stop the penetration of youthful offenders into the system.[37]

In 1996, three communities—Lee and Duval Counties in Florida and San Diego County in California—collaborated with the OJJDP to apply the processes and principles that were described in the *Comprehensive Strategy for Serious, Violent and Chronic Juvenile Offenders.* Initial evaluations of the three pilot projects found that each of the sites has benefited significantly from the comprehensive planning process. Although it was deemed premature to assess any long-term impact on juvenile delinquency, several short-term indicators of success were found.[38] The following are among the pilot programs' accomplishments:

- Enhanced community-wide understanding of prevention services and sanctions options for juveniles
- Expanded networking capacity and better coordination among agencies and service providers
- Institution of performance measurement systems
- Hiring of staff to spearhead the ongoing *Comprehensive Strategy* planning and implementation efforts
- Development of comprehensive five-year strategic action plans.[39]

What Is the Role of Diversion?

In the late 1960s and early 1970s, **diversion programs** sprung up across the nation. *Diversion,* which refers to keeping juveniles outside the formal justice system, can be attempted either through the police and the courts or through agencies outside the juvenile justice system. The main characteristic of diversion initiated by the courts or police is that the justice subsystems retain control over youthful offenders. A youth who fails to respond to such a program usually will be returned to the juvenile court for continued processing within the system.

In the 1990s, new forms of diversion developed in the United States and included community courts, alternative dispute resolution, gun courts, youth courts, and drug courts. Youth courts and drug courts are described next in more detail. See Figure 9–2.

Youth Courts

Youth courts, also known as *teen courts, peer courts,* or *student courts,* are juvenile justice programs in which youths are sentenced by their peers. Established and administered in a variety of ways, most youth courts are used as a sentencing option for first-time offenders

FIGURE 9–2
Diversion Programs

ages eleven to seventeen who are charged with misdemeanor nonviolent offenses. The offender typically acknowledges his or her guilt and participates in a youth court voluntarily, rather than going through the more formal juvenile justice procedures.[40] See Figure 9–3 for a timeline covering the history of youth courts. In 2005, more than 110,000 youths volunteered to hear more than 115,000 juvenile cases, and more than 20,000 adults volunteered to be facilitators for peer justice in youth court programs. Also, in 2005, there were 1,158 youth court programs in forty-nine states and the District of Columbia providing restorative justice for youthful offenders.[41]

Four possible case-processing models are used by these courts:

- *Adult judge.* An adult serves as judge and rules on legal terminology and courtroom procedures. Youths serve as attorneys, jurors, clerks, bailiffs, and so forth.

- *Youth judge.* This is similar to the adult judge model, except that a youth serves as the judge.

- *Tribunal.* Youth attorneys present the case to a panel of three youth judges, who decide the appropriate disposition for the defendant.
  A jury is not used.

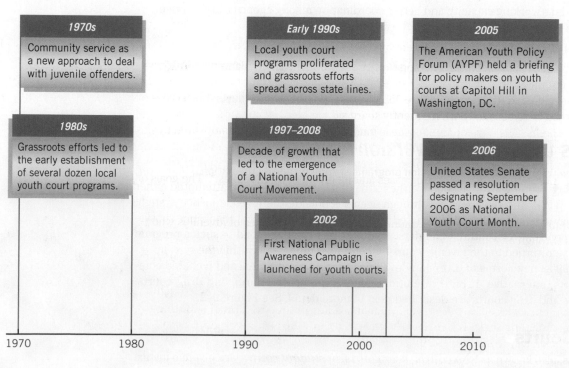

FIGURE 9–3
Timeline of the Development of Youth Courts

Source: Scott B. Peterson and Jill Beres, *Report to the Nation 1993-2008*, published by Scott B. Peterson, 2008.

- *Peer jury.* This model does not use youth attorneys: the case is presented to a youth jury by a youth or adult. The youth jury then questions the defendant directly.[42]

Youth courts usually handle first-time offenders who are charged with offenses such as theft, misdemeanor assault, disorderly conduct, and possession of alcohol. The majority of these teen courts (87 percent) reported that they rarely or never accepted any juveniles with prior arrest records. The most common disposition used by these courts is community service. Following this disposition in level of use are victim apology letters (86 percent), apology essays (79 percent), teen court jury duty (75 percent), drug/alcohol classes (59 percent), and monetary restitution (34 percent).[43]

The Juvenile Drug Court Movement

By 2007, approximately two thousand juvenile drug courts had opened. The juvenile drug court movement is part of an expanding adult drug court movement that is dedicated to juveniles and that has been stimulated by Title V of the Violent Crime Control and Law Enforcement Act of 1994, an act that authorizes the attorney general to make grants to various agencies to establish drug courts. These agencies include states, state and local courts, units of local government, and Indian tribal governments.[44]

A number of strategies are common to juvenile drug courts compared with traditional juvenile courts:

- Much faster and much more comprehensive intake assessments
- Much greater focus on the functioning of the juvenile and the family throughout the juvenile court system
- Much closer integration of the information obtained during the assessment process as it relates to the juvenile and the family
- Much greater coordination among the court, the treatment community, the school system, and other community agencies in responding to the needs of the juvenile and the court
- Much more active and continuous judicial supervision of the juvenile's case and treatment process
- Increased use of immediate sanctions for noncompliance and incentives for progress for both the juvenile and the family.[45]

In 1998, six states operated juvenile drug courts, with the greatest activity in California and Florida. By January 1, 2008, there were 2,148 drug courts operating throughout the United States; included in this number are 455 juvenile and 301 family courts. Both types of courts are noted here because both frequently share similar types of clients and, indeed, often the same clients. The development of these innovative approaches was motivated by the spike in the crack cocaine epidemic in the late 1980s and the early 1990s and the difficulty regular courts had in handling the resulting increased caseloads. The innovation was also fueled by the increasing numbers of drug cases among juveniles and families.[46] The goals of the juvenile drug courts are to:

- Provide immediate intervention treatment, and structure in the lives of juveniles who use drugs through ongoing, active oversight and monitoring by the drug court judge.
- Improve juveniles' level of functioning in their environment, address problems that may be contributing to their use of drugs, and develop/strengthen their ability to lead crime- and drug-free lives.
- Provide juveniles with skills that will aid them in leading productive crime- and drug-free lives—including skills that relate to their educational development, sense of self-worth, and capacity to develop positive relationships in the community.
- Strengthen families of drug-involved youth by improving their ability to provide structure and guidance to their children.
- Promote accountability of both juvenile offenders and those who provide services to them.[47]

Unfortunately, little research exists today that addresses how successful youth courts are in reducing drug use and criminal recidivism. We may, nevertheless, perhaps learn some lessons from the successes of the adult courts, keeping in mind that extrapolating findings from adult drug courts to juvenile courts is extremely risky. Huddleston et al. summarize adult drug court research by noting that some programs reduce recidivism by 7 to 14 percent and others by up to 35 percent. The programs also are cost effective because successfully treated offenders remain free from law enforcement activities, judicial case processing, and the victimization that occurs as a result of repeat criminal activity.[48]

Juvenile Mediation Program

The purpose of the Juvenile Mediation Program is for all involved parties to join together to resolve differences without court involvement. It began in Brooke County, West Virginia, and spread to Hancock, Marshall, Ohio, Tyler, and Wetzel counties. The program works with school-age children and adolescents, ages six to eighteen, and their families or guardians.[49] Status and nonviolent offenders from the aforementioned five counties are eligible to participate in this program. A mediator is used whose responsibilities include determining the sincerity of remorse of the accused juvenile, deciding a fair and just penalty for his or her wrongdoing, and concluding whether any services are necessary. Before proceeding to the mediation hearing, the juvenile must have admitted that he or she is guilty of a crime and signed a waiver of rights. This waiver relinquishes the right to have witnesses or lawyers present.[50]

The program is designed to last no more than ninety days and is terminated under one of the following conditions: (1) successful: juvenile completed the required contractual agreement in ninety days; (2) unsuccessful: juvenile failed to meet the required agreement and is referred to the probation department for formal proceedings; or (3) dismissal: the mediator recommends dismissal prior to disposition. As of September 30, 2000, the rate of successful contract resolutions was 93 percent, or 625 of the first 670 participants. As of July 1, 2001, all 625 juveniles had remained nondelinquent and status offense–free.[51]

Community/Residential Treatment Programs

The three types of community/residential treatment programs discussed next are day treatment programs, group homes, and wilderness programs (Figure 9–4).

How Do Day Treatment Programs Operate?

Day treatment programs, in which youngsters spend each day in the program and return home in the evenings, have been widely used in community-based juvenile corrections. These court-mandated programs are popular because they are more economical than residential placements, do not need to provide living and sleeping quarters, make parental participation easier, require fewer staff members, and are less coercive and punishment oriented.

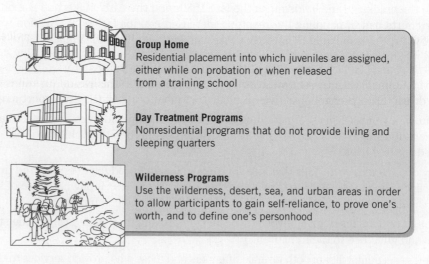

Group Home
Residential placement into which juveniles are assigned, either while on probation or when released from a training school

Day Treatment Programs
Nonresidential programs that do not provide living and sleeping quarters

Wilderness Programs
Use the wilderness, desert, sea, and urban areas in order to allow participants to gain self-reliance, to prove one's worth, and to define one's personhood

FIGURE 9–4
Three Types of Community Programs

Nonresidential programs generally serve male juveniles, although California has operated two programs for girls and several coeducational ones. Nonresidential programs have been used widely by the California Treatment Project, the New York Division for Youth, and the Florida Division of Youth Services. Nonresidential programs in New York, which are called STAY, are similar to many other nonresidential programs in that they expose youths to a guided-group interaction experience.

Day treatment programs, similar to diversion programs, were used less in the 1980s and early 1990s than they were in the 1970s, but two of the most promising programs—the Associated Marine Institute (AMI) and Project New Pride—continue to thrive. The AMI is described here.

Associated Marine Institute

The original Associated Marine Institute (AMI) was a privately operated program funded jointly by state and private donations. It tailored its programs to the geographical strengths of each community, using the ocean, wilderness, rivers, and lakes to stimulate productive behavior in youths referred by the courts or by the Division of Youth Services. Of the forty schools and institutes of the AMI, twenty-five were nonresidential. The fourteen- to eighteen-year-old male and female trainees in the nonresidential programs lived at home or in foster homes.[52]

The Marine Institutes, which constituted most of the schools, set individual goals for the training period in a dozen categories, including diving, ship-handling skills, ocean science, lifesaving, first aid, and such electives as photography and marine maintenance. In a nationally broadcast television program, in which he announced his crime bill, President Bill Clinton said, "These [AMI] programs are giving young people a chance to take their future back, a chance to understand that there is good inside them."[53]

Today AMI is renamed AMIkids and operates fifty-six programs in eight states. The reorganization and new name reflect the fact that the program now includes many different types of programs across the nation that formerly operated independently. Rather than just operating marine programs, today's AMIkids programs provide probation services including community service, wilderness programs, substance abuse counseling, varied after-school programs, and volunteering their services to veterans, the homeless, senior citizens, shoreline cleanups, and other types of community service supporting President Obama's call for community service.[54]

How Do Group Homes Operate?

The group home, the group residence, and the group foster home are all used in juvenile corrections in this country. The term **group home** generally refers to a single dwelling owned or rented by an organization or agency for the purpose of housing offenders. Although it is not part of an institutional campus, this facility provides care for a group of about four to twelve children, and staff are viewed as houseparents or counselors rather than as foster parents. The administrative, supervisory, and service responsibility for the group home rests with the parent agency or organization. Usually indistinguishable from nearby homes or apartments, the group home reaches out to the community for resources and service.

The terms *group residence* or *halfway house* are used in some parts of the country to identify a small facility serving about thirteen to thirty-five youths. It usually houses two or more groups of youths, each with its own child care staff. This residence tends to use agency rather than community services, and its architecture and large size differentiate it from nearby homes and apartments.

Group homes fulfill several purposes in juvenile corrections. First, they provide an alternative to institutionalization. Dependent, neglected, and other noncriminal youths, especially, are referred to them. Second, group homes may be used as short-term residences. The communities in which they are located provide the youths with the resources to deal with such problems as family conflict, school difficulties, and peer interactions. Third, group homes can be used either as a "halfway-in" setting for offenders who are having difficulty keeping to the conditions of probation or as a "halfway-out" setting for juvenile offenders who are returning to the community but do not have adequate home placement.

▲ This is a halfway house for young women who are battling problems of addiction to alcohol and drugs. Some have been ordered here by the courts; others are brought directly here by police and probation officers if they find the women in trouble on the streets.
Kathryn O'Lare

Voices of Delinquency: Pat Lutz: The Turning Point

Group home programs tend to vary from home to home because they have been developed to meet the varying needs of different populations and communities, and standard guidelines do not exist. Consequently, group homes often reflect the personal philosophies of their founders or directors. Intake criteria, length of stay, treatment goals, target population serviced, quantity and quality of staffing, services offered, physical facilities, location in relation to the rest of the city, and house rules are extremely diverse in group homes in this country. This diversity need not be a problem, however, if additional support services are available. One of the most important studies of juvenile justice found a significant reduction in recidivism in Massachusetts when community-based programs had an integrated network of services.[55]

Many group homes are treatment oriented. Group therapy often is used as a treatment modality. These group sessions are largely supportive; they do not probe very deeply, and discussion usually is limited to problems as they arise. Guided Group Interaction (GGI) is probably the most popular treatment method; the members of the group are expected to support, confront, and be honest with one another so that they may be helped in dealing with their own problems. The role of the therapist in GGI is to help the members develop a more positive and prosocial group culture. Some group homes deliberately avoid a comfortable climate, and staff may even try to arouse anxiety. The treatment philosophy behind this is that without a relaxed atmosphere, youths are more likely to become unsettled and thereby more receptive to personality change.

One of the most innovative programs is the House of Umoja (HOU) project, which was founded in 1968 and was officially organized in 1970 as a youth development agency. When she became aware that one of her six sons had joined a gang, Sister Falaka and her husband, David Fattah, took the bold step of inviting the gang to become a part of their family. Sister Falaka saw possible solutions to the violence of gangs in "the strength of the family, tribal concepts, and African value systems." She and her husband created an African-style extended family in which members of the gang could find alternative values to those of their street-life culture. Residents are required to be drug free and are encouraged to maintain good grades. Since its establishment, three thousand adolescents belonging to seventy-three different street gangs have passed through the HOU doors. The success of the Umoja concept has led to its duplication in Bridgeport, Connecticut, and Portland, Oregon. The principles of this resident program are part of the National Center for Neighborhood Enterprise's highly successful Violence-Free Zone initiative that has been instituted in five cities.[56]

Yet innovative programs still are not typical of group homes across the nation. In too many group homes, vacancies are hard to find and many even have long waiting lists. Staff are notoriously underpaid, believe that they have not been properly trained, and have high rates of turnover.[57] Residents also typically have longer stays than they would have in training schools, and this raises real questions about whether group homes are a less punitive placement than juvenile institutions. The evaluations of residential programs further make it difficult to support the conclusion that residential programs in the community result in lower rates of recidivism than do institutional programs. Nevertheless, a convincing case

Focus on Offenders 9–3
What Quakerdale Meant to Me

I spent an entire day thinking about what Quakerdale really means to me. I didn't want to just write a bunch of meaningless prose—I wanted to capture the truth of Quakerdale's impact on my life. As I was thinking, [I] realized that I could probably write an entire novel about my experiences there and what it has done for me. Quakerdale taught me tolerance, patience, respect, self-restraint, and communication.

When I was admitted to Quakerdale, I was a lost, hopeless, self-serving seventeen year old. I had recently attempted suicide, run away from home, dropped out of high school, gotten into marijuana, was a self-mutilator, and didn't understand the meaning of "impulse control." Throughout my six months there, I worked intensively with staff and participated whole-heartedly in groups and peer activities, as well as actively "working my program."

I learned patience when dealing with others and when working through my own problems. I learned that sometimes, I will not get what I want or expect, but that it's still okay.

I learned respect. I did not need to learn to respect others so much as to respect myself. I came to realize that my behavior was hurting no one worse than it was hurting me. It was destroying me physically and, especially, emotionally. And I deserved a lot better than that. I opened my eyes to the ways in which I was treating myself. I realized that I would hope to never allow another person to treat me the way I was treating myself. I saw that the worst relationship I had in my life was my relationship with me. For example, I would never dream of murdering someone, but that's exactly what I tried to do to myself. I realized that I could not hope to be happy if I continued my present, self-hating relationship.

If I was to ever learn to love myself, I needed to learn self-restraint. Quakerdale taught me this, as well. Sometimes, it's better to delay gratification for a more permanent, safer sense of gratification. Impulse control is still something that I work on daily, but I think it is obvious from my present life-circumstances versus my "pre-Quakerdale" life-circumstances that I learned a great deal about self-control. I think that a big part of what helped me learn self-control was Quakerdale's "open door" policy. I had the option to run away, but every day that I chose to remain, I gained more responsibility and privileges. After only four months at Quakerdale, I was allowed to walk to and from East High School every day by myself. This showed me that staff trusted me, which made me *want* to be trustworthy. I received positive reinforcement for acting and reasoning appropriately, which built up my confidence in myself and [the] staff's ability to help me.

I learned communication. I had family sessions once a week, and I had group [sessions] many times a week. We were always encouraged to hold others accountable, hold ourselves accountable, and be honest. I learned that telling the truth can be much more rewarding than trying to "stay out of trouble" by lying. If I did something wrong or lied to staff, I was positively reinforced if I confessed on my own. I learned that it is my responsibility to be honest, and *others'* responsibility to react to my honesty in an appropriate way. It is not my responsibility to keep everyone happy, especially if it ruins me inside. However, I also learned to "pick my battles."

What it all comes down to is that: before Quakerdale, I was literally taking my life in my hands and not even caring if I dropped it. Since Quakerdale, I have gone on to graduate from Dowling High School with a 3.89 cumulative grade point average, made [the] National Honor Society, received the Aquinas Key, [and] received an Academic medal, and [a] letter in academics. I was accepted to all three colleges to which I applied, and I now attend the University of Minnesota, where I have a cumulative grade point average of 3.48, made the Dean's List second semester, and am majoring in English and taking a minor in psychology. I am by no means completely "cured" of the emotional difficulties that I had before Quakerdale, but I can honestly say that I have learned how to live a wonderful life, despite, and sometimes due to, my trials and difficulties. Thank you, Quakerdale, for helping me grow into the woman I have become [italics included in the original].

CRITICAL THINKING QUESTIONS

Why do you think this program was so successful with this young woman? What would it take for us to have more House of Umoja and Quakerdale programs?

Source: Letter received from Rita Fernau, director of the Quakerdale program, and used with permission of the author.

---

can be made that residential programs are at least as successful as training schools, with far less trauma to youths and usually at less cost to the state. In Focus on Offenders 9–3, a former resident writes a letter to the director of Quakerdale, a residential program for girls, expressing her appreciation for what the program has meant to her life.

Voices of Delinquency: Ruth Fernau, Social Worker at Quakerdale

What Are Wilderness Programs?

Outward Bound is the best-known wilderness, or survival, program. All of the outdoor **wilderness programs**, whether they take place in the mountains, canoe country, the forest, the sea, or the desert, conclude that the completion of a seemingly impossible task is one of the best means to gain self-reliance, to prove one's worth, and to define oneself as a person.

Outward Bound

Outward Bound programs were first used in England during World War II. The first Outward Bound school in the United States was the Colorado Outward Bound School, which was established in 1962 and accepted its first delinquents in 1964. This program, situated in the Rocky Mountains at an altitude of 8,800 feet, consists of mountain walking, back-packing, high-altitude camping, solo survival, rappelling, and rock climbing. Other Outward Bound programs soon followed in Maine, Minnesota, North Carolina, Oregon, and Texas. A similar program, a Homeward Bound school, was opened in 1970 in Massachusetts. Several community-based wilderness programs that begin and end in the community but include sessions in a nearby wilderness area are also in operation.[58]

Today, Outward Bound has twelve regional schools: Alabama, Baltimore, California, Hurricane Island, New York City, North Carolina, Northwest, Omaha, Philadelphia, Rock Mountain, Thompson island, and Voyageur. They offer 750 wilderness courses serving adults, teens, and youths. Courses include rock climbing, kayaking, dogsledding, sailing, rappelling, back-packing, and more. Over ten thousand students have participated in wilderness courses. Outward Bound also offers multiyear partnerships with 150 schools across the United States. It encourages over thirty thousand students and four thousand teachers to reach high levels of achievement and to discover their potential.[59]

Are Community-Based Programs Effective?

Increasing numbers of studies demonstrate empirically that many community-based correctional programs reduce recidivism and are less expensive than confinement. So what more needs to be done? It would appear that improving the effectiveness of community-based corrections ultimately requires breaking down community resistance and obtaining greater citizen involvement in community-based programs, while at the same time developing a broader continuum of services in the community for juveniles who need such services.

To break down community resistance and to obtain greater citizen involvement in community-based programs, departments of juvenile corrections must develop and implement a certain plan of action. A well-developed plan should (1) establish programs and (2) decide who will be placed in community facilities. Unfortunately, no agreement has been reached on how to implement either of these strategies.

Careful planning is obviously necessary to gain greater public support for community-based programs. A department should mount a massive public education effort through the communications media, should seek support for the project from the various subcommunities of the community—ethnic, racial, and special interest groups—and should develop a sophisticated understanding of the decision-making processes in society. But should this be done before or after a program has been initiated in the community?

Advocates of keeping the community informed as soon as a site for a program is chosen claim that to do otherwise is dishonest. Opponents of this approach argue that advance information will permit the community to mobilize resistance against the proposed community program. They claim that the community is more likely to accept an already established and successful program than one that exists only on the drawing board.

Widespread controversy also exists over the selection of youths to be placed in community-based programs. One approach is conservative: if the wrong youth is put in the wrong place at the wrong time and commits a serious or violent crime, such as rape or murder, the adverse publicity may destroy the best-planned and implemented program. Therefore, to preserve the viability of community-based programs, only juveniles most likely to be helped should be kept in the community. The opposite approach argues that all but the hard-core recidivist should be retained in the community, for it is there that the youth's problems began in the first place. Advocates of this position believe that institutionalization will only make more serious criminals out of confined youths. Some of these supporters even propose leaving many of the hard-core or difficult-to-handle youths in the community.

Finally, improving the continuum of services for juveniles in a community usually requires a strong deinstitutionalization emphasis. The programs that have this integration of services are more likely to have positive effects on youthful offenders assigned to them. Another advantage of these continuum-of-service programs is that they are not as likely to experience the fragmentation and duplication of services that are found so frequently in other programs in the juvenile justice system.

Juvenile Justice Videos

RESIDENTIAL FACILITY TOUR

In *Residental Facility Tour* the important aspects of a residential facility are highlighted. The social worker at the beginning of the video discusses a youth within the facility. Why is this child in the facility? Are the young girl's actions delinquent? The director of admissions at the facility gives a detailed description of how the facility handles the individualized needs of the children. What are some of the treatments that are available to the children within the facility? Discuss the "individual program plans" as mentioned by the director of admissions. Based on the video and the readings from this chapter, compare and contrast the residential facility with other community-based programs.

SUMMARY

LEARNING OBJECTIVE 1: Summarize the philosophy and objectives of community-based corrections.

The three philosophies that are guiding community-based programming are reintegration, the necessity for a continuum of sanctions, and restorative justice and peacemaking.

LEARNING OBJECTIVE 2: Explain how community-based programs are administered.

The three types of organizational structures in community-based programs are comprehensive state-sponsored, locally sponsored, and privately administered programs.

LEARNING OBJECTIVE 3: Explain the importance of delinquency prevention.

The importance of delinquency prevention is that it attempts to thwart youths' behavior before it becomes delinquent. Many promising delinquency programs exists.

LEARNING OBJECTIVE 4: Describe diversion and various diversion programs.

Diversion programs aim to keep juveniles outside the formal justice system. One of the most celebrated of these diversionary programs is youth courts. Another type is juvenile drug courts.

LEARNING OBJECTIVE 5: Describe residential programs in the community.

Three common types of community/residential treatment programs are day treatment programs, group homes, and wilderness programs.

LEARNING OBJECTIVE 6: Evaluate the effectiveness of community-based programs.

- The effectiveness of community-based programs is controversial. Even in studies that have found lower recidivism rates for youths left in the community, the criticism is often made that juveniles who were more likely to succeed were selected for the experimental group and that the authorities altered the results by giving the experimentals more chances than the controls before returning them to the juvenile court. Even though it is difficult to substantiate the widespread conclusion that community-based programs lower the recidivism rate, a good case can be made for the assumption that community-based corrections programs are at least as successful as institutional confinement is, with far less trauma to youngsters and less cost to the state.

- Community-based programs continue to face several challenges, especially those posed by the reduction of federal funding and the public's preference for getting tough on youth crime. Yet the cost effectiveness of these programs, as opposed to the prohibitive expense of long-term institutions, should continue to lead to an increased use of alternative programs in the community.

KEY TERMS

community corrections acts, p. 185
continuum of sanctions, p. 185
day treatment programs, p. 194

delinquency prevention, p. 187
diversion programs, p. 191
group home, p. 195

reintegration philosophy, p. 184
restorative justice, p. 185
wilderness programs, p. 197

REVIEW QUESTIONS

1. Why have delinquency prevention programs generally been so ineffective?
2. Why is the widening criticism of many of the delinquency prevention programs a serious indictment?
3. Of the programs discussed in this chapter, which do you feel is the best for helping offenders reintegrate into the community?
4. What specific strategies can departments of juvenile corrections pursue to enlist greater support from the community for community programs?
5. What are the main types of residential and nonresidential programs for juvenile delinquents?
6. How effective are community-based corrections? What is the essential link in increasing the effectiveness of community-based corrections?

GROUP EXERCISES

1. **Group Work:** First identify Ann Newton's three levels of delinquency prevention. Then develop the specific kinds of variables identified by Newton's three types of delinquency.
2. **Group Work:** Describe all of the different programs implemented in community-based corrections. Which of Newton's levels does each program represent and why?

3. **Writing to Learn Exercise:** Write approximately two paragraphs that identify the different model prevention programs and their rates of success—with the textbook closed. Critique and revise after reviewing the rates of success of each of the programs as cited in the text.

NOTES

1. Joseph Heinz, Theresa Wise, and Clemens Bartollas, *Successful Management of Juvenile Residential Facilities: A Performance-Based Approach* (Alexandria, VA: American Correctional Association, 2010), 35–36.
2. Patricia M. Harris, Rebecca D. Petersen, and Samantha Rapoza, "Between Probation and Revocation: A Study of Intermediate Sanctions Decision-Making," *Journal of Criminal Justice* 29 (2001), 308.
3. Ibid., 175.
4. For more information on Project Craft in Florida and Connecticut, visit the Project Craft website at http://www.hbi.org/page.cfm?pageID=129.
5. Robin Hamilton and Kay McKinney, "Job Training for Juveniles: Project CRAFT," *OJJDP Fact Sheet* (Washington, DC: Office of Juvenile Justice and Delinquency Prevention, 1999), 1.
6. Steve V. Gies, *Aftercare Services* (Washington, DC: Office of Juvenile Justice and Delinquency Prevention, September 2003), 18–20. Accessed at http://www.ncjrs.gov/pdffiles1/ojjdp/201800.pdf.
7. For an expanded treatment of delinquency prevention, see Clemens Bartollas, *Juvenile Delinquency*, 8th ed. (Englewood Cliffs, NJ: Pearson, 2011).
8. Anne M. Newton, "Prevention of Crime and Delinquency," *Criminal Justice Abstracts* (June 1978), 4.
9. Marylyn Bibb, "Gang-Related Services of Mobilization for Youth," in *Juvenile Gangs in Context: Theory, Research, and Action*, edited by Malcolm W. Klein (Upper Saddle River, NJ: Prentice Hall, 1967), 175–82.
10. For a description of the various prevention programs, see Bartollas, *Juvenile Delinquency*, 521–51.
11. For a review of these studies examining the effectiveness of prevention programs, see ibid., 524.
12. Sharon Mihalic et al., *Successful Implementation: Lessons from Blueprints* (Washington, DC: Office of Juvenile Justice and Delinquency Prevention, 2004), 1.
13. Sharon Mihalic et al., *Blueprints for Violence Prevention* (Washington, DC: Office of Juvenile Justice and Delinquency Prevention, 2004), 55.
14. D. E. McGill, S. Mihalic, and J. K. Grotpeter, "Big Brothers Big Sisters of America," in *Blueprints for Violence Prevention: Book 2*, edited by D. S. Elliott (Boulder: University of Colorado, Institute of Behavioral Science, Center for the Study and Prevention of Violence, 1997).

15. Mihalic et al., *Blueprints for Violence Prevention*, 30–31.
16. M. A. Pentz, S. Mihalic, and J. K. Grotpeter, "The Midwestern Prevention Project," in *Blueprints for Violence Prevention: Book 1,* edited by D. S. Elliott (Boulder: University of Colorado, Institute of Behavioral Science, Center for the Study and Prevention of Violence, 1997).
17. Mihalic et al., *Blueprints for Violence Prevention*, 26–27.
18. J. E. Alexander et al., "Functional Family Therapy," in *Blueprints for Violence Prevention: Juvenile Justice Bulletin,* edited by D. S. Elliott (Boulder: University of Colorado, Institute of Behavioral Science, Center for the Study and Prevention of Violence, 2000).
19. Mihalic et al., *Blueprints for Violence Prevention*, 22–23.
20. C. Webster-Stratton et al., "The Incredible Years: Parents, Teachers and Child Training Series," in *Blueprints for Violence Prevention: Book 11*, edited by D. S. Elliott (Boulder: University of Colorado, Institute of Behavioral Science, Center for the Study and Prevention of Violence, 2001).
21. Mihalic et al., *Blueprints for Violence Prevention*, 47.
22. G. Botvin, S. Mihalic, and J. K. Grotpeter, "Life Skills Training," in *Blueprints for Violence Prevention: Book 5*, edited by D. S. Elliott (Boulder: University of Colorado, Institute of Behavioral Science, Center for the Study and Prevention of Violence, 1998).
23. Mihalic et al., *Blueprints for Violence Prevention*, 31–33.
24. Pentz et al., "The Midwestern Prevention Project."
25. Mihalic et al., *Blueprints for Violence Prevention*, 56–58.
26. P. Chamberlain and S. Mihalic, "Multidimensional Treatment Foster Care," in *Blueprints for Violence Prevention: Book 8,* edited by D. S. Elliott (Boulder: University of Colorado, Institute of Behavioral Science, Center for the Study and Prevention of Violence, 1998).
27. Mihalic et al., *Blueprints for Violence Prevention*, 27–28.
28. S. W. Henggeler et al., "Multisystemic Therapy," in *Blueprints for Violence Prevention: Book 6*, edited by D. S. Elliott (Boulder: University of Colorado, Institute of Behavioral Science, Center for the Study and Prevention of Violence, 2001).
29. Mihalic et al., *Blueprints for Violence Prevention*, 47–48.
30. Ibid., 48.
31. Ibid., 46.
32. James C. Howell, ed., *Guide for Implementing the Comprehensive Strategy for Serious, Violent, and Chronic*

Juvenile Offenders (Washington, DC: Office of Juvenile Justice and Delinquency Prevention, 1995), 10.

33. Ibid., 3.
34. Ibid., 5.
35. Ibid.
36. Ibid., 9–10.
37. Ibid., 11.
38. Kathleen Coolbaugh and Cynthia J. Hansel, "The Comprehensive Strategy: Lessons Learned from the Pilot Sites," *Juvenile Justice Bulletin* (2000), 1.
39. Ibid., 10.
40. Scott B. Peterson and Jill Beres, *The First Report to the Nation on Youth Courts and Teen Courts* (published by Scott B. Peterson, 2008).
41. Ibid.
42. Ibid.
43. T. M. Godwin, *Peer Justice and Youth Empowerment: An Implementation Guide for Teen Court Programs* (Lexington, KY: American Probation and Parole Association, 1998).
44. Marilyn Roberts, Jennifer Brophy, and Caroline Cooper, *The Juvenile Drug Court Movement* (Washington, DC: Office of the Juvenile Justice and Delinquency Prevention, 1997), 1.
45. Ibid., 1–2.
46. C. West Huddleston III, Douglas B. Barlowe, and Rachel Casebolt, *Painting the Current Picture: A National Report on Drug Courts and Other Problem Solving Court Programs in the United States* (Washington, DC: Bureau of Justice Statistics, 2008), 1–16.
47. *Juvenile Drug Courts: Strategies in Procedure* (Washington, DC: Bureau of Justice Statistics, March 2003). Accessed at http://www.ncjrs.gov/pdffiles1/bja/191866.pdf.
48. Huddleston et al., *Painting the Current Picture*.
49. Robert R. Smith and Victor S. Lombardo, "Evaluation Report of the Juvenile Mediation Program," *Corrections and Compendium* 26 (October 2001), 1.
50. Ibid., 2.
51. Ibid.
52. Information on the Associated Marine Institute was supplied in a 1995 phone conversation with Magie Valdés.
53. Unpublished mimeographed statement circulated by AMI, n.d.
54. For additional information on AMIkids, see Jasmine Ouhrt, "New Name, Same Mission: AMI Lakeland Is Now AMIkids," accessed at http://www.theledger.com/article/20090725/NEWS/907255003?Title=New-Name-Same-Mission-AMI-Lakeland-Is-Now-AMIKids. Also see Links on AMIkids on Facebook at http://www.facebook.com/posted.php?id=108818992527.
55. B. Krisberg, J. Austin, and P. Steele, *Unlocking Juvenile Corrections* (San Francisco: National Council on Crime and Delinquency, 1991).
56. For the House of Umoja, see http://www.volunteersolutions.org/volunteerway/org/1236595.
57. One of the authors has had a number of former students who were employed in group homes, and they consistently make these criticisms.
58. Joshua L. Miner and Joe Boldt, *Outward Bound USA: Learning Through Experience* (New York: Morrow, 1981).
59. For Outward Bound USA, see http://www.outwardbound.org.

10 Juvenile Institutionalization

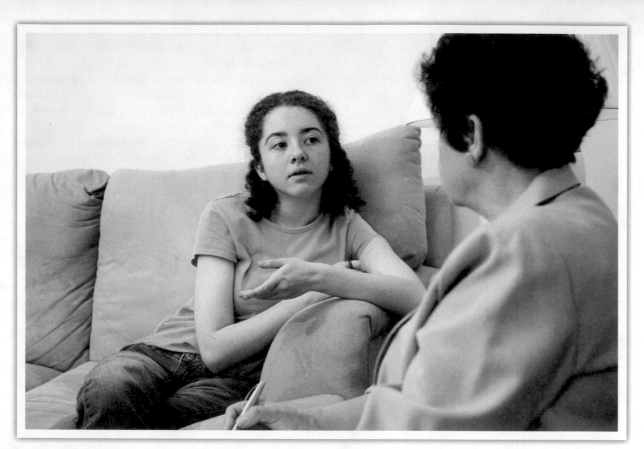

Lisa F. Young/Fotolia

Learning Objectives

1. Describe the purpose and operation of short-term confinement facilities, including jails, detention centers, and shelter care facilities.

2. Describe the purpose and operation of various long-term juvenile correctional facilities, including boot camps, reception and diagnostic centers, and ranches/forestry camps.

3. Describe the goals, programs, and operation of training schools.

4. Summarize the rights of juveniles who are institutionalized.

5. Summarize the factors that should be taken into consideration when implementing a confinement policy for juveniles.

The conditions under which juveniles are housed in institutional care have met with harsh criticism. California juvenile facilities, according to a recent report, are failing the state's children. The children have little chance of leaving improved, the report says, and some are worse off than when they arrived.[1] In March 2007, responding to the reports of sexual abuse of youths at Texas Youth Commission institutions, Texas Governor Rick Perry placed the Texas Youth Commission under conservatorship to guide reform of the agency. A report documents the violence, sexual abuse, and lack of accountability in the juvenile facilities of the state.[2] The Connecticut Juvenile Training School has been a headache for state authorities since its opening in 2001. The high-security perimeter fence, thick steel doors, and small cells with slits for windows make it feel more like a prison than a rehabilitation center for juveniles. The problems increased in 2010 as Connecticut raised the maximum age for juvenile offenders from fifteen to seventeen years old, moving many of the 250 to 300 sixteen- and seventeen-year-olds who previously went to adult prisons each year to juvenile facilities.[3]

The U.S. Department of Justice has filed lawsuits against juvenile facilities in eleven states as a result of supervision that is either abusive or negligent. In addition, the Associated Press contacted each state agency that oversees juvenile correctional centers and asked for information on the numbers of allegations and confirmed cases of physical, sexual, and emotional abuse by state members from January 2004 through 2007. According to this survey, more than thirteen thousand claims of abuse were identified in these facilities during this time period—a disturbing number given that the total population of detained youth was about forty-six thousand at the time the states were surveyed.[4]

The juvenile justice system often is accused of being too lenient, yet youths who are believed to be dangerous or who show little sign of mending their ways frequently find themselves locked up behind walls. The facilities in which these youths are placed are divided into two general categories: temporary-care facilities and correctional facilities. Jails, detention centers, and shelters are temporary-care facilities; boot camps, reception and diagnostic centers, ranches/forestry camps, and training schools are long-term correctional facilities. The primary differences between these two categories of facilities are the absence of correctional programs and the shorter lengths of stay in temporary-care facilities. Temporary-care facilities frequently house both males and females in the same general location, whereas correctional facilities often separate them. Juveniles waived to the adult court can also be sentenced to adult prisons, or they can be transferred to mental health placements. This chapter focuses on the training school because of the length of time it holds youths and because of the special role it has played in juvenile justice. See Focus on Policy 10–1.

What Types of Short-Term Confinement Are Used for Juveniles?

Juvenile offenders are placed in jails, detention centers, and shelter care facilities for short-term confinement.

Jails, as suggested in an earlier chapter, were one of the reasons that motivated reformers to establish houses of refuge. It was commonly agreed that the jails were no place for a juvenile. Overcrowded conditions and idleness fostered a lawless society, one in which the juvenile was frequently a sexual victim. Juveniles also had alarming rates of suicide in jails.

Still, partly because so few alternatives were available, large numbers of juveniles continued to be confined in county jails and police lockups. Estimates vary, but about 100,000 youths were locked up in jails each year during the 1970s.[5]

The numbers appeared to decline in the 1980s and 1990s, chiefly because of the Juvenile Justice and Delinquency Prevention Act (JJDPA) of 1974. This act provided restrictive

Focus on Policy 10–1
Good News in Juvenile Corrections

In the midst of the bad news about juvenile institutionalization, there is good news from California. In the past decade, California has closed eight of its eleven juvenile facilities and successfully turned the responsibility for its nonviolent offenders over to the counties. Governor Jerry Brown also wants to complete the transformation by phasing out the three remaining state facilities, that hold a thousand serious offenders. The state realized that it needed to develop different facilities for managing violent young offenders. Spending on the system has dropped by almost half, from nearly $500 million to about $245 million and the state has cut its juvenile population from about ten thousand in the mid-1990s to about a thousand today. Some critics are concerned that without a state juvenile system to hold violent offenders prosecutors may try more young people as adults, but the state can prevent this by monitoring and penalizing counties that overprosecute juveniles, and by allowing for extended custody in local facilities for those juveniles who have committed more serious crimes.

The Department of Corrections and Rehabilitation's Division of Juvenile Facilities, the former California Youth Authority, is still under a consent decree due to abusive conditions, systemic mismanagement, and ineffectual services (*Farrell v. Cate*, 2004). The closure of the state juvenile facilities would eliminate the state's obligation under the *Farrell* litigation, resulting in a potential $5 million budget reallocation to assist counties with the realignment and reduce the state's current deficit.

CRITICAL THINKING QUESTIONS

Is this good news? Is this something that would help reform the operation of juvenile institutions?

Source: Catherine McCracken and Selena Teji, *An Update: Closing California's Division of Juvenile Facilities: An Analysis of County Institutional Capacity* (Sacramento: Center on Juvenile and Criminal Justice, October 2010), accessed at http://www.cjcj.org.

criteria governing the confinement of juveniles in adult facilities. Congress amended the JJDPA in 1980, requiring participating states to remove all juveniles from adult jails and lockups by the end of 1985 if they wanted to receive federal funding for juvenile justice. The 1985 deadline was extended to 1988 and then again was amended in 1989 because so few states had achieved full compliance.[6] Over the years, the number of youths in adult jails has been dramatically reduced. At the same time, with an increasing number of states sending juveniles to adult court, the percentages of youths in adult jails is increasing.

According to data published in 2006, an estimated 6,159 youth younger than age eighteen were held in adult jails on June 30, 2004. These inmates accounted for 1 percent of the total jail population, as in 2003. In 2004, 87 percent of the jail inmates younger than eighteen were held as adults; this proportion was greater than the 80 percent in 2000 and the 76 percent in 1994.[7] Figure 10–1 contains the data related to the confinement of juveniles in adult jails.

FIGURE 10–1

Juveniles in Adult Jails by Year and Percentage

Source: Howard N. Snyder and Melissa Sickmund, *Juvenile Offenders and Victims: 2006 National Report* (Washington, DC: National Center for Juvenile Justice and Office of Juvenile Justice and Delinquency Prevention, 2006), 236; adapted from Beck's *Prison and Jail Inmates at Midyear 1999*, Beck and Karberg's *Prison and Jail Inmates at Midyear 2000*, Harrison and Karberg's *Prison and Jail Inmates at Midyear 2002*, and Harrison and Beck's *Prison and Jail Inmates at Midyear 2004*.

- Between 1990 and 1999, while the adult jail inmate population increased 48%, the jail inmate population under age 18 increased more than 300%.
- Between 1999 and 2004, the adult jail inmate population increased 19%, while the jail inmate population under age 18 decreased 25%.
- The number of jail inmates younger than 18 held as adults was 6,159 in 2004— up 21% from 1994.
- The number of jail inmates younger than 18 held as juveniles in 2004 was 924— down 42% from 1994.

Several reasons exist why removal of juveniles from jail continues to remain a distant goal. First, juveniles who are transferred to adult court and are waiting criminal trials make up an increasingly large category of youths confined in jail. Second, many states continue to resist full compliance with the JJDPA jail-removal mandate. The claim is frequently made that the states lack the necessary resources and alternatives to implement the jail-removal mandate.[8] Third, the belief is widely held that separating juveniles from adult inmates is sufficient to protect the juveniles against the harmful effects of jail confinement.

What is hopeful is that a number of states have taken a strong stand against the jailing of juveniles. California and Utah have made it unlawful to jail a youthful offender.[9] Illinois, Missouri, North Carolina, Tennessee, and Virginia enacted legislation in the 1980s, either prohibiting the jailing of minors or restricting the number of admissions.[10]

Detention Centers

Established at the end of the nineteenth century as an alternative to jail for juveniles, **detention centers**, also called *juvenile halls*, are intended to be temporary holding centers. The court administers the majority of juvenile detention centers, although state agencies, city or county governments, welfare departments, and juvenile courts also manage these facilities. The state governments of Connecticut, Delaware, Vermont, and Puerto Rico assume responsibility for administering juvenile detention centers. Georgia, Maryland, Massachusetts, New Hampshire, and Rhode Island operate regional detention facilities.

▲ The Shuman Detention Center in Pittsburgh is a modern facility designed primarily for more violent and troubled youths. Associated with the center are a shelter for minor offenders and many local agencies that provide support and assistance to youths and their families.
Kathryn O'Lare

The traditional detention center has sparked many horror stories, and on more than one occasion, former residents have described to the authors the toxic environment of these facilities. Fortunately, detention in the United States has experienced marked improvement in the past two decades. A nationwide movement to develop standards for detention and more innovative detention programs has provided the impetus to improve detention practices in the United States.

Attention homes were initiated in Boulder, Colorado, and have spread to other jurisdictions. Their stated purpose is to give juveniles *attention* rather than *detention*. These facilities have no fences, locked doors, or other physical restraints. They also provide more extensive programming and encourage more interaction among residents and staff. Home detention, as previously discussed, is a nonresidential approach to confinement. It was first used in St. Louis, Missouri; Newport News and Norfolk, Virginia; and Washington, D.C., and is now being used throughout the nation.

In spite of the overall improvement, detention practices still exhibit many disturbing features in the United States. The most serious concerns are that over half of the facilities offer no treatment program and that an increasing number of detention centers have turned to mechanical restraints and isolation to control their populations.[11]

Shelter Care Facilities

Shelter care facilities were developed in the early 1970s to provide short-term care for status offenders and for dependent or neglected children. Although only twenty-three public shelters existed in 1975, they quickly increased in number because of the funding mandate of the JJDPA, which requires that noncriminal youths be placed in such facilities.

The length of stay in these nonsecure facilities with no locked doors varies from overnight to a few days. Occasionally, a juvenile must stay several weeks because of difficulty in scheduling court-required family therapy sessions or because of hearing delays in the juvenile court. Delinquent youths may be placed in shelter care facilities if the county has no detention center and the juvenile judge is reluctant to detain the youth in the county jail, or if a judge decides to reward a delinquent youth's positive behavior in detention by transferring him or her to the more open shelter care. Shelter care facilities do permit residents to enjoy home visits on weekends and field trips into the community during the week.

Voices of Delinquency: Ms. Lynette Drawn-Williamson, Reflections on Detention

TABLE 10–1
Short- and Long-Term Confinement Facilities for Juveniles

Training schools tend to be state facilities, detention centers tend to be local facilities,
and group homes tend to be private facilities

Facility operation	Total	Facility type						
		Detention center	Shelter	Reception/ diagnostic center	Group home	Ranch/wilderness camp	Training school	Residential treatment center
Number of facilities	2,458	734	167	64	661	85	210	847
Operations profile								
All facilities	100%	100%	100%	100%	100%	100%	100%	100%
Public	47	86	31	67	22	52	89	29
State	19	20	4	59	11	12	73	16
Local	27	66	26	8	10	40	15	13
Private	53	13	69	33	78	48	11	71
Facility profile								
All facilities	100%	30%	7%	3%	27%	3%	9%	34%
Public	100	55	4	4	13	4	16	21
State	100	31	1	8	16	2	32	28
Local	100	72	7	1	10	5	5	17
Private	100	7	9	2	40	3	2	46

- Detention centers, reception/diagnostic centers, and training schools were more likely to be public facilities than private facilities; however, a substantial proportion of reception/diagnostic centers were private.

- Most shelters were private facilities, as were group homes and residential treatment centers.

- Detention centers made up the largest proportion of all local facilities and approximately half of all public facilities.

- Training schools constituted 32% of all state facilities.

- Group homes accounted for 40% of all private facilities.

Note: Counts (and row percentages) may sum to more than the total number of facilities because facilities could select more than one facility type category.

Source: Author's analysis of Juvenile Residential Facility Census 2008 [machine-readable data file].

Source: Sarah Hockenberry, Melissa Sickmund, and Anthony Sladky, *Juvenile Residential Facility Census, 2008: Selected Findings* (Washington, DC: U.S. Department of Justice; 2011), 3.

The openness of these settings, not surprisingly, creates problems with runaways and makes it difficult to control use of contraband drugs among residents. Another problem for staff is that these facilities have their share of disciplinary problems among residents, who often have difficulty controlling their attitudes and actions. See Table 10–1 for numbers on the different types of short-term confinement facilities for juveniles just discussed and the long-term facilities discussed next.

What Types of Long-Term Confinement Are Used for Juveniles?

Boot camps, reception and diagnostic centers, ranches and forestry camps, and training schools are the main forms of long-term juvenile correctional institutions (see Table 10–2). Juveniles also may be transferred to mental health placements or sentenced to youthful offender facilities and adult prisons.

Boot Camps

Boot camps received increased attention in juvenile justice in the late 1980s and 1990s. Emphasizing military discipline, physical training, and regimented activity for periods that typically range from 30 to 120 days, the intent of these programs is to shock youthful offenders to prevent them from committing further crimes. Boot camp programs generally are designed for offenders who have failed with lesser sanctions such as probation. The Orleans Parish program, established in 1985, was the first boot camp for juveniles in the country.

TABLE 10–2
Types of Juvenile Placements

Type	Goals	Characteristics
Boot Camps	Shock treatment	Short term and emphasizes military discipline
Reception and Diagnostic Center	Evaluation and placement	Used to evaluate juveniles for possible placement in other facilities
Forestry Camps and Ranches	Minimum-security	Involves informal contact with staff, and a less secure placement than training schools
Public and Private Training Schools	Longer and more secure stays	Larger physical facilities, longer terms of stay, and sometimes violent residential life institutional placement

This program accepts anyone who is sentenced by the juvenile judge, but most programs generally exclude sex offenders, armed robbers, and violent offenders.[12]

The rationale for juvenile boot camps is consistent with the juvenile justice system's historical emphasis on rehabilitation, usually incorporating explicit assumptions about the needs of delinquent youths and providing remedial, counseling, and aftercare programs necessary to address these needs.[13] All of the programs employ military customs and courtesies, including uniformed drill instructors, a platoon structure, and summary punishment of participants, including group punishment under some circumstances. Although there are differences in emphasis, juvenile boot camp programs generally have discovered that they must tailor their environment to participants' maturity levels.[14]

Boot camps for juveniles are generally reserved for midrange offenders; those who have failed with lesser sanctions such as probation but who are not yet hardened delinquents. The shock aspect of the boot camp experience includes incarceration as suggested by the environment within which the program takes place.[15] Only a few programs limit themselves to youths who are nonviolent, have committed their first serious offense, or are being confined for the first time.[16]

Three programs—located in Cleveland, Denver, and Mobile—were funded through the OJJDP, which launched a three-site study of boot camps for youthful offenders in 1991. The program guidelines of these three experimental programs identified six key components to maximize their effectiveness: education and job training and placement, community service, substance abuse counseling and treatment, health and mental health care, individualized and continuous case management, and intensive aftercare services. A 1994 evaluation of the three sites found that the sites were unable to implement the program guidelines fully. Each program "experienced considerable instability and staff turnover" and was unable to "implement and sustain stable, well-developed aftercare services."[17]

Boot camps for juveniles include some type of work detail; most allocate more than half the day to educational and counseling activities, and most include some form of drug and alcohol counseling. In addition, most of the boot camp programs assign graduates to a period of intensive community supervision.[18]

A fair assessment may be that the quality of boot camps depends largely on how much they tailor their programs to participants' maturity levels and how effective they are in implementing and sustaining effective aftercare services. Doris McKenzie and colleagues completed a study of twenty-six juvenile boot camps, comparing them with traditional facilities (the experiences of 2,668 juveniles in twenty-six boot camps were compared to 1,848 juveniles in twenty-two traditional facilities).[19] They found that overall, juveniles in boot camps perceived their environments as more positive or therapeutic, less hostile or dangerous, and more structured than how juveniles in traditional facilities perceived their environments. Moreover, this study revealed that, over time, youths in boot camps became less antisocial and less depressed than did youths in traditional facilities.[20]

Almost all other follow-ups on juvenile boot camps have found recidivism rates of boot camps to be slightly higher or about the same as those of traditional juvenile facilities.[21] Charges of abuse in boot camps have taken place in almost all states with boot camps. In a 2007 federal report that examined the cases of 10 adolescents who died while at programs in six states, it was found that there was "significant evidence of ineffective management" and "reckless or negligent operating practices." The report revealed evidence that teenagers were forced to eat their own vomit, were starved, and were required to wallow for hours in their own excrement.[22]

The disappointing recidivism results, combined with the charges of abuse, have prompted Arizona, Florida, Georgia, Maryland, and South Dakota to shut down or reevaluate the "get tough with juveniles" approach popularized in the early 1990s. Arizona removed fifty juveniles. Maryland shut down one boot camp and suspended the military regimens at its other two facilities after reports of systematic assaults. The charges of abuse in Maryland led to the ouster of the state's top five juvenile justice officials.[23] In March 2006, Florida closed all of its boot camps after charges of abuse and the beating to death of a juvenile by boot camp staff.

Panaceas die hard in juvenile corrections, and this highly publicized approach of the past two decades will likely continue to be used in some states across the nation. The recent criticisms and disappointing recidivism data surrounding boot camps will probably result in fewer new programs being established and more scrutiny of existing programs.

Reception and Diagnostic Centers

The purpose of **reception and diagnostic centers**, which are both publicly and privately administered, is to determine which treatment plan suits and which training school is the best placement for each adjudicated juvenile. See Focus on Practice 10–2.

A few of the larger states have reception and diagnostic centers, but for most states, this diagnostic process takes place in one of the training schools. Although staff are more concerned about short-term diagnosis than long-term treatment, youths frequently receive more attention during this period than at any other time during their confinement. A psychiatrist usually will evaluate the youth and will see him or her several times if the youth is confined for a violent crime. A clinical psychologist, or a person with skills in administering psychological tests, frequently will subject the youth to a battery of tests to determine intelligence, attitudes, maturity, and emotional problems. A social worker, meanwhile, completes a case study of each youth. Equipped with background material from the court, which sometimes takes a week or two to arrive at the reception center, the social worker primarily investigates the youth's family background. Academic staff identify any learning problems

---

Focus on Practice 10–2
Indiana Implements a Faith- and Character-Based Housing Program

During the 2005 session, the Indiana General Assembly passed a new law, House Bill 1429 Transitional Dormitories that permit the Indiana Department of Correction (IDOC) to operate faith-based transitional dormitories at any facility operated by the agency. Before the bill was signed into law, IDOC began developing curricula for pilot programs, named Purposeful Living Units Serve (PLUS), at three facilities, one of which was a juvenile one—the Plainfield Juvenile Correctional Facility. Since the opening of the three pilot sites, this program has expanded to sixteen facilities. The PLUS program is available at female and male facilities, juvenile and adult facilities, and at all security levels.

The Juvenile PLUS program takes sixteen weeks to complete. In addition to their appropriate treatment program, those in the PLUS program participate in additional programming from a faith- or character-based perspective. The PLUS curriculum focuses on helping students integrate the core values of respect, responsibility, honesty, tolerance, and compassion into the education they are already receiving. PLUS program staff members, along with volunteer members, assist the students in this reflection process.

The following topics are used with juvenile participants from a faith or character perspective: religious/cultural diversity, community service projects, mentoring from a community volunteer, and victim impact/restorative justice. The major goals of PLUS are:

* Better behavior which is measured by fewer conduct reports
* Better adjustment as measured by fewer grievances
* Restitution in the form of community service
* Smoother transition back to home
* Reduced recidivism rates.

CRITICAL THINKING QUESTION
What are the advantages and disadvantages of using faith or character-based juvenile facilities in juvenile corrections?

Source: Stephen T. Hall, "Indiana Implements a Faith- and Character-Based Housing Program," *Corrections Today* (March 2008), 62–67.

and determine the proper school placement. Physical and dental examinations also are frequently administered. Finally, cottage or dormitory supervisors evaluate the youth's institutional adjustment and peer relationships. A case conference on each resident is held once all the reports have been prepared, the needs and attitudes of the youth are summarized, and recommendations are made as to the best cottage or institutional placement.

Although previously staff had evaluated residents over a period of four to six weeks, this process has been condensed today to an average length of stay of thirty-four days.[24] The youth is then transferred to the approved institutional placement, and the diagnostic report goes with him or her. It is not uncommon for this report to receive little attention, so the youth often must repeat a similar process in the admitting institution.

Ranches and Forestry Camps

Ranches and forestry camps are minimum-security institutional placements that are normally reserved for youths who have committed minor offenses or who have been committed to the department of youth services or private corrections for the first time.

In these camps, residents typically do conservation work in a state park, cutting grass and weeds, cleaning up, and doing general maintenance. Treatment programs generally consist of individual contacts with social workers and the child care staff, group therapy, and an occasional home visit. Residents may be taken to nearby towns on a regular or weekly basis to make purchases and to attend community events.

These facilities generally have a minimum amount of security, and only about 20 percent have one or more confinement features other than locked sleeping rooms. They contrast with detention homes and long-term secure facilities, roughly 90 percent of which have one or more confinement features beyond locked sleeping rooms. Unlike in the past, when ranches and camps tended to be populated by white youths, today's ranch and camp residents are 76 percent minority offenders; 12 percent of the residents are female. Also, in keeping with today's concerns, it is important to note that 68 percent of secure facilities screen incoming youth on their first day for suicide risk.[25]

The Hennepin County Home School, one of the most innovative juvenile institutions in the nation, combines features of camps and ranches. Except for a fourteen-bed security unit, it is an open facility, located in a beautiful 160-acre wooded site approximately seventeen miles from downtown Minneapolis. The 164-bed facility is coeducational and holds youths who range in age from thirteen to seventeen, with an average age of fifteen. The school receives no status offenders; instead, the population is made up of those who have committed a variety of property and personal offenses. The typical resident has had at least five prior court involvements, and far more than half the residents have been involved in some type of out-of-home placement before their commitment to the Hennepin County Home School.[26]

The institution comprises three juvenile male offender cottages, two juvenile sex offender cottages, one cottage for female offenders, and one Beta cottage for short-term restitution offenders. The residents remain in the Beta program for three to eight weeks and in other cottages for as long as a year. Each resident of the juvenile sex offender cottages would have received an indeterminate sentence, while residents of the other cottages would have received a determinate sentence. The institution's sophisticated treatment program uses such modalities as an educational program that focuses on those with learning disabilities, family therapy, transactional analysis, behavior modification, and reality therapy. Horseback riding and canoeing are favorite recreational activities.[27]

Residents are typically more positive about a placement at a forestry camp or ranch than about placement in a training school. They like the more relaxed security, the more frequent community contacts, the shorter stays, and the better relations with staff. Yet some youths cannot handle these settings. They may be too homesick or too victimized by peers, so they repeatedly run away until they are transferred to more secure facilities.

Training Schools

In 2008, there were a total of 2,458 juvenile facilities, holding 81,015 offenders. There were 1,150 public facilities, holding 56,157 juvenile offenders, and 1,300 private facilities, holding 24,757 offenders.[28] Table 10–3 lists the numbers of juveniles detained and in custody in each state.

TABLE 10-3
Juveniles Detained and in Custody in Each State, 2008

On October 22, 2008, 47% of juvenile facilities were publicly operated; they held 69% of juvenile offenders

State	Juvenile facilities			Juvenile offenders			State	Juvenile facilities			Juvenile offenders		
	Total	Public	Private	Total	Public	Private		Total	Public	Private	Total	Public	Private
U.S. total	2,458	1,150	1,300	81,015	56,157	24,757	Missouri	68	63	5	1,226	1,196	30
Alabama	66	13	43	1,328	632	696	Montana	16	8	7	161	114	30
Alaska	18	8	10	249	178	71	Nebraska	16	4	12	773	438	335
Arizona	40	16	20	1,488	1,198	240	Nevada	23	17	6	1,052	841	211
Arkansas	32	11	21	836	286	550	New Hampshire	8	2	6	157	86	71
California	215	117	98	13,309	12,056	1,253	New Jersey	49	39	10	1,564	1,428	136
Colorado	55	13	43	1,688	853	835	New Mexico	19	15	4	409	397	12
Connecticut	12	3	9	303	180	123	New York	169	40	129	3,157	1,470	1,687
Delaware	7	6	1	256	239	17	North Carolina	52	22	30	1,014	557	457
Dist. of Columbia	10	3	7	236	174	62	North Dakota	9	4	5	85	73	12
Florida	118	37	81	5,895	2,210	3,685	Ohio	87	66	21	3,871	3,521	350
Georgia	40	26	14	2,692	2,168	524	Oklahoma	46	16	29	923	626	276
Hawaii	8	3	5	130	118	12	Oregon	47	25	22	1,437	1,106	331
Idaho	28	15	13	683	540	143	Pennsylvania	152	34	118	5,034	1,263	3,771
Illinois	42	28	14	2,440	2,141	299	Rhode Island	10	1	9	291	168	123
Indiana	76	37	39	2,422	1,561	861	South Carolina	33	13	20	1,258	794	464
Iowa	66	15	51	1,060	297	763	South Dakota	23	7	14	507	233	261
Kansas	41	17	24	973	682	291	Tennessee	43	30	18	1,151	836	315
Kentucky	39	29	10	944	873	71	Texas	109	85	24	5,831	5,192	639
Louisiana	43	17	26	1,294	909	385	Utah	35	18	17	770	384	386
Maine	7	2	5	215	189	26	Vermont	4	1	3	48	24	24
Maryland	35	14	21	787	615	172	Virginia	61	56	5	2,114	2,022	92
Massachusetts	58	18	40	961	343	618	Washington	37	31	6	1,382	1,302	80
Michigan	82	37	45	2,659	1,252	1,407	West Virginia	26	11	15	565	376	189
Minnesota	76	21	55	1,332	697	635	Wisconsin	69	20	49	1,395	834	511
Mississippi	16	14	2	413	351	62	Wyoming	21	2	19	247	34	163

Notes: "State" is the state where the facility is located. Offenders sent to out-of-state facilities are counted in the state where the facility is located, not the state where they committed their offense. Totals include 8 tribal facilities (holding 101 juvenile offenders) located in Arizona, Montana, Oklahoma, and South Dakota.

Source: Authors' analysis of Juvenile Residential Facility Census 2008 [machine-readable data file].

Source: Sarah Hockenberry, Melissa Sickmund, and Anthony Sladky, Juvenile Residential Facility Census, 2008: Selected Findings (Washington, DC: U.S. Department of Justice; National Report Services Bulletin, 2011), 2.

Twenty-five percent of facilities reported that the number of residents they held on the 2008 census date put them at or over the capacity of their standard beds or that they relied on some makeshift beds. The largest facilities were the most likely to be crowded. Overall, the juvenile offender custody population dropped 12 percent from 2006 to 2008. In fact, forty-five states held fewer juvenile offenders in 2008 than in 2006.[29]

The 2006 report *Safety and Welfare Plan: Implementing Reform in California* reveals the skyrocketing average cost of juvenile institutional care and the average length of stay in months. California spends $115,129 per year to institutionalize a resident, which is greater than the cost in five other states for which data were available (see Figure 10–2). California's length of stay, in 2004, was 25.9 months, which was nearly three times as long as the average of the nineteen states that participated in a nationwide survey (see Figure 10–3). Note that California is one of only six states that have an extended age of jurisdiction that goes beyond the age of twenty. California's length of stay for a juvenile offender goes up to

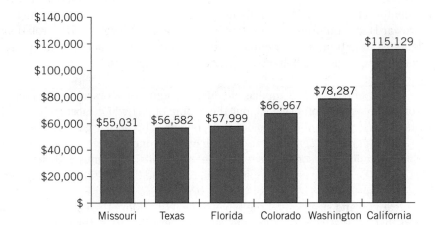

FIGURE 10–2
Comparison of Cost per Youth per Year in Some States

Source: Christopher Murray, Chris Baird, Ned Loughran, Fred Mills, and John Platt, *Safety and Welfare Plan: Implementing Reform in California* (Sacramento: California Department of Corrections and Rehabilitation, Division of Juvenile Justice, 2006), 5.

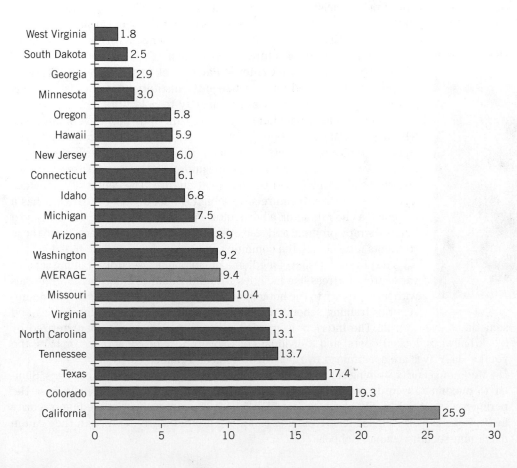

FIGURE 10–3
Average Length of Stay in Months for Males, 2004

Source: Christopher Murray, Chris Baird, Ned Loughran, Fred Mills, and John Platt, *Safety and Welfare Plan: Implementing Reform in California* (Sacramento: California Department of Corrections and Rehabilitation, Division of Juvenile Justice, 2006), 2.

twenty-four years of age, and this has contributed to the lengthy stay for those sentenced to juvenile facilities in California.[30]

California, Illinois, Michigan, New York, and Ohio each has several **training schools**. Smaller states have one training school for boys and another for girls, and Massachusetts and Vermont have no training schools. Although coeducational institutions gained some acceptance in the 1970s and North Carolina even converted all of its training schools into coeducational facilities, that trend seems to have passed.

Organizational Goals and Security Levels

Organizational goals vary among training schools. David Street, Robert D. Vinter, and Charles Perrow's classic study of several public and private training schools identified three basic organizational goals: obedience/conformity, reeducation/development, and treatment. They found that staff in obedience/conformity institutions kept residents under surveillance and emphasized rules. They were also punitive with residents and did not become involved with them. Although staff in reeducation/development institutions demanded conformity, hard work, and intellectual growth, they were more willing to give additional rewards for conformity to positive behavior and to develop closer relationships with residents. Staff in treatment-oriented training schools were much more involved with residents as they worked with, helped, and permitted residents to become more emotionally involved with them.[31]

The philosophy of *parens patriae* has encouraged administrators at training schools to claim rehabilitation as their official goal, but the overall objective for most training schools is to provide a safe, secure, and humane environment. The actual goal depends on the security level of the training school. States that have only one training school for boys and one for girls must enforce all security levels in the one facility, but states with several training schools have the option of developing minimum-, medium-, and maximum-security institutions.

Security features and size vary by the types of facilities. More than 38 percent of facilities reported that at least some of the time residents are locked in their sleeping rooms. Seventy-six percent of public facilities and 62 percent of state facilities reported that they locked residents in sleeping rooms. Few private facilities locked residents in sleeping rooms (5 percent). Among facilities that locked youth in sleeping rooms, most did this at night (85 percent) or when a youth was out of control (77 percent).[32]

▲ Security is a must for correctional facilities. This facility has three layers of security at just the entrance. The first layer consists of a metal detector, the second has a revolving door that can lock, and the third is a door that must be electronically opened by a staff member. Inside are more locked doors throughout the facility.

Kathryn O'Lare

The Lighthouse Youth Center at Paint Creek in southern Ohio is one of the most widely hailed minimum-security institutions in the nation. This privately operated facility has the capacity to hold thirty-three residents but generally has a population of twenty-six or twenty-seven. Juveniles who have committed serious offenses from the southern counties of the state are typically committed to this facility. The facility features a comprehensive and integrated therapeutic approach that emphasizes accountability, social learning, and positive peer culture. The center also includes a school where youth can receive a high school diploma or GED. It has a choir and a choir director, a horticulture program, a pottery program, and a family therapy program and also offers intensive aftercare services to those residents returning to the community.[33]

The physical design of medium- and maximum-security training schools varies from fortress-like facilities with individual cells to open dormitories with little privacy to the homelike atmosphere of small cottages. Maximum-security training schools usually have one or two fairly high fences and sometimes even a wall. The interiors in maximum-security schools are characterized by bleak hallways, locked doors, and individual cells covered by heavy screens or bars; the youths' daily lives are constrained by rules (see Focus on Practice 10–3).

Medium-security training schools usually are designed as dormitories or cottages. Similar to maximum-security institutions, medium-security training schools usually have the perimeter security of a six- or seven-foot-high fence. The atmosphere in medium-security institutions is more relaxed, and residents can move around more freely than they can in maximum-security training schools.

Institutional security is the primary emphasis in medium- and maximum-security training schools. Administrators' jobs typically depend on their success in preventing runaways. The account of a runaway incident from a maximum-security facility, for example, may receive statewide media coverage. If a runaway commits a violent crime, then even more pressure is placed on institutional administrators and their staff. Fortunately, the federal courts' recent involvement in juvenile institutions has eliminated some of the past abuses that sometimes took place to punish those who attempted to run away and those who actually did but were caught and returned.

Programs

The programs in medium- and maximum-security training schools are much more adequate than those in jails or detention homes and more varied than those in camps and ranches. Most of the larger training schools have a full-time nurse on duty and a physician who visits one or more days a week. Such services as the removal of tattoos are sometimes made available if residents desire them.

Most medium- and maximum-security training schools provide educational programs for residents. These may be accredited by the state for granting high school diplomas, and most offer classes to prepare for a GED test. In addition to the regular academic courses, training schools usually offer basic skills classes consisting of a review of the necessary techniques for reading, writing, and arithmetic; some programs have laboratories and programmed instruction as well. Classes are usually small, and pupils are permitted to progress according to their own rate of learning. The Indiana Boys School is an example of one training school that focuses on the learning disabilities of residents, because Indiana correctional officials believe that learning disabilities are closely linked to delinquent behavior.

Well-equipped male training schools offer vocational training in automobile repair, printing, welding, carpentry, woodworking, barbering, machine shop skills, drafting, and food service. Training schools for girls generally are more limited and offer training programs in sewing, food service, secretarial skills, and beauty care.

As a rule, this vocational training does not help residents secure jobs after release for several reasons: they have difficulty gaining admission to the necessary labor unions; they

---

Focus on Practice 10–3
Rules of Youth Conduct

1. You will not be allowed to fight with peers or staff.
2. You will follow the direct orders of staff.
3. You will treat others with courtesy by avoiding the use of profanity, disrespectful language, or physical gestures.
4. You will avoid sexually inappropriate language or gestures toward staff and other youth.
5. You will avoid horseplay, rowdy-rough play, body punching, shadow boxing, verbal taunting, running, [and] wrestling, which could lead to more serious behavior.
6. You will avoid destroying, defacing, or altering state property or the property of others.
7. You will avoid the use of and/or passing of any form of tobacco, alcohol, and drugs.
8. You will avoid the use of and/or possession of contraband.
9. You will avoid leaving trash on tables, chairs, or floors by placing it in proper receptacles.
10. You will maintain personal grooming, hygiene, and clothing at all times throughout the institution. Appropriate dress includes shirttails in pants, pants zipped and uncuffed (not pegged), belt fastened, shoes tied, and socks on.
11. You will refrain from borrowing, lending, buying, trading, betting, selling, and gambling with peers, staff, or visitors.
12. You will play radios only in acceptable areas and at acceptable times.
13. You will not enter any office or restricted areas without staff permission.
14. You will avoid interfering with staff members' duties.
15. You will report any injury or any change in a medical condition to a staff member immediately.
16. You will not steal.
17. You will adhere to all movement instructions.
18. You will not spit.
19. You will not use any phone without staff supervision.
20. You will not use the restroom without permission.

CRITICAL THINKING QUESTIONS
Do you believe all these rules are necessary? What rules would you substitute? How would you feel if restricted by these rules?

Source: The Ohio Department of Youth Services, Training Institution, Central Ohio, 1990.

lack the necessary credentials, such as a high school education; or they simply choose not to pursue the skills they learned. Yet some residents leave the institution and acquire excellent jobs with their acquired skills.

Recreation has always been popular in training schools. Some staff emphasize it because they believe that a tired youth is a well-behaved one or, in the words of one recreation leader, "If we wear them out during the day, they won't fool around at night." Other staff advocate a heavy dosage of recreation because they believe that teaching residents a competitive sport builds self-respect and self-confidence. Still other staff know that juveniles like to play, and recreation is simply a good way for them to entertain themselves and to work off excessive energy. Male residents can compete in softball, volleyball, flag football, basketball, and sometimes even boxing. Cottages usually compete against one another, and the institution may even have a team that competes with other institutions or with teams in the surrounding community. Nonathletic recreational activities include movies, building model cars, painting, decorating the cottages (especially at Christmas), and playing ping-pong, pool, checkers, and chess. Female residents also have recreational possibilities such as softball, volleyball, and basketball. In addition to the nonathletic recreational activities that the boys have access to, girls perform in talent shows or dramatic productions, and occasionally, they have dances with boys from nearby training schools.

Religious instruction and services are always provided in state training schools. Larger training schools usually have a full-time Protestant chaplain and a part- or full-time Roman Catholic chaplain. Smaller training schools contract for the services of clergy from a nearby community. Religious services generally include Sunday mass and morning worship, confession, baptism, instruction for church membership, choir, and the participation of community groups. Yet, few residents have much interest in organized religion, and they are usually quite resistant to compulsory attendance at these religious services.

The most widely used treatment modalities are transactional analysis, reality therapy, psychotherapy, behavior modification, guided group interaction, positive peer culture, and drug and alcohol treatment. The errors-in-thinking modality, models to deactivate gangs, and law enforcement education are new forms of treatment recently implemented in a number of private and public training schools across the nation (see Chapter 11 for an examination of these modalities).

Volunteers are an important adjunct to institutional programs, and an institution that has an active volunteer program can greatly enrich the stay of its residents. Some states have better developed volunteer programs than others and have volunteer coordinators in their major institutions. Confined offenders frequently are receptive to services rendered by unpaid volunteers who do not represent authority figures, but who can present the needs of youth and become their advocates in the community. Among the many services that volunteers provide for institutionalized youths are the following:

1. Education—tutoring and supplying books
2. Entertainment—arranging choral programs and other means of entertainment provided by community groups
3. Chaperones—escorting selected youths to community events
4. Counseling—providing one-to-one contact with offenders
5. Family service—contacting and reassuring parents on the progress of their children
6. Financial aid—providing money for youths' canteen accounts
7. Gifts—supplying Christmas and birthday remembrances
8. Job-finding—assisting youths in locating community jobs while they wait to be released or in securing permanent jobs after release
9. Letter writing—helping youths to correspond with family and friends
10. Recreation—playing basketball, softball, and other sports with residents.

Finally, prerelease programs are a desired component of institutional activities. These programs typically occur more in minimum- than in medium- or maximum-security facilities. In some training schools, residents are transferred to another cottage or to another location to begin a formal program of community reintegration, including exposure to experiences designed to prepare them for a full return to the community. Techniques of interviewing for a job, instruction in reading the help-wanted section of a newspaper, and assistance in money management are important elements of these programs.

Home furloughs, afternoon trips off campus, and permission to work in the community are typical of the privileges given to residents of prerelease cottages or to those who are just a step or two away from release. Home furloughs are probably the most widely used. Some staff believe that reintegrating youths gradually to the community after a long absence of perhaps several years will help ease the shock of release. Home visits also provide opportunities for residents to interview for jobs and visit with family members. Some training schools allow trips off campus for several hours with parents. This enables parents and children to spend time together away from the institution and possibly to shop for clothing or to eat in a restaurant. Community jobs generally are reserved for those youths who are only two or three months from release and who need financial resources before they return to community living. Staff members are very careful in choosing the residents who are permitted to work in the community. Prerelease programs usually have a positive impact on residents, but home visits, especially, result in a high percentage of runaways.

Social Control of Institutional Residents

Until the last ten years or so, most training schools still employed cottage parents. These individuals often were a retired couple who were attracted to this work because of their interest in young people. Cottage parents sometimes provided a strong parental model for the youth placed in their care. The cottage parents system was continued so long simply because institutional administrators felt that cottage parents created more of a homelike atmosphere for confined delinquents than did staff members who worked eight-hour shifts and lived in the nearby community. But the appearance of increasingly difficult-to-handle delinquents and efforts to develop more efficient institutional management techniques resulted in the replacement of cottage parents with staff members who are commonly called *youth supervisors, youth leaders, cottage supervisors, group supervisors,* or *group-care workers.*

The emerging nature of this role has left a number of questions unanswered: How much of a homelike atmosphere should these supervisors establish in the cottages? How involved should they become with residents? Are they to be only custodial agents, or do they also have treatment responsibilities? What are they to do if residents refuse to cooperate? What personal fulfillment can they expect to achieve in their jobs? Although encumbered by these and other questions, the role of youth supervisor is well established in juvenile correctional settings in this country. For increased control of residents, see Focus on Technology 10–4.

The youth supervisors wake residents in the morning, see to it that their charges wash and dress for breakfast, supervise the serving of breakfast in the cottage or escort residents to a central dining facility, and conduct a brief room inspection. They also ensure that those youths enrolled in the academic and vocational programs go to school and that those who work on the grounds, in the kitchen, or in the community go to their jobs. In medium- and maximum-security training schools, residents are usually escorted to their particular assignments, but on many honor farms, and in conservation camps and ranches, they are permitted movement without staff supervision.[34] A number of recommendations for the management of a juvenile facility are listed in Focus on Policy 10–5.

Cottage parents typically remained in the cottage to prepare lunch and to take care of other cottage tasks, but youth supervisors are generally assigned duties that keep them occupied until they pick up their residents for lunch. These duties may include school patrol, inspection of the rooms of residents on restriction, and outside patrol of the recreation field.

Residents are met at the academic area and escorted back to the cottage for lunch, after which they are returned to school or to other assigned duties. The afternoon shift of supervisors picks up the youths in school and brings them back at the end of the day. If the institution has an active group program and youth supervisors are involved, they usually hold several group meetings a week after school. Guided group interaction, positive peer culture, and transactional analysis are the most popular group modalities used in these

Focus on Technology 10–4
Technocorrections

Compared with only a few years ago, institutional correctional technologies are not only better and more reliable today, but they are also cheaper. Technology provides innovations that offer substantial savings in staffing and operations costs. A few of the more intriguing technological developments are listed below. These are obviously more widely used in adult corrections, but they appear to be the wave of the future in juvenile corrections as well.

- *Ground-penetrating radar.* Ground-penetrating radar (GPR) is able to locate tunnels inmates use to escape. GPR works almost like an old-fashioned Geiger counter, but rather than detecting metal, the system detects changes in ground composition, including voids such as those created by a tunnel.

- *Heartbeat monitoring.* Now it is possible to prevent escapes by monitoring inmates' heartbeats! The Advanced Vehicle Interrogation and Notification system (AVIAN) works by identifying the shock wave generated by the beating heart, which couples to any surface the body touches. The system takes in all of the frequencies of movement, such as the expansion and contraction of an engine or rain hitting the roof, and determines if there is a pattern similar to a human heartbeat.

- *Nonlethal electrified fences.* Nonlethal electrified containment fences stop inmates without causing severe harm or death. If an inmate tries to climb or cut through the perimeter fence, he or she will receive a nonlethal jolt of electricity, which causes temporary immobilization. At the same time, the system both initiates an alarm to staff that an escape attempt has occurred and identifies its location.

- *Backscatter imaging system for concealed weapons.* This system utilizes a backscatter imager to detect weapons and contraband. The primary advantage of this device over current walk-through portals is that it can detect nonmetallic as well as metallic weapons. It uses low-power X-rays equal to about five minutes of exposure to the sun at sea level. Although these X-rays penetrate clothing, they do not penetrate the body.

- *Body-scanning screening system.* This is a stationary screening system to detect nonmetallic weapons and contraband in the lower body cavities. It uses simplified magnetic resonance images (MRI) as a noninvasive alternative to X-ray and physical body-cavity searches. The stationary screening system makes use of first-generation medical MRI.

- *Transmitter wristbands.* These wristbands broadcast a unique serial number via radio-frequency every two seconds so that antennas throughout the prison can pick up the signals and pass the data via a local-area network to a central monitoring station computer. The wristbands can sound an alert when an inmate gets close to the perimeter fence or when a prisoner does not return from a furlough on time; they can even tag gang members and notify guards when rivals come into contact with each other.

- *Personal health status monitor.* The personal health status monitor uses acoustics to track the heartbeat and respiration of a person in a cell. More advanced health status monitors are now being developed that can monitor five or more vital signs at once, and based on the combination findings, can produce an assessment of the inmate's state of health. This more advanced version of the personal health status monitor may take another decade to develop, but the current version may already help save lives that would otherwise be lost to suicide.

- *All-in-one drug detection spray.* Drug detection sprays can determine whether someone possesses marijuana, methamphetamines, heroin, or cocaine. A specially made piece of paper is wiped on a surface; when sprayed with one of the aerosol sprays, it changes color within fifteen seconds if as little as four to twenty micrograms of the drug is present. A new detection device is now being developed that uses a single spray that will test for all drugs at once. The test paper will turn different colors depending on which drugs the spray contacts, and several positive results will be possible with a single use of the spray.

- *Radar vital signs monitor/radar flashlight.* The handheld radar flashlight can detect the respiration of a human in a cell from behind a twenty-centimeter hollow-core concrete wall or an eight-inch-thick cinder block wall. It instantly gives the user a bar-graph readout that is viewed on the apparatus itself. Other miniature radar detectors give users heartbeat and respiration readings. The equipment is expected to be a useful tool in searches for people who are hiding, because the only thing that successfully blocks its functioning is a wall made of metal or conductive material.

- *Personal alarm location system.* It is now possible for prison employees to carry a tiny transmitter linking them with a computer in a central control room. In an emergency, they can hit an alarm button and transmit a signal to the computer that automatically records whose distress button has been pushed. An architectural map of the facility appears onscreen, showing the exact location of the staff member in need of assistance.

- *Under-vehicle surveillance system.* An under-vehicle surveillance system utilizes a drive-over camera that records a video image of the license plate and the underside of any vehicle entering or leaving the secure perimeter of the prison. This system allows prison staff to check each vehicle for possible escape attempts and keeps a digital recording of every vehicle that enters or exits the prison.

- *Biometric recognition.* A new biometric system, the facial-recognition system, utilizes facial recognition by matching more than two hundred individual points on the human face with a digitally stored image. The system is currently used to control access to buildings and rooms inside buildings, and it will become more and more common in the near future.

Source: Jeff Goodale, Dave Menzel, and Glen Hodgson, "High-Tech Prisons: Latest Technologies Drive Cost Savings and Staff Efficiencies," *Corrections Today* 67 (July 2005), 78; John Ward, "Jump-Starting Projects to Automatic Correctional Processes," *Corrections Today* 66 (2006), 82–83; John Ward, "Security and Technology: The Human Side," *Corrections Today* 66 (2004), 8; Frank Lu and Laurence Wolfe, "Automated Record Tracking (SWMART) Application," *Corrections Today* 66 (2004), 78–81; Gary Burdett and Mike Rutford, "Technology Improves Security and Reduces Staff in Two Illinois Prisons," *Corrections Today* 65 (2003), 109–10; and Tony Fabelo, "Technocorrections: The Promises, the Uncertain Threats," in *Sentencing & Corrections: Issues for the 21st Century Series*, no. 5 (Washington, DC: National Institute of Corrections, May 2000).

Focus on Policy 10–5
Recommendations for Juvenile Facility Management

- *Pursue excellence in the facility.* Successful administrators set high standards. They not only expect excellence, they demand it.
- *A meaningful institutional program requires a carefully thought-out plan of action or strategy.* Administrators must determine where they want to go (their vision) and understand how they are going to get there (implementing the vision).
- *Management should be proactive.* An anticipatory and preventive approach is fundamental in maintaining institutional control.
- *Professionalism should be held up as a goal to all staff.* Staff development and training are important steps in staff seeing themselves as professionals.
- *Cleanliness and orderliness of the facility are absolute necessities.* Cleanliness shows that the staff are in control.
- *The institutional environment must be safe for youths and staff.* If an institution is not a safe environment, little positive can be accomplished.
- *Both residents and staff must be treated with dignity and respect.* The norm for staff is that they treat residents as they would want their own sons or daughters to be treated.
- *Good programming by committed staff must be available for those youths who want to make positive changes in their lives.*

Treatment programs must be delivered effectively to those interested residents, especially those with additions and anger management.

- *An effective system of accountability for both staff and youths is necessary.* Sufficient consequences are required for inappropriate behavior, especially when rules are broken.
- *The services that are promised must be delivered to youths when they are scheduled to be delivered.* It is important for the system to be predictable and trusted to do what was promised.
- *Facilities, as much as possible, should have the following characteristics.* They should be as close as possible to juveniles' families; offer smaller, personalized services; be family friendly; and be managed in a caring manner.
- *The administrator must be a model of integrity in every way, both inside and outside the facility.*
- *Accreditation is an important process in a juvenile residential facility offering humane confinement and mission effectiveness.*

Source: Joseph Heinz, Theresa Wise, and Clemens Bartollas, *Successful Management of Juvenile Residential Facilities: A Performance-Based Approach* (Alexandria, VA: American Correctional Association, 2010), 43–44.

---

sessions. Time generally is structured after school because many administrators believe that problems arise when youths have a great deal of free time, but in some institutions the period from the end of school until the evening meal is a free one.

After the evening meal, especially during warmer weather, residents are permitted to engage in outside recreational activities. They may participate in organized activities or may choose to throw a football, shoot a basketball, pitch a softball, or talk with a friend. Staff must at this time be particularly alert, because runaway attempts often take place during these outside activities. Following a shower and a little television, residents are usually sent to their rooms and lights are out around 10 P.M.

The night shift, normally consisting of one person, takes over at 11 or 11:30 P.M. This person's job basically is to make certain that youths do not escape from the cottage during the night and to be available if a problem such as an illness or escape attempt occurs. The youth supervisor generally spends the greater part of the eight-hour shift sitting at a desk in the staff office and responding to a periodic phone check on cottage security.

As part of their daily tasks, youth supervisors also intervene in conflicts among residents, respond to emergency situations, search residents and residents' living quarters, orient new residents, advise residents concerning personal or institutional progress, and assign tasks to residents and monitor their performance.

Differences Between Public and Private Training Schools

A little more than half (53 percent) of juvenile facilities holding offenders in 2008 were private, but public facilities held over two-thirds (69 percent) of the juvenile offenders. Compared with public facilities, private facilities hold a smaller share of delinquents and a larger share of status offenders.[35] Table 10–3 compares the various types of juvenile custody facilities and shows how the numbers and profiles of these facilities have changed. Public facilities hold more than three-quarters of those confined for homicide, robbery, aggravated assault, weapons possession, and technical violations of probation or aftercare. Nevertheless, as noted in the *2006 Juvenile Offenders in Correctional Facilities*, "public and private facilities had fairly similar offense profiles in 2003."[36]

David Shichor and Clemens Bartollas's examination of the patterns of public and private juvenile placements in one of the larger probation departments in southern California, however, revealed that few offense differences existed between juveniles sent to public and private facilities. Although juveniles placed in private facilities had more personal problems and those in public institutions were somewhat more delinquent, placements in private facilities included delinquents with serious offenses.[37]

Second, privately administered training schools are probably better known to the public than are state facilities because of their public solicitation of funds. Boys' Town in Nebraska and Glen Mills School in Pennsylvania (near Philadelphia) are two private institutions that are well known to the public.[38] Private training schools also have avoided most of the scathing critiques faced by public training schools during the past two decades.

Third, proponents of private training schools claim that they are more effective than public training schools because they have a limited intake policy that allows them to choose whom they want to admit; they have more professional staff; they have better staff–client ratios; they are smaller; and they are more flexible and innovative.

Gaylene Styve Armstrong and Doris Layton MacKenzie examined forty-eight residential juvenile correctional facilities in nineteen states (sixteen private and thirty-two public facilities). Using both self-report surveys and data from facility records, they found that private facilities had a more extensive admission process, had a higher percentage of juvenile delinquents incarcerated for property offenses, were smaller, and held a higher percentage of males than female offenders. Yet they found that there were no significant differences between private and public juvenile facilities in terms of the quality of their environments.[39]

The advantage of private over public rehabilitation programs may have been more true in the past than in the present. The increased use of interstate compact of children has resulted in some private schools taking as many children as they can get. Indeed, some private institutions exploit the inadequate licensing procedures of the states to warehouse youths as cheaply as possible and thereby reap good profits.[40] It is also true that private training schools are smaller than public ones, but even so, half of the private institutions hold one hundred or more children; these are still too large to effectively rehabilitate juveniles. It is probably accurate to say that private institutions offer greater flexibility of programs because private institutions are relatively free from political processes and bureaucratic inertia. Yet Bartollas and Shichor's comparison of the attitudes of staff and residents at a state training school for adolescent males in the Midwest and at a private facility in the same state found that the enforcement of excessive rules in the private placement created a rigid cottage structure and living environment.[41] Moreover, Shichor and Bartollas found that private placements in southern California do not always provide the services of professional treatment personnel that they purport to provide.[42] Perhaps the old adage is true after all: the best institutions are private ones and the worst institutions are also private ones.

Juvenile Victimization

Institutionalization is a painful process for most youthful offenders, though it is clearly more painful for some than for others. Juvenile victimization is one of the most troubling aspects of juvenile institutionalization.

Many studies of training schools for boys reflect an inmate society in which the strong take advantage of the weak:

- In their study of the State Industrial School for Boys in Golden, Colorado, Gordon E. Barker and W. Thomas Adams found two types of residential leaders: one held power through brute force and the other ruled through charisma. According to these researchers, residents were involved in an unending battle for dominance and control.[43]

- Howard W. Polsky studied a cottage in a residential treatment center in New York. The staff in Cottage Six were unable to keep residential leaders from exploiting peers. The social hierarchy the researchers identified in this cottage had a pecking order; those at the bottom of the status hierarchy found life so debilitating that most of them ended up in mental hospitals.[44]

- Sethard Fisher studied a small training school in California and identified victimization and patronage as two of the major behaviors taking place. He defined **victimization** as

Voices of Delinquency: Doing Your
Own Time

Voices of Delinquency: Juvenile Homicide
Offender and Adjustment to a Training
School

"a predatory practice whereby inmates of superior strength and knowledge of inmate lore prey on weaker and less knowledgeable inmates."[45] *Patronage* referred to youths' building of "protective and ingratiating relationships with others more advantageously situated on the prestige ladder." Fisher also saw victimization as being made up of physical attack, agitation, and exploitation.[46]

- Clemens Bartollas, Stuart J. Miller, and Simon Dinitz's *Juvenile Victimization: The Institutional Paradox,* examined the culture that end-of-the-line delinquents established in a maximum-security institution in Columbus, Ohio (TICO). In this training school, dominant youths exploited submissive ones in every possible way. Ninety percent of the one hundred fifty residents were involved in this exploitation matrix; 19 percent were exploiters who were never themselves exploited, 34 percent were exploiters and victims at different times, 21 percent were occasionally victims and never exploiters, and 17 percent were chronic victims. Ten percent of the residents were neither victims nor exploiters.[47]

- In a fifteen-year follow-up evaluation of this training school, Miller, Bartollas, and Dinitz found that the negative youth culture described in the 1976 study still thrived and that the strong still victimized the weak. Staff members were more disillusioned than they were at the time of the first study. They also were more fearful of victimization from residents.[48]

- Martin Forst, Jeffrey Fagan, and T. Scott Vivona, relying on data collected in both juvenile facilities and adult correctional facilities, found that 1.7 percent of youth in training schools reported having been sexually attacked while in the facility and 8.6 percent (five times as many) of juveniles in adult correctional facilities reported such victimization while incarcerated during the previous twelve months.[49]

- Following the passage and signing of the Prison Rape Elimination Act of 2003, three major government-sponsored research effectors have provided additional insights about the conditions and scope of sexual victimization of confined juveniles. The first drew on a nationally representative sample of 7,073 youths held in 203 facilities and found that 3.6 percent (1 in every 28) of juveniles in residential facilities reported having been sexually victimized at least one time.[50] A second study based on the administrative records data collected by the Bureau of Justice Statistics as part of the PREA-mandated study of sexual violence incidence and prevalence in U.S. correctional institutions found that in 2004 the rate of sexual victimization reported by authorities in juvenile institutions was more than 5 percent of confined juveniles.[51] The third study was conducted in twelve facilities during 2007 that were located in six states and included nine male facilities, one female facility, and two coeducational facilities. According to the study, 19.7 percent of responding youth reported at least one incident of sexual victimization during the previous twelve months of confinement.[52]

Voices of Delinquency: Blood in the Hood, Part III

See the Evidence-Based Practice feature for more about sexual victimization in juvenile facilities.

In sum, although many exceptions to the lawless environment described in these studies exist, an environment in which the strong take advantage of the weak, the fact is that the quality of life for male residents in too many training schools is extremely problematic. Even more troubling are the high rates of staff involvement in the sexual victimization of residents.

What About Facilities for Females?

The **social roles** in training schools for girls are generally based on a family or **kinship social structure**:

- Rose Giallombardo's examination of three training schools for girls in various parts of the United States found that aggressive girls tended to adopt the male sexual roles ("butches") and put pressure on new residents to adopt the female sexual roles ("fems").[53]

- Christopher M. Sieverdes and Bartollas's study of six Southeastern coeducational training schools also revealed the presence of the family social structure in the girls' cottages. This study further divided the seven social roles found in these living units into aggressive, manipulative, and passive roles.[54]

Evidence-Based Practice
Sexual Victimization in Juvenile Facilities

In a 2010 report, *Sexual Victimization in Juvenile Facilities*, the Bureau of Justice Statistics (BJS) conducted the first nationally representative survey of sexual abuse in residential juvenile facilities. This BJS study surveyed 26,550 adjudicated youth held in state-operated and large local or privately operated juvenile facilities; overall 91 percent of the youth in these facilities were male and 9 percent were female. It was found that an estimated 12 percent of youth in state facilities and large nonstate facilities (representing 3,220 youth nationwide) reported one or more incidents of sexual victimization by another youth or facility staff member in the previous months or since admission.

- About 2 percent of youth (700 nationwide) reported an incident involving a peer and, alarmingly, 10.3 percent (2,730) reported an incident involving facility staff.
- About 4.3 percent of youth (1,150) reported having sex or other sexual activity with facility staff as a result of some type of force, 6.4 percent of youth (1,710) reported contact with facility staff without force or threat.
- Approximately 95 percent of all youth reporting staff sexual misconduct said they had been victimized by female staff. In 2008, 42 percent of staff in state juvenile facilities were female.
- Rates of sexual victimization varied among youth: 9.1 percent of females and 2.0 percent of males reported unwanted sexual activity with other youth.

- Youth with a sexual orientation other than heterosexual reported significantly higher rates of sexual victimization by another youth (12.5 percent) compared to heterosexual youth (1.3 percent).
- Youth who had experienced any prior sexual assault were more than twice as likely to report sexual victimization in the current facility (24.1 percent), compared to those with no sexual assault history (10.1 percent).
- Among youth victimized by another youth, 20 percent said they had been physically injured, and 5 percent reported they had sought medical attention for their injuries.
- Among youth victimized by staff, 5 percent reported a physical injury, and fewer than 1 percent had sought medical attention.

CRITICAL THINKING QUESTION

If a juvenile facility must be safe for residents, then this BJS report, as well as other recent ones, is a serious indictment of this nation's policy of juvenile institutionalization. How can juveniles be better protected from each other as well as from exploitative staff?

Source: Allen J. Beck, Paige M. Harrison, and Paul Guerino, *Sexual Victimization in Juvenile Facilities Reported by Youth, 2008–2009* (Washington, DC: U.S. Government Printing Office, Bureau of Justice Statistics, 2010), 1.

- Alice Propper examined three coeducational and four girls' training schools scattered through the East, Midwest, and South, five of which were public and two of which were private Catholic facilities. In contrast to previously held assumptions, she found little overlap between pseudo-family roles and homosexual behavior; participation in homosexuality and make-believe families was just as prevalent in coeducational as in single-sex institutions, and homosexuality was as prevalent in treatment—as in custody—oriented facilities.[55]

In sum, similar to institutions for adolescent males, those for adolescent females also provide an environment in which strong girls take advantage of weaker ones and where aggression is the dominant force in the living environment.

Do Institutionalized Youths Have Rights?

The rights of juveniles is a major issue in juvenile justice. The Children's Rights Movement, as well as proponents of due process rights of children within the juvenile justice system, challenges whether institutionalized youths have sufficient legal protection. They argue that confined juveniles ought to receive three basic rights: the right to treatment, the right not to be treated, and the right to be free from cruel and unusual punishment. The rights of confined offenders have been examined by the federal courts and the Civil Rights of Institutionalized Persons Act.

Right to Treatment

Several court rulings have found that a juvenile committed to a training school has a right to treatment. In the Illinois' *White v. Reid* (1954) case, the court ruled that juveniles could not be held in institutions that did not provide for their rehabilitation.[56] In a Rhode Island case, the *Inmates of the Boys' Training School v. Affleck* (1972) decision also stated that juveniles have a right to treatment because rehabilitation is the true purpose of the juvenile court.[57] In *Nelson v. Heyne* (1974), Indiana's Seventh Circuit agreed with the district court that inmates of the Indiana Boys' School have a right to rehabilitative treatment.[58]

Moreover, in the 1973 *Morales v. Turman* decision, the U.S. District Court for the Eastern District of Texas held that a number of criteria had to be followed by the state of Texas in order to ensure that proper treatment would be provided to confined juveniles. These criteria included minimum standards for assessing and testing children committed to the state; minimum standards for assessing educational skills and handicaps and for providing programs aimed at advancing a child's education; minimum standards for delivering vocational education and medical and psychiatric care; and minimum standards for providing a humane institutional environment.[59] This finding was overruled by the Fifth Circuit Appeals Court on the grounds that a three-judge court should have been convened to hear the case. On *certiorari* to the U.S. Supreme Court, the Court reversed the court of appeals and remanded the case. What may affect future considerations of confined juveniles' right to treatment is whether the order of the district court can withstand the assault against it.

Right of Access from the Courts and to Refuse Treatment

Juveniles committed to training school have a constitutional right of access to the courts. They can petition the juvenile court for relief from earlier judicial decisions. Institutionalized juveniles also have a right to refuse treatment. In addition, treatment should be voluntary and should not be related to the length of institutional confinement. The standards of the Institute of Judicial Administration of the American Bar Association (IJA-ABA), for example, propose that children may voluntarily refuse services except in three cases: "services juveniles are legally obliged to accept (as school attendance), services required to prevent clear harm to physical health, and services mandated by the court as a condition to a nonresidential disposition."[60]

Right to Be Free from Cruel and Unusual Punishment

Some courts have applied the Eighth Amendment, barring cruel and unusual punishment, to juvenile institutions to forbid the use of corporal punishment in any form, the use of Thorazine and other medications for the purpose of control, and the use of extended periods of solitary confinement.[61] The *Pena v. New York State Division for Youth* (1976) decision held that the use of isolation, hand restraints, and tranquilizing drugs at Goshen Annex Center was punitive and antitherapeutic and, therefore, violated the Eighth Amendment.[62] In the case of *Inmates of the Boys' Training School v. Affleck*, the court also condemned such practices as solitary confinement and strip cells, and it established minimum standards for youths confined at the training school.[63] In the *Morales v. Turman* decision in Texas, the court found instances of physical brutality and abuse, including staff-administered beatings and tear gassings, homosexual assaults, excessive use of solitary confinement, and the lack of clinical services.[64] In *Morgan v. Sproat,* a 1977 Mississippi case, the court found that youths were confined in padded cells with no windows or furnishings and only flush holes for toilets and were denied access to all programs or services except a Bible.[65] Finally, in *State v. Werner*, the court found that residents were locked in solitary confinement; were beaten, kicked, slapped, and sprayed with mace by staff; were required to scrub floors with a toothbrush; and were forced to stand or sit for prolonged periods without changing position.[66] In each of these cases, the courts condemned these cruel practices.

CRIPA and Juvenile Correctional Facilities

As of November 1997, the Civil Rights Division had investigated three hundred institutions under the Civil Rights of Institutionalized Persons Act (CRIPA). Of these, seventy-three institutions, or about 25 percent, were juvenile detention and correctional facilities.

FIGURE 10–4
The Three Major Rights of Juveniles

The Civil Rights Division is monitoring conditions in thirty-four juvenile correctional facilities through consent decrees in Kentucky, New Jersey, and Puerto Rico. The consent decree filed in Kentucky covers all thirteen juvenile facilities in the state; the decree in New Jersey is for one facility, and in Puerto Rico, for twenty facilities.[67]

Figure 10–4 illustrates the three major rights of juveniles.

Juvenile Justice Videos

LIFE INSIDE

Life Inside follows youths as they give a "tour" of a juvenile institution. The juveniles interviewed give their perspective on how the institutions function as well as giving a personal account of future plans. Based on the interviews in the video, how did the juvenile institutions have an impact on the goals of the youths? What are some of the programs that juvenile institutions offer and what are the goals of these programs? Using information from the video, discuss whether the institution in the video focuses on retribution or rehabilitation. Why? What would be different if the center operated through the some other treatment model?

THE PROFESSIONAL PERSPECTIVE

The Professional Perspective interviews the superintendent of a juvenile institution. Discuss the differences between the juveniles' perspective of the happenings within the institution from the *Life Inside* video and the perspective of the superintendent. How do the points of view differ? How are the perspectives similar? The superintendent speaks about recruiting and retaining staff members within the institution. According to the superintendent, what characteristics make up a good staff member for an institutional environment? Discuss the impact a staff member can have on the lives of institutionalized juveniles.

SUMMARY

Learning Objective 1: Describe the purpose and operation of short-term confinement facilities including jails, detention centers, and shelter care facilities.

More than seven thousand juveniles continue to be placed in the problematic settings of adult jails. Detention centers that are temporary holding centers for juveniles vary from the traditional detention centers to model facilities for youth. Shelter care facilities are more open settings in which youths in trouble, often status offenders, are placed for a short period of time

Learning Objective 2: Describe the purpose and operation of various long-term correctional facilities, including boot camps, reception and diagnostic centers, and ranches/forestry camps.

Boot camps were widely regarded in the early 1990s, and supporters often viewed them as a panacea for juvenile corrections. More recently, high recidivism rates, as well as charges of abuse, have persuaded some states, including Arizona, Florida, Georgia, Maryland, and South Dakota, to shut these programs down or to reevaluate them. Reception and diagnostic centers found in larger states are used to determine the best treatment plan for delinquents adjudicated to long-term institutional care. Ranches and forestry camps are minimum-security institutional placements that are normally reserved for youths who have committed minor offenses.

Learning Objective 3: Describe the goals, programs, and operation of training schools.

Disagreements on social policy for training schools range from arguing for an increase in the number of these facilities to arguing for closing all training schools. There are those who believe that with proper staff–resident ratios and improved programs, these facilities can provide well for juveniles in trouble. Others assert that training schools are violent, inhumane, and damaging to all children. Some believe that these facilities should be located in

the community, and still others recommend isolating them in rural areas. Beyond these disagreements is the reality that the number of youthful offenders confined in residential facilities increased 27 percent between 1991 and 2006. Private training schools were usually reserved for status offenders, while delinquents were adjudicated to public training schools; but the offense backgrounds of those placed in private and public training schools are quite similar now.

Learning Objective 4: Summarize the rights of juveniles who are institutionalized.

Juveniles have three basic rights: the right to treatment, the right not to be treated, and the right to be free from cruel and unusual punishments. The rights of confined offenders have been examined by the federal courts and the Civil Rights of Institutionalized Persons Act (CRIPA).

Learning Objective 5: Summarize the factors that should be taken into consideration when implementing a confinement policy for juveniles.

- If at all possible, youths should be kept in their home communities.
- If confinement is necessary, the detention home or training school (jails should never be used for children) should be in or very near the home community.
- The facilities should remain small, with detention home populations not exceeding thirty and training school populations not exceeding fifty.
- The facilities should be pleasantly furnished and security features provided only after adequate staffing, programming, and a satisfactory, safe physical plan have been developed. If such facilities are absolutely necessary, they should be completely committed to full use of community resources and, wherever possible, should integrate residents into community programs.

KEY TERMS

attention homes, p. 205
boot camps, p. 206
detention centers, p. 205
jails, p. 203

kinship social structure, p. 219
ranch and forestry camps, p. 209
reception and diagnostic centers, p. 208
shelter care facilities, p. 205

social roles, p. 219
training schools, p. 212
victimization, p. 218

REVIEW QUESTIONS

1. How would you describe the social structure of residents in training schools?
2. Why are training schools damaging to some youths?
3. How can training schools be improved?
4. What are the major shocks a juvenile faces upon release to the community?

5. On the basis of everything you have read and heard about boot camps, would you recommend their continued use? Why or why not?

GROUP EXERCISES

1. *Group Work:* Identify the different types of short-term care facilities, their characteristics, and their clientele.
2. *Group Work:* Identify the different types of long-term care facilities, their characteristics, and their clientele.

3. *Writing to Learn Exercise:* Write a paragraph on each of the following: the characteristics of short- and long-term confinement facilities, their goals, and the types of programs likely to be found in each.

4. **Group Work:** Discuss the characteristics of both private and public juvenile facilities. How is the life of residents structured in these facilities?

5. **Writing to Learn Exercise:** Each student is to write a paragraph on the social organization of inmates in cottages

and the roles inmates play in that structure. Critique and revise.

6. **Group Work:** Discuss the legal rights of youths in juvenile facilities.

NOTES

1. Christopher Murray, Chris Baird, Ned Loughran, Fred Mills, and John Platt, *Safety and Welfare Plan: Implementing Reform in California* (Sacramento: California Department of Corrections and Rehabilitation, Division of Juvenile Justice, 2006).

2. David W. Springer, *Transforming Juvenile Justice in Texas: A Framework for Action* (Austin, TX: Blue Ribbon Task Force Report, 2007).

3. "Juvenile School Would Grow," *Hartford Courant,* February 10, 2008; Alison Leigh Cowan, "New Connecticut Law May Save a Troubled Prison for Juveniles," *New York Times,* July 30, 2007; Christine Smart, "Juvenile Injustice," *CJ News Junkie,* July 19, 2006; and Nan Schnitzler, "Connecticut Juvenile Training School to Close," *New England Psychologist,* October 2005.

4. "Abuse Claims Plague Juvenile Detention," *Star Bulletin* 63 (March 3, 2008).

5. According to Rosemary C. Sari, the number of youths confined in jail each year during the 1970s ranged from 90,000 (Children's Defense fund) to 100,000 (Fund to National Council on Crime and Delinquency). See Sari, "Gender Issues in Juvenile Justice," *Crime and Delinquency* 29 (1983), 390.

6. Howard N. Snyder and Melissa Sickmund, *Juvenile Offenders and Victims: A National Report* (Pittsburgh: National Center for Juvenile Justice, 1995), 72.

7. Ibid., 236.

8. Charles E. Frazier and Donna M. Bishop, "Jailing Juveniles in Florida: The Dynamics of Compliance to a Sluggish Federal Referral Initiative," paper presented at the annual meeting of the American Society of Criminology, Baltimore, MD, November 1990, 4.

9. Ira M. Schwartz, Linda Harris, and Laurie Levi, "The Jailing of Juveniles in Minnesota: A Case Study," *Crime and Delinquency* 34 (1988), 146; David Steinhart, "California's Legislature Ends the Jailing of Children: The Story of a Policy Reversal," *Crime and Delinquency* 34 (1988), 169–70.

10. David Steinhart and Barry Krisberg, "Children in Jail," *State Legislature* 13 (1987), 12–16.

11. Dale G. Parent et al., *Conditions of Confinement: Juvenile Detention and Corrections Facilities* (Washington, DC: Office of Juvenile Justice and Delinquency Prevention, 1994), 180–81. For other criticisms of detention practices, see Ira M. Schwartz and William H. Barton, eds., *Reforming Juvenile Detention: No More Hidden Closets* (Columbus: Ohio State University Press, 1994).

12. Roberta C. Cronin, *Boot Camps for Adult and Juvenile Offenders: Overview and Update*, Final Summary Report (Washington, DC: National Institute of Justice, 1994), 37.

See also Mark Jones and Steven Cuvelier, "Are Boot Camp Graduates Better Probation Risks?" paper presented at the annual meeting of the American Society of Criminology, New Orleans, LA, November 1992; and Thomas W. Waldron, "Boot Camps Offer Second Chance to Young Felons," *Corrections Today* 52 (1990), 144–69.

13. Jean Bottcher, "Evaluating the Youth Authority's Boot Camp: The First Five Months," paper delivered to Western Society of Criminology, Monterey, CA, February 1993; Institute for Criminological Research and American Institute for Research, *Boot Camp for Juvenile Offenders: Constructive Intervention and Early Support—Implementation Evaluation Final Report* (New Brunswick, NJ: Rutgers University Press, 1992).

14. Cronin, *Boot Camps for Adults and Juvenile Offenders.*

15. Anthony W. Salerno, "Boot Camps: A Critique and a Proposed Alternative," *Journal of Offender Rehabilitation* 20 (1994), 149.

16. Ibid., 37.

17. Michael Peters et al., *Boot Camps for Juvenile Offenders: Program Summary* (Washington, DC: Office of Juvenile Justice and Delinquency Prevention, 1997), 3, 35.

18. Ibid.

19. Doris Layton MacKenzie et al., "The Impact of Boot Camps on Traditional Institutions of Juvenile Residents: Perceptions, Adjustment, and Change," *Journal of Research in Crime and Delinquency* 38 (August 2000), 279–313.

20. Ibid., 279.

21. Brent Zaehringer, "Juvenile Boot Camps: Cost and Effectiveness vs. Residential Facilities," Koch Crime Institute White Paper Report, accessed at http://www.hrf.uni-koeln.de/sitenew/content/e/filejuvbootcamps.pdf.

22. For this report, see Diana Jean Schemo, "Report Recounts Horrors of Youth Boot Camps," *New York Times,* December 11, 2007, accessed September 20, 2012, at http://www.nytimes.com/2007/10/11/washington/11report.htm.

23. Marks, "States Fall Out of (Tough) Love with Boot Camps," *Christian Science Monitor,* December 27, 1999, 1.

24. For the classification system in California, the most highly developed in the nation, see Murray et al., *Safety and Welfare Plan*, 12–18.

25. For the most recent data on ranches and camps, see Snyder and Sickmund, *Juvenile Offenders and Victims: 2006 National Report*, 208, 221–27; Sickmund, "Juvenile Residential Facility Census, 2002: Selected Findings."

26. A basic description of this program is included in a brochure developed by the Hennepin County Home School (n.d.). See also the website of the Hennepin County Home School.

27. One of the authors has interviewed Teresa Wise and other administrators of the Hennepin County Home School and was given this information. See also http://www.co.hennepin.mn.us/portal/site/HCInternet/menuitem.14c0cacfe630405b258caf10b1466498/?vgnextoid=393ebe2f09b7c010VgnVCM1000000f094689RCRD.

28. Sarah Hockenberry, Melissa Sickmund, and Anthony Sladky, *Juvenile Residential Facility Census, 2008: Selected Findings* (Washington, D.C.: U.S. Department of Justice, Juvenile Offenders and Victims: National Report Series Bulletin, July 2011).

29. Ibid., 6.

30. Murray et al., *Safety and Welfare Plan,* 2.

31. David Street, Robert D. Vinter, and Charles Perrow, *Organizations for Treatment: A Comparative Study of Institutions* (New York: Free Press, 1966).

32. Hockenberry et al., *Juvenile Residential Facility Census, 2008,* 4.

33. "Youth Center at Paint Creek Provides Opportunities," *Lighthouse Views,* Winter 2008, 1.

34. Experiences of one of the authors in several juvenile institutional systems have revealed these activities of youth supervision.

35. Snyder and Sickmund, *Juvenile Offenders and Victims: 2006 National Report,* 197.

36. Ibid.

37. David Shichor and Clemens Bartollas, "Private and Public Juvenile Placements: Is There a Difference?" *Crime and Delinquency* 36 (April 1990), 286–99.

38. Glen Mills School, for example, was featured in Bill Howard, "Florida Tries to Clone Preppy Glen Mills," *Youth Today: The Newspaper on Youth Work* 5 (July–August 1996), 1, 12, 13.

39. Gaylene Styve Armstrong and Doris Layton MacKenzie, "Private versus Public Juvenile Correctional Facilities: Do Differences in Environmental Quality Exist?" *Crime and Delinquency* 49 (October 2003), 542–63.

40. Shichor and Bartollas, "Private and Public Juvenile Placements."

41. Clemens Bartollas and David Shichor, "Juvenile Privatization: The Expected and the Unexpected," paper presented at the annual meeting of the American Society of Criminology, Baltimore, MD, November 1990.

42. Shichor and Bartollas, "Private and Public Juvenile Placements," 286–99.

43. Gordon E. Barker and W. Thomas Adams, "The Social Structure of a Correctional Institution," *Journal of Criminal Law, Criminology and Police Science* 49 (1959), 417–99.

44. Howard W. Polsky, *Cottage Six: The Social System of Delinquent Boys in Residential Treatment* (New York: Russel Sage Foundation), 69–88.

45. Sethard Fisher, "Social Organization in a Correction Residence," *Pacific Sociological Review* 5 (Fall 1961), 89.

46. Ibid., 89–90.

47. Clemens Bartollas, Stuart J. Miller, and Simon Dinitz, *Juvenile Victimization: The Institutional Paradox* (New York: Sage Publications, 1976), 131–50.

48. Stuart J. Miller, Clemens Bartollas, and Simon Dinitz, *Juvenile Victimization Revisited: A Fifteen-Year Follow-Up at TICO* (unpublished manuscript).

49. Martin Forst, Jeffrey Fagan, and T. Scott Vivona, "Youth in Prisons and Training Schools: Perceptions and Consequences of the Treatment–Custody Dichotomy," *Juvenile and Family Court Journal* 40 (1989), 1–14.

50. Andrea Sedlack, "Sexual Assault of Youth in Residential Placement," presentation at Bureau of Justice Statistics Workshop, Washington, DC, January 18, 2005.

51. Allen J. Beck and Timothy A. Hughes, *Sexual Violence Reported by Correctional Authorities 2004* (Washington, DC: Bureau of Justice Statistics, 2005).

52. Cited by Richard Tewksbury, "What We Know About Sexual Violence in Juvenile Corrections," paper presented at the 2007 Winter Conference, Grapevine, TX.

53. Rose Giallombardo, *The Social World of Imprisoned Girls: A Comparative Study of Institutions for Juvenile Delinquents* (New York: Wiley, 1974).

54. Christopher M. Sieverdes and Clemens Bartollas, "Social Roles, Sex, and Racial Differences," *Deviant Behavior* 5 (1982), 203–18.

55. Alice Propper, *Prison Homosexuality: Myth and Reality* (Lexington, MA: D. C. Heath, 1981).

56. *White v. Reid,* 125 F. Supp. 647 (D.D.C. 1954).

57. *Inmates of the Boys' Training School v. Affleck,* 346 F. Supp. 1354 (D.R.I. 1972).

58. *Nelson v. Heyne,* 355 F. Supp. 451 (N.D. Ind. 1972).

59. *Morales v. Turman,* 364 F. Supp. 166 (E.D. Tex. 1973).

60. H. Swanger, "Juvenile Institutional Litigation," *Clearinghouse Review* 11 (1977), 22.

61. See *Lollis v. N.Y. State Department of Social Services,* 322 F. Supp. 473 (S.D.N.Y. 1970) and N. N. Kittie, *The Right to Be Different: Deviance and Enforced Therapy* (Baltimore: Johns Hopkins University Press, 1971), for more information on this subject.

62. *Pena v. New York State Division for Youth,* 419 F. Supp. 203 (S.D.N.Y. 1976).

63. *Inmates of the Boys' Training School v. Affleck.*

64. *Morales v. Turman.*

65. *Morgan v. Sproat,* 432 F. Supp. 1130 (S.D. Miss. 1977).

66. *State v. Werner,* 242 S.E.2d 907 (W. Va. 1978).

67. Patricia Puritz and Mary Ann Scali, *Beyond the Walls: Improving Conditions of Confinement for Youth in Custody Report* (Washington, DC: Office of Juvenile Justice and Delinquency Prevention, 1998), 4–7.

ZUMA Press/Newscom

Learning Objectives

1. Describe the goals of aftercare.
2. Describe the rules of those on aftercare who are released to the community.
3. Summarize why so many youths fail on aftercare.
4. Describe the role of the aftercare officer.
5. Describe means by which aftercare can be improved.

Marco, a 19-year-old Latino, was incarcerated for being the "trigger man" on a drive-by shooting. As he neared the end of his sentence, Marco vowed that he was finished with gang violence, telling me: "I'm not putting in any more work, though … no more drive-bys." He did intend to sell drugs when he was back in the community, but he had thought carefully about how to reduce the risk. He said that he would not take a lot of risk and would not be a visible dealer out on the street corner. Instead, he planned to make his deals with a pager; with a pager, he said, "You know who is calling you, and you can arrange to meet in a safe place." He also said that he would not carry the drugs in plastic baggies, because "baggies are used to prove intent to sell/deliver," which would carry a longer, more severe sentence.[1]

Release is the prime goal for a confined youth. The days, weeks, months, and sometimes years spent in confinement are occupied by thoughts and fantasies of release or even escape. For many youths, the thoughts and desires of release become all-consuming passions and govern every action of theirs. Youths who have been intractable become compliant, the weak feign strength, the ill pretend health, and the worst become the best. Every action becomes a show for the benefit of those who can expedite release—the staff, social workers, teachers, chaplains, and others.

An estimated one hundred thousand youthful offenders are released each year from secure correctional institutions, including jails, juvenile facilities, and adult prisons. Many juveniles who leave these facilities have multiple risk factors and are struggling with co-occurring mental health and alcohol and drug issues and also have difficulty succeeding in school.[2] These problems, all too typically, are not sufficiently addressed in residential facilities. Specifically, researchers found shortcomings in substance abuse, mental health, and education programs provided to juveniles held in residential services.[3] In addition, some juveniles may be exposed to violence and trauma that leave them even more troubled when they are released to the community.[4]

These problems are further compounded when unprepared juveniles are sent back to surroundings that may have contributed to their delinquent acts in the first place—communities that have high rates of poverty and crime, poorly performing schools, and few community health and social services. Crossover youth are particularly vulnerable to future difficulties because they frequently come from abusive or neglectful families. To successfully rejoin their families and communities, these youths need aftercare services that can assist them in developing the skills and protective factors they need to resist further risky and unlawful behavior and, ultimately, to avoid return to custody.[5]

Despite this need, many state and local juvenile justice and child welfare systems fail to focus on or provide aftercare or reentry programs for juvenile offenders. Much of the current work in juvenile justice is focused on the front-end issue of confinement, rather than on the back end of reentry. As a result, little is known about the effective reentry of juveniles.[6]

This chapter explores juvenile aftercare, the final episode in the correctional endeavor. Beginning with a definition and a discussion of the release process and considering it from the perspectives of resident, staff, and society, the chapter reviews the problems and the opportunities facing the youth on aftercare status, the aftercare officer, and society once a youth is released. General operational problems are considered, and, finally, the issue of improving aftercare is discussed.

What Is Aftercare and What Are Its Objectives?

Aftercare can be defined as "as reintegrative services that prepare out-of-home placed juveniles for reentry into the community by establishing the necessary collaborative arrangements with the community to ensure the delivery of prescribed services and supervision."[7] The term *aftercare* is a misnomer because aftercare involves much more than "after an offender is released." It ideally begins at or after sentencing and continues through confinement and a youth's release to the community. It requires a seamless set of systems across formal and informal social control networks and a continuum of community services to prevent the reoccurrence of delinquent behaviors. Public–private partnerships are often involved in expanding the capacity of youth services.[8]

A major concern in juvenile justice in the past forty years has been the development of a workable philosophy and concept of aftercare. A number of objectives for juvenile aftercare, or **parole**, have been developed through the years:

1. Release residents from confinement at the most favorable time for community adjustment.

2. Prepare youths for their successful reintegration into the community on completion of aftercare.

3. Reduce the crimes committed by released juveniles.

4. Reduce the violent acts committed by released offenders.

5. Increase community confidence in parole.

6. Alleviate overcrowding of training schools.

7. Monitor youthful offenders as they refrain from abusing or trafficking drugs.

8. Discourage the return of youths to street gangs.

The achievement of these objectives requires extensive planning and research. For example, to determine the most favorable time for release requires far more knowledge than is presently available. Many new and innovative techniques for prediction can be developed; research must enable releasing authorities to compare the costs of leaving juveniles in institutions with the possible harm to society if they are released.

Planning must clearly take place in each institution. Such planning is necessary if the functions of the various community agencies are to be articulated with institutional services. Evaluation procedures must be developed to assist institutions and agencies to determine their success. Realistic goals and objectives must be spelled out. Thus, the necessary guidelines for implementing a more effective aftercare policy can be formulated so that the number of arbitrary, whimsical, and idiosyncratic aftercare revocations by individual aftercare officers can be reduced.

Who Is Responsible for Releasing Youths from Training Schools?

Juveniles released from training school are placed on aftercare or parole status. The bases on which they are released from these schools vary, and so do those individuals responsible for making the release decision. In forty-four states the authority for making this decision for juveniles rests with the executive branch of state governments. In four states the decision is made by probation or parole officers, and in three states other board agencies make the decision.[9] In Illinois and several other states, juvenile judges have the authority to remove juveniles from training schools.

At present, some controversy exists about who should make the aftercare decision. Some believe that staff who work with the residents know them best and are, therefore, the best judges of when they should be released. The staff see their charges daily, work with them in therapy, interact with them informally, and observe their interaction with peers. The twenty-four-hour living experience should, according to the proponents of institutional decision making, make the institution and its staff outstanding experts on the progress and character of their youths. Such experience, it is believed, will enable institutional officials to know better than anyone the optimum time for release.

This argument has been countered by another: the institutional officials and staff are prone to overreact to residents' inability to get along in the institution. If offenders can stay out of institutional problems and can remain on the good side of the staff members, or if they reach a certain age, or if the institution becomes overcrowded, they are deemed ready for release. But if a youth has a personality conflict with a particular staff member or fights to protect himself or herself, he or she may not be able to get out. According to this view, staff members sometimes are prejudiced or opposed ideologically to what the youth believes. The accusation also is made that staff members occasionally release troublemakers just to get them out of the institution.

Many believe that the decision to release residents should be made by independent agencies and boards that are not swayed by what happens in institutions. One major advantage of setting up independent agencies and boards is that no longer would release be based on factors irrelevant to a resident's ability to get along in the community. Release would be decided impartially, regardless of whether or not a few rules were violated or a resident did talk back to staff from time to time.

Institutional staff members, however, believe that those independent agencies and boards are too far removed from institutions to know what is going on within them. Staff members further believe that autonomous boards are unrealistic and uninformed about the problems that staff members and other officials face in working with difficult and troublesome youths. They also believe that important aspects of various cases are ignored by independent boards, resulting in inappropriate decisions at times. Moreover, staff members believe that the establishment of these boards downgrades their own professional competence and introduces an unnecessary complication. See Table 11–1 for arguments concerning the release decision for youths released from training school.

Some question whether any method is effective in assessing when to release an institutionalized youth. For example, a study of 16,779 juveniles in Florida released from confinement programs to the community found that no consistent relationship existed between length of confinement and recidivism. The length of confinement, this 2008 study found, was only significant for youths released from high-risk facilities and male offenders.[10]

States that use determinate or mandatory sentencing for juveniles usually have determined the time of institutional release when the youth is committed to training school. A variation of this approach is for the length of confinement to be determined within the department responsible for institutional care, using such guidelines as offense severity, previous offense history, and, perhaps, other criteria. For example, in the late 1980s, the Ohio Department of Youth Services established an Office of Release Review in order to provide a structured, centralized, objective release decision-making process. The goal of this office was to set a length of institutional stay for each juvenile felony offender proportionate to the severity of his or her offenses and the impact on the victims. A parole hearing officer scored each youth using a specialized worksheet. In most cases, the score established the length of stay unless overriding conditions were present, as determined by an administrative committee within the office.[11] Today, Ohio and other states are moving toward a decision tree or logical analysis framework to broaden the number of youthful risk and need factors that can be considered in making the release decision.[12]

In Minnesota, the release of a juvenile from a training school has been until recently the responsibility of a juvenile aftercare hearing officer who used a scale incorporating the severity of the offense history (see Figure 11–1). For example, a youthful offender who committed first-degree burglary would have a severity level of 3. If his or her delinquent history factors equaled 3, this offender would normally be paroled somewhere between the

TABLE 11–1
Controversy About Training School Release Decisions

Decision Makers	Support For	Arguments Against
Support for institutional	Are the best judge for when youths are ready for release.	Make inappropriate decisions, staff based on factors, unreleased to community adjustment
Independent agencies	Decisions are not based on irrelevant factors.	These boards are too far removed from institutions to know what is going on within them.
Determinate or mandatory sentencing	Guidelines of offense severity, previous offense history	Personal factors pertinent to a juvenile's case are not considered.

FIGURE 11–1
Projected Institution Length of Stay in Months

Severity Level	Most Serious Current Offense*	Delinquent History Factors			
		0	1	2	3
I	Violation of Probation Contempt of Court Prostitution Assault—4th & 5th Degree Driving Under Influence of Alcohol Negligent Fires Burglary—3rd & 4th Degree Damage to Property—$2,500 or less Forgery—$2,500 or less Possession of Controlled Substance Receiving Stolen Goods—$2,500 or less Theft—$2,500 or less Unauthorized Use of Motor Vehicle Dangerous Weapons (not including firearms) Trespass All Other Misdemeanors and Gross Misdemeanors	4–3	5–3	6–4	7–5
II	Assault—2nd & 3rd Degree Burglary—2nd Degree Damage to Property—Over $2,500 Forgery—Over $2,500 False Imprisonment Receiving Stolen Goods—$2,500 Felony Possession/Sale of Controlled Substance Theft from Person Theft—Over $2,500 Arson—3rd Degree Criminal Sexual Conduct—3rd & 4th Degree Simple Robbery Terroristic Threats Criminal Vehicular Homicide Dangerous Weapons—Firearms	6–3	7–4	8–5	9–6
III	Burglary—1st Degree Criminal Negligence Resulting in Death Aggravated Robbery Arson—1st & 2nd Degree Criminal Sexual Conduct—1st & 2nd Degree Kidnapping Manslaughter Assault—1st Degree	10–6	11–7	12–8	13–9
IV	Murder (all degrees)**	**	**	**	

*Commitment offenses not specifically listed shall be placed on the grid at the discretion of the hearing officer at the time of the initial institution review.
**Murder shall be dealt with on an individual basis.

ninth and thirteenth months. This scale, consistent with other sentencing structures for juveniles in Minnesota was based on the justice model.[13] Minnesota, too, is reworking the state's procedures for release.

Early release from training school due to overcrowding conditions has complicated this decision-making process. In six states, a parole board appointed by the governor considers early release for institutionalized juveniles. This is not done as frequently as in adult corrections, especially because youths are serving much shorter sentences in juvenile institutions than would be true in adult corrections.

This impasse on decision making for institutional release will not be easily resolved. Institutional officials and staff deserve the wide criticisms they have received. Little evidence exists that juvenile parole boards have been sharply criticized in recent years. The recent move in juvenile justice to use formalized and structured instruments to make release decisions also has its share of problems. Unless researchers can predict with some accuracy the risks and needs of youths before release to facilitate the success of those released on aftercare or parole, this approach becomes extremely questionable.

Characteristics of Those on Aftercare

Unlike adult corrections, in which an article, *Probation and Parole in the United States*, reveals each year the characteristics of adults on probation and parole, the listing of the characteristics on aftercare lacks up-to-date data.[14]

Howard N. Snyder has contributed to our understanding more of the portrait of juveniles returning to the community. He reported that nearly one hundred thousand juvenile offenders are released annually from juvenile facilities. These youths have spent a considerable proportion of their adolescent years in custody. Most are male, minority, and nonviolent offenders. About half live in single-parent families and about one-fourth have a sibling. In addition, about one-fourth have a father who has been incarcerated. Most have not completed eighth grade, which can be compared to one-fourth of similarly aged youth across the nation. The prevalence of the presence of a learning disability is higher than that in the general adolescent population. Excluding alcohol, two-thirds indicate regular drug use. Two-thirds of youths adjudicated to training school have a mental health disorder, with the rate for females being higher. The majority of females leaving a correctional facility have a history of physical or sexual abuse. Finally, a majority of these juveniles will be returning home to an impoverished family and neighborhood.[15]

In a more recent 2010 study, authors Laura S. Abrams and Susan M. Snyder reported that the vast majority of this population is made up of older (81 percent) members of an ethnic minority group (36.6 percent non-Hispanic white, 39.4 percent African American, and 19.8 percent Hispanic). The majority came from single-parent homes (56 percent) or did not live with a parent (26 percent) prior to confinement and approximately one out of eleven were parents themselves.[16] See Table 11–2 for the characteristics of youths returning to the community.

TABLE 11–2
Empirical Portrait of Youths Returning to the Community

Size of Returnees	About one hundred thousand per year
Gender	Mostly male. The majority of females have a history of physical or sexual abuse
Race/Ethnicity	Mostly minority
Offense Background	Most are nonviolent offenders
Age	Mostly older
Family Background	About half live in single-parent households, one-fourth have a father who has been incarcerated, and about 10 percent are parents themselves
Educational Background	Most have not completed eighth grade and have high rates of learning disabilities
Mental Health	Two-thirds of youth have a mental health disorder
Previous Custodial Experience	Most have spent the majority of their adolescence in custody
Economic Background	The majority will be returning home to an impoverished family and neighborhood

Source: Howard Snyder, "An Empirical Portrait of the Youth Reentry Population," *Youth Violence and Juvenile Justice* (2004), 39–55; and Laura S. Abrams and Susan M. Snyder, "Youth Offender Reentry: Models for Intervention and Directions for Future Inquiry," *Children and Youth Services Review* 12 (December 2010), 1787–95.

Risk Control and Crime Reduction

The current emphasis in aftercare, as in juvenile probation, is on short-term behavior control. Consequently, we can assume that, even if more states adopt determinate sentencing statutes for juveniles, the likelihood is that mandatory aftercare services will continue to be provided for those released from public and private placements; indeed, some cities and states are beginning to use the terms *aftercare probation* or *probation aftercare* to emphasize the necessity of planning early for the release of juveniles. These efforts are directed, for the most part, to **intensive supervision programs**. Nevertheless, these in-house detention and electronic monitoring programs still have not received the attention that they have in adult probation. Juvenile aftercare also emphasizes drug and alcohol urinalysis (sometimes called *drug drops*) and turned toward "boot camp" programs in the 1980s and 1990s as a means of releasing juveniles early from training school.

Intensive Aftercare Supervision

Intensive aftercare supervision (IAS) can be conceived as operating "in the context of decision making and planning for the *early release* of juveniles from secure confinement" and as "imposing higher levels of supervision on youth(s) being released after serving a *full* institutional term."[17] In terms of intensive aftercare supervision, three populations of juveniles can be targeted: all parolees, medium- to low-risk parolees, and high-risk parolees.[18]

More than eighty intensive aftercare supervision programs were active across the United States in the 1980s and 1990s. The most noteworthy of these intensive programs were those in the thirty counties of Pennsylvania; the Lifeskills '95 program, which was the Violent Juvenile Offender Research and Development Program in Boston, Memphis, Newark, and Detroit; the Skillman Intensive Aftercare Project; the Michigan Nokomis Challenge program; the PARJO program in New York; and the Office of Juvenile Justice and Delinquency Prevention (OJJDP) IAP project.

One recent concern has been to develop an integrated theoretical framework for guiding intensive supervision of chronic juvenile offenders. The Intensive Aftercare Program (IAP) model is a combination of social control, strain, and social learning theories, and it focuses on the reintegrative process. Its basic assumptions are that serious and chronic delinquency is related to weak controls produced by social disorganization, inadequate socialization, and strain; that strain is produced by social disorganization independent of weak controls; and that peer group influences intervene as a social force between youths with weak bonds and/or strain on one hand and delinquent behaviors on the other.[19]

The IAP project has been implemented in four pilot programs: Colorado (Arapahoe and Jefferson counties), Nevada (Clark County), New Jersey (Camden and Essex counties), and Virginia (Norfolk County). The participation of New Jersey counties ended in 1997, but the other programs carried through on preparing high-risk offenders for progressively increased responsibility and freedom in the community. The well-developed transition components that begin shortly after a youth is adjudicated to an institution and continue through the early months of community adjustments are particularly strict about these programs. The results of the first five years of implementation (1995–2000) reveal a dramatically improved level of communication and coordination between institutional and aftercare staff as well as the ability to involve parolees in community services almost immediately after institutional release.[20]

Intervention Programs

Intervention strategies, such as counseling, behavioral programs, probation, restitution, employment, and academic and vocational programs, seek to prevent delinquency by changing youthful offenders' behavior. Successful treatment approaches appear to have a number of characteristics in common:

- They target specific dynamic and criminogenic characteristics. Research indicates that dynamic criminological factors include attitudes, cognitions, behavior regarding education, peers, employment, authority, substance abuse, and interpersonal relationships.[21]

- They implement a plan, which is strictly adhered to, by trained personnel. Programs must have therapeutic integrity, which means that they must be delivered according to a specific plan and design.
- They require staff and offenders to make frequent contact. Frequent and quality interaction between service providers and offenders is essential for effective intervention.
- They use cognitive and behavioral treatments. A widely observed program evaluation finding is that the most effective intervention programs use structured, focused treatment based on behavioral, skill-oriented, and multimodal methods rather than less structured, less focused approaches.
- They target offenders with the highest risk of recidivism. Several programs have found that the treatment for delinquent behavior is most effective when it is provided to juveniles with the highest risk of recidivism.[22]

What Are the Downsides of the Current Reentry Process?

The juvenile justice system gives some attention to the juvenile's preparation for return to the community. Home visits, especially in private facilities, are frequently made available to juveniles before their release. In Minnesota and other states, parole, or aftercare, officers will visit institutionalized juveniles to help them plan for their community reintegration. Home placements and usually school or job assignments must also be finalized in most jurisdictions before the juvenile is released.

Yet, as with adult corrections, few training schools place much emphasis on prerelease programs that attempt to prepare residents for community experiences. Those that do typically include information and instruction on such matters as job opportunities and employment aids; the importance of being on time; motor vehicle driver training; legal problems and contacts; basic financial management; personal health practices and proper diet; perspectives on family responsibilities; human relations; and the dangers of alcohol, drugs, and cigarettes.

Nor are many juveniles provided the opportunity to work in the community before their release. Private facilities appear to be more concerned than public institutions about juveniles having a work experience prior to their release, but the obstacles to such programs include the security risks involved, the lack of staff to locate jobs and supervise residents, and the inability of residents to handle jobs constructively for more than a short period of time. In juvenile facilities providing such programs, residents leave the facility in the morning, usually with lunch and enough money for transportation, and return at the end of the work day. Some residents are provided transportation to and from work; others depend on public transportation.

Furthermore, in contrast to the number of halfway-in placements for juvenile probationers, relatively few halfway-out houses exist for juvenile parolees. The negative response that juveniles frequently had to such placements in the past apparently has discouraged this movement in juvenile corrections. What has taken the place of halfway-out facilities for juveniles are independent-living placements. Although such placements usually are made for juveniles who lack adequate placements with families or relatives, they do not offer a gradual transition to release that halfway-out residential facilities would permit.

It can be argued that juveniles who have been confined for only a few months in training school do not need **reentry programs** as much as do adults who may have spent years within prison walls. Some adults experience an unexpected jolt when released suddenly and without preparation. They may feel disoriented and confused by the transition from controlled living to life in free society. In contrast, this disorientation and confusion appears much less frequently with the released juveniles. In addition to the much shorter period of confinement, the openness of many training schools permits juveniles to move back and forth between the institution and the community.

Yet a convincing case can be made that juveniles need more of these reentry programs than they usually experience. Confined juveniles often have distorted ideas of what awaits them in the community. They anticipate that long-standing problems with family member will no longer exist. As one aptly put it, "I'm more mature now; I can handle my mom." They also believe that their school adjustment will go more smoothly than it usually does. Moreover, juveniles typically underestimate the difficulty of returning to the same community and peer relationships. Finally, nearly all juveniles entering the job market dramatically overestimate how much they will earn and what standard of living they will be able to maintain with that income.

What Is the "Continuum of Care" and How Does It Work?

Voices of Delinquency: The Day They Told Me I Could Go Free Was the End of Trouble for Me

One of the major challenges of aftercare services rests in the need for transition and reentry programs for youths committed to juvenile institutions. Those who had worked in institutions in the past were aware that once a youth was released, staff were prohibited from having contact with the youth. Staff members were sometimes reprimanded if they responded in any way to a released youth seeking contact and advice.

At the same time, the need to connect institutional and aftercare services has long been recognized. A few programs across the nation attempted to provide a continuum between institutional and aftercare services. More recently, an increasing number of jurisdictions are providing what we can call a *continuum of care* model. See Focus on Practice 11–1.

In sum, while the recidivism rates of these and other "continuum of care" models may not be impressive, they clearly provide services that youths need and desire. The reality is that services in the best institutional–community aftercare models cannot begin to match those factors, discussed in the following section, influencing many youths to continue with delinquent behaviors. Still, for some youths these aftercare services make the difference in helping them to desist from delinquency.

Focus on Practice 11–1
Examples of a Continuum of Care Model

- This *continuum of care* model is found in the Intensive Aftercare Program (IAP) model developed by the OJJDP. This model includes six intertwined phases: assessment, case planning, institutional treatment, prerelease, transition, and community reintegration. The follow-up evaluation of the three IAP sites found no differences between IAP and controls on measures of recidivism and in the severity of their offenses. It was found that some indicators of positive impact were lower numbers of misconduct reports during confinement and decreased length of institutionalization for IAP program participants.[23]

- A six weeks, transition services (TLP) for incarcerated youth in a public correctional institution for felony-level juvenile offenders in the Midwest focused on independent living skills. In this specific program, youths spend the night in the TLP cottage but are released to the community during the day to attend work or school. Gradually, they spend more time over the weekends in their home settings. Case managers work closely with youth to work out their daily schedules and plans for release. Participants in this program viewed the transitional living program as having many benefits, especially independent-living skills training, but it appeared to have no positive effect on reducing recidivism rates.[24]

- The Thomas O'Farrell Youth Center (TOYC) is located in Woodstock, Maryland, and is operated by the North American Family Institute under contract with the Maryland Department of Juvenile Justice. Youths spend on average eight months in this residential facility, followed by nine months

in the specialized aftercare component. Once youths have completed phase 1, in which they demonstrate a number of competencies, they enter the aftercare component. During this phase, each TOYC resident receives postrelease services from two aftercare workers; youths are contacted at least twelve days per month for six months. An evaluation of the TOYC program showed promising results; the first fifty-six TOYC graduates had no further court referrals in the year following their release.[25]

- The Bethesda Day Treatment Center in West Milton, Pennsylvania, is a private nonprofit corporation. The center, consisting of several facilities in eighteen Pennsylvania counties, offers an array of intervention options. The center also includes an intensive aftercare component designed to reintegrate residents released from institutional placement. This component uses a needs assessment to determine youths' clinical needs, and once these needs have been determined, aftercare staff refer the youths to the appropriate agencies. A preliminary evaluation revealed a low recidivism rate in the first year after discharge, but this low rate must be view cautiously because of the small sample size ($n = 5$).[26]

Source: Steve V. Gies, "Aftercare Services," *OJJDP: Juvenile Justice Bulletin* (Washington, DC: U.S. Department of Justice, 2003); Richard G. Wiebush et al., *Implementation and Outcome Evaluation of the Intensive Aftercare Program: Final Report* (Washington, DC: National Council on Crime and Delinquency, 2005); Laura S. Abrams, Sarah K. S. Shannon, and Cindy Sangalong, "Transition Services for Incarcerated Youth: A Mixed Methods Evaluation Study," *Children and Youth Services Review* 30 (2008), 522–35.

Community Experience

In spite of the various institutional and parole programs, many youths do get into trouble after release. The reasons for the failure of aftercare range from organizational factors to the lack of support in the community, and to the personal traits of youths themselves. Organizational factors include the extreme fragmentation encountered in the system, the dubious and even destructive nature of institutional life, and sometimes arbitrary decision making by aftercare officers. The lack of support systems in the community, including the inability to get a job, the stigma associated with being a "bad" person, and the lack of mentors to guide and encourage the youths, also makes it easy to return to crime. Finally, personal factors include an appetite for drugs and alcohol; an inability to walk away from gang involvement; and conflict with parole officers, school authorities, and parents.

Peer groups have considerable impact. Most youths go back to their old group within a day or so of their return, and groups are usually ready to accept them. This return to an old group is particularly true if youths belonged to a gang before their institutional commitment. If the old groups no longer exist, youths then seek new ones. If the family has moved, the problem of influence of antisocial peers is solved by a slowly decreasing rate of interaction with the old groups and the gradual establishment of new friends in the new area.

Parolees face major, sometimes monumental, problems in returning to school and getting jobs. Aftercare officers look upon school attendance and jobs as signs that the youths are performing successfully. Yet many of the youths who did not do well in school before their incarceration do not find it any easier after their return. They usually were behind their classmates when they entered the training schools and are still behind when they come out. Their classmates have changed, principals are leery of accepting these labeled youths, teachers remember them unfavorably, and the training schools have failed to change their attitudes toward academic courses.

The job situation is not any better. Training school programs are often either of a make-work type or otherwise irrelevant to actual jobs available in the home community. In some other cases the training schools prepare the youths for jobs that are available in the area where the training school is located but not in the youths' home communities. The youths may be able to do odd jobs, but their immaturity, lack of desire for a job, and inexperience preclude them from looking for anything more substantial.

These factors, then, provide the matrix within which the youths must operate. What leads them to become delinquent again? For some time it has been known that younger parolees are more likely to fail than older parolees; that persons who were involved in crime for longer periods of time are more likely to fail than individuals with short records; that those who begin early are more likely to continue; that individuals more heavily involved in crime are more likely to fail than those not so heavily involved; that persons frequently confined are more likely to fail than those who have not been confined; and that crimes-against-property offenders fail more than violent offenders. Some attributes, however, seem to separate recidivists and nonrecidivists:

- Recidivists have more difficulty adjusting to their prosocial peers than do nonrecidivists.
- They are more likely than nonrecidivists to be in groups to which it is difficult to adjust.
- They are more likely than nonrecidivists to maintain interaction with older groups that have a history of delinquency.
- They receive less effective antidelinquent teaching than do nonrecidivists.[27]

What Are the Main Responsibilities of Aftercare Officers?

The youths placed on aftercare require supportive counseling, delivery of certain services, and supervision. But frequently they receive only supervision, because the caseloads tend to be high for each officer.

Supervision

Aftercare officers have all the role conflicts of a probation officer described in Chapter 8 and, in fact, they are frequently probation officers with youths on aftercare on their caseloads. In addition, they are looked on even more often as law enforcement figures because they can return offenders to institutional confinement. The director of court services for a large Midwestern probation department compares juveniles on probation and those on aftercare:

> The main difference between the child on probation and the child on aftercare is that the child who has been further in the system and who has already received some sort of primary treatment has identified his or her sets of problems. Staff also are aware of these problems, and so we will more carefully scrutinize them. We are also a little more leery about those further in the system because they are more aware how to manage the system to their advantage. But they don't necessarily pose more danger either to the officer or to the community because those early in the system may be unaware of the impact or the consequences of their actions.[28]

To understand the resentment toward some aftercare officers, it is necessary to examine some of the rules to which youths are subject. A Pennsylvania county uses the rules set down in Focus on Practice 11–2, modified according to each parolee's needs. These rules are read by the juvenile, who then signs the statement, "I, the undersigned, have received a copy, read and understood the aforementioned rules and agree to abide by them." The rules are neither hard to agree to nor hard to break, for many of them are not relevant to anything in the lifestyle of offenders. Enforcement of the rules drives youths even farther from genuine communication with officers. Lack of enforcement of a formal set of rules, however, gives juveniles the impression that they are free to do as they wish, and aftercare officers are left in a bind.

Some youths on release to the community will skip school, talk back to parents, get involved in minor traffic violations, or violate curfew. Most aftercare officers realize that many nondelinquent youths behave in the same manner, but one would not consider confining them for such behaviors. Revocation generally is based on the attitudes of the youths. For example, an expression of hostility toward the officers sometimes results in recommitment,

---

Focus on Practice 11–2
Aftercare Rules of One Pennsylvania County

COUNTY JUVENILE PROBATION/SUPERVISION REGULATIONS

Child's name: _____   Docket # _____

Current Charge(s): _____   Probation Officer: _____

Hearing Date: _____   Probation
                             Officer Phone: _____

You have been placed under the Supervision of the County Juvenile Court. You are expected to obey the conditions placed upon you. Should you have any questions regarding these conditions, it is your responsibility to contact your probation officer for clarification. A violation of these conditions may result in your reappearing before Juvenile Court.

Probation/Supervision Period: _____

While under Court Supervision, I will abide by the following conditions regarding community protection, offender accountability and competency development.

COMMUNITY PROTECTION CONDITIONS
1. I will obey all Federal, State and Local laws.
2. I will give my probation officer prior notice of any changes of address, phone number, education or employment.
3. I will adhere to the following curfew: _____

4. After curfew hours, I will be in the company of a parent or guardian, any exceptions, I will have prior approval of the Probation Office.
5. I will not leave the County without the permission of the Probation Office.
6. I will report to my Probation Officer as directed and permit a PO to visit my residence.

   Where: _____   **When:** _____
   I will give my Probation Officer prior notice for any reasons I cannot meet this requirement.
7. I will not use or carry a firearm in my possession without the express permission of my Probation Officer.
8. _____
9. _____
10. _____
11. _____

CRITICAL THINKING QUESTIONS

Do you believe that these are reasonable rules for a juvenile on aftercare status? If you were an aftercare officer, would you add to these rules?

even if the offenses and behavior are insignificant. The likelihood of revocation is increased as the severity of behavior increases. The commission of misdemeanors, the continuation of drug use, and a pattern of delinquency suggest that more serious offenses may follow. Aftercare officers may decide at this point that for the protection of both the youth and the community, revocation is necessary. Finally, if felonies are committed, little doubt exists in the minds of most officers that the youth should return to the institution.

Officers who take a supervisory stance in relation to youths and their behaviors sometimes consider any violation of the rules as sufficient grounds for revocation. In the past, they simply picked up such offenders and took them back to paroling institutions, ignoring due process. The stepping over of an arbitrary line by the youths was sufficient to warrant taking them into custody. The line often was ill or vaguely defined, and the youths had no idea whether their behavior was within acceptable limits. In addition, since they seldom see the officers, the youths would usually count on getting away with anything they tried, but often the parole officer would suddenly appear and the youth would be sent back to the training school. Revocation depended on chance, the attitude of the youth, and the personal whim of the aftercare officer.

One study of the Kentucky Department of Juvenile Justice's Juvenile Intensive Supervision Team Program, which focused primarily on gang violence among inner-city youth, found that officers perceived rehabilitation as the least important function of their program, behind the functions of ensuring community safety, deterrence through sanctioning infractions, and detecting violations through monitoring. Technical violations, not surprisingly, were the most frequently committed violation and weighed heavily in revocation decisions. Other factors given weight included seriousness of prior and current offenses as well as substance abuse.[29]

Some of the problems faced by youths on aftercare status are possibly different from the problems faced by juvenile probationers. Youths who are confined face the shock of complete isolation from their communities. They are exposed to many degrading experiences, are sometimes "messed over" by staff and residents, learn behavior that allows them to survive, are not permitted to practice the decision making they would have to practice in the community, and are stigmatized by their stay in the institution. The world they left is changing, and perhaps so are they. Consequently, when youths are ready for release, they are not necessarily ready to reenter the community. As the concept of aftercare changes, however, more and more aftercare officers and training schools are increasingly giving youths prerelease counseling and are allowing home visits to ease their return to normal life.

Revocation of Aftercare

The revocation of aftercare is the early termination of a youth's aftercare program, which usually takes place after one or more program violations. Several outcomes are possible when a youthful offender's aftercare is terminated. The youth can be returned to training school. A less severe option is to shift the youth to a different graduated outcome sanction. For example, a youth who is on regular supervision status can be shifted to an intensive supervision caseload. Or an offender may be placed on home confinement, coupled with electronic monitoring.

Aftercare revocation for juveniles is not as clear-cut as parole revocation for adults. Indeed, the U.S. Supreme Court has not yet ruled how juvenile aftercare revocation actions should be conducted. This sometimes has led to prejudicial, whimsical, arbitrary, and irrational actions on the part of the aftercare officers. But the court decisions in *Mempa v. Rhay* (1967), *People ex rel. v. Warden Greenhaven* (1971), *Murray v. Page* (1970), *Morrissey v. Brewer* (1972), and *Gagnon v. Scarpelli* (1973) have been applied to juveniles.[30] The U.S. Supreme Court in the *Mempa* case stated that state probationers have the right to a hearing and counsel when accused of probation violations. In *People v. Greenhaven*, it was stated that inmates are permitted to have counsel at revocation hearings. But the case that set the rationale for the requirement of due process was *Murray v. Page*:

> Therefore, while a prisoner does not have a constitutional right to parole, once paroled he cannot be deprived of his freedom by means inconsistent with due process. The minimal right of the parolee to be informed of the charges and the nature of the evidence against him and to appear to be heard at the revocation hearing is inviolate. Statutory deprivation of this right is manifestly inconsistent with due process and is unconstitutional; nor can such a right be lost by the subjective determination of the executive that the case for revocation is "clear."[31]

In the 1972 *Morrissey v. Brewer* decision, the Supreme Court first ruled on parole revocation procedures.[32] Morrissey had been paroled from the Iowa State Penitentiary. Seven months after his release, his parole was revoked for a technical violation, and he was returned to prison. In a related case, Brewer was returned to prison on a technical parole violation. Both prisoners petitioned for habeas corpus on the grounds that they had been denied due process law and returned to prison without opportunities to defend themselves at an open hearing. The two cases were consolidated for appeal and eventually reached the Supreme Court.

In his opinion, Chief Justice Warren Burger laid down the essential elements of due process for parole revocation. The first requirement was a hearing before an "uninvolved" hearing officer, who might be another parole officer or an "independent decision maker," who would determine whether there was reasonable cause to believe that a parole violation had taken place. If so, the parolee might be returned to prison, subject to a full revocation hearing before the parole board. Due process in such a proceeding was outlined as follows:

> Our task is limited to deciding the minimum requirement(s) of due process. They include (a) written notice of the claimed violation of parole; (b) disclosure to the parolee of evidence against him; (c) opportunity to be heard in person and to present witnesses and documentary evidence; (d) the right to confront and cross-examine adverse witnesses (unless the hearing officer specifically finds good cause for not allowing confrontation); (e) a "neutral and detached" hearing body such as a traditional parole board, members of which need not be judicial officers or lawyers; and (f) a written statement by the fact finders as to the evidence relied on and reasons to revoking parole.[33]

Gagnon v. Scarpelli involved an offender, Scarpelli, whose probation was revoked in Wisconsin without a hearing. Scarpelli had been sentenced to fifteen years in prison for armed robbery in Wisconsin, but his sentence was suspended and he was placed on probation for seven years. He was given permission to reside in Illinois, where he was later arrested for burglary. His probation was then revoked without a hearing. This case was appealed on the grounds that probation revocation without a hearing and counsel violated Scarpelli's due process rights.

The Supreme Court held that the right to counsel should be decided on a case-by-case basis and that considerable latitude must be given to the responsible agency in making the decision. The Court did indicate that counsel should be provided on request when the probationer claims that he or she did not commit the violation and when the reasons for the violation are complex or otherwise difficult to present. The significance of this case is that it equated probation with parole in terms of a revocation hearing. Although the Court did not rule that all probationers and parolees have a right to be represented by counsel in revocation hearings, it did say that the counsel should be provided when the probationer or parolee makes a good case for contesting the allegations. Table 11–3 summarizes the legal cases involved in the revocation of aftercare.

TABLE 11–3
Revocation of Aftercare

Case	Decision
Mempa v. Rhay (1967)	State probationers have the right to a hearing and counsel when accused of probation violations.
People ex rel. v. Warden Green-Haven	Inmates are permitted to have counsel at (1971) revocation hearings.
Murray v. Page (1970)	Once paroled, ex-offender cannot be deprived of freedom by means inconsistent with due process.
Morrissey v. Brewer (1972)	Requirement was a hearing before an "uninvolved" hearing officer who would decide if a parole violation had taken place.
Gagnon v. Scarpelli (1973)	Counsel should be provided on a case-by-case basis and considerable latitude should be provided in making the decision. The significance of this case was also that it equated probation with parole in terms of a revocation hearing.

What Are Interstate Compacts?

It becomes apparent to some juveniles with dysfunctional families that a home placement with a relative in another jurisdiction would probably increase the likelihood of their successful reintegration to society. They would then need to persuade their aftercare officers of the feasibility of such placement. Or an institutional social worker or aftercare officer might come to this same conclusion, and if the youth agrees with such a placement, an **interstate compact**, if needed, would be initiated with the appropriate authorities in this other jurisdiction.

Basically, the compact is an agreement among the states to deal with both the mobility of youths and the need to keep them under supervision. The compact recognizes four basic areas in which the need for cooperation is evident:

1. Cooperative supervision of delinquent juveniles on probation or parole
2. The return, from one state to another, of delinquent juveniles who have escaped or absconded
3. The return, from one state to another, of nondelinquent juveniles who have run away from home
4. Additional measures for the protection of juveniles and of the public, which one or more of the party states may find desirable to undertake cooperatively.[34]

Interstate compacts are also drawn up when youths are wanted for crimes in several states at the same time. In addition, youths facing possible arrest, adjudication, sentencing, confinement, or aftercare supervision sometimes flee to another state to escape being held fully accountable for their offenses. The problems for the jurisdictions involved can become quite complicated. For example, an offender may have arrest warrants against him or her in several states at once, several states may wish to prosecute the youth at the same time, or one state may be attempting to rehabilitate him or her while other states are requesting transfer for prosecution. As a result of the implementation of interstate compacts, parents, police, judges, probation officers, and institutional officials can, by going through the appropriate procedures, facilitate the return or supervision of wanted youths.

If a juvenile is to be sent to another state for treatment or rehabilitation, the states within the compact can enter into supplementary agreements that stipulate the rates to be paid for the care, treatment, and custody of out-of-state delinquent youths; that specify that the referring state shall at all times retain jurisdiction over these juveniles; and that ensure that the state receiving the youths into one of its institutions shall be the sole agent for the referring state.

How Can Aftercare Be Improved?

Aftercare programs too frequently are either underdeveloped or nonexistent. In many jurisdictions, the primary program is one in which probation or aftercare officers see their clients periodically but have few services to offer them. Many youths are required to do no more than send in monthly written reports to the parole officer or to report for a weekly "drug drop" (urinalysis).

The challenge to improving aftercare is even greater today because of the demise of traditional treatment approaches in so many training schools across the nation. As a result, juveniles released from training schools are even less prepared for community living than they were in the past.

The desire to lower recidivism has led to a number of experiments based on the assumption either that the institutions are not doing their job or that conditions in the community prevent parolees from staying out of trouble. The most widely used program provides intensive supervision to high-risk youthful offenders, but, as previously discussed, these programs have had mixed results in terms of reducing recidivism.

Lifeskills '95, one of the more promising aftercare programs, is geared to chronic, high-risk juvenile offenders and is designed to assist these offenders when released from secure confinement. This program begins with a thirteen-week reintegration treatment program that attempts to improve offenders' basic socialization skills, to stop their use or abuse of drugs, and to provide them with employment and/or an educational opportunity. An evaluation of 125 experimentals and 125 controls released to either San Bernardino or Riverside County from a secure California youth authority facility found that Lifeskills '95 was successful in reducing recidivism rates during the period of program participation.[35]

"Aftercare for the Incarcerated through Mentoring" (AIM) is a juvenile reentry program based in Indiana. AIM incorporates the principles of the IAP model and focuses primarily on connecting incarcerated youth and adult mentors. This program seeks to steer juveniles toward productive and successful futures by fostering healthy positive relationships with effective role models.[36] AIM has been carefully evaluated with results reflecting dramatic differences in the likelihood of reincarnation—four years after release, juveniles participating in AIM were 63 percent less likely to have returned to a correctional facility than those who did not participate in the program.[37]

David M. Altschuler, Troy L. Armstrong, and Doris L. MacKenzie recommended the following reforms and changes to improve the effectiveness of aftercare services:

- Community-based aftercare is one part of a reintegrative corrections continuum that must be preceded by parallel services in the corrections facility and must include careful preparations for the aftercare to follow.

- Aftercare is frequently funded and staffed at levels far below what is required to provide truly intensive supervision and enhanced service delivery.

- Intensive aftercare, in contrast to "standard" aftercare, requires close attention via formal assessment procedures to determine which offenders are in need of a level of intervention that includes both highly intrusive supervision and enhanced treatment-related services. See also the Evidence-Based Practice feature below.

- It is clear that a reduction in caseload size and intensification of level of contacts are widely accepted operational principles for intensive aftercare programming.[38]

The 2010 Federal Advisory Committee on Juvenile Justice (FACJJ) made the following recommendations to the president and Congress:

- "The FACJJ recommends that the President and Congress prioritize the importance of reentry in all areas of juvenile justice programming, including solicitation efforts, policy

Evidence-Based Practice
Missouri's Comprehensive Strategy

Missouri has developed a continuum of graduated sanctions and services that sets a high standard for other states to follow. Guided by the Comprehensive Strategy for Serious, Violent, and Chronic Juvenile Offenders, Missouri has created a structured decision-making model that uses a risk and needs assessment and a classification matrix. See Figure 11–2.

The Missouri system has three tools:

- An actuarial risk assessment tool, completed before court adjudication, that classifies youth into three categories—high, moderate, or low—based on their probability of reoffending
- A classification matrix that recommends sanctions and service interventions that seem to be appropriate to the youth risk level and most serious adjudicated offense
- A needs assessment instrument that recommends services that will reduce the likelihood of a juvenile's reoffending by reducing risk factors linked to recidivism.

In more recent reforms, Missouri's Division of Youth Services now serves youthful offenders who cannot be maintained in community settings in small, dormitory-style rehabilitative facilities close to their homes. These facilities focus on (1) individualized and group treatment with a clear treatment model; (2) supervision, not correctional coercion; (3) skill building; (4) family partnership and involvement during confinement; and (5) aftercare.

Only 9 percent of juveniles discharged from the Division of Youth Services were sentenced to adult prison within three years of release, and just 15 percent were reincarcerated within two years of release.

Source: Mark W. Lipsey, James C. Howell, Marion R. Kelly, Gabrielle Chapman, and Darin Carver, Improving the Effectiveness of Juvenile Justice Programs: A New Perspective on Evidence-Based Practice (Washington, DC: Georgetown University, 2010), 44–46; and Annie E. Casey Foundation, The Missouri Model: Reinventing the Practice of Rehabilitation of Youthful Offenders: Summary Report (Baltimore: The Annie E. Casey Foundation, 2010), accessed at http://www.aecf.org/KnowledgeCenter/~/media/Pubs/Initiatives/Juvenile%20Detention%20Alternatives%20Initiative/MOModel/MO_Summary_webfinal.pdf.

Offense Severity	Group 1 Offenses	Group 2 Offenses	Group 3 Offenses
Risk Level	Status Offenses Municipal Ordinances/ Infractions	Class A, B, & C Misdemeanors/ Class C & D Felonies	A & B Felonies
Low Risk	A) Warn & Counsel B) Restitution C) Community Service D) Court Fees & Assessments E) Supervision	A) Warn & Counsel B) Restitution C) Community Service D+) Court Fees & Assessments E) Supervision	B+) Restitution C+) Community Service D+) Court Fees & Assessments E) Supervision F) Day Treatment G) Intensive Supervision H) Court Residential Placement I) Commitment to DYS
Moderate Risk	A) Warn & Counsel B) Restitution C) Community Service D) Court Fees & Assessments E) Supervision	A) Warn & Counsel B) Restitution C+) Community Service D+) Court Fees & Assessments E) Supervision F) Day Treatment	B+) Restitution C+) Community Service D+) Court Fees & Assessments E) Supervision F) Day Treatment G) Intensive Supervision H) Court Residential Placement I) Commitment to DYS
High Risk	A) Warn & Counsel B) Restitution C) Community Service D) Court Fees & Assessments E) Supervision	B+) Restitution C+) Community Service D+) Court Fees & Assessments E) Supervision F) Day Treatment G) Intensive Supervision H) Court Residential Placement I) Commitment to DYS	H) Court Residential Placement I) Commitment to DYS

† Mandatory certification hearings are required by statute for all Class A Felonies. In the event the juvenies not certified, the juvenile officer should refer to this column of the matrix for classification purposes.
+ This symbol indicates options that should never be used as a sole option for youths who score in that cell, but only in conjunction wilth other options.

FIGURE 11–2
Missouri Risk and Offense Case Classification Matrix

Source: Annie E. Casey Foundation, *The Missouri Model: Reinventing the Practice of Rehabilitating Youthful Offenders: Summary Report* (Baltimore, MD: Annie E. Casey Foundation, 2010).

development, and program monitoring. Effective reentry planning should begin upon system entry and should directly involve youth, appropriate family members, positive peer supports, and an array of community assets (such as mentoring) to ensure that effective connections are in place upon a juvenile's exit from confinement."

- "FACJJ recommends that the President and Congress provide funding for the OJJDP Administrator to use to create training and technical assistance content focused on the development of comprehensive reentry tools and approaches consistent with national models to ensure effective implementation and evaluation in state and local jurisdictions."

- "FACJJ recommends that the President and Congress strongly emphasize that states develop effective community-based reentry services that use a system-of-care model and provide funding and training specific to mental health and substance abuse services for youth and families."

- "FACJJ recommends that the President and Congress strongly encourage states to design, develop, and implement reentry approaches that ensure the successful transition of juvenile offenders in secure facilities and crossover youth to adulthood. Such approaches should address education, life skills, work readiness, and community integration."[39]

Juvenile Justice Videos

JUVENILE PROBATION AND PAROLE 2

A youth comes before the Administrative Review Committee to discuss his past criminal behavior and future plans. The committee focuses on the impact that the crimes have had on the victims and the community. Why is this? Discuss the decision of the committee with regard to this youth. What aftercare opportunities might be available to the youth once released from the institution? Explain.

SUMMARY

LEARNING OBJECTIVE 1 Describe the goals of aftercare.

Aftercare, or parole, is one part of the corrections continuum, which has traditionally been the least developed segment of juvenile corrections. Aftercare can be defined as reintegrative services that prepare out-of-home placed juveniles for reentry into the community.

LEARNING OBJECTIVE 2 Describe the rules of those on aftercare who are released to the community.

Typical rules are as follows: Obey all federal, state and local laws, and obey your parents. Maintain a satisfactory adjustment within an employment, educational, or vocational setting. Do not leave the county without permission and avoid places where alcohol is sold or consumed. Do not use, sell, or possess any illegal drug.

LEARNING OBJECTIVE 3 Summarize why so many youths fail on aftercare.

Fragmentation and lack of coordination pervade this relatively unknown phase of the treatment of juvenile offenders. Most states have neither developed comprehensive guidelines for coordinating agencies that work with released youths nor implemented a comprehensive plan for overseeing the administration of parole. Once youths have been released from institutions, community forces often negate the effect of any positive programs in which the youths participated.

LEARNING OBJECTIVE 4 Describe the role of the aftercare officer.

Aftercare officers, much like probation officers, have paperwork to do, supervise offenders, and, when necessary, may initiate the revocation process to return juveniles to an institution. Juvenile aftercare, probably even more than juvenile probation, holds to a risk control and crime reduction approach.

LEARNING OBJECTIVE 5 Describe means by which aftercare can be improved.

As a number of programs have done, it is reasonable to assume that if juveniles were provided with comprehensive and integrated complements to institutional programs, their chances of failure while on aftercare would be far less. This continuum of care, from institution to community, is essential to improve aftercare and to contribute to the reduction of recidivism.

KEY TERMS

aftercare, p. 227
intensive supervision programs, p. 232
interstate compact, p. 239

parole, p. 228
reentry programs, p. 233

REVIEW QUESTIONS

1. What are the major shocks a juvenile faces upon release to the community?
2. What is the purpose of aftercare?
3. What programs appear to have the most promise for juvenile aftercare?
4. How might community factors interfere with a youth's chances of success on aftercare?
5. Using the information in the chapter, draw up a set of rules that juveniles on aftercare would consider reasonable and that would contribute to reducing recidivism.

GROUP EXERCISES

1. *Writing to Learn Exercise:* In one or two paragraphs, describe the different methods states use to release youths from training schools. What are the issues involved in the different types of aftercare release decisions? Critique and revise.
2. *Writing to Learn Exercise:* Write two paragraphs describing determinate and indeterminate types of aftercare release. Critique and revise.
3. *Group Work:* Describe what is meant by risk control and crime reduction in aftercare. Then describe each of the types of intensive aftercare supervision and their treatment goals as described in the chapter.
4. *Writing to Learn Exercise:* Discuss the due process rights of juveniles on aftercare. Critique and revise.

NOTES

1. Michelle, Inderbitzin, "Lessons from a Juvenile Training School: Survival and Growth,' *Journal of Adolescent Research* 21 (2006), 19.

2. *Federal Advisory Committee on Juvenile Justice: Annual Report 2010* (Washington, DC: U.S. Department of Justice, Office of Justice Programs, Office of Juvenile Justice and Delinquency Prevention, 2010), 31.

3. A. J. Sedlak and K. S. McPherson, *Youth's Needs and Services: Findings from the Survey of Youth in Residential Placement: Bulletin* (Washington, DC: U.S. Department of Justice, Office of Justice Programs, Office of Juvenile Justice and Delinquency Prevention, 2010).

4. See the research in Chapter 10 on juvenile victimization.

5. *Federal Advisory Committee on Juvenile Justice: Annual Report 2010.*

6. Ibid.

7. David M. Altschuler and Troy L. Armstrong, "Reintegrating High-Risk Juvenile Offenders into Communities: Experiences and Prospects," *Corrections Management Quarterly* 5 (2001), 79–95.

8. Steve V. Gies, "Aftercare Services," *OJJDP: Juvenile Justice Bulletin* (Washington, DC: U.S. Department of Justice, 2003), 1.

9. Hunter Hurst IV and Patricia McFall Torbet, *Organization and Administration of Juvenile Services: Probation, Aftercare, and State Institutions for Delinquent Youth* (Pittsburgh, PA: National Center for Juvenile Justice, 1993).

10. Kristin Parsons Winokur et al., "Juvenile Recidivism and Length of Stay," *Journal of Criminal Justice* 36 (2008), 126–37.

11. *Mission Statement, Office of Release Review* (Columbus, OH: Department of Youth Services, n.d.), 1.

12. For civil action taken against the state of Ohio, see S.H. et. al., vs. Tom Stickrath, "Joint Plan for Reforming Release Authority Pursuant to Stipulation for Injunctive Relief" (Doc. 118, para. 32). United States District Court Southern District of Ohio Eastern Division, 4/3/2008. http://www.childrenslawky.org/index/files/92_draft_notice.pdf. To examine some of the principles and processes involved with decision tree analysis see, Danida, M. "Logical Analysis Framework: A Flexible Tool for Participatory Development" (Asiatisk Plads, DK-1448 Copenhagen K. Denmark; Technical Advisory Service, February 1996).

13. Materials received from the department.

14. Lauren e. Glaze and Thomas P. Bonczar, *Probation and Parole in the United States, 2009* (Washington, DC: Bureau of Justice Statistics, 2010), Tables 17–19.

15. Howard N. Snyder, "An Empirical Portrait of the Youth reentry Population," *Youth Violence and Youth Justice* 2 (January 2004), 39–55.

16. Laura S. Abrams and Susan M. Snyder, "Youth Offender Reentry: Models for Intervention and Directions for Future Inquiry," *Children and Youth Services Review* 32 (December 2010), 1787–95.

17. David M. Altschuler and Troy L. Armstrong, "Intensive Aftercare for the High-Risk Juvenile Parolee: Issues and Approaches in Reintegration and Community Supervision," in *Intensive Interventions with High-Risk Youths: Promising Approaches in Juvenile Probation and Parole*, edited by Troy Armstrong (Monsey, NY: Criminal Justice Press, 1991), 49–50.

18. Ibid., 50.

19. Gies, "Aftercare Services."

20. Ibid.

21. L. W. Sherman et al., *Preventing Crime: What Works, What Doesn't, What's Promising.* Report to the U.S. Congress (Washington, DC: U.S. Department of Justice, 1997).

22. Gies, "Aftercare Services."

23. Richard G. Wiebush et al., *Implementation and Outcome Evaluation of the Intensive Aftercare Program: Final Report* (Washington, DC: National Council on Crime and Delinquency, 2005).

24. Laura S. Abrams, Sarah K. S. Shannon, and Cindy Sangalong, "Transition Services for Incarcerated Youth: A Mixed Methods Evaluation Study," *Children and Youth Services Review* 30 (2008), 522–35.

25. Gies, "Aftercare Services."

26. Ibid.

27. Richard G. Wiebush, Betsie McNulty, and Thao Le, *Implementation of the Intensive Community-Based Aftercare Program* (Washington, DC: Office of Juvenile Justice and Delinquency Prevention, 2000).

28. David M. Altschuler, Troy L. Armstrong, and Doris L. MacKenzie, "Reintegration, Supervised Release, and Intensive Aftercare," *Juvenile Justice Bulletin* (Rockville, MD: Juvenile Justice Clearinghouse, 1999), 8–9.

29. Nathan C. Lowe et al., "Understanding the Decision to Pursue Revocation of Intensive Supervision: A Descriptive Survey of Juvenile Probation and Aftercare Officers," *Journal of Offender Rehabilitation* 46 (2008), 155.

30. *Mempa v Rhay*, 389 U.S. 128 (1967); *People ex rel. v. Warden Greenhaven*, 318 N.Y.S.2d 449 (1971); *Murray v. Page,* 429 F.2d 1359 (10th Cir. 1970); *Morrissey v. Brewer*, 408 U.S. 471 (1972); *Gagnon v. Scarpelli*, 411 U.S. 778 (1973).

31. *Murray v. Page*, 429 F.2d 1359 (10th Cir. 1970).

32. *Morrissey v. Brewer*, 408 U.S. 471 (1972).

33. Ibid.

34. Purdon's Pennsylvania Statutes Annotated 62 PS. Paragraph 731, 1968, 82.

35. Don A. Josi and Dale K. Sechrest, "A Pragmatic Approach to Parole Aftercare: Evaluation of a Community Reintegration Program for High-Risk Youthful Offenders," *Justice Quarterly* 16 (March 1995), 51–80.

36. *Federal Advisory Committee on Juvenile Justice: Annual Report 2010,* 35.

37. G. R. Jarjoura, *Mentoring as a Critical Tool for Effective Juvenile Reentry.* Written testimony submitted to the Congressional Briefing on youth reentry from Out-of-Home Placement to the Community, November 16, 2009.

38. Altschuler et al., "Reintegration, Supervised Release, and Intensive Aftercare," 11, 15.

39. *Federal Advisory Committee on Juvenile Justice (FACJJO, 36.*

12 Treatment Technologies

Mangostock/Shutterstock

Learning Objectives

1. Summarize the different viewpoints concerning treatment in juvenile justice.
2. Describe the treatment modalities used most frequently in juvenile justice.
3. Evaluate the juvenile justice treatment modalities.
4. Identify suggestions for improving treatment in juvenile justice agencies.

The following tells the story of a man named Derrick Thomas—of his troubled early years and his later success in life. (Unfortunately, Thomas died on February 8, 2000, from complications following an automobile accident.)

Tears streamed down his eyes as his mother cradled 14-year-old Derrick Thomas, already over 6 feet tall, in her arms. After years of beating the system, of committing crimes and not getting caught, of conning adults with his engaging smile and winning personality, Thomas' number had finally come up. He was going to juvenile jail.

Placed on home confinement while awaiting trial on a burglary charge, his first juvenile court referral, Thomas repeatedly left the house. His pretrial services officer had reached her breaking point. She pulled Thomas out of class and summoned him and his mother to her office to break the bad news. For the next thirty days, Thomas would be locked up.

At the time, "Getting locked up seemed like the worst thing that could happen to me," said Thomas, who went on to become a ten-time All-Pro linebacker for the Kansas City Chiefs and one of the National Football League all-time sack leaders. But getting involved in the juvenile justice system actually turned out to be "one of the most important breaks I ever got." Through the court, Thomas met several people who helped him turn his life around. His juvenile court up experiences led him to set up his own foundation for troubled inner-city youths and inspired him to use his life to make a difference with other trouble kids.

In public speaking engagements, Thomas told audiences the same thing he said in testimony before the United States Congress and the Missouri General Assembly, words that are a fitting epilogue to this profile: "I come to you today to say you can make a difference and to tell you that there are any number of success stories in the juvenile justice system, just like mine."[1]

During his lifetime, Derrick Thomas was always quick to say that there are many successes in the juvenile justice system, like himself, and that it is possible to make a difference in working with troubled youngsters. In the midst of this possible affirmation, juvenile offenders are confronted and almost overwhelmed by the various methods used to treat, save, rehabilitate, remodel, remake, or otherwise "recycle" them. Juvenile corrections, far more than adult corrections, has as its guiding premise the rehabilitation of youths before they become hardened criminals. To that end, researchers from every discipline have looked for the key that will modify the behavior of youthful offenders.

Punishment was believed to be the answer for a long period of time. But in the 1700s, the founding fathers of our country substituted a religious orientation as the proper approach to working with wayward children. By the second half of the nineteenth century, this moral and religious emphasis slowly gave way to firm discipline and rigorous work training. The study of the character and mental condition of individual lawbreakers was the accepted treatment during the first four decades of the twentieth century. Sociology began to dominate treatment efforts in the 1950s and 1960s with the use of predelinquency community programs, detached workers (social workers whose jobs are on the streets with juvenile gangs), group interaction, job training, and community reorganization. Indeed, during this period, a new idea sprang up nearly every day, each one heralded as the panacea for youth crime. In the 1970s, as discussed in the next section, correctional treatment was bombarded with criticism from all sides and still has not fully regained its former popularity.

Approaches to treatment range from individual to group methods. This chapter presents a general discussion of treatment in juvenile justice, describes and evaluates the treatment modalities that are most popular today, and emphasizes that many treatments have evidence supporting them.

Where Is Treatment Today?

Correctional treatment has experienced several stages since the mid-twentieth century: (1) The "rehabilitation is not appropriate" stage, (2) the "nothing works" stage, (3) the "some treatments work" stage, and (4) the "numerous programs and innovations work" stage.

"Rehabilitation Is Not Appropriate" Stage

Under the leadership of psychiatrists who were well established in juvenile and adult corrections by the 1920s, a medical model was implemented in correctional institutions throughout the nation. However, by the end of the 1960s, the medical model had largely been discredited in American corrections. Critics argued persuasively that rehabilitation's assumptions conflict with basic human values, that rehabilitation philosophy does not work, and that rehabilitation is a disaster in practice.

The "Nothing Works" Stage

Correctional treatment came under increased empirical criticism in the late 1960s and early 1970s. In 1966, reporting on the results of one hundred empirical evaluations of treatment, Walter C. Bailey concluded that there seemed to be little evidence that correctional treatment was effective.[2] Then, in 1974, the late Robert Martinson startled both correctional personnel and the public with the pronouncement that "with few and isolated exceptions, the rehabilitative efforts that have been reported so far have had no appreciable effect on recidivism."[3] The media quickly simplified Martinson's statement to the idea that "nothing works" in correctional treatment. In 1975, Douglas Lipton, Robert Martinson, and Judith Wilks published *The Effectiveness of Correctional Treatment*, which critically evaluated the effectiveness of correctional treatment programs.[4] In that same year, Martinson announced on *60 Minutes* that "there [was] no evidence that correctional rehabilitation reduces recidivism."[5] A spirited debate on the "nothing works" thesis continued to rage from the late 1970s up through the turn of the century.

The "Some Treatments Work" Stage

Ted Palmer, a correctional researcher in California, challenged Lipton and his colleagues' research by tabulating eighty-two studies mentioned in the book and showing that thirty-nine of them, or 48 percent, had positive or partly positive results on recidivism.[6] Palmer used Martinson's own words to reject the "nothing works" thesis:

> These programs seem to work best when they are new, when their subjects are amenable to treatment in the first place, and when the counselors are not only trained people, but "good people" as well.[7]

Paul Gendreau and Robert Ross reviewed the literature published between 1973 and 1978 and found that 86 percent of the ninety-five intervention programs studied reported success.[8] According to Gendreau and Ross, this success rate was "convincing evidence that some treatment programs, when they are applied with integrity by competent practitioners in appropriate target populations, can be effective in preventing crime or reducing recidivism."[9] In the late 1970s, Martinson conceded that "contrary to [his] previous position, some treatment programs *do* have an appreciable effect on recidivism. Some programs are indeed beneficial."[10] But, despite Martinson's recantation of his "nothing works" thesis and Palmer's and Gendreau and Ross's defense of correctional treatment, the general mood regarding offender rehabilitation in the late 1970s and early 1980s was one of pessimism and discouragement.

In the late 1980s, Gendreau and Ross reviewed the offender rehabilitation literature for the period between 1981 and 1987 and again found that the number and variety of successful reported attempts at reducing delinquent behavior contradicted the "nothing works" hypothesis.[11] Moreover, the rehabilitative evidence in the 1980s grew at a much higher rate than it did during the 1970s and suggested several strategies for developing more effective programs.[12]

Several meta-analyses have evaluated the effectiveness of correctional treatment. The statistical tool of meta-analysis has been developed to enable reviewers to combine findings from different experiments. Meta-analysis undertakes the "aggregation and side-by-side analysis of large numbers of experimental studies."[13] One of the advantages of meta-analysis is that it can "incorporate adjustments for the fact that studies

Evidence-Based Practice
Using Meta-Analysis

The statistical tool of meta-analysis has been developed to enable reviewers to combine findings from different experiments. In meta-analysis, compatible information and data are extracted and pooled. When analyzed, the group data from several different studies provide a more powerful and valid indicator of relationships than is provided by a single study. These more sophisticated techniques have allowed correctional experts to examine some of the most important issues involving the effectiveness of correctional treatment.

Lipsey's comprehensive 2009 analysis of the effects of delinquency interventions consisted of 548 studies that spanned the period from 1958 to 2002. These studies represented all of the intervention research that could be located through an extensive search for published and unpublished reports of research. An overall finding of Lipsey's meta-analysis is that some interventions show relatively large positive effects on the juveniles who participate. What do these programs look like?

- *Risk factors.* One would assume that correctional treatment would be most effective with low-risk, nondangerous offenders. However, meta-analyses do not support this conclusion. Considerable research has found that programs targeting offenders who are higher risk are more effective in reducing recidivism than those that target lower risk offenders; this is referred to as the "risk principle."
- *Program completion.* One would assume that the rehabilitation programs most successful in retaining clients would work the best. And they do. Bernadette Pellisier and colleagues investigated nineteen programs and found that dropouts were, not surprisingly, the least likely to succeed, and that dropouts from treatment were more likely to be women and those who enter treatment with lower levels of motivation. Inmates who were disciplinary discharges from treatment were always more likely to be young, have a history of violence, and have been diagnosed as having an antisocial personality.
- *Voluntariness.* One would assume that inmates who volunteer for treatment would be more successful than those who were coerced into rehabilitation programs. However, a meta-analysis in the United States showed that this is not always the case. Overall, the evidence suggests that coerced clients do at least as well as those who voluntarily enter programs. When Michael L. Pendergast and colleagues examined the psychological functioning and social functioning between those who voluntarily or involuntarily entered the treatment program of a facility in California, they found that regardless of voluntary or involuntary admission status, treatment participants exhibited significant change during treatment on most measures of psychosocial functioning. Significant change was more often observed on measures of psychological than social functioning.
- *Amount and quality of service.* The quality of the program implementation was an important feature related to the magnitude of the effects.

In sum, while Martinson widely rumored review casts doubt on the effectiveness of correctional treatment, more recent reviews have found that programs can be highly effective under particular circumstances and with specific populations, especially for those residents who complete the programs. In the midst of these hopeful possibilities for treatment, there are at least two deterrents today that discourage the wider use of institutional programs: (1) overcrowded facilities, filled with violence, racial conflict, and sometimes gangs require that the focus be on security and institutional survival; and (2) the "no-frills" institutional emphasis found in adult corrections and in some part in juvenile corrections cuts back on program and treatment as much as constitutionally is permitted.

Source: See Mark W. Lipsey, James C. Howell, Marion R. Kelly, Gabrielle Chapman, and Darin Carver, *Improving the Effectiveness of Juvenile Justice Programs: A New Perspective on Evidence-Based Programs* (Washington, DC: Center for Juvenile Justice Reform, Georgetown University, 2010), 22; Bernadette Pellisier, Scott D. Camp, and Mark Motivans, "Staying in Treatment: How Much Difference Is There from Person to Person," *Psychology of Addictive Behavior* 17 (2003), 134, 141; and Michael L. Pendergast, David Farabee, Jerome Cortier, and Susan Henkin, "Involuntary Treatment Within a Prison Setting—Impact on Psychosocial Change During Treatment," *Criminal Justice and Behavior* 29 (2002), 5, 26.

vary considerably in the degree of rigour of their experimental design." Thus, taking all of these meta-analyses together, the net effect of treatment is an average reduction in recidivism rates of between 10 and 12 percent.[14] See the Evidence-Based Practice feature.

The "Numerous Programs and Innovations Work" Stage

Today, arguing that rehabilitation has staged a comeback is easy. More empirical support for the various treatment modalities, such as drug treatment, cognitive therapy, and therapeutic communities (TCs), exists than in the past. And several promising innovations are increasingly being used:

- *Risk/needs assessments* This refers to the attempt to offer treatment-relevant information when residents are classified into a new facility.

TABLE 12–1
Responses to Treatment Today

Treatment has received several responses in the late twentieth century to the present:

- *"Rehabilitation is not appropriate" stage:* Critics charged that rehabilitative philosophy was in conflict with basic human values, did not work, and was a disaster in practice.
- *"Nothing works" stage:* The research conducted by Robert Martinson and his colleagues was hailed by critics of treatment as evidence that "nothing works."
- *"Some treatment works" stage:* A number of studies found positive effects from conducting treatment.
- *"Numerous programs and innovations work" stage:* Much greater support is now found for treatment, but supporters do argue from their analysis of treatment studies that programs with multiple modalities must be used, the intensity of contact must be increased in most programs, and greater attention must be given to offenders' needs and characteristics so that they can be matched with particular programs.

- *Responsivity principle* This maintains that programs should consider offenders' situations as well as characteristics that may become barriers to success in a correctional program.
- *Best practice principle* Principle that states what is done should be based on previous research and successful programming.

In a 2007 article, Mark W. Lipsey and Francis T. Cullen, two highly respected scholars, state this position, as well as the challenges for correctional treatment, clearly:

> The mean recidivism effects found in studies of rehabilitation treatment, by comparison [to supervision and sanctions] are consistently positive and relatively large. There is, however, considerable variability in those effects associated with the type of treatment, how well it is implemented, and the nature of the offenders to whom it is applied. The specific sources of that variability have not been well explored, but some principles for effective treatment have emerged. The rehabilitation treatments generally found effective in research do not characterize current correctional practice and bridging the gap between research and practice remains a significant challenge.[15]

Proponents of intervention's new direction or emphasis largely agreed on the following principles for working with serious offenders: (1) programs with multiple modalities must be used; (2) intensity of contact must be increased in most programs; and (3) greater attention must be paid to offenders' needs and characteristics so that they can be matched with particular program elements.[16] Table 12–1 summarizes the various responses to treatment.

How Are Youthful Offenders Classified?

Throughout the twentieth century, classification was considered the first step of treatment in juvenile correction. Psychiatric evaluations and psychological workups of juvenile delinquents were being conducted in child guidance clinics by the second decade of the twentieth century. A number of reception and diagnostic centers were built in the 1930s and 1940s so that delinquents could be assigned to programs compatible with their psychological, educational, and vocational needs. Classifying youths in terms of their personality dynamics, worldview, and behavior were the three most popular schemes in the 1960s and 1970s. But in the past two decades, classification systems for treatment purposes in juvenile corrections have lost much of their former popularity.

Increasingly popular today are the various risks/needs assessments that are administered to youths as part of pre- and postadjudication case planning. These include the YLS/CMI, J-RAT, YASI, SAVRY, MAYSI-2, and PCL-YV, as discussed in Table 12–2.

Some of these assessment tools are more developed than others, and some are more frequently used in juvenile justice agencies than others. Still, the number of these assessment

Voices of Delinquency: Dr. James Eisenberg, A Forensic Psychologist Explains Assessment

TABLE 12–2
Risk Assessments Instruments

Assessment Tool	Purpose of Assessment
YLS/CMI (Youth Level of Service/Case Management Inventory)	This is the youth version of the widely used adult assessment—the Level of Service Inventory Revisited (LSI-R). This instrument is based on three principles of case management: • "Risk principle"—Services should reflect level of risk present. • "Need principle"—Services should be matched with the delinquent needs of the youth. • "Responsivity"—Decisions about interventions should consider other characteristics of the youth and his or her circumstances that may affect responses to the interventions.
J-RAT (Juvenile Risk Assessment Tool)	This is intended for the initial assessment of male juvenile sexual offenders. As of October 2007, the Stetson School in Florida, which treats sexually reactive children was using the J-RAT Version 3.
YASI (Youth Assessment and Screening Instrument)	This is a method for placing youths in categories that correspond to their likelihood of future arrests and violent offenses. It is being used in New York, Illinois, Washington, Virginia, and Mississippi. It assesses risk, needs, and protective factors and helps develop case plans for youths.
SAVRY (Structured Assessment of Violence Risk in Youth)	With its emphasis on dynamic factors, SAVRY is useful in intervention planning and ongoing progress monitoring, including the formulation of clinical treatment plans, conditions of community supervision, or release/discharge.
MAYSI-2	The MAYSI-2 is a paper-and-pencil self-report inventory of fifty-two Yes/No questions designed to assist juvenile justice facilities in identifying youths ages twelve to seventeen who may have special mental health needs.
PCL-YV (Psychopathy Checklist–Youth Version by Robert Hare)	This is a twenty-item assessment of psychopathic traits in male and female offenders ages twelve to eighteen. It is adapted from the *Hare Psychopathy Checklist Revisited (PCL-R)*, the most widely used measure of psychopathy in adults.

Source: Data accessed at http://www.stetsonschool.org/Clinical_Materials/Assessment_Tools/IM-RAT-V3.pdf; http://www.hare.org/scales/pclyv.html; http://www.djj.virginia.gov/Initiatives/YASI.aspx; and http://www.stoeltingco.com/stoelting/2294/1467/1497/Psychological/Structured-Assessment-of-Violence-Risk-in-Youth-SAVRY.

tools, as well as others, testifies to the importance of needs and assessment as a means of classifying offenders in the juvenile justice system today.

What Are the Main Treatment Modalities?

This section presents a selection of therapeutic methods—both individual and group—that have been used nationally in juvenile correctional facilities and identifies some of their more salient features.

Individual-Level Treatment Programs

The number of different individual techniques include insight therapy, behavior therapy, and cognitive-behavior therapy. These are reviewed below.

Insight-Based Therapy

It is common for training schools today to employ **insight-based therapy** techniques for the treatment of mental and emotional disorders. There are many different types of insight-based

Focus on Treatment 12–1
Insight-Based Therapies

Type	Treatment Goal	Qualifications of Therapist	Length of Treatment Period	Response from Offenders
Psychotherapy	Lead inmates to insight	Psychiatrist, psychologist, social worker	Long-term	Will examine individual problems with therapist
Transactional analysis	Lead inmates to insight	Psychiatrist, psychologist, trained nonprofessional, staff	Usually several months	Will examine individual problems in a group context and will learn a new approach to interpersonal relationships
Reality therapy	Help inmates to obtain basic needs	Psychiatrist, psychologist, trained nonprofessional, staff	Short period of time	Will learn to cope with reality, model responsible behavior, and determine right from wrong

therapy techniques, but in general the therapist utilizes insight, persuasion, suggestion, reinsurance, and instructions so that residents can see themselves and their problems more realistically and can develop a desire to cope effectively with their fears and problems (see Focus on Treatment 12–1).

Psychiatrists, clinical psychologists, and psychiatric social workers have used various forms of insight-based therapies in training schools since the early twentieth century. Residents are encouraged to talk about past conflicts that cause them to express emotional problems through aggressive or antisocial behavior. The insight that residents gain from this therapy supposedly helps resolve the conflicts and unconscious needs that drove them to crime. As a final step, the resident becomes responsible for his or her own behavior.

Insight-based therapy techniques have some fundamental limitations in a training school context. Residents usually do not see themselves as having emotional problems and are reluctant to share their inner thoughts with their therapists. There are also staffing problems. Professional mental health staff make up a small part of agencies' staffs, yet they are expected to provide a wide range of mental health services.

Behavior Therapy

A second form of individual treatment, behavior therapy, rests on the assumption that desirable behaviors are rewarded immediately and will therefore systematically increase, and undesirable behaviors that are not rewarded or punished will diminish and eventually be extinguished. Behavior therapy uses positive and negative reinforcement to encourage desirable and extinguish undesirable behavior. **Behavior modification** is the principal behavior therapy technique and is still practiced informally in a great many training schools. It works like this: residents receive additional privileges as they become more accepting of the institutional rules and procedures and as they exhibit more positive attitudes.

Cognitive-Behavior Therapy (CBT)

Cognitive-behavior therapy (CBT) for offenders is based on the assumption that the foundations for criminal behavior are dysfunctional patterns of thinking. The intent is that by altering routine misinterpretations of life events, offenders can modify antisocial aspects of their personality and consequent behavior. The goal of these interventions is to identify cognitive deficits linked to delinquency. These cognitive deficits are expressed in a concrete thinking style that impinges on the ability to appreciate the feelings and thoughts of others, impairments leading to self-defeating behavior, impulsivity, egocentricity, inability to reason critically, peer interpersonal problem-solving skills, and a preoccupation with self.[17] See Focus on Programs 12–2.

CBT in offender treatment targets the thoughts, choices, attitudes, and meaning systems that are associated with antisocial behavior as well as deviant lifestyle. It generally uses a training approach to teach new skills in areas where offenders showed deficits, such as generating alternative solutions, rather than reacting on first impulse; interpersonal problems awareness; opening up and listening to other perspectives; evaluating consequences;

Focus on Programs 12–2
Definition of Thinking Errors

1. Closed Channel—The criminal communicates from a closed position.
   a. When he talks, he controls what others know about him.
   b. When he listens, he lacks receptivity.
   c. When he evaluates, it is from a position of self-righteousness, faulting or blaming others.
2. Fragmentation—Fluctuations in interests, attitudes, and goals . . . result in the criminal making good starts and poor finishes.
3. Uniqueness—The criminal tends to think about himself as different than others, usually superior.
4. Superoptimism—The criminal tends to think that he will be successful in all he undertakes because of his uniqueness; therefore, preparation and effort are not needed. Superoptimism is absolutely essential prior to and during criminal activity.
5. Pride—The criminal takes pride in his ability to live by his wits, to do what others are fearful of doing and [in] his "tough guy" view of himself.
6. Pretentiousness—[There is] a component of power and control whereby the criminal displays his inflated, "big shot" image in an effort to impress the world.
7. Failure to Assume Obligations—The criminal views an obligation as something that controls him. Failing to assume an obligation results in hardship for people who depend on him, i.e., child, spouse, employer.
8. Ownership—[There is] an attitude whereby the criminal assumes possession of other people's property and domination over other people.
9. Failure to Make an Effort or Endure Adversity—Because of his uniqueness thinking, and superoptimism thinking, the criminal doesn't believe he should have to put forth effort or endure hardship to accomplish a goal.
10. Lack of Time Perspective—The criminal's time frame is mainly in the present. There is little learning from the past or using the present to prepare for the future.
11. Poor Decision Making—[This is] the outcome of poor reasoning, failure to find out facts or consider the future from a responsible perspective.
12. Lack of Trust—The criminal demands [that] others trust him but objects to trusting others.
13. Anger—The criminal [uses] anger to control and regain control of others.
14. I Can't—The criminal [says] "I can't" when he really means "I don't want to" or "I am not going to," [which] results in rejecting responsible behavior.
15. Victimstance—The criminal uses this thinking pattern when being held accountable for wrongdoing in an attempt to avoid punishment.

CRITICAL THINKING QUESTIONS

How would you go about identifying these thinking errors in youthful offenders? What would you recommend a youth do to change his or her thinking errors?

Source: Materials used as part of staff training at Four Oaks, Inc., in Iowa.

---

resisting; soliciting feedback; taking the person's well-being into account; and deciding on the most beneficial course of action.[18]

The CBT therapists act as teachers, and lessons are usually taught to groups in classroom settings. The lessons may include group exercises involving role-play, rehearsal, homework assignments, and intensive feedback and generally follow detailed lesson plans and structured curriculum.[19] People taking part in CBT learn specific skills that can be used to solve the problems they confront all the time as well as skills they can use to achieve the legitimate goals and objectives. CBT first concentrates on developing skills to recognize unrealistic or distorted thinking when it happens, and then works toward changing that thinking or belief to modify or eliminate problematic behavior.[20]

The most widely adopted of the cognitive-behavioral interventions is the **Cognitive Thinking Skill Program (CTSP)** developed by Robert Ross and Elizabeth Fabiano, which is now a core program in the Canadian correctional system and has been implemented in the United States, New Zealand, Australia, and some European countries.[21]

CTSP was developed through a systematic review of all published correctional programs that were associated with reduced criminal recidivism. The researchers identified one hundred evaluations of effective programs and discovered that they all were designed to target offenders' thinking. Rigid thinking could be minimized by teaching participants creative thinking skills and providing them with prosocial alternatives to use when reporting or responding to interpersonal problems. Core components of CTSP are that teaching offender techniques of self-control could improve social adjustments.[22]

▲The resident receives advice that it will be necessary for him to have a positive program to shorten institutional stay.
© ZUMA Wire Service/Alamy

A review of the literature leads to the conclusion that combining elements of cognition and behavior approaches is found in the principle of self-reinforcement. This concept says that behavior and cognitive changes reinforce each other. When cognitive changes lead to changes in behavior, what takes place is a sense of well-being that strengthens its change in thought and, as a result, further strengthens behavioral changes. This self-reinforcing feedback process is a key of the CBT approach and provides a basis for helping offenders understand the cognitive behavior process.[23]

Cognitive-Behavior Therapy Effectiveness   A considerable amount of research indicates that CBT approaches have positive effects with offenders[24]:

- A meta-analysis of sixty-nine studies covering both behavior and cognitive-behavioral problems determined that the cognitive-behavior programs are more effective in reducing rates of recidivism than behavior programs. The mean reduction was about 39 percent for treated offenders.[25]

- Other meta-analyses of correctional treatment concluded that cognitive-behavioral methods constituted critical aspects of effective correctional treatment.[26]

- Another study determined that the most effective interventions are those employed by cognitive-behavioral techniques to improve cognitive function.[27]

- There is strong evidence that positive results are more likely to take place among certain subgroups. For example, CTSP seems to be more effective with offenders over age twenty-five and with property offenders.[28]

See Figure 12–1 for the recidivism effect associated with skill-building programs.

Group Programs

In addition to therapies at the individual level, most training schools maintain group counseling programs. The most popular of these programs are drug and alcohol treatment programs, guided group interaction, positive peer culture, drug and alcohol treatment programs, and intervention with juvenile sex offenders.

Guided Group Interaction

Guided group interaction (GGI) is probably the most widely used treatment modality. It has been used in at least eleven states: Florida, Georgia, Illinois, Kentucky, Maryland, Michigan, Minnesota,

FIGURE 12–1
Mean recidivism effects for the generic program types within the skill building category

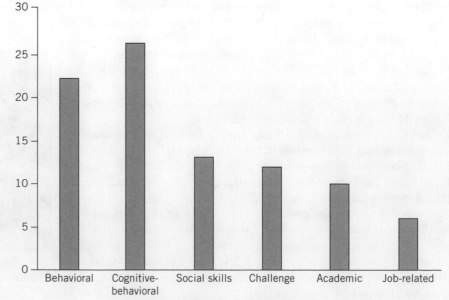

Percent recidivism reduction from .50 baseline

Mean Recidivism Effects for Skill-Building Programs

Source: Mark W. Lipsey, James C. Howell, Marion R. Kelly, Gabrielle Chapman, Darin Carver, *Improving the Effectiveness of Juvenile Justice Programs,* Center for Juvenile Justice, © 2010.

New Hampshire, New Jersey, South Dakota, and West Virginia. Since the 1950s, when this modality was first used, it has been based on the assumption that youths could confront their peers and force them to face the reality of their behavior more effectively than could staff.

The GGI approach is characterized by a nonauthoritarian atmosphere, intensity of interaction, group homogeneity, and an emphasis on group structure. The most important characteristic is the nonauthoritarian atmosphere. Residents in many residential GGI programs, for example, are given considerable say in when a group member will be released, granted a home furlough, or approved for off-campus visits; in how a group will be punished; and in whether the outside door will be locked or left open at night.

Giving residents responsibility for decision making, of course, is a different approach to child care from that followed in most correctional settings. The adult leader constantly refers the decision making back to the group. When informed by a youth that a group member planned to run away, for example, one staff member retorted: "So what do you want me to do? He's your buddy; he's part of your group. You can talk to him if you have to; but it's up to all of you to help one another."[29]

A great strength of GGI is its determination to circumvent the values of the delinquent-peer subculture. This modality, in urging residents to be honest and open with one another, attempts to move group participants toward a more positive, prosocial stance. Another advantage is that it represents a comprehensive strategy for dealing with troubled youth. In effect, it is a total system for mitigating the impact of a delinquent subculture. A third advantage is that GGI seems to have gained acceptance on the state level. Also important is the fact that GGI can be led by line staff, thereby increasing staff involvement in the treatment process. A final advantage is that responsibility is given to offenders; thus, in interacting with peers, offenders become aware of their problems and are directed toward resolutions.

A major problem in using GGI is the shortage of trained group leaders. Also, since this approach to group work lacks a single spokesman, a number of versions and designs of the basic principles have emerged. As a consequence, no clear and consistent philosophy guides the process of working with offenders in groups. The emphasis of GGI on peer group norms and values further tends to slight the importance of individualism. Extreme care must be taken to ensure that peer-group norms established and monitored by institutional staff do not repress the youthful offenders' needs for self-identity and autonomy. Finally, peer-group norms created by GGI may not always be transferable to the actual life situations that will be encountered upon release.

Although the research findings on GGI have been mixed, the general picture that emerges is that a GGI experience in a nonresidential program is at least as effective as and much less costly than confinement in a state facility and that a GGI experience in an institutional program seems to have a more positive impact on less delinquent youngsters.[30]

Positive Peer Culture

The concept of **positive peer culture (PPC)** generated considerable excitement in juvenile corrections, especially in the 1970s. Developed by Harry Vorrath and associates as an outgrowth of GGI, PPC has been implemented in all of the juvenile state institutions in Michigan, Missouri, and West Virginia.[31]

Vorrath believes that PPC "is a total system for building positive youth subcultures."[32] The main philosophy of PPC is to "turn around" the negative peer culture and to mobilize the power of the peer group in a positive way. PPC does this by teaching group members to care for one another; caring is defined as wanting what is best for a person. Vorrath believes that once caring becomes "fashionable" and is accepted by the group, "hurting goes out of style."[33]

PPC involves the same stages as in GGI, but it places more emphasis on positive behavior. Group members learn to speak of positive behaviors as "great," "intelligent," "independent," "improving," and "winning." In contrast, negative behaviors are described as "childish," "unintelligent," "helpless," "destructive," "copping out," and "losing."

PPC is developed through ninety-minute meetings five times per week. Characterized by trust and openness, PPC focuses on the direct and immediate problems of the lawbreaking youth. Believing that groups function most effectively when they are homogeneous, leaders try to include youths who are similar in age, sex, maturity, and delinquency sophistication. Coeducational groups are believed to be counterproductive.

Vorrath believes that the group has to be involved in decision-making processes, such as whether to give a youth a home visit or when to release a resident. Although he acknowledges that institutional staff ultimately must make these decisions, he states that the recommendations initially should come from the group members. The group, in discussing the possibility of releasing a member, concerns itself with both the member's present problems and those he or she will experience once back in the community.

In sum, although Vorrath believes that the basic assumptions of these youths can be changed, few people change many of their background assumptions over the period of a lifetime—much less when they are stripped of their freedom and are in therapy. For this modality to be properly evaluated, more research is needed. But its present successes should remind both followers and critics that PPC remains one of the most promising ways to treat, change, correct, and rehabilitate juvenile offenders.

Drug and Alcohol Abuse Interventions

Drug and alcohol abuse by juveniles, as well as their involvement in drug trafficking in the community, constitutes a serious social problem today. A director of guidance in a training school acknowledged the seriousness of the problem when he said, "Rarely do we get a boy who doesn't have some history of drug or alcohol abuse in his background."[34]

Drug and alcohol abuse interventions increasingly are being developed in community-based and institutional settings to assist those who need help with such problems. These groups are being conducted in training schools in at least three ways: First, institutionalized juveniles assessed to have a problem with alcohol and/or drugs are placed in a separate cottage or in a chemical abuse group. Specialized staff are hired to work in these cottages or lead these groups. Second, in other training schools, the social worker or another cottage staff member conducts ongoing drug and alcohol abuse groups. Third, outside groups, such as Alcoholics Anonymous (AA) or Narcotics Anonymous (NA), come into the institution and hold sessions for interested residents.

Considering the extensiveness of the problem of drug use and trafficking among juvenile offenders, there are still too few programs being offered in juvenile placements. The programs that are offered tend to be relatively unsophisticated and lack adequate theoretical design, treatment integrity, and evaluation follow-up.

Treatment studies done on prison populations have found that when drug programs are well integrated and their effective program elements are implemented carefully, these programs:

- Reduce relapse.
- Reduce criminality.
- Reduce inmate misconduct.
- Reduce mental illness.
- Reduce behavioral disorders.
- Increase the level of the inmates' stake in societal norms.
- Increase levels of education and employment upon returning to the community.
- Improve health and mental health symptoms and conditions.
- Improve relationships.[35]

Unquestionably, development of effective alcohol and drug abuse programs represents one of the most important challenges of juvenile justice today.

▲ A dangerous development with the internet is the "sexploitation" of young boys and girls by sexual predators online. This young girl could well be in extreme danger since her parents apparently did not monitor her online activities.
Valeriy Velikov/Shutterstock

Intervention with Juvenile Sex Offenders

Violent sex crimes often shape the public's perception of sex offenders and sex offending. The view that immediately comes to mind is that of an adult male who by force, guile, or cunning persuades a young person to perform sexual acts deemed inappropriate or illegal by society.[36] This image of adult offenders is assumed to be true of all youthful sex offenders

Focus on Law 12–3
The Teen Sex Offender

The victims of sex offenders frequently are scarred for life. Coercive or violent rape by family members, friends, serial offenders, or members of the same sex devastates victims emotionally. In addition to the physical pain and suffering they experience, these victims wrestle with depression, sleepless nights, and fear of others; many are never able to form normal emotional relationships with others they love. These reasons alone are sufficient to incur society's wrath, but when murder accompanies the act, members of society become particularly incensed, and legislators succumb willingly to public pressures to take up the charge for action. Often knee-jerk reactions take the place of reason, and the laws that are passed have unintended consequences.

Teenage boys often are the unwitting victims of legislators' zeal. Not that what the boys do is right, but consider the following: sixteen- and seventeen-year-old boys frequently have sex with their fourteen- and fifteen-year-old girlfriends—both of whom intend to marry each other. Some youths engage in "heavy" petting and sexual experimentation with members of the opposite sex on dates. In one case, a boy was dared by his friends at a football game to touch a girl's breast. He did, and he, along with the other youths noted above, are now registered as sex offenders by their state.

The consequences of this registration are enormous. Some of these youths may be tried in juvenile or adult courts and remanded to juvenile or adult institutions. They are placed on extended supervision when they get out. Their names are kept on police "watch" lists. People living in their neighborhoods or parents who have children in schools will not want them anywhere near them. The "offenders'" names may be published on informal sex offender lists on the Internet and be available to all. Many states publish formal lists and may require youths to register for periods of time ranging from ten to twenty-five years to life. These youths will be unable to get into the military or obtain private security jobs; they cannot become doctors, nurses, school teachers, scout masters, or band directors or coach youth sports teams; some companies will not hire them. The youths are labeled for life.

CRITICAL THINKING QUESTIONS

In your opinion, is justice served concerning juvenile sex offenders? What should be done with boys responding to dares or having sex with their girlfriends? Develop a system of classification for sex offenders.

Source: Prepared for this volume by the authors.

---

as well; the result is that pressure is put on legislators to "pass a law" that somehow will punish youthful sex offenders severely and that will deter others from committing sex offenses (see Focus on Law 12–3). Adolescents who are growing up, learning how to develop age-appropriate relationships, and assimilating the rules of society often become surprise victims of overzealous citizens, legislators, and prosecutors. Given this perspective, just what is the reality of juvenile sex offending, and how accurate is the imagery?

Much juvenile sexual behavior is concealed in the confines of family, community, and school and remains hidden. Even if it is discovered, children, parents, and teachers may be confused as to what really happened and are often ashamed or embarrassed by their own behavior and by that of their own children, relations, and family friends. Many victims will not report sexual victimization because they believe they deserved what happened, feel guilty, do not want to get others in trouble, or somehow believe that what happened was normal. Yet, the victims often end up psychologically distraught and damaged; sleeplessness, anxiety, depression, sexual dysfunction, and suicide can result. Damaged emotions and fear destroy their ability to form lasting relationships, and many victims' marriages are filled with violence or do not last. The cost to individuals and society often is perpetuated because many imprisoned adolescent and adult sex offenders report having been abused as youths. The cost of a sex offense early in life often extends into adulthood.

Are all sex offenders alike? No. Their relationships with their victims and their personal motives vary widely, making them a diverse lot. The offending behaviors range from noncontact offenses such as voyeurism and exhibitionism to contact offenses such as touching and fondling to sexual penetration with body parts or foreign objects. Most sex offenders also commit nonsexual offenses at rates similar to those of other juvenile offenders. For example, children who experience neglect and physical abuse and who witness family violence are more likely to commit sexual offenses than those who do not, although at an only modestly higher rate.[37] Also, sex offenders who have had prior consensual sexual experiences have higher rates of offending than those without such experiences.

How Do We Treat Sex Offenders?

The treatment goals of many programs for sex offenders include breaking the sex offense cycle. Youths are encouraged to assume responsibility for their abusive behavior and to increase their positive and constructive behaviors in both thinking and relations to others.

Voices of Delinquency: Domenick Lombardo, Former Supervisor of Psychological Services

These goals are designed to prevent further sexual misconduct and the emergence of psychosexual problems and, conversely, to help youths develop appropriate relationships with peers of their own age. Therapists attempt to achieve these goals through individual, group, and family interventions.[38]

Gender-Specific Services in the Juvenile Justice System

Sara Goodkind, in referring to the Juvenile Justice and Delinquency Prevention Appropriations Authorizations, states that "the term 'gender-specific services' means services designed to address needs unique to the gender of the individual to whom such services are provided." She adds that "the term gender specific has been interpreted to mean 'for girls' and that gender-specific programming refers to a comprehensive approach to female delinquency rooted in the experience of girls."[39]

The purpose of a gender-specific approach is to enable each girl to focus on her individual needs, to understand how risk factors have shaped her development, and to address issues that arise in her relationships with others.[40] See Focus on Practice 12–4 for the programming, in terms of gender-specific services, at the Iowa Juvenile Home/State Training School for Girls.

Why Is Treatment Effectiveness So Difficult to Attain?

The increased amount of evidence of best programs in juvenile justice is an indication that there is support for effective treatment in juvenile justice. Unfortunately, the frequent

---

Focus on Practice 12–4
Gender-Specific Services at the Iowa Juvenile Home/State Training School for Girls

Programs for boys are more successful when they focus on rules and offer ways to advance within a structured environment. But programs for girls are more successful when they focus on relationships with other people and offer ways to master their lives while keeping these relationships intact.

ELEVEN POINTS OF BEST PRACTICES FOR SERVICES TO GIRLS

Programs must:

1. Provide emotional and physical safety. They must give girls a "safe space" in which they can talk about their issues—be aware of relational aggression.
2. Be culturally appropriate by being beware of different cultural perspectives. Attempt to respond to diversity as much as possible.
3. Be relational based. Develop alignment and partnerships with youth. The strength of a relationship will support youth who are trying new things—trust takes time to develop.
4. Provide positive female role models and mentors.
5. Address the abuse in girls' lives. Counsel them, provide groups, and teach skills like assertion. Give them practice using those skills.
6. Be strength based, not deficit based. Come from a perspective of resiliency and identify skills already present.
7. Address sexuality, including pregnancy and parenting. Many girls have a great deal of experience and a very small amount of accurate information. In seeking out relationships, girls often put themselves at great risk.
8. Provide equitable education and vocational opportunities. Education plus skills add up to a fair playing field.
9. Address the unique health needs of females, including nutritional concerns and regular physical activities. Teach healthy lifestyle practices, downplay appearance, address girls about media, and address eating disorders.
10. Nurture the spiritual lives of participants. Provide opportunities for spiritual expression: writing groups, poetry groups, journaling, and so forth. Volunteers are a great resource here. Encourage values clarification—discuss issues within the context of self, others, and community.
11. Involve individual members of girls' families. Family issues also need to be resolved. Family involvement will help with transition and carryover of skills to the real-world environment

CRITICAL THINKING QUESTIONS

Why has so little headway been made in developing gender-specific services in training schools?

Source: This statement was initially developed in 1999 but is contained in a more developed framework in *Promising Directions: Programs that Serve Iowa Girls in a Single-Sex Environment* (Des Moines, IA: Iowa Commission on the Status of Women, 2005).

criticism that offender rehabilitation is defective in theory and a disaster in practice is true in too many programs. Program designs have often given little consideration to what a particular program can realistically accomplish with a particular group of offenders and have frequently relied on a single cure for a variety of complex problems. In addition, programs generally have lacked integrity, because they have not delivered the services they claimed with sufficient strength to accomplish the goals of treatment. Furthermore, the research on offender rehabilitation has generally been inadequate, with many projects and reports on rehabilitation almost totally lacking in well-developed research designs.[41]

To improve the quality of institutional treatment even further, three basic steps appear to be necessary: (1) more programs must include the ingredients of effective interventions; (2) more programs must be based on better program design, ensure higher program integrity, and be evaluated by more rigorous research methods; and (3) research must provide more information on what works for whom and in what context.

Ingredients of Effective Programs

Effective programs usually have a number of ingredients in common. They usually are set up by an inspired individual or group of individuals, have developed a unified-team approach among staff, have a transmittable philosophy of life, trust offenders with decision-making responsibilities, help offenders develop needed skills, are regarded as unique and different by offenders, and provide an integrated treatment model.[42]

The Inspired Leader Who Means Business

The inspired individual or group of individuals who is seriously dedicated to setting up a program has been found time after time to be one of the chief ingredients of effective programs. In Outward Bound, Kurt Hahn was able to generate enthusiasm and support among those who contacted him.[43] Sister Falaka Fattah and her husband set up the House of Umoja in Philadelphia, which is committed to dealing with the gang problem in that urban community.[44] The inspiration of Clifford Shaw continues to influence the Chicago Area Projects long after his death.

Unified Treatment Team

A program is more likely to have an impact on offenders if the treatment team is unified. In a unified treatment team, all staff members become treatment agents as they design the program, develop short- and long-range goals for the program, and involve themselves with offenders.

Philosophy of Life That Is Transmittable

Effective programs also generate a sense of mission or purpose among offenders by transmitting a philosophy of life. Martin Groder has noted, "It's not that the guy has to adopt the philosophy of the program, but he's got to learn it well enough to integrate it with his own life experience and come out with his own version."[45] Clemens Bartollas, Stuart J. Miller, and Simon Dinitz reported that having a mission or purpose in life is one characteristic of hard-core offenders who are later successful in the community.[46]

Involvement of Offenders in the Decision-Making Process

Effective programs also frequently provide decision-making responsibilities for juvenile offenders. Although many correctional interventions treat these offenders as helpless children incapable of making decisions for themselves, the more noteworthy programs encourage decision making and then make participants responsible for their choices. The more offenders are permitted to make choices concerning what happens to them, the more likely they are to be involved in a treatment program and to seek to benefit from it.

Skill Development

Effective programs include **skill development**, which helps offenders learn new tasks that prepare them for adjustment in the community. These skills range from educational and vocational to interpersonal and problem-solving skills. Such abilities make offenders believe that they can accomplish something or that they have acquired important insights about themselves or about life.

Uniqueness

The most distinguishing characteristic of effective interventions is sometimes their uniqueness. That is, the components of these programs that make them different from other correctional interventions are sometimes the most important factors in grabbing the attention of youthful offenders and getting them involved in these interventions.

Integrated Treatment Model

The states of Colorado, Texas, and Washington have developed integrated treatment models, and California is in the process of developing such a model. These programs based their treatment philosophy and intervention on cognitive-behavioral treatment. The **integrated treatment model** provides the central guiding vision that unites screening, assessment, case planning, treatment, transition, and aftercare. These concepts are used across all parts of the juvenile correctional system, including the core treatment program, special treatment programs, work, education, recreation, mental health, and parole. All staff members, including administrators, treatment providers, support staff, and line staff, receive training in the model. This not only helps structure the environment to promote success in changing behavior but also creates a common treatment vocabulary for all parts of the agency. Another advantage of this integrated model is that it provides adequate community follow-up in order for offenders to sustain positive changes in their lives.[47]

Strategy for Improving the Effectiveness of Correctional Programs

Improving program effectiveness requires that program designs be based on theoretical premises, that programs be implemented with integrity, and that programs be evaluated with rigorous research methods.

Program Design

The theoretical premises, or constructs, of programs must be examined in order to determine whether they are appropriate for particular groups of offenders. The processes by which any set of interventions will change antisocial behavior must also be examined in order to determine whether the treatment has sufficient strength to produce the desired behavior or attitudinal change. Finally, the theoretical constructs must be meshed with the setting in which treatment takes place to ensure that programs are implemented in appropriate settings.[48]

Program Implementation

Juvenile offenders must be placed in the right program at the optimal time for them to benefit from treatment. Effective interventions must actually deliver the services they claim to deliver, with sufficient strength to accomplish the goals of treatment. In addition, program integrity requires that personnel be equipped to deliver the specified services; thus, treatment personnel must have some degree of expertise in what they are doing, must have sufficient training to do it, and must receive adequate supervision. Finally, it must be possible to modify interventions according to changing interests and needs of offenders.[49]

Program Evaluation

The Panel on Research on Rehabilitative Techniques concluded after nearly two years of examining offender rehabilitation that "the research methodology that has been brought to bear on the problem of finding ways to rehabilitate criminal offenders has been generally so inadequate that only a relatively few studies warrant any unequivocal interpretations."[50] Sample sizes must be large enough to measure subtle effects, such as changes in interactions. True randomized experiments must be conducted whenever feasible because they permit some certainty about causal relationships. Researchers need to identify the common elements of effective programs and to determine how these elements affect success with particular groups of offenders. In addition, researchers need to determine how effective programs can be replicated in other settings. Finally, more empirical work must be done on measuring the outcomes of correctional treatment.[51]

What Works for Whom and in What Context?

Correctional treatment must discover what works for which offenders in what context. In other words, correctional treatment could work if amenable offenders were offered appropriate treatments by matched workers in environments conducive to producing positive effects.[52]

To match individual offenders with the treatments most likely to benefit them will be no easy task. Only through well-planned and soundly executed research will the necessary information be gained. The Panel on Research of Rehabilitative Techniques recommends the use of the "template-matching technique."[53] This technique creates a set of descriptors, or a *template*, of the kinds of people who are most likely to benefit from a particular treatment according to the theory or basic assumptions underlying it.[54] Because of the scarcity of treatment resources, matching programs to those offenders most likely to profit from them is only sensible. See Table 12–3 Treatment Technologies.

TABLE 12–3
Treatment Technologies

Type	Treatment Goal	Qualifications of Therapist	Length of Treatment	Frequency of Treatment	Expected Offender Response
Individual or group psychotherapy	Lead youths to insight	Psychiatrist, psychologist, psychiatric social worker	Frequently extensive or long term	Several times per week if possible	Will examine individual problems with therapist
Transactional analysis	Lead youths to insight	Psychiatrist, psychologist, trained nonprofessional staff	Usually several months	Once or more per week	Will examine individual problems in a group context and will learn a new approach to interpersonal relationships
Reality therapy	Help youths to fulfill basic needs	Psychiatrist, psychologist, trained nonprofessional staff	Short period of time	Once or more per week	To learn reality, responsible behavior, and right from wrong
Behavior modification	Help youths to react positively	Anyone who can assume role of therapist	Usually long term	Continuous rather than interwoven with nontreatment	To continue their reinforced, positive behavior
Guided group interaction	Develop prosocial norms and values	Anyone trained in GGI	Several months	Four or five times per week	Will become responsible for others in the group
Positive peer culture	Develop prosocial norms and values	Anyone trained in PPC	Several months	Four or five times per week	Will genuinely care for other group members
Drug and alcohol abuse programs	Help youths to overcome addiction	Anyone who has understanding of problem	Extensive or long term	Once or more per week	Will gain skills and knowledge to overcome substance abuse
Errors in thinking approach	Insight into individual behavior	Psychiatrist, psychologist, psychiatric social worker	Extensive or long term	Once or more per week	To learn responsible and prosocial behavior
Skill development programs	Personal empowerment	Anyone who can assume role of staff member	Short or long term	Daily	Will gain skills and knowledge to pursue positive behavior

Palmer's approach is somewhat different in determining what works for which offenders in what contexts. He suggests that effective intervention for each offender must take seriously skill deficits, external pressures and disadvantages, and internal difficulties:

1. *Skill/Capacity Deficits:* various, often major, developmental challenges—frequently including life and social skills deficits in such areas as educational and vocational abilities

2. *External Pressures/Disadvantages:* Major environmental pressures and/or major social disadvantages, including comparatively limited or reduced family, community, and other supports or social assistance

3. *Internal Difficulties:* Long-standing or situational feelings, attitudes, and defenses; ambivalence regarding change; particular motivations, desires, and personal and interpersonal commitments.[55]

Juvenile Justice Videos

PEACE LEARNING PROGRAM

In the *Peace Learning Program* video, a female juvenile facility is shown where the Peace Learning Program was established to handle the youths' needs. What is the Peace Learning Program? What are the goals of the Peace Learning Program? The coordinator of the program discusses the situation of one of the youth's and her involvement with the program. How is the program helping the youth with her individualized treatment needs? Can the values learned through the Peace Learning Program be transferred from the care facility to the real world? Why or why not?

FUTURE SOLDIERS PROGRAM

The *Future Soldiers Program* follows a youth offender through a specialized treatment program aimed at training youths in military fashion to promote discipline and set future goals for military service. What are other goals of the Future Soldiers Program? The video displays the admissions process for entering the Future Soldiers Program. What are some of the questions asked by the committee? Why are these important factors in assessing whether a juvenile will be able to handle the intense program? Based on the video and the readings, compare and contrast the Future Soldiers Program to other treatment models. For which types of juveniles might the Future Soldiers Program be more effective?

SUMMARY

LEARNING OBJECTIVE 1 Summarize the different viewpoints concerning treatment in juvenile justice.

(1) The "rehabilitation is not appropriate" stage, (2) the "nothing works" stage, (3) the "some treatments work" stage, and (4) the "numerous programs and innovations work" stage.

LEARNING OBJECTIVE 2 Describe the treatment modalities used most frequently in juvenile justice.

This chapter discusses and evaluates the basic treatment modalities in juvenile justice.

These therapies can be grouped under individual-level treatment programs (insight-based therapy, behavior therapy, and cognitive-behavior therapy) and group therapy (guided group interaction, positive peer culture, drug and alcohol treatment, and intervention with juvenile sex offenders).

LEARNING OBJECTIVE 3 Evaluate the juvenile justice treatment modalities.

It can be argued that we may have expected too much from correctional treatment. Long-term training schools are among the least promising places for treatment to take place. But even in community-based programs, the lack of resources or overworked staff, clients' histories of failure, and drug and alcohol addictions result in far more failures than successes. The danger, however, is to expect too little from correctional treatment. The gathering evidence of best programs is a reminder that treatment technologies are improving and promise to have more positive outcomes and lower rates of recidivism in the future.

LEARNING OBJECTIVE 4 Identify suggestions for improving treatment in juvenile justice agencies.

The future effectiveness of correctional treatment in juvenile justice may be contingent on three conditions:

1. Funding research so that more effective technologies can be developed.

2. Identifying what works for which group of offenders so that youthful offenders interested in treatment can be given the interventions most compatible with their needs and interests.

3. Creating more humane environments, where residents are treated with dignity and respect, so that environmental conditions will not negatively interfere with the treatment process.

KEY TERMS

behavior modification, p. 250
cognitive-behavior therapy (CBT), p. 250
Cognitive Thinking Skill Program
    (CTSP), p. 251
drug and alcohol abuse interventions, p. 254

guided group interaction (GGI), p. 252
insight-based therapy, p. 249
integrated treatment model, p. 258
positive peer culture (PPC), p. 253
psychotherapy, p. 250

reality therapy, p. 250
skill development, p. 257
transactional analysis (TA), p. 250

REVIEW QUESTIONS

1. Do you agree that no treatment is effective for juvenile offenders?
2. If you were superintendent of a training school, which treatment methods would you use? Why? What treatment technologies would you use in a residential program for juvenile probationers?
3. What type of staff member would be effective in carrying out the treatment method you chose in Question 2? Why?

4. Would you hire ex-offenders to work in your community-based or institutional facility? Why or why not?
5. Do you feel that the goals of PPC are realistic?
6. How would you treat youths who do not respond to the rules of your prescribed treatment method?

GROUP EXERCISES

1. *Group Work:* Discuss the stages through which the U.S. correctional system has gone in utilizing the idea of rehabilitation in correctional facilities.
2. *Writing to Learn Exercise:* Write a paragraph each on reality therapy and behavioral modification, indicating how each varies from the others. Critique and revise.
3. *Writing to Learn Exercise:* Write a paragraph describing positive peer culture and its goals and processes. Then, write a second paragraph to describe the cognitive-behavior, or

the thinking errors, approach and cognitive-behavior therapy interventions.
4. *Class Presentations:* Groups of three or four each are to research and analyze a different therapeutic modality and then report their findings to the class during the next session.
5. *Group Work:* Discuss what has to happen for treatment modalities to work.
   - **Research Center:** check out the Cybrary and MySearchLab for even more resources

NOTES

1. Office of Juvenile Justice and Delinquency Prevention, "Second Chances: Giving Kids a Chance to Make a Better Choice," in *Juvenile Justice Bulletin* (Washington, DC: U.S. Department of Justice, 2000), 21–23.
2. Walter C. Bailey, "Correctional Outcome: An Evaluation of 100 Reports," *Journal of Criminal Law, Criminology, and Police Science* 57 (June 1966), 153–60.
3. Robert Martinson, "What Works?—Questions and Answers About Prison Reform," *Public Interest* 35 (Spring 1974), 22–54.
4. Douglas Lipton, Robert Martinson, and Judith Wilks, *The Effectiveness of Correctional Treatment* (New York: Praeger, 1975).
5. CBS Television Network. Excerpted from *60 Minutes* segment, "It Doesn't Work" (August 24, 1975).
6. Ted Palmer, "Martinson Revisited," *Journal of Research in Crime and Delinquency* 12 (July 1975), 133–52.
7. Ibid., 137.
8. Paul Gendreau and Robert Ross, "Effective Correctional Treatment: Bibliotherapy for Cynics," *Crime and Delinquency* 27 (October 1979), 463–89.

9. Robert R. Ross and Paul Gendreau, eds., *Effective Correctional Treatment* (Toronto: Butterworth, 1980), viii.
10. Robert Martinson, "New Findings, New Views: A Note of Caution Regarding Sentencing Reform," *Hofstra Law Review* 7 (Winter 1979), 244.
11. Paul Gendreau and Robert R. Ross, "Revivification of Rehabilitative Evidence," *Justice Quarterly* 4 (September 1987), 349–407.
12. Ibid. For a review of the meta-analyses of correctional treatment in the 1980s, see Ted Palmer, *The Re-Emergence of Correctional Intervention* (Newbury Park, CA: Sage Publications, 1992), 50–76.
13. James McGuire and Philip Priestley, "Reviewing 'What Works': Past, Present, and Future," in *What Works: Reducing Reoffending—Guidelines from Research and Practice*, edited by James McGuire (New York: Wiley, 1995), 7–8.
14. Ibid.
15. Mark W. Lipsey and Frances T. Cullen, "The Effectiveness of Correctional Rehabilitation: A Review of Systematic

Reviews," *American Review of Law and Social Science* 3 (2007), 297–320.

16. Ibid., 4.

17. Gerald G. Gaes, Timothy J. Flanagan, Lawrence L. Motiuk, and Lynn Steward, "Adult Correctional Treatment," in *Crime and Justice, 26th Edition: Prisons*, edited by Michael Tonry and Joan Petersilia (Chicago: University of Chicago Press, 1999), 374–75.

18. Harvey Milkman and Kenneth Wanberg, *Cognitive-Behavior Treatment: A Review and Discussion for Correctional Professionals* (Washington, DC: National Institute of Corrections, 2007), 5.

19. Ibid.

20. Sesha Kentineni and Jeremy Braithwaite, "The Effect of a Cognitive-Behavioral Program for At-Risk Youth: Changes in Attitudes, Social Skills, Family and Community and Peer Relationships," *Victims and Offenders* 6 (2011), 93–116.

21. Patricia van Voorhis, Lis M. Spruance, P. Neal Richey, Shelley Johnson Listwan, and Renita Seebrook, "The Georgia Cognitive skills experiment: A replication of Reasoning and Rehabilitation," *Criminal Justice and Behavior* 31 (2004), 282–305.

22. Ibid.

23. Ibid.

24. Ibid.

25. Frank S. Pearson, Douglas S. Lipton, Charles M. Cleland, and Dorline S. Yee, "The Effects of Behavioral/Cognitive-Behavioral Programs on Recidivism," *Crime and Delinquency* 48 (2002), 476–96.

26. Milkman and Wanberg, *Cognitive-Behavior Treatment,* xix.

27. Ibid.

28. Pearson et al., "The Effects of Behavioral/Cognitive-Behavioral Programs on Recidivism."

29. Interview with Harry Vorrath quoted in Oliver J. Keller, Jr., and Benedict S. Alper, *Halfway Houses: Community Centered Correction and Treatment* (Lexington, MA: D. C. Heath, 1970), 55.

30. Ibid.

31. These materials are adapted from Harry H. Vorrath and Larry K. Brendtro, *Positive Peer Culture* (Chicago: Aldine, 1974).

32. Ibid.

33. Ibid.

34. Interviewed in 1986 in a Midwestern training school.

35. See the Federal Bureau of Prisons, *Substance Abuse Treatment,* accessed May 18, 2012, at http://www.bop.gov/inmate_programs_substance.jsp.

36. Materials for this section are drawn largely from Sue Righthand and Carlann Welch, *Juveniles Who Have Sexually Offended: A Review of the Professional Literature* (Washington, DC: Office of Juvenile Justice and Delinquency Prevention, 2001). Wherever appropriate, the authors of this text refer the reader to the original sources from which Righthand and Welch have drawn their materials.

37. C. Bagley and D. Shewchuk-Dann, "Characteristics of 60 Children and Adolescents Who Have a History of Sexual Assault Against Others: Evidence from a Controlled Study," *Journal of Child and Youth Care* (Fall Special Issue, 1991), 43–52.

38. For a more extensive examination of the treatment of juvenile sex offenders, see the statement by Domenick A. Lombardo in the *Voices* (of offenders and professionals) *in the Juvenile Justice System* supplement.

39. Sara Goodkind, "Gender-Specific Services in the Juvenile Justice System: A Critical Examination," *Affifia: Journal of Women and Social Work* 20 (Spring 2005), 52–70.

40. Office of Juvenile Justice and Delinquency Prevention, "Policy and Program Development for Serving Female Juvenile Delinquents," Chap. 2 in *Guiding Principles for Promising Female Programming: An Inventory of Best Practices* (Washington, DC: Office of Juvenile Justice and Delinquency Prevention, October 1998), accessed at http://ojjdp.ncjrs.org/pubs/principles/ch2_6.html).

41. Lee Sechrest, Susan O. White, and Elizabeth D. Brown, eds., *The Rehabilitation of Criminal Offenders* (Washington, DC: National Academy of Sciences, 1979); Susan Martin, Lee Sechrest, and Robin Redner, eds., *Rehabilitation of Criminal Offenders: Directions for Research* (Washington, DC: National Academy of Sciences, 1981).

42. These elements of effective programs are suggested by the work of Martin Groder and of Alden D. Miller, Lloyd E. Ohlin, and Robert B. Coates. See "Dr. Martin Groder: An Angry Resignation," *Corrections Magazine* 1 (July–August 1975), 3; and Alden D. Miller, Lloyd E. Ohlin, and Robert B. Coates, *A Theory of Social Reform: Correctional Change Processes in Two States* (Cambridge, MA: Ballinger, 1977).

43. Joshua L. Miner and Joe Boldt, *Outward Bound USA: Learning Through Experience in Adventure-Based Education* (New York: William Morrow, 1981).

44. Robert L. Woodson, *A Summons to Life: Mediating Structure and the Prevention of Youth Crime* (Cambridge, MA: Ballinger, 1981).

45. Groder, "Dr. Martin Groder," 33.

46. Clemens Bartollas, Stuart J. Miller, and Simon Dinitz, "Boys Who Profit: The Limits of Institutional Success," in *Reform in Corrections: Problems and Issues*, edited by Harry E. Allen and Nancy J. Beran (New York: Praeger, 1977), 18–19.

47. Christopher Murray et al., *Safety and Welfare Plan: Implementing Reform in California* (Sacramento, CA: Safety and Welfare Planning Team, 2006), 42.

48. Sechrest et al., eds., *The Rehabilitation of Criminal Offenders*, 35–37.

49. For the development of these various aspects of intervention, see Palmer, *The Re-Emergence of Correctional Intervention*, 151–57.

50. Sechrest et al., eds., *The Rehabilitation of Criminal Offenders*, 3–4.

51. Martin et al., eds., *Rehabilitation of Criminal Offenders*, 6.

52. Sechrest et al., eds., *The Rehabilitation of Criminal Offenders*, 45.

53. The template-matching technique was originally proposed in D. Bem and D. Funder, "Predicting More of the People More of the Time: Assessing the Personality of Situations," *Psychological Review* 85 (1978), 485–501.

54. Martin et al., *Rehabilitation of Criminal Offenders*, 82.

55. Palmer, *The Re-Emergence of Correctional Intervention*, 113.

13   Juvenile Gangs

Stockbroker/Glow Images

Learning Objectives

1. Outline the development of gangs in the United States.
2. Describe the behaviors and activities of gangs.
3. Identify the primary types of gangs.
4. Identify the seven stages of emergent gang development.
5. Summarize efforts to prevent and control gangs.

The road to success is a hard one. It begins in the family unit. It is in the family that parents plant the seeds for a young person to succeed. This young person is taught morals and ethics and learns behavior patterns.

By the age of seven or eight, this young person has learned whether he will be loved, whether his needs will be met, and how fair life is. What he thinks will have an effect on his behavior. If he feels he is on the short end of the stick, he may wake up angry as hell in the morning. He will seek elsewhere to have his needs met. He is not in a good place to compete with peer pressure.

It is not long before he is in gangs, doing drugs, and hurting people. It is also not long before he is serving time in the "joint." When he comes out, it is even harder to achieve success. It is a lot easier to go back to crime than to stay away from it.

For those of us who are determined not to go back to a life of crime, we may make it. It takes determination. It takes the opportunity to stand on your own feet. It takes support from others. It takes luck. But we are never out of the woods because it is real easy to go back.

What I am saying is that if we want to deal with youth crime, adult crime, and street gangs, we must go back to the family unit, must improve our schools, must make our neighborhoods more desirable, and must [provide] other alternatives to gangs and drugs.

—Fred "Bobby" Gore[1]

In the chapter-opening quote, Fred "Bobby" Gore explains why the social context is important to understanding youth crime and street gangs. Gore became one of the most influential leaders of the Conservative Vice Lords gang, the largest division of the Vice Lord Nation. That was thirty years ago. Until recently, he was the program director of the SAFER Foundation, a community integration program for ex-offenders. He may be retired now, but he continues to be a positive force against youths becoming involved in gangs.

Beginning in 1988 and continuing through the early 1990s, an upsurge in youth gangs suddenly occurred throughout the United States. Some of these youth gangs used the names of the national **urban gangs**, such as the Bloods and Crips from Los Angeles or the Gangster Disciples, Vice Lords, or Latin Kings from Chicago. Other gangs made up their own names, based on neighborhoods or images they wanted to depict to other peers and the community. By the mid-1990s, nearly every city, many suburban areas, and even some rural areas across the United States experienced the reality of youths who have banded together to form a youth gang.

The good news is that from 1996 to 2003, the estimated numbers of youth gangs and youth gang members in the United States decreased, as did the number of jurisdictions reporting gang problems. Then, however, the numbers steadily increased to 28,100 gangs with 731,000 gang members by 2009. More than one-third of the jurisdictions in the *National Youth Gang Survey* experienced gang problems in 2001, which is the highest annual estimate since before 2000 (see Figure 13–1). Overall, an estimated 3,500 jurisdictions served by city (population of 2,500 or more) and county law enforcement agencies were experiencing gang problems in 2009.[2]

The continuing bad news is that too many juveniles, especially at-risk youths, are involved in gangs; that gang involvement is likely to lead to further involvement in delinquency and drug use; that gang involvement increases the likelihood of the carrying and use of weapons; and that gang involvement increases the probability of going on to adult crime and of spending time in prison.[3]

How Have Gangs Evolved in the United States?

Youth gangs may have existed as early as the American Revolution.[4] Some researchers have suggested that they first emerged in the Southwest following the Mexican Revolution in 1813.[5] In the early 1800s, youth gangs seemed to have spread in New England, with the

Law Enforcement Agency Reports of Gang Problems, 1996–2009

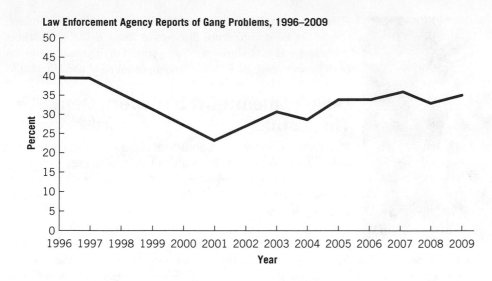

FIGURE 13–1
Law Enforcement Agency Reports
of Gang Problems, 1996–2009

shift from an agrarian to an industrial society. Youth gangs began to flourish in Chicago, New York, and other large cities in the nineteenth century as immigration and population shifts reached record levels.

Youth gangs were primarily Irish, Jewish, and Italian, but this changed in the twentieth century.

Gangs and Play Activity: The 1920s Through the 1940s

A pioneering work on youth gangs was Frederick Thrasher's *The Gang: A Study of 1,313 Gangs in Chicago.*[6] Thrasher viewed these gangs as a normal part of growing up in ethnic neighborhoods. He found that youths who went to school together and played together in the neighborhood naturally developed a strong sense of identity leading to their forming close-knit groups. Evolving from these neighborhood play groups, Thrasher found, they bonded together without any particular purpose or goal. These transitory social groups typically had fewer than thirty members. The youth gangs studied by Thrasher were usually organized in three concentric circles: a core made up of a leader and lieutenants, the rank-and-file membership, and a few youths who drifted in and out of the gang. Each gang was different, but what was universally expected was the protection of turf.[7]

West Side Story Era: The 1950s

Youth gangs became established in Boston, New York, and Philadelphia from the late 1940s through the 1950s. These youth gangs spent time "hanging out" and partying together; when deemed necessary, they fought other gangs. The musical later made into a movie, presented two 1950s New York youth gangs dancing, singing, and battling over turf. It focused on the Sharks, recent immigrants from Puerto Rico, defending their neighborhood ethnic boundaries.

These urban gangs of the 1950s were not the lethal weapons they have become in recent decades, but they were capable of violent behavior. In 1960–1961, one of the authors was hired to work with a white gang in Newark, New Jersey. This job became available because his predecessor, who had been on the job for two weeks, had a knife held to his chest, cutting his shirt and drawing a little blood. Warned that bad things would happen if he did not quit, he chose to resign.

The gangs of the 1950s attracted considerable attention among researchers and policy makers. Millions of dollars in federal, state, and local money were spent on projects and programs designed to prevent and control gang behavior. One of the most widely funded efforts was the detached workers' program. This program sent professional workers into the community to work with gang youths, but this effort proved to have little or no positive

▲ Youth gang's members represent the gang by demonstrating gang signals that are recognized by other gang members and that distinguish it from other gangs.

Steve Skjold/Alamy

effect on reducing their rates of delinquent activities. Indeed, one of the most consistent findings of these detached workers' programs was that workers' efforts ended up increasing the size of the youth gang, as well as the commitment of participants.[8]

Development of the Modern Gang: The 1960s

The 1960s are known as a decade of rapidly changing social and political climates. The development of **supergangs** in Chicago and Los Angeles, the involvement of gangs in social betterment programs, and their participation in political activism were the most significant changes in youth gangs during the 1960s.

The major supergangs developed when neighborhood gangs became larger and more powerful than other gangs in surrounding neighborhoods, and they forced the small groups to become part of their gang organization. Eventually, a few gangs controlled the entire city of Chicago. During this decade, three African American supergangs, the Vice Lords, the Blackstone Rangers, and the Disciples, either had their beginnings or developed into supergangs. See Focus on Offenders 13–1 for a discussion about the development of these Chicago supergangs. In the 1960s, the Crips, an African American supergang, began as a small clique in a section of Los Angeles.[9] It was not long before the Bloods, another African American supergang in Los Angeles, arose to challenge the Crips.

During the late 1960s, the Vice Lords and the Blackstone Rangers, two of Chicago's supergangs, became involved in programs of community betterment. Their social action involvement began in the summer of 1967 when the Vice Lord leaders attended

---

Focus on Offenders 13–1
Origins of the Chicago "Supergangs"

THE VICE LORD NATION

In the late 1950s, Edward "Peppilow" Perry was a fifteen-year-old youth who was sent to the St. Charles reformatory for boys. He persuaded Leonard Calloway, Maurice Miller, and four others to form a new gang when they got out. They played with names. It was Calloway who thought of lords, and vice came to mind. He looked both words up in the dictionary and found vice to mean "having a tight hold." He knew he had it. They would be called "Vice Lords."

It was not until 1964 that the name "Conservative Vice Lords" became well known. Maurice Miller was a conservative type, and he wanted *conservative* added to the name. They did that for him, ending up with Conservative Vice Lords.

As the Conservative Vice Lords grew in number and power, they began to take over other youth gangs in their neighborhood and in surrounding neighborhoods. One of the reasons for the success of this gang's development is that while it was annexing groups to the Conservative Vice Lords, this gang allowed other groups to retain their own identity and to become part of the Vice Lord Nation.

For example, Willie Lloyd became a member of the Vice Lords in the mid-1960s and was put in charge of the Peewees, a junior division of the Conservative Vice Lords. But when the Peewees evolved into another youth gang, Willie was not selected as an officer, nor was his suggested group name accepted. He was

able to persuade two friends at that point to begin a new youth gang, which they called the "Unknown Conservative Vice Lords." This new gang, in spite of the opposition it initially received from established Vice Lord groups, eventually was accepted as a major division of the Vice Lord Nation.

Alfonso Alford became chief of the Lords in the mid-1960s. Tired of humbugging, he began to search for meaning in a world where fighting was the only honor known. Too old to go back to school and with few jobs available, Al suggested the Lords try to open a business, moving toward construction rather than destruction. The Lords just shook their heads. It just didn't sound right. They enjoyed the partying, the drinking, and the fights. But Al kept insisting that together they could make it happen. They had to try.

Between 1965 and 1967, the Lords stopped the gang wars. They opened businesses and ran community programs for the hungry, the unemployed, the homeless, and the young with nothing to do. They reached out to show the people on the streets that there was a thing called hope. For a moment in time they made a difference, but the forces working against them do not remember the moment. They are all dead now. All but Bobby Gore, who continues to have hope and to fight for his brothers and sisters on the streets.

As the decade came to an end, the Vice Lords had twenty-nine branches. In addition to the Conservatives, the largest groups included the Unknown, Four Corner Hustlers, Mafia Insane, 21st Street Executioners, Travelers, and Maniac Vice Lords, but they were still all Lords.

BLACKSTONE RANGERS

Jeff Fort was a scrawny young man who lived in Woodlawn on the west side of Chicago. He and a few friends began to steal hubcaps and groceries, dividing the proceeds among themselves. As others were attracted to this group, they came to be named the Blackstone Rangers. Fort selected twenty-one leaders, giving them responsibility and power. They became known as the Main 21, and their major role was to enforce the rules of the Blackstone Rangers.

The Reverend John Fry, minister of the First Presbyterian Church in Chicago, permitted this gang to hold its meetings in the gymnasium of the church. The meetings captured the emotions of a religious revival. The Blackstones filled the gym, and the Main 21 were seated in a semicircle across the stage at the end of the gym.

Jeff Fort appeared out of nowhere, going to the microphone and podium. He raised his fist, jerking it back hard, with power they all knew him to have. He yelled, "Blackstone," and together the thunderous roar resounded back, "Blackstone."

Fort whipped the Blackstones into a frenzy. In a deep, booming voice that sent static flying across the gym, he demanded, "Stones run it!" Thousands of bodies extended their right fists like banners hammering the winds and responded, "Stones run it!" Over and over the thunder filled the gym, "Blackstones, Blackstones, Blackstones."

The Stones soon spread beyond their neighborhoods throughout Chicago. It was not long before they were known as America's most powerful gang. Some drug sales took place in the 1960s, but gang arrests were typically for crimes ranging from resisting arrest to armed robbery and murder.

THE DISCIPLES

David Barksdale was a self-directed leader who defied anyone; he was accustomed to reaching out and taking what he wanted. During his frequent trips as a teenager to the Illinois Youth Commission, he recruited youths from the south, west, and east sides, organizing a domain that was to extend his field of influence beyond that of just the south side. The movement spread.

He was stocky at age fifteen, standing about 5' 10" tall. He was stoic, quiet, and always serious, with a charisma that instilled fear and awe at the same time. Well mannered with few words, he dressed to perfection, looking fine with processed hair. But above all else he was an excellent boxer, one of the very best.

It was Barksdale's boxing skill that led to the development of the Disciples gang. Champ Harris was the nineteen-year-old leader of the Devil Disciples, which had a membership of about four hundred youths. Champ's girlfriend, Linda Samuels, was pursued by Barksdale, and Champ challenged his rival to a boxing match. By the time Harris hit the floor, he had lost his girlfriend and control over his gang.

Barksdale surrounded himself with leaders he could trust. They fought the Egyptian Cobras, led by Charlie Adkins, and the Supreme Gangsters, led by Martin Givens and Larry Hoover. Barksdale looked around for the small, unknown groups just coming up and recruited them easily most of the time; at other times they had little choice, if any.

With Barksdale on the run a couple of years later, Robert Allen, known to most as Old Timer, assumed responsibility for the leadership of the Devil Disciples. He made the decision to offer Larry Hoover an opportunity to coexist with him as leader of this gang. They would coexist together in one land, two kings ruling one nation, each with equal power. David Barksdale would be king of the Devil Disciples, and Larry would be king of the Gangster Disciples. They were allies, six thousand strong.

In the early 1970s, David Barksdale was wounded and then died a couple of years later. His side of the kingdom was taken over by Jerome Freeman and became known as the Black Disciples. Imprisoned Larry Hoover used the magic of the name "Gangster Disciple" to become a legend and to build one of the largest gang organizations in the United States. Known as the King and Chairman of the Board, he is the head of the vast Gangster Disciples nation.

Source: Linda Dippold Bartollas researched and wrote this material. She was assisted by Nehemiah Russell and Samuel Dillon.

---

meetings at Western Electric and Sears and Roebuck. Operation Bootstrap, which resulted from these meetings, formed committees for education, recreation, and law, order, and justice. A grant from the Rockefeller Foundation in February 1967 enabled the Vice Lords to fund a host of economic and social ventures. The Vice Lords also worked with Jesse Jackson on Operation Breadbasket and, in the summer of 1969, joined with the Coalition for United Community Action to protest the lack of African American employees on construction sites in African American neighborhoods.

The supergangs in Chicago became involved in political activism when they joined together to work against the reelection of Mayor Richard Daley's Democratic machine. This activism brought increased strain to their relationship with the Democratic Party organization. With Daley's reelection, gangs in Chicago began to experience what they perceived as harassment from the police. As soon as he began a new term, Daley announced a crackdown on gang violence, and State's Attorney Edward Hanrahan followed his lead by appraising the gang situation as the most serious crime problem in Chicago. The courts complied with this crackdown on gangs by increasing dramatically the number of gang members sent to prison in Illinois.

Expansion, Violence, and Criminal Operations: The 1970s, 1980s, and 1990s

A number of changes took place with gangs in the last three decades of the twentieth century. Among the most important were that gangs became increasingly made up of adults; that street gangs became responsible for a large portion of urban crime, including violent crime; that urban gangs grew in the 1970s and expanded dramatically throughout the nation in the late 1980s and early 1990s; and that crack cocaine hit the streets in the mid-1980s.

What became evident by the late 1960s was that juveniles were not leaving the urban gangs to which they belonged when they became adults. One of the major reasons for this was that these gangs supplied certain needs that were not being met in other social groups or traditional rites of passage into adulthood. Another reason was that the increased imprisonment of gang members fostered the development of prison gangs that kept their allegiance to these gangs while in prison and subsequent to being released from prison. This pattern remains true today—more than half of all gang members are over the age of 18.[10]

In the 1970s and 1980s, urban gangs became responsible for a major portion of muggings, robberies, extortions, and drug-trafficking operations in the United States. With leadership increasingly assumed by adults, gangs were more intent on making money from crime. With legal weapons more readily available than in the past, gangs became much more violent.

The mid-1980s were a turning point for many ghetto-based gangs, for crack cocaine had hit the streets. These urban street gangs competed with each other for the drug trade. Several Los Angeles gangs established direct connections to major Colombian smugglers, which ensured a continuous supply of top-quality cocaine. In some Chicago neighborhoods, heavily armed teams sold drugs openly on the street corners, using gang "peewees" (youngsters) as police lookouts.

In the period from 2000 to the present, some gangs have decreased in number and violence, while other gangs, especially ethnic ones, have rapidly spread. Gangs also have spread worldwide. See the timeline shown in Figure 13–2 for the development of gangs in the twentieth and twenty-first century.

Definition of Gangs

Thrasher's 1927 gang study was one of the first attempts to define a youth gang. He saw the gangs as formed spontaneously and then integrated through conflict. These gangs were

TIMELINE

1920s–1940s	1940s–1950s	1960s
Gangs were largely transitory social groups in Chicago and elsewhere, and gang membership was a type of rite of passage.	**Teenage gangs** became established in Boston, New York, and Philadelphia. Members hung out together, partied together, and gangs fought each other over "turf."	**Drugs began** to influence gang activity, "supergangs" in Chicago and Los Angeles emerged, and some Chicago gangs became involved in social betterment programs.

1970s–1988	1989–1999	2000–present
Leadership of gangs was assumed by adults, street gangs became involved in more unlawful behaviors and drug trafficking, and gangs became increasingly more violent.	**The number of** youth gangs exploded across the United States.	**Gang membership** and the number of gangs have begun to slightly decline, with some ethnic gangs skyrocketing in numbers. Gangs have spread worldwide.

FIGURE 13–2
Timeline: Development of Gangs in the Twentieth and Early Twenty-First Centuries

TABLE 13–1
Definition of a Youth Gang

Researcher	Contribution
Thrasher	Group interaction
Esbensen and others	Illegal activity
Esbensen	Group demographics (age range, sense of identity, and permanence in a given area)

characterized by such behaviors as movement through space as a unit, conflict, and planning. One result of this behavior was the development of tradition, esprit de corps, morale, solidarity, and attachment to local territory.[11]

Thrasher does not specify that a gang's definition must include illegal activity, but Finn-Aage Esbensen and most other gang researchers do. Whereas Thrasher's definition focused on group interaction, Esbensen was interested in clarifying group demographics (age range, sense of identity, and permanence with a specific area).[12] Combining all three definitions could provide a useful and comprehensive definition of a youth gang. See Table 13–1.

Profiles of Gang Members

Gang profiles have at least three important dimensions: age of gang members, size of the gang, and attraction of the gang.

Age of Gang Members

The smaller the community, the more likely it is that its gang members will be juveniles. Sample surveys of urban street gang members indicate that 14 to 30 percent of adolescents join gangs at some point.[13] Nonetheless, the percentage of gang members who are juveniles has decreased over time. In 1996, 50 percent of all gang members were reported to be age 18 years or older, but by 2001, the number had grown to 67 percent. Juvenile gang members make up 70 percent of all gang members in small communities—a statistic that steadily declines as community size increases.[14]

Juveniles become involved in gangs as young as eight years of age, running errands and carrying weapons or messages. They are recruited as lookouts and street vendors and join an age-appropriate junior division of the gang. Gangs use younger and small members to deal cocaine out of cramped "rock houses," which are steel-reinforced fortresses. Gangs have long known that youngsters are invaluable because their age protects them against the harsher realities of the adult criminal justice system.[15]

Size of the Gang

Gangs vary in size depending on whether they are traditional or specialty gangs in urban areas or emerging gangs in small cities or communities. Large and enduring traditional (territorial) gangs in urban areas average about one hundred fifty members, whereas drug-trafficking gangs average about twenty-five members. Some urban gangs (for example, the supergangs of Chicago) have thousands of members, but gangs in emerging areas usually number fewer than twenty-five or so members.[16]

Attraction of the Gang

Why do young people join gangs? Willie Lloyd, legendary leader of a gang called the Almighty Unknown Vice Lords, explained why he became involved in gangs:

> I grew up on the streets of Chicago. When I was growing up, the Lords had a big impact on me. I never saw it as a gang but a cohesive unifying principle by which a person could organize his life. Even as a kid of nine, I was intrigued by the Lords when I first saw them outside of the Central Park Theater. It was the first time I've ever witnessed so many black

TABLE 13–2
Attraction of Gangs

Why Gangs Form	What Gangs Offer	Why Youths Join
Social discrimination or rejection	Acceptance	To avoid being discriminated against and to seek acceptance and a sense of belonging
Absence of a family and its unconditional love, positive adult role models, and proper discipline	Surrogate family	To be in a family and to have unconditional love, positive adult role models, and discipline
Feelings of powerlessness	Power	To overcome their powerlessness
Abuse, fear, and lack of security	Security	To reduce their feelings of fear and to feel secure
Economic deprivation	Means of earning money	To gain economically
School failure and delinquency	Alternative to school	To vent their frustration
Low self-esteem	Opportunities to build high self-esteem	To acquire high self-esteem
Lack of acceptable rites of passage into adulthood	Rite of passage to adulthood	To accomplish their passage from childhood to adulthood
Lack of legitimate free-time activities	Activity	To keep from being bored
Pathological needs	Setting in which to act out aggression	To vent their anger
Influence of migrating gang members	Any of the aforementioned	To get any of the aforementioned
Mass media portrayals of gangs and gang members	Any of the aforementioned	To get any of the aforementioned
Choice to follow in others' footsteps	Any of the aforementioned	To follow tradition and to gain acceptance
Ability to join	Any of the aforementioned	To get any of the aforementioned

Source: Adapted from Michael Carlie, *Into the Abyss: A Personal Journey into the World of Street Gangs.* http://people .missouristate.edu/MichaelCarlie/what_i_learned_about/gangs/whyform/why_gangs_form.htm#top. Reprinted with permission from Michael K. Carlie.

people moving so harmoniously together. They were motored by the same sense of purpose and they were all wore similar dress and insignia. They were over a hundred guys, all in black, with capes and umbrellas. To my young eyes, it was the most beautiful expression I had ever seen. They all seem so fearless, so proud, so much in control of their lives. Though I didn't know one of them at the time, I fell in love with all of them. In retrospect, I made up my mind the first time I saw the Vice Lords to be a Vice Lord.[17]

Mike Carlie, in his national overview of youth gangs, expanded on the question of why gangs form and what gangs offer to those who join them (see Table 13–2).

Theories of Gang Formation

The classical theories about the origins of youth gangs and gang delinquency date from research done in 1950s and formulated by Herbert A. Bloch and Arthur Niederhoffer, Richard Cloward and Lloyd Ohlin, Albert K. Cohen, Walter B. Miller, and Lewis Yablonsky:

- Bloch and Niederhoffer's theory was based on the idea that joining a gang is part of the experience that male adolescents need to grow up to adulthood, so the basic function of the gang is to provide a substitute for the formalized puberty rites that are found in other societies.[18]

- Cloward and Ohlin's theory used the notion that lower-class boys interact with and gain support from other alienated individuals and that these youngsters pursue illegitimate means to achieve the success they cannot gain through legitimate means.[19]

- Cohen's theory stated that gang delinquency represents the subcultural collective solution to the problems that face lower-class boys of acquiring status when they find themselves evaluated according to middle-class values and the schools.[20]

- Miller held that there is a definite lower-class culture and that gang behavior is an expression of that culture; he saw gang leadership as based mainly on smartness and toughness and viewed the gang as very cohesive and highly conforming to delinquent norms.[21]

- Yablonsky suggested that violent delinquent gangs arise out of certain conditions, which are found in urban slums, that encourage the development of the sociopathic personality in adolescence, and such sociopathic individuals become the core leadership of these gangs.[22]

More recently, **underclass theory** has been widely used to explain the origins of gangs.[23] In the midst of big-city ghettos and barrios filled with poverty and deprivation, it is argued, gangs are a normal response to an abnormal social setting.[24] Part of the underclass plight according to Jeffery Fagan is being permanently excluded from participating in mainstream labor market occupations, so members of the underclass are forced to rely on other economic alternatives, such as low-paying temporary jobs, part-time jobs, some form of welfare, or involvement in drug trafficking, prostitution, muggings, and extortions.[25] Martin Sánchez Jankowski contended that gang violence and the defiant attitudes of young men are connected with a competitive struggle in poor communities and, being a product of their environment, they adopt a "Hobbesian view of life in which violence is an integral part of the state of nature."[26] Table 13–3 summarizes the theories of why juveniles join gangs.

TABLE 13–3
Theories of Why Juveniles Join Gangs

Type of Theory	Proponents	Brief Description
Normal Part of Growing Up	Block and Niederhoffer	Joining the gang is part of the experience adolescents need to grow up to adulthood.
Strain Theory	Cloward and Ohlin	Youngsters pursue gangs to achieve the success they cannot achieve through legitimate means.
Subcultural Affiliation and Strain Theory	Cohen	Gang delinquency represents a subcultural and collective solution to the problems racing lower-class boys.
Subcultural Affiliation	Miller	There is a definite lower-class culture and gang behavior is an expression of that culture.
Social Disorganization	Yablonsky	Violent delinquent gangs arise out of certain conditions, which are found in urban slums.
Underclass Theory	Fagan and others	Excluded from participation in labor market occupations, members of the underclass are attracted to other economic alternatives, such as gangs.

What Is Important to Know About Urban Street Gangs?

Important features of urban street gangs include their types, organizational features, participation in drug trafficking, their behavior in school, and the degree of law-violating behaviors for juveniles involved in these groups. Juveniles may be a minority in urban street gangs, but they have certain role expectations (usually drug "runners" and lookouts for crack houses) and frequently remain in the gang even after they become adults.

Types of Urban Gangs

Detroit urban gangs, according to Carl S. Taylor, can be classified as scavenger, territorial, and corporate. **Scavenger gangs** lack goals, purpose, and consistent leadership and prey on those unable to defend themselves. **Territorial gangs** define an area as belonging exclusively to them and attempt to defend this space from outsiders. They become the controllers of the streets and defend their territory to protect their narcotics business. Organized or **corporate gangs,** which Taylor views as organized crime groups, have as their main purpose the participation in illegal money-making ventures, especially the trafficking of **crack** cocaine. Different divisions of the gang handle sales, distribution, marketing, and enforcement.[27]

C. Ronald Huff's examination of gangs in Cleveland and Columbus, Ohio, identified informal hedonistic gangs, instrumental gangs, and predatory gangs. The basic concerns of informal **hedonistic gangs** were to get high (usually on alcohol, marijuana, or other drugs) and to have a good time. These gangs were more involved in property crimes than in violent personal crimes. The main focus of **instrumental gangs** was economic gain, and they committed a large number of property crimes. Most of these gang members used drugs, including crack cocaine; some members also sold drugs, but doing so was not an organized gang activity. **Predatory gangs** committed robberies, street muggings, and other crimes of opportunity. Members of these gangs were likely to use crack cocaine and to sell drugs to finance the purchase of more sophisticated weapons.[28]

Fagan identified four types of gangs in his analysis of the crime–drug relationships in three cities. Type 1 gangs were involved in a few delinquent activities and only alcohol and marijuana use. These gangs had low involvement in drug sales and appeared to be social gangs. Type 2 gangs were heavily involved in several kinds of drug sales, primarily to support their own drug habits. They were also heavily involved in vandalism. Type 3 gangs had the highest levels of member participation, including extensive involvement in both serious and nonserious offenses. Another feature of this type was less involvement in both drug sales and the use of such substances as cocaine, heroin, PCP, and amphetamines. Type 4 gangs were extensively involved in both serious drug use and serious and nonserious offenses and had higher rates of drug sales. This cohesive and organized type, according to Fagan, "is probably at the highest risk for becoming a more formal criminal organization."[29] Table 13–4 summarizes the types of urban gangs.

Organizational Features of Urban Gangs

Jankowski, who spent more than ten years studying thirty-seven gangs in Los Angeles, New York, and Boston, suggested that the most important organizational features of urban gangs are leadership, recruitment, initiation rites, and migration patterns.[30]

Leadership

Jankowski observed three varieties of **gang leadership**:

1. The *vertical/hierarchical* structure divides leadership hierarchically into several different levels. Power and authority are related to one's position in the line of command.

2. The *horizontal/commission* structure consists of several officeholders who share about equal authority over members. The leaders share the duties as well as the power and authority.

> **TABLE 13–4**
> **Types of Urban Gangs**

Scavenger gangs: Prey on those unable to defend themselves.

Territorial gangs: Defend an area in which they claim ownership.

Corporate gangs: Organized crime groups whose main purpose is participation in illegal money-making ventures.

Hedonistic gangs: Basic purpose is to get high and have a good time.

Instrumental gangs: Focus is on economic gain.

Predatory gangs: Commit a variety of crimes, use and sell cocaine, and purchase more sophisticated weapons to achieve their purposes.

Type 1 gangs: Involved in minor delinquent activities and drug use.

Type 2 gangs: Heavily involved in several types of drug sales.

Type 3 gangs: Little involvement in drug sales but more involvement in both serious and nonserious offenses.

Type 4 gangs: Extensively involved in drug use, drug sales, and serious and nonserious offenses.

---

3. The *influential* structure assigns no written duties or titles to the leadership positions. This type of system has two to four members who are regarded as the leaders of the gang. The authority of the influential leaders is derived from charisma.[31]

The most conspicuous example of the vertical/hierarchical type of leadership is found in the Gangster Disciples, the Vice Lords, the Black Disciples, and the El Rukns, whose leaders have become legends. The Bloods and the Crips, the most notorious Los Angeles gangs, are representative of the horizontal/commission type. In a real sense, they are not gangs at all but confederations of hundreds of subgroups, or sets. Sets are established along neighborhood lines, and most sets have twenty to thirty members. The emerging youth gangs across the nation, described later in this chapter, would be examples of influential type of leadership structure.[32]

Recruitment

Gangs regularly go on recruiting parties, and the recruitment of young members, or soldiers, is easy because the life of a gang member looks glamorous. If a prospective member is not receptive, then coercion or threats can be made concerning the consequences of not joining.

Methods of Initiation

The **methods of initiation** into some gangs include some or all of the following:

- A new member may be *blessed-in* to a gang. Those who are blessed-in to a gang usually have older brothers, fathers, mothers, or other relatives who are already in the gang.

- A new male member more typically must be *jumped-in*, or fight other members. He may have to fight a specified number of gang members for a set period of time and demonstrate that he is able to take a beating and fight back. Or he may have to stand in the middle of a circle and fight his way out, or run between lines of gang members as they administer a beating. Under such circumstances, he is expected to stay on his feet from one end of the line to the other. Recently, there has been a movement away from jumped-in initiations in urban gangs, unless there is some question about the initiate's courage.[33]

- A female often is initiated into male-dominated gangs by providing sexual services for one or more gang members.

- A new member in some gangs has been expected to play Russian roulette. Russian roulette involves loading a pistol's cylinder with one bullet, spinning the cylinder, closing it, then pointing the gun to one's head and pulling the trigger. If the player wins, he's in the gang. If he loses, well …

- A new member is often expected to participate in illegal acts, such as committing thefts or larcenies.
- A new member frequently is expected to assist in trafficking drugs.
- A new member in some gangs is expected to participate in "walk-up" or "drive-by" shootings.
- A new member is sometimes expected to commit a gang-assigned murder. Completing the procedure has sometimes been called a *blood-in*, but is rarely part of initiation rites today.[34]

Migration

A final organizational feature of urban gangs is **migration**. Gang migration can occur in the establishment of satellite gangs in another location, in the relocation of gang members with their families, and in the expansion of drug markets. Cheryl L. Maxson, Malcolm W. Klein, and Lea C. Cunningham surveyed law enforcement agencies in more than 1,100 cities nationwide. Of these, 713 reported some gang migration. The most frequent pattern of gang migration was the relocation of gang members with their families (39 percent); the next most common pattern was the expansion of drug markets (20 percent). But their survey failed to offer much support for gangs attempting to establish satellites in other communities across the nation.[35] Indeed, most jurisdictions surveyed for the *National Youth Gang Survey of 2007* indicated that either no or a very small percentage of the gang members with whom they were familiar were migrants to their area. The primary reasons for migration were social reasons (e.g., as mentioned, their family moved), rather than illicit purposes.[36]

Voices of Delinquency: The Blood in the Hood

Drug Trafficking and Gangs

Beginning in the mid-1980s, street gangs with origins in the urban centers of Los Angeles, Chicago, New York, Miami, and Detroit became criminal entrepreneurs in supplying drugs, especially crack cocaine, to urban communities. They had begun by the late 1980s and early 1990s to develop intrastate and interstate networks to expand their illegal drug market sales.

The Crips and Bloods of Los Angeles have been the most active in **drug trafficking** nationwide. In a 1988 report, the Drug Enforcement Administration claimed that Los Angeles street gangs were identified with drug sales in forty-six states.[37] The Miami Boys of South Florida, the Jamaican Posses of New York and Florida, and the Vice Lords and Gangster Disciples in Chicago are also among the street gangs that have entered the field on the largest scale.[38]

The depth of gang involvement in drugs is documented in the *1997 National Youth Gang Survey*. Respondents to the survey estimate, on the average, that 42 percent of the drug sales across jurisdictions are conducted by gangs. Gangs are responsible for 43 percent of drug sales in suburbs, 35 percent in rural areas, 31 percent in small cities, but 49 percent in large cities.[39]

When ranking gangs according to their involvement in drug sales at low, moderate, or high levels, data indicate that more than half (53 percent) of gang members were reported to be involved at the low level of drug sales, 18 percent at the moderate level, and 29 percent at the high level.[40] The highest proportion of youth gangs involved in drug sales was in large cities, and the lowest was in small cities. Larger cities apparently have more opportunities for the individual entrepreneur. Table 13–5 summarizes the organizational features of urban gangs.

Gangs in School

Urban schools have become fertile soil for the violence of youth gangs. The percentage of high school students who reported the presence of street gangs at school varied by the type of school and whether the school was public or private. Urban schools had a significantly

TABLE 13–5
Organizational Features of Urban Gangs

Features of Urban Gangs	Types
Leadership	
Vertical/hierarchical structure	Divides leadership hierarchically into several different structures.
Horizontal/commission structure	Consists of several officeholders who share about equal authority over members.
Influential structure	Assigns no written duties or titles to the leadership position.
Recruitment	
Friendly	Appeal can be made to join because of the glamor or advantages of gang membership ("we will have your back").
Coercive	Pressure and threats are made. Prospective members are warned about the consequences of failure to join.
Methods of Initiation	
"Blessed-in"	Usually comes because siblings or other relatives are already in the gang.
"Jumped-in"	Must fight other members.
Females' initiation into male-dominated gangs.	Must provide sexual services for one or more gang members.
Must participate in illegal acts.	These include trafficking drugs or even participating in "walk-up" or "drive-by" shootings.
Migration	
Relocation of gang members with their families	This is the most frequent form of migration.
Expansion of drug markets	Second most common pattern.
Urban gangs' attempt to establish satellite gangs in other communities	Little evidence for this.

larger percentage of students who reported the presence of gangs at school than did suburban or rural schools. Indeed, more than twice as many students in urban schools compared with students in rural schools reported the presence of gangs. This same pattern was true of public schools, but it was less true of private schools. Figure 13–3 shows the percentage of students ages twelve through eighteen who reported the presence of street gangs at school during in 2007 and again in 2009.[41]

Gangs perpetrate school violence in a number of ways. Gang members are likely to bring concealed weapons into the school. They are constantly recruiting new members, and nongang youths who refuse to join may be assaulted. Also, when more than one gang is present in a school, conflict among these gangs takes place on a regular basis. Furthermore, conflict among rival gangs in different schools perpetrates violence.

Youths involved in gangs also are known to be disruptive in the classroom, to do poorly in their academic work, to intimidate nongang youth on the way to and from school, to frequently be absent, to be suspended or even expelled from school, and to drop out of school. When an urban high school has a large percentage of gang youths, the culture of that school tends to be chaotic, out of control, and dangerous. A visitor to a typical urban high school is likely to feel very uncomfortable.

FIGURE 13–3

Percentage of Students Ages Twelve to Eighteen Who Reported That Gangs Were Present at School during the School Year, by Urbanicity, 2007 and 2009

Source: Bureau of Justice Statistics, *School Crime Supplement (SCS) to the National Crime Victimization Survey, 2007 and 2009* (Washington, DC: U.S. Department of Justice, 2011).

Law-Violating Behaviors and Gang Activities

Despite the fluidity and diversity of gang roles and affiliations, experts commonly agree that core members are involved in more serious delinquent acts than are situational or fringe members.

Studies in Aurora, Colorado; Broward County, Florida; and Cleveland, Ohio, found some major differences between the behavior of gang members and that of at-risk youths.[42] Individual gang members in these studies reported that they had stolen more cars, that they had participated in more drive-by shootings, that they were far more likely to own guns, that they owned guns of larger caliber, and that they were more involved in selling drugs as compared to the sample of at-risk youths.[43] Of those youths selling drugs, "gang members reported doing so more frequently, having fewer customers, making more money from the sales, and relying more on out-of-state suppliers than nongang youths who sold drugs." This study added that "both gang members and at-risk youths reported that gangs do not control drug trafficking in their communities."[44]

In Rochester, gang members, who made up 30 percent of the sample, self-reported committing 68 percent of all adolescent violent offenses, which was about seven times as many serious and violent acts as committed by nongang youths.[45] In Seattle, gang members, who made up 15 percent of the sample, self-reported committing 85 percent of adolescent robberies.[46] In Denver, gang members, who made up 14 percent of the sample, self-reported committing 89 percent of all serious violent adolescent offenses. Gang members committed about three times as many serious and violent offenses as did nongang youth.[47]

These Rochester, Denver, and Seattle studies showed that the influence of gang membership on levels of youth violence is greater than the influence of other delinquent peers.[48] Youths commit more serious and violent acts while they belong to a gang than they do after they leave the gang.[49] In addition, the effects of gang membership on a propensity toward violence seem to be long lasting. In all three sites, even though gang members' offense rates dropped after leaving the gang, they still remained fairly high.[50]

The overall number of youth gang homicides has declined since the late 1990s and through 2003. The rate has since remained relatively stable with rates spiking up in some isolated cities and down in others. The *National Youth Gang Survey* analysis documents that larger cities and suburban counties are more likely than smaller cities and rural areas to experience gang homicides. One in ten larger cities reports ten or more gang homicides, and one in five larger cities reports from three to nine. A significant majority of smaller cities and rural counties have no gang-related homicides, a distinction that is not found in larger cities and suburban counties.[51] See Figure 13–4.

A final dimension of law-violating behaviors of urban street gangs is an examination of the extent to which they are becoming **organized crime groups**. Scott H. Decker, Tim Bynum, and Deborah Weisel interviewed members of African American and Hispanic gangs in San Diego and Chicago and found that only the Gangster Disciples in Chicago are assuming the attributes of organized crime groups.[52] Several commentaries have spelled out the

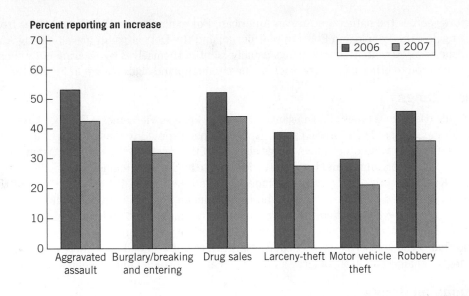

FIGURE 13-4
Changes in Reported Gang Related
Crime, 2006-2007

organizational features of the Gangster Disciples, including a chairman of the board, two boards of directors (one for the streets and one for prisons), governors who control drug trafficking on the streets, regents who supply the drugs, area coordinators who collect revenues from drug-selling spots, enforcers who punish those who violate the rules, and "shorties" who staff drug-selling spots and execute drug deals.[53]

It can be argued that aspects of organized crime groups are found in such drug-trafficking gangs as the Bloods and Crips of Los Angeles, the Miami Boys of South Florida, and the Jamaican Posses of New York and Florida. Beginning in the mid-1980s, these street gangs appeared to become criminal entrepreneurs in supplying illicit drugs. In a brief period of several years, many of these street gangs developed intrastate and interstate networks for the purpose of expanding their illegal drug market sales. As mentioned above, the Crips and Bloods of Los Angeles have been the most active in drug trafficking across the United States.[54] A study by the U.S. Congress concluded that during the latter part of the 1980s the Crips and Bloods controlled 30 percent of the crack cocaine market across the nation.[55]

Racial and Ethnic Gangs

Hispanic/Latino, African American, Asian, and Caucasian constitute the main types of racial and ethnic gangs in the United States. Hispanic/Latino and African American gangs are generally more numerous and have more members that other racial and ethnic gangs.

Hispanic/Latino Gangs

Hispanic/Latino gangs are divided into Mexican American or Chicano, Cuban, Puerto Rican, Dominican, Jamaican, and Central American members. According to the 2005 National Gang Threat Assessment, enforcement agencies across the nation reported that the most prominent Hispanic/Latino gangs in their jurisdiction were the Los Surenos (Sur 13), Latin Kings, MS-13, 18th Street, Nortenos, and La Raza, with more than 50 percent of reporting agencies indicating that Sur 13 was present in their jurisdiction and nearly 40 percent reporting moderate to high Sur 13 gang activity.[56] Currently, the MS-13 Hispanic gang is found throughout the nation and claims to have one hundred thousand members.[56] Hispanic Latino gang members frequently dress distinctly, display colors, communicate through graffiti, use monikers, and bear tattoos.

African American Gangs

African Americans have received more attention in this chapter than any other racial or ethnic group because most of the ghetto-based drug-trafficking gangs that have established

▲ Leaders of gangs command considerable respect in their "hoods." The result is that a member of another gang—or even his own gang—may seek to gain status by killing this man. Indeed, the word on the streets is that this individual is still a target even after serving time in prison.
Constinia Charbonnette

FIGURE 13–5
Gang Tattoos

networks across the nation are African American. For example, the Bloods and Crips from Los Angeles, the People and Folks from Chicago, and the Detroit gangs are all mostly African American. African American gangs usually identify themselves by wearing certain colors in addition to other identifiers, such as the common hand signs shown in Figure 13–5.

Asian Gangs

California has various types of Asian gangs, including Chinese, Vietnamese, Filipino, Japanese, and Korean groups. The Chinese gangs, especially, have spread to many major cities in the state, and some of the other Asian gangs also are active outside of California. Asian gangs tend to be more organized and have more identifiable leadership than is true of other street gangs. Ko-Lin Chin's examination of Chinese gangs found them involved in some of the worst gang-related violence as well as heroin trafficking, but unlike other ethnic groups, Chinese gangs are closely tied to the social and economic life of their rapidly developing economically robust communities.[57] A study of Vietnamese youth gangs in Southern California found that these youths experience much marginality but attained the American dream by robbing Vietnamese families of large amounts of cash that such families keep at home.[57]

Caucasian Gangs

Until the closing decades of the twentieth century, most gangs were made up of Caucasian youths. Today, according to Reiner, Caucasian adolescents make up about 10 percent of the gang population in the United States.[58] In the 1990s, the West Coast saw a consolidation of lower and middle-class Caucasian youth into groups who referred to themselves as *stoners*. These groups frequently abused drugs and alcohol and listened to heavy metal rock music, and some members practiced Satanism, which includes grave robbing, desecration of human remains, and sacrifice of animals. Stoner groups can be identified by their mode of dress: colored T-shirts with decals of their rock music heroes or bands, Levis, and tennis shoes. The emerging Caucasian gangs across the nation have used many of the symbols of the stoner gangs, especially the heavy metal rock music, but they are not likely to call attention to themselves with their dress, may refer to themselves as neo-Nazi skinheads, and are involved in a variety of hate crimes in addition to drug trafficking.[59]

Gang Behavior Among Female Adolescents

Traditional sociologists once considered the female gang almost a contradiction in terms. However, research in recent decades has brought an increased awareness of adolescent girls joining gangs:

- A few studies have identified female gangs in Philadelphia and New York. Some of the gangs are extremely violent.[60]

- A number of studies have found that adolescent females are connected to adolescent male gangs. The planning is done by the males, who usually exclude the females. But the female gang members would participate in violent crimes and drug-related gang activities.[61]

- Loyalty to the gang rivaled loyalty to the family, and most friends came from within the gang. The gang, according to John C. Quicker, offered "warmth, friends, loyalty, and socialization" as it insulated its members from the harsh environment of the barrio.[62]

- Finn-Aage Esbensen, Elizabeth Piper Deschenes, and L. Thomas Winfree, Jr., found from their analysis of the Denver Youth Survey that girl gang participants committed a wide variety of offenses and at only a slightly lower frequency than did boys involved in gangs.[63] Carl S. Taylor found in Detroit that women frequently were represented in drug-trafficking gangs.[64] Beth Bjerregaard and Carolyn Smith found that involvement in gangs for both females and males was associated with increased levels of delinquency and substance abuse.[65] Joan Moore and John Hagedorn's 2001 summary of the research on female gangs reports that delinquency rates of female gang members are lower than those of male gang members but higher than those of nongang females and males. Female gang members are likely to be involved in property crimes and status offenses, but they commit fewer violent crimes than do their male counterparts. Female gang members are also heavily involved in drug dealing.[66]

- Esbensen and colleagues' findings also failed to support the notion that girls involved in gangs were mere sex objects and ancillary members. This study also showed that girls aged out of gangs before boys and that girls received more emotional fulfillment from their involvement with gang activity.[67]

- Jody Miller, in several articles and in her 2001 book, *One of the Guys* has contributed to what is known about gender dynamics in gangs.[68] From research conducted in St. Louis, Missouri, and Columbus, Ohio, Miller found that a female in a mixed-gender gang, an environment that supports gender hierarchies and the exploitation of young women, must learn to negotiate to survive in the gang milieu.[69] Gang involvement does expose young women to risks of victimization. Young women can choose to be "one of the guys" and expose themselves to higher risks of being arrested, injured, or even killed in conflicts with rival gangs. Or they can use gender to decrease their risk of being harmed by not participating in "masculine" activities such as fighting and committing crime. However, females who opt out of violence and crime are often viewed as lesser members and may expose themselves to greater risks of victimization within their gangs.[70]

In sum, most studies have found that girl gangs still serve as adjuncts to boy gangs. Yet an increasing number of important studies show that female gangs provide girls with the necessary skills to survive in their harsh communities while allowing them a temporary escape from the dismal future awaiting them.[71] What these studies reveal is that girls join gangs for the same basic reasons that boys do—and share with boys in their neighborhood the hopelessness and powerlessness of the urban underclass.[72]

Voices of Delinquency: The Transformer

What Are Emergent Street Gangs?

In the late 1980s and early 1990s, gangs began to appear in most communities of this nation. In G. David Curry and colleagues' 1992 survey of law enforcement departments in the seventy-nine largest U.S. cities, 91 percent of respondents reported the presence of gang problems. These researchers estimated that there were 4,881 gangs with 249,324 gang members; forty cities reported a total of 7,205 gang members. Twenty-seven cities reported that there were eighty-three independent female gangs. Significantly, these cities with emerging gangs reported that juveniles made up 90 percent of the gang membership.[73]

Emergent gangs have been examined in Denver, Colorado; Kansas City, Missouri; Rochester, New York; and Seattle, Washington. These studies generally found that gang members were involved in levels of delinquent activity that were much greater than those of nongang youth, that the participation in gangs increased each year from the late 1980s to the early 1990s, and that these emerging gangs brought new levels of violence to a community.[74] Seven stages of gang development could be identified at the time[75]:

Stage 1: Gang leaders are aware of the ripe drug markets outside the major urban areas throughout the nation. They are also aware that crack cocaine in these new markets would bring a higher price than it does in the saturated urban areas. A plan is developed—which varies little from one drug-trafficking urban gang to another—for a gang member to go to a city without gangs. When he arrives, either by plane or auto, he goes to a low-income minority neighborhood and recruits several juveniles to sell crack cocaine. As part of his sales pitch, this ghetto-based gang member assures these juveniles that the mother gang intends to develop a connection, or satellite, in their community. The recruited juveniles are promised a percentage of the money they make from the drug sales. The adult gang member agrees to return on a regular basis to supply more drugs, to pick up the money, and to check on operations. It is not long before a second and sometimes a third representative of urban-based gang arrives to recruit youths to sell crack cocaine.

Stage 2: By stage 2, the adult gang member has told the youths selling drugs enough about the gang that they are able to identify with it. They can wear the proper clothing,

1. Implementation

2. Expansion and conflict

3. Organization and consolidation

4. Gang intimidation and community reaction

5. Expansion of drug markets

6. Gang takeover

7. Community deterioration

FIGURE 13–6
Stages of Emerging Gangs

can represent the gang signs, and can come together as a group. But their basic activity remains that of selling crack cocaine. One Midwestern youth claimed that he was making $40,000 a month selling crack cocaine for the Almighty Unknown Vice Lords when he was arrested and institutionalized. Competition between these youths who claim to be part of the rival street gangs inevitably results in conflict and sometimes violence. Fights are likely to break out during school functions, at athletic events, and in parks. Weapons may be discharged at this time. Police also become aware that increasing numbers of weapons are being brought into the community.

Stage 3: The organization of the gangs develops during stage 3. Gang membership increases as more youths are brought into the core group. Leadership of the gang is usually assumed by a member of the initial core group, as well as by young adult members of the community. Gang members become more visible at school and at school functions, usually by the colors or clothing they wear and by the gang signs they represent. It is not long before a sizable number of "wannabes" are considering themselves gang members. The process of initiation begins at this time, and pressure is placed especially on African American males to join a gang. White youths also frequently are accepted as part of these developing gangs.

Stage 4: The competition between rival gangs erupts in open conflict in school, at school dances, at athletic events, and in shopping centers. Drugs also are increasingly sold in the school environment. White gangs often appear at this time, but African American gangs are more likely to wear their colors and to demonstrate gang affiliation.

Stage 5: Drugs are openly sold in the school, on street corners, and in shopping centers. Extortion of students and victimization of both teachers and students occurs widely in the public schools. Moreover, the gangs are led by adults who remain in the community, and the organizational structure and numbers of gang members show a significant increase.

Stage 6: The gangs are clearly in control in minority neighborhoods, in the school, at school events, and in shopping centers. The criminal operations of the rival gangs also become more varied during stage 6, including robberies, burglaries, aggravated assaults, and rapes. Citizens' fear of gangs dramatically increases, and the police express the inability to control drug trafficking and violence.

Stage 7: The final stage is characterized by the deterioration of the city as a result of gang control. Citizens move out of the city, stay away from shopping centers, and keep their children home from school. See Figure 13–6.

The Toxicity of Gang Involvement

Youths involved in emergent gangs are sounding more and more like those who are members of urban gangs. Both talk about justice. Justice means that honor is revenged. "I feel that what we did that night wasn't enough. Justice, to me, would have been killing seven or eight of them. Even though only one guy shot my brother, there were three guys there."[76]

Both talk about how gang "bangin'" becomes a way of showing that a youth is "bad." "Shootin' guns and stabbin' people" is how a gang youth shows heart and courage, and killing to many gang youths "ain't nothing." The violence of this substitute family makes a youth feel powerful and connected to something worthwhile. To youths who must deal with hopelessness in so many areas of their lives, the fear of dying makes them feel alive.

Beyond gang youths attempting to make sense of their social world is the reality that gangs are destructive to their members. First, gang youths become involved in dangerous, even deadly, games. As one former gang leader put it, "I've gone to more gang funerals than I can even count."[77] Second, although joining a gang may be a normal rite of passage for a youth, gangs minister poorly to such basic adolescent needs as preparation for marriage and employment and learning to adapt to the adult world. Third, juvenile males who join gangs for protection are exposed to dangers that most nongang juveniles are able to avoid. Fourth, gang youth frequently are victimized by both juvenile and adult members of street

Focus on Offender 13–2
Institutionalized Juvenile Who Went Home and Killed

One of the authors was doing a research project comparing a state and a private facility when he was approached by staff members who inquired whether he would like to talk to all the gang kids. Word quickly got around that this coauthor knew Willie Lloyd, the leader of the Unknown Vice Lords, and so all the gang youths wanted to talk to him, especially the Vice Lords. One young man came into the office to talk when this researcher was interviewing staff youth leaders. They were having a good talk, when suddenly the gang youth announced that he had to go home and kill the Crip who had recently killed his nephew.

He would be released the next week and planned to take care of business.

The researcher tried to talk him out of it, with a variety of reasoning ploys. Nothing worked. He went home the next week, and was soon involved in the killing of a Crip on a drive-by shooting. He is presently doing life without parole for this crime.

CRITICAL THINKING QUESTION

If you were in place of this researcher, what would you have said to this young man?

gangs.[78] Adolescent females who often are exploited sexually by male gang members are an apt example of how gangs victimize younger members. Finally, although joining a gang may provide status and esteem in the present, it also increases the likelihood of incarceration in juvenile and adult facilities.[79] See Focus on the Offender 13–2.

Juveniles who belong to urban street gangs or emerging youth gangs are involved in more serious delinquent acts than are youths who do not belong to gangs. The influence of gang participation on violent behavior has been documented by a number of studies. The studies of gangs in Rochester, New York; Denver, Colorado; and Pittsburgh, Pennsylvania, all found that gang youths committed more violent behaviors than did nongang delinquents and that youths commit more serious and more violent acts when they are gang members than they do after leaving the gang.[80] James C. Howell's examination of youth gang homicides found that the recent growth in youth gang homicides has been driven by increased access to firearms. Yet it appears that gang-related homicides are generally not about drugs but are personal, vendetta-like, and motivated primarily by self-protection.[81]

What Can Communities do to Prevent and Control Youth Gangs?

Communities across the United States have had a tendency to deny that they have gangs even when gang youths are causing serious problems at schools and in the neighborhoods. When an incident takes place, such as the killing of an innocent victim or a shootout, and one or more youths are killed, communities tend to substitute repression for denial. The problem is turned over to the police with the directive to make gangs invisible. Gang units are sometimes established in police departments to focus on getting rid of the gang problem and very often turn to repressive measures that are of little long-term significance.

Attorney General Eric Holder has recently pushed for more innovation- and evidence-based programs in combating the violence of youths and youth gangs. He has urged communities to find out what does work, using the programs that are successful as well as going "outside the box" to solve problems. High Point, North Carolina, has been cited as using a model developed by David Kennedy to target the most violent offenders for prosecution, then going to lower-level drug offenders and saying "This is what will happen to you if you don't get your act straight." The young drug dealers are shown videotapes of them dealing drugs and informed that indictments are being prepared for them unless they change their ways. Job training and mentoring are provided to those who are willing to make the adjustments needed in their lives. As a result, Holder reports, the violent crime rate in High Point dropped 57 percent.[82]

Another example of a successful program is the Summer Night Lights Program in Los Angeles. The city, with the cooperation of community leaders and organizations, keeps the lights on in potentially dangerous parks at night and offers recreational, artistic, and educational programs for youths. Gang violence has decreased in the targeted areas by 40 percent.[83] These programs illustrate some of the principles developed below.

What Does Not Work and What Might Work Very Well?

Irving Spergel and colleagues' 1989 survey of forty-five cities with gang problems identified five strategies of intervention: (1) community organization, including community mobilization and networking; (2) social intervention, focusing on individual behavioral and value change; (3) opportunity provision, emphasizing the improvement of basic education, training, and job opportunities for youth; (4) suppression, focusing on arrest, incarceration, monitoring, and supervision of gang members; and (5) organizational development and change, or the creation of special organizational units as well as procedures.[84]

In examining the implementation of these strategies, Spergel and colleagues found that suppression (44 percent) was most frequently used, followed by social intervention (31.5 percent), organizational development (10.9 percent), community organization (8.9 percent), and opportunity provision (4.8 percent). Community organization was more likely to be used with gang programs in emerging gang cities, whereas social intervention and opportunity provision tended to be primarily the strategies of programs in cities with chronic gang problems. But in only seventeen of the forty-five cities was there any evidence of improvement in the gang situation.[85]

Evidence-Based Practice
Planning and Implementing the Comprehensive Gang Model

With funding that the U.S. Department of Justice provided in March 1993, Spergel began implementing the initial version of the comprehensive Gang Model in the Little Village neighborhood of Chicago, a low-income and working-class community that is about 90 percent Mexican American.

Called the Gang Violence Reduction Program, the project lasted five years. The program focused on providing services to individual gang members, rather than to the gangs as groups. It targeted mainly older members (ages seventeen to twenty-four) of two of the area's most violent Hispanic gangs, the Latin Kings and the Two Six. The program actually targeted more than two hundred of the "shooters," the most influential members or leaders of the two gangs. As a group, these two gangs accounted for about 75 percent of felony gang violence in the Little Village community—including twelve homicides in each of the two years before the start of the project.

The primary goal of the project was to reduce the extremely high level of gang violence among youth who were actively involved in the two gangs. Outreach youth workers—nearly all of whom were former members of the two target gangs—attempted to prevent and control gang conflicts and to persuade gang youth to leave the gang as soon as possible. Outreach activities included a balance of services, such as brief family and individual counseling and referrals for services, crisis intervention, and surveillance and suppression activities.

The process evaluation of the Gang Violence Reduction Program revealed that it was implemented very well. Spergel, in examining the effects of the Little Village project on the approximately two hundred hard-core gang youth during the five years, found the following results:

- Self-reports of criminal involvement revealed that the program reduced serious violent property crimes, as well as the frequency of various types of offenses including robbery, gang intimidation, and drive-by shootings.
- The program was more effective with older, more violent gang offenders than with younger, less violent offenders.
- Active gang involvement was reduced among project youth, mostly for older members, and this change was associated with less criminal activity.
- Most youth in both targeted gangs improved their educational and employment rates during the program period.
- Employment was seen to be associated with a general reduction in youth's criminal activity, particularly in regard to reductions in drug dealing.
- Program youth had significantly fewer total violent crime and drug arrests.
- The project had no significant effect on total arrests, property arrests, or other minor crime arrests.
- Gang violence was on the upswing during the project period of 1992–1997, but the increase in homicides and other serious violent gang crimes was lower among the Latin Kings and Two Six compared with other Latino and African American gangs in the area, which is one of the deadliest gang-violent areas of the city.

Source: *Best Practices to Address Community Gang Problems: OJJDP's Comprehensive Gang Model* (Washington, DC: Office of Justice Programs, Office of Juvenile Justice and Delinquency Prevention, 2012), 37–38, Appendix A.

Spergel and colleagues, in developing a model for predicting general effectiveness in dealing with gang problems, stated:

> A final set of analyses across all cities indicate that the primary strategies of community organization and provision of opportunity along with maximum participation by key community actors is predictive of successful efforts at reducing the gang problems.[86]

What this research by Spergel and colleagues has demonstrated is that only an integrated, multidimensional, community-oriented effort is likely to have any long-term effect in preventing and controlling gangs in the United States. This gang prevention and control model must have several components: (1) the community must take responsibility for developing and implementing this model; (2) this structural model must take seriously the hopelessness arising from the unmet needs of underclass children; (3) prevention programs, especially in the first six years of school, must receive a major emphasis; (4) those who support this model must coordinate all of the gang intervention efforts taking place in a community; and (5) sufficient financial resources must be available for implementing the model. See the Evidence-Based Practice feature.

Juvenile Justice Videos

GANG COUNSELING

Gang Counseling depicts a specialized gang unit within a detention facility. What is the perspective of gang involvement from the correctional officer? From the child psychiatrist? From the juveniles in the facility? Based on the video and the readings from this chapter, what types of programs are available to handle youths associated with gangs? The psychiatrist explains that early intervention is a key aspect in keeping youths out of gangs. From the readings, what early diversionary programs are set up to prevent juveniles from entering gangs?

FORMER WHITE SUPREMACY MEMBER

The *Former White Supremacy Member* video features a former gang member within a juvenile institution. How did the youth become involved with the gang? The youth explains the benefits of being locked up. According to the youth what are some of the "upsides" of being incarcerated? Another juvenile in the institution compares the juvenile facility to the adult facility. Why does the youth say he would rather be in the adult prison? Discuss. Based on the video and the readings from this chapter, do institutions offer treatment programs for gang members who plan on being released back into the public? Discuss.

SUMMARY

LEARNING OBJECTIVE 1 Outline the development of gangs in the United States.

Gangs started out in the 1920s as transitory groups; gangs in the 1950s in urban areas in the east became groups of youth fighting each other and protecting "turf"; the supergangs developed in Los Angeles and Chicago in the 1960s; the 1970s, 1980s, and 1990s were the decades when urban gangs were taken over by adults, accompanied by drug trafficking and violence; and the 2000s to the present have seen a decrease in some gangs and but the growth of ethnic gangs. Much is the same and much is new about youth gangs.

LEARNING OBJECTIVE 2 Describe the behaviors and activities of gangs.

Adolescents who find that their needs are not met in social contacts with family members, teachers, and leaders and participation in churches, school activities, and community organizations are more likely to be attracted to street gangs and youth gangs. These gangs become quasi-families offering acceptance, status, and esteem. Most gang activity consists of simply "hanging out," but some focus also takes place on committing unlawful acts. What is new is the widespread use of gun violence, particularly involving automatic and semiautomatic handguns; the juvenile drug trafficking that takes place now much more than in the past; and the frequency with which youth gangs become street gangs with adults as leaders. Juveniles are often in the minority in these urban street gangs. Gangs have thrived because of the poverty in urban neighborhoods. The hopelessness of these environments makes drug trafficking attractive and gang membership desirable even with the high possibility of being injured, killed, or imprisoned.

LEARNING OBJECTIVE 3 Identify the primary types of gangs.

Scavenger gangs: Prey on those unable to defend themselves.

Territorial gangs: Defend an area in which they claim ownership.

Corporate gangs: Organized crime groups whose main purpose is participation in illegal money-making ventures.

Hedonistic gangs: Basic purpose is to get high and have a good time.

Instrumental gangs: Focus is on economic gain.

Predatory gangs: Commit a variety of crimes, use and sell cocaine, and purchase more sophisticated weapons to achieve their purposes.

Type 1 gangs: Involved in minor delinquent activities and drug use.

Type 2 gangs: Heavily involved in several types of drug sales.

Type 3 gangs: Little involvement in drug sales but more involvement in both serious and nonserious offenses.

Type 4 gangs: Extensively involved in drug use, drug sales, and serious and nonserious offenses.

LEARNING OBJECTIVE 4 Identify the seven stages of emergent gang development.

The seven stages of emergent gang development are (1) implementation, (2) expansion and conflict, (3) organization and consolidation, (4) gang intimidation and community reaction, (5) expansion of drug markets, (6) gang takeover, and (7) community deterioration.

LEARNING OBJECTIVE 5 Summarize efforts to prevent and control gangs.

The number of gang members, as well as the number of youth gangs, decreased from the late 1990s to the present. Youth gangs remain a problem throughout the United States; even small towns and rural areas often must contend with the presence of youth gangs. Grassroots community groups seem to make the most sense in reducing the spread of gangs, but gang reduction actually depends on providing at-risk children with more positive options than they have today.

KEY TERMS

corporate gangs, p. 272
crack, p. 272
drug trafficking, p. 274
emergent gangs, p. 279
gang leadership, p. 272
hedonistic gangs, p. 272

instrumental gangs, p. 272
methods of initiation, p. 273
migration, p. 274
organized crime groups, p. 276
predatory gangs, p. 272
scavenger gangs, p. 272

supergangs, p. 266
territorial gangs, p. 272
underclass theory, p. 271
urban gangs, p. 264

REVIEW QUESTIONS

1. Why are adolescents likely to become involved in youth gangs?
2. How have youth gangs changed throughout the years?
3. If you had the opportunity to teach a class of high school students, most of whom were in youth gangs, what would you say to them?

4. Why is community participation the most effective means of gang prevention and control?
5. Why do you believe gang participation and membership decreased in the final years of the twentieth century?

GROUP EXERCISES

1. *Class Presentation:* Have class groups use the Internet to look up the different ethnic group gangs in the United States such as the Jamaican Posse and Chinese and Vietnamese gangs. Have each group choose one of the ethnic group gangs and report to class on the gang's itinerary, age of members, numbers, and modes of operation.
2. *Group Work:* Discuss the different types of urban gangs as described by researchers. Identify the different classifications described.

3. *Writing to Learn Exercise:* Write a paragraph or two describing the organizational features of urban gangs. Critique and revise.
4. *Writing to Learn Exercise:* Discuss in two paragraphs the different toxic effects of gangs on the community and the school. Critique and revise.
5. *Group Work:* Discuss the seven stages involved in the development of emergent street gangs.
   - **Research Center:** check out the Cybrary and MySearchLab for even more resources

NOTES

1. Interviewed in 1995.
2. Arlen Egley, Jr., and James C. Howell, *Highlights of the 2009 National Youth Gang Survey* (Washington, DC: Office of Juvenile Justice and Delinquency Prevention, 2011).

3. See the section on law-violating behaviors of juveniles for studies supporting these conclusions.
4. Luc Sante, *Low Life: Lures and Snares of Old New York* (New York: Vintage Books, 1991).

5. Robert Redfield, *Folk Culture of Yucatan* (Chicago: University of Chicago Press, 1941).

6. Frederick Thrasher, *The Gang: A Study of 1,313 Gangs in Chicago* (Chicago: University of Chicago Press, 1927).

7. Ibid.

8. See Walter B. Miller, "The Impact of a Total Community Delinquency Control Project," *Social Problems* 10 (Fall 1962), 168–91.

9. John C. Quicker and Akil S. Batani-Khalfani, "Clique Succession Among South Los Angeles Street Gangs, the Case of the Crips," paper presented at the annual meeting of the American Society of Criminology, Reno, NV, November 1989.

10. National Youth Gang Center, *National Youth Gang Survey Analysis 2007* (Washington, DC: Office of Juvenile Justice and Delinquency Prevention, National Youth Gang Center, 2007), at http://www.jjr.com/nygc/nygsa.

11. Thrasher, The Gang p.57

12. Finn-Aage Esbensen and David Huizinga, "Gangs, Drugs, and Delinquency in a Survey of Urban Youth," *Criminology* 31 (1993), 565–89.

13. James C. Howell, *OJJDP Fact Sheet* (Washington, DC: Office of Juvenile Justice and Delinquency Prevention, 1997). For an update, see James C. Howell, *Gangs in America's Communities* (Los Angeles: Sage, 2012).

14. See Arlen Egley, Jr., James C. Howell, and Aline K. Major, *National Youth Gang Survey, 1999–2001* (Washington, DC: Office of Juvenile Justice and Delinquency Prevention, 2006), 18. For an update, see Howell, *Gangs in America's Communities*.

15. For the role behavior of juveniles in gangs, see Mike Carlie, *Into the Abyss: A Personal Journal into the World of Street Gangs,* at http://people.missouristate.edu/MichaelCarlie.

16. James C. Howell, "Youth Gangs: An Overview," *Juvenile Justice Bulletin* (Washington, DC: Office of Justice Programs, Office of Juvenile Justice and Delinquency Prevention, 1998). See also Scott H. Decker and B. Van Winkle, *Life in the Gang: Family, Friends, and Violence* (New York: Cambridge University Press, 1996).

17. Interviewed in 1982 at the Iowa State Penitentiary in Ft. Madison, Iowa.

18. H. A. Bloch and A. Niederhoffer, *The Gang: A Study in Adolescent Behavior* (New York: Philosophica Library, 1958).

19. Richard A. Cloward and Lloyd E. Ohlin,

20. Albert K. Cohen, *Delinquent Boys: The Culture of the Gang* (Glencoe, IL: Free Press, 1955).

21. Walter B. Miller, "Lower-Class Culture as a Generating Milieu of Gang Delinquency," *Journal of Social Issues* 14 (1958), 5–19.

22. Lewis Yablonsky, *The Violent Gang* (New York: Macmillan, 1962).

23. See William Julius Wilson, *The Truly Disadvantaged: The Inner City, the Underclass, and Public Policy* (Chicago: University of Chicago Press, 1987).

24. G. David Curry and Irving A. Spergel, "Gang Homicide, Delinquency, and Community," *Criminology* (1988), 381–405.

25. J. E. Fagan, "Gangs, Drugs, and Neighborhood Change," in *Gangs in America*, edited by C. Ronald Huff (Newbury Park, CA: Sage Publications, 1990), 39–74.

26. Martin Sánchez Jankowski, *Island in the Streets: Gangs and American Urban Society* (Berkeley: University of California Press, 1991), 138.

27. Carl S. Taylor, *Dangerous Society* (East Lansing: Michigan State University Press, 1990), 4–7.

28. C. Ronald Huff, "Youth Gangs and Public Policy," *Crime and Delinquency* 35 (October 1989), 528–29.

29. Jeffrey Fagan, "The Social Organization of Drug Use and Drug Dealing Among Urban Gangs," *Criminology* 27 (1989), 633–64.

30. Jankowski, *Islands in the Streets*, 5.

31. Ibid., 64–67.

32. Joan Moore, Diego Vigil, and Robert Garcia, "Residence and Territoriality in Chicago Gangs," *Social Problems* 31 (December 1985), 182–94.

33. Conversations with urban gang chiefs in 1996.

34. Carlie, Island in the Streets

35. Cheryl L. Maxson, Malcolm W. Klein, and Lea C. Cunningham, "Street Gangs and Drug Sales," report to the National Institute of Justice (1993).

36. National Youth Gang Center, *National Youth Gang Survey Analysis 2007*.

37. Drug Enforcement Administration, *Crack Cocaine Availability and Trafficking in the United States* (Washington, DC: U.S. Department of Justice, 1988).

38. Shay Bilchik, *1997 National Youth Gang Survey* (Washington, DC: Office of Juvenile Justice and Delinquency Prevention, December 1999), 25.

39. Ibid., 24.

40. Ibid., 40.

41. Arlen Egley, Jr., and Aline K. Major, *Highlights of the 2002 National Youth Gang Surveys* (Washington, DC: U.S. Government Printing Office), 1.

42. See C. Ronald Huff, *Criminal Behavior of Gang Members and At-Risk Youths: Research Preview* (Washington, DC: National Institute of Research, 1998), 1.

43. Ibid., 1–2.

44. Ibid., 1.

45. Terence P. Thornberry, "Membership in Youth Gangs and Involvement in Serious and Violent Offending," in *Serious and Violent Juvenile Offenders: Risk Factors and Successful Intervention*, edited by R. Loeber and D. P. Farrington (Thousand Oaks, CA: Sage Publications, 1998), 147–66.

46. Sara R. Battin-Pearson et al., "Gang Membership, Delinquent Peers, and Delinquent Behavior," *Juvenile Justice Bulletin* (Washington, DC: Office of Justice Programs, Office of Juvenile Justice and Delinquency Prevention, 1998).

47. David Huizinga, "Gangs and the Volume of Crime," paper presented at the annual meeting of the Western Society of Criminology, Honolulu, HI, 1997.

48. Sara R. Battin et al., "The Contribution of Gang Membership to Delinquency: Beyond Delinquent Friends," *Criminology* 36 (February 1998), 93–115.

49. Finn-Aage Esbensen,

50. James C. Howell, "Youth Gangs."

51. National Institute for Intergovernmental Research, *National Youth Gang Survey Analysis* (2009), at http://www.iir.com/nygc/nygsa/measuring_the_extent_of_gang_problem.htm.

52. Scott H. Decker, Tim Bynum, and Deborah Weisel, "A Tale of Two Cities: Gangs as Organized Crime Groups," *Justice Quarterly* 15 (September 1998), 395–425.

53. James McCormick, "The 'Disciples' of Drugs and Death," *Newsweek* (February 5, 1996), 56–

54. For an excellent examination of the Bloods and Crips and other California gangs, see Howell, *Gangs in America's Communities*

55. U.S. General Accounting Office, *Nontraditional Organized Crime* (Washington, DC: U.S. Government Printing Office, 1989).

56. Robert Walker, "Maria Salvatrucha MS-14 or US," at http://www.gangsorus.com/mariasalvatrucha13.html.

57. James Diego Vigil and Steve Chong Yun, "Vietnamese Youth Gangs in Southern California," in *Gangs in America,* 146–62

58. Reiner, *Gangs, Violence, and Crime in Los Angeles*.

59. See Pete Simi, Lowell Smith, and Ann M. S. Reiner, "From Punk Kids to Public Enemy Number One," *Deviant Behavior* 29 (2009), 753–74.

60. Freda Adler, *Sisters in Crime: The Rise of the New Female Criminal* (New York: McGraw-Hill, 1975); W. B. Miller, "The Molls," *Society* 11 (1973), 32–35; E. Ackley and B. Fliegel, "A Social Work Approach to Street Corner Girls," *Social Work* 5 (1960), 29–31; Peggy C. Giordano, "Girls, Guys and Gangs: The Changing Social Context of Female Delinquency," *Journal of Criminal Law and Criminology* 69 (1978), 130.

61. Lee Bowker and Malcolm W. Klein, "Female Participation in Delinquent Gang Motivation," *Adolescence* 15 (1980), 509–19; John C. Quicker, *Home Girls: Characterizing Chicano Gangs* (San Pedro, CA: International University Press, 1983).

62. Quicker, *Home Girls*.

63. Finn-Agee Esbensen, Elizabeth Piper Deschenes, and L. Thomas Winfee, Jr., "Differences between Gang Girls and Gang Boys: Results from a Multi-site Survey," *Youth and Society* 31 (1999), 27–53.

64. Carl S. Taylor, *Girls, Gangs, Women and Drugs* (East Lansing: Michigan State University Press, 1993), 48.

65. Beth Bjerregaard and Carolyn Smith, "Gender Differences in Gang Participation, Delinquency, and Substance Abuse," *Journal of Quantitative Criminology* 9 (1993), 347–48.

66. Joan Moore and John Hagedorn, "Female Gangs: A Focus on Research," *Juvenile Justice Bulletin* (Washington, DC: Office of Juvenile Justice and Delinquency Prevention, 2001).

67. Finn-Aage Esbensen, Elizabeth Piper Deschenes, and L. Thomas Winfree Jr., "Differences Between Gang Girls and Gang Boys: Results from a Multi-Site Survey," paper presented at the Annual Meeting of the Academy of Criminal Justice Sciences in Albuquerque, NM, 1998, 20–21.

68. Jody Miller, "Gender and Victimization Risk Among Young Women in Gangs," *Journal of Research in Crime and Delinquency* 35 (November 1998), 429–53; Jody Miller and Rod K. Brunson, "Gender Dynamics in Youth Gangs: A Comparison of Males' and Females' Accounts," *Justice Quarterly* 17 (September 2000), 420–47; Jody Miller and Scott Decker, "Young Women and Gang Violence: Gender, Street Offending, and Violent Victimization in Gangs," *Justice Quarterly* 18 (March 2001), 115–39; Jody Miller, *One of the Guys: Girls, Gangs, and Gender* (New York: Oxford University Press, 2001).

69. Miller and Brunson, "Gender Dynamics in Youth Gangs," 443–45.

70. Miller, "Gender and Victimization Risk Among Young Women in Gangs"; Miller

71. Karen Joe and Meda Chesney-Lind, "Just Every Mother's Angel: An Analysis of Gender and Ethnic Variations in Youth Gang Membership," paper presented at the annual meeting of the American Society of Criminology, Phoenix, AZ, November 1993, 9.

72. Ibid.

73. G. David Curry, Robert J. Fox, Richard A. Ball, and Darryl Stone, "National Assessment of Law Enforcement Anti-Gang Information Resources," report to the U.S. Department of Justice, National Institute of Justice (1993).

74. For a review of gang research, including that of emergent gangs, see James C. Howell, "Recent Gang Research: Program and Policy Implications," *Crime and Delinquency* 40 (October 1994), 491–515. For the study in Denver, see Finn-Aage Esbensen and David Huizinga, "Gangs, Drugs, and Delinquency in a Survey of Urban Youth," *Criminology* 31 (1993), 565–89. For the study in Kansas City, Missouri, and Seattle, Washington, see Mark S. Fleisher, "Youth Gangs and Social Networks: Observations from a Long-Term Ethnographic Study," paper presented at the annual meeting of the American Society of Criminology, Miami, FL, November 1994. For the study in Rochester, New York, see Terence P. Thornberry et al., "The Role of Juvenile Gangs in Facilitating Delinquent Behavior," *Journal of Research in Crime and Delinquency* 30 (1993), 55–87.

75. These stages were developed as a result of one of the authors' examination of these emerging gangs.

76. Howell, "Recent Gang Research."

77. Ibid.

78. One of the authors interviewed gang members in 1996.

79. For example, see Felix Padilla's *The Gang as an Ethnic Enterprise* (New Brunswick, NJ: Rutgers University Press, 1992) for the way the youths who traffick drugs for the gang are victimized. For a discussion of the destructiveness of gangs to their members, see James F. Short, Jr., "Gangs, Neighborhood, and Youth Crime," *Criminal Justice Research Bulletin* 3 (1990), 3.

80. Thornberry, "Membership in Youth Gangs and Involvement in Serious and Violent Offending," 147–66.

81. James C. Howell, "Youth Gang Homicides: A Literature Review," *Crime and Delinquency* 45 (April 1999), 208–41.

82. Attorney General Eric Holder, *Remarks Prepared for the White House Conference on Gang Violence Prevention and Crime Control* (Washington, DC: The White House, August 24, 2009), http://www.usdoj.gov/ag/speeches/ag-speech-090824.html.

83. Ibid.

84. I. A. Spergel et al., *Survey of Youth Gang Problems and Programs in 45 Cities and 6 Sites*. Tech. Report No. 2, National Youth Gang Suppression and Intervention Project (Chicago: University of Chicago, School of Social Service Administration, 1989), 211.

85. Ibid., 212.

86. Ibid., 211.

14 Drugs and Youthful Offending

Simone van den Berg/Shutterstock

Learning Objectives

1. Describe how much drug use there is among adolescents in the United States.

2. Identify the main types of drugs used by adolescents.

3. Describe the different types of drug users, drug traffickers, and the relationship of drug use and delinquency.

4. Discuss the theoretical explanations related to the onset of drug use.

5. Summarize what can be done to prevent and control drug use among adolescents in the United States.

A 2011 report by the Office of Juvenile Justice and Delinquency Prevention (OJJDP) draws attention to the fact that research has consistently found that substance abuse among adolescents is linked to serious juvenile offending.[1] That finding was additionally supported by research from the ongoing OJJDP-sponsored Pathways to Desistance Study. The Pathway study is a large collaborative, multidisciplinary project that is currently following 1,354 serious juvenile offenders (both male and female) ages fourteen to eighteen for seven years after their adjudication as delinquent. The study is exploring factors that lead juveniles who have committed serious offenses to continue offending or to desist from offending. Some of these factors include individual maturation, life changes, drug use, and involvement with the criminal justice system. A significant major finding of the study to date is that substance abuse treatment reduces both the use of illegal substances and criminal offending. The adolescent offenders profiled in the Pathway to Desistance Study initially self-reported very high levels of substance use and substance abuse problems. The use of illegal substances was linked to other illegal activities that were also engaged in by the study participants. As such, substance abuse was found to be a strong, prevalent predictor of offending. The presence of a drug or alcohol disorder and the level of substance use were both shown to be strongly and independently related to the level of self-reported offending and the number of arrests. "The good news," say researchers involved in the study, "is that treatment appears to reduce both substance abuse and offending." According to these authors, "Youth whose treatment lasted for at least 90 days and included significant family involvement showed significant reductions in alcohol use, marijuana use, and offending over the following 6 months.[2]

I n addition to the news cited in the chapter-opening vignette, other good news comes from findings that substance abuse among adolescents had dropped dramatically since the late 1970s.[3] The bad news is that drug use has significantly increased among high-risk youths and is becoming commonly linked to juvenile lawbreaking. More juveniles are selling drugs than ever before in the history of this nation. Furthermore, the spread of AIDS within populations of intravenous drug users and their sex partners adds to the gravity of the substance abuse problem.

Adolescent drug use becomes abuse only when the user becomes dysfunctional (e.g., is unable to attend or perform in school or to maintain family and social relationships; exhibits dangerous, reckless, or aggressive behavior; or endangers his or her health). The drug-dependent compulsive user's life generally revolves around obtaining, maintaining, and using a supply of drugs.[4] See Focus on Offender 14–1 for the story of one adolescent whose drug use was out of control.

Drug Use Among Adolescents

Society tends to focus on juveniles' use of harder drugs, although alcohol remains the drug of choice for most adolescents. Drug use among adolescents was extremely high during the late 1960s into the 1970s, reaching epidemic proportions. Overall rates of illicit drug use

Focus on Offenders 14–1
They Call Me Spacey

I started using drugs when I was eight years old. It makes you feel like you can beat anything that comes along. I thought, "Wow, this is great!" When I was nine, someone asked me if I wanted to take some acid. I figured, sure, why not? This was really great because I could sit around and watch the walls melt. My English teacher deteriorated in her chair one time at school. As the years went by, I started to peddle a lot of speed and acid. Pretty soon, I was drug dependent. I needed speed in the morning, and I had to take speed in school to make it through the day. I got to the point that I couldn't handle speed anymore. I was too juiced up. Now I regret doing so many drugs because I can't remember simple things that I should remember, like talking with someone over the phone the night before. I became spacey; in fact, people have called me spacey for two years now.

Source: Interviewed by one of the authors.

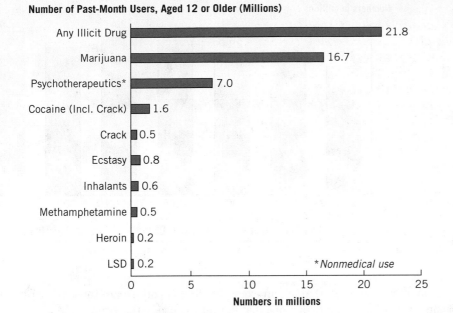

Number of Past-Month Users, Aged 12 or Older (Millions)

FIGURE 14–1
Users of an Illicit Drug in the Past Month in 2010

*Nonmedical use

TABLE 14–1
Percentages of High School Students Reporting Drug Use, 2009

Student Drug Use	Eighth Grade	Tenth Grade	Twelfth Grade
Past-month use	8.1%	17.8%	23.3%
Annual use	14.5	29.4	36.5
Lifetime use	19.9	36.0	46.7

Source: Adopted from Lloyd D. Johnston, Patrick M. O'Malley, Jeraid G. Bachman, and John E. Schulenberg, *Monitoring the Future: National Results on Adolescent Drug Use* (Washington, DC: National Institutes of Health, 2010), Tables 5, 6 and 7.

Voices of Delinquency: I Just Got Caught Up

appeared to peak sometime around 1979 and then leveled off, but even with the leveling off that took place, rates of illegal drug among juveniles remained high for some time. Then, in 2001, there was a significant downturn in drug use levels.[5] According to the 2010 *Mentoring the Future* study, overall illicit drug use by youths continued to decline until 2008, after which increased use of some drugs began to occur.[6]

According to the *2010 National Survey on Drug Use and Health*, an estimated 22.6 million adolescents ages twelve or older were current illicit drug use users, which means they had used an illegal drug during the month prior to the survey interview. Illicit drugs include marijuana/hashish, cocaine (including crack), MDMA (Ecstasy), methamphetamine, heroin, hallucinogens, inhalants, and prescription-type psychotherapeutic drugs.[7] The survey documented increases in the specific categories of prescription drugs, marijuana, Ecstasy, and methamphetamine. The increasing use of illegal drugs was driven by a significant increase in current use of marijuana (from 5.8 to 6.9 percent). See Figure 14–1.

Table 14–1 lists the 2010 percentage of students reporting drug use in the past month, in the past year, and over their lifetime.

What Are the Main Types of Drugs?

The licit and illicit drugs that are used by adolescents, in decreasing order of frequency, are alcohol, tobacco, marijuana, cocaine, methamphetamine, inhalants, sedatives, stimulants (amphetamines and hallucinogens), and heroin. The licit drugs are permitted for users age eighteen and older (for tobacco) and twenty-one and older (for alcohol). The illicit drugs

FIGURE 14–2
Past-Year Cigarette Initiates Among
Persons Ages Twelve or Older, by Age
at First Use, 2002–2008

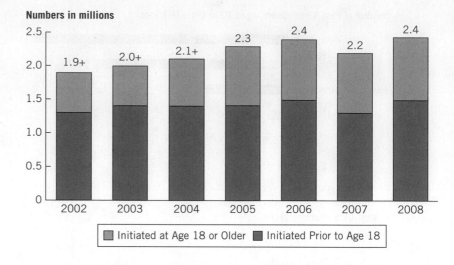

Numbers in millions

Legend: ■ Initiated at Age 18 or Older   ■ Initiated Prior to Age 18

are forbidden by law. Drugs that are an exception to this pattern are those prescribed by a physician, or marijuana in jurisdictions that permit the use of this drug.

Alcohol and Tobacco

What makes **alcohol** so dangerous is that it relaxes inhibitions, and adolescents participate in risky behavior while under its influence. Adolescents' alcohol use is further linked to fights, property damage, academic failure, occupational problems, and conflicts with law enforcement officials.[8] Juveniles who are under the influence of alcohol may commit unlawful acts that they otherwise would not.

Tobacco is often neglected in a discussion of drugs. Even though nicotine is not considered a mind-altering drug, considerable evidence exists that tobacco users suffer severe health consequences from prolonged use and also subject others to the same consequences. A 2000 analysis quantified the major factors contributing to death in the United States and found that tobacco contributed to 435,000 deaths annually, whereas alcohol contributed to 85,000 deaths, whereas all illicit drugs combined contributed to 20,000 deaths.[9] See Figure 14–2.

Marijuana and Hashish

Marijuana is produced from the leaves of *Cannabis sativa*. Hashish (hash) is a concentrated form of cannabis made from unadulterated resin from the female plant. The main active ingredient in both marijuana and hashish is tetrahydrocannabinol (THC), which is a mild hallucinogen. One indication of the popularity of marijuana is the many names given to it, including *Acapulco Gold, A-bomb, Aunt Mary, baby, ashes, African black bammy, California red, birchwood, Columbian gold, gigglewood, golden leaf, dope, grass, hay joints, Mexican green, pot, reefer, Panama gold, reefer weed, shit stinkweed, seaweed, weed,* BC and *Texas tea.*[10]

Debates have been going on for some time concerning the hazards of using marijuana. In the short run, smoking small amounts produces an early excitement ("high") that can lead to drowsiness. In the long run, smoking large amounts of pot can cause distortions in visual and auditory perception. Research in the 1980s documented more ill effects of long-term marijuana use than had been recognized before. For example, several studies concluded that marijuana smoking combines the hazardous features of alcohol and tobacco, as well as containing a number of pitfalls of its own. These studies further suggested that long-term marijuana use can have harmful effects on the vital systems of the body, on the brain, on immunity and resistance, and on sex organs and reproduction.[11]

▲ Marijuana.
Drug Enforcement Administration

Cocaine

Cocaine is the powder derivative of the coca plant. When it was introduced in 1860, it was considered a medical breakthrough that could relieve depression and fatigue, and it quickly became a staple of patent medicines. When its addictive qualities and dangerousness became apparent, its use was controlled by the Pure Food and Drug Act of 1906.

Street names for cocaine include *coke, lady, snow, nose candy, toot,* and *Super Fly.* The main source of cocaine is Colombia, and its distribution has become a diplomatic issue in many Central and South American countries. At one time, cocaine was believed to be less addicting than other illegal drugs. However, users crave the extreme mood elevation, elation, grandiose feelings, and heightened physical prowess that cocaine induces. When these begin to wane, a corresponding deep depression is experienced. Users feel strongly motivated to use the drug again to restore the euphoria.

Snorting (inhaling) is the most common method of using cocaine. Freebasing became popular in the 1980s. Freebase cocaine is derived from a chemical process in which the purified cocaine is crystallized. The crystals are then crushed and smoked in a special heated glass pipe. Smoking freebase cocaine provides a quicker, more potent rush and a more powerful high than does regular cocaine. The intravenous use of cocaine produces a powerful high, generally within fifteen to twenty seconds. A related method is the intravenous use of cocaine along with another drug, which is known as *speedballing.* Speedballing intensifies the effect but can be extremely dangerous. It was speedballing that killed actor-comedian John Belushi in 1982.[12]

Crack is processed street cocaine. Its manufacture involves using baking soda (sodium bicarbonate) or ammonia to remove the hydrochlorides to create a crystalline form of cocaine that can be smoked. Crack gets its name from the fact that the sodium bicarbonate frequently emits a crackling sound when it is smoked. It is known by users as *bricks, boulders, eight-ball* (large rocks), *doo-wap* (two rocks), and *crumbs.* Crack is generally smoked in special glass pipes or makeshift smoking devices. It is also smoked with marijuana in cigarettes, which are called *pin joints, geek joints,* or *lack joints.* A *shotgun,* which is secondary smoke exhaled from one crack user into the mouth of another, also can provide the desired high.

Methamphetamine

Methamphetamine is a synthetic drug otherwise known by its street names *meth, crank, ice, chalk, glass,* and *crystal meth,* to name just a few. This highly addictive stimulant can be snorted, smoked, or injected. Its effects last for up to eight hours (with an initial rush at the beginning and a less intensive high for the duration). Use of this drug makes an individual feel awake, aware, and happy, but also agitated and paranoid.

According to the *2002 National Household Survey on Drug Abuse,* 12.3 million (5.3 percent) of Americans over the age of twelve had used methamphetamine in their lifetime. About 1.5 million (0.7 percent) had used it in the previous year (2001–2002), and 597,000 (0.3 percent) had used it in the previous month.[13] The use of meth stabilized in the United States in 2007 and its domestic manufacture has dropped since 2004.[14] It was formerly concentrated in California (especially in the San Diego area) but has spread to other states in the West and to states in the South and the Midwest. See Table 14–2.

Inhalants

Adolescents use many types of **inhalants**, but what these drugs have in common is that youths have to inhale the vapors to receive the high that they seek.

▲ Cocaine.
Drug Enforcement Administration

▲ Crystal methamphetamine.
Drug Enforcement Administration

▲ The judge holding this photo of a crystal meth user is trying to impress upon her the devastating effects of this exceedingly dangerous drug. The woman is being confronted with a photo of her both before and after her use of the drug.
ZUMA Press/Newscom

TABLE 14–2
Percentage of Students Reporting Methamphetamine Use, 2004 and 2010

	Eighth Grade		Tenth Grade		Twelfth Grade	
	2004	2010	2004	2010	2004	2010
Past-month use	0.6%	0.5%	1.3%	0.67%	%	1.2%
Past-year use	1.5	1.2	3.0	1.6	3.4	1.0
Lifetime use	2.5	1.6	5.3	2.8	3.4	2.4

Source: Adapted from Lloyd D. Johnston, Patrick M. O'Malley, Jerald K. Bachman, and John E. Schulenberg, *Monitoring the Future: National Survey Results en Drug Use,* 1975–2010, Volume I (Washington, DC: National Institutes of Health, 2011), Tables D-84.

Butyl nitrite, commonly called *RUSH*, is one frequently used inhalant. It is packaged in small bottles and can often be found in adult bookstores, as well as on the street. Chlorohydrocarbons and hydrocarbons—which can be inhaled directly from gasoline, paint thinner, glue, or aerosol cans—are other inhalants that are easier for youthful drug users to obtain.

The use of these drugs can bring a feeling of excitement that is frequently followed by a disorientation accompanied by slurred speech and a feeling of sleepiness. The use of inhalants can also be followed by mild to severe headaches as well as nosebleeds. Chronic use of some inhalants is associated with injury to the liver and kidneys and other neurological damage.[15]

Sedatives

Many different forms of **sedatives**, or barbiturates, are used by youth. What is common to all of these barbiturates is that they are taken orally and affect the user by depressing the nervous system and inducing a drowsy condition. On the street, barbiturates are known by the color of their capsule. Seconal pills are known as *reds,* Amytas are called *blue devils,* and Tuinals are known as *rainbows.* Methaqualone, another popular sedative, is known as *Quaaludes* or *ludes* on the street.

Adolescents frequently abuse prescription drugs. Benzodiazepines (minor tranquilizers or sedatives) are among the most widely prescribed drugs. Libriu and Valium are commonly prescribed for anxiety or sleep disorders, and adolescents can obtain them by simply raiding their parents' medicine cabinets. When used in combination with other controlled substances, these prescription drugs produce effects similar to those of alcohol and barbiturates.[16]

The overuse of these and other legitimate drugs have caused a number of celebrity deaths over the years including those of Anna Nicole Smith, Heath Ledger, and Michael Jackson.[17]

Amphetamines

Amphetamines were first made in Germany in the 1880s, but it was not until World War II that they were first used in the United States. All of the military branches issued Benzedrine, Dexedrine, and other amphetamines to relieve fatigue and anxiety, especially in battle conditions. Amphetamines became more readily available after the war and were used widely by truck drivers who had to stay alert for extended periods of time, by people attempting to lose weight, by students studying for examinations, and by people seeking relief from nasal congestion. Street names for amphetamines included *bennies, black beauties, King Kong pills, pinks,* and *purple hearts.*[18]

By the early 1990s, MDMA and methamphetamine arrived on the drug scene in the United States. MDMA, which had been used by psychiatrists and other therapists because of its therapeutic benefits, had become a Schedule I drug by 1986, which meant that its manufacture, distribution, and sale violated federal law. Yet it maintained some popularity among undergraduate

▲ Ecstasy (MDMA)
Drug Enforcement Administration

populations across the nation. **Ecstasy**, the common name for MDMA, became popular on college campuses and with adolescents; it was widely used at parties, sometimes called *raves* in the United States but more often in the United Kingdom. Ecstasy usually is ingested orally in tablet or capsule form, sometimes snorted, and occasionally smoked. MDMA is reported to produce profound pleasurable effects, such as acute euphoria and positive changes in self-confidence and attitude.[19] Ecstasy and various other substances are often called *club drugs*.

Hallucinogens

A variety of hallucinogens have been available over the years to adolescents interested in embracing mind-expanding experiences. Leading the parade has been D-lysergic acid diethylamide, usually known as *LSD*. Public reaction in the late 1960s against LSD and other psychedelic substances resulted in a dramatic decline in their use in the 1970s.

PCP, or phencyclidine, a nervous system excitant that has analgesic, anesthetic, and hallucinogenic properties, was introduced in the late 1960s and became popular during the 1970s. First marketed as the Peace Pill, PCP was also known as *angel dust, animal tank, aurora borealis, buzz, devil dust, DOA, dummy dust, elephant, elephant juice, goon, THC,* and *rocket fuel*. The use of PCP began to decline in 1979, as it became apparent just how dangerous this drug was, and continued to decline until 2004, when it reached its lowest prevalence point to date at 0.7 percent.[20]

Heroin

Opium, which is derived from certain species of poppy, is the source of **heroin**, morphine, paregoric, and codeine, some of which are used medically. Heroin, a refined form of morphine, was introduced at about the turn of the twentieth century and has such street names as *horse, shit, smack, H, harry, henry, boy, brown,* and *black tar*.[21]

The danger of heroin overdose has for several decades marked heroin as a very dangerous drug. Although chronic heroin use, unlike the use of most other drugs, appears to produce relatively minor direct or permanent physiological damage, street heroin users typically neglect themselves and, consequently, report such disorders as heart and lung abnormalities, scarred veins, weight loss, malnutrition, endocarditis (a disease of the heart valves), strokes, gynecological problems, hepatic problems, local skin infections, and abscesses.[22]

Anabolic Steroids

Adolescents, college athletes, and professional athletes use highly dangerous **anabolic steroids** to gain muscle bulk and strength. Baseball players, such as Mark McGuire, Sammy Sosa, and Barry Bonds, all of whom have become baseball's greatest homerun hitters, have been accused of steroid use. Black-market sales of these drugs approach $1 billion annually. Long-term users may spend up to $400 a week on steroids. Steroids have a number of health problems associated with their long-term use: liver ailments, tumors, kidney problems, sexual dysfunction, hypertension, and mental problems such as depression. Also, steroid users frequently share needles, which puts them at high risk for contracting human immunodeficiency virus (HIV), the virus that causes AIDS.[23] See Table 14–3.

▲ Anabolic steroids.
Drug Enforcement Administration

TABLE 14–3
Reported Steroid Use by Grade Level

	Eighth Grade	Tenth Grade	Twelfth Grade
Past-month use	0.4%	0.59%	1.0%
Past-year use	0.8	0.8	1.5
Lifetime use	1.4	1.4	2.0

Source: Adapted from Lloyd D. Johnston, Patrick M. O'Malley, Jerald G. Bachman, and John E. Schulenberg, Monitoring the Future: National Results on Adolescent Drug Use (Washington, DC: National Institutes of Health, 2010), Tables 1, 3, and 7.

FIGURE 14-3
Percentage of Twelfth Graders Reporting Past-Year Use of Pharmaceuticals and Other Drugs

Source: University of Michigan, *2011 Monitoring the Future Study*.

▲ Prescription drugs.
Kathryn O'Lare

Prescription Drugs

Prescription drug abuse is a growing problem in the United States. After marijuana and synthetic marijuana use by teenagers (both of which appear to be growing among all age groups), prescription drugs follow in frequency of use. These drugs are illicit if not being used by the person to whom they are prescribed or for the reasons prescribed for that person's disorder. Across all age groups, roughly 6.3 million people use these drugs for their effects. Juveniles find these drugs easily available in their parents', grandparents', or other relatives' medicine chests, are sometimes given these drugs by their friends or, as often happens, buy them from peers. Some drugs ease their emotional pain, others pick them up from depression, and yet others provide them with unique hallucinatory experiences. These drugs have the same type of effects as do other illicit drugs purchased on the streets. The risk juveniles take is becoming addicted to these drugs because the drugs act on the brain and, in other cases, they can have harmful effects on the kidneys, liver, and other organs of the body. Taken in combination with other drugs, legal and illegal, the drugs have synergistic or compounding effects on the body—that is, 1 + 1 does not equal 2; 1 + 1 may equal 4 or 5 and cause serious damage or death to the person. See Figure 14-3.

The recent deaths of Michael Jackson and Whitney Houston have been attributed to the abuse of multiple drugs in combination.

What Is the Relationship Between Drug Use and Delinquency?

One of the important issues in the juvenile delinquency/juvenile justice field is whether drugs cause delinquency or delinquency leads to drug use, or whether the use of other drugs precedes both delinquency and the onset of drug use.[24] Research has found that delinquency tends to precede the use of drugs.[25] Other research proposes that what might appear to be a causal association is actually a product of shared antecedents.[26] A common factor may underlay both the frequency and type of drug use.[27] Furthermore, a number of researchers have found that substance abuse is just one of an interrelated and overlapping group of adolescent problem behaviors, including delinquency, teen pregnancy, school failure, and dropping out of school.[28] According to this position, substance abuse is one of the problem behaviors developed by adolescents during their early life course. See Table 14-4.

TABLE 14–4
Drug Use by Decreasing Order of Frequency

Type of Drug	Description
Alcohol and Tobacco	Both are considered licit drugs because their use by juveniles is prohibited. Their wide use is considered a serious social problem.
Marijuana	The most frequently used illicit drug, marijuana is known by a variety of street names and is usually smoked.
Cocaine	Snorting (inhaling) is the most common method of using cocaine, but freebasing (smoking) cocaine has gained some popularity.
Methamphetamine	This highly addicted stimulant can be injected, smoked, or snorted. This is one of the many so-called club drugs.
Inhalants	With these drugs, youths need to inhale the vapors to receive the high they seek.
Sedatives	The common factor of sedatives is that they are taken orally and depress the nervous system, inducing a drowsy condition.
Ecstasy	Sometimes called a club drug, Ecstasy can be ingested orally, is sometimes snorted, and is occasionally smoked.
Hallucinogens	LSD was used in the 1960s and 1970s, but PCP, a nervous system excitant has been more recently used by adolescents.
Anabolic Steroids	It is believed that steroids can produce an effect on muscle size; the 100 different types can be taken orally, injected intramuscularly, or robbed on the skin in the form of creams or gels.

These signs began appearing on streets near schools about a generation ago when drugs and violence became more frequent near schools. Are the signs effective, in your experience?
Kathryn O'Lare

Consensus is increasing on three findings that explain the onset and continuing use of illicit drugs:

- First, widespread agreement exists that a sequential pattern of involvement in drug use takes place during adolescence.[29] Denise B. Kandel and colleagues, using cross-sectional research and longitudinal data, proposed a developmental model for drug use involvement. This model suggests that alcohol use follows a pattern of minor delinquency and exposure to friends and parents who drink. The use of marijuana follows participation in minor delinquency and adoption of beliefs and values that are consistent with those held by peers but are opposed to parental standards. Finally, an adolescent's use of marijuana proceeds to other illicit drugs if relationships with parents are poor and the youth experiences an increased exposure to peers who use a variety of illegal drugs.[30]

- Second, a number of risk factors seem to be related to delinquency and drug use. Preperinatal risk factors consist of in-the-womb difficulties, minor physical abnormalities, and brain damage. Early developmental risk factors are found in the family environment, including a family history of alcoholism, family conflict, and poor family management practices. Other risk factors are related to early antisocial behavior and academic failure. Community risk factors include living in disorganized neighborhoods. According to J. David Hawkins, Richard E. Catalano, and Devon D. Brewer, the more of these risk factors a child has, the more likely he or she will become involved in drug abuse.[31]

- Finally, youths who use hard drugs are more likely to engage in chronic delinquent behavior.[32] Delbert Elliott and David Huizinga found that nearly 50 percent of serious youthful offenders were also multiple-drug users. Eighty-two percent of these offenders reported use, beyond experimentation, of at least one illicit drug.[33] David M. Altschuler and Paul J. Brounstein's examination of drug use and drug trafficking among inner-city adolescent males in Washington, D.C., found that the use and sale of drugs affected the frequency and seriousness of delinquent behavior. The heaviest users were significantly more likely than nonusers to commit property offenses; those who trafficked in drugs were significantly more likely to commit crimes against people than were youths who did not sell drugs; and juveniles who both used and sold drugs were the most likely to commit offenses against property and persons.[34]

What Are the Different Types of Drug and Alcohol Users?

Voices of Delinquency: I Started Young

As indicated by the statistics in this chapter, drug use is pervasive and increasing among some young people, especially those involved in antisocial behaviors. One group of juveniles includes experimental users; these youths are curious about drugs and occasionally use the drugs to test their effects. Another group consists of social or recreational users who occasionally take drugs to socialize with friends. In a third group are youths who spend considerable time and money obtaining drugs, and these substances play an important role in the users' lives. Despite heavy and regular use, however, adolescents in this group are still functional and able to meet social and academic responsibilities. The lives of juveniles in a fourth group are dominated by drugs, and the process of securing and using drugs interferes with their everyday functioning. These four groups fit into two clusters: (1) social or recreational users and (2) those whose lives are dominated by drugs—**addicts**. Some of these users are plagued by internal demons.

Social or Recreational Users

Adolescents generally prefer substances that are not too costly. Beer and marijuana meet this criterion better than hard drugs do. Availability and potency are also important in drug use, for these substances are likely to be used as a means to other ends, especially for achieving excitement. For example, marijuana, alcohol, and other drugs used at football games, rock concerts, parties, outings, dances, and similar activities provide additional excitement already inherent in such activities or, in some cases, produce excitement when it seems to be lacking. In addition to excitement, experience-enhancing substances serve the purpose of exploration. They enable the youth to experience new social orbits, mating relations, and unfamiliar places. Narcotic substances are further used to escape or retreat from the external world into a private inner self.

Voices of Delinquency: It Was the Fear

The fact is that drug and alcohol use among American adolescents is increasing, with no good news on the horizon. Alcohol use is continuing to rise among *all* American adolescents, rich as well as poor, nonoffenders as well as offenders. It constitutes a serious social problem that currently is attracting national attention. More bad news is that the use of marijuana has experienced a major increase among American adolescents in the past decade.[35]

Voices of Delinquency: Drugs Are Cool, Man

Addicts

Too many adolescents' lives are dominated by drugs. Many of these drug-dependent youths need speed in the morning, and they require speed in school to make it through the day. Others become intoxicated several evenings a week and may even drink at school. Still others use so much marijuana that they become known to their peers as *pot heads*. Even sadder, other youths, especially high-risk females, become addicted to crack cocaine. These girls are likely to be unable to give up this addiction even when they become pregnant. Further, drug-dependent youths typically are multiple-drug users.

The factors that place a youth at **high risk** for later substance abuse include the following:

1. *Early initiation:* use of any substance by the age of ten or twelve
2. *School problems:* low expectation that school will be a positive experience, low grades, disruptive behavior in school, and truancy
3. *Family problems:* lack of parental support and guidance
4. *Peer influences:* relationships with peers who use substances, and an inability to resist their influences
5. *Personality:* nonconformism, rebellion, or a strong sense of independence.[36]

Those who work with juvenile offenders argue that rarely is a youth institutionalized or placed on probation who does not have some history of alcohol or narcotic abuse.[37] As one director of guidance noted, "We only have one or two youths a year admitted to this institution who don't have a problem with substance abuse."[38]

The use of drugs, especially on a daily basis, increases the likelihood that a youth will be arrested and referred to the juvenile justice system. Other short-term consequences are vulnerability to other drugs, loss of interest in school, and impaired psychological functioning. Long-term consequences include respiratory problems, drug dependence, chronic depression and fatigue, and social and financial problems. A long-term risk of taking intravenous drugs today is exposure to AIDS.[39]

What About Drug-Trafficking Juveniles?

Some evidence exists that independents sell drugs as frequently as, or even more frequently than, drug-trafficking gangs do.[40] Some adolescents also sell drugs independently of any gang affiliation, particularly in suburban settings.

Personal interview data add to this portrait of juveniles involved in drug trafficking. In urban settings, juveniles are members of drug-trafficking gangs, and as part of their membership responsibilities, are supposed to assist in selling drugs. These youths, who can be as young as eleven or twelve, may be given a firearm and told to stand watch at a crack house. If anyone tries to enter who is not supposed to be there, they are told to shoot and kill. As these youths get a little older, they are given the job of what is usually called a *mule*, delivering drugs to specific locations. Older juveniles are placed on street corners where they sell drugs, usually crack cocaine, to regular customers and people driving by.

In the cities and in settings made up of what in Chapter 13 is called *emerging gangs*, those juveniles selling crack cocaine may be working for someone from an urban setting who may or may not be a representative of an organized gang in that setting. They usually get a percentage of the profits from the sale of these drugs. Interviewees have reported that this is up to 10 percent and that they make a fair amount of money selling drugs. They like to talk about how much money they have made selling drugs throughout the years; a couple of the stories in the *Voices* address this issue.

Typically, those who made considerable amounts of money from selling drugs have trafficked in other drugs besides crack cocaine. Those juveniles selling marijuana sometimes make a lot of money. They are able to purchase several cars and have a closet full of expensive clothing. They also buy all kinds of presents for their girlfriends, and always have money to purchase "toys" and any entertainment they want for themselves.

In *Voices* the stories of youth who spent their lives trafficking drugs and had authority over others who were trafficking drugs are reviewed. In this account, the tragic consequences of drug trafficking, both to those who traffic in drugs and to those who get caught up in this victim and addict cycle of buying drugs, are revealed. Juveniles, especially those who sell drugs, are inevitably caught by the police, quickly processed by the courts, and sent to prison. Sometimes, they end up in training school first, but at other times they are sent directly to prison.

What Explains the Onset of Drug Use?

A number of theories have attempted to explain the onset and escalation of juveniles' drug use:

- *Cognitive-affective theories.* A number of theories have focused on how perceptions about the costs and benefits of drug use contribute to juveniles' decisions to experiment with these substances. Hence, the decision to use substances rests in substance-specific expectations and perceptions held by adolescents.[41]

- *Addictive personality theory.* Another theory for the onset and continued use of drugs is that the typical addict has an addiction-prone personality and suffers from some deep-rooted personality disorder.

FIGURE 14-4
Explanations for the Onset
of Drug Abuse

Source: Adapted from Lloyd D.
Johnston, Patrick M. O'Malley,
Jerald G. Bachman, and
John E. Schulenberg, *Monitoring
the Future: National Results on
Adolescent Drug Use* (Washington,
DC: National Institutes of Health
2010), Tables 1, 3, and 7.

Types of Explanation Description

Cognitive-Affective Theories—These theories relate to how the perceptions about the costs and benefits of drug use contribute to adolescents decision to experiment with these substances.

Addictive-Personality Theory—The typical addict has an addiction prone personality and suffers from deep-rooted personality disorder or emotional problems.

Stress Relief Theory—The desire to get high as a means to relieve stress, depression, or boredom of everyday life is common in adolescent culture.

Social Learning Theory—This theory postulates that an adolescent's involvement in substance abuse begins with observation and imitation of substance specific behaviors, continues with social reinforcement, and cultivates in a juvenile's expectation of positive social and physiological consequences from continued drug use.

Social Control Theories—Emotional attachment to peers who use substances is a primary causes of substance use.

Social Disorganization Theory—The bleak economic environment has resulted in those situated in these settings to experience doubt, hopelessness, and uncertainty, and, as a result, they seek relief in drugs.

Integrated Theories—Elliott and colleagues use strain, social control, and social teaming theories to form a perspective that accounts for delinquent behavior and drug use.

- *Stress relief theory.* The desire to get high, which is seen as a way to relieve stress, depression, or the boredom of everyday life, is common in adolescent peer culture.

- *Social learning theory.* Some argue that drug use begins and continues chiefly because juveniles or adults have contact with peers who use drugs. Peers then provide role models, as well as social support, for drug use. Of course, once peers persuade a person to begin using drugs, a pattern of use can be established that may lead eventually to addiction and continued use.[42]

- *Social control theory.* Travis Hirschi's social control theory and Hawkins and Weiss's social development model both assume that emotional attachment to peers who use substances is a primary cause of substance abuse. Unlike social learning theories, however, these two approaches pay specific attention to weak conventional bonds to society and to the institutions and individuals who might otherwise discourage deviant behavior.

- *Social disorganization theory.* This theory explains the onset and escalation of adolescents' drug use by claiming that a bleak economic environment for certain disenfranchised groups has created a generation of young adults in urban inner cities who regularly experience doubt, hopelessness, and uncertainty.

- *Integrated theories.* Elliott and colleagues offer a model that expands traditional strain, social, and social learning theories into a single perspective that accounts for delinquent behavior and drug use.[43] See Figure 14-4.

Solutions to the Drug Problem

Prevention programs, treatment programs, strict enforcement, and harm reduction are all possible means of controlling drug use among adolescents.

Prevention Programs

The 1990s saw dramatic developments in drug prevention programs. The Center for the Study and Prevention of Violence at the University of Colorado began an initiative called Blueprints for Violence Prevention, in which researchers evaluated six hundred programs designed to prevent violence and drug abuse and to treat youths with problem behavior.[44] The investigators were able to identify eleven model programs and twenty-one promising programs. Effective programs need to incorporate early childhood and family interventions, school-based interventions, and comprehensive community-wide efforts. The important dimension of drug prevention intervention is use of a multidimensional approach that centers on the family, school, and community.

Treatment Programs

Treatment for drug abusers takes place in psychiatric and hospitals settings for youngsters whose parents can afford it or have the needed insurance benefits. Other youths, particularly those substance abusers who have committed minor forms of delinquency, receive treatment in privately administered placements, which vary tremendously in the quality of program design and implementation. Substance-abusing youths with multiple typical problems may be more malleable than adult offenders, but there is little evidence that the majority of substance abuse programs are any more successful than those for adult substance abusers. For an exception, see the Evidence-Based Practice feature.

Strict Enforcement

The "war on drugs" has not been won with juveniles anymore that it has with adults. A disastrous consequence of the strict enforcement policies that accompany this "war" is the increasing number of minority youths who, having been involved in using or selling crack cocaine, have been brought into the justice system for extended periods of time. Strict enforcement, however, has seemed to make a difference in several ways:

- The destruction of overseas drug-producing crops has no doubt had some impact on the availability of drugs in the United States, raising prices and making some drugs harder to find.
- Heavy penalties associated with the sale of illicit drugs seem to have been somewhat effective in deterring both juvenile and adult offenders.

Evidence-Based Practice
Are Drug Courts Effective?

Drug courts are currently being established throughout the nation and the initial evaluations have been favorable. A number of evidence-based evaluations conducted in Miami, Philadelphia, and Las Vegas reveal that adult drug courts can comparatively lower rates of recidivism. Using a nationally representative sample (including all drug courts that had been in operation for at least one year and had at least forty program graduates), the National Institute of Justice and the Drug Court Program Office found that within one year 16 percent of drug court graduates had been arrested and charged with a serious offense (84 percent success rate), and within two years, 28 percent had been arrested and charged with a serious offense (73 percent success rate). The programs seem to work best for high-risk offenders who might normally have been sent to prison.

Although general research findings are that drug courts can reduce recidivism and promote other positive outcomes such as cost savings, several factors affect a drug court program's success: proper assessment and treatment, the role assumed by the judge, and the nature of offender's interactions with the judge. Other variable influences include drug use trends, staff turnover, and resource allocation.

There is reason to believe that juvenile drug courts will work as effectively as adult drug courts. A quasi-experimental 2010 study of juvenile drug courts compared 1,120 youths in juvenile drug courts in multiple jurisdictions with 1,120 youth not in juvenile drug court, but who participated in adolescent outpatient treatment. The juvenile drug courts appeared to do a better job (compared to treatment alone) of helping youth reduce symptoms of their emotional problems and reduce their substance use as measured six months post-intake.

Other findings of this study included the following:

- Using evidence-based treatment matters.
- Juvenile drug court proceedings were less likely than youth in treatment-only to begin treatment within two weeks of intake, which is significant because it has been found that initiation of treatment within two weeks is a major protective factor against relapse and recidivism.
- Contrary to concerns about net widening, juvenile drug courts are one of several ways of getting significantly impaired youths into treatment and reliably achieving positive outcomes.

CRITICAL THINKING QUESTIONS

Why is it important that drug courts, both adults and juveniles, appear to be effective? What types of youthful offenders do you believe juvenile drug courts would be more effective with?

Source: Douglas B. Marlowe, "Evidence-Based Policies and Practices for Drug-Involved Offenders," *Prison Journal* 9 (2011), 27–47; Michael W. Finigan, Shannon M. Carey, and Anton Cox, "Impact of a Mature Drug Court over 10 Years of Operation: Recidivism and Costs," NPC Research, Inc., 2007; National Institute of Justice, "Do Drug Courts Work? Findings from Drug Court Research," at http://nij.gov/nij/topics/courts/drug-courts/work.htm (accessed February 20, 2012).

Michelle L. Dennis, Michelle K. White, and Melissa L. Ives, "Individual Characteristics and Needs Associated with Adolescents and Young Adults in Addiction in Treatment." *Children and Family Lives* 9 (2009), pp. 45–72.

- Law enforcement's targeting of drug dealers has had some success in getting those dealers off the streets.
- The policing of the sale of tobacco products, especially cigarettes at convenience stores and other places, has made it more difficult for minors to purchase or obtain tobacco products.

Harm Reduction

Harm reduction is an approach designed to reduce the harm done by drug use and by the severe penalties resulting from drug use and sales. A number of harm reduction strategies have been employed:

- Programs in which health professionals administer drugs to addicts as part of a treatment and detoxification regimen
- Drug treatment facilities that are available for those drug addicts who desire treatment
- Needle exchange programs that are intended to slow the transmission of HIV and that provide educational resources about how HIV is contracted and spread.

Juvenile Justice Videos

ENTERING THE JUVENILE JUSTICE SYSTEM

Entering the Juvenile Justice System follows a juvenile with a record of arrests as he enters the juvenile justice system through the intake process. The intake officers are very concerned with the youth's drug use; why is this an important factor at the intake process? Notice the questions asked by the officer when filing the intake report. Discuss the importance of these questions and how they relate to the youth's criminal record, medical history, and drug and alcohol habits. Does the intake process do a reliable job in assessing the juvenile's immediate needs? Why or why not? How would the intake process be handled if the juvenile admitted to being on drugs at the time? Discuss.

SUMMARY

LEARNING OBJECTIVE 1 Describe how much drug use there is among adolescents in the United States.

Drug and alcohol abuse is a problem behavior for many juveniles in the United States. Drug use appears to have increased considerably since the late 1970s, but today appears to be declining.

The bad news is that high-risk children are becoming increasingly involved in substance abuse.

Although the use of crack cocaine may be declining across the nation, it remains the drug of choice for disadvantaged youth.

LEARNING OBJECTIVE 2 Identify the main types of drugs used by adolescents.

The licit and illicit drugs used by adolescents, in decreasing order of frequency are alcohol, tobacco, marijuana, cocaine, methamphetamine, inhalants, sedatives, stimulants (amphetamines and hallucinogens), and heroin.

LEARNING OBJECTIVE 3 Describe the different types of drug users, drug traffickers, and the relationship of drug use and delinquency.

There are three types of drug users: social or recreational users, addicts, and drug trafficking juveniles. It is the latter two groups that most frequently come to the attention of the juvenile justice system.

LEARNING OBJECTIVE 4 Discuss the theoretical explanations related to the onset of drug use.

The main theoretical explanations are cognitive-affective theories, addictive personality theory, stress relief theory, social learning theory, social control theory, social disorganization theory, and integrated theories.

LEARNING OBJECTIVE 5 Summarize what can be done to prevent and control drug use among adolescents in the United States.

Solutions to the drug problem include prevention programs, treatment programs, strict enforcement, and harm reduction.

KEY TERMS

addicts, p. 296

alcohol, p. 290

amphetamines, p. 292

anabolic steroids, p. 293

cocaine, p. 291

crack, p. 291

Ecstasy, p. 293

heroin, p. 293

high risk, p. 296

inhalants, p. 291

marijuana, p. 290

sedatives, p. 292

REVIEW QUESTIONS

1. What explains the popularity of drug use in the United States?

2. "Just say no" is a common saying when it comes to drugs. Will that approach work? Why or why not? Under what conditions will it work or not work? If a friend you know is a user, what can you say to him or her? Would you turn in a friend if you believed you could help this person? Where would you go for help?

3. What do you think is the relationship between drug use and delinquency?

4. Why do college students drink as much as they do? How is their drinking related to the subject matter of this chapter?

GROUP EXERCISES

1. *Group Work:* Without looking in the text, list and describe as many drugs as possible and their effects. After about five to ten minutes, review the drugs noted in the text and fill in the gaps.

2. *Group Work:* Think back to your days in junior high and high school. What are your best recollections of the amount of drug use by students in school (include alcohol), why students did it, and the effect of the drugs? Which drug categories noted in the text did the various students fall into?

3. *Group Work:* Read through three or four of the stories in *Voices* about people who were involved in drugs. What reasons do the addicts give for getting involved with drugs?

4. *Group Work:* Go online and look up the characteristics of addiction. During the next class period, discuss with other members of your groups what addiction is and how it takes over the lives of individuals.

   • **Research Center:** check out the Cybrary and MySearchLab for even more resources

NOTES

1. Jeff Slowkowski, *Highlights from Pathways to Desistance, A Longitudinal Study of Serious Adolescent Behavior* (Washington, DC: Office of Juvenile Justice and Delinquency Prevention, 2011).

2. Ibid.

3. Results from *The 2010 National Survey on Drug Use and Health: National Findings* (Rockville, MD: Substance Abuse and Mental Health Services Administration, 2012).

4. Howard Abadinsky, *Drug Use and Abuse: A Comprehensive Introduction,* 6th ed. (Belmont, CA: Thomson Learning, 2008).

5. *Juveniles and Drugs* (Washington, DC: Office of National Drug Control Policy, 2004).

6. Lloyd D. Johnson et al., *Monitoring the Future: National Results on Adolescent Drug Use. Overview of Key Findings, 2010* (Bethesda, MD: National Institute on Drug Use, 2011).

7. Office of National Drug Control Policy, *2009 National Survey on Drug Use and Health Highlights Fact Sheet* (Washington, DC: Office of National Drug Control Policy, 2010), 1.

8. U.S. Public Health Service, *Healthy People 2000: National Health Promotion and Disease Prevention Objectives—Full Report with Commentary* (Washington, DC: Department of Health and Human Services, 2001).

9. Ali H. Mokdad et al., "Actual Causes of Death in the United States, 2000," *Journal of the American Medical Association* 291 (March 2004), 1238, 1241.

10. For many other names, see James A. Inciardi, *The War on Drugs II* (Mountain View, CA: Mayfield, 1992), 62.

11. For a review of these studies, see Joseph M. Rey, Andres Martin, and Peter Krabman, "Is the Party Over? Cannabis and Juvenile Psychiatric Disorder: The Past Ten Years," *Journal of the American Academy of Child and Adolescent Psychiatry* 43 (October 2004), 1194–1208.

12. Inciardi, *The War on Drugs II*, 94.

13. U.S. Department of Health and Human Services, *2002 National Household Survey on Drug Abuse* (Washington, DC: U.S. Department of Health and Human Services, 2003).

14. National Drug Intelligence Center, *National Methamphetamine Threat Assessment, 2008* (December 2007), at http://www.usdoj.gov/ndic/pubs261/26594/index.htm#overview.

15. T. M. McSherry, "Program Experiences with the Solvent Abuser in Philadelphia," in *Epidemiology of Inhalant*

Abuse: An Update, edited by R. A. Crider and B. A. Rouse, Research Monograph 85 (Washington, DC: National Institute on Drug Abuse, 1989), 106–20.

16. Howard Abadinsky, *Drugs: An Introduction*, 4th ed. (Belmont, CA: Wadsworth/Thomson Learning, 2001), 82.

17. See the following websites: http://www.casapalmera.com/articles/how-20-prominent-people-died-as-a-result-of-drug-use; http://www.nytimes.com/2008/02/07/nyregion/07ledger.html; http://artsbeat.blogs.nytimes.com/2009/10/01/doctor-reveals-details-of-michael-jacksons-autopsy-report.

18. Inciardi, *The War on Drugs II*, 39.

19. Abadinsky, *Drugs: An Introduction*, 143–44.

20. Lloyd D. Johnson et al., *Monitoring the Future: National Survey Results on Drug Use, 2004* (Bethesda, MD: National Institute on Drug Abuse, 2005), 148.

21. Inciardi, *The War on Drugs II*, 63.

22. For the medical complications associated with heroin addiction, see Jerome J. Platt, *Heroin Addiction: Theory, Research, and Treatment* (Malabar, FL: Robert E. Krieger, 1986), 80–101.

23. Paul Goldstein, "Anabolic Steroids: An Ethnographic Approach," unpublished paper (New York: Narcotics and Drug Research, Inc., March 1989).

24. David M. Altschuler and Paul J. Brounstein, "Patterns of Drug Use: Drug Trafficking and Other Delinquency Among Inner-City Adolescent Males in Washington, DC," *Criminology* 29 (1991), 590.

25. Lloyd D. Johnson et al., "Drugs and Delinquency: A Search for Causal Connections," in *Longitudinal Research on Drug Use: Empirical Finds and Methodological Issues*, edited by Denis B. Kandel, Ronald C. Kessler, and Rebecca Z. Margulies (Washington DC: Hemisphere, 1978), 137–56.

26. Altschuler and Brounstein, "Patterns of Drug Use."

27. Marc Le Blanc and Nathalie Kaspy, "Trajectories of Delinquency and Problem Behavior: Comparison of Social and Personal Control Characteristics of Adjudicated Boys on Synchronous and Nonsynchronous Paths," *Journal of Quantitative Criminology* 14 (1998), 181–214.

28. Richard Jessor and Shirley L. Jessor, *Problem Behavior and Psychosocial Development: A Longitudinal Study of Youth* (New York: Academic Press, 1977).

29. U.S. Bureau of Justice Statistics, *Drugs, Crime, and the Justice System* (Washington, DC: U.S. Government Printing Office, 1993), 23.

30. Kandel et al., eds., *Longitudinal Research on Drug Use.*

31. J. David Hawkins, Richard F. Catalano, and Devon D. Brewer, "Preventing Serious, Violent, and Chronic Juvenile Offending," in *A Sourcebook: Serious, Violent and Chronic Juvenile Offenders,* edited by James C. Howell et al. (Thousand Oaks, CA: Sage Publications, 1995), 48–49.

32. Delbert S. Elliott, David Huizinga, and Suzanne S. Ageton, *Explaining Delinquency and Drug Use* (Beverly Hills, CA: Sage Publications, 1985).

33. D. S. Elliott and D. Huizinga, "*The Relationship Between Delinquent Behavior and ADM Problem Behaviors*," paper prepared for the ADAMHA/OJJDP State of the Art Research Conference on Juvenile Offenders with Serious Drug/Alcohol and Mental Health Problems, Bethesda, MD, April 17–18, 1984.

34. Altschuler and Brounstein, "Patterns of Drug Use," 587.

35. See the statistics on the rise of marijuana use earlier in this chapter.

36. Joy G. Dryfoos, *Adolescents at Risk: Prevalence and Prevention* (New York: Oxford University Press, 1990), 54.

37. A statement made to one of the authors by several training school staff in the early 1990s.

38. Interviewed during the early 1990s.

39. Dryfoos, *Adolescents at Risk*, 48.

40. Malcolm Klein, Cheryl Maxson, and Lea C. Cunningham, "Crack, Street Gangs, and Violence," *Criminology* 29 (November 1991), 623–50.

41. David B. Henry and Kimberly Kobus, "Early Adolescent Social Networks and Substance Use," *Journal of Early Adolescence* 27 (2007), 346–62.

42. For the positive relationship between peers and drug use, see Thomas J. Dishion and Rolf Loeber, "Adolescent Marijuana and Alcohol Use: The Role of Parents and Peers Revisited," *American Journal of Drug and Alcohol Abuse* 11 (1985), 11–25.

43. Elliott et al., *Explaining Delinquency and Drug Use.*

44. Sharon Mihalic, Katherine Irwin, Abigail Fagan, Diane Ballard, and Delbert Elliott, *Blueprint for Violence Prevention, Book 5* (Boulder: University of Colorado, Institute of Behavioral Sciences, Center for the Study and Prevention of Violence, 1998).

ASSOCIATED PRESS

Learning Objectives

1. Understand the Beijing Rules, their content, and the proposed model rules for juveniles for all nations.

2. Illustrate how the social organization of different types of countries affects how the countries treat children.

3. Describe Somalia, a failed state, and the plight of children in that country.

4. Explain how three emerging countries with extreme social, population, and economic problems—China, India, and Brazil—deal with troublesome youth.

5. Explain the basic approaches used by three developed nations—Canada, England/Wales, and Sweden— in dealing with troublesome youth.

A Safe Childhood Is a Human Right

Across the World, Children Are Denied Their Human Rights

They miss out on their right to education. They are abandoned and left to fend for themselves on the street. They are recruited into armed forces and are subjected to the death penalty, are disappeared, are punished by cruel and inhumane methods and suffer many other forms of violence.

Child Soldiers

Worldwide, hundreds of thousands of children under 18 are affected by armed conflict. These youths are recruited into government armed forces, paramilitaries, civil militia and a variety of other armed groups. Often they are abducted at school, on the streets, or at home. Others enlist "voluntarily," usually because they see few alternatives or are forced to join. Yet international law prohibits the participation in armed conflict of children under age 18.

Juvenile Life Without Parole

At least 2,500 people in the US are serving life imprisonment without the possibility of parole for crimes committed when they were under 18 years old.

Right to Education

Everyone has the right to education—which should be available free to all at least at the primary level. Education is also indispensable in realizing other human rights.

Convention on the Rights of the Child

The United Nations Convention on the Rights of the Child (CRC), adopted in 1989 to protect the rights of children, is the most widely ratified human rights treaty in history. It encompasses civil rights and freedoms, family environment, basic health and welfare, education, leisure and cultural activities and special protection measures for children. The CRC establishes a comprehensive set of goals for countries to achieve, guided by the best interests of the child.[1]

One of the most exciting developments in juvenile justice during the past two and a half decades is a growing international awareness of the problems faced by youths. The world's media, child care experts, national governments, and international organizations are for the first time looking at the problems of children in a broader context. Their findings are both illuminating and sobering. Stark contrasts exist in how countries in different parts of the world and in different stages of economic development treat children. Industrialized and democratized countries, so often held up as models of rational and responsible systems of justice, often fall far short not only of their own ideals but also of those of the international community.

Voices of Delinquency: Trauma in Bosnia

Arguments about what to do about juveniles and juvenile crime in countries around the world are similar to those prevalent in the United States, Canada, and England. Discussed throughout the industrialized world, particularly, are the age of criminal culpability, diversion from the system, due process, the role of the police in dealing with juveniles, the separation of the dependent and neglected from the delinquent and criminal, the severity of sanctions, the efficacy of community-based programs and institutionalization, probation and parole, and the death penalty. Countries vary widely in how they handle these issues. Some governments ignore juveniles totally, while others engage in serious study and debate what works best. This diversity has a number of sources.

Some of the variation is related to each country's stage of economic, social, and political development (see Focus on Economic Development 15–1). Failed and weakened states are characterized by sometimes nonexistent or weak governments incapable of governing. These countries are politically disorganized and can neither draw up nor enforce their

Focus on Economic Development 15-1
HDCs, MDCs, and LDCs

Countries around the world are ranked on a number of criteria, some quantitative and some qualitative. Three levels are often used throughout the academic world and the media to refer to the countries. Let's look at the three levels and their general descriptions:

HIGHLY DEVELOPED COUNTRIES (HDCs)

Citizens in these countries have a per capita income above $16,000. The countries have constitutions, democratically elected governments that are able to govern the country, well-formed and functioning institutions, adequate resources, industrial capacity, and are able to support all of their citizens. Women and children have rights for the most part in law, but not necessarily in practice.

MODERATELY DEVELOPED COUNTRIES (MDCs)

Per capita incomes range between $600 and $16,000. Those near the top of this category have constitutions, may have popularly elected officials, and can govern most of the country most of the time. Institutions such as education and health care that support their populations are limited in number and quality; birth rates and poverty are high compared with the HDCs. The countries have weak but often growing industrial output, struggle at times to feed all of their people, and often experience conflict among the national government, regional controlling bodies, and indigenous peoples. Countries near the bottom of this category have weaker governments, lack the ability to control all of their population groups, and frequently struggle to provide citizens with basic needs. Countries near the bottom often are called weakened states. Women and children clearly are second-class citizens.

LESSER DEVELOPED COUNTRIES (LDCs)

Per capita income averages in the neighborhood of $600; most of the population makes around $1 a day. Governments and institutions tend to be very weak and cannot provide their populations with basic necessities. Life in these countries is a struggle, with indigenous groups running themselves, much conflict among competing groups and the government, and extensive brutality toward women and children. The countries have very few and underdeveloped industrial capabilities and agricultural systems are short of land, water, modern crop seed, and machinery. Agricultural products are often exported and the money goes to the rulers of the countries. Families often break up with men going to cities and women running the gardens they have planted in order to try to survive. Women and children are third-class citizens.

---

laws; citizens often view the government as illegitimate, and warlords, religious clerics, terrorist groups, and pro and con government forces battle with one another for control of the state.[2] The lack of political organization is matched by economic failures and, because many countries lack sufficient natural resources, the absence of agricultural and business infrastructures means that large percentages of the county's population also lack educational facilities, hospitals, routine medical care, disease control, and jobs; what money is in the country is funneled up to those who govern. Ruling parties usually do not care what happens to their citizens. In the case of complaints, demonstrations, or protests by the population, the rulers will brutally put down those who are organizing as was occurring in Syria well into 2012 and has been going on in Somalia for over two decades now. Security for the general population, in other words, is nonexistent and target groups find themselves being starved, mutilated, and the victims of genocide. Basic human needs are not met. Children are the saddest victims of all as they are just beginning their lives and have lost parents, siblings, friends, and neighbors and are themselves the victims of abuse by the existing government and conflicting powers.

Developing countries with **indigenous populations** frequently rely on the internalized and long-standing folkways and mores of **traditional cultures**. Rules in these countries are enforced by parents and by religious and community leaders and very likely are more effective than the formalized methods of democratic nations. Sometimes the two systems collide. Nations colonized by Western countries even centuries ago often still experience social strains as traditional ways conflict with modern methods, thereby setting the stage for mistrust, acrimony, and sometimes violent conflict between the governing and the governed. These countries are far better developed than failed states, although many are quite weak and threatened with failure. The developing countries, however, are generally much better organized politically, economically, and socially and many are making serious efforts to follow world norms, including the rights of children. Others are so concerned with economic development that the

▲ Child soldiers as young as seven and eight years old are found throughout the lesser developed countries by governments, militias, and terrorist groups. Some of these youths are simply killed when no longer useful to their captors. Almost all suffer long-term psychological damage.
eye ubiquitous/Robert Harding World Imagery

rights of children are ignored and, indeed, children often end up in industrial sweat shops servicing the advanced nations of the developed world; an education is an impossibility. The lack of control over armed forces, police departments, and militias in developing countries results in children being treated brutally and sometimes killed on the streets at night, raped, and conscripted into violent gangs and terrorist groups. Children often are put in jails and prisons that are in deplorable, unsafe, and unsanitary prison systems run by brutal staff.

Democratized and **industrialized countries** usually base their criminal and juvenile law on constitutionally derived formal rules and procedures. Well-developed educational systems provide these states with trained police, judges, and professional child care workers capable of giving juveniles needed help. Nevertheless, these countries, too, often do not care for children properly. Some states in the United States, for example, are criticized internationally for being "failed states" and children in many regions of the county are subjected to understaffed schools, poor teachers, and a lack of resources; some live on impoverished Indian reservations, experience violent and degrading impoverishment in ghetto areas, and have extreme difficulty trying to obtain medical and dental care. Simply because a nation is called a developed nation does not mean that all of its children are granted their full human rights. See Figure 15–1.

Attitudes of governmental leaders in both failed states and developing countries toward citizens also contribute to overall confusion and conflict. More than a few countries are governed by political, religious, or ideological despots who care only about wealth, power, and control. Indeed, police, military, and civilian authorities in these countries often engage in beatings, torture, sexual assault, and murder. The methods of suppression used are so horrific that worldwide condemnation is directed at the guilty police, paramilitary security forces, terrorist groups, and others. International media, United Nations white papers, U.S. Department of State reports, and **nongovernmental organizations (NGOs)** such as Amnesty International constantly urge those responsible to cease their human rights violations. Yet the leaders of these countries continue to ignore even the most fundamental rights of their citizens. Nevertheless, momentum is building, pushing leaders everywhere to carefully

FIGURE 15–1
Relative Income Poverty
Percentage of children, ages zero to seventeen years, in households with equivalent incomes of less than 50% of the median.

Source: Child Poverty in Perspective: An Overview of Child Well-Being in Rich Countries, Innocenti Report Card No. 7, (2007) UNICEF Innocenti Research Centre, Florence, p. 6.

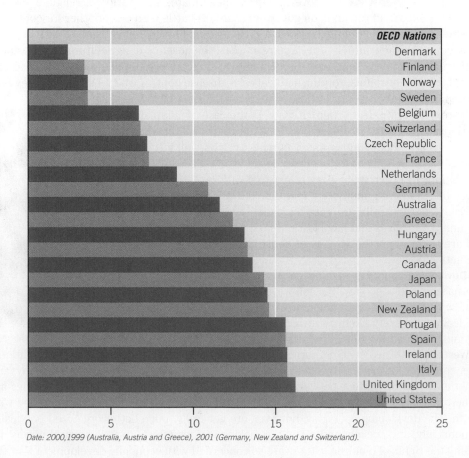

Date: 2000,1999 (Australia, Austria and Greece), 2001 (Germany, New Zealand and Switzerland).

consider their actions and the consequences of their actions before they condone violence against their citizens.

This chapter briefly addresses the first major effort by the United Nations to set standards for the treatment of children—the *Beijing Rules*. Then the focus of the chapter turns to its primary emphasis: justice systems in a number of other countries. These countries were chosen either for their similarity to the United States or because of their total lack of adherence to international norms. We discuss what it is about their population, culture, or state of socioeconomic development that makes them unique. First examined is Somalia, a failed state. We then turn to Brazil, China, and India, three countries that are developing or emerging economically. These are the world's largest nations in terms of population; all are extremely poor and represent different areas of the world with diverse cultural traditions. In India and Brazil, the laws of colonial nations, usually the **common law**, replaced the traditional native laws of indigenous peoples . The common laws were eventually replaced by formal **statutory law**. Today, years after the end of colonization, the formal statutory laws remain in place, but long-discarded indigenous practices of native populations are reemerging as challenges to the statutory laws. Brazil has the largest population in South America and a colonial history that includes the disenfranchisement of native populations; its problems are characteristic of many South American countries. China has a huge population, numerous ethnic groups, ideological conflicts, and problems that accompany a changing socioeconomic structure. India's population matches that of China. India faces abject poverty and has fewer resources than China.

Last we turn to three postindustrial countries: Canada, England, and Sweden. The modern, statutory legal systems of these English-speaking countries evolved from English common law. Canada, like the United States, disenfranchised its indigenous populations several centuries ago.

What Are the Beijing Rules?

One outcome of the emerging world order is the setting of international standards for the administration of juvenile justice. The earliest standards, which were developed in 1955 as the *United Nations Standard Minimum Rules for the Treatment of Prisoners*, did not

---

Focus on Policy 15–2
The Beijing Rules: Fundamental Perspectives

1. Member States shall seek, in conformity with their respective general interests, to further the well-being of the juvenile and her or his family.
2. Member States shall endeavour to develop conditions that will ensure for the juvenile a meaningful life in the community, which, during that period in life when she or he is most susceptible to deviant behaviour, will foster a process of personal development and education that is as free from crime and delinquency as possible.
3. Sufficient attention shall be given to positive measures that involve the full mobilization of all possible resources, including the family, volunteers and other community groups, as well as schools and other community institutions, for the purpose of promoting the well-being of the juvenile, with a view to reducing the need for intervention under the law, and of effectively, fairly and humanely, dealing with the juvenile in conflict with the law.
4. Juvenile justice shall be conceived as an integral part of the national development process of each country, within a comprehensive framework of social justice for all juveniles,

thus, at the same time, contributing to the protection of the young and the maintenance of a peaceful order in society.
5. These Rules shall be implemented in the context of economic, social and cultural conditions prevailing in each Member State.
6. Juvenile justice services shall be systematically developed and coordinated with a view to improving and sustaining the competence of personnel involved in the services, including their methods, approaches, and attitudes.

CRITICAL THINKING QUESTIONS

How does the operation of juvenile justice in the United States fare in terms of the Beijing Rules?
How is the United States strong? Weak? Explain.
What changes do you think should be made in terms of juvenile justice in the United States to make it more humane, just, and efficient?

Source: United Nations, *United Nations Standard Minimum Rules for the Administration of Juvenile Justice: The Beijing Rules* (New York: United Nations Department of Public Information, 1986), 1–15.

directly address the issue of children.[3] The **Beijing Rules** were the first to do this but should be placed alongside two other sets of rules adopted in 1990, the *United Nations Guidelines for the Prevention of Juvenile Delinquency* (the Riyadh Guidelines) and the *United Nations Rules for the Protection of Juveniles Deprived of Their Liberty* (the JDL Rules). These three sets of rules cover the prevention of delinquency, the due process required for processing offenders through justice systems, and the reintegration of offenders into their communities after confinement and/or rehabilitation. The *Beijing Rules* set standards for all countries (see Focus on Policy 15–2).

The fundamental perspective of the Beijing Rules is based on the broader human rights movement. The actual rules state "musts" and "shoulds" that sound much like the modern due process requirements of the United States, Canada, England, and Australia. For example, the framers of the Beijing Rules emphasize the well-being of all youths as the fundamental principle behind the rules. The term "juveniles" includes all youths from ages seven to eighteen, although the age may vary according to local customs. The rules mandate that authorities not overreact to either the offender or the offense and that all youths be presumed innocent until fair hearings are held. Rule 7.1, for example, states:

> Basic procedural safeguards such as the presumption of innocence, the right to be notified of the charges, the right to remain silent, the right to legal representation, the right to the presence of a parent or guardian, the right to call and cross-examine witnesses and the right of appeal to a higher authority shall be guaranteed at all stages of the proceedings.[4]

The rules call for training juvenile justice officials to exercise proper discretion when working with youths. "No intervention" is considered the best policy for many children, and authorities should divert youths from the system at all stages of the proceedings. Youthful offenders should be placed with local families, schools, or agencies capable of providing the youths with appropriate care and protection. If juveniles are taken into custody, authorities must notify their parents at the earliest possible moment. Youths have the right to privacy when in custody, and their identities must be kept confidential at all stages of the proceedings. A youth should not be confined unless absolutely necessary, and no juvenile should ever be harmed.

The rules go on to state that youths must be permitted to express themselves freely and without fear of recrimination. Juveniles have the right to an attorney and free legal aid; they should have confidence that the courts are informed accurately of their special social, educational, and emotional backgrounds through preadjudicatory and presentencing reports by trained court officers. The courts, in addition, should have access to a wide range of dispositional alternatives including "various care orders, probation, community service orders, compensation to the victim or financial penalties, group counseling and foster care or other educational establishments."[5] Confinement is the last resort, and confined youths must be released as soon as possible and must be placed in programs for reintegrating them back into the community. Corporal punishments are prohibited, and no youth under the age of eighteen should be put to death.

Importantly, the laws of all nations "shall be applied to juvenile offenders impartially, without distinction of any kind, for example as to race, colour, sex, language, religion, political or other opinions, national or social origin, property, birth or other status."[6] Few, if any, nations in the world today meet the standards set by the Beijing Rules.

What Can Happen to Children in a Failed State?
Somalia: A Failed State*

Somalia experienced a total collapse of the central government in the early 1990s, which led to political instability. This economically poor country in the Horn of Africa remains politically and socially disorganized in spite of efforts by the international community to establish a new governmental structure; one has yet to materialize, and many citizens remain with very few, if any, decent governmental systems, educational facilities, hospitals, housing, banks, or potable water supplies. Whatever police and military forces are to be found are

---

*Special thanks are due to Mr. Corey Young of Clemson University for his research and writing on Somalia.

inadequate, ineffective, corrupt, or under the control of local warlords or religious groups; human rights are largely unknown.

In the absence of a central government and unifying laws, many Somali communities have formed ad hoc governing bodies to provide for the needs of citizens.[7] These ad hoc bodies are typically conglomerates of formal and informal power structures and represent collaboration among business groups, local clan elders, community leaders, and clergymen who sometimes exercise control over splintered police and military forces; the country is further hindered by the existence of terrorist groups such as Al Shabaab. Equally as dangerous to children are the forces of the Transitional Federal Government formed to help solve the problems of the state. International organizations such as the United Nations and the African Union, along with numerous NGOs are trying to help stabilize the country and assist Somalia citizens to survive. The political landscape of Somalia, then, resembles a loosely defined web of local, regional, autonomous, and semiautonomous governing bodies with no one in control of the country as a whole.

▲ Orphaned children are common in countries where AIDS, government troops, or terrorists kill their parents. Justice for many depends on NGOs that focus on the human rights of these children and their families and set up schools such as the one shown in this photo.
eye ubiquitous/Robert Harding World Imagery

Perhaps the most important impetus and function of the ad hoc bodies for their formation is the establishment of order and the rule of law throughout Somalia. No national codified law exists; consequently, each local or regional government assumes complete legislative control.[8] Because of the influence of Islam and the prominence of clergymen within the governments of Somalia, many locales have turned to Islamic teachings or *Shari'ah* law for guidance in establishing local order.[9] In many instances, *Shari'ah* law is strict—mandating harsh penalties for even minor infractions by children as well as adults.

Despite the strict nature of laws and the harshness with which they are often applied, lawlessness persists. Rule of law is limited only to areas in which governing bodies exist, thus creating pockets of crime and conflict. Furthermore, ethnic tensions, clan violence, and antigovernment militarism have all thwarted efforts to maintain order, even at the local level.[10] In effect, Somalia is caught in a vicious cycle. That is, no central government can get a foothold because of the persistence of violence—and violence persists primarily as a result of the absence of a central government.

Treatment of Juveniles and Juvenile Offenders

In the absence of the rule of law in some areas of Somalia and the influence of *Shari'ah* law in others, juveniles and juvenile offenders are subject to violence and mistreatment on a large scale. One of the first major problems is that many children are subjected to or have become a part of the armed conflict ravaging Somalia. Al Shabaab, a terrorist group, recruits children as young as age ten, offering them or their parents as few as twenty dollars for their services. In some cases, Al Shabaab commanders and officials kidnap girls in their teens and make them their wives. In one instance, a Al Shabaab commander kidnapped a sixteen-year-old girl from her school to become his wife. After she refused to marry him three times, he beheaded her and took her head to her school classroom where he paraded the head in front of her classmates, telling them that if they didn't cooperate, this could happen to them also. In addition to Al Shabaab, the Transitional Federal Government militias also use child soldiers in its fight against opposing forces. Children who are not killed in conflict may be executed when caught and others are put in prisons along with adults. Among the most egregious violations of children occur when both sides of the conflicting forces use the gang rape of females, including children, as a power strategy in inflicting their wills on opposing populations.

A second problem is that families may give up on their ability to control their children and will request that the youths be placed in prisons alongside adult criminals. The prisons are filthy and infested with disease and vermin and the youths are often physically and sexually victimized, in some cases killed, and many times are infected with HIV/AIDS. The extreme poverty in the country-side and cities and the death of parents from political conflict and AIDS result in other youths having to abandon their homes to attempt to survive alone in the cities. In their attempts to survive, some boys shine shoes and girls may have to turn to prostitution; older youths then rob them of their earnings. In many cases, girls are raped at night and some sleep with bags over their lower extremities in the hopes that they can escape rape. Needless to say, some of the homeless children get caught in the cross fire between warring factions and are wounded or killed. Yet other problems stem from the low status of women in society. Both wives and daughters experience physical and sexual abuse in their families. Girls from the ages of four or younger to fourteen and older are subjected to female genital mutilation throughout Somalia and suffer pain and death from the mutilations. Both male and female youths are unfairly punished, imprisoned, or even killed for minor infractions at home and in the community. Such common mistreatment of children and other at-risk groups, including but not limited to women, ethnic minorities, and displaced persons, has created an outright human rights crisis in Somalia.

Finally, the religious community is also a player in the maltreatment of children. If families are unable to control their children, the focus of control moves to local governing bodies, which are often run by the religious community; here, the rules by which children must abide are often dictated by *Shari'ah* law. However, interpretations of *Shari'ah* law vary, and thus the rules and sanctions adopted by each locale also vary. Furthermore, the system in which offenders are tried and sanctions determined is highly idiosyncratic. Because few individuals serving as law enforcement officials and judges have any formal training, arrests, detainments, and sentences are in many cases arbitrary, show a disregard for the age, sex, or circumstances of the offender, and are disproportionately harsh given the transgression. Thus, families rely heavily on local governing bodies for disciplinary action even for their own children.

However, such practices lead to the incarceration of children for even minor infractions. Hundreds of teens in Somalia are imprisoned on minor charges of disobedience to parents and truancy. Sentences for such infractions can range from a couple of days to several years. Like their counterparts in the makeshift prisons of many warlords, juvenile offenders in prisons sanctioned by the regional and local bodies are subjected to harsh treatment and poor conditions. Detention centers typically lack adequate sanitation, are infested by lice and rodents, supply inadequate food and water to prisoners, and provide few if any health services. As noted, juvenile offenders are not segregated from adults and little attention is paid to the safety of juveniles within the general prison population.[11]

Somalia and the International Community

The deterioration of human rights in Somalia, specifically the mistreatment of children, has not gone unnoticed by the international community. Today and in the past, groups and organizations such as the United Nations, Amnesty International, and Human Rights Watch have been actively involved in promoting stability in the country and improving human rights conditions. However, measures taken by these groups have been hampered by the inability to establish a national government. Efforts in Somalia, then, have either proven ineffective over time or been limited in scope to only a handful of regions and locales.

As a defunct state, Somalia has ratified neither the United Nations' Convention on the Rights of the Child, nor the African Charter on the Rights and Welfare of the Child. The first of these treaties was developed by the United Nations and established the importance of protecting children and providing special assistance to ensure that each child's basic needs are met (Convention on the Rights of the Child). Only two nations, Somalia and the United States, have yet to ratify the treaty.[12] Somalia has been unable to do so because no recognized government exists to represent the nation at the United Nations. The second treaty, the African Charter on the Rights and Welfare of the Child, is similar to the treaty passed by the United Nations but addresses a number of concerns unique to Africa.[13] Although Somali leaders have signed the African treaty, they have been unable to ratify it, again because of the lack of a national government.

Having ratified neither of the treaties concerning the treatment of children, Somalia has no official obligation to discontinue its harsh treatment of children and active recruitment of child soldiers. The failure to ratify these measures only further highlights the pervasive nature of the central government (or lack thereof) in the protection and improvement of human rights.

Steps Toward Improvement

With the help of international organizations like the United Nations Development Program (UNDP), Somalia is making little, if any, headway in addressing the mistreatment of juveniles and juvenile offenders. Most notably, Somaliland, a region with a semiautonomous government within Somalia, developed a Juvenile Justice Law in 2008 with the help of the UNDP's Rule of Law and Society (ROLS) Program.[14] By passing the law, that government exhibited a commitment not only to improving the lives and welfare of children, but also a commitment to the promotion of social order through the official codification of law.

The 2008 law came about as collaboration between the ministry of justice in the region, judges, police, religious leaders, street children, and numerous other parties involved in the disciplinary process. The primary aim was to collaborate and establish new institutions to deal with juvenile offenders in a fair and consistent manner. The result was the establishment of special courts, rehabilitation centers, and detention centers for children. The law further stipulates that criminal liability be limited to those between fifteen and eighteen years of age and that punishment be proportionate to the severity of the offense. A maximum sentence of fifteen years was established, and life imprisonment and the death penalty were abolished for juvenile offenders.[15]

Despite the efforts of officials and the United Nations in Somaliland, much work remains in the way of addressing the grave human rights violations against children in Somalia. The law does nothing to address the involvement of children in armed conflict. Furthermore, the law established in Somaliland is limited to only one of many governing bodies within the state. Violence against children and the mistreatment of juvenile offenders persists in other regions of the country.

How Do Emerging Nations Handle Juvenile Crime?

Most nations around the world either have economies based on agriculture or are just beginning to industrialize. Their per capita incomes are extremely low, most citizens are impoverished, and life is a desperate struggle for survival. The three countries discussed here were chosen in part because of the regions of the world they represent; combined, their populations constitute close to one half of the world's population.

China

The People's Republic of China is the world's most populous nation today, with approximately 1.3 billion people crowded into a land area roughly the size of the United States. Slightly more than 43 percent of China's population is under the age of thirty-four, with 25 percent under the age of eighteen.[16] Whereas China relied historically on traditional family, school, and community structures and processes to control its youth, China today is attempting to shift the responsibility for the social control of juveniles to the state. This shift accompanies a general weakening of local family, neighborhood, and factory controls as China permits some horizontal mobility of its citizens and more individual entrepreneurism in its quest for an economically productive and competitive society.

Historical Periods

Children in feudal China were ranked by family, sex, and age. Males were ranked higher than the females, who were raised as child bearers and servants. Children were expected to serve their families by working on the farms and rice paddies, and their role was one of subservience and helpfulness. The family's responsibility was to ensure the conformity of its children, and when the family failed in its mission, the school and the community intervened. In addition, most eras in Chinese history were characterized by such desperate living conditions that social upheaval, unrest, and wars resulted; as a consequence, thousands of children were neglected or abused, and were wandering the streets in need of care.[17] Not until after World War II did the first serious efforts to aid juveniles occur.

The first era in modern Chinese juvenile justice extends from 1949 to 1965. Following the seizure of control by Mao Zedong and the Communist Party in 1949, the government cracked down on "criminals" left over from pre-Mao days. The government also initiated efforts to improve the welfare of dependent and neglected children by setting up welfare services and institutions for juveniles and by eliminating the thousand-year-old practice of child labor.[18] The purpose was to rescue millions of children from the sex trade and to provide youths in need with proper care and attention. Emergency shelters, educational facilities, orphanages, and child welfare houses were set up to get children back to their families, adopted, or in foster homes.[19] The primary concern of governmental agencies was with children's needs, their susceptibility to an abusive upbringing, and their dependence on others. Particular attention was paid to holding parents responsible for the way they raised their children.

The second era, from 1966 to 1976, was a period of social chaos as China underwent a "cultural revolution." In the process, Chinese rulers attempted to rid the nation of all enemies of the proletariat class. During this time, the operations of all criminal justice institutions, including those directed toward juveniles, were suspended.

The third era extends from shortly after Mao's death in 1976 to the present. Authorities wrote a new constitution in 1982 and took appropriate steps toward strengthening the legal system.[20] Authorities also recognized that its justice institutions were flawed and that crime rates among the young were increasing. Steps were taken to deal with the problem. Youths who are guilty of minor behavioral problems such as incorrigibility or who commit minor offenses are sometimes required by parents, schoolteachers, or community leaders to go to work-study schools called *gongdu* schools.[21] Youths guilty of more serious offenses most frequently are confined, without trial, in reformatories or penal institutions that focus on "Education through Labor" and "Reform through Labor."[22] Both types of youths, in other words, are dealt with administratively rather than processed through the system. Although no national statistics are published, available data suggest that 75 percent of all crime in China is committed by individuals under age twenty-five.[23] Chinese youths' problem behaviors cover the spectrum from major to minor, yet the number of major offenses in China appears to be low compared with those in more industrialized nations.

The Police

Youths receive four chances. The first chance is when the neighborhood faction of the Communist Party comes to the child's home, discusses potential or real problems with his or her parents, and asks the parents for their help; neighbors and neighborhood organizations also may be approached. The second chance is when assistance is sought from schoolteachers and other authorities such as the police. The third chance is when the youth is sent to a work-study school, and the fourth comes when the youth is sent to a reformatory, with or without court action.[24]

On the negative side, police are permitted to use coercion, torture, beatings, and violence against citizens, depending on the situation.[25] On the positive side, the police role is to provide service and order maintenance to communities. Thus, police actually may become aware of a youth's problems at any of the above times and, in fact, counsel, mediate, and negotiate with juveniles and work with the community to help children solve their problems. In this regard, police act more like social workers than crime fighters. When the rare juvenile who does commit a serious crime comes to the attention of the police, he or she is taken into police custody, where interrogation must be undertaken within twenty-four hours; remand to the prosecutor's office must occur within four days. By law, police may detain the youth only in juvenile facilities or an adult facility if no juvenile facility is available. As in other countries, police may not release a child's name, address, or photo to the media. See Focus on Practice 15–3.

The Courts

Most juveniles with problems are dealt with by parents, local citizens, and neighborhood groups, but China's central government today is attempting to expand the more formal methods of handling juvenile offenders. The Beijing Rules standard of defining a juvenile as anyone under age eighteen is now accepted as the age of majority for Chinese youth, although for some purposes the age of majority is twenty-five. Age, in other words, is a mitigating factor in Chinese juvenile justice. For example, serious offenders under the age

Focus on Practice 15–3
Informal Justice in China

China is much more oriented toward informal juvenile justice than most industrialized nations. In China, the police's role with juveniles primarily involves either order maintenance or service activities, rather than law enforcement.

The informal role of the police, especially, is oriented toward crime prevention and services. Police precincts assign their officers to different neighborhoods or large dwelling complexes to work closely with the neighborhood committees and schools, and to oversee the safety and welfare of those neighborhoods. The behavioral problems of children are quickly identified at the first sign of trouble by an informally organized coalition consisting of parents, schoolteachers, neighborhood committee volunteers, and police officers. The lower expectation for family privacy in the Chinese cultural tradition permits police officers to penetrate the community and family lives. It is not at all unusual for police officers to make casual visits to members to whom children have been adjudicated by the court and have been placed under parents' custody or in which juveniles have been released from juvenile institutions for postrelease supervision.

Most police officers in China carry neither a gun nor a baton, therefore they appear more like social workers than police officers. In fact, the police generally devote about 90 to 95 percent of their time and resources to serving the community's various social and human needs. Arrest of juvenile offenders is rare and considered as a last resort. Only when a juvenile commits a serious crime would he or she be taken into police custody and be adjudicated by the court. Otherwise, police usually work with parents, schools, or neighborhood committees to counsel children in trouble.

CRITICAL THINKING QUESTIONS

What would trouble you if the powers of the U.S. police were expanded with children in trouble? What would be the advantages of increasing police control over children? What should the police be doing in the United States that they are not doing to prevent and control juvenile crime?

Source: Xin Ren, "People's Republic of China," in *International Handbook on Juvenile Justice*, edited by Donald J. Shoemaker (Westport, CT: Greenwood Press, 1996), 63–64.

of eighteen actually are tried in adult courts, but these trials are closed to the public in deference to the youth's age. Youths between the ages of fourteen and sixteen may be held criminally liable for crimes, but no youth under the age of eighteen may be executed for a crime unless the crime is extremely serious. Juveniles ages sixteen or seventeen who commit a capital crime and who are given the death penalty are held until the age of eighteen before execution.

Crimes in China are classified according to whether they are intentional or negligent and whether the offender violated a criminal law or committed minor violations not deemed criminal.[26] Once juveniles' cases are turned over to the procurator, the courts must either render a decision or dismiss the cases within thirty days. Typically, the courts decide on the adequacy of police evidence, but juveniles have no rights in the proceedings and are assumed to be guilty. The state's responsibility, under the inquisitory system, is to prove the guilt of the offenders by presenting the facts of the cases to the judges, one of whom is from the formal court system and two of whom are lay judges from the community. Typically, the courts decide whether the juveniles should be dealt with in the community by their parents or by a community agency; given criminal detention in a jail or another facility; placed in Institutions of Management and Education for Juvenile Offenders; or given a fixed-term imprisonment, life imprisonment, or death penalty.[27] In recent years, more youths have been placed on probation in community organizations than confined in institutions, because the Chinese prefer that all youths under the age of fourteen be worked with intensively by parents, neighborhood organizations, local police, and schools.

Institutionalization

Some youngsters are not placed with families or treated by community organizations or schools. These youths are likely to be between the ages of fourteen and sixteen and guilty of serious criminal law violations, or to have parents deemed incapable of taking care of them; this latter group includes youths up to the age of twenty-five. Both of these groups of youths are subject to confinement in juvenile facilities such as the *gongdu* schools; some are placed in adult institutions. Yet another classification of youths is sometimes confined; these are juveniles sentenced by local police, schools, and neighborhood committees for up to three years in educational camps through the Labor Department under what is called "administrative commitment."[28] Educational camps are reformatories guarded by armed guards who march uniformed youths from one assignment to the next in double time.

Two basic types of institutions designated for juveniles exist: community-based facilities and Institutions of Management and Education for Juvenile Offenders. Sixty percent of juveniles are placed in institutions for five years or less. Regardless of the length of stay, the emphasis in institutions is on "persuasion and salvation," with reintegration of the youth into their family with a better education and newly developed values.[29]

Current Concerns

China's massive population, limited resources, increasing inflation, and rapidly increasing unemployment rate pose significant problems to all Chinese who want a higher standard of living. Chinese rulers, in an effort to improve productivity and increase the number of jobs, are encouraging individual entrepreneurial activity as well as industrial growth.[30] The consequence is that parents work harder for longer hours and spend less time socializing with their children. In addition, two-thirds of today's Chinese high school students are rejected by colleges, thereby shaming their parents and guaranteeing themselves a bleak economic future; considering these trends, the reasons for juvenile offending become clear.[31] With weakening family, neighborhood, and social controls, youths are freer today than at any time in recent history. All of these factors together result in an increase in delinquency that must be brought under control.

Furthermore, the Chinese central government has stated that it desires to bring the country into compliance with the Beijing Rules. Thus, for juveniles at least, it would appear that China is moving slowly away from traditional methods of social control to a more formal system of justice. Still, tradition is strong, and the Chinese place heavy emphasis on informal community services and organizations to keep youths in line. Parents, schoolteachers, trade union representatives, neighborhood committees, Juvenile Scouts, police officers, special schools, and many others try to rehabilitate youths both in the community and in juvenile institutions. Of considerable interest is the fact that while China seems slowly to be moving *away* from these informal methods of control, many countries in other parts of the world are moving *toward* such methods.[32] Given that much of the industrialized world is trying to reintegrate youths into their families and communities, some question exists as to whether China is going in the right direction.

Another important consideration is that China is notorious for its human rights violations. Police apparently are permitted to use certain types of torture; charges of abuse are not condemned; rights violations are not investigated; and youths are tried without being indicted, not permitted effective legal representation, or given fair trials. If the Chinese government is to win the respect of other countries, due process of justice must be developed in all thirty of China's administrative units.

India

India's population is projected to surpass that of China's by the year 2025.[33] Birth rates now hover around 3.2 children per woman of childbearing age. Of the projected population of more than 1.4 billion (in 2025), more than three hundred million will be juveniles. Still, even with more than several hundred million youths, only a tiny fraction of these youths are arrested each year for all national Indian Penal Code violations and local code violations combined. The low arrest rates are explained by a combination of factors, including that the crime rate is, in fact, low and that most offenders are handled informally; a major factor, however, is the extensive police corruption found throughout India.[34]

The first major Indian acts identifying juveniles as a special category of offenders came about with the Apprentice Act of 1850, which granted special protection to young people. An 1860s act established the age of responsibility as seven. An 1861 act called for separate trials for youths under age fifteen, and an 1897 act permitted the confinement of males under age fifteen in reformatories in place of exile or confinement in adult prisons.[35] Separate judicial and confinement systems were established for juveniles and adults in the early 1920s.[36] In 1960, a national Children's Act was passed for use by all nationally governed territories and as a model for India's states, a goal that has only been partially met thus far.

The most recent major change in Indian juvenile justice law is based on that 1960s national Children's Act. In 1986, some fifty-five political jurisdictions passed laws facilitating

Voices of Deliquency: Abusive Treatment in More than One Culture

the treatment and rehabilitation of neglected and delinquent youths.[37] *Delinquent* and *neglected* were defined in this act, as were the procedures to be used in processing each through the system. In India, a juvenile is any male under the age of sixteen and any female under the age of eighteen. A delinquent, as might be expected, is anyone who violates one of India's codes, and a neglected youth is any youth who might be classified as a status offender in the United States. The act also describes the types of residential and correctional facilities each type of youthful offender is to be confined in and the qualifications of correctional staff. Within the formal system, the first stop for youths is either the welfare boards or courts, although a semiofficial agency, the *Panchayat*, recently has reemerged as an agent of social control in Indian society.[38]

An important consideration relates to the traditional methods of social control in Indian society. Custom and tradition enforced by the family were long used to maintain order. Equally important as a social control factor was the fact that the family's position in the caste or subcaste (or *jati*) was based on its reputation in that *jati*. Youths who engaged in deviancy of any type threatened the reputation of their families and therefore also threatened the family's ability to obtain jobs, the family's ability to arrange good marriages for their daughters, and the family's overall socioeconomic status. Also important is that a deep distrust still is directed at the police and courts as a result of British rule. Indians today still prefer traditional methods of social control, with the consequence that few youths ever come to the attention of the police and courts.[39]

Panchayats

Panchayats are quasi-governmental organizations at the community level. These groups have their roots in ancient India but were eliminated at the time of British colonization. With the return of the nation to Indian rule, the *Panchayats* have again emerged. They consist of elected members of the community, usually village elders, who understand community traditions and who are able to deal with all aspects of youthful misbehavior. *Panchayats* hear cases, levy fines, order youths to stop associating with others, and, in extreme cases, compel youths to undergo corporal punishment.[40]

The Police

Police in India generally are viewed with suspicion because of the way the British used them to maintain control. Police today continue to control, but often in the name of the upper classes or whoever happens to have power. Thus, child labor and bondage and female and child prostitution are often overlooked by the police in deference to the ruling parties. Police are also known to engage in extralegal beatings, arrests, "disappearances," and, in some parts of the country, rapes, tortures, and murders. Nevertheless, we should point out, police behavior varies widely in the different cities, states, and political jurisdictions throughout India.

Police officers have the option of taking juveniles before either the welfare boards or the juvenile courts, depending on the characteristics of the offenders, their situations, and their offenses. Most of the offenses for which police make arrests under the Indian Penal Code are property crimes and gambling, whereas offenses under Local and Special Laws consist primarily of alcohol prohibitions; the number of drug violations is very small. The distrust of police and formal law leads most communities to deal with the problems of the juveniles informally and in *Panchayats*.

The Courts

Delinquent youths come before special juvenile courts whose membership is mandated by the state to be either metropolitan or judicial magistrates. Each court has a panel of two honorary social workers, one of whom, as in the case of the welfare boards, must be a woman.[41] Citizens appointed to the welfare boards or courts must have some understanding of the psychology and needs of youths. A wide range of sentences is available to judges. Youths may be sent home after consultation; released to parents; placed on probation or with responsible persons in the community; fined; or confined in community facilities, special homes, jails, or prisons.[42]

The Indian point of view is that both the courts and the police are to be avoided at all costs. Nevertheless, police do occasionally bring juveniles before the courts for violation of both the Indian Penal Code and the Local and Special Laws. Court hearings are closed to the public, although either the juvenile or the court may request anyone relevant to the case to appear.

Institutions

Although the Children's Act of 1960 and the Juvenile Justice Act of 1986 state that juveniles may not be held in the same facilities as adults, youths are confined with adults in both jails and prisons across India. The problems of confined youths are undoubtedly increased in that prisoners are classified by their social status. Wealthy prisoners and prominent citizens are classified as Class A prisoners. They are held in private rooms and government guest houses and may have their food supplemented by their families. Class B prisoners consist of college students and taxpayers and are held in less auspicious facilities with poorer support services. Class C prisoners often are held in overcrowded cells with dirt floors, no furnishings, and poor-quality food.[43] Juveniles from the lower castes and *jatis* are most frequently found in facilities for Class C prisoners.

Only a minority of youths are ever confined, because most are either acquitted of the charges, released to their parents, or placed under supervision in the community. Some children are placed in observation homes or "places of safety" until their cases are decided. Youths who are considered neglected or incorrigible may be placed in juvenile homes for a period of time up to age twenty for males and age eighteen for females.[44] Children who violate their probation often end up in these special homes.

Current Concerns

India's expanding population, lack of natural resources, and abject poverty characterize the struggle of its citizens for survival. Children growing up under these conditions, especially those in the remnants of the lower castes and *jatis*, find themselves hungry and disease ridden. A nationwide shortage of jobs means that most children have no economically viable future. If they are poor, and most are, children must attempt to survive in any way possible. The options for most are child labor, wandering the streets, prostitution, begging, and crime. Estimates are that India has some five hundred thousand street children nationwide and another three hundred thousand who are bonded, that is, forced to work for others to help pay back their parents' debts. Trafficking in young females for purposes of prostitution and begging is common.[45] Dramatically, an estimated 34 percent of all primary schoolchildren drop out of school, many of whom then enter the illegal labor markets. Given the economic importance of children to the ruling classes, little incentive exists for the central government to crack down on those who violate child labor laws and even less incentive for police and local authorities to try to dissuade youths or those who exploit them from undesirable activities.

The plight of females in India also must not be overlooked. Already noted is that females are sold into prostitution, and they frequently are the victims of infanticide. In some parts of India, females also are given as child brides to males; payment of dowry to the male's family is often part of the marriage deal. When these dowries are considered inadequate, the brides, more than one-half of whom are under the age of sixteen, are often beaten and/or killed. The assumption in some states of India is that any girl who dies under the age of sixteen is the victim of murder by either her husband or his family.[46]

The Indian government is trying to improve its justice system. Nevertheless, the challenge for the government is to generate the financial resources necessary to expand and professionalize its police forces. Resources must also be found to train professionals in child care, rehabilitation, and the administration of justice. Facilities exclusively for juveniles must be built and staff sensitive to the needs of children hired. Finally, the ethnic and social class divisions found throughout India result in almost unlimited sources of conflict between the rulers and the ruled.

Brazil

Brazil has the largest population of any country in South America and is the fifth most populous nation in the world, with 174 million people.[47] Its legislative history in dealing with children has its roots in European law, particularly the Napoleonic and Rocco Codes, and has long called for differential treatment of juveniles and adults. The Penal Code of the Empire and the First Penal Code of the Republic, for example, differentiate between adults and juveniles by focusing on the ways minors' degree of "moral responsibility" and "discernment" exempt them from criminal culpability. The Penal Code of 1940 established that minors under the age of eighteen lack criminal responsibility entirely, and this assumption was continued through the enactment of a juvenile code in 1979 and the Statute of the Child and Adolescent (SEA) in 1990. The latter act specifically identifies a "child" as any person up to the age of twelve and an "adolescent" as any youth between the ages of twelve and seventeen.[48] The main thrust of Brazilian laws and codes is on the "protection of fundamental rights to physical, intellectual, emotional, social, and cultural development."[49] In 1988, the SEA called for the government to protect the rights of children. Reform groups and the government continue to call for human rights for children and for setting up a wide range of social service facilities throughout the country.[50] The first stop for a child in trouble is often a guardianship council.

▲ Slums such as these are common throughout the world. Here, children suffer poverty, disease, and malnutrition that will remain with them throughout their lives. Storms, tsunamis, and floods take a terrible toll on their lives.
eye ubiquitous/Robert Harding World Imagery

Guardianship Council

Guardianship councils are composed of five members chosen by local citizens of local communities. The proceedings of these councils begin upon the referral of a youth by a judge to the council. The charge of these agencies is to guarantee that any youth who gets into difficulties receives any of a number of protective measures. The councils may, for example, recommend that children be placed under the care of their parents, basic education schools, government or community programs for youths or their families, hospitals, shelter foster families, or treatment.[51] Adolescents, in addition to being subject to protective measures, may be reprimanded, required to pay restitution or perform community service, or placed on probation. Youths caught committing serious crimes are subject to the deprivation of liberty if approved by the proper judicial authority.[52]

The Police

Police officers vary widely in how they handle juveniles. Reports of police brutality and vigilante murders continue to shock the world—three children are estimated to be murdered in Brazil each day. A disturbing number of these children are murdered on the streets and in custody by both on- and off-duty police officers.[53] Youths of African descent, mixed parentage, and Native Indian heritage are the primary targets, with males outnumbering females by a ratio of seven to one. Estimates are that many impoverished youths engage in begging, petty theft, shoplifting, loitering, and prostitution in an attempt to supplement family incomes.

In an effort to reduce police arbitrariness in dealing with juveniles, it is mandated that police must take any youth caught in the act of committing a crime directly to a guardianship council or a juvenile court judge as soon as possible. In rural areas, the youth usually is taken to a regular police station and often is confined with adult offenders. Once the police investigate the offense as well as the needs of the minor, the youth may either be released or, if the evidence warrants, sent to the prosecutor.

The Courts

Once a prosecutor decides how to dispose of a case, it is sent to either a juvenile judge, if one is available, or, more likely, to a judge of the adult court who handles the review. This judge then evaluates the characteristics of the juvenile, the juvenile's family situation, and the seriousness of the behavior. If the judge agrees with the prosecutor's procedures and decisions, the judge then calls for the sentence to be carried out. If the judge does not agree, the case is sent back to the chief prosecutor's office for another hearing.

The courts work closely with the guardianship councils to maintain the juvenile's ties to the family and community and to provide juveniles with the proper educational experiences. Like the councils, judges have available to them such mechanisms as enrolling youths and parents in specialized schools and programs in order to assist them in solving their problems.[54]

Institutions

New laws provide for community centers for youths and include integrated screening centers, which are open twenty-four hours a day and are available to all street youths who need help. Also available are training centers that operate as day care centers and shelters that offer children a safe place to sleep. Actual penalties include reprimands, requiring the payment of restitution, performing community service, or, in more extreme instances, depriving youths of their liberty.[55] This latter sanction may involve either semiliberty, in which youths work or go to school during the day and return to a facility at night, or internment, which is confinement in a juvenile institution.

Maximum-security institutions are used only as a last resort for youths who are guilty of particularly serious offenses, who are repeat offenders, and who are capable of understanding and evaluating their own behavior. In fact, all types of youths, including the dependent and neglected, status offenders, and minor offenders, are often institutionalized. Once confined, juveniles are supposed to be evaluated every six months and are confined for no more than three years. In spite of today's welfare orientation, children are beaten, sexually abused, and packed in small cells without bathrooms or ventilation. In a 1999 riot in a juvenile institution in São Paulo, four inmates were killed, one of whom was beheaded. Forty other people were injured, including sixteen guards.[56] Life in institutions is often as brutal as life on the streets.

Current Concerns

Brazil is a society of extremes. Industrially and agriculturally based wealth qualifies Brazil to be listed in some reports as an emerging nation. Yet Brazil has poverty and discrimination as deep as those in any country in South America. In addition, wild economic fluctuations during the past several decades have frequently destabilized Brazilian society to the point that few have confidence that their economic status will remain stable for long. The poor do not have these concerns, because their status at the bottom of the Brazilian socioeconomic structure remains unchanged.

How Do Industrialized Nations Handle Juvenile Crime?

This section focuses on three industrialized, English-speaking countries: Canada, England, and Australia. All share common social, cultural, and legal backgrounds.

Canada

The development of Canadian juvenile justice parallels that of the United States in that juveniles in colonial Canada were tried in the same courts and held in the same prisons as were adults. Then, in the early 1800s, some houses of refuge were built, and a few reformatories were constructed in the mid-1800s. Most juveniles were tried in adult courts and confined in adult prisons throughout the nineteenth century. Whether youths had the mental capacity to understand their actions, however, was debated as much then as it is today. Child savers of the late 1800s maintained that youthful offenders were misdirected children who required assistance more than punishment. Reformers of this era further believed that juveniles needed to be tried in separate juvenile courts and confined in facilities separate from those for adults, a clear shift in thinking from that in the past.[57]

The consequence was that a Juvenile Delinquents Act (JDA) was passed in 1908 at the federal level, calling for Canada's provinces and territories to implement a new approach to juvenile justice. This law called for a **welfare model** approach to juvenile justice similar to that of the 1899 act that created the juvenile court in Chicago.[58] Provinces and territories developed their own facilities and set the age of jurisdiction at sixteen, seventeen, or eighteen, depending on the prevailing philosophy in the particular political jurisdiction. The system that was developed called for informal practices with officials free to exercise great discretion. This approach dominated Canadian juvenile justice until the 1960s, when reformers questioned whether juveniles actually were being rehabilitated.

A 1965 report on juvenile delinquency in Canada criticized the informal and often arbitrary procedures of the 1908 act, but Canada continued to follow the ideals of the welfare model. After a number of unsuccessful tries, a new reform act, the **Young Offenders Act (YOA)**, was passed in 1982. This act set the age of eighteen as the upper limit of jurisdiction across Canada and called for a modified justice model approach to juvenile crime.[59] Youths began to be held accountable for their crimes, to be provided with many of the same due process rights as adults, and to receive sentences proportionate to their offenses. Nevertheless, the YOA principles calling for welfare services for youths in need remained strong, but they emphasized that these needs should not be addressed in the criminal justice system.[60] Thus, the YOA was a compromise between the welfare and justice models, although the C.19 Bill of 1995 removed some of the treatment objectives of the YOA and strengthened justice and due process responses to serious and violent offenders.[61] These last two changes moved Canadian juvenile justice toward a **crime control model**. The results were such that procedural protections were inadequate, too many young and minor offenders were confined—often with adult offenders—and disparities and unfairness in sentencing existed. In addition, the proposed interventions were not appropriately targeted to individuals, victims, and offenders.[62]

The YOA was repealed with the passage of the **Youth Criminal Justice Act (YCJA)** on April 1, 2003. The new act statutorily directs the most serious sanctions to the more serious older offenders, and increases extrajudicial sanctions options for police, prosecutors, and judges for the less serious and younger offenders. Unlike the Young Offenders Act, the YCJA's principles call for extrajudicial sanctions proportionate to the youth's age, maturity, offense, and behavior in the community. At the front end, the new act's principles specify conditions under which youths may be processed formally through the courts. The statute also encourages police, prosecutors, and judges to caution or warn youths about the consequences of continued misbehaviors. "Conferencing" with victims, offenders, and families is encouraged as is directing the youths to appropriate community programs. The extrajudicial sanctions are used at all stages of the processing of youths.[63]

The Police

The police function in Canada with regard to juveniles is to respond to and investigate youth crime. Upon apprehending a juvenile, police must inform the youth of his or her rights, which include consulting parents or counsel and remaining silent. In the event that the juvenile is willing to talk to the police, police must obtain a written statement that the youth agrees to waive these rights before the police are permitted to take a statement or conduct an interview.

Police officers diverted youths to community agencies, but the ambiguities of the YOA resulted in an increasing number of youths being pushed into the system and, eventually, an increase in confinements. The YCJA was designed to reverse this trend and provide police and prosecutors with specific discretionary guidelines to get younger and minor offenders with special needs into extrajudicial programs, and older and more serious offenders into the courts; both types of offenders are placed in programs that rehabilitate, but in which offenders are held accountable for their behaviors.[64] Since the passage of the YCJA, police are diverting more younger and less serious offenders in need to community agencies for these extrajudicial interventions. Information sharing also is improved under the YCJA and youths at all offending levels have their names entered into national databases accessible by other agencies with a need to know. Police share information with probation officers to facilitate the filing of new charges in the event that a youth violates probation.[65]

Prosecution

The prosecution's role is most comprehensive in British Columbia and Quebec where prosecutors make all decisions relating to intake, diversion, and filing charges. The prosecutor, just as the police, follows statutory guidelines for diverting youths to extrajudicial sanctions, and may do so after police charge youths to them.[66] In other provinces, police still are responsible for filing charges, although their charges, the evidence, and the possibility of conviction are reviewed by Crown counsel before the youth is taken to court. In all provinces, Crown counsel must "show cause" before remanding a youth to a juvenile facility before trial.

In addition, Crown counsel no longer decides whether to transfer youths to adult court. Prosecutors may under the YCJA, however, notify the youth court that prosecutors will seek an adult sentence in youth court for youths over the age of fourteen charged with murder, attempted murder, manslaughter, and aggravated sexual assault; if the prosecutor does not notify the youth court that an adult sentence is sought, judges are prohibited from giving the youth an adult sentence.[67]

Probation Officers

Under the YOA, probation officers who played supervisory and law enforcement roles were expected to apply due process rules rigorously, and were to remain neutral in the courtroom. Under the YCJA, probation officers continue to consult with police officers on the referral of juveniles to the proper community agencies. Probation officers also continue to interview police, offenders, families, employers, and school officials when developing presentencing reports for prosecutors and judges. Another primary role is to manage offenders referred to community agencies. Juveniles who are adjudicated and found guilty of offenses may be sentenced directly to probation or, as frequently happens, given a custodial sentence that includes probation as part of judges' sentences. Probation officers are case managers, directing offenders to the proper community agencies, tracking and supervising them, conducting "conferencing sessions," and implementing other options available in the different provinces.[68]

The Courts

Juvenile judges under the YOA received many younger, less serious and "child in need" cases as police and prosecutors funneled large numbers of youths through the system. The result was the confinement of many youths whose needs called for extrajudicial sanctions rather than confinement. Under the YCJA, judges receive primarily the older, more serious and repetitive offenders who, citizens and criminal justice professionals believe, should be held accountable for their actions. Nevertheless, judges are permitted to refer eligible youths to extrajudicial sanctions, either before adjudication or after, but the more serious offenders are likely to be confined in a juvenile facility of some type. Typically, the youths are required to serve two-thirds of their sentences before being sent to community agencies on probation. In addition, judges may not assign adult sentences in which a juvenile serves time in an adult facility. Rather, youths receive an adult sentence to be served in juvenile confinement, thus keeping alive the principles of the YCJA that juveniles, even murderers, are not adults and must be treated according to their maturity levels.[69]

Juvenile Facilities

Throughout the era of the YOA, the traditions initiated by the JDA and the philosophy of the juvenile court that existed at its beginning continued to influence Canadian juvenile justice. Community-based corrections were founded in all provinces and included community service, intensive supervision, and counseling services. Also used were private-sector programs, such as wilderness camps, and public-sector initiatives, such as foster care, alternative schools, drug and alcohol abuse centers, and counseling centers. Under the YCJA, the number and types of these programs for extrajudicial sanctions have increased throughout Canada.[70]

Canada's juvenile institutions vary by security level and by province as much as juvenile facilities do in the United States. Some open facilities tend to lack fences and walls, while others, depending on the province, have all the security features of a U.S. maximum-security juvenile facility. Facilities focus on security, health, education, and recreation, with treatment provided when requested by youths; most treatment is delivered by outside contractors, and Canada, under the YCJA, is focusing more attention than ever before on reintegrating offenders into their communities after confinement. Unfortunately, reports of physical and sexual assault by peers and staff continue to filter out of Canada's juvenile facilities.

Current Concerns

Canadian officials are committed to improving the fairness, justice, and effectiveness of the juvenile justice system. Due process rules and modern efforts of crime control continue to be emphasized, but in modified form. The focus today is on formalizing the structure of discretion involved in extrajudicial sanctions so that police, prosecutors, and judges can get young offenders the needed help outside the justice system; rules are much clearer, and inconsistent discretion is reduced to a great extent.

A major issue is whether the police and courts discriminate against minority youths. Police and court activity does vary from province to province, but evidence exists that Native Indians are prosecuted four times as often as nonnatives in British Columbia. In other provinces, more than half of the confined youths are Native Indians. Government reports state that the discrepancy between natives and nonnatives is the result of widespread discrimination, but some studies find no evidence of such discriminatory practices.

England and Wales

As noted in earlier chapters, English common law helped set the stage for criminal and juvenile law in the United States. The concept of *parens patriae* was of particular importance because it justified the intervention of the king in the lives of, first, all citizens and their families and, later, children. To review, children under the age of seven seldom faced any legal sanctions for misbehavior; children between the ages of seven and fourteen could face criminal sanctions, depending on the seriousness of the crime, their intent, and their ability to determine right from wrong.

Children who met one or more of these latter criteria faced the possibility of being punished as adults—often by imprisonment or **corporal punishment** such as whipping and branding. English law also called for **capital punishment** (the death penalty) for close to two hundred offenses and for the transportation of youthful offenders to British colonies in Australia, New Zealand, and North America. Many of those sentenced to death were pardoned or transported, but according to Leon Radzinowicz, eighteen of twenty people executed in London in 1785 were under the age of eighteen.[71]

In the late 1700s, the English and U.S. methods for handling juveniles roughly paralleled each other. The English initiated the use of private homes to house minor offenders, and lower courts were set up to adjudicate minor offenses. In 1847, the Juvenile Offenders Act permitted summary trials of youths under the age of fourteen. Then, in 1854, the first Reformatory Schools Act was passed; this act called for placing youths in reformatories separate from adult prisons. In 1879, summary trials for youths under the age of sixteen were permitted for most offenses, and in a significant reform, the number of juveniles imprisoned with adults was reduced.

The first juvenile court was established in England under the Children Act of 1908.[72] This court's criminal jurisdiction was for *children* under age fourteen and for *young persons* between fourteen and sixteen, and civil jurisdiction was for youths in need of welfare services.[73]

The early acts did not emphasize special training for judges, nor did they focus on the special needs of youths—unless the youth's needs were exceptional. In the Children and Young Persons Act of 1933, the principle that the court "should always act in the best interests of the welfare of the child was affirmed as was the principle of *in loco parentis.*"[74] The philosophy behind this act clearly was based on positivism and a welfare model rather than a punishment model of justice. Also established were changes in the ages of youths under the jurisdiction of the courts; "the age of criminal responsibility was raised from seven to eight (Sec. 50) and sixteen-year-olds were placed under the criminal jurisdiction of the juvenile court."[75] Thus, the court had both criminal and civil jurisdiction.

The Children and Young Persons Act of 1969 reemphasized the importance of treating delinquents the same way as any other youths in need. The age of minimum responsibility was raised from eight to ten, and juveniles who formerly were treated as criminals were handled through civil proceedings. Police were required to consult social work personnel about decisions concerning youths, and children under the age of seventeen were not to be confined in juvenile facilities or detention centers.[76] Nevertheless, the ideals of the welfare model were not met, and the juvenile court took on the form of a criminal court that emphasized punishment.[77] A hard line emerged in England at this time paralleling the development of a similar hard line in the United States. Even so, the Criminal Justice Act of 1982 empowered magistrates to place delinquent youths in custody, issue care orders with residential requirements, and require community service; this act reflected a blend of treatment and punishment.[78] In 1989, the Children Act affirmed an existing philosophy that youths should be prosecuted only as a last resort; care cases were transferred to the civil courts.

The Criminal Justice Act of 1991 renamed the juvenile court the youth court, broadened the court's jurisdiction to include youths as old as age seventeen, emphasized individualized sentencing based on the maturity of youths, placed more emphasis on parental responsibility, called for more interagency cooperation in dealing with youths, and developed new procedural guidelines for the police and courts. In 1994, the Criminal Justice and Public Order Act was passed. It called for longer custodial sentences and a "secure training order" for juveniles.[79] The hard line was in place.

In 1998, England's response to juveniles shifted direction with the passage of the Crime and Disorder Act, which set up a Youth Justice Board (YJB) for England and Wales.[80] Under the auspices of the Secretary of State, the YJB had the broader goals of reducing the numbers of youths in custody by emphasizing community prevention and treatment, and monitoring the performance of the Youth Justice System, the organizational entity responsible for overseeing the actual purchases of places for the placement of children, the promotion of effective practices, and the commissioning of research.

The Police

In England, the police departments are usually among the first formal agencies to make contact with juveniles in trouble. Depending on the behavior of youths and the evidence, English Bobbies (police officers) are expected to exercise discretion in determining whether to hold youths for further action. Youths under the age of ten are almost always sent into community programs by the police; the only exceptions are juveniles who commit heinous crimes such as murder. For most crimes, youths and their parents must go to the police station, where most juveniles are released to their parents. Information about the children is collected by the juvenile bureau and is used by the chief inspector to determine whether to prosecute, issue a formal caution, or drop the case. If a formal reprimand is decided on, the juveniles are warned about their behavior and informed that further offenses will result in court action. According to David Farrington and Trever Bennett, "A caution can only be administered if the juvenile admits the offence, if the parents agree that the juvenile should be cautioned, and if the complainant or victim is willing to leave the decision to the police."[81] Cautions are used widely to minimize the penetration of youths into the system.

The ability to issue cautions has resulted in "net widening" in that officers are now bringing increasing numbers of youths into stations to reprimand them. At the court level, the number of youths diverted from the juvenile court increased and the number of youths sentenced to confinement declined.[82] A large number of these youths are sent to youth court.

Juvenile Courts

Youth courts in England usually are presided over by three lay magistrates or, less frequently, one magistrate. These magistrates are citizens who are believed to be well qualified for working with juveniles and who undergo twelve months of special training in courtrooms, in juvenile institutions, and with juvenile probation and parole officers.[83] The youth court sessions are more informal than adult trials and are conducted by the magistrates at different times and places than the adult courts when possible; youth court proceedings are closed to the public. Juveniles do not have jury trials. The media may be present, but must keep all information about the juveniles confidential. In England, unlike in the United States, juveniles have the right to bail.

Whereas only police officers prosecuted cases in the past, today a representative from the Crown Prosecution Service tries cases. Whereas in the past the courts relied on the presumed fairness of the police in presenting cases, the system today is moving toward the representation of juveniles by lawyers.

Once in the courtroom, juveniles and their parents must be present as the charges are read. If the magistrate is not convinced that the parent or child understands the charges, the magistrate may enter a "not admit" (not guilty) plea on behalf of the family and throw the burden of proof on the prosecution.[84] The prosecution then presents the information available about the case to the magistrate(s), who asks the youth and his or her parents if the information is accurate. The child's parents or counsel may cross-examine the police officer and any available witnesses.[85] If the youth is found guilty, a predisposition report is prepared, and, once completed, the juvenile and his or her parents are called back before the magistrate for sentencing.

Magistrates, depending on the seriousness of the offense, have a range of sentences available to them. They may discharge cases, issue fines, require offenders to pay recognizance (which is refunded if the offenders complete their "binding over" successfully), place juveniles under supervision (probation), require community service or the payment of compensation to the victim(s), or defer sentences for six months to see how well the youths behave during that time.[86] Magistrates attempt to avoid imposing the maximum custodial sentence of six months on offenders, although two consecutive sentences of six months each may be handed out if necessary. For more serious offenses, juveniles over the age of fifteen may be tried in Crown court, where sentences, including life sentences for murder, may be handed down.

Juvenile Institutions

Juveniles were housed with adults in local jails, prisons, and galleys in the late 1700s and early 1800s. The violence and disease in these facilities attracted the attention of reformers, who began to look for safer alternative placements for juveniles. One of the first reforms involved putting some juveniles with minor problems into private homes. Then the Juvenile Offenders Act of 1847 was passed, and the first reformatories for juveniles under the age of sixteen were built. Not until the early 1900s did the Borstal system develop, with a heavy emphasis on aftercare. Borstals lasted until the 1980s, when they were turned into youth custody centers in which sentences were determinate and youths received shorter confinements. These centers emphasize cleanliness, order, discipline, and hard work.[87] See Focus on Practice 15–4 for the development of the Borstal system.

Current Concerns

A hard-line consensus appears to dominate the thinking of both the Conservative and Labour Parties in England. Nevertheless, critics of the English system continue to argue that detention and other custodial facilities are "schools of crime" and that a return to treatment and the welfare model is in order. On another level, more specific issues are of concern. The murder of a two-year-old boy by two ten-year-old youths in 1993 generated national soul-searching and debate similar to that resulting from the Columbine High School massacres in Colorado in the United States. The emergence of a "rave culture" and the fact that one-half of all males and one-third of all females have tried drugs suggest to many that drug use is increasing among British youths.[88] Particularly disturbing to the middle class is that it is middle-class children, not lower-class children, who are involved with drugs, particularly Ecstasy. Finally, extreme reservations are being expressed about the increased use of guns by disadvantaged youths. Whether a lack of jobs in England will result in problems of violence becoming more endemic and comparable to that in the United States is in the back of many minds. Concern, too, is expressed about reports that British police are using unjustified violence among the immigrant minority populations that make up an increasingly large part of the British population.

Sweden: The Most Humane State?[*]

Juvenile crime in Sweden looks a lot like youth crime in other parts of the West. Youth crime began to increase dramatically in the years following World War II, and throughout the 1950s a strong increase in reported crime among juveniles became evident and continued up through the beginning of the 1970s.[89] Since then the annual number of juvenile offenders has stabilized. The crime most commonly committed by juveniles is theft, which has remained relatively stable in regards to the annual number of prosecutions since the 1980s. The use of illegal drugs is also a frequent crime by juveniles within the fifteen- to sixteen-year-old age group; however, studies show that from 1971 to 1997 the proportion of juveniles who admit to using an illegal drug on a regular basis has decreased. The proportion

*Special recognition to Mr. James Schrecengost and Lauren Horning of Washington & Jefferson College.

Focus on Practice 15–4
The Borstal System

The principles of the Borstal system are important to outline because they became influential in setting up similar programs in the United States and in the British overseas dominions. Briefly, the Borstal system called for the lad's reform by "individualization," mentally, morally, and physically. There would be physical drills, gymnastics, and technical literacy training. Good conduct would be rewarded. The staff were selected for characteristics that were likely to influence youths of the kind that a Borstal had to work with. Soon after the beginning of the program, it was decided that the minimum period of exposure to the Borstal should be at least a year.

The Borstal system proceeded on this fairly austere plan until 1921, when the remarkable personality of Alexander Paterson (1884–1947) was added to the Prison Commission. He was one of a kind. The son of an affluent family, he attended a public school and went on to Oxford University like hundreds of others headed for conventional careers in the civil service or politics. At the age of twenty-one, he graduated from Oxford and settled in Bermondsey, one of London's worst slums, as a member of the staff of the Oxford Medical Mission. He lived in Bermondsey for twenty years, organizing boys' clubs and recruiting Oxford students to work with him in the clubs and, later, when he became a prison commissioner, to take on assignments in the Borstal system.

Paterson's work in the Borstal system was notable for at least four achievements. First, as far as possible, he removed the appearances and the procedures of the British prisons from the Borstals. The governor was still called the governor, but the assistant governors were housemasters serving, as far as possible, the roles of housemasters in an English public school. The prison officials were taken out of uniform, and so were the lads, who were allowed to wear civilian clothes instead of the convicts' demeaning uniform.

Second, having removed as many of the earmarks of prison as he could, he went on to bring in young university men to fill the posts of governors and housemasters. To induce scions of the upper and middle classes to choose a career in penology was an astonishing innovation. The governor in one of the largest prisons in England tells how he was recruited to work in the Borstal system. He had worked in Paterson's settlement house in Bermondsey during a university vacation. Shortly after his return to Oxford, there was a knock on the door of his college room, and there was Paterson. He said, "I need you as a housemaster at a new Borstal. I want you to report to my office in London next

Monday." The startled young student protested that he was only in his second year at Oxford but perhaps could work during the next vacation. "That's not soon enough," Paterson replied. "I need you full time, beginning next Monday." To the mystification of the college authorities and the dismay of his parents, he left Oxford, reported the following Monday, and continued in the Borstal system and later in the Prison Commission for the succeeding 40 years.

Paterson's third innovation was a training school for prison and Borstal staff at Wakefield in the north of England. The prison staff college was opened in 1935 to train likely candidates for promotion—not a popular new departure among prison officers accustomed to promotion by seniority. Eventually, the training program was expanded to include a six-week curriculum for all new recruits for prisons and Borstals and a six-month course for new assistant governors and housemasters.

Paterson's fourth and surely his most significant contribution was the Borstal mystique. He had a flair for aphorisms: "You cannot train a man for freedom in conditions of captivity." He added:

> The Borstal System has no merit apart from the Borstal Staff. It is men and not buildings who will change the hearts and ways of misguided lads. Better an institution that consists of two log huts in swamp or desert, with a staff devoted to their task, than a model block of buildings . . . whose staff is solely concerned with thoughts of pay and promotion.

American prison reformers took a considerable interest in the Borstal model. In 1940 the American Law Institute made a long and comprehensive study of the problem of delinquency that culminated in a model Youth Correction Authority Act, recommended for adoption by each state; it also called specifically for new institutions patterned on the Borstal system. The system was adopted in California and in modified form by several other states.

CRITICAL THINKING QUESTIONS

Do we have such charismatic and dedicated leaders as Paterson today in juvenile justice in the United States? Can such a person still make a real difference? Do you believe that you can make a difference in juvenile justice in this nation? How?

Source: Sir Evelyn Ruggles-Brise, *The English Prison System* (London: Macmillan, 1921), 85–87.

of juvenile suspects involved with illegal narcotics-related crimes has decreased by 75 percent from 1970 to 1996.[90] In 2008, the most common offenses made by juveniles older than age fifteen and younger than twenty-one were stealing (36 percent), crimes against another individual (28 percent), traffic-related offences (18 percent), narcotic/drug-related crimes (17 percent), and crimes inflicting damage to property (12 percent).[91]

Juvenile violence data collected through police reports, victimization and self-report surveys, and hospital statistics show relatively small amounts of increase from the 1930s until the 1980s when a dramatic spike in prosecutions for juvenile assault occurred. In 1986 the media was abuzz with "youth violence," causing many politicians to focus campaigns on the issue and push for new legislation dealing with young offenders. Victimization surveys show that while an increase of youth violence occurred in the 1980s the levels dropped and stabilized in the 1990s to reflect the pre-1980s level. Self-report studies on violence by schoolchildren indicate that the overall levels of children participating in violence remained generally stable during the past few decades.[92]

Since the 1960s Sweden has kept hospital records that, among other things, track the number of patients admitted to medical facilities for injuries obtained due to violent assault. Although there has not been a clear increase or decrease in the data obtained overall, the records do show a small drop in the number of knife wounds between the early 1970s and the latter 1990s and early 2000s, with an accompanying increase in gun wounds also occurring throughout the 1990s and into the 2000s. Medical records indicating the number of fatal injuries due to youth violence has also not shown any significant change since the 1970s; approximately 16 individuals die annually as a result of youth violence.[93] How does Sweden handle these crimes? Are institutions a major part of the picture?

The Rationale Against Institutionalization

The limited use of institutions as well as an added focus on social welfare are major factors in what sets Sweden's juvenile justice system apart from other nations. Throughout the entire twentieth century, numerous reforms took place in the institutionalizing of juvenile offenders, but the returning theme was that juveniles should be kept separate from adults at all costs to protect the innocence of the child. Rather than sending impressionable youths to the harsh realities of the adult prison, Sweden began introducing alternative punitive measures to allow for a focus on diversion and rehabilitation and the preparation to return to society. In 1902, "forced care" facilities were made available for children between the ages of fifteen and seventeen to replace the adult prisons, and this system was made available for juveniles up to age twenty through the Act on Child Care in 1935.[94]

Youth prisons were established in the 1930s to handle children who were amenable to treatment by the social welfare system. Sentences to these youth prisons were mandated to be for indeterminate sentences; this way, the individual characteristics of the needs of the child were given greater importance than the act he or she committed. After World War II, the public became aware of the cruel environment of youth prisons and the harmful impact the institutions had on confined offenders. Because of this realization, sentencing offenders to the youth prisons became a last resort in the handling of deviant children while youth welfare and diversionary programs became the primary methods for dealing with juvenile offenders.[95]

Throughout the 1950s and into the 1960s, public opinion and new legislation favored a more humane treatment approach over the classic punishment models. Youth prisons still existed as an option for eighteen- to twenty-year-olds and youths who committed crimes for which the mandated punishment was incarceration. Only in rare and special circumstances did youths under age eighteen enter the youth prison system because the goal was now to direct youths between the ages of fifteen and seventeen through the child care system and prevent these youngsters from entering further into the criminal justice system. These new treatment methods were grouped under a penalty labeled "commitment to special care."[96]

The 1970s continued the trend of avoiding placing juveniles in the youth prison systems until these youth prisons were abolished in 1980 after Swedish officials decided that children within the prisons did not improve sufficiently enough to remain there. The Social Services Act (SoL) of 1982 made youth welfare a system based on voluntary commitment and an understanding between the juvenile and the officials that together promoted better treatment for the child. Further legislation was set forth by the Act with Special Provisions in the Care of Young People that, in accordance with the SoL, was based on what was considered to be in the best interest of the child. Community homes became Special Approved Youth Homes, the goals of which were to keep the child close to home near his or her family, friends, and other support groups that would benefit his or her progress through treatment.[97]

Institutionalization is now regulated by the National Board for Institutional Care (SiS) which was established in 1993. The SiS is responsible for juveniles under age eighteen who are sentenced to institutional treatment. The amount of time a juvenile spends in institutional care is based on the crime and his or her individual needs; the length of confinement is no shorter than fourteen days and no longer than four years. While prison sentences still exist under exceptional consequences for youths between the ages of eighteen and twenty-one, the SiS strives to replace prison sentences with alternative care for any individual under the age of eighteen.[98]

By 1999 only about sixty juveniles under the age of eighteen were being sentenced to prison annually, while an added twenty-five youths were sentenced to a probation that began with a short prison sentence. Since the enactment of the Secure Youth Care sanctions in 1999, even fewer youths have been sentenced to prison; the annual total is approximately four juveniles per year.[99]

How Does the System Work?

The criminal justice system of Sweden is both very successful and different from many of other nations' programs. Sweden is a welfare-focused nation and employs an extremely humane approach in regards to young offenders. The juvenile system rejects the concept of punishment for children under the age of twenty-one and instead turns to social services and diversionary programs to prevent delinquent behavior. Swedish laws are designed to keep criminal and at-risk children out of the prisons or the adult court systems and instead place the youths in social welfare communities. It is helpful to note here that the concept of delinquency as used in the United States does not have a comparable concept in the Swedish language. Those who are called status offenders in the United States are handled totally outside the criminal justice system since they are not violating criminal law. This approach helps define the progressive nature of Sweden's approach to juvenile crime and helps the country keep from placing all but a very few juveniles into the criminal justice system.

The Police

Sweden's juvenile policy works through three aspects of the judicial system: the police, the prosecution, and the courts. Each must follow the laws and legal code set forth by the government but is also gifted with a great amount of discretion when dealing with juveniles. The duty of the police according to Swedish law is to prevent, discover, and investigate criminal activity. Like the police in the United States, Swedish police must be aware of at-risk children within communities while keeping an eye out for suspicious behavior. Under normal circumstances, police are expected to handle crimes that are committed by individuals over the age of twelve but must do so in partnership with social services to ensure that the social needs of the child are met. Swedish law states that police may only investigate crimes committed by children younger than twelve under special circumstances.[100] Social services have the right to request that police investigations be suspended in cases involving individuals under the age of fifteen, but where the youth is over fifteen the case is passed from the police to the prosecutor.

The Prosecutor

A prosecutor's goal is to decide what steps and processes should be taken in the case after the police investigation has concluded. The prosecutor is responsible for deciding whether it is necessary to arrest the offender or to make a plea to the courts for a detention order. In cases involving juveniles, these steps are rarely used and when they are implemented the steps are tailored to the needs of the youth. The prosecutor works closely with social services to declare the seriousness of the offense and what sanctions the juvenile should be subjected to. In minor cases where the offender has confessed to his or her crime, the prosecutor has the right to determine the sanction necessary, most of which are day fines based on the offender's socioeconomic standing. Of the fifteen- to seventeen-year-olds convicted of offenses in 2001, 61 percent received sanctions from a prosecutor while the rest were remanded to a public court.

The Courts

The courts come into play when a prosecutor prosecutes an individual for his or her crime but allows the public court system to decide the necessary sanction. Approximately 47 percent of cases brought to the courts involving juveniles between the ages of fifteen to seventeen are sentenced day-fines.[101] Other measures the court can take include but are not limited to suspended sentences and probation. The courts also work closely with social services to discover what sanctions or treatment will best suit the young offender and will facilitate the youth's progress in his or her return to society.

Supportive Legislation: Age Divisions

The way juveniles are defined by age also helps keep the numbers in prisons low. In Sweden, the definition of a young offender is an offender who has reached age fifteen but is still under twenty-one years of age. Sweden divides juveniles into three age categories: under the age of fifteen, fifteen to seventeen, and eighteen to twenty years old.[102] The age of criminal liability in Sweden is age fifteen; any individual under fifteen who commits a criminal act cannot be sentenced in a criminal court but is instead dealt with solely by social services.[103] The responsibility of implementing corrective measures for individuals under age fifteen falls to the social welfare board, which can put the child in a special care environment such as a family home or a home with supervision.

Both social services and judicial authorities deal with young offenders, youths between the ages of fifteen and seventeen. This age group is considered to be more responsible than their younger counterparts in both maturity and forming criminal intent, and as such are subject to criminal sanctions. Many of the proceedings in a case involving a youth in this age group rely heavily on the individual circumstances involving the juvenile, the crime, and any other mitigating factors as well as the discretion of the police and the prosecutor.

The Swedish Young Offenders Act grants prosecutors numerous powers in handling youth offenders under the age of eighteen. In minor or nonviolent cases, prosecutors may issue prosecution waivers to youths that exempt the child from any further court proceeding as long as the child does not take part in further criminal activity; waivers can be revoked if the child continues taking part in crime. The prosecutor also has the duty of deciding whether a youth should be detained during an ongoing investigation, but Swedish law states that "exceptional cause" must be present in detaining a youth in this manner.[104] The prosecutor must decide if the criminal action deserves further legal proceedings and if so the courts may issue criminal sanctions in accordance with the Act with Special Provisions in the Care of Young People (LVU). Juveniles under age eighteen cannot be sentenced to prison except in rare and exceptional circumstances.[105]

Offenders from the last age group, eighteen to twenty, are handled mainly by the judicial authorities rather than the social services. These offenders are still treated as juveniles rather than adults but are less protected by laws such as the LVU than the younger age groups. An offender older than age eighteen but under twenty-one may be subject to sentences such as prison based on the mitigating factors of the case, but no individual under twenty-one years of age may receive life imprisonment.[106]

Defining Legislation: Social Services Act

The Social Services Act (SoL) was passed in 1982 with the intention to increase voluntary and preventive measures available to children through social services. The SoL dictates that any social service measures that attempt to remove or diminish an individual's criminal behavior must be approached with cooperation between the juvenile, his or her parents, and the social service. Prior to this legislation the Child Welfare Act mandated that at-risk children engaging in deviant behavior would be issued a warning, followed by an order, to stop engaging in the activity. If both measures failed, a supervisor would be assigned to the child; if the child continued his or her delinquency, the juvenile would be taken into care.[107]

The SoL replaced this process in that social services will set up meetings with the child and his or her family to establish whether there are any issues in the household such as internal conflicts between family members or severe economic problems. If problems exist social services will take the necessary steps to rectify the situation in the best interest of the child by offering economic support or different forms of group therapy.[108] A contact person is also assigned to the family to provide support on a voluntary and preventive basis.[109] SoL also establishes social welfare boards, which are separate from the court system and made up of local politicians who make the decisions regarding children and the social services available to assist them. The key aspect to the SoL is that all social services must hold the concept of acting in the child's best interest above everything else.

Defining Legislation: Act with Special Provisions in the Care of Young People

Much like the Social Services Act, the Act with Special Provisions in the Care of Young People (LVU) is legislation aimed at introducing social services to individuals in severe need. LVU contains measures that social services can take to intercept children with extreme antisocial behavior that may be detrimental to his or her own growth and development. The social welfare boards set up by the Social Services Act are used to declare if a juvenile can be forcibly taken out of unfavorable living situations by social services and placed into a family home, treatment household, or other institutions. A similar act is the Act on the Care of Drug Abusers in Certain Cases, where social services can step in and require compulsory treatment to assist juveniles who may suffer from substance abuse.[110] The LVU, like the SoL, allows social services to take the measures that will improve the living conditions of juveniles and prevent youths from entering the world of crime. The three measures that LVU can take are submitting the child to a short-term out-of-home care; long-term or permanent out-of-home care; or an assignment of a contact person to assist the family in preventive measures.[111] For the lack of effectiveness of compulsory treatment in a number of nations, see the Evidence-Based Practice feature.

Defining Legislation: Closed Youth Detention

In 1999 closed youth detention became a common sanction in the sentencing system for juvenile offenders who have committed serious crimes and have an extensive criminal record. Closed youth detention takes the form of a treatment model but it is a sentence and is mandated by a public court. This sanction takes place in specialized youth detention centers rather than prison environments and aims to prevent the detrimental influence prison time can have on juveniles. The length of the sentence is based on the seriousness of the crime and varies from two weeks to four years. The average stay for a juvenile in closed youth detention is approximately ten months. In 2008, ninety-three juveniles were sentenced to closed youth detention with robbery or assault being the most common charges.[112]

Closed youth detention centers focus on individually adapted care to assist the juvenile depending on his or her needs. Many of the young offenders inside these detention centers

---

Evidence-Based Practice
Quasi-Compulsory Treatment of Drug-Dependent Offenders: An International Review

LITERATURE REVIEW

This paper reports on a review of the literature on the quasi-compulsory treatment (QCT) of drug-dependent offenders in four languages: English, French, Italian, and Dutch. The findings of this review on previous Anglophone reviews have typically presented positive outcomes from QCT, but problems do exist with this research. QCT is increasingly available internationally, but may be applied at different stages of the criminal justice process and to different types of offenders. Research on the process of QCT is reported to be comparatively rare. The available research does suggest problems of system integration between criminal justice and treatment agencies in implementing QCT.

The research in languages other than English reveals a wider range of outcomes (including negative effective effects) for QCT than was found in the English literature. It can be concluded from the evidence from the international community that QCT

does not inevitably produce better or "no worse" outcomes than voluntary treatment, but more multimethod, multisite studies of QCT are needed in order to inform policy and practice, which is presently being made in the absence of reliable evidence in many countries.

This evidence of best programs raises a critically important issue in juvenile justice: Does coercive or nonvoluntary treatment have no worse outcomes than voluntary treatment? Research results in the United States would suggest that this is true, but research done in other nations would suggest otherwise. This research in languages other than English would remind us that this issue still needs more investigation.

Source: Alex Stevens, Daniele Berto, Wolfgang Heckman, Victoria Kerschl, Kerralie Oeuvray, Marianne Ooyen, van Eldriede Steffan, and Ambros Uchtenhagen, "Quasi Compulsory Treatment of Drug Dependent Offenders: An International Review," *Informal Health Care* 40 (2005), 269–83.

suffer from a history of substance abuse, relationship issues, and schooling problems that are treated through individualized programs. After the youth has served his or her sentence, the aim of closed youth detention is to return the juvenile to society where he or she may be admitted into an aftercare program to prevent recidivism.[113]

Continuing Issues

Critics within Sweden lament several features of the Swedish system. Some are concerned that youths who commit crime are not punished. They believe in the appropriateness of punishment because of the wrongful nature of the youths' acts and that punishment will deter youths from further crime, and also, that youths need to learn from their crime. Second, at the very least, critics believe that punishments should be proportionate to the crimes committed in an eye-for-an-eye fashion. Thirdly, some critics do not believe that rehabilitation works. They argue that no data exist to support the effectiveness of treatment and that in the lieu of a lack of data, rehabilitation should not be the focus of the system. The counterarguments against changing the system are so far prevailing. One is the belief that rehabilitation works; secondly that abuses are prevented by the current system; and third that youths should not be exposed to the brutalities of prison life. On this last point, both sides agree.

Juvenile Justice Videos

UNICEF RADIO–SOMALIA

In this UNICEF radio interview, the blight of the conflict in Somalia is discussed in regards to the harsh living conditions as well as the aggressive and deceptive recruitment of children into the armed forces. As the conflict in Somalia increases, so does the number of children recruited. How does socioeconomic status correlate with the recruitment of children? What are some of the methods for recruiting children? Discuss the impact that involvement with armed conflict may have on a child.

SUMMARY

LEARNING OBJECTIVE 1 Understand the Beijing Rules, their content, and the proposed model rules for juveniles for all nations.

The Beijing Rules emerged out of the international recognition that children around the world are victims of many injustices. Concerns culminated in 1985 with the development of the Beijing Rules and continued in 1990 with two other sets of rules, one calling for the prohibition of children in armed conflict and the other one protecting children from being sold, forced into prostitution, or used in the pornography industry.

The Beijing Rules specifically call for member states to enable all their children to develop a meaningful and purposeful life in the community through education and to be free from crime and delinquency. The full force of family and community groups should be employed in these efforts so that juveniles' contacts with the law are fair, humane, and, wherever possible, unneeded. These efforts should be national in scope and directed to all children without regard to race, sex, ethnicity, class, or religion so that all in society are guaranteed safety, peace, and order. While states may vary in terms of economic, social, and cultural characteristics, children are to be protected and their lives enhanced to the fullest extent possible. This means that institutions must train their personnel in the skills, values, and attitudes required for the effort.

LEARNING OBJECTIVE 2 Illustrate how the social organization of different types of countries affects how the countries treat children.

Social organization refers to how individuals, groups, organization, and institutions hold together. To operate, a country needs to have natural resources, a means of extracting and marketing them, and the ability to receive financial resources through which the needs of its citizens can be met. Weakened and failed states (lesser developed countries) lack the financial ability to manufacture goods and to develop markets that allow the development of decent financial strength and adequate personal finances for the society to do well in a global or even local context. Governments, business organizations, religions, tribes, ethnic groups, and military forces end up battling over who controls the nation and its resources. With the exception of outside nongovernmental organizations, few in these societies are able to exert positive influence over the care and support of children.

As a country moves up the ladder toward greater and more effective forms of organization at the governmental levels and in various financial sectors, laws supported by the population become more evident and dysfunctional activities diminish. Yet, even these countries suffer from large segments of the population being disenfranchised and making up their own rules and regulations and enforcing them. Conflicts continue among the various factions until some are able to either conquer one another or compromises are reached that help the competing parties agree on rules and more equality in the distribution of power. These developing nations generally have more resources and closer knit relationships among these countries' constituencies than are found in weakened or failed states. Products are manufactured that can be sold as can agricultural products that are exported for profits. Again, as countries move further up the ladder, more and more resources are available and, if power sharing and egalitarian distribution of goods are viewed as fair, countries begin to develop internally in a way that benefits greater and greater portions of their citizens.

LEARNING OBJECTIVE 3 Describe Somalia, a failed state, and the plight of children in that country.

Failed and weakened states are among the most dangerous states in which women and children can find themselves. The Somalian government collapsed in the early 1990s and it lacks law in everything but name. The institutions of law, religion, politics, and economics are fragmented from each other, and each attempts to provide order by declaring the existence of laws and enforcing them by militias under their control. Religious, tribal, governmental, and ethnic militias do whatever their leaders want and the result is disorganization, conflict, and chaos.

Undermanned armed forces and militias conscript young males and females to serve their causes resulting in the infamous use of young males and females from the ages of seven and up. These children are exposed to and forced to engage in horrendous maiming, rapes, and murders of which they may be the victim as well as the offender. Those who survive may be damaged for life; with good luck, some will be rescued and placed in orphanages. With bad luck, the children are killed, forced by circumstances to live on the street, starved in ghettos or rural areas, or placed in prisons with adults where they continue to be brutalized.

LEARNING OBJECTIVE 4 Explain how three emerging countries with extreme social, population, and economic problems—China, India, and Brazil—deal with troublesome youth.

China, India, and Brazil are among the top five in the world in population numbers. Their per capita incomes are in the $600 to $16,000 range and, in all cases, the bulk of their population lives in poverty while those at the top of the socioeconomic structure are very, very well off financially.

In an effort to prove their worthiness as world leaders, governments in all three nations have indicated verbal as well as legislative support for the Beijing Rules, but all three countries receive criticism from human and children's rights watch groups such as Amnesty International. In all three countries, police and officials ignore complaints of the children being raped, murdered, tortured, and sold as sex slaves both within the country as well as across international borders; many are beaten and tortured and find their rights to speech, religion, due process, and fairness in judicial proceedings violated. Youths are subject to cruel and unusual punishment and placed in juvenile and adult prisons where they are subject again to beatings, rape, devastating diseases, and murder. Unfortunately, many governmental officials' attitudes indicate that they either do not care about the outcomes for children, or are in denial about the importance of problems faced by their country and children, in particular.

Yet, all three nations' have many officials who are aware of the problems and trying to make progress in enforcing laws. Other government officials simply ignore the needs of children and many participate in and condone the youths' victimization. Progress is spotty in many emerging nations and totally absent in others. However, all three have fairly strong local and traditional means of dealing with children. The heterogeneity of these massive populations in terms of indigenous tribes, ethnic groups, religions, and isolated geographical location is accompanied by long-standing traditions of local mechanisms of control. Community elders, officials and interested citizens come together on local boards and informal judicial groups—some supported by the state—to bring together the youths, their families, and local authorities to determine how to handle particular problems. In other words, some emerging nations are rediscovering long defunct informal methods of control, while others, like China, are beginning to substitute formal methods of control for the informal.

LEARNING OBJECTIVE 5 Explain the basic approaches used by three developed nations—Canada, England/Wales, and Sweden—in dealing with troublesome youth.

These nations attempt to follow the rule of law. All are constitutional democracies and have the resources to develop governmental institutional structures at national, state, and local levels that are responsible for guaranteeing juveniles their due process rights.

- Countries like Canada, England/Wales, and Sweden (and the United States), permit youths to have lawyers, expect parents to be present at all stages of criminal justice processing, protect the youths from self-incrimination, have the right to keep their cases confidential and their names out of the press, and the right to be free from inappropriate search and seizure and cruel and unusual punishment.

- Juveniles, depending on the country, have to be proven guilty beyond all reasonable doubt and, if further decisions are to be made regarding the youths' confinement, hearings and due process must occur.

Differences do exist at other levels, however. The resources held by economically and governmentally modern nations permit them to educate and train legal and professional law enforcement personnel about how the system works, its rules and regulations, and how to respond to youths with different types of needs. These states over the years have attempted to rectify the needs of juveniles by placing them in training schools and other secure facilities that exemplify the punishment model. While the institutions are built with the purported goal of putting youths in facilities as punishment, the training schools also claim they are providing youths with safe and nurturing environments to handle problem youths on the basis of their needs. At this point, these techniques are recognized as unworkable.

As a result of greater understanding of human behavior and experimentation, experts in these societies now are beginning to take the position that youths are not simply "bad" and need punishment, but that multiple factors result in youths engaging in misbehaviors and crime. Now, professionals increasingly believe that youths are the victims of unfortunate biology and neurology and inadequate families and neighborhoods—and immaturity in general. The modern states, especially Sweden, try to initially deal with almost all children outside the criminal justice system because youths are now viewed as changing, impressionable, impulsive, and in need of strong family relationships, counseling, skills training, therapy, and the opportunity simply to grow up. Some of these views are found in the United States because this country seems to be experiencing a growth of probation and community-based programs geared to keep kids out of the system—as are other developed nations.

KEY TERMS

Beijing Rules, p. 308
capital punishment, p. 321
common law, p. 307
corporal punishment, p. 321
crime control model, p. 319
developing countries, p. 305

indigenous populations, p. 305
industrialized countries, p. 306
jati, p. 315
nongovernmental organizations (NGOs), p. 306
Panchayats, p. 315

statutory law, p. 307
traditional cultures, p. 305
welfare model, p. 318
Young Offenders Act (YOA), p. 319
Youth Criminal Justice Act (YCJA), p. 319

REVIEW QUESTIONS

1. What are the major differences and similarities between the U.S. approach to juvenile justice and those of the countries discussed in this chapter?
2. What is the influence of the different historical backgrounds of the countries discussed in this chapter on their delinquency rates and their juvenile justice systems?
3. How are the changing social and economic conditions of the countries discussed in this chapter likely to influence both their delinquency rates and the way they approach juvenile justice?
4. Should the United States try to develop some informal methods of social control of youths similar to those found in other countries?
5. Should states in the United States follow, or be required to follow, the Beijing Rules?
6. Do you believe that the techniques of juvenile justice used by other countries would work in the United States? Why or why not?

GROUP EXERCISES

1. ***Writing to Learn Exercise:*** Write two paragraphs describing the nature of the Beijing Rules. Critique and revise.
2. ***Class Presentation:*** Each group in class will evaluate one of the countries discussed in the chapter. The fundamentals of juvenile justice in that country are to be presented to the class and each group is to field questions about the country chosen.
3. ***Class Presentation:*** Identify countries around the world in which students are interested. Have groups in the class choose a country for class presentation and research that country's juvenile justice system for a report to class.
4. ***Group Work:*** Discuss the Beijing Rules and the extent to which the United States does or does not conform to the recommendations of the rules.

NOTES

1. Amnesty International, *A Safe Childhood Is a Human Right,* AI DOC: AMR 19/014/2000 (New York: Amnesty International, December 7, 2000, at http://www.amnestyusa.org/our-work/issues/children-s-rights.
2. See Susan E. Rice and Stewart Patrick, *Index of State Weakness in the Developing World*, Foreign Affairs at Brookings, 2008, at http://www.brookings.edu/research/reports/2008/02/weak-states-index.
3. United Nations, "United Nations Standard Minimum Rules for the Administration of Juvenile Justice: The *Beijing Rules*" (New York: United Nations, 1986), 1–15. For a synopsis of the rules, see Geraldine Van Bueren and Anne-Marie Tootell, "United Nations Standard Minimum Rules for the Administration of Juvenile Justice: *Beijing Rules*," at http://childhouse.uio.no/childrens_rights/dci_html, 1–28.
4. United Nations, "United Nations Standard Minimum Rules: *Beijing Rules*," Rule 7.1, 6; see also Van Bueren and Tootell, "United Nations Standard Minimum Rules," 4.

5. Van Bueren and Tootell, "United Nations Standard Minimum Rules," 5.
6. United Nations, "United Nations Standard Minimum Rules: *Beijing Rules*," Part 1, Rule 2.1.
7. Ken Mekhaus, "Governance Without Government in Somalia: Spoilers, State Building, and the Politics of Coping," *International Security* 31, no.3 (Winter 2006/07), 74–106.
8. U.S. Department of State, *Somalia: Country Specific Information* (2007).
9. Mekhaus, "Governance Without Government."
10. Ibid.
11. U.S. Department of State, *Somalia.*
12. J. D. Mujuzi, 'The Constitutional Court of Uganda and Women's Right to Equality: The Adultery Judgment' 16:2 *East African Journal on Peace and Human Rights* (2010), 477.
13. Ibid.

14. Priyadharshini Dias, "Somaliland Launches New Juvenile Law" (New York: UNICEF), accessed May 24, 2012, at http://www.unicef.org/somalia/reallives_5434.html.

15. Dias, 2008

16. John R. Weeks, *Population: An Introduction to Concepts and Issues*, 7th ed. (New York: Wadsworth, 1999), 14, 461.

17. Xin Ren, "People's Republic of China," in *International Handbook on Juvenile Justice*, edited by Donald J. Shoemaker (Westport, CT: Greenwood Press, 1996), 55–79.

18. Judge Emily Baker, "People's Republic of China Today: A View of Its Juvenile Justice System," *Juvenile and Family Court Journal* 37 (1986), 51; Xin Ren, "People's Republic of China," 57.

19. Xin Ren, "People's Republic of China," 57–59.

20. Dorothy Bracey, "'Like a Doctor to a Patient, Like a Parent to a Child'—Corrections in the People's Republic of China," *Prison Journal* 68, no. 1 (1988), 25.

21. *Gongdu* schools are middle schools that administer to children ages twelve to seventeen. For a discussion of these facilities, see Daniel J. Curran and Sandra Cook, "Growing Fears, Rising Crime: Juveniles and China's Justice System," *Crime and Delinquency* 39, no. 3 (July 1993), 296–315.

22. Baker, "People's Republic of China Today," 51–57.

23. Curran and Cook, "Growing Fears, Rising Crime," 302.

24. Baker, "People's Republic of China Today," 54. Curran and Cook, in "Growing Fears, Rising Crime," state that the juveniles face a five-stage hierarchy of control: education assisted by the community, education through work and study, reeducation through labor, reform through labor, and discipline in the reformatory.

25. Amnesty International, "China: Gross Human Rights Violations Continue," *Amnesty International Report* (February 1996), 3.

26. Baker, "People's Republic of China Today," 52.

27. Bracey, "Like a Doctor to a Patient," 24–33.

28. Baker, "People's Republic of China Today," 55.

29. Ibid., 55.

30. Xiaogang Dent and Ann Cordilia, "To Get Rich Is Glorious: Rising Expectations, Declining Control, and Escalating Crime in Contemporary China," *International Journal of Offender Therapy and Comparative Criminology* 43, no. 2 (1999), 211–28. See also Curran and Cook, "Growing Fears, Rising Crime," 307–09.

31. Curran and Cook, "Growing Fears, Rising Crime," 304–05.

32. Ren, "People's Republic of China," 72–75.

33. Weeks, *Population*, 17–23.

34. Arvind Verma, "Cultural Roots of Police Corruption in India," *Policing: An International Journal of Police Strategies and Management* 22, no. 3 (1999), 264–79; see also Clayton Hartjen, "Legal Change and Juvenile Justice in India," *International Criminal Justice Review* 5 (1995), 6.

35. For a list of acts related to juveniles, see K. S. Shukla, "Role of the Police in Juvenile Justice," *Indian Journal of Criminology* (September 1981), 163.

36. Hartjen, "Legal Change and Juvenile Justice in India," 2–3.

37. Ibid.

38. Clayton A. Hartjen and G. Kethineni, "India," in *International Handbook on Juvenile Justice*, 184–87.

39. Ibid.

40. Ibid., 185.

41. Hartjen, "Legal Change and Juvenile Justice in India," 4.

42. Ibid.

43. U.S. Department of State, "India Report on Human Rights Practices for 1997" (Washington, DC: Bureau of Democracy, Human Rights and Labor, January 30, 1998), 10.

44. Hartjen, "Legal Change and Juvenile Justice in India," 5.

45. U.S. Department of State, "India Report on Human Rights," 21, 25–26.

46. For more information, see http://www.cnn.com/world/9608/18/bride.burn.

47. Weeks, *Population*, 17–23.

48. Annina Lahalle, "Modern Legislation for a Country of Contrasts: The Example of Brazil," in *Juvenile Delinquents and Young People in Danger in an Open Environment*, edited by Willie McCarney (Winchester, NM: Waterside Press, 1966), 177–83.

49. Ibid., 180.

50. Chuck Pfister, "Not for Kids," September 1995, at http://www.brazil-brazil.com/cvrsep95.htm.

51. Lahalle, "Modern Legislation for a Country of Contrasts," 182.

52. Ibid., 182–88. This legislative act also calls for programs that offer assistance to parents.

53. Vincent A. Keeton and Michael P. McConnell, "Street Children in Brazil: The Policy Issue, Policy Background, and Current Policy and Programs," Chap. 11 in *PRP Papers, 1994–1995*, at http://lanic.utexas.edu/project/ppb/papers94–95/mcconnel.html.

54. Lahalle, "Modern Legislation for a Country of Contrasts," 182–83.

55. Keeton and McConnell, "Street Children in Brazil," 16.

56. Reuters, "Brazil Youth Riot Ends with Four Boys Dead," October 25, 1999, at http://www.nytimes.com/reuters/international/international-brazil-html.

57. Maureen McGuire, "C.19: An Act to Amend the Young Offenders Act and the Criminal Code—Getting Tougher?" *Canadian Journal of Criminology* 39, no. 2 (April 1997), 186.

58. John A. Winterdyk, "Juvenile Justice and Young Offenders: An Overview of Canada," in *Juvenile Justice Systems*, edited by John A. Winterdyk (Toronto: Canadian Scholars Press, 1997) 141. See also McGuire, "C.19: An Act to Amend the Young Offenders Act.".

59. McGuire, "C.19: An Act to Amend the Young Offenders Act."

60. For a listing of some of the major juvenile justice legislation leading up to the YOA as well as the major tenets of the YOA, see Winterdyk, "Juvenile Justice and Young Offenders," 143–46.

61. McGuire, "C.19: An Act to Amend the Young Offenders Act."

62. Department of Justice, Youth Justice, Canada "Why Did the Government Introduce New Youth Justice Legislation," modified December 13, 2008, at http://www.justice.gc.ca/eng/pi/yi-jj/ycja/why-pourq.html.

63. Ibid.
64. Ibid.
65. Ibid.
66. Ibid., 41; Department of Justice, Canada, "Youth Criminal Justice Act: Extrajudicial Sanctions Programs," May 20, 2008, at http://www.justice.golv.ab.ca/criminal_pros/default.aspx?id=5649.
67. Department of Justice, Canada, "The Youth Criminal Justice Act: Summary and Background," modified December 13, 2008, at http://www.justice.gc.ca/eng/pi/yj-jy/ycja—lsjpa/back-hiwst.html.
68. Guy Lemire, "Probation and Parole," *The Canadian Encyclopedia*, at http://www.thecanadianencyclopeia.com/index.cfm?PgNm=TCE&Params=A1SEC826719.
69. Ibid.
70. Raymond Corrado and Alan Markwart, "Canada," in *International Handbook on Juvenile Justice*, 48.
71. Leon A. Radzinowicz, *A History of English Criminal Law and Its Administration from 1750–1833* (London: Stevens and Sons, 1948).
72. Chris Cunneen and Rob White, *Juvenile Justice: An Australian Perspective* (Melbourne: Oxford University Press, 1995), 18–20. For a detailed discussion of the history of English juvenile law as it relates to competing British conservative and labor ideologies, see Loraine Gelsthorpe and Mark Fenwick, "Comparative Juvenile Justice: England and Wales," in *Juvenile Justice Systems*, 79–80.
73. William Wakefield and David Hirschel, "England," in *International Handbook on Juvenile Justice*, 94.
74. Gelsthorpe and Fenwick, "Comparative Juvenile Justice."
75. Wakefield and Hirschel, "England."
76. Ibid., 95.
77. Michael Cavadino and James Dignan, *The Penal System* (London: Sage Publications, 1992).
78. Gelsthorpe and Fenwick, "Comparative Juvenile Justice," 96.
79. Wakefield and Hirschel, "England," 97.
80. Youth Justice Board, "About the YJB: Mission, Vision and Values," n.d., at http://tb.gov.uk/en-gb/mission vision and values.
81. David P. Farrington and Trever Bennett, "Police Cautioning of Juveniles in London," *British Journal of Criminology* 21 (1981), 123–35.
82. Bryan Gibson et al., *The Youth Court: One Year Onwards* (Winchester, England: Waterside Press, 1994).
83. Wakefield and Hirschel, "England," 99–100.
84. B. F. Harrison and A. J. Maddox, *The Work of a Magistrate*, 3d ed. (London: Shaw and Sons, 1975).
85. Wakefield and Hirschel, "England," 101.
86. Ibid., 102–03.
87. Ibid., 104.
88. Gelsthorpe and Fenwick, "Comparative Juvenile Justice," 103–04.
89. Felipe Estrada and Jerzy Sarnecki, *Juvenile Crime in Sweden: A Trend Report on Criminal Policy, the Development of Juvenile Delinquency and the Juvenile Justice System.* (Stockholm: Rep. Stockholm University, Department of Criminology, 2004), 13, at http://www.esc-eurocrim.org/files/youth_crime_in_sweden_sarnecki_estrada_final_version.doc.
90. Durrant, Joan E., *A Generation Without Smacking: The Impact of Sweden's Ban on Physical Punishment* (London: Save the Children, 1999), 19. at http://www.endcorporalpunishment.org/pages/pdfs/GenerationwithoutSmacking.pdf.
91. Erik Axelsson, *Young Offenders and Juvenile Justice in Sweden* (Stockholm: Riksdag Research Service, 2002), 3.
92. Estrada and Sarnecki, *Juvenile Crime in Sweden,* 10.
93. Ibid., 12.
94. Ibid., 2.
95. Ibid., 3.
96. Ibid., 4.
97. Ibid., 4.
98. Ibid., 5.
99. Ibid., 18.
100. Ibid., 13.
101. Ibid., 17.
102. Ibid., 1.
103. The Swedish System of Sanctions—Det svenska pafoljdssystemet.
104. Ibid., 13–14.
105. The Swedish System of Sanctions.
106. Durrant, *A Generation Without Smacking.*
107. Ibid., 19.
108. Ibid., 19.
109. Estrada and Sarnecki, *Juvenile Crime in Sweden*, 19.
110. Durrant, *A Generation Without Smacking.*
111. SIS, "Closed Institutional Care," at http://www.stat-inst.se/om-webbplatsen/other-languages/the-national-board-of-institutional-care/closed-institutional-youth-care.
112. Durrant, *A Generation Without Smacking*, 20.
113. Axelsson, *Young Offenders*, 5.

16 Juvenile Justice in the Twenty-First Century

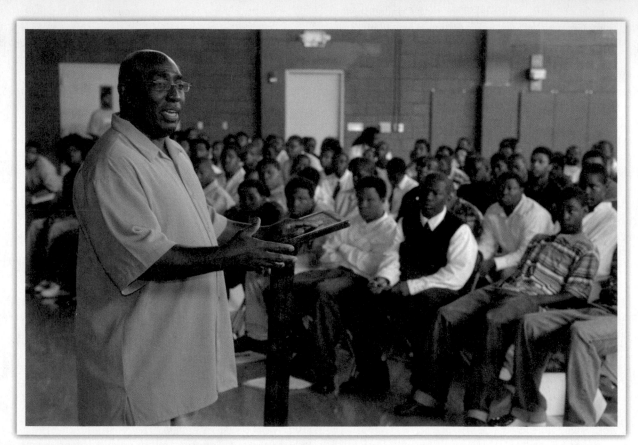

© Jeff Greenberg/Alamy

Learning Objectives

1. Summarize how the problems of modern society affect juveniles.
2. Summarize the major issues facing juvenile justice at the present time.
3. Describe the changing face of juvenile justice.
4. Explain what professionalism is and how it affects juvenile justice.
5. Describe what juvenile justice will look like in years to come.

Kids are kids, not adults . . . . But it troubles me deeply that our focus is on juvenile justice and not juvenile education. It's about trials and not about schools or discipline. It's about punishment and not about mentoring. No, I can't understand it and I don't agree with it. We will never, in my view, solve our problems on the back end with punishment. We will solve our problems only if we are united with a higher purpose of doing better on the front end with day care, preschool, schools, churches, other institutions and yes, families. Kids are our future and we need to invest in them. Treating kids as adults solves very little; it's another quick-fix solution to a complex problem that took years to reach and will take years to resolve.

—Barry Glick and William Sturgeon[1]

Barry Glick and William Sturgeon, in the chapter-opening quote, do not deny that juvenile crime is both a serious matter and a common phenomenon today.[2] Yet they contend that what is needed is more effective front-end programs, including day care, preschool, schools, and community programs. They believe that such an investment in youngsters will have far greater success than punishment programs on the back end have.

The long-standing mission of juvenile justice is to correct youthful offenders so that they will neither return to the juvenile justice system nor continue on into the life of an adult criminal. Indeed, the opposite often appears to be true, for once trouble-making youths are processed through the correctional system, the chances of their returning are increased, not reduced. Juvenile corrections often breeds rather than reforms offenders.[3] A more recently recognized mission is to provide justice to juveniles who are referred to the juvenile justice system.[4] As this book repeatedly documents, the United States has a long way to go to achieve the goals of either rehabilitation or justice.

Many intervention methods have been tried in order to accomplish the mission of rehabilitation. These include diversion, community-based corrections, radical nonintervention, the closing of training schools, mandatory sentencing, punishment, transactional analysis, guided group interaction, positive peer culture, behavior therapy, work release, home furloughs, and coeducational institutionalization. Although we know that some things work in some situations with some offenders, overall these strategies fall short of accomplishing the goal of preventing youngsters from returning to the system.

The juvenile justice system is under attack from all quarters. Few support keeping the system as it has been. Some urge the decriminalization of status offenders; others want to increase the number of youths transferred to the adult court. An increasingly vocal minority even propose merging the juvenile system into the adult justice system.

This chapter depicts the major issues and challenges facing juvenile justice; it gazes into the crystal ball to see what the future of juvenile justice might look like; it provides a glimpse of what takes place during rehabilitation, discusses professionalism, and examines juvenile justice as a possible career choice.

How Do the Problems of Modern Society Affect Youths At Risk?

The problems of juveniles start well before they come to the attention of juvenile justice authorities. Accordingly, for real progress to be made in understanding the problems of high-risk youths, the larger social context of their lives must be examined.

The Family

The American family has changed rather dramatically in recent decades. Inflation has eroded the economic support of the traditional family. Even in intact families, both parents often must work to make ends meet. Single parents experience greater financial difficulties because they have only one source of income; some qualify only for unskilled and minimum-wage jobs. The result in too many families is that children find themselves on their own for significant portions of the day as parents attempt to survive financially.

To add to their problems, many children are members of dysfunctional families, in which neglect, emotional abuse, physical abuse, and sexual abuse are regular occurrences. Dysfunctional families also have more than their share of parents who are emotionally disturbed, alcoholics, drug users, or in prison. Children in some dysfunctional families may have no contact with one parent or may not even remember that parent. But even in what appear to be stable family units, parents may be struggling with problems stemming from long-repressed violence, neglect, or sexual or emotional abuse from their own childhood. The result is that many youths never receive the love, affection, and acceptance they need from parents.

The Socioeconomic Structure

The American social class structure has come under increased scrutiny during the past decade. Such headlines as "The Rich Get Richer" and "Income Disparity Between the Rich and Poor Increases" frequently are found in the media. Increased references to a "shrinking middle class" and the "development of the underclass" are also found. These media trends reflect statistics indicating that a rather small percentage (20 percent) of the population controls more than 86 percent of the wealth in the nation and receives more than 45 percent of the income. The bottom 20 percent of the population controls less than 1 percent of the wealth and receives less than 5 percent of the income. The gap between the bottom 20 percent and the top 20 percent is increasing. In addition, the middle class has more people moving down than up in the social class structure.

The rapidly expanding underclass is one of the most serious social problems facing the United States. The underclass is made up of the poorest of the poor. Joblessness pervades the inner cities, as young males find employment increasingly difficult to find. The lack of suitable jobs tends to make the underclass welfare dependent, but its members do not receive enough welfare support to escape the ravages of poverty—high rents, dilapidated and inadequate housing, deteriorated neighborhoods, and ineffective schooling for their children. Another feature of underclass life is the tendency of adolescent females to have children out of wedlock, which only extends the welfare and poverty cycle to another generation. Drugs, especially crack cocaine, are readily available as an escape from this dreary existence.

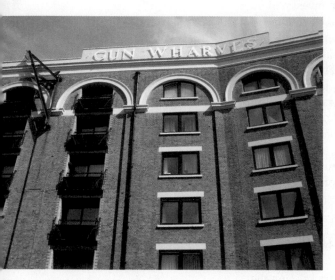

▲ These apartments,which formerly overlooked industrial waterfront docks in London were remodeled—not for the poor who needed them, but for the affluent who wanted a gentrified way of life.
David Burrows/Shutterstock

The Neighborhood

As children reach an age that allows them to spend time outside the home and away from direct supervision of parents or guardians, the neighborhood becomes an important focus of their expectations. For urban children, exploration of the neighborhood brings them in contact with a variety of social groups and institutions. Unfortunately, they find their inner-city neighborhoods too frequently to be battlegrounds where wars are waged among different ethnic groups. The battles are fought for reasons of misunderstanding, for imagined slights, and sometimes to protect the markets in which drugs are the sole means of making a living.

These neighborhoods reflect the downside of American society. Residents of such communities are poor, face prejudice, and feel powerless. On a daily basis, they must deal with an absence of jobs, vermin-filled housing, untreated diseases, scarcity of food, unwanted pregnancies, and a lack of community political and social organization. Weighed down with such problems, residents come to believe in fate rather than in their ability to bring positive change to their lives.

The School

Inner-city schools, especially, are under increased criticism. Although such schools have long been targeted as in need of reform, society has yet to take more than a piecemeal approach to the problems of uninterested and bored students, disillusioned and detached teachers, antiquated facilities, and inadequate curriculums. The gang battles of the streets are often carried into the halls of the schools, and innocent youths have been beaten and killed on school steps, hallways, classrooms, and playgrounds. Not surprisingly, these schools have become dens of fear and frustration for the remaining students and teachers. Drugs are frequently available, even as police and security staff attempt to bring some semblance of order to the disorder. Too frequently, juveniles caught up in the environments of these schools make poor grades, become disruptive, skip school, are suspended, assault others, join gangs, traffic in drugs, and drop out. These problems help ensure that this nation has more uneducated citizens, higher dropout rates, and more people with minimal reading skills than do most of the industrialized countries in the world. African American, Hispanic, and Native American students are particularly vulnerable to these problems.

The Gang

Almost all adolescents are members of peer groups. This grouping together with peers is a normal rite of passage to adulthood. What is not normal from society's viewpoint is the weaponry and violence, drug trafficking, and other antisocial behaviors of urban and emerging gangs. Measures taken to deal with these gangs are often repressive and fail to recognize the major functions of the gangs for their members.

Many juveniles, especially those from the inner cities, see gangs as substitutes for their families. Gangs provide their members with roots, respect, and identity, which they can carry either to an early grave or into prison—the only futures on the horizons of many gang youths. For the first time in their lives, many feel a sense of respect and belonging they can get nowhere else. The gang gives them a sense of loyalty and an identity marked by the turf of their neighborhood. Finally, the gang offers the belief that only in this social group can they really belong to something and attain what is missing in their lives.

But gang participation is ultimately as self-defeating or destructive as, or perhaps even more than, the family and school have been. Gang involvement thrusts a youth into dangerous and deadly games. Gang members are more likely than nongang members to commit offenses and to become victims. Gang involvement also is one of the best ways for a juvenile to increase the likelihood of confinement in juvenile and adult facilities. Moreover, gangs poorly prepare a youth for marriage, employment, or learning to adapt to the adult world.

Youth Attitudes

Juveniles can be divided into high-risk, middle-risk, and low-risk groups. High-risk children, making up about one-fourth of the adolescent population, frequently are involved in problem-oriented behaviors. Middle-risk children, making up another one-fourth of the population, occasionally become involved in problem behaviors, especially minor forms of juvenile lawbreaking, drug and alcohol use, and sexual behaviors. Low-risk children, constituting the other 50 percent of the adolescent population, become involved in few problem behaviors. The high-risk children are those with the most problematic social contexts shaping their lives. Middle-risk children have some problems in their social backgrounds but usually have positive forces balancing the negative ones. Low-risk children tend to have positive social and family backgrounds.

High-risk children frequently come out of their experiences with families, neighborhoods, and schools with the self-concept of being a loser. Told all of their lives that they are dumb, worthless, and troublemakers and that they will never amount to anything, they tend to be self-absorbed, look down on themselves, and resent anyone who confronts them. Once immersed in alcohol and drugs, they may assume that no legitimate avenues of success will ever open to them and that a life of trouble and an early death are their inevitable future. These youngsters blame society and others for their failures and have no confidence in themselves or in their ability to turn their lives around.

What Are the Major Issues Facing Juvenile Justice?

The most serious issues facing juvenile justice today are (1) continued reliance on the get-tough approach and what that means; (2) the fiscal challenges facing juvenile justice agencies today; (3) the high rates of recidivism; (4) the discrimination found among race/ethnicity and gender in juvenile justice processing; and (5) the victimization of weak or passive youth in juvenile institutions.

Reliance on the Get-Tough Approach

Although reform may remain as the official policy in most jurisdictions, the get-tough approach for serious juvenile offenders has characterized the sentencing policies of the juvenile court in recent decades and is likely to remain so throughout the twenty-first century. Probation and aftercare agencies are further influenced by risk control and crime reduction strategies. A new probation or aftercare officer quickly finds out that the safety of society comes first and close behind is the protection of the agencies against public or political embarrassment.

It is also contended that the get-tough approach has resulted in referring more youths to the adult court, some of whom have been sentenced to adult correctional facilities. Although used since the formation of the United States, the death penalty can no longer be given to youths or young adults who have committed a murder prior to their eighteenth birthdays. But today, with the death penalty no longer a possibility for juveniles, individuals who committed crimes while they were juveniles are being sent to prison for the remainder of their lives. However, the U.S. Supreme Court is presently considering the constitutionality of life without parole for juveniles, with the ruling to come in 2012.

Fiscal Challenges Facing Juvenile Justice

All agencies of government, including the criminal justice and juvenile justice systems, have experienced fiscal austerity during the past few years. Those who work in the justice system have found that they must do more with less. Some justice practitioners have risen to the occasion and been able to find creative solutions to their budget shortfalls. The use of volunteers has helped fill the gap between what agencies need and what they are presently receiving from governmental agencies. But budgetary challenges remain a major issue.

The High Rates of Recidivism

Every study that has ever been done on juveniles released from institutions has found extremely high rates of recidivism. These rates vary from 50 to 70 percent. Fortunately, studies that have taken place in the community have had more positive rates of success from some of these programs. Evidence-based studies are beginning to show more positive and hopeful signs.

One of the problems with the high rates of recidivism is that juveniles, according to a wide body of empirical research, often get worse rather than better as a result of their exposure to the juvenile justice system. This is a serious indictment, when it takes place, and represents a major concern for juvenile justice policy makers.

What is troubling is that many who begin a pathway of juvenile crime tend to continue on to adult crime. This is called delinquency across the life course, and it places the seriousness of youth crime in the context that too many youngsters will spend the remainders of their lives in and out of the juvenile system, some remaining in prison for most of their adult years.

Discrimination Based on Race/Ethnicity and Gender in Juvenile Justice Processing

One of the major issues is the disproportionate representation of minorities in the juvenile justice system. The Juvenile Justice and Delinquency Prevention Act and its various modifications, however, have contributed to the reduction of minority youth in the justice system.

In the same light, as discussed elsewhere in this text, females have also been victimized in that they have been sentenced to training school for lesser offenses than males who have been adjudicated to training school, remained in custody longer than males for similar offenses, and have been denied programs and services needed for their rehabilitation and restoration.

Juvenile Victimization

For those who are familiar with what goes on in training schools and many residential centers, they have been aware of the extent of victimization of weaker youth. Far too frequently, as one youth informed one of the authors, "Only the strong survive in here." What is particularly disconcerting is the number of staff who have been predators of institutional residents. Fortunately, a number of studies during the past few years have identified the extent of the problem, and it is hoped that training schools and all types of residential settings for juveniles will be much safer places in the future.

The Changing Face of Juvenile Justice

The greater use of technology, the expanding use of restorative justice, the ever increasing use of evidence-based principles, an emphasis on reentry, and the attention given to professionalism in juvenile justice are affecting the face of juvenile justice in the United States.

Increased Use of Technology

Rather than relying on traditional methods of security and control, the correctional system is now entering a new phase of **technocorrections**, which involves using technology rather than personnel to monitor probation, aftercare, and institutional populations. Today, **technology-driven security** is designed to maintain security both in the community and in the institutions. Examples include the use of motion detectors at the perimeters of institutions that transmit movement to a centralized command center for immediate response; infrared image detectors that use handheld devices no bigger than a flashlight; and better and stronger physical barriers that make escape nearly impossible.[5]

▲ Security cameras are symbols of our times. Schools, buses, hospitals, and streets are being wired for constant surveillance in an attempt to maintain order in a constantly changing and complex society.
Kathryn O'Lare

Technical experts are now identifying numerous areas in both community-based and secure settings in which correctional management can be aided by information technology (IT), including reception and commitment, sentence and time accounting, classification, caseload management, security, discipline, housing-bed management, medical treatment, grievances, programs, scheduling, investigations/gang management, property, trust accounting, visitation, release and discharge, and community supervision. Because IT can be applied in so many areas within community and institutional settings, administrators have begun to take advantage of the potential offered by these new technologies.

The Dangers of Technocorrections

Although technocorrections holds the promise of providing greater security and control, it also brings with it a unique set of problems. The danger is that increasingly technology-driven corrections will provide a sterile and isolated environment for inmates, in which contact with staff is greatly reduced or even nonexistent. Correctional institutions, it is true, will be more secure, in both external and internal security, but they may also be less humane, and it is hard to imagine that this environment will not have an adverse effect on prisoners as they return to the community. Technology can also provide a false sense of security in both community-based and institutional settings. For example, knowing where someone is does not mean that it is possible to know what that person is doing.

Ever-Expanding Use of Restorative Justice

The expansion of restorative justice, as discussed in several chapters of this text, is one of the most exciting movements in corrections today. Restorative justice has recently been coupled with intermediate sanctions. From the grassroots level to state and local headquarters, restorative justice is rapidly gaining momentum within the United States. Victim–offender conferencing (sometimes called mediation) is the oldest and most widely used expression of restorative justice, with more than 1,300 programs in eighteen countries.[6] While stressing accountability for offenses committed, restorative strategies operate with

Evidence-Based Practice
Ten Evidence-Based Principles

- *Principle 1: Target Criminogenic Needs.* Good programs target factors related to offending that can be changed.
- *Principle 2: Target Thorough Assessment of Risk and Need and Target Programs to High-Risk Offenders.* Risk assessment provides a measure of the risk principle, which states that higher risk offenders are likely to reoffend if not treated, and that low-risk offenders are not likely to reoffend even without treatment. The Level of Service Inventory–Revised (LSI-R) provides insight into which youthful offenders should receive the highest priority for treatment, regardless of their specific problem areas.
- *Principle 3: Base Design and Implementation on a Proven Theoretical Model.* Effective programs work within the context of a proven (evidence-based) theory of criminal behavior. Proven theories include social learning and cognitive-behavioral theories.
- *Principle 4: Use a Cognitive-Behavioral Approach.* Thinking and behavior are linked: youthful offenders behave like offenders because they think like them; changing thinking is the first step toward changing behavior. Effective programs attempt to alter the cognitions, values, attitudes, and expectations of an offender that maintain antisocial behavior. They emphasize problem solving, decision making, reasoning, self-control, and behavior modification, through role playing, graduated practice, and behavioral rehearsal.
- *Principle 5: Disrupt the Delinquency Network.* Effective programs provide a structure that disrupts the delinquency network by enabling offenders to place themselves in situations (around people and places) where prosocial activities dominate. Effective programs also help offenders to understand the consequences of maintaining friendships with criminals. Role playing can help them practice building new prosocial friendships.
- *Principle 6: Provide Intensive Services.* Effective programs offer services that occupy 40 to 70 percent of the youthful offender's time while in the program and last three to nine months. The actual length of the program needs to be driven by the specific behavioral objectives of the program and specific needs of the individual inmate.
- *Principle 7: Match Offender's Personality and Learning Style with Appropriate Program Settings and Approaches.* This is known as the "responsivity" principle. There are important interrelations between the learning and personality style of the youth and their settings or situations.
- *Principle 8: Include a Relapse Prevention Component.* Relapse prevention should be offered, both in training school and in the community, when possible, and should include (1) rehearsal of alternative prosocial responses, (2) practicing prosocial behaviors by rewarding improved competencies in increasingly difficult situations, (3) training family and friends to provide reinforcement for prosocial behavior, and (4) providing booster sessions to youthful offenders following the formal phase of treatment.
- *Principle 9: Integrate with Community-Based Services.* Effective programs refer youths to other programs with good track records.
- *Principle 10: Reinforce Integrity of Services.* Effective programs continually monitor program development, organizational structure, staff development and training, and other core organizational processes. An important part of this effective offender intervention treatment approach is program evaluation.

Source: Lawrence W. Sherman, David P. Farrington, and Brandon Welsh, *Understanding and Implementing Correctional Options That Work* (Harrisburg: Pennsylvania Department of Corrections, 2003).

the goal of repairing injuries to victims and to communities in which crimes have taken place. Whether these conferences occur before, during, or after adjudication, they promote education and transformation within a context of respect and healing. These models are neither mutually exclusive nor complete in and of themselves. They can be combined or adapted depending on the special situation at hand.[7]

Greater Use of Evidence-Based Principles and Rehabilitative Approaches

Evidence-based practice principles are used increasingly in juvenile justice today. Professionals contend that programs that follow these principles have a better chance of succeeding than those that do not. Consider the ten principles described in the Evidence-Based Practice feature.

Emphasis on Reentry

The high rates of recidivism of juveniles being released from training school has been one of the stimulators for an increased emphasis on reentry. The importance of a continuum of services for youth being released from an institution to the community has gained support, as have aftercare services for these youth.

Growth of Professionalism in Juvenile Justice

One of the developments in juvenile justice is that signs of **professionalism** began to appear in both state and private agencies. State corrections training academies were established across the nation. Accreditation, spearheaded by the American Correctional Association, was developed and spread throughout community-based agencies and correctional institutions throughout the nation. Affirmative action policies were developed and implemented throughout corrections. The abuse of residents began to be replaced with actions based on the belief that youths are to be treated with dignity and respect. Some states moved more quickly than others, but this spirit of professionalism is now found throughout the nation. The characteristics and attitudes of what it means to be a juvenile justice professional can be summarized, as follows:

- To see oneself as a person of integrity and to live at integrity level. A definition of integrity is to do the right thing when no one else is around.

- To treat offenders with dignity and respect. As one corrections professional put it, to treat inmates as you would want your father or brother to be treated in a correctional setting.[8]

- To model positive behaviors. One way that this can be done is to adhere to the ethical principles set forth by the American Correctional Association, the organization that accredits juvenile institutions.

- To be a person committed to a learning model and to be open to new ways of doing things. This person seeks to learn throughout his career and is always willing to pursue all the training opportunities available.

- To believe that it is possible to make a difference. This person believes that he or she can have an impact and, as a result, is not limited by what others have done.

- To keep your personal stuff from getting in the way; that is, not to permit one's personal problems or issues to interfere with doing an effective job.[9]

- To refuse to accept unethical behavior from fellow staff members.

- To stay positive and to do what is possible to create a workplace that is safe, healthy, and free of harassment in any form.[10]

What Remains to Be Done?

- Correctional organizations must develop greater clarity about their purpose: Why the organization exists—its mission; why it is needed to support the purpose and mission; what should be the future direction of the organization.

- The growing trend toward getting accreditation must continue in both community-based and institutional facilities.

- There needs to be a nationally applicable set of principles and philosophy on what is acceptable behavior toward residents in community-based programs and inmates in prisons. Accreditation provides the broad map of what is expected in correctional care, but the subtle things expected from staff need further clarity and explanation.

- The quality of juvenile institutions has improved compared to those in the past, but there seems to be a movement in juvenile corrections to make training schools into juvenile prisons. This is a movement that must be discouraged.

- The level of professionalism is very much affected by the ability to recruit the right staff and, once they are recruited, to explain the principles and behaviors that are expected of them.

- Rehabilitative programs for those who desire them must be based on the most effective design, delivery of services, and follow-up in the community.

- The residential staff's inclination to a culture that sanctions abuse and mistreatment of youths must be eradicated. One way that this can be done is to videotape any disciplinary interaction between correctional staff and residents and to remind officers that charges will be brought in court if they violate the rights of residents.

- The use of restraints in institutional settings must be carefully supervised, because of the possibility of abusive treatment of difficult-to-handle residents.

- The salaries of correctional personnel in the community and institutional contexts need to be revised periodically. The salaries of these staff in some jurisdictions are still far too low. One advantage of increased salaries is that college-educated applicants will be attracted to these positions in higher numbers.

- Administrative correctional staff must be willing to step forth when colleagues are out of line. This may come to the point of termination if that should be necessary.

- Private correctional care, which has always played and still plays an important role, can pose a problem because too frequently privately run institutions pay inadequate salaries to staff, have poorly constructed corrections facilities, and fail to provide needed services for inmates. Private companies, if they intend to be in the corrections business, must maintain the standards of county and state corrections.

Is Juvenile Justice a Good Career?

This text has attempted to present a realistic analysis of juvenile justice, both in the community and in the institutional settings. At times this analysis had to be critical, as shortcomings and abuses of youths are clearly present and must be corrected. But at the same time, a clear underlying message has been that juvenile justice is an excellent career choice. A number of interviewees in the text, as well as in *Voices in the Juvenile Justice System*, make three points: (1) I really like my job, (2) I feel like I am making a difference, and (3) I am glad that I pursued my career choice.

A number of exciting jobs are available to those who want to work with youths in trouble. Some of them are:

- Juvenile court judge
- Public defender for youth
- Prosecutor of youth for a governmental jurisdiction
- Administrator in the central office, including director of a youth agency
- Treatment staff or residential staff in a community-based program
- Forensic psychologist
- Probation officer
- Substance abuse counselor
- Detention worker
- Superintendent of a juvenile correctional facility
- Middle-level manager or treatment agent in a training school
- Social worker in a training school
- Recreational therapist
- Aftercare officer
- Chaplain

What Will Juvenile Justice Look Like in the Twenty-First Century?

Much will remain the same in juvenile justice in the years to come, but there will also be much that is different:

- The U.S. Census Bureau estimates that the population of juveniles under the age of eighteen will increase 14 percent between 2000 and 2025—about one-half of 1 percent per year. By 2050, it is estimated that the juvenile population will be 36 percent larger than it was in 2000.[11] Given this population growth of juveniles in the years to come, it is likely that juvenile justice will have greater demands placed on it.

▲ Teaching children in the home and at school how to be responsible citizens is a never-ending challenge to all societies. The first lessons must begin in homes by parents and other caregivers. Children need this care and direction for them to be successful in their own lives.
Washington County Juvenile Probation Services

- Many members of this increased population of juveniles will come from impoverished homes headed by single mothers. In 2012, African American and Hispanic juveniles were more than three times as likely to live in poverty as were non-Hispanic white juveniles. Since juvenile poverty appears to be associated with juvenile crime, it is likely that minority juveniles will continue to be the focus of social control in American society.[12]

- With this increased population of poor juveniles, the rate of juvenile violence, including homicide, may again grow, as it did in the late 1980s and early 1990s.

- The widespread feeling today that more troubled teenagers exist now than in the past will be even more pronounced in the next twenty years. Adolescent psychiatry will be more frequently called on to treat youths who experience problems in early childhood, but it will be the children of the haves who will benefit the most, as their wealthy parents place their children in private hospitals and treatment centers.

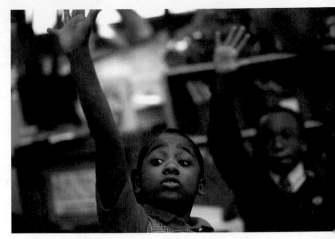

▲ Some schools across the nation are trying seriously to bring the excitement of learning to their students. These young men demonstrate the enthusiasm that ideally should be found in every classroom.
Getty Images

- The *Roper v. Simmons* decision reveals that the debate about the death penalty for juveniles under the age of eighteen has been resolved at least for now, and it is unlikely that any changes will take place in the near future.[13]

- The Roper and *Graham v. Florida* decision may be the first two of one or more decisions determining the fate of the life-without-parole sentence for juveniles.

- The trilogy of gangs, drugs, and guns will continue to be a social problem. Youth gangs are increasingly becoming a minority problem, and this trend is likely to increase in the decades to come.

- The drug choices of juveniles may well change in the future, but there is no evidence that drug use will be less of a problem than it presently is. There is currently a widespread movement among juveniles away from the use of crack cocaine to the use of methamphetamine.

- Cigarette smoking among adolescents will likely continue to decrease.

- Juveniles will continue to drink alcohol, and there is no reason to believe that the use of alcohol will be less of a problem than it is at present.

- The issue of gun control will remain a serious problem facing the juvenile justice system.

- The current tendency to create uniformity and reduce discretion in juvenile sentencing procedures is likely to continue.

- The deinstitutionalization movement is likely to continue and even expand, given the high costs of institutionalization and the successful outcomes of many community-based correctional programs.

- Drug courts, teen courts, and gun courts for juveniles will likely continue to increase.

- The use of restorative justice will continue to spread throughout the United States.

- The use of private programs will continue to be an important part of the landscape of juvenile corrections.

- State legislatures will become increasingly involved in passing laws related to the social control of juveniles.

- A structural change that will likely be implemented in those states that do not have it is the removal of serious crimes from the jurisdiction of the juvenile court. What will probably be developed is an increased number of mechanisms for the direct referral of juvenile crimes to the adult court.

- Disproportionate minority confinement, in spite of the efforts of the Juvenile Justice and Delinquency Prevention Act will remain a problem, and juvenile institutions will become even more sought out as dumping grounds for poor and minority children.

- The number of juveniles in adult prisons will probably not greatly decrease. Wardens and their staff will view the protection of these youngsters as one of their most difficult management problems.

- The dissatisfaction with the juvenile justice system will probably continue. Those who want to eliminate the juvenile justice system and the juvenile court will be more vocal and will receive much greater support.

- Yet it remains unlikely that this nation will give up, any time in the near future, on the more-than-a-century-long experiment with a separate system for juveniles.

One of the underlying themes of this text is that working in the juvenile justice system is an exciting job and a fulfilling career. We hope that the student shares our enthusiasm and aspirations about the possibility of creating a better day for youngsters in our society.

If we care for children, we will increase our efforts to diminish the negative effects of the hard-line and punitive approaches to youth.

If we care for children, we will see to it that our ideas are presented forcefully and clearly to policy makers.

And if we care for children, we will not wait until the system finally works; instead, we will reach out and help those youths seeking to find themselves.

Juvenile Justice Videos

RUNAWAY STATUS OFFENDER

The *Runaway Status Offender* video features a female juvenile who was arrested for running away. The video depicts how the juvenile court must consider the best interests of the youthful offender while also maintaining public safety. In the case, the youth not only repeatedly runs away but also kidnaps her infant child. How does the court assess the needs for the youth? Based on the readings, videos, and reviews throughout this book, what options are available to the court for dealing with the juvenile? How would the well-being of the infant child impact the decision of the court in sentencing the teenager? What treatment model would best suit the juvenile? What community programs are best suited for this case? Discuss. If you were to recommend a sentence to the judge for this case based on what you have learned from this book, what options would you suggest? Explain.

FORGERY CHARGES

The *Forgery Charges* video covers the initial hearing for a youth who has been charged with forgery as well as other offenses. The child wrote two checks that she forged her foster mother's name on, and stole property from friends and family to pawn at a pawnshop. What rights were granted to the child as listed by the judge? What sentence was recommended to the judge to handle the case? The judge explained that the youth was not a "bad person," but merely engaged in "unacceptable behavior." What decisions does the judge make to handle the juvenile, and what led the judge to come to this conclusion? At the end of the video, the judge speaks to the juvenile and discusses the youth's past behavior, present circumstances, and future plans. Discuss what the goals of the judge may have been in handling the juvenile. If you were to recommend a sentence to the judge for this case based on what you have learned from this book, what options would you suggest? Explain.

SUMMARY

LEARNING OBJECTIVE 1 Summarize how the problems of modern society affect juveniles.

The family, the socioeconomic structure, the neighborhood, the school, the gang, and youth attitudes are all influential in both the lawful and illegal behaviors of juveniles.

LEARNING OBJECTIVE 2 Summarize the major issues facing juvenile justice at the present time.

The major issues facing juvenile justice are reliance on the get-tough approach, fiscal challenges, the high rates of recidivism, discrimination based on race/ethnicity and gender in juvenile justice processing, and juvenile victimization.

LEARNING OBJECTIVE 3 Describe the changing face of juvenile justice.

The changing face of juvenile justice involved an increased use of technology, an expanding use of restorative justice, greater use of evidence-based practices and principles, and an emphasis on reentry.

LEARNING OBJECTIVE 4 Explain what professionalism is and how it affects juvenile justice.

Professionalism in juvenile justice is an approach that maintains the importance of integrity, that sees the importance of treating juveniles with dignity and respect, that believes it is possible to make a difference, and that strives to create a workplace that is safe, healthy, and free of harassment in any form. As the number of professionals in juvenile justice increases, what takes place in agencies and institutions will reflect the principles just listed and other principles of professionalism.

LEARNING OBJECTIVE 5 Describe what juvenile justice will look like in the years to come.

In the years to come, juvenile justice may have an increased juvenile base, whose members will be impoverished and from minority groups headed by single mothers; the rates of violence among juveniles may increase again, so there are likely to be more troubled juveniles in the juvenile justice system; the trilogy of gangs, drugs, and guns will likely to continue to be a problem; drug courts, teen courts, and gun courts are likely to increase in number; and disproportionate minority confinement will remain a problem. Finally, while dissatisfaction will remain with the juvenile justice system, the movement to eliminate this system for juveniles will probably experience no greater in support than it does now.

KEY TERMS

professionalism, p. 341   technocorrections, p. 339   technology-driven security, p. 339

REVIEW QUESTIONS

1. What are the benefits of various technologies? What are their disadvantages? Which technologies do you believe are the most acceptable?
2. What are some strategies you could use to increase the use of evidence-based juvenile programs?
3. What are some methods you could use in your local communities to address the issues of hope, healing, honor, and habilitation?
4. What would you like the juvenile justice system to look like by 2040?
5. After reading this book, what types of education and training should professionals in juvenile justice receive to prepare them for jobs in the system?

GROUP EXERCISES

1. *Writing to Learn Exercise:* Write a few paragraphs identifying various technological innovations in the community and how the innovations work. Critique and revise.
2. *Group Work:* Describe the new types of technology that can be used in secure institutions. Continue discussions after referring to the chapter.
3. *Writing to Learn Exercise:* Write an essay describing what restorative justice is, which sections of the criminal justice system are using it, and how. Critique and revise.
4. *Writing to Learn Exercise:* Write a paragraph or two that reviews the empirical evidence as to which programs do and do not work. Critique and revise.
5. *Writing to Learn Exercise:* Write two paragraphs on what the nature of the juvenile problem will look like in the year 2020 and beyond. Critique and revise.
6. *Large Group Work:* Discuss what appear to be the most important aspects of professional training needed for the future. How do the authors believe that the juvenile system should be modified in the future?

NOTES

1. Barry Glick and William Sturgeon, *No Time to Play: Youthful Offenders in Adult Correctional Systems* (Lanham, MD: American Correctional Association, 1998), 10.
2. Refer to the self-report and cohort studies in Chapter 2.
3. See Lyle Shannon, *Assessing the Relationships of Adult Criminal Careers to Juvenile Careers* (Washington, DC: Government Printing Office, 1982); and Donna Martin Hamparian et al., *The Violent Few: A Study of Dangerous Juvenile Offenders* (Lexington, MA: Lexington Books, 1980).
4. See David Fogel, *We Are the Living Proof: The Justice Model for Corrections* (Cincinnati, OH: Anderson, 1975); and David Fogel and Joe Hudson, eds., *Justice as Fairness: Perspectives on the Justice Model* (Cincinnati, OH: Anderson, 1981).
5. Debbie Mchaffey, "Security and Technology: The Human Side," *Corrections Today* 13 (January–February 2004), 30.
6. M. Coates, R. Coates, and B. Vos, "The Impact of Victim–Offender Mediation: Two Decades of Research," *Federal Probation* 65 (2001), 29–36.

7. Katherine van Wormer and Clemens Bartollas, *Women and the Criminal Justice System* 4sth (Boston: Allyn & Bacon, 2013.

8. Clemens Bartollas, *Becoming a Model Warden: Striving for Excellence* (Lanham, MD: American Correctional Association, 2004), 26.

9. Ibid., 83.

10. Code of Ethics of the American Correctional Association.

11. Howard N. Snyder and Melissa Sickmund, *Juvenile Offenders and Victims: 2006 National Report* (Washington, DC: National Center for Juvenile Justice, 2006), 2.

12. Ibid., 7.

13. *Roper v. Simmons* (No. 03-633) 543 U.S. 551, 161 L.Ed. 2d 1, 125 S.Ct. 1183 (2005).

Act with Special Provisions in the Care of Young People (LVU; Sweden) Allows authorities broad discretion in intervening with youths in severe need.

Ad Hoc Means "for this purpose"; members of a group, specially formed committee, or informal organization of people that is organized to address some issue or problem.

Addict A person who builds up a tolerance to any kind of drug and finds it necessary to keep taking the drug or experience discomfort from withdrawal. Gradually, more and more of the drug must be taken to reduce the withdrawal effects.

Adjudicatory Hearing This hearing for juveniles is equivalent to a trial in adult courts. This is the point when the judge reviews the charges as described in the petition, hears the testimony from the parties involved, and decides whether the youth committed the offense.

Adolescence-Limited Delinquents Individuals who only engage in delinquent behavior during youth and desist from deviant activities around their eighteenth birthday.

Adult Sex Offender An adult male who by force, guile, or cunning persuades a young person to perform sexual acts deemed inappropriate or illegal by society.

African Charter on the Rights and Welfare of the Child (ACRWC) Modeled after the United Nations documents on the rights of the child, this charter addresses African cultural, political, and social concerns about the treatment of children.

Aftercare With the formation of the juvenile court, this became another term for parole.

Aftercare officers Juvenile equivalent of adult parole officers.

Age of onset The age at which a juvenile began law-violating behaviors.

Al Shabaab A terrorist group in Somalia and the Horn of Africa notorious for its rape, torture, maiming, and killing of citizens as well as the conscription of young males and females as child soldiers; recently aligned with Al Qaeda.

Amphetamine See Methamphetamine.

Anabolic Steroids Synthetic testosterone obtained by prescription and often used by athletes and body builders to increase body size and male characteristics.

Antisocial Personality Disorder Child engages in lying, intimidation of others, aggression toward others, ignoring rules and regulations, abuse relationships with those around him or her, and shows no regrets about the harm he or she causes.

Apartheid A formal policy of segregation rescinded by South Africa.

Attention Homes Facilities designed to give attention to the delinquent, not detention. Locked doors, fences, and/or physical restraints are absent.

Autonomy The desire for personal independence is an important concern for lower-class persons because they feel controlled so much of the time.

Bail A security given for the release of a juvenile awaiting hearing. It is not a form of punishment. The purpose of bail is to ensure that the defendant will show up at his or her adjudicatory hearing.

Balanced and Restorative Justice Model A traditional New Zealand approach to juvenile offending. This "balanced" system ensures resources are allocated equally among efforts to ensure accountability to crime victims, to increase competency in offenders, and to enhance community safety.

Balanced Approach to Juvenile Probation The goal of this approach is to protect the community from delinquency, to impose accountability for offenses committed, and to equip juvenile offenders with the required competencies to live productively and responsibly in the community.

Behavior Modification A theory that applies learning theory to problems of human behavior.

Beijing Rules Rules developed by the United Nations in 1985 that established guidelines for all nations to follow in the treatment of children, regardless of background.

Biological Positivism Approach that argues crime is the result of biological differences among people that can be discovered through rigorous scientific measurement.

Bullying A stronger, more aggressive child inducing fear, distress, or harm in a weaker child through physical, verbal, or psychological intimidation.

Capital Punishment The death penalty.

Child Abuse The act of engaging in physical, sexual, verbal, or emotional assaults or neglect of a child.

Chronic Offenders A repeat offender or serious delinquent. Predominant characteristics of these youths are their commitment to crime and their involvement in one crime after another. Chronic offenders may include prostitutes and gang members.

Class Oppression A form of exploitation experienced by some adolescents in which socioeconomic conditions have a direct impact on a youth's criminal behavior are imposed on them that denies lower class youths the ability to live normal lives.

Closed Youth Detention (Sweden) Confinement based on seriousness of offense and in detention centers rather than prison.

Cocaine (Drug Abuse) A stimulant drug used for thousands of years with some legitimate medical use but today is used illegally to help users feel euphoric and mentally alert to sounds, sight, and touch; different users experience extremely variable effects with some users experiencing negative effects such as anxiety and restlessness; a very powerful addictive drug.

Cognitive-Behavioral Interventions Interventions used to identify the errors characteristic of youthful offenders' thinking by changing their thought patterns and thinking.

Cognitive Transformation Theory that the way an individual thinks and views the world plays an integral part in his or her desisting from crime. As a delinquent begins to change his or her personal beliefs and openness to change, the individual is less likely to engage in criminal acts.

Cohort Studies A research methodology in which researchers usually identify every juvenile born in a certain time frame in a particular city and then follow those juveniles for many years to track behavioral patterns.

Commitment A sentence to confinement in a facility for juveniles.

Common Law Unwritten laws that emerge over time in societies to solve problems.

Community Correction Acts Residential and day treatment programs are developed under these acts. The Minnesota Community Correction Act has become a model for others because it provides a state subsidy to any county or group of counties that chooses to develop its own community corrections system.

Concurrent Jurisdiction The right of both juvenile and adult courts to try juveniles for crime. Prosecutors decide which court to try juveniles in.

Conduct Disorder Often a result of child abuse, this mental problem results in a child who has difficulty following rules, gets into fights, bullies others, sets fires, steals, and is aggressive to or brutalizes animals.

Conduct Norms The rules of a group that dictate how its members should act under particular conditions.

Constitutionalists   A group that argues that the juvenile court is unconstitutional because under its auspices the principles of a fair trial and individual rights are denied to juveniles.

Containment Theory   Walter Reckless's theory that explains crimes as being the result of internal factors such as poor self-concept and external factors such as weak family, peer and group controls.

Continuum of Care Model   Provided by a number of jurisdictions, this model provides a continuum between institutions and aftercare services to maintain a nurturing environment for youthful offenders.

Continuum of Sanctions   The system of programs, services, and facilities designed to provide escalating punishment as the severity of a youth's criminal behavior increases.

Corporal Punishment   Punishments that involves violence, whipping, and branding; any punishment of the body.

Cottage System   Juvenile facilities that are placed outside of a city and consist of a series of cottages in which youths live in small numbers. The rationale is that youths in rural areas will be reformed when exposed to the rural values.

Crack   A processed crystalline form of cocaine that can be smoked.

Crime Control Model   This model assumes that offenders have free will and should be punished with harsh penalties, such as long prison sentences, to protect society.

Criminal Opportunity Theory   Philip Cook's theory that criminals tend to be selective in choosing a crime target and are most attracted to targets that appear to offer a high payoff with little effort or risk of legal consequence.

Criminal Recidivism   The act of a youth engaging in further or more severe criminal behavior after already being punished for prior delinquent activity.

Cultural Deviance Theory   Walter Miller's theory that the lower-class culture is characterized by a set of focal concerns, or values, that command widespread attention and a high degree of emotional involvement.

Cyclothyme   One of the two body types in Ernst Kretschmer's body type theory. The cyclothyme individual is soft skinned and lacks muscle, and is less likely to engage in criminal behavior than the counterpart schizothyme body type.

Dangerous Poor   In the mid- to late 1800s and early 1900s, those coming from a poor background were blamed for crime. Many appeared dangerous because they came from different cultural, ethnic, and religious backgrounds.

Day Treatment Programs   Treatment programs in which youngsters participate during the day and return home in the evenings.

Decriminalizing Status Offenders   Removing from the juvenile court's jurisdiction youthful behavior that would not be a chargeable offense if committed by an adult.

Deinstitutionalization   The removal of youths from secure confinement and the placement of all qualified youths in community programs rather than in institutions.

Deinstitutionalization of Status Offenders   To no longer confine status offenders in secure detention facilities or secure correctional facilities with delinquents.

Delinquency Prevention   Any attempt to thwart youths' illegal behavior before it occurs.

Dependent and Neglected Children   These children are young, live in dysfunctional families, and lack the love and the consistent behavior models required to grow up as socially functional adults.

Desistance from Crime   The termination of delinquency, strongly related to the maturation process, as juveniles either come to desire a conventional lifestyle or do not desire continuing unlawful activities.

Detention   Being held in a short-term facility designed specifically for juveniles or, occasionally, in a local jail until a police department, probation officer or judge decides on what to do with them

Detention Center   Juvenile hall; intended to be a temporary holding center.

Detention Hearing   Hearing at which a decision to detain is made. The hearing must be held within a short period of time after taking the juvenile into custody, generally forty-eight to seventy-two hours, excluding weekends and holidays.

Determinate Parole   The length of supervision is clearly specified; often related to the period of commitment specified by the juvenile court and is proportionate to the youth's offense.

Deterministic View   The deterministic view states that individuals cannot help committing criminal or delinquent acts because they are controlled either by internal factors (biological or psychological imbalances) or by external factors (poverty, learning crime from others, strain, or societal labeling).

Developing Countries   Countries in the early to middle stages of industrialization and other social structural changes characteristic of modern societies.

Deviant Sexual Arousal   Frequent and inappropriate thoughts about rape and sexual fantasies.

Differential Association Theory   Edwin H. Sutherland's theory that criminals and youthful offenders learn crime from others in intimate personal groups.

Diminished Responsibility   The belief that youths are less responsible for their actions than adults due to sociobiological circumstances that prevent a juvenile from fully understanding his or her actions.

Discretion   The choice between two or more possible legal means of handling a situation confronting a police officer, prosecutor, probation officer, judge, or other law enforcement official.

Disposition Hearing   Hearing that is equivalent to sentencing in adult courts and is of two basic types. The first may occur at the same time as the adjudicatory hearing and the second occurs at a considerably later date.

Disproportionate Minority Confinement (DMC)   An issue in which individuals belonging to minorities are involved within the justice system at a higher proportion than are whites.

Diversion Programs   Programs that sprouted across the nation in the late 1960s and early 1970s in an effort to keep juveniles outside the formal justice system.

Dopamine (Drug Addiction)   A major neurotransmitter within the brain that regulates movement, emotion, cognition, motivation, and feelings of pleasure. Some drugs mimic dopamine and some drugs result in a flooding of the brain with dopamine, thereby producing pleasure.

Drug and Alcohol Abuse Interventions   These interventions are increasingly developing in community-based and institutional settings to assist those who need help with their drug/alcohol addiction problems.

Ecstasy (MDMA)   Has properties of both stimulants and hallucinations and some users report both time and space distortions; a tablet may contain any of a number of other drugs. Neurotoxicity includes increasing levels of serotonin and dopamine, both neurotransmitters. Hhas adverse long-term effects on higher thought processes.

Electronic Monitoring   Electronic anklets and bracelets are used to verify probationers' presence in the residence in which they are confined.

Emerging Nation   Also called a moderately developed nation (MDC), this is a relatively poor nation with an average per capita income of $6,000 to $16,000 with a large population that is beginning to industrialize, export goods, and treat major sections of the population fairly politically, economically, and socially.

Emerging Youth Gangs   Gangs developing in smaller towns and villages, sometimes as a result of urban street gangs' efforts to expand their drug markets.

Emotionally Disturbed Offender   A type of youth whose emotional problems severely interfere with his or her everyday life such that he or she ends up in the justice system.

Escalation of Offenses   An increase in the number and severity of crimes committed by an individual.

Excitement   The quest for excitement leads juveniles to the widespread use of alcohol and drugs or engaging in sex and gambling.

Experimental Drug User   Someone who tries different drugs to experience their effects; may lead to addiction.

Failed State   A country whose government has collapsed and is incapable of governing and supporting all of its citizens. Such a country often experiences constant violent conflict among many groups competing for power.

Family Conferences   Meetings in which a facilitator, the offender, their families, and a community representative participate; held to solve the offender's problems in the community.

Family Therapy   Therapy aimed at treating the entire family. This has become a widely used method when dealing with a youthful offender's socially unacceptable behavior.

Fate   Lower-class individuals feel that their lives are subject to a set of forces over which they have little or no control.

Felicific Calculus   Human beings are presumed to be creatures governed by their desires to gain pleasure and avoid pain.

Feminist Theory of Delinquency   A theory proposed by Meda Chesney-Lind which states that female delinquency is explained by the relationship between the female's crimes and her sexual and physical victimization.

Fingerprinting   Taking a person's fingerprint for possible identification.

Forestry Camps   Minimum-security institutional camps. Residents engage in conservation work in state parks.

Free Will   Human beings are viewed as rational creatures who, being free to choose their actions, can be held responsible for their behavior.

Gang Deactivation   Removing youths from gang involvements.

Gang Detail   Officers of the traditional police unit assigned to gang problems.

Gang Unit   Units established to work solely on gang problems and that develop extensive intelligence networks with gang members in the community.

Gender-Neutral Position   An approach to explaining male–female delinquency that focuses on social learning, delinquent peer relationships, social bonding, the family, and deterrence and strain rather than gender differences. Advocates of this approach explain that females engage with the criminal world using the same methods as males.

Group Home   A single dwelling owned or rented by an organization or agency for the purpose of housing offenders.

Guardian ad litem   A lawyer who is appointed by the court to take care of youths who need help, especially in neglect, dependency, and abuse cases, but also occasionally in delinquency cases.

Guardianship Councils (Brazil)   Five-member groups of local citizens that protect juveniles assigned to them by judges and make recommendations for youth placement in hospitals, with parents, in shelter foster homes, or treatment.

Guided Group Interaction (GGI)   The most widely used treatment modality in juvenile corrections. The modality is based on the assumption that youths can confront their peers and force them to face the reality of their behavior more effectively than staff can.

Habilitation   To socialize a child into the dominant societal values and norms, and acceptable ways of living in a society.

Healing   To ease the pain of children who have grown up without families, who have experienced the pain or loss of family members, or who have experienced neglect or physical, psychological, or emotional abuse.

Heroin   Highly addictive drug that, when laced with fentanyl, has the potential to cause death within hours. Serious health hazards accompany use. Withdrawal occurs soon after the drug is taken and withdrawal symptoms are severe.

High (Drug Addiction)   a feeling of euphoria or excitement as a result of taking a drug.

Highly Developed Nation (HDC)   A nation with a high per capita average income, usually well above $16,000, and a highly functioning government capable of treating almost all citizens fairly politically, economically, and socially.

Honor   For a youth to have acceptance and respect from his or her peers and society as a whole.

Hope   Adolescents having something to anticipate, a reason to obey the law, to attend school, to avoid drug involvement, to stay out of gangs, and to have a positive outlook on the future.

House Arrest   Home confinement is a program of intermediate punishment whereby youths are ordered to remain confined in their own residences during evening hours, after curfew, and on weekends.

Houses of Refuge   Facilities created for all children in the early 1800s when citizens became concerned about the inhumane living conditions in jails and prisons.

Illicit drug   Any compound defined by law to be illegal for any category of people; includes prescription drugs used for any purpose other than that for which they were prescribed.

Indigenous Population   The people native to an area.

Industrialized Countries   Nations that have economies based more on industries than on agriculture. Usually these democratized nations tend to base criminal and juvenile law on constitutionally derived formal rules and procedures.

Infancy   From birth to approximately two years of age.

Inhalants   Substances that produce a loss of sensation, and even unconsciousness. Irreversible effects include hearing loss, limb spasms, central nervous system or brain damage, or bone marrow damage. Sniffing high concentrations of inhalants may result in death from heart failure or suffocation (inhalants displace oxygen in the lungs).

Insight-Based Therapy   A therapy model employed by training schools to treat mental and emotional disorders. The therapist uses insight, persuasion, suggestion, reassurance, and instructions to provide residents with a realistic view of their problems and can establish a desire to cope in a healthy and effective manner.

Intake   The point at which a probation officer conducts a preliminary investigation that includes an interview during which a youth is advised of his or her legal rights and the officer decides on the next step for the youth.

Intake Process   When probation officers evaluate whether a juvenile offender needs help from the juvenile court; the intake process controls detention, reduces caseloads, and keeps minor cases out of juvenile court.

Intensive Supervision Program (ISP)   Juveniles are placed in small caseloads and receive frequent contacts (up to five or six a day) from their aftercare officers.

Interpersonal Maturity Level (I-Level) Classification System   Developed by J. Grant and M. Grant in the late 1950s, an I-Level classification assumes that personality development follows a normal sequence and attempts to identify the developmental stage of offenders by focusing on their perception of themselves, others, and the world.

Interrogation   Occurs when an individual is formally questioned by the police.

Interstate Compact   An agreement among certain states to deal with both the mobility of youths and the need to keep them under supervision. Interstate compacts may be drawn up when youths are wanted for several crimes in several states at the same time or when a state has a specialized treatment program appropriate to specific offenders.

Investigation   Background check of a the juvenile. Probation officers are usually given up to sixty days to do background checks on a juvenile, but if the court combines the adjudicatory and disposition stages, the social study must be completed before the youth appears in front of a judge.

Jails   A local institution for individuals being held for trial or for short-term confinements for sentences of a year of less.

jati   A Hindu caste or distinctive social group of which there are thousands throughout India; a special characteristic is often the exclusive occupation of its male members (such as barber or potter).

Judicial Waiver   The most widely used transfer mechanism for moving a juvenile case to adult court. This involves the actual decision-making process that begins when the juvenile is brought to intake.

Just Desserts   A concept promoted by David Fogel, who believes that the punishment given to juvenile and adult offenders must be proportionate to the seriousness of the offense.

Justice Model   A punishment model promoted by David Fogel, who believes that both juvenile and adult offenders are volitional and responsible human beings and deserve to be punished proportionately to the seriousness of their offenses if they violate the law.

Juvenile Court Officer   Usually a probation officer.

Juvenile Court Statistics   First published in 1929, the purpose of this publication was threefold: to furnish an index of the nature and extent of the problems brought before courts with juvenile jurisdiction, to show the nature and extent of services given by these courts in such a way that significant trends could be identified, and to show the extent to which service given by courts has been effective in correcting social problems.

Juvenile Justice and Delinquency Prevention Act (JJDP)   Main policy changes brought about by the act include (1) status offenders must be separated from delinquents in secure detention and (2) institutionalization facilities for adults that hold juveniles may not receive federal funding.

Labeling Perspective   Labeling theory contends that society creates the deviant by labeling some juveniles as "different" from others.

Law-Related Education (LRE)   An educational program designed to promote the development of character that leads to healthy behaviors. LRE is designed to teach students the fundamental principles and skills needed to become responsible citizens in a constitutional democracy.

Least-Restrictive Approach   The "go soft" approach to minor offenders found guilty of a crime. This first became popular in the 1960s and called for keeping juveniles from penetrating any further than necessary into the system.

Lesser Developed Countries (LDCs)   Nations that are weakened or failed states whose per capita is around six hundred dollars or less.

Life without Parole Sentence   Sentencing used to incarcerate juveniles for the rest of their natural lives.

Lineup   Situation in which a number of people, including a suspect, are lined up in front of witnesses or victims who try to identify the person who committed a crime against them.

Mandatory Sentencing   Sentences that impose specific sanctions for specific actions regardless of mitigating factors.

Marijuana   Leaves from the cannabis plant are used to achieve "highs"; its use is correlated with anxiety and other mental problems, particularly in very young users. Research is mixed on its effects on brain and health, but it is known to increase heart rate; contains many carcinogens. Prolonged use may reduce I.Q.

Marxist Perspective   Perspective that views the state and the law itself as ultimate tools of the economic interests of the ownership class.

Masculinity Hypothesis   A hypothesis suggesting that as females become more male-like in their social roles and became more masculine as a result they also become more delinquent.

Medical Model   The first treatment model to develop from the *parens patriae* philosophy, which argues that youth crime is caused by factors that can be identified, isolated, and treated as in the case of a disease.

Medicalization of Deviance   Attributing deviancy to medical causes and treating deviancy as a disease instead of delinquent behavior.

Mental Health Placements   Keeping juveniles with mental illnesses out of institutions in the justice system and placing them in mental health systems instead.

Methamphetamine   A major addictive stimulant; long-term use can lead to mood disturbances, violent behavior, anxiety, confusion, insomnia, and severe dental problems.

Minor   A defendant under the age specified as an adult for legal purposes.

Miranda Rights   Established by the 1966 Supreme Court case *Miranda v. Arizona*, these rights must be read by law enforcement officers to individuals prior to arrest. The Miranda rights fully explain the rights the arrested individual is entitled to throughout the justice system and prevents the individual from unknowingly giving up his or her rights or incriminating his or herself.

Missouri Plan   Adopted by a dozen states, this plan involves a commission being appointed to nominate candidates for judicial vacancies; an elected official, generally the governor, makes judicial appointments from the list submitted by the commission, and nonpartisan and uncontested elections are held to give incumbent judges an opportunity to run on their records.

Naive Offenders   These types of offenders can be divided into three groups of adolescents: youths who are mentally deficient, those who simply are unaware that they are violating the law, and those who are naïve risk-takers.

National Board for Institutional Care (SiS; Sweden)   Board that regulates institutionalization based on the crime and individual needs and limits confinement to no less than fourteen days or more than four years.

National Council of Juvenile and Family Court Judges   Located in Reno, Nevada, this organization has done a great deal to upgrade the juvenile court judiciary. It has sponsored research and continuing legal education efforts.

National Crime Victimization Survey   Analysis of data from this survey is done by the U.S. Bureau of the Census to determine as accurately as possible the extent of crime in the United States by interviewing victims.

Neonatal   From birth to approximately one month after birth.

Nerve Synapses   Spaces between the neurons of the brain and central nervous systems that must be crossed for messages to be sent.

Neurons   Specialized cells of the brain and central nervous system that carry messages throughout the body.

Neurotransmitters   Chemicals that carry messages between the neurons through the nerve synapses.

Nongovernmental Organizations (NGOs)   Privately funded organizations that attempt to address world, national, and local issues in various countries.

Objective Research   A method of research that uses quantitative data and is acquired through collecting numerical and statistical data.

Official Statistics   Three main sources of official or governmental statistics pertaining to juvenile delinquency are uniform crime reports, juvenile court statistics, and national victimization studies; any other data collected by governmental as opposed to private agencies.

Oppositional Defiant Disorder   Excessive refusal to cooperate with others; characterized by being angry, swearing, and deliberately hassling others and is a problem if these behaviors last longer than six months. Some of these behavioral symptoms are normal for the "terrible twos" and some teenagers.

Panchayats   Based on traditional Indian methods of working with troublesome youths in the community, the Panchayat is reemerging in Indian society. These are quasi-governmental organizations supported by the government and run by elected elders of the community.

Parens Patriae   A philosophical basis of the treatment model that emerged in the United States with the founding of the juvenile court. The philosophy of the juvenile court is that the state has the right to guardianship over a child found under adverse social/individual conditions that encourage development of crime or other problems. This philosophy has been challenged by due process philosophy since its founding.

Parole   The period of time after institutional release when offenders are still under control of the courts or state.

Perinatal   Any time from roughly one month prior to birth until one month after birth.

Petition   An indictment.

Petitioner   A prosecutor.

Photographs   Pictures taken of offenders for identification and law enforcement files.

Plea Bargain   A deal made between the prosecutor and the defense attorney to reduce charges so the juvenile will receive a lesser sentence.

Positive Peer Culture (PPC)   Developed by Harry Vorrath, PPC is a total system for building positive youth subcultures. Its main philosophy is to turn around the negative peer culture and to mobilize the power of the peer group in a positive way.

Positivism   The dominant philosophical perspective of juvenile justice that argues that human behavior is determined and that the causes of crime can be discovered through rigorous scientific measurement.

Postindustrial Society   Countries moving away from industrial and factory production to a service, communications, and financially based economy.

Predictor Items   These items, based on relevant offender backgrounds, are used to determine whether offenders will remain law abiding or get into trouble after release.

Prescription Drugs (Drug Addiction)   Drugs prescribed for a specific reason to a specific person. Use of the drug for any other purpose by that person or by others for any reason is illegal.

Presumptive Minimum   Involves the assumption that aftercare should terminate after the youthful offender completes a commonly accepted minimum period of time on supervised release.

Preventive Detention   Confinement that is proactive, not punitive, for a specific offense.

Probation   A judicial disposition under which youthful offenders are subject to certain conditions imposed by the juvenile court and are permitted to remain in the community under the supervision of a probation officer.

Probation Subsidy Program   Used in states such as California, Nevada, Oregon, and Washington, these programs encourage a decreased rate of commitment of offenders by counties to state institutions by reimbursing the communities for confining youths locally.

Problem-Oriented Policing   A policy police departments are currently turning to in which police respond to the circumstances that create juvenile problems rather than to the incidents themselves.

Proportionality   The practice that all sanctions must be proportioned according to the seriousness criminal act. A punishment must not be excessive in nature when compared to the crime the individual committed.

Prosecutorial Discretion   The right of a prosecutor to determine whether juveniles are to be tried in adult or juvenile court.

Psychoanalysis   Developed by Sigmund Freud, this therapy helps patients understand their internal emotional states.

Psychotherapy   Therapy based on Freudian psychoanalysis. It is based on the concepts of id, ego, and superego and the oral, anal, and phallic stages of psychosexual development used to understand youths' emotional development.

Qualitative Research   Research data that is based on verbal descriptions and characteristics rather than quantitative data.

Quay Classification System   This system evaluates delinquents in terms of their behavior rather than their worldview and is based on five personality types: inadequate-immature, neurotic-conflicted, unsocialized aggressive or psychopathic, socialized or subcultural delinquent, and subcultural-immature delinquents.

Ranches   Privately or publicly administered minimum-security institutional placements that are normally reserved for youths who have committed minor offenses, who have been committed to the department of youth services or private corrections, or who have been released from confinement in a facility. Widely used in California, these tend to hold primarily white youths.

Rational Choice Theory   An extension of the deterrence doctrine found in the classical school that focuses on the rational calculation of payoffs and costs before delinquent acts are committed.

Rave Culture   An outgrowth of music and drug use in the 1960, today's rave culture builds on the use of psychedelic and other drugs, electronic music, and dancing through the night, sometimes with tens of thousands of youths involved.

Reality Therapy   William Glasser and G. L. Harrington assume that irresponsible behavior arises when a person is unable to fulfill his or her basic needs. According to this approach, the basic human needs are relatedness and respect, and one satisfies these needs by doing what is realistic, responsible, and right.

Reception and Diagnostic Centers   Run by both private and public administrations, these centers provide evaluation for youths to determine which treatment plans or facilities would serve the juvenile in the best way possible based on characteristics and needs for the youth.

Reentry Programs   After being confined within facilities, when they are released, juveniles may feel disoriented and confused by the transition from controlled living into free society; reentry programs are used to help them reenter society.

Referee   In some jurisdictions this individual takes the role of a judge in the juvenile court.

Reformatories   Also known as training schools or industrial schools. Developed in the mid-nineteenth century, reformatories were similar to houses of refuge but also provided schooling half of the day as well as harsh industrial labor for juveniles.

Reinforcement Theory   The theory that behavior is governed by its consequent rewards and punishments as reflected in the history of the individual.

Reintegration Philosophy   {Philosophy that assumes both the offender and the receiving community must be brought together in formal programs.

Reliability   One of the two goals of data collection. Reliability is achieved when researchers can produce the same results using the same instruments numerous times. Reliability goes hand in hand with validity to provide accurate data.

Repeat Offender   Individuals who commit criminal behavior even after being charged with previous crimes.

Representing   Secret handshakes, hand signs, and colors used by gang members to identify the gangs to which they belong.

Respondent   A defense attorney.

Restitution   A disposition that requires offenders to pay back their victims or the community for their crime. This began to be used widely in probation during the 1970s and 1980s.

Restorative Justice Model   The purpose of this model is to reconcile the interests of victims, offenders, and the community through common programs and supervision practices that meet mutual needs.

Risk/Needs Assessment   Tests and evaluations that are used to assess an offender's psychiatric and psychological complications. The results of these assessments are used to find which treatment programs will best suit the offender. Popular risk/needs assessments include the YLS/CMI, J-RAT, YASI, SARY, and MAYSI-2.

Routine Activity Approach   This approach links the dramatic increase in crime rates since 1960 to changes in the routine activity structure of U.S. society and to a corresponding increase in target suitability and decrease in the presence of "guardians."

Schizothyme   One of the two body types in Ernst Kretschmer's body type theory. The schizothyme individual is strong and muscular, and is more likely to engage in criminal behavior than the counterpart cyclothyme body type.

School Safety   Drugs, alcohol, suicide, rape, robbery, assault, arson, and bomb threats combine with knives and guns to change the atmosphere of schools and generate fear in parents about student's safety today.

School Searches   Courts have ruled that schools do not need to obtain a warrant or have probable cause that a crime took place to conduct a search of students or their belongings. The legality of the search depends on its reasonableness, the scope of the search, the student's gender and age, and the student's behavior at the time.

Search and Seizure   U.S. citizens are protected by the Fourth Amendment to the Constitution against being searched without probable cause and without a proper search warrant.

Self-Report Studies   Studies used to measure hidden youth crime. Their purpose is to obtain a fuller and more accurate picture of the amount of crime by asking youths what offenses they have committed.

Sensation Seeking   The behavior of an individual who takes extreme risks and engages in new and novel activities. Many youths who take part in sensation seeking turn to delinquent behavior to fulfill these desires.

Sex-Role Socialization   The social phenomenon in which a youth learning his or her sex m Females tend to be supervised by parental figures more than males are, resulting in these gender roles causing females to be less delinquent than males.

Sexual Assault Cycle   Sex offenders are believed to engage in a cycle of emotional and thinking processes that lead them to sex offending, punishment, depression, and sex offending again, which must be broken if offenders are to be helped with their problems.

Sharia Law   Islamic law that governs the everyday lives of followers of Islam including marriage, divorce, sexual relations, business and religious practices, inheritance, and the custody and treatment of children. The law varies widely around the world.

Situational Offenders   Those who do not normally look upon themselves as committed to youth crime. They drift in and out of crime because of boredom, group pressure, financial need, and the opportunity to commit crime.

Skill Development Programs   Programs that help offenders learn new skills such as reading and interpersonal communication that prepare them for adjustment in the community.

Smartness   A value among the lower class that involves the desire to outsmart, outfox, con, and dupe others.

Social Control Theory   A theory by Travis Hirschi that linked delinquent behavior to the bonds individuals have with conventional social groups such as the family and school.

Social Disorganization Theory   A theory by Clifford R. Shaw and Henry D. McKay that views crime as resulting from the breakdown of social control by the traditional primary groups such as family and the neighborhood because of the social disorganization of the community.

Social Roles   Found in training schools for boys; the roles are classified as aggressive, manipulative, passive, and other roles.

Social Services Act (SoL; Sweden)   This act was passed in 1982 because of the inadequacy of prisons. The act emphasized a social welfare system in which offenders and officials cooperated in finding the best treatment for a child.

Social Study Report   This report is ordered by a judge in a bifurcated hearing when a youth is found delinquent at the fact-finding stage of court proceedings.

Sociobiologists   Researchers who investigate the relationship between antisocial behavior and biological factors and the environment, through studies including, but not limited to, twins, adoption, intelligence, chromosomal activity, and chemical imbalances in the body.

Sociopath   A sociopath or psychopath is a person with a lack of affect, ability to empathize, and who commits crimes in a cold-hearted unemotional manner; normally not diagnosed before age 17; some authors distinguish between the two.

Somalia   A nation in the Horn of Africa considered a failed state because its government, religions, businesses, and territorial groups vie for power are fragmented, and commit atrocities against each other.

Specialization of Offenses   The tendency to repeat one type of crime.

Status Offender   A legal description applied to juveniles who commit acts that are law violations only for juveniles, not adults.

Statute of the Child and Adolescent (Brazil, SEA)   A 1990 act that identifies a child as any person up to the age 12 and adolescents as youths between ages 12 and 17.

Statutorial Exclusion   Some state legislatures automatically mandate that the perpetrators of specific offenses be tried in adult court.

Statutory law   Laws passed by legislatures that are written down and that police and courts enforce.

Strain Theory   Robert K. Merton's theory that cultural goals and the means to achieve these goals must be reasonably well integrated if a culture is to be stable and smooth running.

Street Gang Members   Any youths who join gangs.

Supervision   Once a youth has been placed on probation, the probation officer is required to provide the best supervision, including surveillance, casework services, and counseling or guidance, available. This also involves careful monitoring of the minor's adjustment to the community.

Swedish Young Offenders Act (LUL)   Act that grants prosecutors wide discretion in how to handle youths and in keeping youths out of court.

Synergistic Effect (Drugs)   When the combined effect of more than one drug is greater than the sum of the drugs taken together, a multiplier effect occurs.

Taking into Custody   Arresting a suspect.

Teenage Prostitution   A form of chronic sexual offending in which females are more involved than males.

Tolerance (Drug Addiction)   Occurs when a person needs to use more and more of a drug to produce the same effects as already experienced with a smaller amount of the same drug.

Toughness   The ideal personality trait in the eyes of lower-class males; the "tough guy" is hard, fearless, undemonstrative, and a good fighter.

Traditional Cultures   Cultures that still use internalized and long-standing folkways and mores.

Training Schools   Public and private schools that are used to confine youths for long periods of time.

Transactional Analysis (TA)   Method that focuses on interpreting and evaluating interpersonal relationships and tries to teach youthful lawbreakers to relate to others in an "adult," mature way instead of as a "parent" or a "child."

Transfer Process   Process used to move juveniles who violate criminal codes from the juvenile justice system to the adult justice system to be tried in adult criminal court.

Transition to Adult Crime   Occurs when groups of youthful offenders continue to commit offenses into their adult years.

Treatment Model   Including the medical model, a model based on the belief that the basic mission of juvenile justice is to rehabilitate youthful offenders. It proposes that juveniles should be treated by specialists for those factors that caused them to commit offenses.

Trouble   Getting into and out of trouble represents a major preoccupation of the lower class; fighting, drinking, and sexual adventures are basic causes of trouble for them.

Underclass Theory   An explanation for the origin of gangs, this theory states that gangs are a normal response to the abnormal social setting in which underclass (impoverished) youths are exposed to the point that delinquent behavior may be the only means of gaining economic success.

Uniform Crime Reports (UCR)   Compiled from police statistics by the FBI. The FBI classifies crimes into Part I and Part II offenses based on their seriousness.

Urban Gangs   Gangs found in urban areas that are capable of extremely violent behavior.

Validity   One of the two goals of data collection. Validity is achieved when researchers are studying what they believe they are studying. Validity goes hand in hand with reliability to provide accurate data.

Victimization   The exploitation of youths not able to protect themselves by predatory peers.

Waiver Hearing   A hearing held to decide whether an offender should be sent to adult court.

Welfare Model   In Canada, a model that focuses on treating, curing, and helping offenders.

Wilderness Programs   Wilderness or survival programs are similar to ranches. Two of the best known are Outward Bound and VisionQuest.

Wisconsin System   Under this system, a risk/needs assessment is conducted for each probationer at regular intervals to see what level of supervision to place him or her under.

Young Offenders Act (YOA; Canada) of 1982 This bill set the age of maturity as eighteen for juvenile offenders.

Young Offender Teams Made up of representatives of community agencies that plan and program extrajudicial sanctions for young offenders in England.

Youth Criminal Justice Act (YCJA; Canada) Replaced the Young Offenders Act in Canada in 2003. The YCJA statutorily emphasized the use of extrajudicial sanctions for different ages and specific offenders.

Youth Service Board A nongovernmental group that advises the Home Secretary in England on the youth justice system and the implementation of extrajudicial sanctions in local areas.

Youth Service Program (United States) Programs comprised of regular police officers; some are known as Youth Service Bureaus. Such a program is formed to deal with a specific gang problem and is not a permanent unit within the police force.

Youthful Offender System (YOS; United States) Proposed for young adults (sixteen to nineteen years old). Programs in these institutions emphasize work readiness, job training, and work experience.

Table of Cases

Arizona v. Gant, 556 U.S. 332 (2009)—The U.S. Supreme Court ruled that police may search the passenger compartment of a vehicle incident to a recent occupant's arrest only if it is reasonable to believe that the arrestee might access the vehicle at the time of the search or that the vehicle contains evidence of the offense of arrest.

Atkins v. Virginia, 536 U.S. 304 (2002)—The Supreme Court ruled that juveniles who are mentally retarded cannot be executed for their offenses.

Breed v. Jones, 421 U.S. 519, 95 S. Ct. 1779 (1975)—The Supreme Court ruled that Jones's hearing in the juvenile court was an adjudicatory hearing and that his trial in adult court constituted double jeopardy.

Brown v. Mississippi, 297 U.S. 278 (1936)—The Supreme Court ruled that force may not be used to obtain confessions.

Ciulla v. State, 434 S.W. 2d 948 (Tex. Civ. App. 1968)—A youth confined to a Texas training school after police found marijuana in his car was ordered released by an appellate court because the search took place too late to be related to the arrest.

Commonwealth v. Fisher, 213 P. 48, 62 A. 198 (1905)—The Court ruled that the juvenile court "is not for the punishment of offenders but for the salvation of children ... whose salvation may become the duty of the state."

Commonwealth v. Guyton, 405 Mass. 497 (1989)—A Massachusetts motion appeals judge held that no other minor, not even a relative, can act as an interested adult in a juvenile's initial hearings.

Davis v. Mississippi, 394 U.S. 721 (1969)—The Supreme Court ruled, among other things, that fingerprints taken by the police at the youth's initial interrogation could not be used as evidence against him in this case. The Court also ruled that the police should not have detained the youth without authorization by a judicial officer, that the youth was unnecessarily fingerprinted a second time, and that the youth should not have been interrogated at the first detention when he was fingerprinted.

Eddings v. Oklahoma, 102 S. Ct. 869 (1982)—The Supreme Court was able to avoid directly addressing the constitutionality of the juvenile death penalty by ruling that "the chronological age of a minor is itself a relevant mitigating factor of great weight."

Ex parte Crouse CASES OF THE SUPREME COURT OF PENNSYLVANIA. EASTERN DISTRICT-DECEMBER TERM, 1838 (Philadelphia, January 5, 1839)—The Pennsylvania Supreme Court formalized the idea of *parens patriae*, meaning that the court could serve as a guardian in the absence of a responsible parent. *Ex parte Crouse* also dictated that, unlike adults, juveniles were not protected by the Bill of Rights found in the Constitution.

Fare v. Michael C., 442 U.S. 23, 99 S. Ct. 2560 (1979)—The Supreme Court ruled that Michael seemed to understand his rights and that even when his request to talk with his probation officer was denied, he still was willing to waive his rights and continue the interrogation.

Farrell v. Cate (Super. Ct. Alameda County, 2004, No. RG03079344)—A complaint made towards the California Youth Authority (CYA), regarding the conditions within their facilities, resulted in the signing of a consent decree in which expressed that the program needed to provide effective treatments, programs, services, and care for juveniles; in order to correct behavior within their system.

Gagnon v. Scarpelli, 411 U.S. 778 (1973)—The Supreme Court held that the right to counsel should be decided on a case-by-case basis. The Court did indicate that counsel should be provided on request when the probationer denies that he or she committed the violation or when the reasons for the violation are complex.

Gallegos v. Colorado, 370 U.S. 49, 82 S. Ct. 1209 (1962)—The U.S. Supreme Court had prohibited the use of confessions coerced from juveniles. —A defendant who was held five days without seeing a lawyer, parent or other amenable adult, including his mother, signed a written confession that he had assaulted an elderly man five days before the victim died and prior to the defendant's being seen by a judge. The Supreme Court ruled the confession was obtained in violation of due process, and the judgment sustaining his conviction was reversed.

Graham v. Florida, 08-7412 982 So. 2d 43 (2010)—The U.S. Supreme Court ruled that individuals under the age of eighteen could not be sentenced to life without the possibility of parole for nonhomicide offenses.

Gregg v. Georgia, 48 U.S. 153 (1976)—The U.S. Supreme Court ruled that the death penalty did not violate the Eighth Amendment's prohibition against cruel and unusual punishment.

Haley v. Ohio, 332 U.S. 596 (1948)—The Supreme Court ruled that neither an adult nor a child can be interrogated without counsel present or the requirements of the due process of the law fulfilled.

Inmates of the Boys' Training School v. Affleck, 346 F. Supp. 1354 (D.R.I. 1972)—The Court ruled that juveniles have a right to treatment because rehabilitation is the true purpose of the juvenile court.

In re Barbara Burrus, 403 U.S. 528, 91 S.Ct. 1976, 29 L.Ed.2d 647 (1967)—The Supreme Court ruled that juveniles do not have a constitutional right to a jury trial. Some states do permit jury trials for juveniles.

In re Gault, 387 U.S. 1,18,1,18 L.Ws.2d 527, 87 S.Ct.1428 (1967)—The U.S. Supreme Court ruled that juveniles have the right to due process safeguards during confinement; these rights include receiving notice of the charges, the right to be represented by counsel, the right to confront and cross-examine witnesses, and the right to avoid self-incrimination.

In re Holley R.I. 615; 268 A.2d 723; 1970 R.I—The court's decision was that "the presence of [defendant's] counsel is necessary to preserve[his] basic right to a fair trial as affected by his right meaningfully to cross-examine the witnesses against him and to have effective assistance of counsel at the trial itself." —Also, that a lineup is a critical stage of a prosecution and denial of the right of counsel at a lineup renders the identification made at that time inadmissible."

In re Terry, 438 pa., 339, 265 A.2d 350 (1970)—The Supreme Court ruled that juveniles do not have a constitutional right to a jury trial. Some states do permit jury trials for juveniles.

In re Winship, 357 U.S. 358, 90 S.Ct. 1968, 25 L. Ed. 2d 368 (1970)—The Supreme Court ruled that juveniles are entitled to proof "beyond a reasonable doubt." The preponderance of evidence standard was thrown out when youths committed acts for which adults would be charged with a criminal offense.

Jackson v. State, 359 Ark. 87, 194 S.W.3d 757 (2004) (10-9647) (2012)—Ruled along side *Miller v. Alabama,* the Supreme Court ruled that a mandatory sentence imposing life imprisonment without the possibility of parole for juveniles is unconstitutional.

Kent v. United States, 383 U.S. 541, 86 S.Ct. 1045, 16 L. Ed. 2d 84 (1966)—The Court ruled that Kent had the right to a transfer hearing in which evidence was presented, that Kent had the right to be present at a waiver hearing, that Kent's attorney had the right to see the social service reports, and that the judge had to state the reasons for the transfer.

Kirby v. Illinois, 406 U.S. 682, 92 S.Ct. 1877 (1972)—Following the *United States v. Wade* decision, the Court went on to say that the defendant's right to counsel at postindictment lineup procedures goes into effect as soon as the complaint or the indictment is issued.

Mapp v. Ohio, **367 U.S. 643 (1961)**—The Supreme Court affirmed Fourth Amendment rights for adults. The decision stated that evidence gathered in an unreasonable search and seizure was inadmissible in court.

McKeiver v. Pennsylvania, **403 U.S. 528 (1971)** —The decision denied the right of juveniles to have jury trials.

Mempa v. Rhay, **389 U.S. 128 (1968)**—The Court upheld that the Sixth Amendment's right to counsel applies to the sentencing hearing because it is an important step in criminal prosecution.

Miller v. Alabama, **(10–9646) (2012)**—The Court ruled that a mandatory sentence imposing life imprisonment without the possibility of parole for juveniles is unconstitutional.

Morales v. Turman, **364 F. Supp. 166 (E.D. Tex. 1973)**—The U.S. District Court for the Eastern District of Texas held that a number of criteria had to be followed by the state of Texas in order to ensure that proper treatment would be provided to confined juveniles.

Morgan v. Sproat, **432 F. Supp. 1130 (S.D. Miss. 1977)**—The Court condemned the cruel practices of confining youths to padded cells with no windows or furnishings, and only flush holes for toilets, and denying access to rehabilitation programs or services.

Morrissey v. Brewer **408 U.S. 471 (1972)** —The Court ruled that a hearing must be provided to determine the facts for a parole violation.

Murray v. Page **429 F.2d 1359 (1970)**—The court stated that once a prisoner is paroled he cannot be deprived of his freedom by means inconsistent with due process. The minimal right of the parolee to be informed of the charges and the nature of the evidence against him and to appear and to be heard at the revocation hearing is inviolate.

Nelson v. Heyne, **355 F. Supp. 451 (N.D. Ind. 1972)**—Indiana's Seventh Circuit agreed with the district court that inmates of the Indiana Boys' School have a right to rehabilitative treatment.

New Jersey v. T. L. O, **469 U.S. 325 (1985)** —The U.S. Supreme Court held that the Fourth Amendment right against unreasonable searches and seizures does not apply to the school setting. School searches do not have to be based on a search warrant or probable cause; the search, however, must be reasonable.

Pena v. New York State Division for Youth, **419 F. Supp. 203 (S.D.N.Y. 1976)**—The Court held that the use of isolation, hand restraints, and tranquilizing drugs at Gosheen Annex Center was punitive and antitherapeutic and, therefore, violated the Eighth Amendment.

People v. Lara, **62 Cal. Rptr. 586 (1967), cert. denied 392 U.S. 945 (1968)**—The state of California upheld the confession of two Spanish-speaking youths, one of whom had a mental age of slightly over ten years.

Roper v. Simmons, **543 U.S. 551 (2005) 112 S.W. 3td.397**—In 2005 the Supreme Court ruled, in a four-to-five decision, that no juveniles who committed their crimes under the age of eighteen could be executed.

Safford Unified School District v. Redding, **557 U.S. (2009)**—The Supreme Court ruled that schools do not have unlimited search and seizure rights. The June 2009 Supreme Court decision in *Safford Unified School District v. Redding* placed limitations on strip searches of students. School officials in Safford, Arizona, strip searched a thirteen-year-old girl, forcing her to expose her breasts and pelvic area in a search for two Advil. The court ruled that the search was unreasonable because school officials had not demonstrated that either the power of the drugs and or their quantity was sufficiently dangerous so as to warrant a search that was intrusive, humiliating, frightening, and embarrassing.

Schall v. Martin, **467 U.S. 253 (1984)**—The Supreme Court held that preventive detention upholds a legitimate interest of the state.

Stanford v. Kentucky, **492 U.S. 361 (1989)** —The Supreme Court upheld the constitutionality of the death penalty for juveniles under the age of eighteen but older than sixteen.

State v. Lowery, **230 A.2d 907 (1967)**—The Supreme Court applied the Fourth Amendment ban against unreasonable searches and seizures to juveniles.

State v. Werner, **242 S.E.2d 907 (W. Va. 1978)** —The Court condemned as cruel practices the locking of residents by staff in solitary confinement; beating, kicking, slapping, and spraying them with mace; requiring them to scrub floors with a toothbrush; and forcing residents to stand or sit for prolonged periods without changing position.

Terry v. Ohio, **392 U.S. 1, 20 L.2d 889, 911 (1968)**—Police having a specific and articulable suspicion that a juvenile is armed and possibly dangerous, the youth's presence in a high-drug-dealing area of town, an obvious bulge in clothing, or the presence of another officer who may have arrested the youth previously and found a weapon on the youth may all lead to the reasonable suspicion justifying a pat down. An officer may do a *Terry* search, that is, patting down the youth's outer clothing, in a search for weapons only.

Thompson v. Oklahoma, **487 U.S. 815 (1988)** —The Court ruled by a five-to-three vote that "the Eighth and Fourteenth Amendment[s] prohibit the execution of a person who was under sixteen years of age at the time of his or her offense."

United States v. Wade, **338 U.S. 218, 87 S.Ct. 1926 (1967)**—The Supreme Court ruled that the accused has the right to have counsel present at postindictment lineup procedures.

White v. Reid, **125 F. Supp. 647 (D.D.C.) (1954)**—The court ruled that juveniles could not be held in institutions that did not provide for their rehabilitation.

Wilkins v. Missouri, **109 S.Ct. 2969 (1989)** —The Supreme Court decided that the death penalty was appropriate and sentenced Wilkins to die. The Missouri Supreme Court later upheld this decision.

Name Index

O

Oeuvray, K., 328
Office of Juvenile Justice and Delinquency
    Prevention, 261n.1
Ohio Department of Youth Services, 213, 229,
    243n.11
Ohlin, L., 271, 285n.19
Ohlin, L. E., 57, 58, 67n.48, 262n.42
Olds, D., 200n.30
O'Malley, P. M., 89n.48, 289, 292, 293, 298,
    301n.6, 302nn.20,25
Ooyen, M., 328

P

Padilla, F., 286n.79
Palmer, T., 182nn.21,28, 246, 247, 260,
    261nn.6,7,12, 262nn.49,55
Parent, D. G., 224n.11
Parsons, T., 89n.24
Pastore, A. L., 144n.63
Paternoster, R., 46n.53
Paterson, A., 324
Patrick, S., 331n.2
Pearson, F. S., 262nn.25,28
Pellisier, B., 247
Pendergast, M. L., 247
Pentz, M. A., 200nn.16,24
Perrow, C., 225n.31
Perry, D., 45n.30
Perry, E., 266
Peters, M., 224nn.17,18
Petersen, R. D., 200nn.2,3
Petersilla, J., 182n.5
Peterson, R. D., 136, 144nn.69,70,71, 144
Peterson, S. B., 192, 201nn.40,41,42
Pfister, C., 332n.50
Phelps, J. R., 77
Phillipson, M., 66n.5
Pines, A., 77, 89n.52
Pink, W. T., 45n3
Piquero, A. R., 64, 68n.81, 149
Pisciotta, A. W., 24n.11
Platt, A., 5, 13, 18, 24nn.28,32
Platt, J., 211, 224nn.1,24, 225n.30
Platt, J. J., 301n.22
Polsky, H. W., 225n.44
Pope, C. E., 85, 90nn.101,102
Porter, P. K., 39
Priestley, P., 261nn.13,14
Propper, A., 225n.55
Puritz, P., 225n.67
Puzzanchera, C., 143n.49

Q

Quicker, J. C., 278, 284n.9

R

Radzinowicz, L., 24n.4, 321, 323n.71
Rapoza, S., 200nn.2,3
Reckless, W. C., 59, 67n.51
Redding, R. E., 155, 156, 163nn.26,31
Redfield, R., 285n.8

Redner, R., 262nn.41,51,54
Rehnquist, W., 130
Reimer, D. J., 46n.37
Reiner, 278, 286n.58
Reiner, A. S., 286n.59
Ren, X., 313, 332nn.17,18,19,32
Rennie, Y., 66nn.7,9
Rey, J. M., 301n.11
Rice, S. E., 331n.2
Richey, P. N., 262nn.21,22,23,24
Riester, D., 20
Righthand, S., 262n.36
Rindels, B., 88n.10
Rittenhouse, R., 89n.24
Robers, S., 45nn.24,25,26, 27
Roberts, M., 201nn.44,45
Robins, L. N., 55, 67nn.39,40, 87nn.40,41
Rodriguez,, 77
Rodriguez, O., 90n.90
Rogers, K. O., 89–90n.64
Romig, D., 24n37
Romig, D. A., 169, 170, 182nn.10,11
Rosner, L., 143n.50
Ross, R. R., 246, 261nn.8,9,11,12
Rothman, D., 24nn.5,11,12,29,30
Rothman, D. J., 55nn.16,17
Rouse, M., 143n.25
Rubin, T. H., 143nn.34,41
Rudd, K., 42
Rudolph, J. L, 68n.85
Ruggles-Brise, E., 324
Rumbaut, R., 83
Russell, N., 267
Rutford, M., 216
Ryerson, E., 142n.8

S

Sabol, W., 163n.34
Saldana, L., 170
Salerno, A. W., 224nn.15,16
Sampson, R. J., 63, 68nn.75,76,77,78, 81, 82,
    90nn.78,79,80,81,82,83,84,85,86,89
Samuels, L., 267
Sanborn, J. B., Jr., 143n.44
Sangalong, C., 234, 243n.24
Sante, L., 284n.4
Sarnecki, J., 333nn.89,92,93,94,95,96,97,98,
    99,100,101,102,109
Sarri, R. C., 79, 224n.5
Scali, M. A., 225n.67
Scarpitti, F. R., 89n.25
Scham, P., 182n.4
Schemo, D. J., 224n.22
Schewe, P. A., 170
Schneider, A. L., 182n.16
Schnitzler, N., 224n.3
Schrecengost, J., 323
Schulenberg, J. E., 89n.48, 289, 292, 293, 298,
    301n.6, 302nn.20,25
Schur, E. M., 24nn.26,27
Schuster, D., 89n.45
Schwaibe, C. S., 182n.9
Schwartz, I. M., 224nn.9,11
Scott, E., 147
Sechrest, D. K., 243n.35, 262nn.41,48,50,52
Sedack, A., 225n.50
Sedack, A. J., 243n.3

Seebrook, R., 262nn.21,22,23,24
Segrave, J. D., 89n.25
Segura, L., 161
Sellin, T., 46n.45, 60, 67n.62, 89n.44
Senna, J. J., 143nn.37,45
Shannon, L., 345n.3
Shannon, L. W., 46n.45
Shannon, S. K. S., 234
Shaw, C. R., 56, 67n.45, 257
Sheldon, R. G., 144n.58
Sheldon, W., 54, 67nn.21,22
Sherman, L. W., 243n.21, 340
Shewchuk-Dann, D., 262n.37
Shichor, D., 218, 225nn.37,40,41,42
Shireman, C., 24nn.33,36
Shoemaker, D. J., 68n.74, 88n.2
Short, J. F., Jr., 46n.40, 286n.79
Shukla, K. S., 332n.35
Sickmund, M., 17, 90nn.106,106,107,108,
    132, 143n.49, 162nn.11,15, 182n.2,
    204, 205, 210, 224nn.6,7,25,28,29,
    225nn.35,36, 243n.15, 346nn.11,12
Siegel, L. J., 143nn.37,45
Sieverdes, C. M., 225n.54
Silbert, M., 77, 89n.52
Silva, P. A., 76, 89n.46
Simi, P., 286n.59
Simpson, J., 89nn.33,34,35,36
Sladky, A., 205, 210, 224nn.28,29
Slee, P., 45n.31
Slowkowski, J., 301nn.1,2
Smart, C., 224n.3
Smith, A. N., 292
Smith, C., 278, 286n.65
Smith, C. P., 143n.51
Smith, D., 90n.71
Smith, L., 286n.59
Smith, R. R., 201nn.49,50,51
Snyder, H. N., 17, 90nn.106,106,107,108, 132,
    162n.11, 182n.2, 225nn.35,36, 231,
    243n.15, 345nn.11,12
Snyder, K., 182n.23,25, 224nn.6,7,25
Snyder, S. M., 231, 243nn.16.24
Snyder, T. D., 45nn.24,25,26, 27
Sommers, I., 64, 68nn.83,84
Soohill, K., 149
Sourander, A., 45n.32
Speck, R., 48
Speers, B., 45n.31
Spergel, I., 282, 283, 285n.24
Spergel, I. A., 286nn.84,85,86
Springer, C. E., 142n.5
Springer, D. W. 224n.2
Spruance, L. M., 262nn.21,22,23,24
Stanford, K., 159
Staples, W. G., 182n.17
Steele, P., 201n.55
Steffensmeier, D., 72, 88n.16
Stein, N., 78, 89nn.56,57,58,59,60
Steinhart, D., 224n.10
Stephenson, R. M., 89n.25
Stevens, A., 328
Steward, L., 262n.17
Stone, D., 286n.73
Street, D., 225n.31
Strieb, V. L., 158, 163nn.39,42
Strong, A., 143n.48
Sturgeon, W., 335, 345n.1
Sutherland, E., 53, 58, 66nn.19,20, 86

Subject Index

Note: The locators followed by "illus", "b", "t" and "f" refer to illustrations, boxes, tables and figures cited in the text.